FYODOR DOSTOEVSKY—THE GATHERING STORM (1846–1847)

A volume in the

NIU Series in Slavic, East European, and Eurasian Studies
Edited by Christine D. Worobec

For a list of books in the series, visit our website at cornellpress.cornell.edu.

FYODOR DOSTOEVSKY—THE GATHERING STORM (1846–1847)

A Life in Letters, Memoirs, and Criticism

THOMAS GAITON MARULLO

NORTHERN ILLINOIS UNIVERSITY PRESS
AN IMPRINT OF CORNELL UNIVERSITY PRESS
Ithaca and London

First published 2020 by Cornell University Press

Library of Congress Cataloging-in-Publication Data

Names: Marullo, Thomas Gaiton, author.
Title: Fyodor Dostoevsky : the gathering storm
    (1846–1847) : a life in letters, memoirs, and criticism /
    Thomas Gaiton Marullo.
Description: Ithaca [New York] : Northern Illinois
    University Press, an imprint of Cornell University Press,
    2020. | Series: NIU Series in Slavic, East European, and
    Eurasian Studies | Includes bibliographical references
    and index.
Identifiers: LCCN 2020003014 (print) | LCCN 2020003015
    (ebook) | ISBN 9781501751851 (cloth) |
    ISBN 9781501751868 (epub) | ISBN 9781501751875 (pdf)
Subjects: LCSH: Dostoyevsky, Fyodor, 1821–1881. |
    Dostoyevsky, Fyodor, 1821–1881—Correspondence. |
    Authors, Russian—19th century—Biography.
Classification: LCC PG3328 .M384 2020 (print) |
    LCC PG3328 (ebook) | DDC 891.73/3 [B] —dc23
LC record available at https://lccn.loc.gov/2020003014
LC ebook record available at https://lccn.loc.gov/2020003015

For Jeff Brooks,
colleague and friend

CONTENTS

NOTE ON THE FIRST VOLUME

Fyodor Dostoevsky—In the Beginning (1821–1845):
A Life in Letters, Memoirs, and Criticism, the first in a three-volume study of
the writer's early life and work, focuses on the images and ideas, and on the
people, places, and events, that influenced Dostoevsky in the first twenty-
four years of his life. It renders the writer in a new and seminal way: a diary-
portrait of Dostoevsky drawn from letters, memoirs, and criticism of the
writer, as well as the witness and testimony of family and friends, readers and
reviewers, observers and participants as he stepped forward into existence.

Each of the three parts of *Fyodor Dostoevsky—In the Beginning* includes a
wide selection of excerpts from primary sources, arranged chronologically
and thematically. Prominent sources include the memoirs or notes of Dostoevsky's brother Andrei, his daughter Lyubov, and his friend and roommate
Alexander Rizemkampf; letters between Dostoevsky's parents, between
Dostoevsky and his older brother Mikhail, and between both siblings and
their father; and quotations from Orest Miller and Nikolai Strakhov's 1883
biography of Dostoevsky and from Dostoevsky's own *Diary of a Writer.*

An important aspect of *Fyodor Dostoevsky—In the Beginning* is the debunk-
ing of clichés and misinformation, particularly about the writer's family,
such as time-honored assertions that Dostoevsky's father was murdered
by the serfs, and that he was so at odds with his sons Fyodor and Mikhail
over money and vocation that they wished him dead. Indeed, from the pan-
tomime villain of legend, Dostoevsky's father emerges from the study of
primary materials as a caring and solicitous parent to his children and as a
tender and loving spouse to his wife.

The first part, "All in the Family," considers Dostoevsky's early formation
and schooling—his time in city and country, and his ties to his family, particularly his parents. The second part, "To Petersburg," features Dostoevsky's
early days in Russia's imperial city, his years at the Main Engineering Academy, and the death of his father. The third part, "Darkness before Dawn,"
deals with the writer's youthful struggles and strivings, culminating in the

success of *Poor Folk*. Each section is introduced by a brief essay on select people and events in the young writer's life.

Fyodor Dostoevsky—In the Beginning seeks to shed light on many dark and unexplored corners of the young writer's life. More important, it strives to render a clear and cohesive picture of the early years of one of the world's greatest writers.

PREFACE

Scholars and students of nineteenth-century Russian literature see the foremost prose practitioners of the period as pursuing a simple if straightforward path to greatness. Evidence for such a view abounds. Between 1820 and 1900, foremost indigenous writers of novels and novellas, short stories, and tales seemed to climb the ladder of success in dizzying, lockstep fashion. Alexander Pushkin progressed from *Tales of Belkin* (1831) to *Eugene Onegin* (1833) to *Queen of Spades* (1834) and *Captain's Daughter* (1836). Nikolai Gogol advanced from *Evenings on a Farm Near Dikanka* (1831–32) to *Arabesques* and *Mirgorod* (1835), "The Nose" (1835–1836), "The Overcoat" (1842), and *Dead Souls* (1842). Also writing works in rapidly ascendant succession was Ivan Turgenev with *Diary of a Superfluous Man* (1850), *Notes of a Huntsman* (1852), *Rudin* (1857), *Asya* (1858), *A Nest of Gentlefolk* (1859), *On the Eve* (1860), *First Love* (1860), and *Fathers and Sons* (1862). Even more destined for upward literary mobility was Leo Tolstoy, first with *Childhood* (1852), *Adolescence* (1854), and *Youth* (1856); then with *Family Happiness* (1859) and *The Cossacks* (1863); next with *War and Peace* (1869) and *Anna Karenina* (1878); and finally with *The Death of Ivan Ilyich* (1886), *The Kreutzer Sonata* (1889), and *Resurrection* (1899).

In charting the steady rise of nineteenth-century Russian writers to greatness, scholars and students of the national written expression note a grand exception: Fyodor Dostoevsky. They are correct to do so. As quickly as Pushkin, Gogol, Turgenev, and Tolstoy ascended to fortune and fame, so did Dostoevsky, Icarus-like, crash and burn when he approached metaphorical suns.

For followers and admirers of Russian literature, Dostoevsky's failure to scale literary heights safely and soundly was especially tragic given two facts. His first literary venture, *Poor Folk* (1845), caused a sensation that far outstripped the fictional debuts of Pushkin, Gogol, Turgenev, and Tolstoy. Also, Dostoevsky had to wait almost twenty years before he reached his literary stride with *Notes from the Underground* (1864) and, at long last, achieved steady and lasting renown with *Crime and Punishment* (1866), *The Idiot* (1869), *Devils* (1872), and *The Brothers Karamazov* (1880). Most assuredly, Dostoevsky did not follow the seemingly simple and straightforward path of Pushkin, Gogol, Turgenev, and Tolstoy. Indeed, it is a measure of the ongoing fascination with the writer and his works that he did not.

Students and scholars of Russian literature agree, though, that the ins and outs, ups and downs, and zigs and zags that mark Dostoevsky's path in the years between *Poor Folk* and *Notes from the Underground* were crucial to his personal and literary growth. They assert rightly that Dostoevsky could not have written *Notes* and subsequent works without the people, places, and events that had let him experience and understand life in ways that none of his literary confreres could or would.

In their studies of Dostoevsky between 1846 and 1864, personal and professional enthusiasts of Russian literature reveal a key flaw. They do not discuss adequately these people, places, and events that influenced Dostoevsky in this period. Not unlike their investigations into the first twenty-four years of the young writer's life, they pass or rush over this material or absorb it into larger, overriding movements and trends.

In so doing, scholars and students of Russian literature miss the many small and momentary, accidental, and incidental issues, images, and ideas that entered into Dostoevsky's mind, heart, and soul, and that served as stimuli and seedbeds for his mature fiction and thought. They also fail to realize the ultimate paradox of investigations into the writer: only by sweating the small stuff can one gain a complete and integral understanding of Dostoevsky's literature and life.

Fyodor Dostoevsky—The Gathering Storm (1846–1847): A Life in Letters, Memoirs, and Criticism, the second of what will be a three-volume study on the writer's early years, rushes in where others feared or failed to tread. Like its predecessor, *Fyodor Dostoevsky—In the Beginning (1821–1845),* it focuses on the prosaics that shaped Dostoevsky and his writing, taken from the letters, memoirs, and criticism of the young writer, as well as from the witness and testimony of family and friends, readers and reviewers, and participants and players who stepped into Dostoevsky's life in the first two years after *Poor Folk.*

With this second volume also, I again note several things. First, I have sought the fullest picture of Dostoevsky in 1846 and 1847, via an exhaustive search and study of all published materials on the writer. No stone has been left unturned in my quest. Second, I have arranged citations both chronologically and from the vantage points of ten, twenty, thirty, even forty years later, interlacing the voices of both the young and the mature Dostoevsky with those of individuals who knew him personally or from his writings, literary and otherwise. In so doing, I seek to inform all the individuals in my study with an artistic and modern allure, presenting them as many-faceted, engaged, and self-determining beings, as well as spontaneous and multiple selves who dialogue about people, places, and events in 1846 and 1847, and who, in a seminal way, show maturity and growth, dualism and conflict, physically, socially, and spiritually. Third, I have given equal opportunity and freedom to all the actors in this tale. Truths and lies, facts and fictions— intimate and disturbing, outrageous and far-fetched—enter the narrative, with notes that provide correctives, counterarguments, and/or pertinent information to set the record straight on Dostoevsky's thoughts, emotions, and actions at this time. Fourth, I have again rejected the still strong urge to measure the people and events of Dostoevsky's first two years after *Poor Folk* against the characters and events of both his early and his mature fiction. Any references to the writer's oeuvre are from the speakers alone.

As I did in *Fyodor Dostoevsky—In the Beginning*, I seek in *Fyodor Dostoevsky— The Gathering Storm* to extend the map of Dostoevsky's physical and spiritual terrain as he moved, tentatively, into the socio-literary life of his time. Again, with this second volume, my purpose is not only to plot the coordinates of Dostoevsky's passage to greatness in the first two years after *Poor Folk* but also to call attention to the many people, places, and events that helped or deterred him in his journey forward.

If in *Fyodor Dostoevsky—In the Beginning* I showed how Dostoevsky moved in upward spirals—he had known a loving family, received an excellent educa- tion, launched a promising career, and scored a runaway hit with *Poor Folk*— I demonstrate in *Fyodor Dostoevsky—The Gathering Storm* how Dostoevsky, sadly, advanced along slippery slopes. In what would be recurring patterns in the young writer's existence, and not unlike his playing with time in his later fiction in which moments become eternities, not only did the events and experiences of the young writer in the first two years after *Poor Folk* remain etched, acid-like, in his consciousness throughout his life but also, perhaps more important, they portended troubles and tribulations that would beset him and his characters in the next three decades or so of his time on earth. In 1846 and 1847, Dostoevsky experienced frustration and anger, doubt and despair, loneliness and isolation in both literature and life. The failures of his second, third, fourth, and fifth works—*The Double*, "Mr. Prokharchin," "The Landlady," and "A Novel in Nine Letters"—threatened oblivion, even extinction as a writer. His difficulties with Vissarion Belinsky, Nikolai Nekra- sov, Ivan Turgenev, Ivan Panaev, and other members of the Russian literary world cast him as a loser and a buffoon for all to mock and scorn.

In retrospect, the triumph of *Poor Folk* was for Dostoevsky a curse, not a blessing. Given the young writer's temperament, it might have been better if he had started his literary career with a whimper, not a bang. Caught between the success of his first work and the failures of his following four pieces, Dostoevsky "split" into warring halves. On the one hand, he was an "extraordinary" being, a lord and master above everyone and everything. On the other hand, he was an "underground" man, a louse and mouse below everyone and everything. Indeed, the personal and professional crises that beset Dostoevsky in 1846 and 1847 so shattered the young writer that they moved him to catastrophe two years later: his implication in the Petrashevsky affair, a plot to overthrow the government, and his subsequent decade-long exile in Siberia.

The dark clouds that hung over Dostoevsky in 1846 and 1847, though, had two silver linings. The first is that the young writer found solace and support in three new families: the Vielgorskys, the Beketovs, and the Maykovs. The second and more important, perhaps, is that Dostoevsky, even in fictional failure, was portending literary success. In his stories he was finding himself as a thinker and an artist, probing human weakness and sin in ways that no one else in Russian or world literature could or would. In his literary laboratory were men, women, and children who, like himself, split into conflicting selves, inhabited multiple realities, and perhaps most important, declared war on themselves and others with murderous glee. Like a mad scientist, Dostoevsky was creating Russian Frankensteins who, within twenty years, would say more about human debasement and deformity than anyone else would care or dare to admit.

Indeed, it can be argued that without the physical and metaphysical trials, travails, and traumas that took root during the first two years after *Poor Folk* and later, Dostoevsky might not have created "extraordinary" qua "underground" men, women, and children who enthrall if unnerve readers and reviewers in the first decades of the twenty-first century in much the same way they did in the last decades of the nineteenth. In a dramatic way, for both himself and others, Dostoevsky embodied the adage "no pain, no gain."

As was the case with the previous volume, *Fyodor Dostoevsky—The Gathering Storm* consists of a preface, an introduction, three parts, a conclusion, endnotes, a directory of names, and notes on sources. The first part, "Pride before the Fall," focuses on Dostoevsky's increasingly tense ties with Vissarion Belinsky, Nikolai Nekrasov, Ivan Turgenev, Ivan Panaev, and other figures of the Russian literary world. The second part, "Havens from the Storms," deals with the reception, often negative, from writers and critics in response not only to the success of *Poor Folk* but also to the failures that followed quickly. The third part, "The Psycho-Spiritual Turn," centers on Dostoevsky's final break with Belinsky and his circle, as well as his increasing struggles to stay afloat, internally and externally.

Furthermore, each section is introduced by a brief essay on select people, issues, and events in Dostoevsky's life at this time. The preface to "Pride before the Fall" is a piece on the writer's tortuous tie to Belinsky, a stance of love and hate that haunted him throughout his life. A sketch on the Vielgorskys, Maykovs, and Beketovs, three families who proved to be Dostoevsky's salvation in this period, heads "Havens from the Storms"; and a unifying analysis of *The Double*, "Mr. Prokharchin," "The Landlady," and "A Novel in Nine Letters" introduces "The Psycho-Spiritual Turn."

For their assistance in *Fyodor Dostoevsky—The Gathering Storm*, I wish to express my deep gratitude to Joseph Lenkart, Annabella Irvine, and especially Jan Adamczyk of the Slavic Reference Service at the University of Illinois, who, with exceptional diligence, endless patience, and exemplary grace and good cheer, found answers to the myriad, complicated, and often outrageous questions that I asked regarding the young Dostoevsky; and who, as has always been the case in my now forty-five-year association with the group, ended their responses with offers of further assistance. If there are heroes and heroines in the academy of Russian studies in America today, it is they. I also thank Bethany Wasik, Karen Hwa, Sarah Noell, Richanna Patrick, Michael Morris, and especially Amanda Heller, the copyeditor of this volume, at Cornell University Press for the exceptional attention and expertise they gave to my book.

Here at Notre Dame, I thank Thomas Merluzzi and Alison Rice, past and present directors of the Institute for Scholarship in the Liberal Arts, for their continued support; Nita Hashil of Interlibrary Loan for supplying materials for research, especially from libraries and institutions in Russia; Randy Yoho and Matthew Pollard, who kept my computers in good working order; and Cheryl Reed, who transformed my chaotic files into a professional document.

It is with special gratitude and warmth that I salute my research assistants Maria Hieber, Ana Miravete, Katherine Mansourova, Charles Sedore, and especially Joshua O'Brien, whom, during his four years as a student at Notre Dame and the two summers after graduation, I drove to the brink and beyond with endless queries on pages and dates; obscure questions on people, places, and events; and torturous searches through newspapers, journals, books, and cyberspace for citations and claims. Truly, and as was the case with *Fyodor Dostoevsky—In the Beginning*, *Fyodor Dostoevsky—The Gathering Storm* would never have seen the light of day without him.

I also acknowledge my wife, Gloria Gibbs Marullo, for forty-one years of unstinting encouragement and support, and my cats, Benedict Joseph,

Francis Xavier, and Agnes Mary, for unconditional warmth and love. (For readers of my scholarly adventures, Bernadette Marie and Bridget Josephine passed from this life at age nineteen and eighteen, respectively, and now watch down on me from heaven.)

With *Fyodor Dostoevsky—The Gathering Storm*, four individuals deserve special acclaim and applause: Irwin Weil, Department of Slavic Languages and Literatures, Northwestern University; Kathleen Parthé, Department of Modern Languages and Cultures, University of Rochester; Jeff Brooks, Department of History, Johns Hopkins University; and Amy Farranto, senior acquisitions editor, Northern Illinois University Press. With painstaking care and concern, they read the manuscript, offered counsel and advice, and cheered me on in my work. I am particularly grateful to Kathleen Parthé for editing the entire study; and to Jeff Brooks for sending email after email, often on a daily basis, with ideas and suggestions to improve my work. A special and affectionate note of thanks is due to Amy Farranto, who oversaw the publication of what is now our third book together with exemplary energy and expertise, graciousness and aplomb. Indeed, if *Fyodor Dostoevsky—The Gathering Storm* qualifies as a work of readable scholarship, it is in no small measure because of the efforts of all four individuals on my behalf.

Finally, it is with special gratitude that I again acknowledge Jeff Brooks for his assistance not only in this work but also in many of my previous studies. He has been a devoted friend and colleague, a gentleman and a scholar, and it is with deep admiration and affection for him as a person and a professional that I dedicate *Fyodor Dostoevsky—The Gathering Storm* to him.

May he and all who have accompanied me in this venture know only happiness, health, and peace.

FYODOR DOSTOEVSKY—THE GATHERING STORM (1846–1847)

Introduction

In early 1846, the young Dostoevsky was the toast of the town. The applause was deafening. Everyone wanted to meet the new writer who, with the publication of *Poor Folk*, was hailed as a savior, a prophet, and an idol whom God had chosen to lead Russian literature from alleged deserts to promised lands. It was a measure of the angst and concern for the fate and future of the national written expression that readers, writers, and reviewers embraced Dostoevsky with such excitement and joy. All wanted to meet the young man, to shake his hand, to talk with him, to introduce him to society, and, most important, to claim him as a colleague, teacher, and friend.

With bated breath, readers, writers, and reviewers waited to see what Dostoevsky would do next. They wondered: Would he write a second *Poor Folk*? Would he, à la Charles Dickens, Victor Hugo, or Honoré de Balzac, pursue the trials and travails of urban denizens? Would he, like Pushkin, Mikhail Lermontov, and Gogol censure inertia and injustice, as well as sanction freedom and change? Would he emulate the Decembrists and challenge Nicholas I and "orthodoxy, autocracy, and nationality," which since 1833 had defined the very foundation of the Russian state?

Two individuals were particularly taken with Dostoevsky. One was Vissarion Belinsky; the other, Nikolai Nekrasov. Both men had been educated in the school of hard knocks. Neither of them had known security and love in their early years. Belinsky's father, Grigory Nikiforovich Belinsky, was a rural doctor who so angered patients with his drunkenness, atheism, and enthusiasm for Voltaire that he feared violence against his person. His equally unstable mother fueled fires. The young Belinsky was subjected not only to violent quarrels between the two but also to abuse at their hands. Formal education was minimal, the lad having been expelled from Moscow University in 1832 for alleged ill health and limited intelligence, but in truth because he had not taken a single examination in his three years at the school. A tragedy, titled *Dmitri Kalinin* and written by Belinsky as a student, captured his frame of mind: a noble soul is driven to suicide by an inscrutable and unjust fate.

Nekrasov fared even worse. The son of a poor and equally violent gentryman, he had been disowned by his father for seeking admission to the university in St. Petersburg. For the next three years, Nekrasov fended off poverty and starvation in the city by begging, tutoring, and writing.

It speaks greatly to the minds, hearts, and souls of both men that despite such setbacks, they were, in 1846 and 1847, key figures in the Russian literary world. At thirty-seven years old, Belinsky had a string of successes to his name. He had turned *The Fatherland Notes* into the leading publication of the day. He was also the foremost champion qua interpreter of Pushkin, Lermontov, and Gogol. A decade younger than Belinsky, Nekrasov had won acclaim for writing poems about Russian provincial life, for publishing *The Physiology of Petersburg* (1845) and *The Petersburg Miscellany* (1846), and, in 1847, for purchasing *The Contemporary* and attracting Belinsky to its ranks.

Although earlier in their careers both Belinsky and Nekrasov were romantics, they were, by 1846 and 1847, staunch realists, as well as avid proponents of progressivism in Russian literature and life. In their view, writers should address political and social ills, and move their country westward, toward democracy and liberalism. Both men took heart that the national written expression, after an embarrassingly slow start, was approaching universal prominence and respect. They were particularly thrilled with what came to be known as the "Petersburg tradition" in Russian literature: fiction about "little" men and women who lived and loved, worked and died, often tragically, in the imperial city. With pride—and, in truth, relief—they pointed to Pushkin's "The Bronze Horseman" (1833); to Gogol's "Nevsky Prospekt" and "The Nose"; and to the so-called "physiological sketches" that appeared in newspapers and journals, almanacs, and anthologies throughout the northern metropolis.

Both Belinsky and Nekrasov realized, though, that when measured against the fiction of western Europe, Russian literature had a long way to go. Nothing in the national written expression could compare with the novels of

Dickens, Balzac, and Hugo. Pieces on native urban life were scarce, short, sour, and ended in madness and death. Heroes and heroines—Pushkin's Yevgeny and Gogol's Akaky and Kovalyov, Pirogov and Piskaryov come to mind—spoke and acted little. More often than not, they moved to type and daguerreotype, into cartoon and cardboard characters, with strings pulled, puppet-like, by their creators.

Both Belinsky and Nekrasov had an additional if not more pressing cause for worry. No one, it seemed, was on hand to carry on their goals for literature and life. Pushkin had died in 1837, Gogol had left fiction and, worse, in 1847 was writing *Selected Passages from Correspondence to Friends*, a bizarre collection of homilies, exhortations, and personal confessions, often of a conservative, even reactionary bent.

Understandable, therefore, was the excitement—and again relief—of both Belinsky and Nekrasov, as well as of writers, readers, and reviewers of Russian literature, over Dostoevsky and *Poor Folk*. At long last they had an indigenous novel of urban life, with flesh-and-blood characters who talked about their unhappy lives in a credible and realistic way. Dostoevsky, they believed, was the answer to their prayers. He was the hope, if not the salvation, of Russia and its literature.

They were in for the shock of their lives. On both counts—the writer and his writing—Dostoevsky failed miserably.

Physically, he could not have made a worse impression. If Russian readers, writers, and reviewers were expecting a strapping Goliath, they got a sickly David. The writer of *Poor Folk* was frail and pale. His clothes were worn and poorly fitting. His surroundings were monastically spartan. Visitors sat on the one dilapidated chair in his home.

Dostoevsky did little to help the situation. When admirers oohed and aahed over *Poor Folk*, he became embarrassed and confused. Conversations were sporadic and brief. Others often did the talking. Also, Dostoevsky kept his cards close to his vest, answering questions in sporadic and evasive ways.

Ironically, personal discomfort only increased public allure. As would be the case with the eccentrics of Dostoevsky's mature fiction—Prince Myshkin of *The Idiot* is a pertinent example—and as in his own time as a student at the Main Engineering Academy in St. Petersburg, Dostoevsky impressed others as somber and strange, but also as attuned to truths of this and other worlds.

Willingly, devotees of *Poor Folk* cut its creator a great deal of slack. Despite the disappointment, if not the shock, of initial encounters, they found—or, more accurately, persuaded themselves to find—Dostoevsky worthy to present in public, if only for their own honor and glory: they were groupies with a genius in tow.

Or so they thought. If Dostoevsky failed in private, he fared even worse in public. Invitations to homes and gatherings were greeted with unease, even fear. It was only after repeated entreaties and threats that Dostoevsky showed himself to the world. To friends and followers, the public Dostoevsky was like an erupting volcano. His body shook and shuddered; his face was stormy and dark. The writer of *Poor Folk* also did not accept people at face value or with good intentions. Rather, he sensed threats and agendas from all. Anxiety and paranoia raised their heads. Before, during, and after meetings, Dostoevsky asked attendees to repeat what they and others had said. Not unlike his fictional clerks, he often eluded scrutiny in nooks and corners and behind screens.

At first glance, Dostoevsky's angst over the beau monde belies the facts. He was hardly déclassé. The writer of *Poor Folk* was a bona fide aristocrat who, as a child, adolescent, and youth, had known only stability and love from parents, teachers, and friends. Values of industry and culture encouraged virtues of confidence and self-respect. Unlike many of the higher-ups he reportedly feared, Dostoevsky was superbly educated in both the sciences and the arts. He was better read in classical and contemporary literature than any of his peers. Furthermore, Dostoevsky was comfortable and convivial with all types and castes. He was particularly enterprising with editors, publishers, and booksellers. With potential patrons, too, Dostoevsky had everything to gain and nothing to lose, particularly with wolves at his door. Reasons for reticence are lacking.

Plausible if problematic reasons for Dostoevsky's standoffishness are fourfold. Most obviously, the young man—having come to St. Petersburg from Moscow less than a decade previously, and by education and training a draftsman and engineer—was shy, if not uncomfortable, with larger-than-life individuals like Belinsky and Nekrasov, as well as with the intellectual and cultural society of the imperial city. He feared, rightly, that he would be seen as little more than a local yokel who would amuse the literati without joining their ranks.

Another apparent reason for Dostoevsky's aloofness—and a characteristic that new acquaintances also noted in the young writer—was pride. They had every reason to do so. If Dostoevsky did not look or act like a genius, he had no trouble seeing himself as one. The success of *Poor Folk* had gone to his head. A legend in his own mind, Dostoevsky had become insufferable. The bragging and boasting were nonstop. The young writer was heir to Lord Byron, Pushkin, and Gogol. He laid claim to a brilliant and lucrative future. By his own (generous) count, he had been cited in articles and reviews thirty-five times in the first three months of 1846 alone. Heady, even intoxicated, with the success of *Poor Folk*, Dostoevsky had even greater hopes for *The Double*. In his view, his second work was ten times better than his first one. It was a worthy successor to Gogol's *Dead Souls*, if not a vanquishing challenger.

Such braggadocio, of course, brought to bear still a third reason for Dostoevsky's remoteness from people: his insecurity as a writer. He was having great difficulty with *The Double*. He also would have grave doubts over "Mr. Prokharchin," "The Landlady," and "A Novel in Nine Letters." Understandably, the young writer wondered if he had had beginner's luck with *Poor Folk*, if he were a flash-in-the-pan sensation who would exit the national written expression as quickly as he had entered it.

Given his uneasiness with high society, his pride over *Poor Folk*, and his doubts about his next four works, Dostoevsky soon alienated everyone. More seriously, he clashed with the very people who not only had introduced him to the Russian literary world but also could and would have advanced his career as a writer. Akin to his fictional down-and-outers who revere and then rebel against patrons and benefactors, Dostoevsky bit hands that fed him. His behavior was often scandalous. Arguably, Dostoevsky was the only person in Russia who told Belinsky to keep still. He fought with Turgenev, Panaev, and Nekrasov. He bolted from parties and gatherings; he shunned confreres in public places. Anything could raise his temper and fists. Whispers and winks provoked sound and fury. Sallies and ribbings triggered war and revenge. Dostoevsky had people walking on eggshells to the point where they rejoiced at his exit or absence. Purposely Belinsky eschewed conversation and contact with the young writer, thereby infuriating his obstreperous protégé by being seemingly callous and cold.

Truth be told, Dostoevsky was only partially responsible for the difficulties. Readers, writers, and reviewers in the Russian literary world drove him wild. With Dostoevsky, Belinsky and Nekrasov overstepped bounds. Having championed *Poor Folk*—wrongly—as sociopolitical exposé, they demanded that new works by the writer be similarly reproachful and accusatory. Men of principle, but also ideologues—not for nothing was Belinsky called "frenzied"—the two brooked no compromise. Mirroring the tortuous ties between man-gods and disciples in Dostoevsky's mature novels, Belinsky and Nekrasov saw Dostoevsky as their creature and captive. Neither man valued Dostoevsky for who he was or for what he was trying to be—or write. Rather, Belinsky and Nekrasov sought to remake Dostoevsky in their own image and likeness, to use him for their own ends, and to bend him to their political, social, and economic wills and worldviews. Whatever the cost, Dostoevsky would be their herald for a progressive, democratic Russia.

It was a recipe for disaster.

Dostoevsky again failed to live up to expectations. Part of the problem was that the young writer, in thrall to editors, publishers, and booksellers, was forced to meet deadlines, to write hurriedly, and, by his own admission, to rush images, issues, and ideas. More seriously, perhaps, Dostoevsky continued to do in his twenty-fifth and twenty-six years of life what he had done in his previous twenty-four. In a move that would have thrilled his headstrong father, Mikhail, he went his own way as an artist and a man.

Despite the cosmopolitan formation of his early years, Dostoevsky was alien or indifferent to sociopolitical discussions. Not once in 1846 and 1847—in oral or written form, or in the witness and testimony of companions and colleagues—did Dostoevsky comment on the burning images, issues, and ideas of the day. He held his tongue on Hegelianism, Fourierism, socialism, and communism. Meetings with Mikhail Petrashevsky, the radical *intelligent* who, in 1849, would bring the young writer to ruin, were sporadic and brief. It was only in *Diary of a Writer*, written from 1873 to 1876, that Dostoevsky addressed the controversy between Westernizers and Slavophiles. The next four works of his literary career—*The Double* and "Mr. Prokharchin" in 1846, "The Landlady" and "A Novel in Nine Letters" in 1847—showed that Dostoevsky heard a different drummer, one who sounded beats from pounding minds and hearts, not prattling forums and public squares.

From the beginning of his fictional foray, Dostoevsky opposed the idea that writers should address civic ills. Rather, he looked internally for causes of human suffering, to unearth in his characters the reasons for their distress. If Belinsky and Nekrasov sought political, social, and economic integration in Russia and the world, Dostoevsky looked to psychological and spiritual disintegration in corners and "depths." If they talked about autocracy, serfdom, and censorship, he discussed schizophrenia, deviancy, and execution of self and others. If they believed that humankind was poor in spirit, he insisted that society was even sicker in body and mind. As conflicted and confused as the young Dostoevsky might have been about everyone and everything in his life, nothing would deter him from his quest to find out what made people tick—and explode.

Predictably, Belinsky and company were furious over what they saw as personal and fictional perfidy. Dostoevsky, they charged, was cultivating thistles and thorns. He was brandishing wooden swords and spears. It was again symptomatic of their misplaced and overblown faith in the young writer that they responded so violently to the four works after *Poor Folk*. The abuse was unending, Nekrasov, Turgenev, Ivan Panaev, and Dmitri Grigorovich leading the way. In their view, Dostoevsky was yesterday's news. He was a traitor, a fop, and a fraud.

In the literary uproar over Dostoevsky in 1846 and 1847, two things are clear. The first is that fans turned foes were remarkably candid about their earlier enthusiasm for the young writer. Unlike the false friends in Dostoevsky's oeuvre who applauded alleged geniuses in surreptitious tête-à-têtes—the specious ovations of the musician B. for Yefimov in *Netochka Nezvanova*, and of Pyotr Verkhovensky for Nikolai Stavrogin in *Devils* are pertinent examples—Dostoevsky's disenchanted followers acknowledged publicly that it was they who had made the man. Confessions came fast and furious. It was Belinsky and company who had proclaimed Dostoevsky a genius. Even more stridently, it was they who had raised the writer to a savior, idol, and god. Powerful literary figures had put Dostoevsky on a pedestal, carried him throughout the city, and demanded that he be worshiped by all. Gladly had they suffered Dostoevsky's failings and flaws to proclaim him the great hope of Russian literature.

Now, with metaphorical egg on their faces, former devotees were as upset with themselves as they were with Dostoevsky over what they now saw as their illusions and delusions about the young writer. Some blamed Belinsky for the fiasco. With Dostoevsky, they said, the critic had extolled a talent that in fact had never existed. Others cried foul, charging that they—sincere, disinterested, and well meaning—had been duped by a master manipulator.

Other emotions fueled the fire. Even as members of the Belinsky circle applauded Dostoevsky's *Poor Folk*, they also envied—and resented—the success of the piece. No one in the group could claim an initial work that had caused the sensation that *Poor Folk* did. Belinsky and company were now seized with schadenfreude. As quickly as their god had ascended into heaven, equally swiftly had he descended into hell.

The anger of Belinsky and company was understandable. A native Russian literature was the sole means by which citizens could discuss the "damned questions." National written expression was also proof that Russians were viable and visionary, that they were moving toward progress and democracy, and that they were contributing to human culture and civilization.

In Dostoevsky, Belinsky and company believed, Russians had their Dickens, Hugo, and Balzac. With the young writer, national literature was alive and well. What Pushkin had done with *Eugene Onegin* in 1833, Lermontov with *A Hero of Our Time* in 1840, and Gogol with *Dead Souls* in 1842, Dostoevsky did with *Poor Folk* in 1845. Like gamblers at a roulette wheel, Belinsky and company staked all their hopes and dreams on the young writer; and when they lost their bets on subsequent works in 1846 and 1847, they were even more furious and fuming than Dostoevsky himself. Portraits of a schizophrenic clerk, a churlish miser, scheming cardsharps, and a head-in-the-clouds intellectual in a ménage à trois with a young maiden and her father, husband, or lover (it is not clear whom) only reinforced stereotypes of Russia and Russians as backward, barbaric, and perverse. Very possibly, Belinsky and company fretted, Russian literature was regressing altogether. Instead of Dickens, Hugo, or Balzac, they had at best a pale imitation of E. T. A. Hoffmann.

Revenge was swift and sweet. For Belinsky and company, the idol and god had shrunk suddenly. He was now "little" as well as ill, physically and mentally. The young writer spoke in strained tones. He fainted before large crowds. His face seemingly disappeared; his body faded into shadows. He had one foot in the grave, the other on a cabbage leaf.

In truth, the former apostles found Dostoevsky loathsome. He obsessed over glory and fame. He demanded adoration and praise. He waved letters from fans, imagined more than real. He insisted that borders surround *Poor Folk* and *The Double* in anthologies and journals to distinguish them from other works. He himself did no wrong. Everyone and everything else had caused his troubles. Rumors titillated and teased, as Dostoevsky's detractors claimed that he was no Casanova but captive to a siren who directed his every move, a socialite who transfixed him with her beauty, and a sibyl who proclaimed him the sun, moon, and stars.

The members of the Belinsky circle also accused Dostoevsky of having multiple faces, personae, and masks. He feigned happiness and humility. He played people like harps. He weaseled his way into social and literary ranks. Privately, local literati derided him. Grigorovich and Panaev spread stories that Dostoevsky was castigating everyone as heartless, insignificant, and jealous, convinced that chance had made him an eagle but had left others grounded, flopping and floundering. Publicly, fellow writers taunted him. Turgenev drove Dostoevsky to the brink. Privately, they went in for the kill with poems and prose that mocked the writer as once the toast of sultans and sovereigns but now a mournful knight scorned by all. Gogol was still king, Turgenev and company proclaimed, but Dostoevsky was only a jester, a knave.

A second issue in the ruckus over Dostoevsky during the first two years after *Poor Folk* was that former admirers conceded that they too had demonstrated shortcomings as lovers of the Russian word. A truism of the national written expression has been that literary circles in Moscow and St. Petersburg served as havens for Russian intellectuals and writers in the 1840s, as places where, behind closed doors, people could discuss political, social, and aesthetic images, issues, and ideas in a free and safe way. No doubt this was so, but contemporaries of Dostoevsky in 1846 and 1847 tell a different story about these cliques, particularly about the members of the Belinsky circle.

If Nekrasov, Panaev, and others are to be believed, the individuals who had gathered about the famous critic were as imperfect as—if not more so than—the object of their scorn. In fact, a case can be made that Nekrasov and others, because of who and what they were, bore partial responsibility for driving the admittedly difficult young man into more radical and dangerous groups, and ultimately into disaster: his involvement, in 1849, with the Petrashevsky affair and his decade-long exile to Siberia.

The lampoons that Nekrasov, Panaev, Turgenev, and others wrote about Dostoevsky reveal as much about themselves as they do their subject. If in public Nekrasov and company appeared solid and serious in politics and art, they were in private like everyone else: mortals with weaknesses that were trivial, motives that were petty, and emotions that were base.

A particular failing of the members of the Belinsky circle was that, like the great critic himself, they also crossed lines, personally and professionally. Mock concerns for body and soul, specious appeals to justice and enlightenment, irksome bursts of mischief and boredom, and naked attempts at despotism and power play were the catalysts by which members of the Belinsky circle curbed everyone around them. Newcomers felt insulted, not instructed; chastised, not cherished; pained, not pleased. With Dostoevsky a prime example, the members of the Belinsky circle often chased out more adherents than they attracted.

As conceded by Nekrasov, Panaev, Turgenev, and others, still another problem with the members of the Belinsky circle was that they looked to votaries as lackeys and minions to do their bidding, not to discuss literature or art. Writers and retainers existed in a symbiosis—a literary ecosystem, so to speak—in which parasites, for a tie to the Russian literary world, did everything and anything to safeguard the peace and happiness of their hosts. If in theory Nekrasov and company objected to serfdom as a sociopolitical evil, they in practice had little problem with exacting servitude from their followers. Master was to man as oppressor was to oppressed. Unrelenting and cruel were the insults and humiliations to which the members of the Belinsky circle subjected their vassals and valets. Devotees were for them *Untermenschen*: dimwitted and dull, with large heads and small minds. They were fictional "little men" come to life. Heads drooped, faces paled, and bodies sagged. Utterances were monosyllabic; voices were gasping and low.

To be sure, the flunkeys and attendants who served the members of the Belinsky circle got what they deserved. Not unlike the fixations of Belinsky, Turgenev, Panaev, Nekrasov, and others on Dostoevsky, their obsession as groupies—their mania to see and be seen with Russian literati-glitterati—caused them not only to tolerate abuse but also to welcome it. In a sense, the servants of the Belinsky circle were the real villains in the story of Dostoevsky in 1846 and 1847. Scraping and bowing to Belinsky and company, they made a bad situation worse—especially for the young writer.

The domestic footmen of the Belinsky circle were literary in name only. They cared little for intellectual and aesthetic concerns. They rarely picked up a book, much less a pen. Beyond engaging writers, they did little other than eat, sleep, and receive the world with apathy and indifference. What these individuals lacked in substance, they made up for in style. The only art they pursued was that of posturing and pose. Consciously and unconsciously, the have-nots of the Belinsky circle parodied the haves. As rendered by Nekrasov in his spoof *The Stone Heart*, their names said it all. There was The Poet in Soul and The Noble Personality. There was The Artistic Nature and The Practical Head. There was The Library and The Newspaper. There was Sputnik, The Element of Good Breeding, and The All-Around (and Also Embracing) Nature.

The attendants to the Belinsky circle kept the writers in the group in good working order. With no other purpose in life, they did their job well. For their literary guests, they ran literary hotels. Star boarders were surrounded with laughter and good cheer; stroked with flattering and fawning; titillated with gossip and news; and regaled with jam, tea, pretzels, books, pillows, money, and cigars. To their lettered clients, also, the maître d' qua managers of the Belinsky circle offered maximum security and comfort. Parroting views and opinions, often conflicting or diametrically opposed, was one service. Helping with correspondence and engaging editors, publishers, and booksellers was a second. Parading as writers and critics extolling geniuses was a third. Nothing fazed the hospitallers of the Belinsky circle. They saw and understood everything. They embraced and relished everyone.

The writers of the Belinsky circle obliged with gusto. Outwardly they proclaimed the moral and aesthetic sensitivities of their sidekicks, but inwardly they looked to more pragmatic virtues. They ran their attendants ragged, seeing them as creditors who supplied funds; caterers who furnished truffles and champagne; and clerks who, like Gogol's Akaky Akakievich, copied manuscripts or who, like Dostoevsky's Devushkin or Golyadkin, suffered insults and injuries. Anything could trigger hazings and dressing-downs, sneers and jeers: a dinner that was not up to snuff, a book that was delivered late, a request that wives or children attend a gathering. Even as the members of the Belinsky circle championed idealistic youth, they did not hesitate to dine at the expense of a boyish sponsor before being ejected by an outraged parent footing the bill. Even as they penned stories about tender marriage and love, they did not waver in salivating over tales of followers in marital distress, of wives beating husbands, even seeking out victims with black eyes with faux-solace and support. The members of the Belinsky circle championed liberalism and democracy, but they did not tolerate images and ideas other than their own. They extolled harmony and peace, but they did not think twice about unleashing adherents on enemies and rivals.

The antics of Nekrasov, Panaev, Turgenev, and others exacerbated the tension and bad feeling between Dostoevsky and the Russian literary world. Already nervous and high-strung, the writer of one success and four failures struggled with demons from both without and within. Dostoevsky began to withdraw from Belinsky and his circle, but he was hardly quiet in his retreat. Seething with anger and bile, the young writer charged subversion and spite. Everyone was laughing at him, he believed, both to his face and behind his back. Not unlike the heroes of his fiction, he was at war with the world.

Critics rubbed salt into wounds. Although reviewers received Dostoevsky's *Poor Folk* along party lines—fiery liberals took on passionate conservatives—members of both camps took Dostoevsky to task for what they saw as the shortcomings of the work.

All agreed that as a writer, Dostoevsky lacked discipline. *Poor Folk*, they charged, was a molehill, not a mountain. It suffered from aimless creativity: pages of trifles. Details were numerous and repetitive, extraneous and tiresome. Language was prolix and long-winded, mawkish and sentimental. Images and ideas smacked of Lermontov, Gogol, and Hryhory Kvitka. Hero and heroine were types and daguerreotypes. To see the clerk Poprishchin in Gogol's *Diary of a Madman*, one critic sniffed, was to see them all. For reviewers of all colors and stripes, the writer of *Poor Folk* ran a distant second to the author of *Dead Souls*. He was Gogol writ small.

Ironically, in their censure of *Poor Folk*, liberal and conservative critics came close to understanding Dostoevsky's motives for the work. Unlike Belinsky or Nekrasov, they were not taken in by the faux pathos and bathos of the narrative. The pictures of poverty in the piece, they maintained, were random and added little to the story. Reviewers also did not see Makar Devushkin and Varvara Dobroselova as insulted and injured. Rather, they indicted hero and heroine as users and abusers with agendas, grudges, and ends.

For both liberal and conservative critics, Makar Devushkin was a loser who deserved life's blows. He was not Gogol's hapless Akaky Akakievich but an individual who could advance in life. For all his aloofness, Makar was also seen by reviewers as an avid social animal. He was consumed by ambition, as well as by the rumors and gossip about him. Furthermore, Makar suffered from wounded pride, taking umbrage at Akaky Akakievich, to whom, he sensed, he was too close for comfort. Varvara caused even greater anger and consternation in that heroine regarded hero as a slave, not a savior. Particularly irksome to critics were the final scenes of *Poor Folk,* in which Varvara not only told Makar of her upcoming marriage in a cold, offhand way but also, even more callously, tormented him with orders for her upcoming wedding to another.

Reviewers were not immune either to the sexual darkness of the work. They noted how Makar called Varvara "little mother" and bore the name Lovelace. They also recorded how Varvara, foreshadowing the heroine in *A Gentle Creature* (1876), opted for a monster for a mate who more than met his match. Even as critics moaned and groaned over hero and heroine— Varvara recalled Shakespeare's Desdemona, one said—they remarked that the two assuaged searing fear and angst with sentimental tenderness and concern.

Reviewers were even more united in their condemnation of *The Double.* Conservative critics were particularly gleeful, rejoicing that they had been right about the so-called genius all along. Dostoevsky had regressed as a writer, both "right" and "left" groups said. The initial blunders of his first work had become enduring mistakes and inadequacies in the second. Dostoevsky, they continued, had grown even more verbose, sterile, and boring. Indeed, the faults and failings of *The Double* were so great that one critic wondered if Dostoevsky had penned an inferior piece to amuse himself at public expense.

What Dostoevsky had done in *The Double,* liberal and conservative reviewers went on to charge, was pathological, nightmarish, and corpse-like. With his second work, they added, Dostoevsky was eating Gogol's dust, his latest effort being no more than a parody of the great writer. Anyone who read *The Double,* critics agreed, merged with the hero and became diminished and destroyed. In their view also, it would have been easier on everyone if author had accompanied hero to the madhouse on the first page of the work, not on the last. Throw in "Mr. Prokharchin," liberal and conservative reviewers concluded, and a former talent like Dostoevsky had to face a bitter truth: he had only stepped out in the clothing of an artist. He had a tragic sense, but only from under piles of manure.

The failures of Dostoevsky's "Mr. Prokharchin," "The Landlady," and "A Novel in Nine Letters" only deepened the anger, confusion, and dismay over the young writer. Dostoevsky, critics agreed, had turned inward. He had retreated from civic realism to gothic romanticism. He had forsaken social exposé for schlock sensationalism. He had repudiated enlightened politics for specious psychology. He had replaced men and women in urban "corners" and "depths" with madmen, misers, and mystics from dark and demented worlds. Like jackals around wounded prey, "left" and "right" reviewers linked arms with members of the Belinsky circle in seeing Dostoevsky as smoke, not fire.

A particularly troubling feature in the darkening assessments of Dostoevsky was the problematic stance of Belinsky toward his former protégé. If memoirists in 1846 and 1847 attested to the great critic's initial praise of *Poor Folk* in private, they also noted his subsequent if almost immediate doubt about the young writer and his works in public. More than anyone else in his circle, Belinsky had had his fill of Dostoevsky's shenanigans. He was particularly incensed that Dostoevsky had rejected him as a mentor, and that the would-be genius wanted success without sweat. He also had grave reservations about Dostoevsky's well-being, wondering, accurately and loudly, if the young writer's instability would get the better of his literature and life. Belinsky loved and valued Dostoevsky; but he also pitied and grieved for the young man, fearing, again presciently, that he would waste or even scotch his talent in self-deception and destruction.

Given Belinsky's growing misgivings about Dostoevsky, it is not surprising that in his articles and reviews, he damned his charge's latest works, and even *Poor Folk*, with faint praise. Platitudes and clichés were the order of the day. The success of *Poor Folk*, Belinsky maintained, was beyond a doubt. It was poetic and creative, humorous and simple, sensitive and tragic. In his first work, Belinsky continued, Dostoevsky shook the souls of readers; he forced them to laugh through tears.

Poor Folk, though, failed in key criteria that Belinsky held dear for art. It did not spring from a knowledge of life. It did not break free from the melodrama of French novelists. Belinsky fretted that if only Dostoevsky had cut *Poor Folk* by 10 percent and rid his piece of repetitions and redundancies, his debut in fiction would have been beyond artistic reproach.

Even worse, perhaps, Belinsky missed Dostoevsky's intentions for the piece. Wrongly he proclaimed Makar Devushkin a model of humanity and Varvara Dobroselova a paragon of virtue. Equally off the mark was Belinsky's avowal that with Varenka, Makar was a knight in shining armor who sought to rescue an imperiled Pauline. Even more outrageous was Belinsky's contention that Makar could have married Varenka, if only because no one other than himself could sacrifice so much on her behalf.

Belinsky had even less use for *The Double*. As with *Poor Folk*, he began with well-meaning if perfunctory praise. Dostoevsky's second work was for him more masterly and bold than the first: a wellspring of intelligence, truth, and art. If *The Double* was not a triumph with the public, though, he knew the reasons why. As with other reviewers of *The Double*, Belinsky charged that what were flaws and failings in Dostoevsky's first novel were now monstrous weaknesses in the second. The young writer had not learned his literary lessons. He was still writing in a slapdash and sloppy way, with little concern for measure, tact, and restraint. Proving his point, Belinsky even added a vicious parody of Golyadkin's utterances in the work.

He was only getting started. If Dostoevsky would have done well to shorten *Poor Folk* by 10 percent, Belinsky complained, he would have done even better to cut *The Double* by a third. The strengths of *The Double*, he continued, only underscored its weaknesses. The piece reached literary heights, but in such a rich and unrelenting way that it left the few readers who finished the piece not only with an aching head and stomach but also with a marked preference for the works of Alexandre Dumas père and Eugène Sue. In a word, *The Double* was a disaster in both content and form.

Belinsky also slammed *The Double* by seeing the hero as a construct that was social, not psychological. In his view, Golyadkin was an exemplar of lower-class urban males who, from frustrated ambition, go off the deep end, courtesy of a sickly if not demonic sensibility and suspiciousness of life. Dostoevsky's bold break-up of Golyadkin into a loser-Senior and a winner-Junior was dismissed as the stuff of mentally illness, the prerogative of doctors, not poets.

Dostoevsky's "Mr. Prokharchin" fared even worse. The sporadic flashes of talent in the work, the critic contended, were mired in darkness and pretense. In a parting blow to Dostoevsky's early fiction, Belinsky claims he had to force himself to finish "A Novel in Nine Letters."

With his misgivings about the four works after *Poor Folk*, Belinsky burst the bubble of Dostoevsky's alleged genius and fame. In no uncertain terms, he declined to anoint Dostoevsky the new messiah of Russian literature, the heir-successor to Pushkin, Lermontov, and Gogol. Such accolades, Belinsky declared, were childish and absurd. They led nowhere and explained nothing. Dostoevsky did not stand higher than his predecessors, the critic continued. He did not even stand alongside them as an equal; rather, he had only had the good fortune to come after them.

Not pulling any punches, Belinsky also proclaimed Dostoevsky's dependence on Gogol. Even more brutally, perhaps, he insisted that the author of *Dead Souls* would remain for the young writer a father figure, a Columbus to help him navigate his way through art. How much, Belinsky lamented, did the writer of *Poor Folk* have to learn from the writer of *Dead Souls* in both substance and style. Gogol was a writer for the masses, but Dostoevsky a dallier for dilettantes. Gogol showed no contradictions in his writing, but Dostoevsky, in his works, had muddled content and form. Belinsky make the ranking painfully clear. Expanding the aesthetic distance further, he insisted that readers and reviewers eschew listing Dostoevsky along with Pushkin, Lermontov, and Gogol.

Needless to say, Dostoevsky was stung deeply by the critics' reviews. He was not stupid. He saw that behind the clamor and delight over his writing, there were serious reservations about his talent. Also rankling to Dostoevsky were charges that *Poor Folk* and *The Double* were boring, flaccid, and difficult if not impossible to read. Even more hurtful, if not insulting, was the claim that there was little difference between him and his ill-fated characters—he and Makar Devushkin shared the same mug.

The pièce de résistance was the assertion of ties, even subservience, to Gogol. Here Dostoevsky's anger knew no bounds. In no way would he acknowledge dependence on the great master. He was more profound than Gogol, the young writer ranted. He analyzed people and things in ways that Gogol never could or would, he raved. Far more than the writer of *Dead Souls*, the author of *Poor Folk* and *The Double* was doing something very new and dramatic in Russian literature. Why else, Dostoevsky reasoned, were people reading and rereading him in such a frenzied way? Why else was *The Petersburg Miscellany* (read: *Poor Folk* as the main attraction in the publication) selling like hotcakes in the provinces? Why were fans treating his works as lavish feasts, reading only a chapter a day so as not to exhaust themselves, but to smack their lips with pleasure? Alexander Herzen and Ivan Goncharov might be nipping at his heels, but he need not worry, Dostoevsky told himself and others. He still held first place among contemporary Russian writers. Indeed, he hoped to stay there forever. Dostoevsky may have been bloodied, but he was unbowed. He would show them all.

Or so he thought.

Ironically, in the two years after *Poor Folk*, the more Dostoevsky swelled externally with self-induced accolades and applause, the more he shrank internally with self-inspired doubt and despair. The devolution was sudden and swift, with sins of omission and commission everywhere in view.

If, consciously or unconsciously, in 1846 and 1847 Dostoevsky entered upon what he later recalled as a sad and fateful time, he had only himself to blame. The sudden success of *Poor Folk* had so inflated the writer's being that he lost contact not only with reality but also with everyone and everything that had afforded him harmony, stability, and peace. Dostoevsky did not forget his roots so much as he ripped them out with his hands. The values and verities instilled in him by father Mikhail and mother Maria stabilized him no longer. The parental lessons of faith, hope, and love that he had internalized during the first twenty-four years of his existence he expunged almost entirely in the following two. For one thing, Dostoevsky forgot God. If, before the success of *Poor Folk*, he had filled letters with appeals to the Almighty, or comments on deific mercy, justice, and goodness, he did not do so now. Not once in his missives in 1846 and 1847 was there the slightest mention of a supreme being. (Professed shock at Belinsky's disparagement of Christ at this time Dostoevsky recalled many years later, in 1873 entries of *Diary of a Writer*, after he had got religion.)

For another thing, Dostoevsky abandoned family and friends. Beyond occasional notes to brother Mikhail, he lost contact with brothers and sisters, uncles and aunts. Members of the clan often had no idea where he was or what he was doing. With the prodigal son or nephew, they rejoiced over rare missives or contacts. Friends, too, were cast aside, recipients of letters that were sporadic, fleeting, and scribbled on scraps of paper. Women also continued to be absent from his purview. At gatherings and events, Dostoevsky engaged members of the opposite sex only in occasional dances or in brief and polite conversations. Even more serious, perhaps, Dostoevsky no longer kept mental company with the theologians and philosophers, writers and artists, who had so excited his childhood, adolescence, and youth. Indeed, he stopped reading them altogether.

The ill-treatment shown to family and friends was extended to others. Not content with alienating members of the Belinsky circle, Dostoevsky also estranged other agents of the Russian literary world. He quarreled with booksellers for bleeding him dry and for withholding his works from the public for better prices and profits. He also ran afoul of editors and publishers, setting high-handed terms for unwritten works, failing to keep promises, and insisting that he and his writing were worth more, much more, than he was offered.

More than ever, Dostoevsky wounded himself. Disorder and dissoluteness claimed heavy tolls. Debts, loans, and IOUs mounted precariously. Illnesses—real and imagined; past, present, and future—promised an early grave. Complaints included a body that was fevered and trembling, nerves that were sick and shot, and a heart that palpitated dangerously. Bouts of apathy and boredom gave way to pipe dreams of life in Italy, to spells of sadness, lethargy, and dread, and to preparations for his wake and funeral.

Even more painful, perhaps, Dostoevsky wondered if the critics were correct in their claims. Increasingly, he found writing difficult. *The Double*, the young writer admitted, had given him fits. With "Mr. Prokharchin," "The Landlady," and "A Novel in Nine Letters," he seemed to be declining, even disintegrating, as a writer. In a rare moment of honesty, Dostoevsky also acknowledged that he had failed expectations, and that exhaustion and haste had ruined *The Double*. It took no arm-twisting on the young writer's part to agree, implicitly, with Belinsky's disavowal of his second work as muddle, foulness, and trash.

More than once in 1846 and 1847, Dostoevsky saw the collapse of projects and plans, leaving him to flop and flounder like the very people he despised. Despite claims to the contrary, he was facing stiff competition from colleagues who had also begun their careers with a bang—admittedly, not with the furor of *Poor Folk*, but with strength and speed in subsequent writing. With or without the author of *Poor Folk*, Russian literature, particularly works of social exposé, was alive and well. In those same two years, Goncharov published *A Common Story*; Grigorovich, *The Village* and *Anton Goremyka*; Alexander Druzhinin, *Polinka Saks*; Ivan Turgenev, "Khor and Kalinych"; and Alexander Herzen, *Who Is to Blame?*, *Mimoezdom*, *Doctor Krupov*, and *The Thieving Magpie*. Dostoevsky ran the danger not just of being outpaced and outclassed but of being forgotten altogether. For the umpteenth time in his now twenty-six years of existence, Dostoevsky questioned if he had what it took to be a writer, if he could endure the difficulties and labor needed to establish himself in the Russian literary world.

In this dark time, though, there were bright spots. If Dostoevsky was anything in 1846 and 1847, he was a survivor who, by sheer will, moved from swamp to sun. He was not entirely downcast. He still had goals. He still needed success. When life was not dreary and cold, it could be warm and rich.

Although the young writer had lost touch with much of his family, he held fast to brother Mikhail—and, by extension, to his sister-in-law Emiliya and their two children. Here Dostoevsky was his old self, with demands for solace and support that were swift and sure, overbearing and outrageous. Would Mikhail be kind enough, Dostoevsky asked boldly, to manage his affairs, support his dreams, and fund his projects? Even more extreme, could his brother kindly take a leave of absence several months before his formal retirement from state service to join Dostoevsky in St. Petersburg earlier than planned? As before, Dostoevsky struck pay dirt. Ever the loyal brother, Mikhail agreed to everything.

Dostoevsky also became friends with Stepan Yanovsky, a physician and himself a character in the cast of the young writer's life. In the first two years after *Poor Folk*, he was a kindred spirit, a guardian angel, a psycho-spiritual brother, and, even more than Mikhail, Dostoevsky's closest friend and contact with reality.

Dostoevsky and Yanovsky had much in common. They were "doubles" in a positive sense. The two were relatively close in age: When they met in late 1846, Yanovsky was thirty-one. Dostoevsky twenty-five. Both came from serf-owning families of petty gentry. Both had spent their early years in provincial Russia. Dostoevsky summered near Tula, some one hundred miles south of Moscow. Yanovsky hailed from Kursk, approximately two hundred miles southwest of Tula, near the border with Ukraine. Both men had studied science. Dostoevsky had taken up engineering at the Main Engineering Academy in St. Petersburg; Yanovsky had turned to medicine at the Surgical-Medical Academy in Moscow, after which he was a teacher of natural history and a doctor for the members of the Forestry Institute and of the Preobrazhensky Regiment in St. Petersburg. In spring 1846, when Yanovsky met Dostoevsky, he had just transferred to the Department of Public Medical Training in the Ministry of the Interior. He had also begun a private practice.

Dostoevsky and Yanovsky loved fiction and had similar aesthetic tastes and worldviews. (While studying medicine, Yanovksy also audited lectures in literature by Stepan Shevyryov.) Both thought empirically. Both shunned cards as well as wine, women, and song. To the mix, Yanovsky added fervent beliefs in God and country, tenets, it will be recalled, set aside by Dostoevsky.

Yanovsky found Dostoevsky in rough shape. Beyond the writer's already noted complaints, Yanovsky diagnosed additional problems. Some were physical; most were mental. Scurvy and anemia wracked the writer's body. Hallucinations, panics, and fears of paralysis and strokes warped his soul. In his newfound friend, Yanovsky encountered an even more disturbing complication. To him Dostoevsky confided that death was no stranger, having come for him more than once. In fact, the young writer often feared that he would die in his sleep.

Treatment by Yanovsky was part conventional science, part common sense. Two or three comforting words were often all that was needed to set the young writer at ease and to convince him that most of his illnesses were in his head. In Yanovsky, too, Dostoevsky found what he cherished most: conversations, intimate and intense, which allowed him to hold forth on literature and life.

Doctor also gained from patient. Dostoevsky was for Yanovsky a mesmerizing teacher, virtuoso, and guide who imparted lifelong values and ideals. Not for nothing did Yanovsky compare Dostoevsky to Socrates.

Several claims Yanovsky made about Dostoevsky during the first two years after *Poor Folk*, though, require clarification. The first was Yanovsky's avowal that in 1846 and 1847 the young writer experienced occasional bouts of "falling sickness" or *"epilepsia"*—several times to a life-threatening degree. The observation must be taken *cum grano salis*, for several reasons. First,

Yanovsky made the remark only as a passing comment in a letter to a Russian newspaper in 1881, almost forty years after they were supposed to have occurred (and two weeks after the writer's death). Absent from the good doctor's allegations were precise details about these afflictions. The two cited instances were maddeningly vague. It was also only in the second one that the young writer was said to have had convulsions. Further undercutting Yanovsky's claim as to Dostoevsky's epilepsy was his admission not only that his patient was a notorious hypochondriac but also that he sensed the onset of "falling sickness" at specific times and places—trips to Haymarket Square, a key setting in his major novels, were a common trigger—a foreboding that Yanovsky himself dismissed as neurosis, not neurology.[1]

Three things complicate matters further. First, Apollon Maykov, an alleged witness to one of Dostoevsky's bouts, never noted such an event in writing. Three others individuals—Alexander Poretsky, Pyotr Tseidler, and Ivan Lkhovsky—who, along with Maykov, were named by Yanovsky as having been informed of Dostoevsky's attack three days later, were also silent about the episode.

Second, independent of the doctor's account was the testimony of Mikhail Yazykov, who, in an article written two weeks after Yanovsky's, claimed that Dostoevsky suffered an epileptic attack at a gathering in his home in the summer of 1847.

Weaknesses in Yazykov's account of Dostoevsky's alleged epilepsy mirrored those of Yanovsky. Yazykov stated that Dostoevsky showed initial symptoms of the attack—a facial expression that was agitated, eyes that were frightened, a voice that was anxious and hollow, together with sudden confusion over his surroundings and mad dashes for air—all in the presence of Panaev, Pavel Annenkov, Turgenev, and possibly Nekrasov. Although these individuals would have delighted in having new ammunition to use against the writer, again, none of them noted such an occurrence in writing then or later. Even more revealing, perhaps, all four men were conveniently gone or exiting the scene (it is not clear which) when the real fun began: Dostoevsky, allegedly doused with cold water, fled the premises and ran down Liteinyi Prospket in central Petersburg before being stopped by Yazykov in a carriage, who now, *mirabile dictu*, found the young writer conscious, calm, and heading for home.[2] Third, and even more serious, perhaps, is the fact that Dostoevsky himself admitted in 1849 that he suffered not from "falling sickness" but from hypochondria three years in a row. Also, looking back on physical failings in this period almost a decade later, Dostoevsky reiterated that he had been seized not with epilepsy but with great spiritual illness and hypochondria, often to a powerful degree.

To return to Yanovsky, it is also conceivable that he held Dostoevsky in such awe that for him the young writer, via "fainting sickness," perceived, if not inhabited, unearthly realms. Just as students at the Main Engineering Academy saw Dostoevsky as a mystic, divorced from everyday persuasions and preoccupations, so could Yanovsky have come to see Dostoevsky-cum-*epilepsia* as a prophet or "holy fool" who embraced more, much more, than others could.

Still another observation by Yanovsky in this period requires discussion. Most certainly, Dostoevsky in 1846 and 1847 was not, as the doctor claimed him to be, a patriot, a believer in Christ, or an advocate for the poor. As has already been noted, in the first two years after *Poor Folk*, God and country were the last things on Dostoevsky's mind. Earlier concerns for the insulted and injured had also fallen by the wayside. If unfortunates did figure in the writer's thoughts and travels at this time, it was only marginally or, as with Ivan Karamazov in Dostoevsky's final work, as constructs that tormented mind, not heart. It should also be recalled that the heroes of his first five works were not from the lower reaches of society. They had jobs, salaries, and skills—even humane superiors. For the young writer, social or economic injustice was not an issue. No liberal or radical was he.

The discrepancy between Dostoevsky during the first two years after *Poor Folk* and Yanovsky's account of him can be explained simply. The Dostoevsky recalled in 1881 was not the young writer thrashing about in literature and life; rather, he was a much older, established, and successful individual who, after years of searing trial and error, believed that only God and Russia promised happiness and salvation. In no way was the Dostoevsky of 1846 and 1847 the Dostoevsky of 1881.

In 1846 and 1847, Dostoevsky did not always have to be the star of the show. He could take comfort in things outside of himself. Music, particularly Italian opera and Russian singers, captured his fancy. So did interests in medicine, crania, nervous systems, spiritual disorders, and illnesses of the brain.

Dostoevsky also enjoyed the company of select families such as the Vielgorskys, the Beketovs, and the Maykovs. Even more revealing, he loved to arrange gatherings with close colleagues and friends. Dinners at restaurants and hotels were modest and cheap—no more than two rubles per person—but embraced merriment and inspired memories long afterward.

At these gatherings, Dostoevsky was the consummate host. True to form, he drank little—a thimble of vodka, a quarter glass of wine—but he was the life of the party. He loved to toast guests, to engage them in an open and sincere way, and to give them hearty send-offs and encouraging words before they reentered the cold, cruel world. In contrast to the get-togethers with the Vielgorskys, Beketovs, and Maykovs, the dinners at restaurants and hotels had an unwashed, bohemian flair. In the writer's idea, all present were self-styled proletarians who eschewed the daily grind and regular paychecks to pursue dreams as writers and students of literature, philosophy, and art. Amidst such company, Dostoevsky held court and continued unimpeded as teacher-mentor to novice writers with ambitions similar to his own.

Equally important, Dostoevsky still had his fans. Alexei Pleshcheev saw the writer as a bright new star. Valerian Maykov deemed Dostoevsky highly original, hardly Gogol's sidekick. Indeed, Maykov hit the nail on the head when he said that Gogol was a social writer, but Dostoevsky was a psychological one. Gogol, Maykov continued, traveled the length and breadth of Russia, whereas Dostoevsky inhabited the even vaster, if more challenging, expanses of the mind. Maykov agreed that Dostoevsky was not an easy read, but that the results were worth the time and effort. It was, he said, only after readers and reviewers explored *Poor Folk* and subsequent stories a second or third time that they could grasp the profundity, perception, and psychology in Dostoevsky's writing. Remarkable also was Maykov's prescience, that is, his striking ability to light upon virtues in Dostoevsky's early works that would be the seedbeds of his later ones. When Maykov called the final encounter between Makar and Varvara tortured, oppressive, and despotic, he unknowingly pointed to the torturous ties between men and women in Dostoevsky's major novels, for example, how Nastasya Filippovna abused Rogozhin and Myshkin in *The Idiot*; or how Katerina Ivanovna and Grushenka assaulted Dmitri in *The Brothers Karamazov*.

Maykov also had high if singular praise for *The Double*. In his second work, he asserted, Dostoevsky was a scientist of the body, a psychologist of the mind, and a seer of the soul. Just as Maykov foreshadowed the battles of the sexes in *The Idiot* and *The Brothers Karamazov* with comments on Makar and Varvara in *Poor Folk*, so now did he foresee the birth of the hero in *Notes of the Underground* and of Raskolnikov in *Crime and Punishment* with claims that Golyadkin was a slave but bent on personhood in life. Given such insights into Dostoevsky's early work, it is a pity that Maykov did not have Belinsky's authority. It is an even greater tragedy that Maykov left life so early—he died of a stroke at age twenty-four while swimming, just before, according to Turgenev, he would have been named Belinsky's successor as a critic[3]—since he might have steered readers and reviewers to see *Poor Folk, The Double,* and other early works in a more positive and accurate light and thus save Dostoevsky from the disastrous mistake, his involvement in the Petrashevsky affair, which almost ended his life, let alone his literary career.

In the first two years after *Poor Folk*, Dostoevsky held fast to his dream as writer. He would not accept failure or a humdrum existence. Thrown from his metaphorical horse, the young writer got back up on his feet, dusted himself off, and started again. He also had scores to settle. Pen in hand, Dostoevsky again waged war on all. Indeed, he seemed almost glad for his quarrels with Nekrasov, Belinsky, and others so that he could burn, if not blow up, bridges behind him and work unimpeded, and independently, for his idea of art.

In his mind at least, Dostoevsky had ample albeit inflated proof for his revolt. He could still tell a good story, spellbinding listeners with tales of drunkards and other "poor folk" that, taken from real life, were merciless, comical, and humane. Ideas and images that he deemed more original, lively, and bright begged for paper. His pen moved to inspiration from his soul. He was swamped with work, writing day and night, and seeing better days ahead. "The Landlady" was as crisp and successful as *Poor Folk*. The beginnings of a novel that would be *Netochka Nezvanova* was giving him no peace. Plans to publish the story, along with *Poor Folk* and a revision of *The Double* as separate and illustrated works, appeared with schemes for a series of translations, courtesy of brother Mikhail. Within two years, Dostoevsky mused, he would have a complete edition of his writings in print. Previous readers, reviewers, and booksellers be damned! Other people would take their place and applaud, defend, and publish him.

Beyond fictional works, Dostoevsky was also trying his hand at feuilleton-style journalism: a series of 1847 articles, titled "The Petersburg Chronicle," in which, via the breezy, gossipy style that would become a hallmark of many speakers in his mature works, Dostoevsky made clear his likes and dislikes in literature and life. It can be argued that more than any other work to date, "The Petersburg Chronicle" was his most significant step as a thinker and an artist. That is, whereas in *Poor Folk*, "The Double," "Mr. Prokharchin," "The Landlady," and "A Novel in Nine Letters," Dostoevsky painted muddy canvases of individuals disaffected with life, he, in "The Petersburg Chronicle," conceptualized, logically and simply, many of the images and ideas that he would sanction or censure in his later fiction.

In "The Petersburg Chronicle," Dostoevsky defended Russian history and nationality against what he saw as the attacks of stupid Frenchmen, armchair intellectuals, and the public at large. Vengeful ridicule of circles and salons merged with insightful musings about beings who shifted, at will, between sinners and saints, oppressors and oppressed.

Equally revealing, in these articles Dostoevsky praised outlooks and views that, later in life, he would condemn with a vengeance. Peter the Great, his city, and his idea for Russia drew only praise and applause from the twenty-six-year-old writer. Indeed, Dostoevsky sounded very much like Belinsky and the other Westernizers of the time when he rejected the worldview of the Slavophiles as dreamy and dead. In its place, the young writer put forth St. Petersburg as model and exemplar for native minds, hearts, and souls. For such a reality, though, Dostoevsky foresaw a rough and rocky road. The Russian window on the West, he said again à la Belinsky, was clouded with garbage and dust; but such disorder was necessary for national renewal and rebirth.

Changing metaphors, Dostoevsky saw St. Petersburg as a sturdy sapling that had been planted in a swamp but spread its roots throughout Russia, to industry, trade, science, education—and, of course, literature. In no way, Dostoevsky continued, were denizens of the northern Venice perishing under European influence. They were not soulless Germans: walking dead. Rather, citizens of St. Petersburg and elsewhere in Russia were experiencing a union of East and West: positive and principled, healthy and whole.

He had ample evidence for such a view. *Peterburzhtsy*, Dostoevsky insisted, were stoic fatalists no longer. Rather, they were curious, analytical, and discerning. Even more revealing and salutary, they were open, even confessional about their failings and faults. It came as small wonder, Dostoevsky went on to say, that Russian readers and reviewers wanted the same in their literature. Equally unsurprising, he added, was the public impatience and ire with contemporary writers. The demand was for literati to pick up pen and paper with no holds barred. Everyone and everything were subjects for them to disclose what people thought, said, and did.

In "The Petersburg Chronicle," though, Dostoevsky was under no illusions as to what he saw as shortcomings in the national character. Particularly annoying to him was the penchant of Russians to become excited by causes and ideas but never to follow through. Rather than pursue meaningful goals, they wasted time and lives in drink, duels, and cards. Presaging the moral monsters of Dostoevsky's mature fiction, they gave in to specious ideas and goals which, after painful, near-fatal trial and error, they later despised as sentimental and silly.

The most important aspect of "The Petersburg Chronicle," however, was Dostoevsky's fascination with dreamers. As he saw it, dreamers were men and women, as well as children, adolescents, and youths, who yearned for action and life but who experienced catastrophe and upheaval.

So intrigued was Dostoevsky with dreamers, though, that in the style of the "physiological" writing of the time, he not only embarked on engaging sketches of such types but also, unwittingly, set in motion characterizations of the wishful thinkers of his later writing. Externally, Dostoevsky saw dreamers as dark and dismal, terse and tense, weary and wan. He deemed such individuals overheated ideologues, burdened by skull-cracking thoughts and impressions, the content of which he, sadly, did not care to define. Additionally, Dostoevsky assessed dreamers as unbalanced dualities who are both happy and sad: egoists and boors.

Dreamers, Dostoevsky went on to say, were also failures and freaks at odds with the world. They withdrew into themselves. They hid from people and life, in corners that were inaccessible, disordered, and dirty. Dreamers also relished idleness and ease. Any effort—physical, mental, and spiritual— was for them anathema.

In Dostoevsky's view, dreamers dwelled between a rock and a hard place. On the one hand, they so feared life that they were submissive and inert. On the other hand, they struck back at their lot by seeing reality not as it was but as it should be—or, more accurately, as they wanted it to be. Such individuals, Dostoevsky insisted, did not plumb existence for ideas; rather, they imposed ideas on existence, to trap the world in structures and systems that were self-fashioned, self-serving, and self-preserving.

With idle minds as devil's workshops, Dostoevsky asserted that dreamers sought life in sensations, impressions, and moods. Sometimes these arose from a book, music, or memory, other times from daily trivia and trifles. More seriously, they often assumed a cerebral form. Indeed, dreamers for Dostoevsky could be so seduced by images and ideas that they lost all sense of reality and self. The thrills and spills that such yearning souls missed outside their bodies they more than relished inside them. They stepped forth as heroes and heroines of stories, novels, and tales. Religious myths competed with romantic intrigues; swashbuckling adventures vied with bloody melodramas; epic struggles contended with charming fairy tales. There were joys and sorrows, heavens and hells. There were captivating women and damsels in distress. There were heroic gestures, activities, and struggles. There were horrors and crimes. There was even an eternal if not apocalyptic flair. Space disappeared. Hours became minutes; eternities turned into moments.

It was also sensations, impressions, and moods that made Dostoevsky's dreamers feel alive, if not resurrected from the dead. With God and Christ not moving them to spiritual joy, and women not bringing them to physical bliss, Dostoevsky's wishful thinkers had only themselves with whom to experience delight. They also encountered alone their version of utopia and Eden. Indeed, for Dostoevsky, dreamers were so aroused by sensations, impressions, and moods that they entered into paradises that were splendid, grand, and filled with peace and love. Once there, they encountered physical and spiritual ecstasy. Their pulse quickened, their eyes filled with tears, and their cheeks became fevered and moist.

Such joy did not last, though. When it was over, it left dreamers hurt and hung over, even more dissatisfied, unfulfilled, and apathetic than previously. They also took away nothing from the experience. They recalled little of what had allegedly transpired, other than the beating hearts that returned them to earthbound and expanded hells.

Tragically, dreamers were for Dostoevsky a stiff-necked lot. Having refused to learn from their mistakes, they—willingly, perversely—committed them anew. It was a measure of their pathos that, in Dostoevsky's idea, not only did wishful thinkers celebrate the anniversaries of their fantasies and adventures but also, after denying efficacy, responsibility, and will for their actions, they marked their calendars for times when they deemed themselves happy and could dream anew. They appealed to existence not for life lessons or truths but for stimuli to reignite minds, hearts, and souls. Chance was a key and crucial factor. A book that fell into their hands, or a woman they saw on the street, was all they needed to fly through the air with the greatest of ease, and to re-create an impotent if self-destructive bliss.

Having lived vicariously as heroes, even as man-gods, Dostoevsky's dreamers refused to accept what the writer saw as a key truth, namely, that life is an endless contemplation of nature and daily being, Such a concept was for Dostoevsky's fantasists too quiet and mundane, too genuine and prosaic, and too dangerous and demeaning to be of value. Reflection on nature and being threatened ego and self. Even worse, it destroyed their view of the world. In no way could or would Dostoevsky's dreamers accept that running the show was God and life, not they. Equally abhorrent to them was the idea that they were specks in the universe, not its core or center. For Dostoevsky, such resistance got dreamers into trouble. It forced them to forsake ethics and morality. Twenty years before the fact, Dostoevsky laid the foundation for "all is permitted."

If Dostoevsky wrote insightfully about dreamers, it was because he—and everyone else—created life in their own image and likeness. Tired of the daily grind and fearful that he would destroy his talent and youth, Dostoevsky also went out on mental limbs, taking as truth self-styled, convoluted, and contradictory versions of people, places, and events. However paradoxically, Dostoevsky believed that the decline in his fame brought him closer to success. Even with a string of failures to his name, Dostoevsky held fast to the view that he held the public's love, fascination, and hope.

He clung fast to a grand view of self. Editors and publishers were inundating him with offers; they were throwing money at his feet. No doubt about it, Dostoevsky told himself (and anybody else in proximity), he would regain fame, even primacy as a writer.

It would not be Dostoevsky if he did not assert internal change as well. Things, distasteful and unpleasant, were giving way to changes that were useful and good. In a move that would make the villains of his later fiction blush, Dostoevsky professed that he was being reborn, physically and spiritually. Never before, he continued, had he experienced such abundance and clarity, equilibrium and health. *Mirabile dictu*, Dostoevsky even claimed to be debt-free!

For all the hoopla and good cheer, Dostoevsky failed to move forward. "The Landlady" was a failure. "The Petersburg Chronicle" ended as quickly as it had begun. Refusing to publish unfinished pieces, Dostoevsky had nothing to give to editors and publishers, from whom he often hid rather than approach them with empty hands. It would not be until 1849 that Dostoevsky published the first three parts of *Netochka Nezvanova*.

The young writer was also hardly secure financially. Even as funds came in from the publication of *Poor Folk*, he simply could not manage money. He owed everyone in town. He succumbed to fanciful schemes. He helped (or was exploited by) one and all. As Dostoevsky was the first to admit, if it were not for the kindness of others—the Maykovs, for one—he would have perished.

Stresses from without triggered strains from within. Despite Yanovsky's counsel and care, Dostoevsky went about in hazes and dazes. He suffered rushes of blood to the head. Existence, he told brother Mikhail, was becoming dual. External realities were overwhelming and fearsome. Internal ones ascended dangerously. Floods of fantasy inundated his being; surges of nerves plunged it into bottomless voids.

With an eye to readers and reviewers, particularly the members of the Belinsky circle, Dostoevsky charged that society championed false prophets and Pharisees, shamans and sages who, useless, repulsive, and vile, upheld the status quo. As with biblical demons, their name was legion. As with folk woodcuts, their message was cheap and mass-produced.

Striking out blindly, Dostoevsky chased away the people he loved—and who loved him—the most. Brother Mikhail was (again) first in line. In the first two years after *Poor Folk*, Mikhail moved from being Dostoevsky's sounding board for his hopes and dreams to a whipping boy for his frustrations and fears. Insult followed injury. In sporadic and scribbled notes, Dostoevsky engaged Mikhail in classic self-projection, chiding his brother for failings and wrongs of which he himself was guilty. Dostoevsky berated

Mikhail for withdrawing in silence and neglect, for eschewing a healthy life-style, for failing to be vibrant and bold, and for disparaging the thought of better times ahead. Even worse were moments when Dostoevsky, not unlike Varvara with Makar in *Poor Folk*, tormented Mikhail with elaborate, outrageous, and costly errands and requests. With Mikhail's wife and children, Dostoevsky could even be cruel. On a visit to his brother and his family in Revel (now Tallinn) in Estonia, Dostoevsky noted that he had been awkward and difficult. To Mikhail's wife, Emiliya, he was rude; to Mikhail's five-year old son, Fedya, spiteful.

Mikhail protested the injustice, but such complaints fell on deaf ears. At times, the young writer challenged Mikhail's objections as unjust. At other times, he engaged in self-recrimination and rebuke. For his misconduct toward Mikhail, Dostoevsky blamed illness and nerves. More revealingly, perhaps, he indicted himself for being repulsive and heartless: a mass of contradictions beyond comprehension and control. Only when external circumstances or incidents wrenched Dostoevsky violently from himself could he show heart and love. At still other times, Dostoevsky sought to mend fences with Mikhail by proclaiming himself to be the lesser of the two and by professing ultimate affection and sacrifice, saying that he was ready to die for his brother and his family.

Dostoevsky, though, had no intention of changing his ways. Akin to the characters in both his early and mature fiction, he regaled Mikhail with confessions that were false. The lists of failings and flaws were too swift and schematic; they lacked moves toward reconciliation, restitution, and true remorse. Indeed, one wonders if with Mikhail—not unlike the villains in, say, *Devils* and *The Brothers Karamazov*—Dostoevsky was boasting of his sins rather than disclosing them. Even more outrageous, perhaps, the young writer demanded that Mikhail—and by implication others—accept him, warts and all. After all, Dostoevsky complained self-pityingly if defensively, if only Mikhail, and the world at large, knew how he had suffered constantly and unjustly. Whatever Dostoevsky thought he was doing—or not doing—in his rapprochements with Mikhail, his breast-beating ended as quickly as it had begun. Other cares and concerns—his despair over *The Double* and his excitement over "The Landlady" and *Netochka Nezvanova* were key examples—diverted his attention. His own Underground Man, Dostoevsky spent days and nights alone. Even more like his infamous hero, he wondered how Mikhail, and anyone else for that matter, could love him. In truth, in 1846 and 1847, few could or would.

It comes as little surprise that when Dostoevsky reflected on his youth in the twilight of his existence, he saw the first two years after *Poor Folk* as a time when he both cursed and embraced the darkness. It is also safe to say that later in life, Dostoevsky came to understand the years 1846 and 1847 as an initial foray into a self-styled, self-imposed, and self-directed Golgotha, during which twelve years of crucifixion were followed by twenty years of gradual resurrection. Whether Dostoevsky attained the latter is a matter of debate; whether he achieved the former, especially in the first two years after *Poor Folk*, is beyond a doubt.

PART ONE

Pride before the Fall

Belinsky and the Aftermath of Poor Folk

When Vissarion Belinsky first met Dostoevsky in May 1845, he was thirty-six years old. He would die of tuberculosis exactly three years later, concluding a decade-long search for truth and meaning in life. Initially, Belinsky had espoused the German romantic idealism of Friedrich Schiller, Friedrich Schelling, and Georg Hegel and their universalist notions about poets, nations, and societies.

Then, in a famed "reconciliation with reality," he had looked to such French socialists as Pierre-Joseph Proudhon, Henri de Saint-Simon, Robert Lamennais, Charles Fourier, Étienne Cabet, Louis Blanc, and Pierre Leroux, who advocated secular worldwide brotherhoods as well as scientific restructurings of reality. More recently, Belinsky had become enamored with such left Hegelians as David Strauss and Ludwig Feuerbach, particularly their ideas on mechanistic and moral determinism, as well as their demands that communist worlds replace Christian ones. In the last two or three years of Belinsky's life, Annenkov wrote, the great critic was "concerned with the emerging definitions of the rights and obligations of man, with the new truths proclaimed by economic doctrines that were liquidating all notions of the old, displaced ideas about the moral, good, and the noble on earth, and, in their place, was putting formulas and theses of a purely rational character."[1]

At the core of Belinsky's quest were two additional, stirring beliefs. The first was his absolute faith in the sanctity and greatness of humankind. The second was his equally unshakeable confidence in the Westernizing path that Peter the Great had chosen for his homeland. Peter was for the eminent critic his "philosophy, [his] religion, [his] revelation to all that concerns Russia."[2]

In his final years, though, Belinsky was in even worse straits than the young Dostoevsky. For one thing, he was trapped in an unhappy marriage. Just a month before his nuptials to Maria Orlova, he confessed to his fiancée on October 13, 1843, that there was "nothing fiery, nothing ardent" in their relationship. Three years later, Belinsky chastised the woman on July 30, 1846, writing, "Nothing, neither living together nor separating [from each other], will teach you to understand my character."[3]

For another thing, Belinsky knew that his days were numbered. "I began to realize with horror and fear that I do not have long to go," he wrote to Vasily Botkin on February 6, 1843. Three years later, he confessed to Herzen his fear not only of death but also of familial ruin. "It is a terrible thing," he wrote, "to leave wife and daughter without a crust of bread."[4]

Even more serious, perhaps, Belinsky was tired of the literary grind. Successful as the great critic was, he struggled to make a living materially and mentally. "The walls of my quarters are hateful to me," he wrote to Botkin on December 9–10, 1842. "Like a prisoner returning to jail, I return to them with despair and repugnance in my soul." On February 6, 1843, he continued, telling Botkin, "Work on *The Fatherland Notes* has come to disgust me to the point of morbidity." Three years later, Belinsky had had his fill of the publication and its editor, Andrei Kraevsky. "Working against a deadline for a journal sucks the living strength out of me," he complained to Herzen on January 2, 1846, "like a vampire . . . ever ready to suck the blood and soul of a person and then to throw him out the window like a squeezed lemon."[5]

His new position at *The Contemporary* only exacerbated his angst. If Dostoevsky had had difficulties with Nekrasov and Panaev, so did Belinsky. He wrote to Turgenev on March 1, 1847, "Nekrasov was one of the worst; perhaps only Panaev is worse." On February 6, 1847, he complained to Botkin: "My repugnance for literature and journalism *as a trade* grows from day to day, and I do not know what will become of it. It is more difficult to fight repugnance than need; it is a disease."[6]

Needless to say, Belinsky felt alone, socially and spiritually; but again, as with the young Dostoevsky, his isolation was self-imposed. The more extreme his convictions, the less he shared them with the few friends he had. The more radical his thinking, the greater his fear and frustration for his country and its citizens. Belinsky was experiencing a Dostoevskian duality all his own. If he was split in mind and soul, it was because of his insistence that art maintain absolute integrity, but also that it serve sociopolitical ends.

Dostoevsky was conflicted deeply over Belinsky, particularly during the eighteen or so months of their close relationship. On the one hand, he saw Belinsky as a personal and professional success. The great critic was a gentleman and a scholar who cared for his family as much as he did for Russia. He was also a being who understood national life better than anyone else. Equally unusual for the young Dostoevsky, Belinsky was a man of thought and action: an individual who not only crashed through walls—political, social, and aesthetic—but also pondered how they stymied Russia and Russians. For Dostoevsky, Belinsky was not "superfluous." He did not yield to apathy; he did not brood about life and fate. Energized by ideas and warmed by progress, he was the happiest man in his homeland. Animated and intense, Belinsky brimmed with confidence and aplomb. Pragmatic and philosophical, he championed men and women, railroads and art. His only sadness was that growth came slowly. "Why not today, why not tomorrow?" was his mantra-like lament.

With hindsight, Dostoevsky saw Belinsky as a mentor and guide, even as a parental figure who extended the life lessons of father Michael and mother Maria in his childhood, adolescence, and youth.

On the other hand, Dostoevsky became increasingly hostile to Belinsky, for straightforward reasons. He chafed against the great critic's attempt to bend him to his aesthetic will and to make him a critic of political and social ills. More to the point, Dostoevsky never forgave Belinsky for the fact that he had applauded *Poor Folk* but castigated *The Double*, "Mr. Prokharchin," "The Landlady," and "A Novel in Nine Letters."

More important, perhaps, with the hindsight of some thirty years after events—a period during which Dostoevsky became increasingly conservative politically and socially, and was also writing his political novel *Devils*—his anger with Belinsky assumed a darker and deeper cast.

Belinsky, he charged, had been the catalyst for personal and national catastrophe. Having appealed to Western liberals, socialists, and communists for deliverance and salvation, Belinsky had led both Dostoevsky and Russia astray. He had moved from God-man to man-gods, from solid and sacred values of the past to seductive and shimmering fantasies of the future. Belinsky, Dostoevsky claimed, deified reason, science, and economics; he had debunked Christ and religion; he had renounced private ownership, traditional values, and individual responsibility. Even as Belinsky foresaw the mess, even monstrosity, he was creating—the dream-turned-nightmare of the sociopolitical ant heap—he carried on with this personal and political madness. Belinsky, Dostoevsky continued, was hardly the solution to Russia's ills. He was part of the problem, shameful and stinking.

The rancor was unending. Belinsky, Dostoevsky declared, was stubborn and spiteful, pushy and proud. He was also petty and powerless, but with a dangerous and destructive streak. On good days, Belinsky was an ideologue, a retrograde, and a traitor. On bad days, he was a louse and a "shitty insect." The man was a host of contradictions: a fanatic who swung wildly between extremist rights and lefts, as well as a nihilist who covered the world with spittle and shame. No one escaped Belinsky's venom and wrath. Westernizers suffered the same reprimands and rebukes as Slavophiles. Russians were chronic basket cases, beyond resurrection and renewal. Indeed, Belinsky believed that if Russia traveled a special path, it was not to a third Rome but over a cliff into an abyss. Even as an émigré, Dostoevsky added, Belinsky would have been Turgenev's Rudin come to life: an empty talker of spurious causes and campaigns.

Given such personal and professional shortcomings, Dostoevsky concluded, it was not surprising that as a critic, Belinsky was so wrong about so many things. His views on Pushkin's *Eugene Onegin* and Gogol's *Dead Souls* topped the list. How could it be otherwise, Dostoevsky noted, when aesthetics concerned Belinsky but little. Literature that indicted and propagandized, that chose fact over fiction, that stressed sensation and scandal, and that grabbed readers by their necks and throttled them was for the critic the stuff of the national literary expression. Anything else was muddle and mess.

Good or bad, Belinsky loomed large in Dostoevsky's life. He was for the writer the father who had given him professional life, but with sins that were visited on his most famous son.

1846 and after
Fyodor Dostoevsky, from *A Writer's Diary*

My entrance onto the literary scene—God knows how many years ago—was for me a sad and fateful time.

1846 and after
Fyodor Dostoevsky, from dictated notes

He first retired [from service] and then wrote his rather large story, *Poor Folk.* . . . Its success was rare in the full sense of the word. But then in the next few years, his lack of health harmed his literary activities.

1846 and after
Fyodor Dostoevsky, from an 1858 letter to Mikhail Katkov

> Work for money and work for art are for me two incompatible things. Because of such a thing, I suffered the entire three years of my literary activity in Petersburg. I did not wish to profane my best ideas, my best plans for stories and novels. I worked hurriedly for deadlines. I so loved [these ideas and plans] that I wanted to create in an unhurried way, with love, so much so that, it seemed, I would rather die than to engage my best ideas in a dishonest way. Always being in constant debt to A. A. Kraevsky (who, by the way, never extorted work from me, but always gave me time [to write]), I was tied hand and foot.

1846 and after
Fyodor Dostoevsky, from his testimony to the Investigatory Commission for the Petrashevsky affair

> I have been sick constantly, suffering from attacks of hypochondria for three years running.

1846 and after
Stepan Yanovsky, from his memoirs

> During the entire time of my acquaintance with Dostoevsky, I never once heard that he was in love or that he loved any woman with passion. Before his exile to Siberia, I never saw him even hint at such things, that is, to study and analyze the character of the women or girls we both knew.

1846 and after
Nikolai Grech, from his memoirs

> A certain freedom in print proved very useful to the government, informing the powers that be who were their friends and enemies. In such a way, the vile *Fatherland Notes* before 1848 could serve as the best telegraph to show what kind of people Belinsky, Dostoevsky, and Herzen (Iskander) were.

1846
Pavel Annenkov, from an article

> The year 1846 was a remarkable one. By strange coincidence there appeared remarkable monuments of Russian literature . . . I. A. Goncharov's *A Common Story,* F. M. Dostoevsky's *Poor Folk,* and D. V. Grigorovich's *Anton Goremyka.*

1846
Anna Dostoevskaya, from her notebook

> From Balzac, Dostoevsky liked *Cousin Pons* and *Cousin Bette*.[7]

January–March 1846
Vera Dostoevskaya-Ivanova, from a letter to Fyodor Dostoevsky

> How guilty I am before you, dear brother, that I did not answer your
> letter right away, but it was not from laziness. Not knowing where to
> send my reply, I decided to wait to write a letter to [brother] Andryusha
> and to include one to you.
>
> I do not know how to thank you, dear brother, for your letter. . . .
> You have brought me to tears of happiness.

January 1, 1846
Vissarion Belinsky, from a review

> This coming year . . . will awaken powerfully the attention of the pub-
> lic to a name that, it seems, is fated to play in our literature a role
> given to extremely few individuals. Who is this name, and why is he
> noteworthy—this we will keep silent for a while, all the more so since
> readers will find out about him in the next few days or so.[8]

January 2, 1846
Vissarion Belinsky, from a letter to Alexander Herzen

> By Easter I am coming out with *Leviathan*, a huge thick almanac. . . .
> Dostoevsky is giving me a story.[9]

Before January 24, 1846
Dmitri Grigorovich, from his memoirs

> During the publication of *Poor Folk* . . . Dostoevsky was in a state of
> extreme nervous excitement.

After January 24, 1846
Ivan Panaev, from his memoirs

> The appearance of any new remarkable talent in Russian literature
> was always a holiday for Sollogub. He did not have the slightest trace
> of that literary envy or unpleasantness over another's success which,
> unfortunately, one often meets with among very talented writers and
> artists. . . . Enthusiastic over Dostoevsky's *Poor Folk*, he kept asking us:
> "But who is this Dostoevsky? For God's sake, show him to me, intro-
> duce me to him!"

After January 24, 1846
Vladimir Sollogub, from his memoirs

Poor Folk featured such talent, such simplicity and force, that it led me to ecstasy. Having read the work, I immediately set out to see the editor of the journal—it seemed it was Andrei Alexandrovich Kraevsky—to find out about the author.[10] He told me it was Dostoevsky and gave me his address. I went there right away and came across a small apartment on one of the far-flung streets of Petersburg. . . .

[There I met] a pale and sickly-looking young man. He wore a rather worn house frock coat with unusually short if seemingly unattached sleeves. When I introduced myself and told him in glowing terms the profound and surprising impression that *Poor Folk* had made on me, that it was unlike anything that had been written at that time, Dostoevsky became embarrassed and confused. He offered me an old-fashioned chair, the only one in the room. I sat down and we talked. To tell the truth, I talked more, a sin that I am always guilty of. Dostoevsky answered all my questions in a modest and even evasive way. Immediately I saw that this was an individual who was shy, proud, and reserved, but to a high degree also talented and pleasant. After twenty or so minutes, I stood up and invited him to my place in an informal way.

Dostoevsky took on a frightened look.

"No, Count, forgive me," he muttered bewilderingly, rubbing his hands one against the other, "but to tell you the truth, I have never been in high society and in no way can I bring myself to. . . ."

"But who is talking about high society, dear Fyodor Mikhailovich? True, my wife and I belong to such circles . . . but we will not let them into our home!"

Dostoevsky burst out laughing, but he remained adamant. It was only two months later that he first visited my home.

January 26, 1846
Vissarion Belinsky, from a letter to Alexander Herzen

[*The Petersburg Miscellany*] is going great guns; more than 200 copies have been sold from January 21st to January 25th.

January 26, 1846
Apollon Grigoriev, from a review

Devushkin and Varvara are a strange pair. They could see each other on a daily basis . . . but they talk in letters . . . so that neighbors will not see them together. . . .

Varvara sees Devushkin not as a mailman but as a mail horse. First she burdens him with orders for her wedding; then she leaves him for her new husband.

January 26, 1846
Nikolai Kukolnik, from a review

> *Poor Folk* has no form. It is founded entirely on details that are tiresome and monotonous, and that induce such boredom the likes of which you have never experienced. . . . It is like a dinner in which sugar is served instead of soup, and sauce instead of beef.

January 30, 1846
Pyotr Pletnyov, from a letter to Yakov Grot

> I did not care for *Poor Folk*, the much-vaunted novel by Dostoevsky. . . . The entire thing sounds like Gogol and Kvitka. . . . One should buy it only for a university library.

January 30, 1846
Leopold Brandt, from a review

> Mr. Dostoevsky's *Poor Folk* is made up of letters—a narrative that demands unusual talent, great experience, masterly exposition . . . and profound emotion so as to remedy the shortcomings . . . of writing of this type. . . .
>
> Mr. Dostoevsky . . . has taken into his head to write a *poema*, a drama. But despite all his pretenses to create something that is profound, highly poetic . . . and artistically simple, he has come up with *nothing*.
>
> Makar Devushkin, an elderly chancellery clerk who, for some thirty years, has been copying papers in some department, and Varvara Dobroselova, a woman of fallen virtue and guilty innocence, are the main and almost only characters of the work. Although the two live in the same building, they daily, sometimes twice a day, write to each other extremely long letters in which they complain bitterly about their poverty and fate. . . . The tie is generous and touching, but where precisely is the drama, the novel? How does one fill up 166 pages on such trifles? Involuntarily, one runs into . . . repetitions, into endless expositions of one and the same thing.
>
> In the personage of an uneducated, simple . . . and stupid old man, the author wishes to give to the world a type of simple-hearted goodness, unconscious nobility, disinterested honesty, and noble "humanity,"

even if this [model of] elevated humanity cannot withstand the blows of fate and sometimes gets drunk, causing the "virtuous" Varvara Alexeevna to issue forth extremely.

Now it is the fashion to seek out by force, to squeeze, so to speak, from the most usual, simple situations, something that is legendary, highly significant, and meaningful; "precisely" (a very sickly precisely) to analyze the "inner world" of the heart and soul; and despite reality and truth, to advance the most ordinary characters to some unattainable ideal—in other words, to make a mountain out of a molehill.

"Here is mystery, here are the heights, here is the triumph of art!" exclaim eccentric critics.[11] Like Varvara Alexeevna, inexperienced youth is deluded by such wise theories. . . .

How does this "naively . . . and profoundly simple" story of *Poor Folk* end? Oh, the surprising conclusion, the "artistic denouement"!

Varvara Alexeevna Dobroselova, crushed by grief, need, and the sufferings of the "noble, but incomprehensible world" of her soul, resolves to marry her vile (but, as you see, still rather honest) seducer. An ill-starred sacrifice! But this "sad, forced" union does not prevent her from thinking about the attire for her wedding (another precise reproach to feminine nature!), and from turning her priceless friend, Makar Alexeevich, into a sacrificial agent who upon her instructions . . . and edifying "notations" . . . runs about like a madman, to jewelers and fashionable stores. . . . Furthermore, this virtuous Varvara Alexeevna, "God knows how seductive" in her youth, gets carried away by games, by extremely feigned roles of oppressed sacrifice and innocence! . . .

Do not the following lines arouse the deepest empathy:

"Tell Madam Chiron that without fail, she [must] change the blond lace to conform to yesterday's patterns. Also tell her that I have changed my mind about the satin, and that it should be embroidered with crochet. Also, the letters for the monograms on the dresses should be done in tambour. Are you listening? In tambour, not smooth work. Make sure that it be done in tambour. One more thing, before I forget. Tell her, for God's sake, that the lapels for the fur coat must be raised and that the collar be done with lace. Please, Makar Alexeevich, tell her these things!"

Unhappy sacrifice! Does such a request not tear at your heart? Are these touching words about lace and trimmings the voice of the most cruel feminine suffering?. . . .

And poor Makar Alexeevich! What has happened to him, this truly virtuous old man, as his name "Devushkin" makes clear?[12] He is in despair that his beloved "little mother" (so he usually calls Varvara) is getting married and leaving him in such sadness that one fears he will not be able to carry on. So the novel ends.

The reader, moved to the depths of his soul, and shedding tears over the fate of these mournful "sacrifices to fate," lets the book fall from his hands . . . but, perhaps, for another reason. . . . It weighs on his arms with its heaviness . . . and a great, great deal of "pathos."

We, of course, would not have gone on at length about this first unsuccessful attempt of a young writer if it were not for the fact that . . . several weeks before the appearance [of *Poor Folk*] . . . people claimed that it was the work of a new and unusual talent, a piece that was great, even greater than the writings of Gogol and Lermontov. Immediately, a hundred rumors carried the pleasant news throughout the "length and breadth of Petrograd." Curiosity, expectation, and impatience were everywhere.

Rejoicing spiritually over a new talent amidst our insipid contemporary Russian literature, we set about [reading] Mr. Dostoevsky's novel greedily; but together with our readers, we were disappointed cruelly. "You will see a model of genuine, noble beauty and a peaceful, profound drama, written in a masterly style!" So we were told on the day it appeared. But alas, after reading the novel with the most complete and sincere goodwill, we, in our obtuseness and lack of taste, saw no such thing.

Would you like to see an example of the false simplicity in Devushkin's letters? Here are several lines: "As soon as it gets dark, my Varenka, I will *run* to you for a tiny hour. Now it is getting dark early, so I *will come running*. I, little mother, will today, without fail, *run* for a teeny-weeny hour. . . . You will now wait for Bykov (the seducer), but as soon as he leaves, I *will come running* to you. But just wait, little mother, I *will come running*."

What is this? Simplicity or humor or comedy? In truth, we do not know. We could put forth twenty examples of similar simplicity, but the size of our newspaper will not admit such long lists. We also note that Devushkin, in a large part of his letters, talks about the poor condition of his shoes and boots. This is his *idée fixe*. . . . He so fusses and fumes over such things that the entire novel, one can say, is written *à propos de bottes*.[13]

In each literary work, we try diligently to find a good side; so we will not say that this new author is not completely without talent, but he gets carried away by the empty theories of "principled" critics who, in our country, are confusing the younger generation [with their ideas].[14] The work has several tolerable places, but they do not make up for the rest. . . .

In future attempts, let Mr. Dostoevsky move away from the temptation of external imitation, from the absurd theories of the magicians of art, and perhaps he will be more successful. But this time, pardon us, the first pancake has turned out lumpy,[15] the mountain has given birth to a mouse, the "rumors" about Mr. Dostoevsky have been false and have even hurt him greatly, since they have led the public to expect something unusual.

Late January 1846
Varvara Dostoevskaya-Karepina, from a letter to Mikhail and Emiliya Dostoevsky

In my letter, dear brother, I saw to my surprise that you still did not know about the marriage of our sister Verochka. . . . The engagement was on December 2, 1845, and the wedding on January 7, 1846. Her husband, Alexander Pavlovich Ivanov, is a very kind and intelligent individual, about thirty-two years old. He so loves and worships sister that it is fun to see the two of them together. He has a mother who also cannot get enough of Verochka. In a word, she is so happy that it seems she cannot want for anything else. Do you know, dear brother, anything about brother Fedinka? We have not seen hide nor hair of him as to whether he is well or not. Write, please, and let us know if he wants to reenter service [to the state].

Circa February 1846 and after
Fyodor Dostoevsky, from an 1867 letter to Apollon Maykov

I have finished with that damned article "My Acquaintance with Belinsky." There was no way I could delay it or set it aside. In truth, I worked on it in the summer, but I found it so torturous to write . . . that I dragged it out to this very moment and, gritting my teeth, finished it. . . . Like a fool, I took on such a piece. As soon as I began the thing, I realized right away that with the *censorship*, there was no possible way I could do it justice (since I wanted to write the entire story). A hundred and fifty pages of a novel would have been easier than those thirty-two pages! The result was that . . . I rewrote the accursed article at least *five times*, then crossed it all out and put it all back together again. Somehow I have come up with an article—but it is such a rotten piece that it makes me sick to my stomach. How much valuable material was

I forced to throw out! As I might have expected, what was left was the most worthless "golden mean." *Garbage!*[16]

Circa February 1846 and after
Anna Dostoevskaya, from her memoirs

> When [in 1867] it was proposed to Fyodor Mikhailovich that he write an article, titled "About Belinsky," he set about this interesting theme with pleasure. He planned to write . . . a serious article on the man, to offer a most elementary and sincere opinion of this individual who in the beginning was dear to him, but who in the end treated him with such hostility.
>
> It became evident, though, that Fyodor Mikhailovich was not yet settled in his thinking [about Belinsky]; that many things needed to be thought through and resolved; and that many doubts remained. The article had to be written at least five times, and in the end Fyodor Mikhailovich was dissatisfied with the piece.

Circa February 1846 and after
Fyodor Dostoevsky, from *A Writer's Diary*

> Belinsky was the most intense person I have ever met.

Circa February 1846 and after
Vsevelod Solovyov, from his memoirs

> [Dostoevsky said:] "Belinsky was not like the others. If he said something, he would also do it. His was a nature that was simple, whole, and for whom word and deed were one. Others got lost in thought a hundred times over before they decided to do something, if they ever decided at all. But Belinsky was not like that."

Circa February 1846 and after
Fyodor Dostoevsky, from a *Writer's Diary*

> Belinsky . . . compared an excessive "concern" [for an audience] to a "depraved talent" and scorned it openly, implying, of course, its antithesis: even in the most ardent poetic mood, [the writer must] keep this concern [for his audience] in check.

Circa February 1846 and after
Fyodor Dostoevsky, from his "Notes" on *Devils*

> One time Dostoevsky met Belinsky at a railroad station under construction. "I cannot wait patiently [for its completion]." he said. "I choose to stroll here every day so I can look at the work that is going on."

Oh, the poor man, if only he knew how many others looked at the railroad with the same glance, how dear the construction was also to them. . . .

Dostoevsky also talked to him . . . about future railroads, about heated coach cars, and about heating [homes] in Moscow, where wood was becoming more and more expensive. [He also talked] about the future, about the crisscrossing of railroads in Moscow, and how much more costly still wood would become. Perhaps, Dostoevsky said, wood would be brought in on railways from countries with forests.

Belinsky laughed long and hard at [what he saw as] such a poor knowledge of life. "Now he wants to bring wood on railways!" he said. Such a thing seemed to him to be monstrous. Imagine that Belinsky thought that only passengers traveled on trains, and that the only goods that moved on rails were the most delicate and costly articles from Paris. That was Belinsky's knowledge of life. But he understood it better than anyone.

Circa February 1846 and after
Fyodor Dostoevsky, from *A Writer's Diary*

This most blessed among men, who possessed a remarkably tranquil conscience, had his occasional sad moments. But his sadness was of a special kind. It came not from doubts or disillusionment—oh, no—but from the questions "Why not today, why not tomorrow?"

In all of Russia there was no one in a bigger hurry [than Belinsky]. Once when I met him near the Znamensky Church[17] . . . he told me:

"I often drop by here to look at how the construction is progressing." (The station for the Nikolaevsky railway was still being built).[18] "It makes my heart rest a bit easier to stand and watch the work: at long last we will have at least one railway. You will never believe how at times such a thing comforts my heart."

This Belinsky said well and with passion: He never put on airs. We set off together. I recall he said, "When they lay me in my grave" (he knew that he had consumption), "only then will they realize whom they have lost."

Circa February 1846 and after
Fyodor Dostoevsky, from *A Writer's Diary*

Belinsky was as good a husband and father as Herzen.[19]

Circa February 1846 and after
Fyodor Dostoevsky, from *A Writer's Diary*

> Were there many genuine liberals [in the 1840s in Russia]? Were there many truly suffering, pure, and sincere people such as Belinsky?

Circa February 1846 and after
Fyodor Dostoevsky, from his 1876–77 *Notebook*

> Belinsky's very errors, if he had any, are higher than any truth, if not everything, that you have created and written.

Circa February 1846 and after
Fyodor Dostoevsky, from *A Writer's Diary*

> Belinsky . . . was no *gentilhomme* at all—oh no. (God knows what his origins were. I think that his father was an army doctor.)

Circa February 1846 and after
Fyodor Dostoevsky, from *A Writer's Diary*

> Given such a warm faith in his ideas, Belinsky was, of course, the happiest of men. People were wrong in writing later that if he had lived longer, he would have joined the Slavophiles. Belinsky would never have ended up a Slavophile. He might have ended by emigrating [from Russia]. . . .
>
> As a small and rapturous man whose former warm faith never permitted him the slightest doubt, Belinsky would have made the rounds of various congresses in Germany and Switzerland; or . . . run errands on behalf of the women's movement.

Circa February 1846 and after
Fyodor Dostoevsky, from an 1868 letter to Apollon Maykov

> I will never believe Apollon Grigoriev's statement that Belinsky would have ended up with Slavophilism.[20] Belinsky could not end up like that. He was just a little louse and nothing more. He was a great poet in his time, but he could not have developed any further. He would have ended up at the beck and call of some local Mme. Goegg[21] as an adjutant for the woman question at meetings and would have forgotten how to speak Russian without having learned German.

Circa February 1846 and after
Fyodor Dostoevsky, from an 1870 letter to Apollon Maykov

> At the time [in exile] I was still under the sway of a mangy, yeast-like Russian liberalism, propagandized . . . [by people] like the shitty insect Belinsky and others.

Circa February 1846 and after
Fyodor Dostoevsky, from an 1871 letter to Nikolai Strakhov

> That stinking insect Belinsky . . . a precisely small, feeble, and power-less individual . . . who cursed Russia and consciously brought to it much harm.

Circa February 1846 and after
Fyodor Dostoevsky, from an 1868 letter to Apollon Maykov

> Recall the best liberals—recall Belinsky: Surely was he not a conscious enemy of the fatherland, a retrograde?

Circa February 1846 and after
Fyodor Dostoevsky, from *A Writer's Diary*

> Belinsky, an individual who, by nature, was passionately carried away [by everything,] . . . was almost the first of the Russians who attached themselves directly to European socialists, who had already rejected the entire order of European civilization, even as at home, in Russian literature, he waged a war to the end against the Slavophiles, apparently for completely the opposite cause.

Circa February 1846 and after
Fyodor Dostoevsky, from *A Writer's Diary*

> For some the Slavophile doctrine even now means only kvass and radishes as it did in the old days of Belinsky. . . . Belinsky *really* went no further than that in his understanding of Slavophilism.

Circa February 1846 and after
Fyodor Dostoevsky, from his 1876–77 *Notebook*

> Truly, Belinsky understood Russia little, or, better to say, he understood it in a prejudicial way and knew it extremely little. He knew Russia factually, although he grasped it terribly via instinct, premonition.

The entire European order Belinsky applied directly to Russia, without pondering the differences [between the two], and it was in such things that he differed from the Slavophiles.

Circa February 1846 and after
Fyodor Dostoevsky, from his 1876–77 *Notebook*

Belinsky saw only order. He loved the people, but he differed from the Slavophiles in that he had no hopes for their transformation and did not believe in and studied little . . . the paths that they had proposed for the rebirth of Russia in the spirit of the folk. Apparently, also, Belinsky read little of the Slavophiles' works. As if in despair, he began to await universal renewal in the nascent social movements in Europe and was carried away by them passionately.

Nonetheless, Belinsky also expressed a serious negation of civilization in rejecting Europe, falling in with the Slavophiles but in a different spirit. In order to explain this curious phenomenon of Russian life, I add that Belinsky was incomparably a more conservative Russian than the Gagarins.[22] But, having adhered to the *extreme left*, he spoke unconsciously as an extreme Russian and thus became close to the Slavophiles, in contrast to Westernizers at the time who worshiped the West over Russia and moved to Catholicism (in its right wing). . . .

I repeat, those who adhered to the left, extreme left, of Europe changed their minds completely and declared themselves to be the most Russian, negating European culture with native revulsion. Belinsky, for example.

Circa February 1846 and after
Fyodor Dostoevsky, from his 1880–81 *Notebook*

Belinsky. An unusual striving for the acceptance of new ideas [along] with an unusual desire . . . to trample on everything that was old with hatred, spittle, and shame. As if thirsting to revenge the old, I burned everything that I had worshiped.

Circa February 1846 and after
Fyodor Dostoevsky, from *A Writer's Diary*

Even well before the Paris revolution of 1848, we were caught up by the fascinating power of . . . ideas. Even in 1846 Belinsky had initiated me into the entire *truth* of this coming "regenerated world," into the entire *sanctity* of the future communistic society.

Circa February 1846 and after
Fyodor Dostoevsky, from *A Writer's Diary*

> I found Belinsky to be a passionate socialist, and with me, he began directly with atheism. That was for me very significant—precisely his amazing feeling and his unusual capacity to penetrate an idea in the most profound way, to become totally inspired by an idea. . . .
>
> Cherishing above all reason, science, and realism, Belinsky understood, more profoundly than anyone, that reason, science, and realism alone could create only an ant heap and not the social "harmony" in which humankind could get on with life. He knew that moral beginnings are the basis of everything. He believed in the new moral foundations of socialism (which, to date, have shown nothing but vile distortions of nature and common sense). He believed [such things] to the point of madness, without any reflection at all.

Circa February 1846 and after
Fyodor Dostoevsky, from *A Writer's Diary*

> As a socialist, Belinsky first had to dethrone Christianity. He knew that necessarily, the revolution must begin with atheism. He had to dethrone that religion from which came the moral foundations of the society he was rejecting. Radically, Belinsky rejected the family, private property, and the moral responsibility of the individual.

Circa February 1846 and after
Fyodor Dostoevsky, from *A Writer's Diary*

> As a socialist, Belinsky was absolutely bound to destroy Christ's teachings and to label them as a false and ignorant philanthropy that was condemned by contemporary science and by economic principles. Still, there remained the most radiant image of the God-man, its moral unattainability, its marvelous and miraculous beauty. But Belinsky, in his endless and unending enthusiasm, did not pause even before this insurmountable obstacle, as did Renan, who proclaimed in his *Life of Jesus,* a book filled with unbelief,[23] that Christ is still the ideal of human beauty, an unattainable type, never to be repeated in the future.

Circa February 1846 and after
Fyodor Dostoevsky, from an 1871 letter to Nikolai Strakhov

> You never knew Belinsky, but I did and understood him fully.
>
> This individual (Belinsky) . . . could not note how much he and others harbored petty ambition, spite, impatience, irritation, and the

main thing, pride. Cursing Christ, Belinsky never said to himself that when we put ourselves in His place, we are so vile. No, he never pondered the fact that he himself was vile. He was extremely satisfied with himself . . . personal, foul-smelling, ignominious, and obtuse.[24]

Circa February 1846 and after
Fyodor Dostoevsky, from his "Notes" on *Devils*

> The deceased Belinsky cursed Christ in an abusive way, but he himself would not harm a chicken.
>
> As to reality and his understanding of real-life things, Belinsky was very weak. Turgenev was right when he said that Belinsky knew very little, even in a scientific way,[25] but he understood things better than anyone else. You laugh because you feel like saying, "But he understood things nonetheless." But, my friend, I do not pretend to understand the pieces of genuine life. . . .
>
> I recall the writer Dostoevsky[26] who was still a youth at that time. Belinsky attempted to turn him toward atheism, but to the objections of Dostoevsky, who defended Christ, he cursed [the Savior] in an abusive way. "When I swore, Belinsky always made such a sad and crushed face . . . [before] he pointed to Dostoevsky with well-meaning and innocent laughter."

Circa February 1846 and after
Fyodor Dostoevsky, from *The Brothers Karamazov*

> [Kolya Krasotkin:] "If you wish, I am not against Christ. He was a completely humane personality. If he had lived in our time, he would have joined the revolutionaries, and perhaps would have played a visible role. . . . Even with failure."
>
> "And where did you pick that up from?" Alyosha exclaimed. "What fool have you been hanging out with?"
>
> "Have mercy. You can't hide the truth. . . . Even old man Belinsky, people say, said such a thing."

Circa February 1846 and after
Fyodor Dostoevsky, from *A Writer's Diary*

> "But do you know," Belinsky screamed one evening (sometimes if he was very excited, he would scream) as he turned to me. "Do you know that one cannot count a man's sins, nor burden him with obligations and turnings of the other cheek when society is set up so basely that a

man cannot help but do wrong, when he is driven economically to do so; and that it is absurd and cruel to demand from a man something which, by the laws of nature, he cannot fulfill, even if he wanted to. . . ."

We were not alone that evening. One of Belinsky's friends, an individual whom he respected highly and listened to often, was present, along with a certain young beginning writer who won fame in literature later.[27]

"It's touching just to look at him," Belinsky said, breaking off his furious exclamations suddenly and turning to his friend as he pointed to me. "Every time I mention Christ, his whole face changes, as if he wanted to burst out crying. . . . But believe me, you naive fellow," he said, attacking me again. "Believe me that your Christ, if he were born in our time, would be the most unremarkable and ordinary of men; he would have faded away among today's science and movers of humanity."

"But no-o-o-o-o!" Belinsky's friend chimed in. (I recall that we were sitting, while Belinsky was pacing back and forth around the room.) "But no. If Christ appeared now, he would have joined the movement and become its head. . . ."

"Yes, yes," Belinsky agreed suddenly, with surprising haste. "He certainly would have joined the socialists and followed them."

Circa February 1846 and after
Anna Dostoevskaya, from her memoirs

Despite Fyodor Mikhailovich's high opinion of Belinsky's critical acumen, and sincere gratitude for the man's encouragement of his literary gifts, he could not forgive Belinsky's mocking and almost blasphemous attitude toward his religious views and beliefs.

Circa February 1846 and after
Fyodor Dostoevsky, from *A Writer's Diary*

The forces that advanced humanity, which [Belinsky believed] Christ was destined to join were all Frenchmen: George Sand,[28] the now totally forgotten Cabet,[29] Pierre Leroux,[30] and Proudhon, who was then only beginning his work.[31]

As far as I can recall, Belinsky held these four in the greatest respect. . . . He would discuss these men for entire evenings at a time. There was also one German to whom Belinsky paid great tribute and that was Feuerbach.[32] (Belinsky, who, throughout his entire life,

could not master a single foreign language, pronounced it "Fierbach.")
Strauss was also spoken of very reverently.[33]

Circa February 1846 and after
Fyodor Dostoevsky, from an 1871 letter to Nikolai Strakhov

> If Belinsky, Granovsky, and that entire bunch of riffraff could take a
> look [at life] now, they would say: "No, we did not dream about that;
> [what is happening now] is a deviation; we will wait further and light
> will appear, progress will rule, and humanity will be rebuilt and will
> be happy!"
>
> In no way would they have agreed that once you have set out on this
> road, you end up only at the Commune and Felix Pyat.[34] They were so
> obtuse that even *now,* after the event . . . they would continue to dream.
>
> I cursed Belinsky more as a phenomenon of Russian life than as a
> person: a most stinking, obtuse, shameful, and inevitable phenomenon
> of Russian life. . . . I assure you that Belinsky would now reconcile him-
> self with the following thought: "Truly, the Commune was a failure
> above all because it was French, that is, it preserved in itself the infec-
> tion of nationality. What is needed are people in whom there is not a
> drop of nationality and who are slapping their mother's (Russia's) face
> in the way I do."
>
> Foaming at the mouth, Belinsky would again have rushed to write
> his vile articles, defaming Russia, denying her great phenomenon
> (Pushkin)[35] so as once and for all to make Russia an *impassive* nation
> capable of leading a *universal cause.*

Circa February 1846 and after
Fyodor Dostoevsky from an 1873 letter to Alexander III

> Our Belinskys and Granovskys would not believe it if they were told
> that they were Nechaev's direct fathers.

Circa February 1846 and after
Fyodor Dostoevsky, from an 1871 letter to Nikolai Strakhov

> You say that Belinsky was a talented individual. Not at all. . . . I recall
> my youthful surprise when I listened to several of his purely artistic
> judgments (for example, on *Dead Souls*).[36] He was outrageously super-
> ficial and careless in the way he related to Gogol's type.[37] He was happy
> only that Gogol *indicted*. During these four years, I have reread his criti-
> cism. He abused Pushkin whenever the writer sounded a false note. . . .
> With amazement, he proclaimed the nothingness of the Belkin tales.[38]

In Gogol's story "The Carriage," he found nothing artistic in the entire composition of the work, but saw it only a comic story.[39] He rejected the ending of *Eugene Onegin*.[40] He was the first to put forth Pushkin as a Gentleman of the Emperor's Bedchamber.[41] . . . He said that Turgenev would not be an artist, and did so during a reading of his extremely remarkable story "Three Portraits."[42] I could put before you many such examples as proof of the falseness of his critical sense and his "impressionable trembling." . . . We still judge Belinsky and many phenomena of our life through a multitude of extreme prejudices.

Circa February 1846 and after
Fyodor Dostoevsky, from an 1870 letter to Apollon Maykov

Do they still give to graduates from high schools books like the complete collection of Belinsky's works in which he cries over why Tatyana remains faithful to her husband?[43] No, long have such things not been eradicated.

Circa February 1846 and after
Fyodor Dostoevsky, from testimony to the Investigatory Commission for the Petrashevsky affair

I often reproached Belinsky for the fact that he tried to give to literature a personal and unworthy significance, and that he lowered it to description . . . only to newspaper facts or scandalous events. Namely, I objected to the fact that bile attracted no one, that it tired everyone in a mortal way, and that it grabbed passers-by the buttons of their frock coats and taught and propagandized by force.

Circa February 1846 and after
Fyodor Dostoevsky, from his novel *The Insulted and Injured*

[Ikhmenev:] "Is B. still writing?"
    "Yes, he is writing," I answered.
    "Ekh, Vanya, Vanya," he concluded, waving his hand, "but what kind of criticism is it?!"

Circa February 1846 and after
Ivan Turgenev, from his memoirs

Occasionally Belinsky treated beginners with great tenderness, getting carried away most charmingly, almost amusingly.
    When he got hold of Mr. Dostoevsky's *Poor Folk*, he was positively delighted. "Yes," he used to say proudly, as though he himself had been

responsible for some terrific achievement, "yes, my dear fellows, let me tell you, he may be a tiny bird," and he would his hand about a foot from the floor to show how tiny he was, "but he's got sharp claws!" . . .

In his paternal tenderness toward a newly discovered talent, Belinsky treated Dostoevsky like a son, just as if he were his own "little boy."

Circa February 1846 and after
Avdotya Panaeva, from her memoirs

Belinsky avoided all serious discussions with Dostoevsky so as not to upset him. Such a response Dostoevsky took for coldness. . . .

When people told Belinsky that Dostoevsky saw himself as a genius, he shrugged his shoulders sadly and said:

"What a misfortune! Dostoevsky has indubitable talent, but if instead of developing it, he imagines himself already to be a genius. His giftedness will not move forward. Without fail, he must receive medical treatment . . . for his terribly unstrung nerves. It must be that life has worn him out, poor soul! These are difficult times, one needs nerves of steel to withstand all the conditions of contemporary life."

Circa February 1846 and after
Stepan Yanovsky, from his memoirs

I know that Fyodor Mikhailovich, by virtue of his mind and the power of his convictions, did not love to submit to any authority. . . . He often told me how he talked to Belinsky: "That's all right, Vissarion Grigorievich, you just keep quiet; there will come a time when you will start talking your head off." (So Fyodor Mikhailovich would say apropos of the fact that Belinsky had praised *Poor Folk* to the skies, but that he had seemingly ignored his other works, and [that] the silence about his [later] writing was more bitter than abuse.)

Circa February 1846 and after
Pavel Annenkov, from his memoirs

Belinsky wanted to do for Dostoevsky what he had done for other writers, for example, Koltsov and Nekrasov, that is, to free his talent from moralizing tendencies and to invest it with strong nerves and muscles so that he could possess his subject immediately, directly, without strain.

But [from Dostoevsky] Belinsky met with a decisive rebuff. . . .

At Belinsky's, the new author read his second story, *The Double*, a sensational depiction of a person who moves between two worlds—real and fantastic—without allowing him the possibility of settling in either one of them.

Belinsky liked the story by virtue of its power and skillful handling of an original and strange theme. It seemed to me, though—(I was present at the meeting)—that the critic also had an ulterior motive which he did not think necessary to articulate immediately at that time.

Belinsky constantly drew Dostoevsky's attention to the necessity of *hitting the nail on the head,* as they say in the literary world, to free oneself from the difficulties of literary exposition, to acquire the ability to render one's thoughts in a free and easy way.

Belinsky apparently could not accustom himself to Dostoevsky's then still diffuse manner of narration with its constant returns to the same old phrases, and its ad infinitum repetitions and rephrasings. Belinsky ascribed this manner to the young writer's inexperience, his failure as yet to surmount the stumbling blocks of language and form. . . .

Dostoevsky heard the critic's recommendations in a mood of affable indifference. The sudden success of his novel had sprouted seeds and germs of high self-regard and self-esteem already in this soul. It more than liberated [him] from the doubts and hesitations that normally accompany the first steps of a writer. It took him to a prophetic dream auguring laurel wreath and chaplets.

With Belinsky, Dostoevsky soon parted company. . . . Life took them in different directions, although for a long time their views and thinking were the same.

Circa February 1846 and after
Fyodor Dostoevsky, from a draft of *A Writer's Diary*

> Mr. Annenkov . . . could not have been a witness to [his claim] of arguments between me and Belinsky as we never did such things.

Circa February 1846 and after
Avdotya Panaeva, from her memoirs

> Dostoevsky was annoyed at Belinsky for playing preference[44] and for not speaking to him about his *Poor Folk.*
>
> "How can such an intelligent individual spend even ten minutes over such an idiotic activity as cards," Dostoevsky said with some bitterness. "Belinsky does so for two or three hours at a time. Truly, one cannot tell the different between bureaucrats and writers: they both spend time in the same dull way."[45]

Circa February 1846 and after
Fyodor Dostoevsky, from *A Writer's Diary*

> Having scrutinized Nekrasov's character . . . [I found him to be] reserved, almost fleeting, cautious, and almost non-communicative.

Circa February 1846 and after
Anna Dostoevskaya, from her memoirs

> [Dostoevsky] considered Nekrasov the friend of his youth and esteemed his poetic gifts.

Circa Feburary 1846 and after
Anna Dostoevskaya, from her memoirs

> Nekrasov figured in memories of [my husband's] youth and of the beginning of his literary career. After all, Nekrasov was one of the first who recognized the talent of Fyodor Mikhailovich and facilitated his success in the intellectual world of that time.

Circa February 1846 and after
Lyubov Dostoevskaya, from her memoirs

> Nekrasov published *Poor Folk* in his journal[46] and it was a great success. Suddenly, my father became famous. Everyone wanted to meet him. "Who is this Dostoevsky?" was heard on all sides. For a long time Father had visited literary salons, but no one had paid any attention to him.[47] This shy individual always took refuge in a corner, on a window seat, or behind a screen.
>
> But now he was no longer allowed to hide. People surrounded him and flattered him; they forced him to speak and found him enchanting. . . . They invited him to their homes and accepted him wholeheartedly.

Circa February 1846 and after
Stepan Yanovsky, from his memoirs

> Fyodor Mikhailovich loved to listen to music, as a result of which, with any opportunity, he attended Italian operas. . . .
>
> He especially loved *William Tell*. . . . With delight he listened to Mozart's *Don Giovanni*, especially the role of Zerlina, and he went into raves over *Norma*. . . . He also went wild over the debut of Meyerbeer's opera *Huguenots* in Petersburg. . . .[48]
>
> About ballet, Fyodor Mikhailovich knew only from hearsay; he never attended performances.

Circa February 1846 and after
Anna Dostoevskaya, from her memoirs

It is possible that many of the unhappy impressions that Fyodor Mikhailovich retained from his tie with Belinsky were the result of gossip and innuendoes, of "friends" who, at first, acknowledged Dostoevsky's talent and spread it hither and yon, but who later, for reasons inexplicable to me, began to persecute the shy author of *Poor Folk*, to write lies about him, to compose epigrams, and to try his patience in every possible way.

Circa February 1846 and after
Lyubov Dostoevskaya, from her memoirs

Dostoevsky's friends, young writers who were setting out on their own path in literature, could not bear his sudden success. They began to envy my father, driving themselves to distraction with the thought that this shy and modest individual had been accepted in the salons of famous personalities to whom they had no access. They could not value *Poor Folk* for its worth. The work seemed to them to be silly. They parodied it in their poetry and prose, and poked fun at the writer in a merciless way. To harm him in society, they spread humorous anecdotes about him.

Dostoevsky's friends insisted that success had gone to his head, and that he demanded that every page of his second novel, which was to appear in Nekrasov's journal, should be surrounded by a border so as to distinguish it from other works in the issue. This was apparently a lie. The novel *The Double* appeared without any borders.[49]

Circa February 1846 and after
Dmitri Grigorovich, from his memoirs

The sudden change from people worshiping and raising the author of *Poor Folk* almost to the level of genius to their cruel rejection of him crushed such an impressionable and proud individual as Dostoevsky.

He began to avoid the people of the Belinsky circle. He became withdrawn completely, and irritable to the highest degree. Unfortunately, whenever Dostoevsky met Turgenev . . . he gave full vent to the indignation that had been welling up inside him, saying that he was not afraid of anyone and that just give him time and he would drown all of them in mud. I do not recall what caused such an outburst . . . but the conversation was seemingly about Gogol.

It was Dostoevsky who was at fault. Turgenev lacked all passion and fervor. He could even be reproached for his gentleness and pliancy.

Circa February 1846 and after
Avdotya Panaeva, from her memoirs

Dostoevsky often visited us in the evenings. His shyness had passed. He even showed a certain passion [for things]. He got into arguments with everyone. Apparently from stubbornness, he contradicted others. From youth and nerves, he could not control himself. In an extremely manifest way, he gave witness to his authorial pride and high opinion of his writing talent.

Stunned by his unexpectedly brilliant entry into the fictional enterprise, and showered with praise from competent people in literature, he, as an impressionable individual, could not hide his pride before other young writers who had set forth modestly into fiction.

As if on purpose, Dostoevsky tore at his colleagues with his irritability and condescending tone, saying that he was an incomparably better writer than they. They responded by making him the object of gossip, by pricking his pride with jibes in conversations.

Circa February 1846 and after
Avdotya Panaeva, from her memoirs

Dostoevsky became terribly suspicious after a friend told him everything that people were saying about him and his *Poor Folk*. . . .[50] Dostoevsky suspected jealousy . . . and believed that everyone wished to ridicule him and belittle his work.

He visited us seething with anger . . . as if to pour on envious peers all the bile that was suffocating him. But our jests, rather than soothing a sick and nervous individual, irritated him more forcefully.

Circa February 1846 and after
Ivan Panaev, from his memoirs

Belinsky said that *Poor Folk* revealed a great and immense talent, and that the author would surpass Gogol. . . .[51] *Poor Folk*, of course, is a remarkable work and fully deserving of the success it enjoyed, but Belinsky's enthusiasm for the novel was extreme.

Circa February 1846 and after
Ivan Turgenev, from his memoirs

The exaggerated praise that he gave to *Poor Folk* was among Belinsky's initial blunders and demonstrated clearly his declining powers.[52]

Circa February 1846 and after
Ivan Panaev, from an 1855 article

Any new appearance in literature, any new talent made for me an indescribably joyful impression. I rejoiced over any literary success; never did the slightest feeling of jealousy possess me. Just the opposite, I needed authorities in literature with all my being . . . and in the absence of genuine heroes, I worshiped little idols who were erected by people close to me, and whom I respected and believed in.

We put little idols on pedestals and worshiped them with genuine enthusiasm. . . . With incense and bowing, we almost lost our minds. One of these little idols made us happier than others. We carried him in our arms around the city gates; we showed him to the public, crying: "Here is a recently born small genius who in time will kill all our present and past literature. Bow to him! Bow to him!" . . .

We heralded him everywhere, in salons, on the streets. One lady, blond and shapely, with airy curls and a brilliant name, read his work. Having heard so much about him, she wanted to meet him. A certain individual . . . brought the man to her, saying with ecstasy: "Here he is! Look! Here he is!"

Gracefully, the lady with the airy curls, moved her lips, licking them with her small tongue. To our idol, she wanted to drop a most charming compliment: one of those accolades which one of my acquaintances, a seminarian, having studied in a noble home, calls a "fragrant, enlightened trifle," and which, always off the mark, he also tells his wife is a *"dear absurdity."*

As soon as the lady with the airy curls gifted our little genius with this fragrant, enlightened trifle, he turned pale suddenly and started to sway. He was carried off to the back room and sprayed with eau de cologne. He regained consciousness but would not return to where the woman with the airy curls was sitting, illumined brightly by oil lamps and candles. . . .

From that time on, our little genius became unbearable. In no way did he want to feel the earth under his feet. . . . Invariably, he demanded that we lift him as high as possible so that everyone could see him. Constantly he raged at us and cried out: "Higher! Higher!" Our arms grew numb as we raised him . . . but still he raged and cried out, "Higher!"

When we tried to cut our little genius down to size, he began to reproach us for being jealous of him, for hating him, for lacking the strength to lift him higher. In a fury, he jumped from our hands, dashed about, raised his head back completely, and in an unusually majestic way, marched through the crowd, surprised that people did not notice him and fall at his feet when they saw him. . . .

Offended by the crowd, he rushed to his small attic, where before him appeared the aristocratic lady with the airy curls who kept telling him: "You are a genius! You are mine! I love you! . . . Together we will go to the cathedral of glory, to our bright and brilliant salons where you will never hear a Russian word. You must meet *our kind of people*, because only our kind will preach genuine glory. . . . The world is divided into two types of people . . . *connus* and *inconnus*, and you will never become famous until you know the first group. . . ."

She wound her downy hand around his and touched his face with her airy curls.

At first, he did not to believe in such a division of people. Involuntarily, his entire nature rose up against such a strange separation. But when her hand touched his, a most shallow and pitiable pride rose up in him and possessed his being. . . .

He imagined himself in gold in a hall, glittering and magnificently lit, in the very center of those people whom the lady with the airy curls had called the *connus*. Although such individuals were coming to shake his hand, she was beckoning him elsewhere . . . to lavish and mysterious boudoirs with diffuse light and elegant couches as in ancient Russian stories . . . [bidding] that he keep following her there, there!

But then the vision disappeared suddenly . . . and again he saw himself in his poor attic, on the coarse Turkish couch which he had bought at a flea market. Having wiped his eyes and glanced around, he sobbed, and in horror covered his face with his hands. . . .

Once, after such a vision, he walked about his room in an agitated way. Suddenly, he ran to the editor of a journal to whom, several days previously, he had given a small article. At that moment he was for the editor the same as he was for everyone else: a little idol.

Our idol demanded that without fail, the piece be published at the beginning or end of the book, and that it make a striking visual impression, being set off from the others with a golden border or edge. The editor agreed to everything, and having patted the man on the shoulder, began to sing:

> "I will make a fuss over you
> I will set forth, a scoundrel on the mend
> I will surround you with a border
> And put you at the end."[53]

From that moment on, our little idol began to rant and rave. Soon he was hurled down from his pedestal and forgotten completely. The poor soul! We ruined him! We made him laughable! He could not keep to the heights to which we had raised him. We ourselves were carried away in a way that was sincere, disinterested, and well meaning. But were we guilty? . . . Can one indict people for their youth, enthusiasm, passions, and delusions?

Circa February 1846 and after
Nikolai Nekrasov, from *The Stone Heart*[54]

On that day at eleven a.m. Trostnikov, gasping for breath, ran with *The Stone Heart* to his friend Mertsalov. With enthusiasm, he said to him:

"Grigory Alexandrovich! Read this, for God's sake, read this manuscript as soon as possible! If I am not mistaken, fate is sending our literature a new brilliant figure! In my opinion, it is a most splendid thing!"

Mertsalov was an individual of precise literary taste. Deservedly did he have the distinction of being an excellent critic. He was a key contributor to a journal that, at the time, enjoyed a widespread and honored reputation, and, one can say without exaggeration, Mertsalov was the reason. A sharp, irritable tone; an impartiality that bowed neither to ties nor to advantage; and an irony, if not always exacting, always wicked and precise—[such things] made the man many enemies who spread God knows what rumors about him. Mertsalov was for them a scourge of everything that was gifted and splendid; a literary bandit who, if only to indulge his youthful boldness, was merciless with anybody and everybody.

In truth, though, there was never a more kind, noble, and delicate individual [than Mertsalov]; and if he sometimes attacked unworthy literary phenomena with greater fervor and indignation than they deserved, it was because of his ardent and passionate love for literature. Like a tender father toward a favorite child, Mertsalov wished to see only virtue in literature. Any untalented, unscrupulous, appalling, or scandalous phenomenon brought him to despair. It aroused in him all manner of bile, which he often expressed in reviews of such works.

As a result, no one greeted new signs of talent with such love, with such warmth and encouragement. Indeed, his enthusiasm for such giftedness was that for one good feature of a piece, he overlooked ten poor ones, In so doing, Mertsalov gave his enemies cause to accuse him not only of exaggerated censure but also of overblown praise, which they called idol worship. Generally speaking, such extremes were for him key in both literature and life. There was no middle. An individual or book that was dear to him today risked arousing his repugnance tomorrow. Such shifts always took place suddenly and sharply, preceded by an inner and painfully burdensome process of thinking which led him to conscious mistakes.

Both orally and in writing, Mertsalov did not hesitate to admit his errors. If he was not always consistent in his views (something that some see as a necessary hallmark of a great mind) . . . his opinions flowed from profound convictions. It should also be noted that in him fate did not observe a particular disposition. He was very unhappy in life, a condition that, naturally, intensified his irritability.

Mertsalov heard Trostnikov's enthusiastic praise of *The Stone Heart* with the mild smile of disbelief with which, typically, experienced critics receive people who take it upon themselves to pronounce positive verdicts on matters belonging exclusively to them. Personal enthusiasms, followed by bitter disenchantments that wounded one's pride, had also taught Mertsalov to be more careful. If he could not change his nature, then at the very least, he tried to greet every new occurrence [in literature] in a calmer and more sober way, and that taught by time and experience, he would not surrender to passion.

Mertsalov was just under forty years old, but—to tell the truth—thanks to rich and perceptive personality, he was younger than any twenty-year-old.

"Oh, you youth, youth!" he said with a grin. "You barely finish reading something, you like it, it begins to stir your heart, and right away, a superb, truly, even a brilliant work."

"First of all, read it—and tell me what you yourself think."

"Read it? Now look here: Is it worth reading? I am very busy now."

"It's worth it, I assure you, it's worth it!" Trostnikov answered enthusiastically. "Only begin to read it—you will not be able to tear yourself away from it!"

"Really? You judge for yourself! But enough! I am not a kid like you. Right now there is not a book that exists which I could not tear away from whenever I please—even for an empty conversation."

"I will stop by," Trostnikov said.

"This evening? Fine, do so."

"And you will give me your opinion."

"Right away? You think that I will drop everything and start reading?"

"But it is an excellent thing. Read it today. . . ."

"I cannot today. I have just begun a splendid book. I have to finish it."

"But when will you read it?"

"Well . . . I will read it sometime," Mertsalov answered lazily.

Trostnikov left. In truth, Mertsalov had no intention of continuing what he had been reading. No sooner had Trostnikov left than, in a lively way, he seized the manuscript of *The Stone Heart*. He read the title, ran past the epigraph, which contained several lines from one of his own critical articles, and began to read. After several lines, his face became inflamed. He put down the manuscript and with quick steps walked around the room. Then he summoned his servant, ordered that he not be disturbed, and began to read again.

Around eight in the evening, Trostnikov, burning with impatience, ran to Mertsalov's home.

When the bell sounded, Mertsalov was lying on the couch. His facial expression was greatly excited. In his hands was the manuscript of *The Stone Heart*. Having heard the bell, he jumped off the couch and met Trostnikov with words that expressed both annoyance and impatience:

"Where have you been?"

"Me? I had supper. . . . I dined with Glazhievsky at the Hôtel de Paris."

"I was waiting for you. I waited and waited. I was even thinking of sending my servant for you. . . . So tell me, is he a young person?"

Seeing the familiar manuscript in Mertsalov's hands, Trostnikov guessed whom he was referring to.

"He is young," he answered.

"How young?"

"I think he is about twenty-four or twenty-five."

"Thank God!" Mertsalov exclaimed with delight and exhaled as if a stone had been lifted from his chest. "Such a question was very much on my mind. I am simply exhausted, waiting for you. So you say that he is only twenty four?"

"In no way is he more than twenty-five!" Trostnikov responded.

"But he is such a genius!" Mertsalov pronounced with emphasis.

"I told you so," a delighted Trostnikov noted.

"You said so? You told me? But could you really tell me? Can one really talk about such a thing? You came, turned around, left a manuscript, and disappeared!. . . . It is a splendid thing, but it is not enough that it is splendid. Such a description could also be attached to a trifling vaudeville, a business file. But this is a brilliant artistic work!" Mertsalov continued, inspired.

"I will tell you, Trostnikov," he went on, his face so inflamed that it turned red, and making a sharp gesture with his hand, he added: "I would not exchange *The Stone Heart* for all of Russian literature!"

He then talked about the merits of *The Stone Heart*, its artistic significance, the profound principles at its base, the unusual composition of its parts, and the complete nature of the whole (such words were in great use in the literary language of the time).

Mertsalov also talked (extremely intelligently, and with great animation) about each character in the novel. In a decisive way, he could not praise the art of the author enough.

"The main thing," Mertsalov said in passing, "is the [author's] remarkable ability to put forth, before the eyes of the reader, a character as if alive, defining him with only two or three words, but in such a way that if another writer had covered ten pages with writing, his character would not step forward in such sharp relief. And what profound and warm sympathy toward poverty, toward suffering! Tell me, he must be a poor individual. Has he suffered much in life?"

Trostnikov told Mertsalov everything that he had managed to learn about Glazhievsky's character and existence. Mertsalov was interested to know even the man's mannerisms and his physiognomy. From everything that Trostnikov told him, he made more or less accurate references to *The Stone Heart*, explaining, as they loved to say at the time, that the author is his work, and the work is its author. If, from a lack of facts, these considerations were remiss in truth, they also showed wit and intelligent subtleties . . . [of which] Mertsalov was a great master and enthusiast. It was enough for him to have the most insignificant fact [about an individual] for his imagination to conjure up the entire personality; or, if the matter concerned an event, it afforded the missing piece. In a masterly and completely logical way, Mertsalov explained the causes of the departure [of someone] from the straight path and its likely outcome. One only had to listen how, on his lips, a scrap of fact, an event or an item in a newspaper . . . took on form and soul, something orderly and whole, like a seed that had been tossed on the ground but that gradually became a tall and splendid tree with a powerful trunk and wide, beautifully spreading leaves. It was amusing to see (and also annoying because Mertsalov developed his points in such a witty way that the listener was always carried away and believed them) how completely he demolished the first half of an idea with the second, destroying the entire edifice he had built in such a painstaking and logical way—an edifice he had come to see as fact, not fiction.

Mertsalov was a great master . . . of developing a thought in a logical way, with the most far-reaching consequences, but he did not always pursue the direction of his thought . . . and sometimes came up with extremely strange conclusions. The faithfulness with which he pursued truth, together with the endless generation of friends who listened to him like an oracle, did not restrain the innate liveliness of his imagination.

Mertsalov told Trostnikov that, while waiting for him in tormented agony (he loved to express himself forcefully), he was on the verge of conjuring up . . . an external portrait of the author of *The Stone Heart*, but that his picture did not accord entirely with the original.

"Most of all, I rejoice," he said, "that he is only twenty-four-years old. If he had been middle-aged, then most likely nothing would have come of him. One would have seen *The Stone Heart* as the result of the entire and best half of the life of an intelligent and observing individual who had experienced and felt a great deal in life. But to write such a thing at age twenty-five, that only a genius could do, someone who, by force of his understanding, has seized upon things in a way that would demand of the average person many years of experience!"

Mertsalov also talked about the shortcomings of *The Stone Heart* (as a precise critic, he could not but notice them; after all, it was his very calling to be enjoined to find them), but such shortcomings—its prolixity, long-windedness, inappropriate repetition of one and the same words, and certain exposing affectations—he attributed to the youth and inexperience of the author, which of course indicted neither him nor his work.

Circa February 1846 and after
Nikolai Nekrasov, from *The Stone Heart*

Deep into the night the friends chattered about *The Stone Heart* and its author. Trostnikov left, promising on the following day to bring the new man of genius. But despite its being so late, Trostnikov ran straight to Glazhievsky's place and openly, with youthful enthusiasm, told him Mertsalov's opinion of *The Stone Heart*.

During his brief acquaintance with Glazhievsky, Trostnikov had many occasions to see joy on the face of the new writer, [an emotion] which stood out even more sharply since Glazhievsky's countenance usually resembled a hazy, grayish autumnal cloud which, at any minute, could end up in rain, sleet, and snow. But never had Trostnikov seen such happiness on Glazhievsky's face as when he told him about

Mertsalov's praise [for *The Stone Heart*]. It was something akin to the fainting spells that greeted Glazhievsky at night.

Several times in the same week, in a nervous and trembling voice, Glazhievsky asked Trostnikov precisely what Mertsalov had said, repeating the critic's observations as if entering into them and weighing the significance of each word. Every minute he broke into a tinkling nervous laugh, struggling in vain to keep a stolid and calm face.

Not without foundation, Trostnikov thought that if there had been witnesses, the man of genius most likely would have danced about happily, as would any mortal in moments of extreme joy. But Trostnikov also noted that his own praise of *The Stone Heart* was no longer received by Glazhievsky in such a happy way. It now seemed so insignificant to him.

Glazhievsky asked offhandedly:

"Is that really what Grigory Alexandrovich [Mertsalov] said?" When Trostnikov added that Mertsalov agreed with what he himself had thought [of *The Stone Heart*], something akin to suspicion appeared on Glazhievsky's face, or so it seemed to Trostnikov.

"But there is also Razbegaev," Glazhievsky noted in passing. "After all, he is a decent fellow with taste and tact. . . . A good soul, an exceedingly good soul, and not the least bit envious! I smiled when he called my *Stone Heart* a work of genius, and now Grigory Alexandrovich says the same thing! And you seem to think so too?"

In this remark, Trostnikov thought he heard a reproach, since, in his first meeting with Glazhievsky, he had never called *The Stone Heart* a work of genius, but he did not deem it important to comment on Razbegaev's praise because to do so would be empty and shameful.

Such a thing surprised him somewhat.

Circa February 1846 and after
Nikolai Nekrasov, from *The Stone Heart*

On the following day, Trostnikov waited for Glazhievsky to take him to Mertsalov's home. The appointed time passed, but he had not appeared. Knowing Mertsavlov's impatient attitude, Trostnikov rushed to Glazhievsky's place.

The man of genius was not dressed. His features bore traces of long indecision, of a struggle of weakness with himself.

"What's the matter with you?" Trostnikov asked reproachfully.

"I'm not going to Mertsalov's," Glazhievsky answered.

"What? Why not? What's going on?"

"Well, just . . . truly. . . . Would it not be better if I didn't go?" He spoke less decisively, having lowered his eyes to the floor.

"But why?"

"I have thought about this. . . . I have thought about it the entire night. . . . After all, you said that he asked about me, even about my face . . . I'm afraid . . . if—"

Here he stopped suddenly, as if he had said something he shouldn't have. Then he added more decisively:

"No . . . I'd better not go . . ."

"What childishness!" Trostnikov exclaimed heatedly. "Are you really afraid that when Mertsalov sees you, the impact of your work will be destroyed?"

"Where did you get that from? How do you know what I am thinking?" the man of genius objected sharply, offended that Trostnikov had guessed the reason for his thoughts. . . .

"I simply will not go because I have decided that I have no reason to be there. What am I to him? What role will I play with him? What do we have in common? He is a learned man, a well-known man of letters, a famous critic, but I . . . who am I?"

"Osip Mikhailovich! Osip Mikhailovich!" Trostnikov noted in sharp rebuke. What humility! And before whom? Have I not read *The Stone Heart*? Has not Mertsalov also read it?"

"So you think there is something in there?" Glazhievsky pronounced quietly and ingratiatingly, restraining a smile of satisfaction.

"As if you did not know, as if you have not been told that even if Mertsalov does not know your personal qualities, there is still your work. . . ."

The face of the man of genius took on a happy look. Every freckle became filled with joy. But seeking to hide such a thing, Glazhievsky interrupted Trostnikov with feigned annoyance and humility:

"Enough! Enough! Perhaps you think so. But does he? Yesterday he praised it . . . but now, perhaps, he has grown cold to it and already thinks something entirely different. . . ."

Once again the shadow of genuine doubt and fear showed on his face which, we have noted, had the habit of changing a thousand times a minute, first suggesting a threatening cloud ready to pour down rain and sleet, but then suddenly shining forth with a bright, playful light like the sun lighting up frost.

"Mertsalov is not that kind of individual, and *The Stone Heart* is not that kind of work [for one] to become disenchanted quickly,"

Trostnikov replied (during which time the face of the genius again changed to frost). "He is accustomed to pronounce judgment in a careful and thought-out way."

"Splendid, splendid!" Glazhievsky countered. "So what else does he need? He has read the novel; he has come to a conclusion about it. So let him write something, even if it be an entire book. As you told me yesterday, he will write something. . . ."

"So you will not go?"

"No . . . perhaps another time when . . . after . . . there will still be time. . . ."

"Well, as you wish!" Trostnikov answered with annoyance, tired of begging him. He also had no desire to come up for a second time with proof why Mertsalov was interested in seeing him [Glazhievsky] or why Glazhievsky should call on him, having added:

"What would he find interesting in a person, who . . . who . . . ?"

"Good-bye!" Trostnikov said in place of an answer and left.

Hardly had Trostnikov take ten steps onto the sidewalk, though, when he heard a cry behind him:

"Tikhon Vasilich! Tikhon Vasilich!"

Trostnikov turned around and saw [the servant] Terentiy, running after him without a hat.

"What is it?"

"The master is calling for you. He has ordered me to tell you that he will go, that he will get dressed right away."

Trostnikov returned.

"I thought," Glazhievsky told him, "what would be the harm in going? Perhaps he is waiting for me. . . . It is all the same; there would be no great harm if I were to make a quick visit there, right?" he asked, as if he were still doubting if there would be any harm in doing so.

"How could there be any harm, when Mertsalov himself has asked and is waiting for you? How many times have I told you that?"

Glazhievsky got dressed and the two took off. All along the way, Glazhievsky kept asking about Mertsalov's habits. He also kept saying that he himself was not a refined man, that he did not know how to make an entrance and how to greet or talk to people he did not know. Trostnikov answered that with Mertsalov, one had to behave simply and nothing more!

They arrived at the staircase, and Trostnikov made for the bell.

"Wait!" Glazhievsky pronounced in such a severe and shuddering voice that Trostnikov became frightened and dropped his hand instinctively.

"Now what?"

"No, truly. . . . No. . . . I have decided that I must not go. I will not go! You go by yourself," Glazhievsky said as if Trostnikov were an emissary from hell who had come to drag him into the kingdom of darkness.

He rushed down the stairs.

"As you wish," a furious Trostnikov answered.

"Will he be angry?"

Trostnikov had not managed to say a final word when Glazhievsky was again standing alongside him, his hand searching for the doorbell. He kept looking for the thing, unaware that the handle was on the other side of the door. Glazhievsky's eyes and, generally speaking, his entire face resembled a stormcloud . . . [with] a strong autumn wind in full force; looking at it, one could hear the shrill and plaintive howling of the gale. . . .

Only then did Trostnikov understand Glazhievsky's prolonged indecisiveness, seeing to what an astounding degree the author of *The Stone Heart* had become timid, imagining himself before the severe eyes of the critic. In moments of extreme shyness, Glazhievsky had the habit of shriveling up, of taking leave of himself to such a degree . . . that it could be characterized by the phrase "to descend into nothingness.". . .[55]

Suddenly, Glazhievsky's entire face became owl-like. His eyes disappeared under his eyelids, his head hung down to his shoulders; his voice, always suffocating, lost all clarity and freedom, as if the man of genius were in an empty barrel without sufficient air. His gestures, words, and glances, as well as his constantly moving lips, expressed suspicion, danger . . . [and] something tragic that precluded all possibility of laughing.

Circa February 1846 and after
Nikolai Nekrasov, from *The Stone Heart*

The simple and tender reception of Mertsalov, especially the accolades he did not hesitate to sprinkle over *The Stone Heart*, returned Glazhievsky to his senses. The young man even went to the opposite extreme, taking it into his head to flaunt an undue familiarity, to purr a line from a song, and to tell an anecdote about his [servant] Terentiy, who, because he could not read or write, once ate some kind of medical plaster which had been prescribed for external use. The anecdote was not funny, but its exposition was marked by affectation and two or three extended sarcasms.

"Well, God be with your Terentiy," Mertsalov said. "But tell me, did it take you a long time to write *The Stone Heart*?"

Glazhievsky became somewhat confused.

"Me? . . . Not long . . ."

"Well, how long?"

After a while, Glazhievsky answered.

"How long? I began it in May . . . and finished, er, put an end to it . . . the same year."

To Trostnikov, such an answer seemed somewhat strange. After all, it was not that long ago that Glazhievsky had told him that he had worked on his novel for four years and that he had rewritten it sixteen times.[56]

"Is he really unashamed to tell Mertsalov the truth?" Trostnikov thought.

"So quickly!" Mertsalov responded. "But in truth, when it comes to creativity, time means nothing. Pushkin wrote several of his pieces in an unusally quick way; by contrast, others cost him a great deal of work. I have happened to see several chapters from *Eugene Onegin*: every word was crossed out and scribbled over ten times. But the result is the same: Whether one of Pushkin's works was written quickly or over a long time, with pronounced effort, it reads easily, with identical delight. They were all works of genius! Byron wrote very quickly. He wrote *Manfred* in twenty-two days, and several verses in *Don Juan* in no more than a single night.[57] The story goes that our Gogol found writing to be so difficult . . . that he paused several times over a single word. His manuscripts were a complete mess, but could one know that such even, flowing, and picturesque prose cost its author such effort? I have the autographs and several manuscripts of many famous writers. Would you like to see them?"

Mertsalov spoke in a good-natured way, not thinking of the impression his words were making. But if he had followed what was transpiring on Glazhievsky's face, he would have seen that it was not his words or the autographs of great people that were engaging his listener so much as that the great Russian critic had begun to talk about Pushkin, Byron, and Gogol. All the more eloquently did the face of the author of *The Stone Heart* show the emotions aroused by such flattering associations. And with this face, Trostnikov, already having begun to understand Glazhievsky, guessed immediately what was going on in the young writer's head!

"What an intelligent man!" Glazhievsky said to Trostnikov when Mertsalov left to get the writers' autographs. "And how remarkable that he understands elegance so precisely! Here is a genuine critic!"

Mertsalov was truly an intelligent individual, but his mind, of course, did not make itself manifest in scenes and circumstances like this one. Very quickly did he move from the role he had thought to assume, having resolved firmly to be moderate in his praise. Sufficient was one phrase to which Glazhievsky responded with unusually gentle humility:

"Are you, perhaps, exaggerating the merits of my novel?"

The kindhearted Mertsalov, having flared at such a remark, began to prove why he considered *The Stone Heart* to be an artistic work of great genius.

From time to time Glazhievsky threw in a word (not without design, as it was beginning to seem to Trostnikov), which had the effect of pouring oil on a fire. Mertsalov became more and more impassioned; he lost all restraint in his expressions, repeating anew and solemnly the phrase of the previous day, that [in exchange] for *The Stone Heart*, he would not take all of Russian literature!

"So you will see: I will write. Only then will the great significance of *The Stone Heart* be revealed. About such a novel, one could write an entire book, twice as thick as the original!"

"Enough, Grigory Alexandrovich! Truly, you have been so kind to me—no matter what you write about my work! I confess that if I were in your shoes, I would not know how to fill even a short review. Praise should be short; if it is drawn out, it will be boring . . ."

"That only goes to show," Mertsalov replied, not without some pride, "that you are not a critic and that you do not know how to engage such a work. To analyze such a piece means to show its essence, its meaning, so much so that one can dispense with praise easily. The matter is absolutely clear and speaks loudly for itself. But the essence and significance of such an artistic creation [as yours] is so profound and significant that one cannot merely allude to such qualities in a review."

"Well, that is your affair, your affair entirely," Glazhievsky replied, letting it be known that the critic's arguments had convinced him completely.

The conversation continued like that for an hour and a half more. . . .

Bidding farewell to Glazhievsky, Mertsalov announced that he hoped to see him again at his place.

"In a few days I will be gathering one or two of my friends and we will introduce you into our literary circle. All the people there are very good. I will prepare for them a good time. We will read *The Stone Heart*."

After three days Glazhievsky indeed received a note with this content:

"Dear Osip Mikhailovich! Today at my place there have gathered several good friends. They will be happy to meet the author of *The Stone Heart*, which you will be so kind and read to us, etc.

"Mertsalov."

After he had read the note, Glazhievsky's face extended into a long question: To go or not?

Circa February 1846 and after
Nikolai Nekrasov, from *The Stone Heart*

With unusual speed, news about the new novel of genius, and about the new literary genius himself, spread in the literary circle where Mertsalov was the center and guiding light.

Friends and visitors always saw him with *The Stone Heart* in his hands, from which he began immediately to read excepts, praising them and paying necessary tribute of surprise at the talent of the author.

The literary circle which had gathered about Mertsalov was made up of everyone who, at that time in literature, was young, talented, and noble. Along with writers, though, were several individuals who had never written anything and most likely never would. Nonetheless, they had no circle other than a literary one in which they could spend all their time, free from work or other activities.

Such individuals were tolerated . . . thanks to the patronage of Mertsalov or another writer with authority, their introduction . . . always being justified by virtues with which their patrons and others had discovered in them.

"Although he does not write poetry, he is a poet in his soul," they said about one of them. "Look how he understands the splendid! How he is able to notice each most precise feature in a poetic work!"

Another was called the noble personality, surprising everyone with his far-reaching ability to sympathize with the splendid, his supporters telling one and the same story about him as proof of his remarkable moral force. A third was hailed for his unusual humor.

In this group were also a great many who were able to feel; that is why they were called "literary sympathizers." In truth, they were good souls, most of them being completely indifferent [to things], but able to be indispensable luminaries by virtue of their connections and riches, or simply by a special obsequiousness and ability to flatter.

The Poet in Soul was rich. Once a week the entire circle dined at his place with truffles and champagne. In important cases, he loaned money to writers of whom, with credit that was moral but not real, he did not hesitate to take advantage.

The Noble Personality distinguished himself by his unusual inclination for sleep, apathy, and corpulence, but he had become a necessity thanks to his untiring ability to fulfill orders. If a member of the circle was . . . a person of substance, and if he needed a book, to get a dress on credit, deal with a bookseller, get hold of funds, or have someone host a dinner and invite precisely so-and-so and such-and-such, the noble personality set aside his personal affairs and with passion, rushed to fulfill his wish. If a writer was leaving for somewhere far away and needed help with correspondence: no one could be more faithful than the noble personality. With incomprehensible fervor, the noble personality took it upon himself to inform you about everything that was going in literature in your absence, to manage your peasants if they were in Petersburg, and to send you your favorite cigars. And he did it all with such readiness and civility, so disinterestedly and so meticulously, that the fame of the noble personality grew with unusual speed. Not content with one literary circle, he soon made his way into other groups . . . [so that] a description of his exploits at his home would take up in our notes several chapters, and perhaps even an entire volume.

The Artistic Nature was like the poet in soul, but with this difference: the dinners that, with heavy heart, he sometimes gave to maintain his dignity were unbelievably poor. With great difficulty, he also lent money in small sums, but with sizable collateral and an eye to respectable profits.

The Practical Head, having left the stock company where he worked "because of an unpleasant turn of events" . . . took it upon himself to help writers . . . to acquire funds when there was no other way to obtain some. Being on good terms with booksellers, and knowing the moral credit of each writer, he was a most practical head.

The Element of Good Breeding was kept on for albeit secondhand news and gossip . . . to which, generally speaking, all writers were extremely susceptible.

The Library furnished writers with rare and expensive editions and all kinds of necessary books.

The Newspaper . . . roamed, from morning to night, the various corners of Petersburg, eavesdropping [on conversations], and writing in his little book everything that he happened to hear on the street.

Finally, *The All-Around (and Also Embracing) Nature* gained entrance into the circle because he knew everything, saw everything, sympathized with everything, and, in a profound way, embraced to his bosom every manifestation of life, every work of pen, chisel, and brush, and, like a bee, collected from them the juice of their delights. So people said about him, noting how worthy of envy was his fortunate ability to delight in everything, understand everything, and sympathize with everything, without giving himself over to anything exclusively. In truth, he was a weighty being because in the three years he had been abroad, he had seen all the famous galleries in Paris and London and, with unusual impudence, talked about everything—even if it be Chinese grammar—sharply, decisively, with the scholarly air of a connoisseur.

Circa February 1846 and after
Nikolai Nekrasov, from *The Stone Heart*

The literary sympathizers included two or three scholars . . . who would be at home in any circle. The rest . . . were kept on because of their ample means and also for their unfailing and ample flattery, servitude, and obsequiousness. . . . Many were happy if a writer ordered them to copy one of his compositions, claiming that in so doing, they felt rapturous tremblings and shed tender tears. Others submitted to voluntary humiliation, enduring rather unpleasant scenes, such as when Mertsalov, having becoming irritated rather suddenly, found himself in momentary disarray. In such moments he did not consider it untoward to tell a literary sympathizer who had come at an inopportune moment, "Get out of here!" or to say something like:

"Where the hell have you been? I have been in desperate need of *Conversational Lexicon*. I have asked you to get it three times. You are never here when I need you, and when I have nothing for you, you always show up! So why have you come? I asked for *Lexicon*, not you. Have you brought it?"

"No, I gave it to Lyukoshin."

"You gave it to Lyukoshin! You always do something like this! Who asked you to give it to him?"

The poor sympathizer was silent, daring not to remind [Mertsalov] that he owned the library and was willing to lend out his books.

If the dinner that a sympathizer gave turned out to be a poor one, he was immediately subject to the most severe judgment:

"This is shoe leather, pal, simply shoe leather!" one would cry out, stabbing his cutlet with his fork and sticking it under the nose of his host.

"This is vinegar!" said another, having tried the sauterne.

"A scandal!" said a third, pouring his red wine on the plate.

Sometimes the dinner ended with the host in tears. But soon the passion for the literary circle imbued him with the most patient submission. Within a week he again invited his friends to dinner.

"Look sharp!" the invited guests told the literary sympathizer in one voice.

"Look sharp!" proclaimed Parutin in a bass voice, speaking to everyone without exception in the familiar "you," and threatening his host with his finger in an expressive way. . . .

A limited individual who, rarely and reluctantly, was admitted into the literary circle (in passionate attempts to attain such happiness, he even traveled abroad despite his complete ignorance of French), sought to draw closer to writers by announcing his desire to host a dinner. Shyly, he informed Parutin of his wish.

"Will there be dinner?" Parutin asked sullenly.

"There will be dinner, there will be dinner."

"With champagne?"

"How can there not be champagne?"

"Make sure that there will be enough champagne."

"There will be enough, believe me, there will be enough. Only allow me to ask: My wife also wishes to be with writers. . . . You understand, she finds it all interesting: So can she come too?"

"Your wife?" Parutin exclaimed. "Your wife! Absolutely not! Not even the slightest trace of her!"

"But she will leave right away. She only wants to take a look. . . ."

"No, no, no!" Parutin objected, moving his pipe about threateningly in his mouth. "No wife, and no kids either. . . . Are you listening?"

So the timid sympathizer chased away his wife and children so as to have only gentlemen writers for dinner.

Young sympathizers, still under the care of their mommies and daddies, also sometimes wished to get together with writers. Long did they fight off such a temptation. But in the end, apparently, everything was arranged well. Fortunately their room was on the second floor, with parents not at home. So the sympathizer hastened to take advantage of the favorable situation and to summon the group.

The feast was in full swing. . . . The champagne flowed like a river, and under its lively influence, the conversation became more and more animated. A passionate debate turned into screams and cries.

Suddenly, amidst the merriment, there arrived an old man, stepping softly, in slippers, robe, and nightcap, and with an irritated, flushed face, and a tallow candle end in his hand. Like a bombshell, he fell upon the merry company, and for a moment, everyone grew silent. He fixed a questioning and unpleasant stare upon the sympathizer, trembling and white as a sheet. A deep silence reigned, followed by the threatening, thundering voice of the old man:

"You brat! What's going on here? And you, gentlemen. . . ."

"Papenka! I have the honor of presenting to you my friends: Mr. Glazhievsky, the author of *The Stone Heart*; our famous critic Trostnikov, Mertsalov, also a critic, Lyukoshin—the translator of Calderón. . . and all kinds of other things. . . ."

The poor soul! He thought that the importance of the guests would soften the anger of his irritated parent. But in a threatening way, the parent interrupted him, exclaiming:

"Quiet! Clear out and get to bed, brat! Obey me. Wine! Lamps! Candelabra!"

He went up to the lamp and candelabra and extinguished the candles. The room became semi-dark, now lit dimly only by the candle in the hand of the old man. . . .

The guests seized their hats and, as a group, took their leave, accompanied by the threatening muttering of the old man, who did not observe any proprieties in his expressions for them or his son, whom he threatened to flog.

"I should do the same thing to your friends!" he cried out loudly, within earshot of the departing guests.

Swearing at the young sympathizer, the guests left, laughing as they did.

For a long time the young sympathizer did not show himself in the literary circle until, finally, he, having performed an important service to Mertsalov, or having brought him some important bit of news, had the doors opened to him anew.

But even more powerful than the dinners, the flattery, and the petty services were the tongues of the sympathizers, which, obedient and insatiable . . . made them indispensable. Through them the luminaries of the circle could exert their will in any and all directions, since they were assured firmly that praise, censure, news, and opinions would enter the mainstream with incredible speed and art. One must not think that such things came about as a preliminary strike. God forbid! Among writers and sympathizers there reigned a spirit of truth, perhaps because the luminary of a circle was distinguished by genuine integrity or, to speak literarily, conscientiousness. Evil acts were subject to the most severe judgment; regularly it was decided not to shake hands with someone who . . . had treated his wife badly. . . .

The newest sympathizer abhorred being the weapon of whoever came by. Everyone wanted his own opinion and, more than anything, to assert his independence. The worship of luminaries was so absolute, though, that it took only one of them to let loose any kind of absurdity that within the hour all the dilettantes would repeat it among themselves and to their acquaintances who came their way on Nevsky Prospekt. Their fervor for the glory of their patrons was so great that when a writer did not agree with the consensus and reviewed an extolled work in a sharp way, he caused sympathizers sometimes to become so impertinent that they attacked the individual and accused him of bias and envy.

Such escapades, infrequent as they were, usually ended up in shame for diligent sympathizers. The writer was driven so insane by their insolence that finally, in a serious way, he took up proving his opinion about the shortcomings of the disputed work. He was joined by other writers and even often by the author of the work himself. Here one had to see the confusion and embarrassment of the poor sympathizers, which, incidentally, did not last for long. Suddenly, they made an about-face, avowing the opposite opinion as seeming to come into view. . . .

Circa February 1846 and after
Nikolai Nekrasov, from *The Stone Heart*

Now for the writers. . . . Let not the reader think that I am going to put forth before his eyes a series of bright, impeccable portraits, edifying examples for non-writing humanity. As one thinking reviewer said profoundly, a man is always a man and will always be a man. . . . Trivial weaknesses, petty motives, and base emotions are part and parcel of the people who write good books, as well as the people who read them. As the most simple mortals, they

gossip and slander
boast and envy.

Their gossip is all the more unforgivable since they know splendidly and understand soundly to what extent such deeds are degrading.

What is even more horrible, under the guise of concern for you, in the name of justice, and/or in the name of new and enlightened ideas, they consider it their duty to interfere in your affairs, to analyze your domestic life. Without permit or permission, they also give advice, at first indirect, but if you are slow-witted, also direct, striking and overwhelming you with coarse and unforgivable frankness and with unceremonious attachment as to such aspects of your life, even those of your heart, on which, even with the most delicate hand, you could not be touched without pain and indignation.

And good God! What these characters who succumb to their influence will not do! . . . Terrible is their lot: They are called dim-witted, backward, almost schismatic. . . . About them writers invent fantastic facts, predict their ruin, count every copeck in their pockets, write caustic remarks and even reprimands without reprieve, and, finally, find fault with their small foreheads unable to accommodate vast minds. . . .

Nowhere is it possible for these poor sacrifices to show themselves. . . .

Ladies with sadness, almost with tears, look into their eyes and then lower their heads slowly.

Sympathizers also droop their heads, sigh, shrug their shoulders sadly, and converse with them more pliantly.

As soon as these poor souls leave, there immediately rises a general cry of sympathy which is so genuine, so warm, that a bystander visitor would inevitably burst into tears. . . .

"Poor, poor Vetugin, or Balakleev, or Trostnikov! What a terrible thing: Such a splendid, intelligent, and educated man B., his wife beats him!"

"She does, she does! I myself saw such a thing! . . . I went to his place, and he came out with red eyes."

"Perhaps he was asleep?"

"No, no! What sleep! One of his cheeks was somewhat swollen."

"I went to his place, no one was in the dining room. . . . I went further—into the dining room, the nursery. Finally, I entered the bedroom, and a terrible picture unfolded before my eyes. He was sitting on the floor, leaning his head against the bed, and Natalya Karpova was beating him around the legs terribly and crying: 'So you don't want this? So you don't want this?' What was wanted, I do not know, but her hair was tousled and her face was aflame, shrew-like."

"Oh, the unhappy man!"

In truth, the situation of the unhappy, sacrificial sympathizer became worse with each passing day. He was the topic of conversation with the Element of Enlightenment, the All-Embracing Nature, the Sympathetic Nature, and the Poet in the Soul. Even the Brat cried out about him, saying how he himself had seen how, in his presence, Lyukoshin had gotten into a fight with his wife and would not show himself in public because he had a black eye. The Noble Personality, setting his friend aside, whispered sadly, shaking his head in a mysterious way:

"My wife and I were not able to fall sleep for the entire night."

"Why?"

"Poor, poor Lyukoshin! . . . and so forth."

The Sympathetic Nature, having feared a rumbling in his stomach and refusing to drink champagne, said:

"I cannot talk about it, my friend, I cannot! Lyukoshin's situation torments me."

"Lyukoshin's situation, Lyukoshin's situation!"—there began anxiety solely about Lyukoshin's situation.

"I wonder what's going on?" remarked the gentleman who loved to give everything a great and mysterious color. "Why is Lyukoshin so silent? Why does he not want to unburden his soul, having revealed the secret to his friends? I hope that he knows that we are his friends, that we wish him well, and that we are ready to do anything we can [for him]. To give advice, even to take action. I will go, I will pay him a visit: let him have his say; what are we and his friends for?"

The gentleman went to see Lyukoshin, and after a brief interlude, said to him:

"Listen here, Lyukoshin: you know how I love you. . . ."

The face of the sympathizer was covered in deathly paleness. He struggled to remain silent, but the inquisitive and obsessive friend had achieved his goal. Certain that he had become an interesting person, he did not waste any time but marched bravely to the wise men of the first order, as well as to each and every one of the sympathizers, to retell Lyukoshin's secret, beginning:

"Well, I was at his place. The scene was a painful one. I cried. Never have I left anywhere with such a burdensome, joyless impression."

Encouraged by his success, others also went to see the unfortunate man. He held out, though, maintaining his silence stubbornly. But the rumors become bolder and more persistent, the sympathy more open, the remarks more straightforward. At the same time, letters flew about to absent wise men and sympathizers with a detailed description of the fight and the disastrous situation of the sympathizer.

After several days, the unfortunate man began to receive letters of an ambiguous and delicate nature in which he was assured that he was loved, that he was respected by everyone, that no one had changed their stance toward him, and that, if he took it into his head to visit, he could expect the most warm welcome. The letters kept ending with all kinds of hints, all straightforward . . . to comfort him and to set his mind at peace!

About such letters people spoke with great importance:

"Trostnikov has written to him. It seems that such a thing has comforted him somewhat. No matter what you say, Trostnikov is a fine fellow!"

The gossip spread to the most incredible degree; people spoke of their sympathy almost in the presence of the victim himself. The poor soul kept seeing that it was already too late to hide, that everything was already known, that friends were attaching themselves to him more and more persistently, and finally, at the conclusion of a lunch or dinner, when the curiosity, warmed by champagne, had become more and more insistent, there occurred the final shameful act of sympathy.

The unhappy man, besieged on all sides, confessed his disgrace to all. Such a stance would have been burdensome even if it were not for the fortunate fact that the unhappy man, noticing that effect he was making and becoming the subject of overall attention, began to tell things about which he should have kept silent. . . .

But then there began another period—a period of overt sympathy, advice, and cavalier interference. But perhaps we would do better if we lowered the curtain which we have scarcely raised.

Circa February 1846 and after
Nikolai Nekrasov, from *The Stone Heart*

Every morning people began to run in droves to Mertsalov, agitated about the rumor of an unusual literary talent. Willingly to each, he told details about the author himself, as well as about his work, enhancing the information with excerpts from *The Stone Heart*, which, as he himself said, had become his bible. In truth he had not let the manuscript drop from his hands, and in conversations, he constantly cited expressions of the new writer, which, incidentally, he did every time he read the remarkable work: such was the impression that it had made on his mind.

In support of his claims, before sympathizers, he read and reread parts of *The Stone Heart*, and in the end, the frequently repeated readings of the work so blunted his taste that he began to find splendid even things that he saw initially as shortcomings of the work.

"In this remarkable composition," he said, "there are no shortcomings. Everything in it is thought out, imagined, and fulfilled in such an artistic way that initially, the work seems somewhat forced, that it does not get to the matter at hand. But look at it more attentively and you will see that such a flaw comes not from the immature talent of the author but from your own inability and limitation to embrace an artistic piece in all its fullness and breadth. Such is the profundity [of *The Stone Heart*] that only via an attentive reading does it reveal itself in all the depth and height of its broad content. . . . Here you will see not just one novel but five, ten, twenty novels; turn to any page and there will pour forth such a splendid thing as to bring fame to an ordinary writer!"

Such opinions were in such great supply as to excite not only sympathizers but also writers for whom Mertsalov's opinion could not but help the new author.

"Have you heard, have you heard?" Balakleev told anybody and everybody who came his way, running with his usual haste along Nevsky Prospekt. "In our literature there has appeared a new genius. Trostnikov and I were the first to discover him, but I have known him even in childhood. We are friends with him. A wonderful thing! Mertsalov said that he has never read a better thing in his life!"

"Have you been to Mertsalov's?" the so-called Noble Personality asked mysteriously, meeting another sympathizer or writer.

"I have."

"Have you heard?"

"I have heard, how can one not hear, it is interesting to read . . ."

"A new epoch in literature: there has never been such a thing like it! Mertsalov says that [in exchange] for it he would not take all of Russian literature. . . . Truly it is an unusual phenomenon. Do you know him?"

"No. Why?"

"My wife is very interested in seeing him. We did not sleep all night."

"How come? Was someone sick at your house?"

"No, thank God, we are well. All night long we talked about *The Stone Heart*. Mertsalov read one scene to me. I told my wife. She has such an impressionable, sensitive nature. She could not fall asleep."

Having bent his ear in a mysterious way toward the sympathizer, the Noble Personality, under strictest confidence, passed on everything that was already known to the literary circle.

"Ach, you will not believe, Lyukoshin, what I will tell you!" the Element of Enlightenment exclaimed in a sweetish, long-drawn-out voice.

"What?"

"Mertsalov has discovered a genius . . ."

And so forth.

When they met among themselves, the sympathizers and writers talked about nothing but *The Stone Heart*."Will you be at Mertsalov's on Friday?"

"I will. And you?"

"How can I not be there! I should say so!"—and so forth.

Finally, Friday came.

Circa February 1846 and after
Nikolai Nekrasov, from *The Stone Heart*

Literary readings are out of fashion in Petersburg. Now it is *du jour* to be indifferent to literature and to run from such gatherings where whispers fly that one or another gentleman will read his story. Indeed, the best way to chase away guests is to let loose with such rumors. Journalists avoid readings, claiming a lack of time. Writers go their separate ways and come together rarely. It was not like earlier, when several homes supposedly flourished solely to serve as a haven for writers, as so-called literary hotels. A writer could go there whenever he felt like it, to do whatever he wanted. If he wanted to eat, even it if be midnight, people began to cook and fry. If he wanted to sleep, people put a soft pillow under his head and walked around on tiptoe and spoke only in whispers. If he wanted to speak, people listened to him with servility and smiled at his every word. The entire family was rushed off its legs, one racing to offer jam; another, favorite small pretzels with tea; still another, cigarettes. If, without rhyme or reason, a writer took it into his heard to sing Italian arias, the family listened to him with rapture, swearing that they would not [have to] go to the opera, and telling acquaintances later that they had had an opera singer in their home.

Literary sympathizers have also become rare and show to writers an indifference to literature. Only in small literary circles do readings still flourish. Literary dilettantes are still great fans of them, but, incidentally, not for completely unselfish reasons. Enticing writers with the news that a remarkable work will be read at their place, they at first yield the floor to the author who is of interest to the writers, but then once this person finishes his piece (sometimes such a thing goes on until midnight), these dilettantes announce modestly that they also have a new small thing which they would like to read so as to hear the advice of such choice and experienced judges. And under the guise of [receiving] such advice, which they do not follow, they begin to torture writers with their own personal works sometimes until three or five in the morning.

But at the time of our story, literary readings were in full swing. The reason for this was in part because Mertsalov, having directed the tastes of the circle, truly loved his job. The appearance of each new talent was for him a holiday. He treated the individual like his own small child—and not only because the talent was ten times ready to listen to him but also in part because most of the circle was made up of young people.

On Friday around seven o'clock everyone who belonged to the circle and who had the right to be there came running to Mertsalov's home. There even appeared several individuals whom Mertsalov was completely displeased with.

At eight o'clock there also arrived Reshetilov with a small, plausible gentleman around twenty years old . . . a gentle, quiet, reliable young man.

This young man was neither a writer not an artist. He was a special type of literary sympathizer.

He accompanied literary and other celebrities . . . and was called Sputnik. God knows how, but no sooner was there a rumor about a new celebrity than Sputnik was already constantly at his side. Even on close terms, the relationship had a strange, somewhat suspicious character. The two were neither friendly nor amiable; rather, the tie recalled the supple pairing of a modest, efficient, and sharp subordinate with his superior. . . .

The genius, in the heat of triumph, glory, and worship, could not but be flattered by the unknown small man. Sputnik, from the very first meeting, became for him a necessary and many-faceted service.

Every morning Sputnik appeared at the genius's home, passing on to him (seemingly not without exaggeration) everything that he had heard yesterday, flattering items about him and unflattering about his rivals, and also relaying gossip and the behind-the-scenes secrets of the literary circle.

He arrived with every journal and newspaper that talked about the genius.

Quickly, Sputnik also memorized and rendered as general property the witticisms and noteworthy sayings which the genius had uttered in a circle of two or three friends.

Sputnik mediated between the genius and those who wished to meet him. He gave dinners precisely for those whom he wanted to engage. . . .

If the genius wished to set in motion an opinion about his work which he felt it awkward to say himself, he told it to Sputnik. The quick-witted man understood what he had to do.

During solemn readings, Sputnik filled in for the genius's weak chest, lending his trembling voice in pathetic places in the work (being read for the twentieth time) as a sign of staggering emotion.

If a new work was being read, he exclaimed in well-known places: "Shh, shh! A splendid scene is about to begin! . . ." And the attention of the listeners doubled.

As if in reward for such disinterested and many-faceted service, the indirect rays of glory that illumined the body of the genius also fell on Sputnik, affording him his own kind of advantage.

"Do you know whom I was walking with?" he asked, having met a writer.

"With whom?"

"With Reshetilov!"

"You are acquainted with him!"

"How could I not be, we are friends. Do you want me to take you to him?"

"Do me the favor!"

"Without fail. When?"

"What about tomorrow?"

In such a way Sputnik landed in the home of a writer who had known him for ten years but who had never invited him to visit.

"Vladimir Petrovich! Vladimir Petrovich!" Sputnik cried out to a journalist who, having spotted him, rushed headlong the other way. "Vladimir Petrovich!"

"What is it?" the journalist asked angrily, turning around without stopping.

"Yesterday I was at Reshetilov's. He is writing a new story."

The journalist stopped.

"I tried to persuade him to give it to your journal."

The journalist approached Sputnik quickly and offered him his hand in a kind way, saying:

"Hello! Where is he now?"

"But I still do not know. If you want, I will tell . . ."

"Be so kind."

"With pleasure! Without fail! I will tell him simply: 'If you do not wish to give your story to Tomashevsky, I will no longer be your friend!'"

"I will be greatly indebted to you. When can I expect an answer?"

"Whenever it is convenient for you. Perhaps tomorrow. Only where will we meet?"

It ended with the severe and haughty journalist inviting Sputnik to dinner.

Having met a famous actor—unknown actors, writers, journalists Sputnik had no need of and responded to with a bitter grimace, in a contemptuous way—he asked:

"Is your performance soon?"

"I still don't know!" the actor answered carelessly, hardly gracing him with a bow.

"Why do you ask?"

"Well, you know, Reshetilov . . ." So began the same story. He promised the actor that he would advise Reshetilov to give him a drama.

In a word, Sputnik took advantage of the fame of his friend in such a masterly way that he came to regret his own lack of personal glory—as sometimes happens when one pities a hungry poor man who discusses in an artificial way the distribution and use of the capital of others. The phrases "Reshetilov and I," "I was working when Reshetilov walked in," "News, important news: Reshetilov is writing a new novel; I have already heard two chapters; it is splendid!" "Do you know what Reshetilov said about your story?" "What a strange character is this Reshetilov"—these and similar phrases slipped from his tongue, affording him a smile, attention, and acceptance from people whose society he was trying to enter. To dine at the home of a journalist or a well-known writer, to stroll with them along Nevsky Prospekt, or to ride around with them in a carriage, such events were bright spots in Sputnik's life since he understood in a prudent way that he did not have what it took to shine with his own light. . . .

Among the unpleasant and prolonged epochs of a great man's life are when he takes to drink or dies . . . or when he descends into the ranks of ordinary mortals.

Thus did Sputnik disappear instantly, leaving the literary circle with one memory, so very vague, just like his personality.

Circa February 1846
Avdotya Panaeva, from her memoirs

One time Dostoevsky wished to speak to Nekrasov. He was in a very aroused state. I left Nekrasov's study and listened from the dining room. Both men became angry. Suddenly Dostoevsky ran out of the study and into the foyer. White as a sheet, he . . . grabbed his coat from the servant's hands and rushed down the stairs. . . .

"Dostoevsky has simply lost his mind!" Nekrasov said in a trembling and agitated voice. "He threatened that I dare not publish my review of his work.[58] Someone has been telling him stories that I am reading a poetic lampoon that I wrote about him. He was beside himself with anger."

Circa February 1846
Nikolai Nekrasov, Ivan Turgenev, and Ivan Panaev, from a poem

A Greeting from Belinsky to Dostoevsky.

A knight of mournful cast,
Dostoevsky, dear, grand, and tall
Like a new pimple on literature's nose
Redly do you glow to all.
Although a new writer
Joyfully you dethrone one and all
The Emperor praises you
Even Lichtenberg is enthralled.

To you the Turkish sultan
Will send his wisest men
But the grand reception before princes
No one knows where and when.
Now a myth and a puzzle
You have fallen like a Finnish star
And sneezed your pug-like nose
At a red-haired beauty from afar.
How tragically inert
You looked at the object of your light
And so close to death.
Did not perish at your artful height.

From the envious cliffs
Bend your ear to my request
Cast your ashen glance
Hurl it at me, your guest.
For the sake of future praise
(Such extremes, you see, are quirks)
But separate *The Double*
From your unpublished works.

I will fuss over you
I will set forth, a scoundrel on the mend
I will surround you with a border
And put you at the end.

Circa February 1846
Dmitri Grigorovich, from his memoirs

"A Greeting from Belinsky to Dostoevsky" was written in 1846, when Turgenev and Nekrasov were friends, and was dedicated to Belinsky, who at that time was raving about Dostoevsky. Dostoevsky demanded constantly that *The Double* be included in Belinsky's *Anthology*, and that the work be surrounded by a border to distinguish it from the other selections in the work.

Circa February 1846
Dmitri Grigorovich, from his memoirs

Turgenev was the master of the epigram. . . . For a good shot, he sometimes would not even spare a friend.

Circa February 1846
Alexei Surovin, from an 1880 article

F. M. Dostoevsky, now residing in Staraya Russa,[59] where he is taking a cure, has asked me to assert in his name . . . that he "never received verses allegedly composed by Nekrasov and Panaev."[60]

Circa February 1846
Pavel Annenkov, from an 1880 letter to Mikhail Stasyulevich

Tell Turgenev to remember to write about Nekrasov's epigram on that wild dog howling in the wind.

Circa February 1846
Nikolai Nekrasov, from an 1856 poem

His voice like a child's, his legs like spokes
His hands, soft and red,
A strand of hair like fluffy down
Marks his beard and head.

Circa February 1846
Stepan Yanovsky, from an 1884 letter to Anna Dostoevskaya

Fyodor Mikhailovich, describing a visit to the salon of Count Vielgorsky, where he had been together with Belinsky, told me, "We were invited there as an exhibit, for show." . . . When Belinsky dropped a glass and a tray . . . Fyodor Mikhailovich told me that he heard . . . how Vielgorsky's daughter said to Count Sollogub, "They are not only barbaric and inept but also dumb."

Circa February 1846
Dmitri Grigorovich, from his memoirs

When, at the Vielgorskys' home, Dostoevsky was introduced to the beauty Mrs. Senyavina, he fainted from excitement.

Circa February 1846
Lyubov Dostoevskaya, from her memoirs

Dostoevsky's friends laughed at his shyness with women and spread the story that allegedly, from agitation, he fainted when he saw the legs of a young woman to whom he had been introduced.

PART TWO

Havens from the Storms

The Vielgorskys, Beketovs, and Maykovs

Disillusioned, if not angry, with the members of the Belinsky circle, Dostoevsky looked elsewhere for solace and support. In 1846 and 1847 he was fortunate to find three Russian families who, for the moment at least, provided the young writer with a haven from personal and professional storms.

The first clan were the Vielgorskys, whom Dostoevsky visited in early 1846. Mikhail Vielgorsky was a wealthy count, composer, and writer of romances. He was also a patron of the arts with ties and connections throughout Russia. Equally important, Mikhail was a *barin* of the old school: kind, moral, educated, easygoing, and notoriously absent-minded, but with a precise feeling for art and the finer things in life. As his son-in-law, the writer Vladimir Sollogub, noted, Mikhail "loved and took advantage not only of all that was good but also of all that was sinful." Food was a particular passion. Friends recalled inviting Mikhail to their homes to sample a wine, a dish, or the fare of a new cook and waiting, often with bated breath, to hear "judgments that were authoritative, always sincere, and often even harsh." Nonetheless, Mikhail enjoyed love and respect from all. As Sollogub remarked, "Rarely have I loved an individual as much as Count Vielgorsky."[1]

Mikhail's wife, Luiza, was even more interesting, if only because she served as a type for the "infernal women" of Dostoevsky's mature fiction. As recalled by Sollogub, Luiza—known to all as *matushka* or "little mother"—had two radically different personalities. One moment the woman showed "unapproachable pride . . . [and] the most extraordinary arrogance"; the next she displayed the "most sincere Christian abasement . . . [with] the most touching goodness and kindness."[2]

Whatever their strengths and weaknesses, Mikhail and Luiza were consummate hosts. Receptions featured legendary dinners, as well as concerts not only with the best musicians in St. Petersburg but also—if Dostoevsky's daughter Lyubov is to believed—poor artists whom Mikhail discovered in the darkest reaches of the city. Luiza's parties welcomed prominent members of society. Mikhail's gatherings took place two or three times a week and embraced novice as well as established writers, journalists, and artists; Gogol, for example, was a frequent guest. It is no surprise that Dostoevsky loved the time he spent with the couple. "Father felt especially comfortable at the Vielgorskys'," Lyubov Dostoevskaya recalled. "There one could hear excellent music. He loved music passionately."[3] (Sadly, Dostoevsky never met Gogol in their home.) Again, according to Lyubov, the musicians whom Mikhail found in the attics and cellars of St. Petersburg served as prototypes for Yegor Yefimov, the mad artist in the first part of *Netochka Nezvanova*. Mikhail himself would appear as Prince X in the second part of the work.

A second group came into Dostoevsky's life in the first two years after the publication of *Poor Folk* in early 1846—the Maykovs. Like the Vielgorskys, the Maykovs were a colorful clan. Nikolai, the head of the household, was a handsome retired officer who painted neoclassical portraits of women, as well as icons for St. Isaac's Cathedral and other churches in the northern capital.[4] His wife, Yevgenya, was an equally attractive, if temperamental, dark-haired poetess and prose writer with an aristocratic figure and face. One son, Apollon, was on his way to becoming an accomplished poet who felt most at home in the ancient and medieval worlds. (He had been introduced to Dostoevsky by Belinsky.) A second son, Valerian, the organizer if not the "soul" of the group,[5] was making a name for himself, and not only as a sociopolitical journalist[6] and an advocate of Feuerbach and the utopian socialists. He was also an early member of the circle that gathered around Mikhail Petrashevsky, and an editor of the first volume of the infamous *Dictionary of Foreign Words*[7] who contributed articles on the social significance of art. A third son, Leonid, was a historian, ethnographer, and academician. A sister-in-law, Natalya, was the daughter of the poet Alexander Izmailov as well as an inspector for the Catherine Institute and a friend of the empress, Alexandra Fyodorovna.[8]

The Maykovs mirrored the Vielgorskys physically and socially. They too loved the good life led in spacious and elegant surroundings. They too were connoisseurs of material pleasures but also caretakers of the soul. Good food and drink took their place alongside contemplation and prayer.

The Maykovs had their faults. At any moment they could be proud and aloof or sentimental and silly. Most often they were kind, progressive, and humane—welcome alternatives to the sham glitterati of St. Petersburg. They were also warm and welcoming. Every Sunday, beginning at seven in the evening, they opened their home to an extended family of young writers, critics, journalists, scholars, musicians, and artists who sought collectively to solve the problems of Russia and the world.

Unlike the members of the Belinsky circle, the visitors to the Maykovs' home were not prima donnas seeking praise and perks. Guests read their articles, proposed projects and plans, and debated science, politics, literature, and art in an atmosphere of trust, equality, and bonhomie. Reluctantly, participants departed from the Maykovs' in the wee hours of the morning, if not later.

At the Maykovs' gatherings, writers also read their works. Indeed, fiction was the primary interest of the group. It was here that Goncharov exposed to public scrutiny his first novel, *A Common Story*. It was also at the Maykovs' that Dostoevsky presented not only his writings—"Mr. Prokharchin" was one—but also "atomic analyses" of Gogol, Turgenev, and others.

A final group to provide solace and support for Dostoevsky were the Beketovs. Even more than the Maykovs, the Beketovs enjoyed personal and professional success. Alexei Beketov, it will be recalled, had been a close friend of Dostoevsky's at the Main Engineering Academy in St. Petersburg. He was a universal favorite: virtuous, intelligent, and energetic. He was also outraged by all kinds of injustice. Alexei had two equally gifted brothers, both university students. Nikolai would become an outstanding chemist, physicist, and member of the Russian Academy of Sciences. Andrei would emerge as a leading botanist, a rector of St. Petersburg University, and the grandfather of Alexander Blok. The Beketovs also kept good company. Along with Grigorovich and the Maykov brothers, frequent if not daily visitors included Nikolai Khanykov, a budding orientalist, and the poet Alexei Pleshcheev.

Gatherings at the Beketovs' were more unstructured and spirited than those at the Maykovs'. Rarely did the conversation focus on a single subject. As soon as someone raised an issue or question—Fourier and utopian socialism were frequent topics—everyone expounded on everything before breaking into smaller groups to continue the chaos. With as many as fifteen high-powered types under one roof, egos collided and clashed. Arguments and debates became heated and sharp; cries and outbursts filled the air. Momentary war gave way to enduring peace under the watchful mediation of elders, or with all-night excursions to forests and lakes where participants made merry with story and song.

Dostoevsky found the Beketovs to be practical and intelligent, noble and kind. He also asserted that the members of the family were his salvation, so much so that in October or November 1846, he lived with all three Beketov brothers, as well as with Pleshcheev, Grigorovich, and Apollon Maykov in an apartment "association," until Andrei and Nikolai left for Kazan in February 1847.

In a sense, the Vielgorskys, Maykovs, and Beketovs were the young writer's link to his early years with his family. All three groups provided oases of security, warmth, and love in which Dostoevsky could pursue interests and ideas among like-minded aficionados of culture and art. They were also among the precious few who supported Dostoevsky as a writer during the first two years after *Poor Folk*. Valerian Maykov was the only critic of the period to applaud *The Double* and to see Dostoevsky as a psychologist who would leave Gogol in his dust. If anything, the Vielgorskys, Maykovs, and Beketovs kept the young Dostoevsky out of social and spiritual trouble. Even as the young writer was beset by what he saw as the failures of the four stories after *Poor Folk*, as well as by the betrayals by Belinsky's circle, he could still take heart in the peace and goodness in the world, in a life worth living.

February 1846
Nikolai Melgunov, from a letter to Mikhail Pogodin

> [Nikolai] Pavlov is in ecstasy over Dostoevsky's *Poor Folk*. He cannot praise it enough. Ask him to write a review about the work. I do not think that he will refuse. . . . After all, it would be a shame if it were overlooked.[9]

February 1846
Lyubov Dostoevskaya, from her memoirs

> Without a doubt, *Poor Folk* was written very well, but it was not an original work. It appeared to be an imitation of a Gogolian novel, which, in turn, imitated the French literature of the time.

February 1, 1846
Fyodor Dostoevsky, from a letter to Mikhail Dostoevsky

> First of all, do not be angry at me that I have not written to you for such a long time. Honest to God, there has been no time, and I will prove that to you right now. The main thing that has been holding me

up was that until very recently, that is, until the 28th of last month, *I was finishing up my scoundrel Golyadkin*.[10] It was terrible! So much for human calculations! I would have liked to finish it before August but dragged it out until February! I am sending you the almanac now.[11] *Poor Folk* came out on the fifteenth. Well, brother! What cruel abuse it has met everywhere! In *Illustration*, read swearing, not criticism.[12] In *The Northern Bee*, there was only the devil knows what.[13] But I remember how Gogol was received, and we all know the reception that Pushkin got for his works. Even the public is in an uproar: three quarters of the readers abuse it, but one quarter (not even that much, really) praise it extravagantly. The debates about it are terrible. People rant and rave, but they still read it. (The almanac is selling in an unnatural, terrible way.) In two weeks, let us hope, not a single copy will remain. That is how it was with Gogol. They kept ranting and raving about him, but nonetheless they read him; now they have made their peace and have even begun to praise him. To all I have thrown a dog bone! Let them gnaw on it—the fools are building my fame. To degrade oneself that way the *Northern Bee* does with its criticism is the height of disgrace. How frantically stupid! But on the other hand, brother, what praises do I also hear! Just imagine, all our people and even Belinsky have found that I have even departed far from Gogol. In *The Library for Reading*,[14] where Nikitenko writes criticism, there will be a huge analysis of *Poor Folk*, in my favor. Belinsky will be ringing the bells about it in March. Odoevsky is writing a separate article about *Poor Folk*. My friend Sollogub is too.[15] I have entered high society, brother, and in about three months, I will tell you about all my adventures in person.

Our public has instinct, but like any crowd, it is uneducated. They do not understand how one can write in such a way. In everything, they have grown accustomed to seeing the author's mug; but I did not show mine. It is beyond them to see that it is Devushkin, not I, who is speaking; and that Devushkin cannot talk in any other way. They also find the novel drawn out, but there is not a superfluous word in it. They (Belinsky and others) find in me a new, original style, that I operate by Analysis, not Synthesis,[16] that is, I go into the depths, but by taking things apart atom by atom, whereas Gogol takes the whole directly, and for that reason is not as profound as I am. You will read and see for yourself. I have a brilliant future, brother!

Golyadkin is coming out today. *Four days ago*, I was still writing him. He will take up eleven signature pages in *The Fatherland Notes*. Golyadkin is ten times better than *Poor Folk*. Our people say that not since

Dead Souls has there been anything like it in Russia, and that it is a work of genius. What do they not say about it! With what hopes do they all view me! Truly, I was unbelievably successful with Golyadkin! You will like it like I don't know what! You will like it even better than *Dead Souls*. That I know. Are people getting *The Fatherland Notes?*[17] I do not know if Kraevsky will give me a copy.

Well, brother, I have not written to you in such a long while that I do not remember where I left off. So much water has flowed under the bridge. We will see each other soon. In the summer, I will definitely come to see you, my friend, and I will be terribly busy writing all summer. I have ideas. I am also writing now. For Golyadkin I got exactly 600 silver rubles.[18] In addition, I have also been receiving a ton of money, so much so that I have spent 3,000 rubles since parting with you. I am living in a very chaotic way—there's no joking about that! I've moved from my apartment and I am now renting two marvelously furnished rooms from tenants. I am enjoying life very much. . . .

For heaven's sake, please write. Write whether you like *Poor Folk*. Give my regards to Emiliya Fyodorovna and kiss all the children. I was really in love with Panaeva, but that is passing now, and I still do not know. My health is in terrible shape. My nerves are sick and I am afraid of a nervous fever or an inflammation. I cannot live in an orderly way. I am so dissolute. If I do not get to swim in the sea this summer, it will simply be a disaster. Good-bye, and for God's sake, write. Forgive me for having written this letter in a vile way. I am in a hurry, I kiss you. Good-bye.

P.S. Well, brother, for God's sake, forgive me for not having sent anything to you. I will bring everything this summer. Well, for the third time, good-bye.

I will bring gifts to all of you.

In the summer, my friend, you and I will pass the time in a merrier way than right now. I will not be rich, but I hope to have 800 or 1,000 rubles. That will be enough for the summer.

Verochka is getting married.[19] Did you know that?

February 1, 1846
Fyodor Dostoevsky, from *A Writer's Diary*

[*The Double*] did not turn well at all, but its idea was rather clear. Never in my writing did I express anything more serious. But I did not succeed at all with the form of the tale. Subsequently, some fifteen years later, when I revised it thoroughly for a *Complete Edition* of my works,

I again was convinced that the thing was a total failure, and if I now were able to take up the idea and expound upon it anew, I would opt for an entirely different form. But in 1846, I had not found this form and could not come to grips with this tale.

February 1, 1846
Vissarion Belinsky, from a review

> In [Nekrasov's] *The Petersburg Miscellany* is *Poor Folk* by Mr. Dostoevsky—a name that is completely unknown and new but, so it seems, is destined to play a significant role in our literature.
>
> In this issue of *The Fatherland Notes*, the public will read still another novel by Dostoevsky, *The Double*—and will be more than convinced that with *such works*, ordinary talents do not begin their career.

February 1, 1846
Vissarion Belinsky, from an article

> What is new in our literature? The latest news is the appearance of a new and unusual talent. We are speaking of Mr. Dostoevsky, whom we recommend to the public with *Poor Folk* and *The Double*—works that would end one's career in a brilliant and glorious way, but with which to begin *so* . . . is something extremely unusual! The public now talks only of Mr. Dostoevsky, the author of *Poor Folk*.
>
> Fame, though, is not without thorns. People also say that mediocrity and a lack of talent eat away at Mr. Dostoevsky's wooden swords and spears. . . . All the better since such thorns do not prick but set a talent in motion. . . . After all, a talent is not a talent if he has no enemies and envious people.

February 1, 1846
Pyotr Pletnyov, from a review

> In [*Poor Folk*] there are two poetic elements: serious and comic. The first is far greater than the second in that it bears the tone of *artistic truth*. . . . The comic, though, is somehow artificial and, in a significant way, imitates the tone and even the colors of Gogol and Kvitka.

February 1, 1846
Faddei Bulgarin, from an article

> All about town people are talking about a new genius named Mr. Dostoevsky—we do not know if this is a pseudonym (most likely) or his real name—and are praising his novel, *Poor Folk*, to the skies. So

we too have read this work and all we can say is: our poor Russian writ-ers! Mr. Dostoevsky is not without talent, but if he wishes to pursue a true path in literature, he should write something decent. Let him not listen to the accolades of the *natural* party and believe that he is being praised at the expense of others.[20] To praise in excess is to obstruct the road to further success.

February 1, 1846
Apollon Grigoriev, from his memoirs

[At that time] two pieces [of *The Petersburg Miscellany*] made an overall powerful impression: [Dostoevsky's] *Poor Folk* and Nekrasov's poem "On the Road."[21]

February 5, 1846
Pyotr Pletnyov, from a letter to Vasily Zhukovsky

Sollogub will send you *The Petersburg Miscellany*. In it is Dostoevsky's novel *Poor Folk*. All the Nekrasovites (people who publish in the alma-nac of a certain Nekrasov) have lost their mind over it. They are also saying that he spells death to Gogol and everyone else. For the time being I do not think this will happen.

February 6, 1846
Vissarion Belinsky, from a letter to Alexander Herzen

[One of your stories] would make a first-rate article for my almanac and share the ecstasy of the public over Dostoevsky's "Shaved Sideburns."[22]

February 6, 1846
Pyotr Pletnyov, from a letter to Yakov Grot

Yesterday . . . we read a thing or two from *The Petersburg Miscellany*. Not everything in it is to our liking. Even Maykov and Turgenev have turned into *Nekrasovites*.[23] . . . Pyotr Ivanovich was indignant over the boredom of Dostoevsky's story *Poor Folk*. So was I.

February 9, 1846
Pyotr Pletnyov, from a letter to Yakov Grot

I forgot to tell you that yesterday at a gathering . . . we read Dosto-evsky's new novel in the second issue of *The Fatherland Notes*. I did not like it, although one could see talent. He is chasing after Gogol. Wish-ing to obliterate Gogol's *Diary of a Madman,* Dostoevsky puts forth [his own type] of lunatic.[24]

February 9, 1846
Apollon Grigoriev, from a review

[With *Poor Folk*], Dostoevsky has made a forceful literary debut . . .
with a work that will be read by not only educated but also everyday
readers . . . with several pages that, we are not ashamed to say, moved
us to tears.

Poor Folk is so simple, so very simple, that only with very great effort
can one regard it as a serious undertaking, to extract from its very poor
content an entire internal drama.

A poor, somewhat old and laughable clerk—Makar Alexeevich
Devushkin—suffers all possible deprivations and needs . . . for Varvara
Alexeevna Dobroselova, one of those unhappy beings who are well
known in Petersburg, someone who is unhappy, but profoundly worthy of sympathy . . . a very simple, noble, and poetic girl . . . who
chooses poverty and suffering over debauchery and vice.

Here are two people who, to the highest degree, are interesting and
enlightened. One is given to human love and suffering; the other . . .
to Christian humility. . . . Despite their monotonous sensations, as well
as their manifestly petty joys and sorrows, they cannot but arouse our
sympathy. . . .

One sees flashes of Gogol . . . but the author analyzes. . . and digs
deeper . . . than the writer of *Dead Souls* and "Nevsky Prospekt." . . .[25]

If one judges by his great talent, Dostoevsky seems fated to be
without limits . . . [and] to be a reconciling link between Gogol and
Lermontov.

February 10, 1846
An anonymous reviewer, from an article

In a terrible, heartbreaking picture, Dostoevsky presents the extreme
unhappiness suffered by the poor in our society. The hero of his novel
is a wretched elderly clerk, Makar Alexeevich, who conducts a correspondence with a poor girl, Varvara Alexeevna Dobroselova, for
whom he nourishes tender fatherly feelings. Nothing that makes our
earthly life luxurious and bright—riches, honors, respect, love, and
earthly delights—exists for these two unhappy people. They live and
are happy only for their mutual friendship. They share with each other
their meager funds. With motherly tenderness they warm each other
with news about their poor circumstances and the secrets of their lacer-
ated hearts; but they also hide anything that could destroy their mutual

peace. Everything around them is gloomy and sad, like an autumn evening in Petersburg with its drizzle and slush. You will read these half-amusing, half-sad pages. Sometimes a smile will appear on your lips; but more often your heart will ache and moan, and your eyes will fill up with tears. You will finish the novel, but in your soul there will remain a heavy, ineffably mournful feeling—one that will recall the death knell song of Desdemona.

February 12, 1846
An anonymous reviewer, from an article

For Mr. Dostoevsky to have complete success [as a writer], he must create his own public. . . . He has hardly entered literature, but already he has met enthusiastic fans on one side, and on the other, quick-tempered detractors. Such an outcome is the best proof of his talent. Does one not recall that Pushkin, Gogol, and Lermontov also began in the same way?

February 15, 1846
Nikolai Melgunov, from a letter to Mikhail Pogodin

Have you read *Poor Folk*? If Shevyryov slams it, I request a spot [in *The Muscovite*] to defend the work . . . and to expound upon its artistic and social significance.[26]

February 16, 1846
Mikhail Pogodin, from his diary

I am reading *The Petersburg Miscellany*. Dostoevsky is not without merit or hope. But in his work are so many repulsive things.

February 18, 1846
Nikolai Yazykov, from a letter to Nikolai Gogol

According to *The Fatherland Notes*, Petersburg has a new genius: one Dostoevsky. You will find his story in Nekrasov's almanac. Read it and tell me your opinion. I myself have not yet found time to do so, but local benefactors are now praising it!

February 19, 1846
Vissarion Belinsky, from a letter to Alexander Herzen

In no way is Nekrasov's poem "On the Road" responsible for the success of the almanac. *Poor Folk* is a different thing and thus the object of earlier rumors.

February 28, 1846
Leopold Brandt, from a review

> This confusion of words, all this senselessness and absurdity are being
> passed off to us as a great talent, as the work of a genius!
>   Along with us, what will you say to this, reader? Do you know what
> kind of genius this Mr. Dostoevsky is, and from what corner he has
> been crowned with *glory*?

February 28, 1846
Leopold Brandt, from a review

> One cannot imagine anything more colorless, monotonous, endlessly
> drawn out, and deathly tiring as the unimpressive "adventures of
> Mr. Golyadkin," who, from the beginning of the story to its end, appears
> insane, and who makes constant stupidities and blunders which are
> neither touching nor humorous, despite the efforts of the author to
> show them as such, with pretenses to some "profound," unsatisfactory
> humor. There is no end to the verbiage—tiresome, annoying, and nerve-
> wracking—as well as to the repetitions and paraphrases of one and the
> same thought, of one and the same words so beloved by the writer. . . .
>   The hero, Mr. Golyadkin Senior, ends his adventures in a madhouse.
> Indeed, it would have been easier for the hero, writer, and readers to
> have begun there.
>   We regret sincerely a talented young man who understands art so
> falsely, and who has been so led astray by the views of the literary
> "coterie" who talk of his remarkable genius.[27]

February 28, 1846
An anonymous reviewer, from an article

> As often happens, Mr. Dostoevsky already has avid detractors and
> adherents who are ready to fight it out to the end. Happy is the author
> if he sees the praises of his friends as less significant than the disclaim-
> ers of his enemies . . . since, to such an individual, the latter is more
> valuable than the former. . . . Indeed, the fans of a new writer can be a
> stumbling block, even a millstone. . . .

March 1, 1846
Vissarion Belinsky, from a review

> In [Nekrasov's] almanac, *Poor Folk*, a novel by Mr. Dostoevsky, is the
> first piece by both place and worth. . . .

In the reading and writing world, the appearance of any unusual talent gives rise to contradictions and discrepancies. If such a talent appears in the early phase of a still unestablished literature, he meets with, on the one hand, enthusiastic cries and unrestrained praise; but, on the other, absolute condemnation, absolute negation. So it was with Pushkin. . . .

Nonetheless, the success of *Poor Folk* is complete. . . .

Upon first glance one can see that the talent of Mr. Dostoevsky is neither satirical nor descriptive but to a great degree creative, and that the predominant characteristic of his talent is humor. Such humor he does not express from a knowledge of life or from a human heart given to observation and experience. No, he knows such things profoundly; but also a priori, in a purely poetic and creative way. His knowledge is his talent and inspiration.

We do not wish to compare Mr. Dostoevsky with anyone because, generally speaking, such comparisons are childish, lead nowhere, and explain nothing. We will only say that this is a talent who is unusual and original; who immediately, from his first work, distinguishes himself sharply from the entire crowd of our writers; and who is more or less indebted to Gogol in character and direction. Hence the success of his talent. . . .

In many parts of both novels of Mr. Dostoevsky (*Poor Folk* and *The Double*), one sees the powerful influence of Gogol, even in his turns of phrase. But in Mr. Dostoevsky there is so much independence that the obvious influence of Gogol will probably not continue and will disappear with other personally characteristic shortcomings. Nonetheless, Gogol will remain with Mr. Dostoevsky forever as, so to speak, a father figure in creativity . . . the Columbus of that immense and inexhaustible realm of creativity which Mr. Dostoevsky must [also] pursue.

Although it is still early to determine decisively what distinguishing features Mr. Dostoevsky will have, so to speak, the individuality and personality of his talent, such things he has, of this we have no doubt.

March 1, 1846
Vissarion Belinsky, from a review

Judging from *Poor Folk*, we are about to conclude that a profoundly human and emotional element, together with a humorous one, makes up a key feature in the character of Mr. Dostoevsky's talent. But having read *The Double*, we have seen that a similar conclusion would be extremely hasty. Truly, in *The Double*, only the morally deaf and blind can fail to see and hear its deeply emotional call, the deeply tragic color and tone. But, as in Gogol's *Diary of a Madman*, humor masks and hides both. . . .

Generally speaking, for all its grandness, Mr. Dostoevsky's talents is still too young to be put forth in a definite way. This is natural: for a writer who introduces everything in his first work, one cannot expect a great deal. . . .

We have said that in both novels of Mr. Dostoevsky, one notices the strong influence of Gogol, but such a claim refers only to parts, to turns of phrase, and nowhere to the conception of the entire piece or the character of the protagonists. In these respects, the talent of Mr. Dostoevsky shines forth with bright independence. If one should think that Mr. Dostoevsky's Makar Alexeevich Devushkin, old man Pokrovsky, and Mr. Golyadkin Senior have something in common with Gogol's Poprishchin and Akaky Akakievich Bashmachkin,[28] then one cannot help but see that the characters in the novels of Mr. Dostoevsky and the stories of Gogol are as different as Poprishchin and Bashmachkin, even though both were created by the same author.

March 1, 1846
Vissarion Belinsky, from a review

One cannot but agree that for a first work, *Poor Folk* and, immediately thereafter, *The Double* are pieces of unusual depth, works with which no [other] Russian writer has begun his literary career. Of course, in no way does this show that as regards talent, Dostoevsky stands higher than his predecessors (we are far from expressing a similar absurd idea), but only that he had the fortune to come after them. With all this, though, such a debut points clearly to the place that, with time, Mr. Dostoevsky will occupy in Russian literature, and that even if he does not stand alongside his predecessors as an equal among equals, we will still have to wait for a long time for a talent that could come close to him. Look how simple is the beginning of *Poor Folk*: after all, there is no story to tell! But necessarily, there is also much to tell if one decides to do so!

A poor elderly clerk of minimal intelligence and without any education, but with an endlessly kind soul and warm heart, relying on an . . . ill-planned or implausible pretext or tie, wishes to tear from the hands of a vile businessman a poor girl of feminine virtue and maidenly beauty. The author does not tell us if love for this girl has forced his clerk to feel compassion, or if compassion has given birth to love. We know only that his feeling for her is not simply paternal or elderly, the feeling of a lonely man who needs to love someone so as not to hate life or . . . to have a being who owes or is obligated to him—an individual to whom he has grown accustomed and who has become accustomed to him. No, the feeling that Makar Alexeevich has for his "little mother, little angel, and little cherub Varenka" is something akin to the emotion of a lover—a feeling which he strives manfully not to recognize in himself, but which against his will, and in time, bursts through the surface, and which he would not begin to hide if he had noticed that *she* regards him as completely inappropriate for her.

The poor soul, though, does not see such a thing, and with heroic self-sacrifice remains in the role of a relative and patron. Sometimes he becomes lazy and spoiled, especially in the first letter, when the talk is about the raised corner of the window curtain, the good spring weather, the birds in the heavens, and that "everything is coming up roses." Having received in answer an innuendo about his age, the poor soul falls into despair, believing that he is being seen as a prankster, and annoyed, asserting that he is not at all an old man. These attitudes, this feeling, this elderly passion merging, in such a wondrous way, with sincere kindness, love, and habit—all this the author develops with remarkable art and inimitable mastery.

Devushkin, helping Varenka Dobroselova, takes advances on his salary, enters into debt, suffers terrible need, and, in intense moments of despair, like any Russian, seeks oblivion in drink. But how delicate is his instinct! Acting as a benefactor, he deprives himself of everything. He robs and pillages his very self—to the last extreme. He deceives his Varenka with his imaginary capital in a pawnshop, and if he lets slip about the truth of his situation, he does so in elderly chatter and in such a simple-minded way! It never occurs to him that with his sacrifices, he has acquired the right to demand the reward of love for love, since, given his limited and narrow understanding, he could foist himself as a husband on Varenka on the natural and extremely just conviction that no one other than himself could love her and make such sacrifices on her behalf.

From Varenka, though, Devushkin does not demand similar sacrifice. He loves her not for himself but for her very self, and to sacrifice everything for her is his happiness. The more limited his mind, the more constricted and coarse his understanding, so it also seems the more noble and delicate his heart. One can say that all of the intellectual capabilities of his head have moved to his heart. Many can think that in the personage of Devushkin, the author wanted to depict an individual whose mind and capabilities have been weighed down and flattened by life. But to think so would be a huge mistake. The intent of the author is much more profound and humane. In the personage of Makar Alexeevich, he shows us how much [that is] splendid, noble, and saintly lies in the most limited nature. Of course, not all poor people of this time are like Makar Alexeevich in his good qualities, and we also agree that such people are rare. At the same time, however, we also cannot help but agree that such people we pay little attention to, are not interested in, and know little of. If a rich person, eating through a hundred, two hundred or more rubles on a daily basis, throws to a beggar twenty-five rubles, such a thing everyone notices and, hoping to get more from him, is moved in his or her soul by such a magnanimous act. But a poor person who gives the same amount to a beggar like himself, the last twenty-five copper copecks, as Devushkin gives to Gorshkov—such an individual does not move one and all, and in the story, written with such mastery, as well as in life, no one wants to see in his deed anything other than something comic. Glory and honor to the young poet who loves people in attics and cellars and talks about them as if they lived in golden palaces. "After all, these people are also our brothers!"

March 1, 1846
Vissarion Belinsky, from a review

[In *Poor Folk*] pay attention to the old man Pokrovsky—and you will see the humane thought of the author. At first the false husband of a seductive, deceitful woman, then the oppressed mate of a reckless shrew, as well as a drunkard and clown, but he is also a *man*. You may laugh at his love for his would-be son, not unlike the shy love of a dog for its master. But if, laughing at such affections, you are also, at the same time, not touched by it, if the picture of Pokrovsky, with books in his pocket and under his arm, without a hat on his head, running in the rain and the cold, looking like a madman, at the coffin of his son [whom] he loved in such a laughable way, if this does not make a tragic impression on you—do not say anything about this to anyone, so that some Pokrovsky, a clown and a drunkard, will not blush for you as a man. . . .

Generally speaking, a tragic element pervades the entire novel in a profound way. This element is all the more remarkable since it is conveyed to the reader not only in the words but also in the thoughts of

Makar Alexeevich. At the same time [it seeks] to amuse and shake profoundly the soul of the reader, to force him to laugh through tears—what skill, what talent! And without melodramatic springs, without anything resembling theatrical effects! Everything is so simple and ordinary, like the everyday, humdrum life that swarms around each of us, as well as the vulgarity that comes to an end with the sudden death of first one, then the other!

All the characters are drawn so fully, so clearly . . . in a word, every character who appears in passing, or is mentioned in absentia, so stands before the reader as if acquainted with him for a rather short period of time.

One should note, and not without basis, that the personage of Varenka is not completely defined or complete; but such is the lot of Russian women. Russian poetry is not on good terms with them, that is all one can say! We do not know who is guilty, Russian women or Russian poetry. We know that only Pushkin, in the character of Tatyana, managed to seize upon several features of the Russian woman . . . to inform her character with definition and independence.[29] Varenka's journal is splendid, but as to mastery of exposition, it cannot compare to Devushkin's letters. Here the author is not completely at home; but he has dealt with a difficult situation in a brilliant way. The memories of childhood, the arrival in Petersburg, the disorder of affairs with Dobroselov, the education in school, especially life in the home of Anna Fyodorovna, the tie of Varenka with Pokrovsky, their rapprochement, the portrait of father Pokrovsky, the gift to the young Pokrovsky for his name day, the death of young Pokrovsky—all this is told with remarkable mastery. Dobroselova talks neither about a single delicate circumstance, nor about the dishonorable views of Anna Fyodorovna about her, nor about her love for Pokrovsky, nor about her subsequent involuntary fall, but the reader sees everything so clearly that no explanations are needed.

It would be superfluous to tell the plot of this novel or to take copious notes on it. . . . Readers, though, should recall their personal impressions [of the work] and summon them as evidence for the justice and accuracy of our opinion of the high worth of *Poor Folk*. This is why we consider it necessary to cite several passages from the letters of Makar Alexeevich. . . . [In so doing] we will force them to reread the work anew and to see that they have understood it only after a second reading. Works like *Poor Folk* are not understood the first time around; they demand not only reading but also study. . . .

In this picture, painted with such a broad and powerful brush . . . are also the melodramatic effects of modern French feuilleton novelists. But with what terrible simplicity and truth! But who is telling this story? The limited and laughable Makar Alexeevich Devushkin! . . .

We will not point further to the splendid parts of this novel. It is easier to reread the entire piece than to retell everything that is wonderful about it because the entire work is remarkable. We need only to note the last letter of Devushkin to his Varvara: the tears, the sobbing, the wails lacerating the soul. Everything is so truthful, proud, and great, and writing it all is still the limited, laughable Makar Alexeevich Devushkin! And reading him, you yourself will want to sob, and at the same time laugh. . . . How much shattering love, grief, and despair in these simple words of an old man who is losing everything that is dear to him in life. "Do you only know what lies there, where you are going, little mother? You, perhaps, do not know, so ask me! The steppe, my beloved, the steppe, open and bare as the palm of my hand! There goes the unfeeling old woman, the drunken illiterate peasant."

March 1, 1846
Vissarion Belinsky, from a review

By the way, we think that now we should say a few words about [Mr. Dostoevsky's] *The Double.* . . . As an unusual talent, the author in no way repeats himself in his second work. Here he presents a completely new world. The hero of the novel—Mr. Golyadkin—is one of those people, sensitive and crazed from *ambition,* whom one often meets in the lower and middling levels of our society. It always seems to him that people offend him in words, looks, and gestures, and that they are undermining and intriguing against him. Such a stance is all the more laughable, since neither by position, nor rank, nor job, nor intelligence, nor capabilities can he arouse envy in anyone. He is neither smart nor stupid; neither rich nor poor. As a character, he is very kind and soft to the point of weakness. He could get on in the world in an absolutely good way, but the sickly sensibility and suspiciousness of his character is the black demon in his life and is fated to make a hell out of his existence. If you look more attentively around you, you will see so many Mr. Golyadkins, both rich and poor, both stupid and smart!

Mr. Golyadkin is in ecstasy over one virtue . . . the fact that he does not wear a mask, that he is not an intriguer, that he operates openly, and that he goes along a straight path. Even in the beginning of the novel, in his conversation with Doctor Krestyan Ivanovich, it is no wonder that Mr. Golyadin is disturbed mentally. Indeed, the hero of the novel is a madman! The idea is bold and done by the author with remarkable mastery! We consider it superfluous to follow the plot of the work, or to point out particular episodes, or to marvel at the entire creation. For anyone privy to the mysteries of art, one can see right away that in *The Double* there is still more creative talent and depth of thought than in *Poor Folk*. But in the meantime, almost the entire general voice of readers in Petersburg have decided that the novel is unbearably long-winded, and for that reason intolerably boring, and furthermore, that the author has been trumpeted in vain and that in his talent there is nothing unusual! . . .

But is such a conclusion just? Without indicting ourselves, we will say that on the one hand, such an assessment is extremely false, and but on the other, there is also a basis [for such a view] as often happens with the judgment of the mob who does not understand its own self.

Let us begin by saying that *The Double* is in no way long-winded, but one cannot also say that it is not tiring for the average reader who does not understand or value the talent of the author in a profound and truthful way. The fact of the matter is that so-called long-windedness is of two types. One is from a lack of talent—that is true long-windedness. The other is from the riches of a particularly young talent who has still not matured. Such a thing one should call not long-windedness but excessive fecundity.

If the author of *The Double* had put a pen in our hands with the unconditional right to exclude from the manuscript of the work everything that seemed to us long-winded and superfluous, we would not be able to put a hand to a single individual place, because every individual place in this novel is the height of perfection. But the fact of the matter is that there are so extremely many superb places in *The Double* which occur one after another that no matter how awesomely superb they are, they tire and bore [readers]. Demyan is famous for his fish soup, and his neighbor Foka eats it to his heart's content; but in the end, he still flees from his host.[30] It is evident that the author of *The Double* still has not mastered the techniques of measure and harmony. This is why, not completely without foundation, many readers reproach the writer for long-windedness even in *Poor Folk*, although such reprimands are less with this work than in *The Double*. The most extreme fecundity only serves as evidence for the greatness and extent of the writer's talent. What should this young author do now? Should he continue on his own path alone, not listening to anyone—or should he wish to accommodate the mob, to try to acquire a premature, and consequently artificial, maturity . . . and a sham sense of proportion? . . .

In our opinion, both extremes are equally destructive. Talent must travel its own path, and in a natural way, with each passing day, rid itself of its key weaknesses, that is, of youth and immaturity. At the same time, however, it must, it is obliged, to *take into account* what particularly dissatisfies the majority of readers. Even more, it must take care to despise their opinion, but also always to seek to discern the basis of such a view, because such a strategy is almost always sensible and just.

If one can consider *The Double* to be long-winded, it is because of the frequent and often unnecessary repetition of one and the same phrase, as, for example: *"I have been reduced to misfortune! Thus I have been reduced to misfortune! . . . Goodness, after all, such misfortune! . . . Goodness, after all, such misfortune has conquered!"* . . . Italicized phrases are also completely superfluous, and there exist a sufficient number of them in the work. We understand their source. A young talent, conscious of his power and gifts, is seemingly amused by humor; but his work has so much genuine humor, the humor of thought and deed, that he can boldly dispense with the humor of phrases and words.

March 1, 1846
Vissarion Belinsky, from a review

Generally speaking, *The Double* bears the imprint of a talent that is great and powerful, but still young and immature. Hence all of its shortcomings, but also all of its strengths. Both are tied together so tightly that if the author would take it into his head to rework his *Double* completely, to keep certain strengths, and to exclude all its weaknesses, we are sure that he would spoil it. The author relates the adventures of his hero from himself, completely in his own language and concepts. On the one hand, this aspect shows a wealth of humor . . . an endlessly powerful ability for the objective contemplation of the appearances of life, the ability, so to speak, of migrating into the skin of another, a being completely different from himself. But, on the other hand, this very same feature also somehow obscures many of the circumstances of the novel. A reader is completely correct not to understand or suspect that the letters of Vakhrameev and of Mr. Golyadkin Junior, Mr. Golyadkin Senior has, in his disordered imagination, written to himself—and even that the surface likeness between Golyadkin Senior and Golyadkin Junior is really not so great and striking as it seems to him in his disturbed mind. Generally speaking, also, about the very madness of Mr. Golyadkin, not every reader would guess quickly. . . .

We have touched extremely lightly on both works of Mr. Dostoevsky, especially the second one. . . . But such an inexhaustible wealth of fantasy one does not often happen to find in talents of great depth and breadth—and this wealth, apparently, both torments and burdens the author of *Poor Folk* and *The Double*. Hence the imaginary long-windedness which people complain about, individuals who love to read but who, incidentally, do not find *Mysteries of Paris*, *The Eternal Jew*, or *The Count of Monte Cristo* long-winded.[31] And, on the one hand, readers of this type are correct. Not everyone can know the mysteries of art . . . or how to feel and think in a profound way. Thus readers have the full right not to know either the cause or the genuine significance of that which they call "long-windedness." They know only that reading *Poor Folk* tires them somewhat but also that they like the work. *The Double*, though, not many have the strength to read to the end. This is a fact. Let the young author understand such a thing and take it as useful information.

May the god of inspiration save Mr. Dostoevsky from the proud thought of despising the opinions even of the profaners of art . . . just as may this deity save him from the degrading idea of reworking his pieces to flatter the taste of the mob. Both these extremes are the Scylla and Charybdis of talent. Aficionados of art, even if they become somewhat tired from reading *The Double*, nevertheless will not tear themselves away from the novel. . . .

Most readers say that *The Double* is a poor work, and that rumors about the unusual talent of the author are exaggerated. . . . But Mr. Dostoevsky has little cause for concern: his talent belongs to those individuals who are not acknowledged and understood right away. . . . There will be many talents who will stand apart from him, but who will disappear and be forgotten at precisely the same time that he will achieve the heights of his fame. When there appears a new story from him, these very people, with unconscious curiosity and greed, will seize upon it, knowingly, wisely, and decisively.

March 1, 1846
Alexander Nikitenko, from a review

The indisputable talent of the author of *Poor Folk* draws from the fact that he cares little for the shallow desire to render *his own* impressions, *his own* abstract or weighty thoughts on life. Rather, he wishes to understand life from personal lessons . . . to probe its cherished mysteries. . . .

We are tired of the endless abuse [in literature] brought about by invented and unimaginative fantasies, the twists and turns of daydreams and apparitions with claims to reality. [We are bored by] humorous stories, essays that give us a slanted or nearsighted view of things . . . [as well as by] dramas, novels, and the like which violate history, distort our mores, and engage in hypocrisy, lies, and exaggerations of everything including virtue and vice. . . .

Mr. Dostoevsky's novel distinguishes itself . . . as an intelligent . . . analysis of people at all levels of society and in all the phases of life. . . . From all this comes truth. . . .

We understand why one kind and intelligent woman . . . having read to the middle of *Poor Folk* said, "I am crying, I cannot finish the work." Such a simple-hearted emotion is worth more than any critical assessment. . . . Having finished the novel, you feel as though you have been on a pleasant but exhausting stroll.

March 1, 1846
Osip Senkovsky, from a review

[In *The Petersburg Miscellany*] is an article, namely, *Poor Folk*, a *novel* by Fyodor Dostoevsky—that is what this little article is called: novels have now become *tone-poems*, and little articles have now become *novels*. Of all the articles [in the anthology] *Poor Folk* is the longest— much longer than the subject of the story—but it is distinguished by a touching interest. Sometimes tiresome, *Poor Folk* is, for the most part, enjoyable. Seemingly, though, the work has frightened many people. Some have seen it as gifted—as art—the horror!—and decided to praise it right then and there. Others have decided to abuse it so as to wipe out every trace of the work altogether. Some say there is no genius [in our literature] and pronounce the author of the article to be the ranks of such individuals. And what individuals they are—the world has seen nothing like it!—it simply beats everything. Others claim that there is nothing truly extraordinary [in it] and begin to downgrade the writer, so bitter are they over the newborn talent of the writer of *Poor Folk*. . . .

The poor young man! . . . Although I confess that at first I thought that the author of *Poor Folk* was not a young person . . . and even now I am not convinced completely that the writer is not a girl—a claim that I ask you take not as a reproach but as its own kind of praise! . . . The poor young man! Why do you praise [Dostoevsky] so cruelly, why do you abuse him in such a flattering way? . . . What has he done to you? . . . He, a most modest, quiet, dear, and comely individual? He who does not even dare to speak *ore rotundo* but expounds on everything in diminutives? . . . "In the grove are *small birds* running about the *small edge of the wood* . . . so *very dear*, even *most merry*. The *little birch tree* was arrayed in such talkative and trembling little leaves . . . forcing you to jump over *the little pond* and across the grass under you *harmonically*."

The ideas are the most tiny, the details are the most minuscule, the sentences are so pristine, the small pen is so repulsive, the observations are so small, the feelings and emotions are so tender and dainty that unwillingly I cry out: this is a very sweet little talent! . . . No matter how many times I have been deceived, I have a weakness for the future of any beginning talent, and I am convinced that soon . . . Fyodor Dostoevsky will force me, with full voice and deep bass, to proclaim him a most dear writer! But meanwhile, his microscopic little words, objects, characters, and details have so narrowed and compressed my lips that I, like he, must also speak in diminutives.

March 1, 1846
Leopold Brandt, from a review

> We would not burden the columns of *The Northern Bee* and the patience of readers with excerpts from assessments from *The Fatherland Notes* if, unfortunately, we were not convinced that this journal, constantly, over the course of several years, has harnessed all its energies toward spreading false and perverse ideas about poetry and art, thereby confusing both the young generation and young writers. An example of the latter we see in Mr. Dostoevsky, a storyteller not without talent but hopelessly carried away by empty and pitiful theories of that group who announces that only the "new school" writes well and that only its works are read by the public.

March 1, 1846
Leopold. Brandt, from a review

> In the crowded confectionary store Izler's, on Nevsky Prospekt, there is on public view a magnificently pictorial advertisement for *The Petersburg Miscellany*.[32] At the top of this superbly drawn advertisement are bright flowers . . . and the large figures of Makar Alexeevich Devushkin and Varvara Alexeevna Dobroselova, the hero and heroine of Mr. Dostoevsky's novel *Poor Folk*. Makar is writing on his knees,

Varvara is reading letters, delighting in their torment. As noted by this advertisement, there is no doubt that *The Petersburg Miscellany*, with its themes of *envy* and *injustice*, will be a great success. . . .

March 3, 1846
Stepan Shevyryov, from a review

One cannot but marvel at the activity of our Petersburg writers! One need only to look around! Was it all that long ago that *The Physiology of Petersburg* appeared in two volumes? Now we have this colossal *Petersburg Miscellany*, so heavy for the table. Five hundred and sixty pages of small and close-set print! There is also a huge story: *Poor Folk* by F. Dostoevsky. This alone is an entire book! . . .

This is a new name in literature—Mr. Fyodor Dostoevsky! With great trumpets, journalistic rumor mills have announced his appearance. Errand boys have traveled the length and breadth of Muscovite living rooms . . . [announcing] that a star of the first magnitude has appeared in the sky of our starless literature.

As we see it, though, not only has all this hustle and bustle been in vain, but also it has harmed this new talent. A writer for one Petersburg journal was extremely just when he said that a "new talent, great or ordinary, can now step forth bravely into literature without the protection of journals and other entities. Now a new writer is acknowledged for who and what he is." So why must he be trumpeted in advance? Let him come forth peacefully: readers themselves can assess his worth. Preliminary praises can raise expectations that are not always in sync with newly arrived glory. . . .

Of course, in the almost barren field of our contemporary graceful literature, *Poor Folk* is a remarkable phenomenon. What is the theme of this work?

In our northern capital beneath the majestic world of European splendor, luxury, and comfort lies a world invisible to the eye . . . Here belong the poor clerk-copyists, the hardly noticeable screws in the big and bulky machine that is government. Nonetheless, they are people in their own right. For all of Russia, they supply an endless amount of documents necessary to run the country. They are also, though, the butt of vaudevilles, comedies, stories, satires, and sketches. . . . Hardly does an evening go by in the theaters in Moscow and Petersburg where the public does not laugh at them. . . .

In his first story, Mr. Dostoevsky . . . depicts one of these poor clerks with the most noble sentiments toward all poor people. Makar

Devushkin lives alone, in a quiet, unassuming way. He has a sheep-like heart. He loves dearly to use diminutives in his speech . . . a sign of his meekness and humility. . . . He has only one concern: he is a copyist, but by both the style of his letters, as well as by his many genuine thoughts and observations, he is, unlike Akaky Akakievch, not at all lacking in ability; indeed, he could do something else with his life.

With a most pure and compassionate love, Devushkin is tied to a another poor being, an educated girl, Varvara Dobroselova. . . .

Dostoevsky surrounds his hero with a poverty-stricken world. Everything that is unfortunate and sad touches Devushkin's heart; such things cling to him instinctively. Here also is the Gorshkov family, the organ-grinder, and the lad with a note asking for alms. . . .

Along with such innate love of humankind, though, is Makar Devushkin's ambition. He fears social opinion, he thinks a great deal about what people will say. He drinks tea only for others, for show, for social airs, because it is shameful not to drink tea. For the sake of [other] people, he wears an overcoat; shoes he needs for his honor and name. That is why he becomes so terribly angry at Gogol's [story] "The Overcoat," which stings him to the quick, touching upon his ambition. Literature which he once loved, he now begins to call trash. Seemingly, when Devushkin reads "The Overcoat," he initiates his downfall. The outrage that makes him unworthy to pursue Varvara Dobroselova he carries to the end. For the first time in his life, he gets dead drunk. . . . His fellow clerks, having learned about his friendship with Varvara via a draft of one his letters, misinterpret the tie and call him a Lovelace.[33]

[In *Poor Folk*] Varvara is an insignificant character. She is brought in as a sacrifice to the hero and arouses little human sentiment, especially at the end of the work when, marrying a gentryman by the name of Bykov, [she] informs her friend in an indifferent way and tortures him to the end with her boring instructions for her wedding.

The story is written in manifest philanthropic tones . . . particularly noticeable in the second part of the work. For this reason, we understand this work from two points of view: artistic and philanthropic.

From an artistic standpoint, we note in this narrative observation and feeling. Much about Makar Devushkin is rendered in a very truthful way. All the episodes about the poor people [in the work] are imbued with feeling, especially the story about the student Pokrovsky and his father—probably the best part of the entire story.

Devushkin's letter about the death of the Gorshkov son forces one to become lost in thought.

But does one see this piece as an original work? Initially, such a question is difficult to answer . . . The form of *Poor Folk* still shows such a sharp, irresistible imprint of Gogol that we do not see any escape from it. But one cannot indict the writer [for such a shortcoming]. The influence of Gogol is seen in a large part of our fictional and especially dramatic literature. Indeed, it is difficult for a beginning writer to escape it. The style of Makar Devushkin often recalls the style of characters put forth by Gogol. The humorous escapades [in the piece] are also so redolent of his humor. . . . In a word, the entire coloring of the story shows such a powerful influence of a teacher that we still cannot say a word about the student. What lies ahead [for Mr. Dostoevsky], we do not know.

The philanthropic aspect of *Poor Folk* is more noteworthy than the artistic one.

March 3, 1846
Stepan Shevyryov, from a review

We do not understand how the author of *Poor Folk*, a work that is so remarkable, could write *The Double*. . . . This work is a sin against artistic consciousness. . . .

[In it] one must appeal constantly to familiar characters from Gogol: Chichikov, the Nose, Petrushka . . . and Selifan.[34] But the work, assuming one gets to the end, is like a most unpleasant and boring nightmare after a rich dinner.

The Double is not without thought. In truth, the motif is that of Makar Devushkin, but only half so: the ambition of the Russian clerk, outraged by life. . . . The theme is a rich one. . . . The Russian values what people say about him as long as they esteem his being and personality, as long as others acknowledge them. . . . [Such a thing] Peter the Great understood, and in the Russian he inculcated *ambition* . . . [when] he founded the Table of Ranks, which, although taken from another land, took hold so strongly in our native beginnings.[35]

Golyadkin, a very decent clerk with an eye on marriage in a certain household, has been thrown out bodily from the place. As a result, he goes insane and sees his double everywhere he goes. Again we repeat: the idea demands an observing talent . . . but without such giftedness, it gives rise only to nightmares. . . . Mr. Dostoevsky will understand what we are saying if his talent is genuine.

March 4, 1846
Pyotr Pletnyov, from a letter to Nikolai Gogol

> Here Belinsky and Kraevsky are raving about someone named Dosto-
> evsky. So far I know nothing about him. Can there be something to it?

March 9, 1846
Faddei Bulgarin, from a review

> From where has come this new genius, the cries about whom drown out
> all previous news? Here has appeared a young writer, Mr. Dostoevsky,
> who had written two extremely weak stories, *Poor Folk* and *The Double*.
> They are works that, if they had come out at any other time, would
> have passed unnoticed in our literature, [like] stories that appear by
> the hundreds in Germany and France, but without finding readers,
> if it were not for a party that has seized upon Mr. Dostoevsky and
> has raised him higher than a standing forest but lower than a passing
> cloud!
>
> Such a thing is laughable but all the more pitiful. What can one
> expect from a literature in which the spirit of a party can go to such an
> extreme, manifestly before the public to proclaim as works of genius
> trifling stories in which there is neither passionate emotion, nor imagi-
> native force, nor a single idea. There is even no allure in the beginning
> or charm in the style!
>
> The two stories of Mr. Dostoevsky cannot even compare to a single
> story by Count Sollogub, I. I. Panaev, Count Odoevsky, or Mr. Pavlov,
> in a word, with a single work by our new and old writers! About them
> we will say no more.

March 18–21, 1846
Anna Vielgorskaya, from a letter to Nikolai Gogol

> With this courier we are also sending you Dostoevsky's story *Poor Folk*,
> which I liked very much. Read it, please, and give me your opinion.

Circa early spring 1846
Dmitri Grigorovich, from his memoirs

> About the Beketovs there gathered, little by little, an entire circle . . .
> thanks to the oldest brother, Alexei Beketov, a former schoolmate [at
> the Main Engineering Academy]. . . . At any one time there gathered a
> great many people, most of them as young as ourselves.

April–May 1846 and later
Fyodor Dostoevsky, from an 1856 letter to Edward Totleben

> For two years in a row I was sick with a strange disease, a moral one. I fell
> into hypochondria. There was even a time when I lost my reason. I was
> extremely irritable, impressionable . . . and capable of distorting the most
> ordinary facts and attach to them different measures and views. But I felt
> that although this illness had a powerfully negative influence on my fate, it
> would be a very poor excuse [for my behavior] and even a humiliating one.

April–May 1846 and later
Fyodor Dostoevsky, from an 1858 letter to Mikhail Katkov

> At that time, in addition to everything else, I was sick with hypochon-
> dria, often to a most powerful degree. Only youth kept me from wear-
> ing myself out, from losing my passion and love for literature.

April–early May 1846 and after
Stepan Yanovsky, from his memoirs

> When I met Dostoevsky . . . I was also treating V. N. Maykov. . . . The
> name F. M. Dostoevsky was on everyone's lips, the result of the smash-
> ing success of his first work, *Poor Folk*. Maykov and I often talked about
> him, and I always expressed my delight over his work. . . .
>
> Maykov informed me that Fyodor Mikhailovich had asked if he
> could see me since he, too, was sick. Of course I was overjoyed at the
> prospect of meeting him. On the following day, Maykov came to my
> office and introduced me to the person whom I would see every day
> until his arrest in 1849. . . .
>
> Dostoevsky was small in stature but big-boned, especially in his
> chest and shoulders. His head was well proportioned to his body. His
> forehead, though, was extremely pronounced and lined. Dostoevsky's
> eyes were small, bright gray, and extremely lively. His lips were thin and
> compressed, but they gave his face an intensely affectionate and kind
> expression. His hair was not so much light-colored as it was almost
> whitish and extremely thin and soft. The hair on his hands and legs,
> though, was considerably thicker.
>
> Dostoevsky was dressed simply but elegantly. He wore a splendid
> black jacket, a black cashmere vest, a stunningly white Dutch-style
> shirt, and a fashionable top hat. Two things disturbed the harmony of
> his appearance: his plain shoes and his awkward demeanor, like semi-
> narians or military students who have finished their course of study.

When I examined Dostoevsky, I found that his lungs were healthy but that his heartbeat was not quite regular. His pulse was also uneven and extremely rapid, as is often the case with women or people of nervous temperament.

On the first meeting and for the next three or four visits, we were doctor and patient. But after that I asked Fyodor Mikhailovich to stop by my office earlier than his scheduled appointment so that I could talk to him at length about topics that had nothing to do with illness. The reason for this was simple. In only a short time, Dostoevsky had fascinated me with his intellect, his unusual humanity, and his extremely precise and profound analysis of people and events.

Fyodor Mikhailovich granted my request. He came by to visit on any and all days not at ten a.m. but at eight thirty; together we drank tea. After several months he started to drop by also at nine in the evening and stayed until eleven. Sometimes he even spent the night at my place. My mornings and evenings with Dostoevsky were for me unforgettable. Never in my life have I ever experienced such joyful and instructive moments.

My treatment of Fyodor Mikhailovich was rather prolonged. When his illness had been cured completely, he continued for three weeks or so to take the home-brewed medicine for the severe scurvy-like anemia that I had observed in him. During the time of his treatment, beginning in late May and continuing to mid-June, Fyodor Mikhailovich visited me on a daily basis, excluding those times when inclement weather kept him at home or when I visited him at his place.

At that time Dostoevsky lived in a very small room with a woman who took in boarders. Every morning, at first around nine a.m. and then exactly at nine thirty, the bell sounded in the foyer. I saw Fyodor Mikhailovich enter the reception room quickly, put his top hat on the first chair that was available to him, and look immediately into the mirror, his hands smoothing down his soft, light-colored hair, cut in the Russian style. Then he turned directly toward me and said:

"Well, it seems that everything is okay. Even today I am doing all right. How are you getting along, old man?" ("Old man" was a favorite and genuinely affectionate expression for Fyodor Mikhailovich, one that he pronounced in an extremely sympathetic way.)

"How does my tongue look?" Dostoevsky continued. "I seem somewhat pale, even nervous. I sleep on and off. I also have been having these hallucinations, old man, and my head hurts."

When Fyodor Mikhailovich told me such things, I examined him in a systematic way. I measured his pulse and listened to his heartbeats. Having found nothing out of place, I sought to set his mind at ease, telling him that everything was fine and that his hallucinations were from nerves. When Fyodor Mikhailovich heard such words, he became happy and content. "Of course, it is nerves," he said. "So there won't be any stroke or paralysis? That's great! After all, if a stroke doesn't strike me dead, I can cope with everything else."

With that, Dostoevsky changed his expression and mood quickly. His intense and frightened look disappeared. His tightly compressed lips relaxed and revealed his strong and healthy teeth. Dostoevsky again went up to the mirror to make sure that he was completely well. He also stuck out his tongue and said: "Yes, of course, it's just nerves. My tongue is white, not yellow! That means I am fine!"

When we sat down for tea, Fyodor Mikhailovich said: "Well, give me just half a cup without sugar. My first cup I will have this way; but my second, I will take it with sugar and a rusk." Every time he said the same thing.

At tea we talked . . . most of all about medicine, social questions, and topics on literature and art. We also spoke a great deal about religion. In such matters, Fyodor Mikhailovich impressed me—and also mutual acquaintances, all of whom were university educated and well read—with his erudition, the singular accuracy of his views, as well as his analysis of people and events in so profound a way that the evidence for his convictions we accepted unconsciously as palpable and concrete.

April–early May 1846 and after
Stepan Yanovsky, from his memoirs

Fyodor Mikhailovich also borrowed books on medicine, especially works that dealt with the nervous system and illnesses of the brain. He was also interested in studies of spiritual disorders and of the development of the cranium à la the fashionable system of Gall.[36] This last item with its drawings so engaged Fyodor Mikhailovich that he often arrived at my place in the evening to talk about the anatomy of the cranium and the brain, the physiological functioning of the brain and nerves, and the meaning of the cranial indentations and elevations to which Gall had attached such significance. Demanding from me an explanation of every nook and cranny of his skull, Fyodor Mikhailovich often extended our conversations deep into the night.

Fyodor Mikhailovich's skull was truly splendid. His broad forehead . . . sharply defined sinuses, equally pronounced edges of his eyelids, and the lack of any elevation in the lower back of his cranium made him look like Socrates. Fyodor Mikhailovich himself was very pleased with such a comparison. . . . He added: "It is a good that there are no elevations on the back of the head. That means that I am not a hat-wearer. I do not like hats at all; but I love bonnets, especially the type that Yevgenya Petrovna wears" (the mother of Apollon and other Maykovs whom we all loved and respected deeply).

April–early May 1846 and after
Stepan Yanovsky, from an 1882 letter to Anna Dostoevskaya

I have had many good, kind, and honest acquaintances [in my life]. Some I have loved in a powerful way and considered them colleagues, even friends, the latter including Apollon Nikolaevich Maykov . . . [and] Mikhail Mikhailovich Dostoevsky.

But none of them were like Fyodor Mikhailovich . . . whom I followed with my heart and soul . . . nourished by the deep humanity and striving for truth which God had endowed him with so lavishly. . . .

We saw each other almost every day and talked without stopping. . . . Thanks to my friend, I have become sensitive to any lie and falsehood, as well as to a sad and burdensome feeling . . . when I come across some everyday picture . . . of our spiritual life in which truth is distorted . . . in a tendentious Khlestakov-type of way.[37]

Here the image of Fyodor Mikhailovich rises before my eyes. I see his lips compressed from moral unease. I notice the movement of his right hand as he first fixes his hair and then twirls his small mustache. I even hear his voice clearly, saying—"oh, pal, how untrue, how vile"— and I, too, feel burdened and vile.

April 1, 1846
Fyodor Dostoevsky, from a letter to Mikhail Dostoevsky

I am sending you a helmet with accessories and a pair of epaulets. The covering on the helmet is not attached because, as I was told, the shako would get ruined on the road. I do not know if I have served you well or not. If not, I am not at fault because about these things I understand absolutely nothing. I am behind the times, my friend.

Now the second question. You ask why I am so late [in replying to you]. But, my dear friend, I have been so very busy that however strange it may seem to you, I could not find time to fulfill your request. Truly, from sheer negligence, I missed two mailings. I am guilty. Do not be angry.

Now to other things, my friend. Most likely you are reproaching me for not having written to you in such a long time. But I agree completely with Gogol's *Poprishchin*: *"A letter is nonsense, letters are written by pharmacists."* What could I write to you? If I were to begin to speak as I would like, I would have to fill entire volumes. Every day in my life there are so many new things, so many changes, so many impressions, and so many things that are good and useful for me; there are also many unpleasant and disadvantageous things that even I myself do not have time to think them through. In the first place, I am always busy. I have tons of ideas and I am writing constantly. Do not think that I am lying completely in a bed of roses. Nonsense. In the first place, I have gone through a lot of money, i.e., exactly 4,500 rubles since we parted and 1,000 paper rubles as an advance on my future. Thus, with that tidiness of mine which you know well, I have robbed myself completely, and again am beginning to live as before, without a copeck.

But that is all right. My fame has reached an apogee. In 2 months, according to my calculations, I have been spoken about 35 times in various publications. In some of them I am praised to the skies, in others I am praised with exceptions, and in still others I am cursed to an extreme. What could be better and more noble? But here is what is vile and tormenting: our people, Belinsky, and everyone else are displeased with me over Golyadkin. The first impression was unrestrained delight, clamor, noise, and talk. The second was criticism. Specifically, everyone in the general clamor, i.e., *our people* and the entire public, have found Golyadkin to be so flaccid, boring, and so drawn out that it is impossible to read it. But what is most comical of all is the fact that everyone is angry at me for long-windedness, but also that everyone is reading and rereading me in a frenzied way. The only thing one of our people does is to spend time reading a chapter a day so as not to exhaust himself. All he does is smack his lips from pleasure. Some of the public yell that my work is quite impossible, that it is stupid both to write and to publish such things; others scream that it is taken and copied from their lives; and from still others I have heard such madrigals that it is even embarrassing to speak of them.

As for me, I was even depressed for a while. I have a terrible vice: boundless vanity and ambition. The idea that I had failed expectations and ruined a thing that could have been a great work was killing me. Golyadkin became repulsive to me. Much of it was written in haste and exhaustion. The first half is better than the last. Along with brilliant pages there is foulness and trash. It is nauseating and one does not want to read it. That is exactly what created a hell for me for a time and I fell ill from misery. Brother, I will send you Golyadkin in about two weeks. You will read it. Write me your opinion.

I am passing over my life and my *studies* and will say a bit about our news. The 1st (enormous news) is that *Belinsky* is leaving *The Fatherland Notes*.[38] He has ruined his health terribly and is heading out for the waters and, perhaps, for abroad. He will not take up criticism for about two years.[39] But to support his finances, he is publishing an almanac of *gigantic size* (60 signature pages in all).[40] For him I am writing two stories: the first, "Shaved Sideburns," and the second, "A Tale about Destroyed Offices," both with stunningly tragic interest and—I am already answering [my critics]—condensed as much as possible. These the public are waiting for with impatience. Both stories are short. In addition, I am writing something for Kraevsky and a novel for Nekrasov. All this will take me a year. I am finishing "Shaved Sideburns."[41]

The second piece of news is that an entire horde of writers has appeared on the scene. Some are my rivals. Of them Herzen (Iskander) and Goncharov are especially remarkable. The former has published, the latter is only starting out and has not yet appeared in print anywhere.[42] People praise them terribly. For the time being I am in first place and I hope I stay there forever. Generally speaking, never before has literature begun to be in full swing as now. That is all for the best.

The third piece of news is that I will visit you either very early or very late, or I will not come at all. I am in debt. I will not have any money (without money I will not come for anything), and in the third place, I am swamped with work.

The fourth piece of news is that Shidlovsky has responded. His brother visited me. I am beginning a correspondence with him.

The fifth piece of news is that if you want, my beloved friend, to earn something in the literary field, there is a chance to show off and produce an effect with one translation. Translate Goethe's *Reynard the Fox*.[43] I was even asked to entrust the translation to you, since Nekrasov needs the piece for his almanacs. If you want, translate it. Do not hurry. Even if I do not arrive by May 15th or June 1st,[44] send what you have ready. Everyone is heading off for the summer; but if it is possible,

I, perhaps, will place it somewhere even in the spring and will bring you the money. If not in the spring, then in the fall—but *definitely, without fail.* There will definitely be money. Nekrasov is a publisher, he will buy it. Belinsky will buy it, Ratkov will buy it, and Kraevsky is completely at my disposal. It is a matter of profit. People here have talked about this translation. So start, if you wish, and I will vouch for its success. If you translate roughly three chapters, send them to me. I will *show* them to the gentlemen and they will give you an advance.[45]

I have never been so rich in activity as I am now. Everything is moving along, in full swing. . . . But what will happen? . . .

Good-bye, my dear. I kiss you all and wish you all the best. I kiss both Emiliya Fyodorovna's hands. The children too. How are you? Write about yourself. Oh, my friend, I want to see you. But what can I do?

P.S. Verochka has been married 3 months already. They say happily so. Uncle [Kumanin] gave her as much as he gave Varya. She married *Ivanov* (His Excellency). He is 30 years old. He is a professor of chemistry somewhere.

April 1, 1846
Vissarion Belinsky, from a review

> *The Northern Bee* has filled [pages] with not entirely calm and collected proof that Mr. Dostoevsky has not an iota of talent. If you so agree, all the better for you. You will say such a thing and you will be at peace. But others will think that you are not sincere, and that—for whatever reason—you are afraid of a new talent. . . . But in so doing, you harm only yourself.

April 15, 1846
Faddei Bulgarin, from an article

> Almost all our writers are like spoiled young ladies, suffering from the *vapors,* hysteria, and appetite.

April 26, 1846
Fyodor Dostoevsky, from a letter to Mikhail Dostoevsky

> I have not written to you because up until today I have not been able to take up pen in hand. The reason for that is that I have been sick and near death in the full sense of the word . . . with an irritation of the entire nervous system. The illness . . . produced a rush of blood and an inflammation of the heart which was remedied barely by leeches and two bloodlettings. I also made myself worse with various concoctions,

drops, powders, and other similar abominations. Now I am out of danger . . . but my recovery will take a long time. My treatment has to be both physical and moral. In the first place, with diet and continual physical deprivations that have been prescribed for me. In the second, with a change of place, abstention from all strong shocks and sensations, a balanced and tranquil life, and finally, order in everything. To this end, a trip to Revel[46] (although not for bathing, since such an activity has been deemed harmful for me) for a change of scene and lifestyle has been prescribed as a drastic remedy. But since I do not have a copeck to my name, and I need huge amounts of money for this trip, not so much for Revel, but for expenses and payments of debt in Petersburg. So practically everything concerning my life and health depends on Kraevsky. If he gives me an advance, I will come; if not, I will not. . . .

I am writing to you in haste and on a business matter. I have a request that you should fulfill with all your energy. Belinsky is going (he left yesterday) to Moscow for the summer. Then together with his friend the actor Shchepkin and a few other people, he is taking a trip to the south of Russia, to Ukraine, and to the Crimea. He is returning in September to take care of his almanac. His wife, however, and her sister and year-old child are setting out for Gapsal.[47] Maybe I will go with them, maybe not. The ship stops at Revel for a few hours. The problem is that their household staff refuses to go to a foreign place, even for the summer. So they are left without a nanny. It is impossible to hire one here . . . except for a huge sum which Mme. Belinskaya is unable to pay. So they ask me most humbly to write . . . that you try with all your might (which I also ask) to find in Revel a nanny, *a German and not a Finn* (that is essential), and if possible an older woman who would agree to go with them to Gapsal until September. The pay will be 15 paper rubles a month. If, however, she agrees to go with them later to Petersburg, then 25 paper rubles. Mme. Belinskaya cannot pay any more than that. It goes without saying that it is quite desirable to find a woman with a good reputation, in a word, a respectable nanny. When you have found her, keep her in readiness from May 5th on, i.e., for departure at a moment's notice because . . . since the ship stops in Revel for four hours, Mme. Belinskaya will come to see you. You will send for the nanny, and the entire business will be taken care of. Everything depends on whether you agree or not. I fall before your knees to do this. I implore you for myself. I like and respect these people. I ask you most humbly that you and Emiliya Fyodorovna try your best.

Mme. Belinskaya is quite weak, aging, and ailing;[48] she is forced to travel all alone, and with a child to boot. No individual could do better than to work for them. They are good people, they live in a contented way, and they treat people superbly. For them a nanny is only a nanny and nothing else. For heaven's sake, brother, please do your best. Also answer me as soon as possible. The Belinskys may be in Revel by the 10th. Write me soon and tell me whether passengers are accepted on the ship that goes from Petersburg to Gapsal via Revel. Otherwise they will not take the nanny on board.

Before my departure I have to finish a short story for the money I borrowed from Kraevsky.[49] Then I will take an advance from him.

The enormous activity in literature is in full swing. . . . I have great hopes. When we see each other, I will tell you all about them, but for now, good-bye.

April 30, 1846
Apollon Grigoriev, from an article

In our humble opinion, *The Double* is a work that is therapeutic and pathological but also literary. It is a story of madness analyzed to an extreme, but also it is as repulsive as a corpse. . . . Having read *The Double*, we think instinctively that the author will pursue this path further. He is fated to play in our fiction the same role that Hoffmann did in German literature. Hoffmann saw . . . German bourgeois life . . . in broken, monstrous, and fantastic forms. In exactly the same way does Dostoevsky delve into the life of a civil servant so that this boring, naked reality assumes a type of raving that is close to madness. . . . We also confess that it will be unfortunate if the goal of Dostoevsky is the same as [that of] the talented but abnormal Hoffmann.

May 1, 1846
An anonymous reviewer, from an article

On Saturday there was again a reading . . . by Mr. Shchepkin. This time we regret to say that the evening was not entirely successful, despite the fact that the audience had filled the room completely. Mikhail Semyonovich was not in his best form. His first piece, Gogol's "Old-World Landowners,"[50] a work that is splendid, full of life, naturalness, and feeling, Shchepkin read in a way that we have never heard from him before. A letter from Dostoevsky's *Poor Folk* went better. But why did Shchepkin read such a thing? Mr. Dostoevsky has inalienable qualities as a writer: a profound view [of life] and a knowledge of the human heart, as well as a masterly brush [to render such things in fiction]. The scene in which Devushkin stands before his kind boss is beyond words! The fact of the matter, though, is that in his faithfulness to life, Dostoevsky comes close to daguerreotype.

May 14, 1846
Nikolai Gogol, from a letter to Anna Vielgorskaya

I have only just started *Poor Folk*. I read three pages and then peeked in the middle to see the makeup and manner of the discourse of the new writer. (You were wrong to tear out only *Poor Folk* and not send me the entire anthology.) . . . In the author of *Poor Folk*, one sees talent. The choice of subject speaks in favor of his spiritual qualities, but also to the fact that he is young. There is much garrulousness and little concentration. Everything [in the story] would have turned out in a much more lively and powerful way if it had been more compressed. Incidentally, my comments draw not from a thorough reading of the work but only from having leafed through it.

Circa mid-May 1846
Stepan Yanovsky, from an 1882 letter to Orest Miller

About ten in the evening, as was our custom, we sat down to tea . . . and Dostoevsky talked about how he was thinking of arranging his life in general . . . about why, not wanting to leave literature, he did not want to be in [state] service, and why he had abandoned his career as an engineer. . . . [He added that he intended] to write and write, and in so doing to defend the humiliated and the injured.

May 16, 1846
Fyodor Dostoevsky, from a letter to Mikhail Dostoevsky

The ladies who have delivered this message to you are Mme. Belinskaya and her most interesting sister. Please receive them well, and if possible, it would not be a bad idea to invite them to dinner. They also asked to be introduced to Emiliya Fyodorovna. As much as possible, nourish their egotism; and, of course, talk about literature as little as possible. But you yourself understand these matters better than I do. Tell them where to stay and what to do. I do not know what is better for them—to stay in Revel or move on to Gapsal.[51]

About myself I will say that I absolutely do not know what is going to happen to me. I do not have a copeck to my name and I also do not know where I can get any money. I cannot leave here unless I have specifically 500 rubles to pay off my debts. So judge for yourself. It is even more than likely that . . . I will not come [to visit you].

I find it boring and burdensome to be here. I am writing but I do not see an end to my work. I send my regards to Emiliya Fyodorovna and ask her graciousness toward the Belinsky ladies. I rely on all her indulgence and kindness. It would also not be a bad idea if for their part, Fedya and Masha[52] showed their cordiality and expressed their opinions openly, to the extent of their well-known solidarity. Well, good-bye, brother, there is no time [to write further]. I absolutely never have had a more difficult time of it [than now]. Boredom, sadness, apathy, and a feverish, convulsive expectation of something better torment me. There is also my illness. The devil knows what it is. If only all of this would somehow pass me by.

After May 16, 1846
Maria Belinskaya, from an 1862 letter to Fyodor Dostoevsky

Fifteen years have passed since the time we last saw each other. Perhaps you have forgotten about my existence, but toward you I have never stopped [having] the most friendly disposition. I have always taken a sincere interest in you.

How often do my sister and I recall you and that time when you were acquainted with my husband. With what attention did my daughter listen to you as you held her in your arms.[53]

After May 16, 1846
Fyodor Dostoevsky, from an 1862 letter to Maria Belinskaya

Your letter made an extremely pleasant impression on me. I so loved and respected your unforgettable husband and [the letter] caused me to recall everything of the best time of my life.

May 24, 1846
Fyodor Dostoevsky, from testimony to the Investigatory Commission for the Petrashevsky affair

My acquaintance [with Petrashevsky] was accidental. If I am not mistaken, I was with Pleshcheev in a candy store . . . and was reading the newspapers. I saw that Pleshcheev had stopped to speak to Petrashevsky, but I had no idea who he was. I left about five minutes later. . . . On the street Petrashevsky caught up with me and asked suddenly, "If I may be so bold as to inquire: what is the subject of your new story?"

Since Petrashevsky had not said a word to me in the candy store, I assumed that he was simply a passer-by . . . not a friend of Pleshcheev. But Pleshcheev, having caught up with us, introduced us. We spoke a bit . . . and parted. So this is how Petrashevsky attracted my curiosity. My first encounter with him was on the eve of a trip to Revel, but I saw him later that winter.

Petrashevsky seemed to [me] a very original individual, not empty. I saw his erudition, his knowledge.

May 24, 1846
Fyodor Dostoevsky, from a letter to Andrei Dostoevsky

Brother. I am leaving right now for Revel. I am sorry that I did not drop by to see you. Recently I have been keeping different apartments, and in general, disorder has overtaken my life because I am uncertain as to whether I will remain in Petersburg. You probably looked for me but did not find me. My health is not bad, but I have not recovered completely. I am leaving to take a cure. I will pass along your regards to our brother. Farewell for now.

June 14, 1846
Vissarion Belinsky, from a letter to Maria Belinskaya

From [Mikhail] Dostoevsky you can find out who are the best doctors in Revel.

June 15, 1846
An anonymous reviewer, from an article

The fabrication of geniuses which the critic of one well-known journal[54] does so successfully must willy-nilly arouse the indignation of well-thinking people. Recently Dostoevsky's prank, his *Poor Folk*, has brought more harm than good to the author of this extremely remarkable but far from brilliant piece.

June 24, 1846
Nikolai Yazykov, from a letter to Nikolai Gogol

Tell me your opinion of Dostoevsky's story [*Poor Folk*]. Piter's[55] critics and scribblers are praising it to the skies. The story is rather long, and I do not feel like reading it for the hell of it. You who are always tormented by a thirst for reading will read it, no matter what. Pletnyov says that Dostoevsky is among your imitators and that the distance between you and him is the same as between Karamzin and Prince Shalikov! That is a devil of a difference!

Circa July 1846 and after
Alexei Pleshcheev, from an 1888 letter to Apollon Maykov

> The distant past breaking into my memory, I, with special pleasure, pause at that time when I, still a beginner, encountered in your family such warm welcome and approval. What a shining time in literature. The usual visitors and friends at your home were I. A. Goncharov and F. M. Dostoevsky, both of whom read their works.

Circa July 1846 and after
Ivan Goncharov, from his memoirs

> The home [of N. A. Maykov] brimmed with life. . . . Young scholars, musicians, and artists . . . crowded . . . in shelter-like rooms. Together with the host and hostess, they were like a family or school in which everyone taught everyone else, exchanging ideas as well as news of science and art that engaged Russian society at the time.

Circa July 1846 and after
Alexander Skabichevsky, from his memoirs

> The members of the Maykov family . . . were severely balanced individuals . . . who housed a private intellectual egoism and, from time to time, an adequate dose of spiritual callousness. [Such shortcomings] they mitigated with societal tact and deportment so that everyone, from the highest to the lowest, found them to be very easygoing and pleasant. Indeed, to us youths, it would have been difficult to find people who were more progressive, idealistic, and humane. Here was the greatest "harmony" of all the elements of human nature . . . the quintessence of a truly enlightened ethics which took the place of the dilapidated, commonplace morality which we had rejected.
>
> To a man [and woman], all the Maykovs were Epicureans, exacting connoisseurs of everything that was graceful and elegant. They were also gourmets who ate and drank in a fairly tasteful way. All the Maykovs were also contemplative types, with a touch of sentimentality. Father Maykov . . . supplied icons for St. Isaac's Cathedral and other churches in St. Petersburg, so much so that he hovered in a world of celestial beings, with eyes that sometimes showed sadness. His eldest son, Apollon, was filled with chaste sounds and prayers. He loved to be

carried away by his own poetic imagination, by classical antiquity and medieval knighthood. He descended . . . into reality only to imitate the love motifs of Heine or to sing the great feats of his world.

The middle son, Vladimir, was also inclined toward introspection. His job as an administrator in the Department of External Trade so seduced him that his wife, who possessed a more lively and passionate temperament . . . ran off to the Caucasus with a nihilist whom Goncharov punished . . . in the person of Mark Volokhov in his novel *The Precipice.* . . .[56]

The younger Maykov brother, Leonid . . . lacked any brilliant or even outstanding gifts. He was a sincere and assiduous researcher-bibliographer . . . who once directed his intellectual gifts at the untalented Tredyakovsky, his prolix *Telemachus.* . . .[57] If he held such visible posts as assistant to the director of the public library, the vice president of the Academy of Sciences, and the chair of the ethnographic division of the Geographical Society . . . it was, for the most part, due to the protection and powerful ties of his brother Apollon . . . who as a youth had achieved glory and fame in the praises of highly placed individuals.

Circa July 1846 and after
Albert Starchevsky, from his memoirs

In all respects, the Maykov family was a model and splendid group, the likes of which people dream about in French novels and stories. . . . It consisted of six people, but almost daily, beginning with dinner until late at night, it embraced a respectful society.

The head of the family, Nikolai Apollonovich Maykov, was the son of Ap. Al. [Apollon Alexandrovich] Maykov, the well-known director of the imperial theaters in the beginning of the century. He was a retired officer, a handsome brunet, with an open and kindhearted disposition. He was married to Yevgenya Petrovna [Maykova] . . . a shapely, beautiful brunette, with an oblong aristocratic face, which was mirrored in her second son, Valerian. After he married, N. A. Maykov retired and lived in Moscow. When the time came to educate his sons, he moved to Petersburg.

While still in Moscow, N. A. Maykov began to take up painting as a lover of art and a self-taught student. In Petersburg he dedicated himself to this undertaking fully. One time he set out for the flea market in Apraksin Court, where formerly masses of ancient small shops housed books, drawings, and pictures in oils, large and small. There he suddenly came across a small picture, cut from a steel form and featuring a well-known Catholic *Virgo immaculata* or something of that kind, with the Most Holy Virgin trampling a snake with her foot. N. A. bought the engraving and from it began to draw a picture in oil colors. Soon there was ready another wondrous image . . . which, with the approval of Tsar Nikolai Pavlovich, was placed behind the altar in the new Troitsky Monastery. . . .[58]

His reputation as an artist solidified . . . N. A. soon painted several more icons for the Troitsky Izmailovsky Cathedral,[59] as well as for the Small Church of the Winter Palace, which had been restored after the famous fire.[60] Finally he completed an order for the left side of the iconostasis for St. Isaac's Cathedral. The colors that N. A. Maykov [used for his icons] were highly singular, and although his drawings and compositions offended many, he was given additional work for St. Isaac's Cathedral.

At that time, all the young Maykovs were students at the university. . . . N. A. Maykov was roughly fifty years old. Yevgenya was about forty. To the highest degree, they were cordial, pleasant, and welcoming. The oldest son, Al. Nik., was still a very young man, a small version of his father. Early in life he showed a poetic talent which later made him famous. The second son, Valerian, was distinguished by a great capacity for sociopolitical journalism, but at that time he was just spreading his wings when accidental death cut short the life of this very gifted and talented youth. The third son, Vladimir Nikolaevich, called the "little old man" because of his quiet and serene nature, was not as gifted and still in high school. The fourth, Leonid Nikolaevich, was still a boy at the time.

The Maykov family also included the younger brother of Nik. Apol., Konstantin Apol., a colonel in the Izmailovsky Regiment[61] and director of the military academy who often visited his brother's home and spent entire evenings with young people there. There was also Natalya Alexandrovna Maykova, the widow of one of N. A.'s brothers[62] . . . the daughter of a well-known writer, poet, and journalist of the twenties,[63] a lady who was superbly educated, well bred, and gifted with superb external features and wit. She was the inspector for the Catherine Institute and was known personally to Empress Alexandra Fyodorovna. . . . There were also people who were engaged in science, art, and literature.

The gentility, openness, humor, and cordiality of the hosts, together with their ability to keep conversations going with lively episodes and digressions . . . greatly affected the young visitors who came to the

Maykov home. . . . In their circle one heard vulgar talk or anecdotes with double meanings. No one was censured, condemned, or ridiculed. Everyone made merry, and they were free, easy, and engaged. Only unwillingly did regular visitors make for their hats at three in the morning to head home.

Also at the Maykovs' home . . . were readings of prominent individuals in contemporary journalism, together with critical and other comments on matters at hand. . . .

Ivan Alexandrovich Goncharov . . . announced once evening that before he published his first piece, *A Common Story*, he wanted to read it at the Maykovs' home for comments . . . that were precise, open, and unrestrained . . . from close friends and well-wishers.

Circa July 1846 and after
Stepan Yanovsky, from a letter to Anna Dostoevskaya

At the salon of the Maykovs . . . Fyodor Mikhailovich prevailed . . . with his characteristic atomic analysis, delving into the character of works by Gogol, Turgenev, and his own Prokharchin, which at that time most readers did not understand.

July 1846
Pyotr Bilyarsky, from a review

Regarding *The Double* by Mr. Dostoevsky . . . never again will we like to see similar abuses of talent and effort. . . . The conversation of the characters in this story transcends all borders of decency . . . a meld of curses and oaths . . . intolerable for educated readers.

July 1, 1846
Valerian Maykov, from a review

[Dostoevsky's] Mr. Golyadkin Senior is as remarkable and as universal as Chichikov or Manilov.[64] A large number of acquaintances and even yourself, you call Golyadkin.

July 12, 1846
Vissarion Belinsky, from a letter to Maria Belinskaya

So, your trip to Revel did not bring you any pleasure or advantage because . . . you hoped, mistakenly, to find in Revel a servant and risked going there without one. . . .

The apprehension of [your sister] Agrafena [Orlova] that I babble on to Dostoevsky that his relatives are wishy-washy is completely unfounded. I would be not a chatterbox but a fool if I did not consider myself correct to laugh at Dostoevsky in the eyes of people who are close to him, and who . . . were kind to you. On this account, I can assure you.

August 15–18, 1846
Ferdinand Loeve, from a review in German

Russian literature, and contemporary Russian life in general, has this advantage, i.e., it has never followed the model of a single people. From the beginning it has found . . . all the riches of the European spiritual soul. From study and assimilation, Russian literature has acquired something universal, but at the expense of originality.

Other European countries have crossed the marked borders of national life. Gradually they have achieved a degree of spiritual linkage and ethical exchange. They have seemingly risen from the personal to the general. The Russian people, though, the leading light of the Slavic tribes . . . has gone backwards. . . . It has returned to its personal essence. Without singing praises, beloved by so many Slavophiles and Slavomaniacs . . . world history has decided on a new experiment.

[With] the entrance of the Slavic tribes in the community of nations, [we see] . . . works of the Slavic spirit . . . [that] have been successful in informing national creativity with . . . European culture. Pushkin is first in poetry. . . . He has penetrated the secret depths of the Russian genius. . . . He has brought Russian literature, adrift in the waves of the European cultural sea, to the shores of national verse. His cultural talent does not fear comparisons with the greatest names [in art]. . . .

We agree fully with [the people at] *The Fatherland Notes* who champion Pushkin, Gogol, and Krylov. . . . The works of this triumvirate are the core, the truthful source of Russian poetry. . . . The author of the novel that we will discuss does not tap into this source in a complete way. In no way, though, . . . [is he] an imitator. . . . Similar to Goethe's *Werther*,[65] the tone and structure of *Poor Folk* are so original that we, without hesitation, align these two works . . . in their sentimentality.

Poor Folk by Dostoevsky is a most successful attempt to represent artistically the [Russian] national character in its current phase of development. . . .

The hero of the novel . . . is a clerk, a titular counselor, a poor individual. . . . The colleagues in his department ridicule him. They pour papers over his head and so forth. He is for them . . . the symbol of the simple soul, a target for the most coarse witticisms. With touching resignation, this hero has become reconciled to his sorrowful situation. . . . He is a copier of documents. . . . His behavior is undistinguished and unnoticed. His demands do not exceed his finances. His external image is extremely unpretentious. . . . What interest can such an individual attract?

The appeal is found in a belated flowering . . . of a highly forceful spiritual existence. At forty-four years old and thirty years of work . . . in his clerk-like soul, in his scrivener-like heart . . . there shines . . . a creative flame that forces his parched and withered soul . . . to burn with new life. . . .

The idea to portray an individual who is despised by all; who is misunderstood by himself and others; and who, in burdensome and depressing circumstances, has managed to preserve in his heart the full force of emotions . . . [and] the spark of love . . . is truly genius-like . . . [as well as] Christian in universal and historical significance. . . .

Varvara Alexeevna Dobroselova is a young orphan whom Makar, from pure empathy, saves from a depraved woman. . . . [but who] beautiful and innocent . . . becomes the object of courting by one Bykov. . . . Can an individual . . . find sufficient strength . . . to defend herself against an unworthy man?

Is it the complexity of the problem that has so attracted the writer? . . .

The first letter of Makar Alexeevich shows his new mood. He is the philanthropic savior of Varvara Alexeevna. . . . He tries to express his spiritual surge. He rejoices in the splendid morning, the bright sun, the singing of the birds, the smells of the spring air, of all nature. Suddenly he lapses into clerk-like prose: "Well, everything is as it should be; everything is in order, in a spring-like way." He comes up with comparisons: "I liken you to a heavenly bird . . . to an ornament of creation." He admits openly that he has run to a book for his lines. . . .

With joy he moves from a comfortable dwelling . . . to his current noisy and dirty little room . . . [so that] he can look at Varvara's windows to see if she is nearby. Makar Alexeevich . . . has begun to live only for her. In complete selflessness, he asks her about her . . . important and unimportant affairs . . . to drop if only one word about some delight so that he may not rest until he acquires it [for her]. . . . He forgets himself to find his being in her. . . .

But the spark that glows warmly in the ashes of everyday and petty cares . . . cannot burst into youthful flame. The love of our Makar moves to a warm and heartfelt sensitivity, to a simple-souled worship of a beloved entity . . . [whose] spiritual beauty he cannot attain. He thirsts to penetrate into the very depths of this feminine soul. . . . It is better for him to receive than give. . . .

Makar Alexeevich understands that Varvara has been given to him only as a friend. . . . The hundred variants . . . of his gentle unhurried-ness, his distinctive tenderness . . . afford him the full and seductive possibility of moving his most passionate feelings to innocent forms of fatherly, kindred attachment. . . . Despite her fleeting requests, he, with most noble delicacy, refuses to meet her other than in a completely innocent place. Such is the modesty of an individual who knows his moral worth. . . .

Makar Alexeevich feels himself to be equal to his friend, although she is the one who helps him to realize such a thing. He expresses this feeling . . . openly and straightforwardly, often with comic pathos. His sole conviction is that he cannot instill passion or offer riches, youth, or rank. . . . He often says that he is an uneducated person, that he has no "style." . . . [Such a view] impedes . . . his declarations of love and his pretenses to marriage to which Varvara would, perhaps, agree if he were not so delicate . . . and remind her that he is her benefactor, her savior. . . .

If Makar Alexeevich had grown up in favorable circumstances, if he had been supported by good people . . . he could have become an excel-lent poet, an artist who would engage life in a practical way. Now he is only a machine for letters. Such a thing he realizes with bitterness. . . . He begins to ask . . . Why do his colleagues mock him while Varvara respects him, she who is better than them all? Did he ever "jump rank"? Did he not, by the sweat of his brow, earn his own bread? Did he always hold himself a bit more aloof from their liberal ideas? . . .

Varvara deserves a crown for her charming femininity. . . . She is offered a post as a governess . . . but she is too independent, too awk-ward, too retiring, and too wounded to live among others. Makar is against such an idea. . . . He explains to her how he will feel abandoned, how he will do everything for her so as not to let her go. . . . But he cannot save his Varenka from poverty . . . from shame. . . . His attack against an unjust world order recalls the behavior of the noble knight from La Mancha. . . .

Our poor friend loses courage. His stance toward Varenka moves to suspicion and taunts. He falls into temptation and despair. For the first time in years of irreproachable service and righteous living, he finds himself in the hands of the police. . . . He carouses in a tavern while she suffers. . . .

On his gloomy horizon, there shines still another saving light—none other than his "excellency" who . . . drops a hundred-ruble banknote in the palm of [the clerk's] hand. . . . Makar Alexeevich writes to Varenka that . . . what is important to him is not the hundred rubles but that "his excellency" has pressed the hand of a "blockhead and drunkard." . . .

In his dreams, Makar paints a radiant future. He asks God for forgiveness for all his sins. . . . He promises Varenka that he will be prudent. He reminds her of the possibility of living in harmony and happiness with the exchange of "happy letters" . . . and with reading literature.

But at the very height of his dreams and hopes, the poor man suffers a final terrible blow.

Bykov comes to Petersburg and offers Varenka his hand and heart. Does she ask advice from her friend? No, she decides her fate herself. . . . She writes to her friend that she has given an affirmative answer [to Bykov] and that her decision is final. . . .

What has forced our Varenka to take this decisive step? . . . Continuation of a tie with Makar Alexeevich is impossible. . . . Her nature is ordered so precisely, her emotions are so noble, that they would disappear in the rather effeminate character of Makar. . . .

Poor Devushkin . . . is crushed. . . . His final letter [to Varenka] is a cry of despair, written in bed, in sickness. . . . Our Russian Werther is a splendid sufferer. . . .

Poor Folk is an outstanding book, full of thoughts and reflections. . . . In it a completely new language has entered Russian literature. It is not the variegated style of Pushkin, nor the wise brevity of Krylov, nor the warm . . . and sharp speech of Gogol. It is everyday communication in the very highest sense of this word. The author has appealed to the language of the people as his personal style. He has discovered in it profoundly new aspects. His heroes speak exactly as would Russians of their rank and station. . . .

Reading Poor Folk—we hope it will become a national work— Russians will hear themselves. In a most elevated and complete way, they will be uplifted. . . . Surely can . . . Dostoevsky not also be called a national poet, since he infuses his subject with the spirit of his nation?

In a decisive way, we affirm this great contribution of Mr. Dostoevsky to the literature of his land. . . . He has shown that he knows
the life of the heart. He can follow the most precise movements of the
soul. . . . He puts forward feeling and thinking people in circles that are
hidden [from public view]. He has opened our eyes to the eternal core
of national morality. . . .

Early September 1846
Konstantin Trutovsky, from his memoirs

Fyodor Mikhailovich once stayed with me at my apartment for a few
days. . . . When he was about to go to bed, he always asked me that if
he fell victim to his lethargy, he not be buried for at least three days.
Thoughts about lethargy always disturbed and terrified him.

September 1, 1846
Valerian Maykov, from a review

What an impression [Gogol's] *Dead Souls* . . . must have made [on Dos-
toevsky]. . . . Indeed, if the writer of *The Double* had been born eight
years earlier, would he be the psychologist he is now?

September 5, 1846
Fyodor Dostoevsky, from a letter to Mikhail Dostoevsky

I hasten to inform you, dear brother, that I somehow made it back
to Petersburg and as I had wished, I am staying with Trutovsky. I did
not experience any seasickness, but on the way and here in Petersburg
I got soaked to the skin and caught one hell of a cold. I have a cough, a
head cold and all of that to the highest degree. In the beginning I was
depressed terribly. . . . A terrible sadness has taken hold of me.

The Belinskys arrived without any problems and since docking
I have not yet seen them. On the next day I dropped by to see Nekrasov.
He and the Panaevs live in the same apartment,[66] and thus I got to see
everyone. . . .

In the next month's issue of *The Contemporary*, Gogol will publish an
article—his spiritual will, in which he rejects all his works and considers them useless and even more than that.[67] He says that he will not
take up the pen for the rest of his life because his business is praying.
He agrees with all the opinions of his opponents. He orders that his
portrait be printed in a huge number of copies and that the profits
from them be designated for financial assistance to travelers to Jerusa-
lem and so forth. So that's that. Draw your own conclusions.

I was also at Kraevsky's. He has begun setting "Prokharchin." It will appear in October. So far I have not spoken about money. He is sweet and playful. . . .

It is raining terribly outside and therefore difficult to go out. I am still living at Trutovsky's, but I am moving to an apartment tomorrow. It also has been absolutely impossible to see about an overcoat [for you] because of all the errands and rain. I want to live in a most modest way. I wish the same for you. One needs to accomplish things little by little. We will live a bit and see. And now good-bye. I am in a hurry. I would like to write a great deal, but sometimes it is better not to speak. Write. I am expecting a reply from you in the shortest possible time. Kiss the children. Give my regards to Emiliya Fyodorovna. Also give my regards to anyone whom you should. I will write you more in the next letter. This is just a note. Good-bye, I wish you all the best, my priceless friend—and most important for the time being, patience and health.

September 11, 1846
Pyotr Pletnyov, from a letter to Yakov Grot

On Tuesday I spent the entire day . . . reading *The Fatherland Notes*. There are only wonders in there. Lermontov is already obsolete. . . . and Dostoevsky stands higher than he.

September 17, 1846
Fyodor Dostoevsky, from a letter to Mikhail Dostoevsky

I am sending you an overcoat. Forgive me for being so late. The delay was not my fault. I was looking for my servant and found him finally. I could not buy it without him. The overcoat has its virtues and inconveniences. The virtue is that it is unusually full, in fact, double the normal size; and the color is good, the best for a uniform, gray; the shortcoming is that the material sells for only 8 paper rubles. There was nothing better. But it cost only 82 paper rubles. The remaining money was used for mailing. There was nothing else I could do. There was material at 12 paper rubles, but the color was bright steel-blue. It was excellent, but you would have rejected it. But I do not think you will dislike the one I am sending you. It's still a bit long, though.

Because of the overcoat, I have not written to you until now. I already announced to you that I have rented an apartment. Things are not bad; only I will have almost no means in the future. Kraevsky just gave me 50 silver rubles, and judging from his look, he will not give me any more. I am going to have to endure a great deal.

"Prokharchin" has been disfigured terribly at a certain place. The gentleman of this certain place forbade even the word *bureaucrat* and only God knows why. Even as it was, everything was extremely innocent and things were crossed out everywhere. Anything living in the piece has disappeared. There remains only the skeleton of what I read to you. I am renouncing my story.

I have not heard anything new. Everything is as before. People are waiting for Belinsky.[68] Mme. Belinskaya sends her regards. All ventures . . . seem to have been put on hold; or perhaps they are being kept a secret—only the devil knows.

We are pooling our resources for dinners. Six friends have gathered at the Beketovs', including Grigorovich and me. Each one contributes 15 silver copecks a day, and we have two simple dishes for dinner and are satisfied. As a result, dinner costs me no more than 16 rubles.

I am writing to you in haste. Because I am running late, and the servant is waiting with the package to take to the post office. I have even more nonsense than when your teeth ache. I am very much afraid that the overcoat will come too late for you. But what can I do? I tried as hard as I could.

I am still writing "Shaved Sideburns." The thing is going so slowly. I am afraid that I will be late with it. I have heard from two gentlemen, from the second Beketov and Grigorovich, that *The Petersburg Miscellany* is known in the provinces exclusively as *Poor Folk*. No one wants to know about the other things in the work, although they snatch it up out there like crazy, outbidding each other and paying a high price from people who have been lucky enough to get a copy. In the bookstores, for instance, in Penza and Kiev,[69] it officially costs 25 and 30 paper rubles. What a strange fact: here it just sits and there you cannot get it.

Grigorovich has written an amazingly good story,[70] through my efforts and those of Maykov, who, by the way, wants to write a long article about me by January 1st,[71] the story will be published in *The Fatherland Notes*, which also, by the way, has become completely impoverished. The people there do not have a single story in reserve.

I am seized by a most terrible angst. . . . Give me something good and with my character I will make it worse. I wish Emiliya Fyodorovna happiness and, most important, health. I want that sincerely. I think about all of you a great deal. Yes, brother, money and security are great things. I kiss my niece and nephew. Well, good-bye. I will write more in the next letter. And now, for God's sake, do not be angry with me. And be healthy and don't eat a lot of beef.

P.S. Try to eat as healthily as possible, and please without mushrooms, mustard, and other similar junk. For God's sake, do not eat so much.

September 17, 1846, and after
Dmitri Grigorovich, from his memoirs

> Everyone, in equal degree, was drawn to Alexei Nikolaevich [Beketov]. He was goodness and straightforwardness incarnate, with a developed mind and passionate soul that was outraged by any injustice and that was open to any noble and honest striving.
>
> For the most part, gatherings [at the Beketovs' home] were in the evening. Among the many guests (sometimes as many as fifteen individuals) . . . rarely did the conversation focus on a single subject. Rather, as soon as someone raised a question, everyone touched upon it in his own way. For the most part, people broke up into groups, each with separate conversations. But no matter who spoke, or what the topic was, or whether it concerned events in Petersburg, in Russia, or abroad, or a literary or artistic question, one felt in everything a burst of fresh power, the living nerve of youth, and the appearance of enlightened thought which was borne suddenly, in an enlarged passionate brain. Everywhere one heard an indignant, noble onrush against oppression and injustice. The arguments were heated, but never wound up in fights, thanks to the older Beketov, who managed immediately to reconcile opposing individuals or groups, to being about peace and agreement. Youth, flaring with singular lightness and carried away with liveliness, added much to the meetings. Often, when people had had their fill of talking and exclaiming to the extreme, someone suggested a walk, a recommendation to which everyone agreed gladly.
>
> One time, we as a group . . . set out on foot to Pargolovo and spent the night on Parnassus Hill overlooking a lake.[72] Everyone had to provide some kind of provisions. . . . Even now I find it pleasurable to recall the trip. All along the way and throughout the night . . . merriment rained down in a stream; happiness was in everyone's heart. . . . One heard songs, witticisms, amusing stories, and incessant laughter. The lake at Pargolovo, I think, never saw such exuberance.
>
> [In our discussions] personal pride always served as the prime motivator. Constantly to keep one's mind on guard, not to appear dumber than others, to pursue a thought, to support or dispute it publicly—all this, to a significant degree, aroused the consciousness, sharpened the mind, and "shook up the brains."

September 17, 1846, and after
Dmitri Grigorovich, from his memoirs

> Until I became a regular member [of the Beketov circle], my intellec-
> tual capacities had developed in a fog. Conversations with Dostoevsky
> never had gone beyond the boundaries of literature; all the interests
> of life had been focused on that alone. . . . I had never thought about
> anything at all seriously; social questions had not interested me in the
> slightest. . . . Many things that had never entered my mind previously
> now began to concern me: the living word, sobering up the mind from
> frivolity, I first heard only here, in the Beketov circle.

September 17, 1846, and after
Dmitri Grigorovich, from an 1853 letter to Mikhail Dostoevsky

> Truly, the Beketov home will be the same fulfilling corner for you as it
> was for many of our acquaintances.

September 17, 1846, and after
Stepan Yanovsky, from an 1882 letter to Anna Dostoevskaya

> A salon to which everyone [came] . . . to talk . . . about literature . . . to
> discuss what they considered necessary to develop fictional writing . . .
> to direct the thoughts of individuals to sober and salutary paths . . .
> to polish talent and creativity . . . was found in the family of Yevgenya
> Petrovna and Nikolai Apollonovich Maykov. . . .
>
> Among its regular visitors were individuals who, in our present time,
> are known not only in Russia but also in Europe. In the group were first
> the accomplished and *do nec ultra* human and attractive hosts with their
> richly talented family, and then I. A. Goncharov, St. Sem. Dudyshkin,
> M. A. Yazykov, or unforgettable Fyodor Mikhailovich, M. M. Dosto-
> evsky, N. A. Nekrasov, and an entire pleiad of friends, contemporaries,
> and colleagues who all at the time worked in our best periodical editions
> and who were developing their talents and gifts and which I have already
> said without thinking were polishing them precisely in this salon.
>
> I learned of the salon of Yev. P. and N. Ap. Maykov in the forties,
> but as people told me, it had existed in Petersburg much earlier. When
> I became acquainted with the Maykovs—the parents—they at that time
> had just lost their elder son Valerian. The sudden and recent passing of
> this especially gifted and still quite young son had such a shattering effect
> on the parents, and especially on the tender and extremely delicate organ-
> ism of his mother, so much so that family and friends feared for her life.

September 17, 1846, and after
Vasily Bervi-Flerovsky, from his memoirs

> [The Beketovs] were extremely serious people who later became
> well-known scholars. Like Petrashevsky, they propagated the study of
> Fourier.[73]

September 17, 1846, and after
Vasily Bervi-Flerovsky, from his memoirs

> The Beketovs were an extremely capable family. One of them was a
> botanist and a well-known rector of Petersburg University. Another
> was a chemist and a member of the Academy of Sciences. A third . . .
> having graduated from the institute of communications entered [state]
> service. One time someone brought him money and said, "This is in
> addition to your salary." "What addition?" he asked. It seems that the
> engineers had a general cashbox which contained bribes paid by vari-
> ous people. The funds were dispersed among the engineers, according
> to rank and occupation. Beketov refused the money, thereby ruining
> his career.

September 17, 1846, and after
Nikolai Beketov, from an 1877 letter to Fyodor Dostoevsky

> I have not forgotten you, although I was only nineteen years old when
> we went our separate ways. Since that time, you have continued your
> tireless study of the human soul. To read your works is to converse
> with one's conscience . . . [to] discern a universal and all-embracing
> meaning. How splendid to share with the public your spiritual under-
> standing of all that is going on around you.

September 17, 1846, and after
Nikolai Beketov, from an 1878 letter to Fyodor Dostoevsky

> How delightful to receive a letter from you and to know that the tie
> between us has not been broken. Like you, I recall . . . in our time
> together . . . your personality standing out in a clear and definite way.

Between September 21 and 26, 1846
Nikolai Nekrasov, from a letter to Vissarion Belinsky

> Dostoevsky has given a story to Kraevsky, but I do not know when he
> will give one to you.[74]

PART THREE

The Psycho-Spiritual Turn

The Double, "Mr. Prokharchin," "The Landlady,"
and "A Novel in Nine Letters"

Fyodor Dostoevsky wrote *The Double* in 1846
and "Mr. Prokharchin," "The Landlady," and "A Novel in Nine Letters" in
1847. Sadly, not one of these works met with the success of his first piece, *Poor
Folk*. Indeed, to readers and reviewers, Dostoevsky seemed to have regressed
as a writer and perhaps to have lost his fictional touch altogether. There were
valid reasons for disenchantment. If the hero and heroine in *Poor Folk* had
captivated audiences with groundbreaking depictions of Russian urban life,
the lead characters in *The Double*, "Mr. Prokhachin," "The Landlady," and
"A Novel in Nine Letters" confused them with timeworn portrayals of mania
and madness, roguery and romance that related little to contemporary life.
Readers and reviewers moved from a clerk, Golyadkin, who, à la E. T. A. Hoffmann, invokes a maddening double; to another clerk, Prokharchin, who, à la
Dickens, is a miser with visions of the past; to a young man, Ordynov, who,
à la fairy tales and courtly novels, seeks to rescue a maiden, Katerina, from
a wizard, Murin; and finally to two cardsharps, Ivan Pyotrovich and Pyotr
Ivanovich, who, à la Pushkin and Gogol, scheme against everyone including
each other.

Making matter worse, readers and reviewers of *The Double*,
"Mr. Prokharchin," "The Landlady," and "A Novel in Nine Letters" had to
slog their way through fractured plots, tortured prose, and bizarre thoughts

and deeds. Readily did they join with Belinsky and company to consign Dostoevsky to oblivion.

It is only when they are measured against Dostoevsky's later works that the value of *The Double*, "Mr. Prokharchin," "The Landlady," and "A Novel in Nine Letters" becomes clear. Each in its own way was a significant exercise in which Dostoevsky probed minds, hearts, and souls to understand human faults and failings. Each in its own way was a link in the admittedly long and weighty chain that brought Dostoevsky to greatness. With apologies to Belinsky and company, Dostoevsky, in these four works, asserted that it was not political, social, and economic injustices that wreaked havoc on society but rather the psychological and spiritual traumas of individuals that, like the steady drop of Chinese water torture, eroded humankind, if not over-whelmed it in biblical floods.

At the basis of *The Double*, "Mr. Prokharchin," "The Landlady," and "A Novel in Nine Letters" are heroes who are alone, adrift, and ambivalent about their place in society. The first three stories are particularly striking vis-à-vis self and other. Golyadkin, Prokharchin, and Ordynov personify paranoia, anxiety, and guilt. They view the world as conspiracy, not com-munity. They rage that they, the meek, do not inherit the earth so much as consume it. They want love, attention, and respect from without to assuage the pain and emptiness from within.

The heroes of *The Double*, "Mr. Prokharchin," and "The Landlady" believe in a good defense as the best offense. Their armor is diverse and intriguing. Money and mask, pose and posturing, camouflage and charade take their place among idées fixes, delusions of grandeur, and aggression, active and passive. Speech is a particular weapon of mass destruction. Ceaseless ora-tions, convulsive outbursts, and numbing repetitions move in sync with syntactic jumbles, lexical breakdowns, and telegraphic ellipses and dashes. Furthermore, the heroes of the four works after *Poor Folk* slash and burn with impunity. They feel no remorse for their sins. They also commit mayhem from bloodlust, without recourse to the theories, manifestos, and ideas that promoted "extraordinary beings," justified ends, and challenged God and creation that moved their counterparts in Dostoevsky's mature fic-tion to crime and punishment.

Unsurprisingly, the heroes of *The Double*, "Mr. Prokharchin," and "The Landlady" fail miserably at mastering their fates. Not knowing whether they want to be in or out of society, at war or at peace with the world, they fall somewhere in between. Physically, socially, and spiritually, they never find a place to call home. They are their own worst enemies. They live lives of noisy desperation. They tilt at windmills and bite hands that feed them. They count and discount what others say about them. They spurn the very people and things they say they desire.

The heroes of these stories come to bad ends—or dead ends. Never do they know a moment's peace. They experience fevers and trances, nightmares and hallucinations. They encounter thunderbolts and bombshells and see specters and ghosts. They engage in sadomasochism and commit sins of omission and commission. They offer brazen excuses, false confessions, and *apologiae pro sua vita*. Hysterics and hyperbole negate sensibility and sense. Eros and fantasy void affection and love.

On good days, the heroes in the next four works after *Poor Folk* engage in endless monologues; on bad days, they drown in streams of consciousness. They die, go insane, or return to their pain and distress, sadder but dumber for their experience. Indeed, they never learn from their mistakes.

The heroes of *The Double*, "Mr. Prokharchin," "The Landlady," and "A Novel in Nine Letters" may have been done for in life but not in literature. Rather, they reappear in Dostoevsky's later fiction. Golyadkin, in his verbal sputtering between Senior and Junior, rants and raves of the hero in *Notes from the Underground*. Prokharchin prefigures Alexei in *The Gambler* and Arkady in *A Raw Youth* in his idea that money conquers all, as well as Raskolnikov in *Crime and Punishment* in his stance as Napoleon, and in his tortured dreams of accusers, real and imagined. Ordynov presages Ivan Karamazov as a philosopher cum "system." He also competes with Murin for Katerina in much the same way Fyodor contends with Dmitri for Grushenka in *The Brothers Karamazov*. Murin, as the first epileptic in Dostoevsky's fiction, sets the stage for the seizure-prone Prince Myshkin in *The Idiot* and Alyosha in *The Brothers Karamazov*. He again comes to the fore in Stavrogin in *Devils* as a dark, demonic figure who destroys all in his path. Ivan Petrovich and Pyotr Ivanovich foretell Luzhin in *Crime and Punishment* and Pyotr Verkhovensky in *Devils* as solid citizens with squalid schemes. Equally important are the narrators in these early stories who portend the tellers of later tales in that they—flippant and fickle, ridiculing and rambling—exacerbate the chaos in the narrative.

It is to be regretted that Belinsky and company, together with other readers and reviewers of "The Double," "Mr. Prokharchin," "The Landlady," and "A Novel in Nine Letters," did not live to see Dostoevsky achieve greatness. If they had, they would likely have set aside their differences with the writer and understood, even applauded, what he had done in his early writing. They would have seen that in these four works, the young Dostoevsky, however slowly and awkwardly, was moving from empiricism to epistemology, from physics to metaphysics, from the terra firma of political, social, and economic concerns to the muck and mire of human anger, rebellion, and despair. They would again have put him on a pedestal not as a creature of their own making but as one of the greatest writers of their land and time.

October 1, 1846
Ivan Panaev, from a letter to Nikolai Ketcher

> Belinsky's anthology (*Leviathan*) will not come to be. . . . Simply, without ceremony, the local gentlemen have announced that they cannot give to Belinsky the articles they promised to him (Dostoevsky, Goncharov, and others). They say that they are poor and need the money right away, but from Belinsky they have only distant hopes for funds.[1]

October 5–8, 1846
Alexander Herzen, from a letter to Nikolai Ogaryov

> Today I saw Dostoevsky. He was here. I cannot say that the impression was a particularly pleasant one.

October 7, 1846
Fyodor Dostoevsky, from a letter to Mikhail Dostoevsky

> Last time I wrote you to say that I am planning to go abroad.[2] The booksellers are offering me four thousand paper rubles for everything. Nekrasov was going to give me 1,500 rubles . . . but it seems that he will renege. . . . So if my price seems low (judging by my expenses) . . . I myself will publish the volume, perhaps even by November 15th. That is even better because the business will take place right before my eyes and others will not mess up the volume. . . . In a word, such an undertaking will have its own advantages. Then by January 1st, I will sell all the copies to booksellers wholesale. Perhaps I will earn 4,000 [rubles], and although that is the same that the booksellers are offering, I will not publish everything in my volume. As a result, if I add a little bit, a second volume will come out after my return from Italy, and I will arrive to money straightaway.
>
> I am going not for a good time but to take a cure. Petersburg is hell for me. It is burdensome, so burdensome to live here! And my health is noticeably worse. Moreover, I am terribly afraid. What will October bring, for instance? So far the days have been clear. I am very much looking forward to your opinion. But for the time being . . . help me, brother, until December 1st at the very latest. Because until that time, I absolutely

do not know where I can get any money. . . . Kraevsky is throwing some at me, but I have already borrowed 100 silver rubles from him; and now I run away from him. . . . In Italy, at my leisure, in freedom I want to write a novel[3] and finally be able to raise my price. But the system of continual indebtedness that Kraevsky fosters is the system of my slavery and literary dependence. So give me some money if you can. In leaving for abroad, I wrote to you that I would repay the 100 rubles; but if you can send me 50 silver rubles now, I will give that money back too. Everything will be straightened out by January 1st. Figure out if you can lend me money until January 1st. Then give it to me. As regards repayment, count on me as if I were a stone mountain. . . .

I need this money for an overcoat. I no longer have people make clothing for me. I am taken up entirely with my system of literary emancipation, and . . . my clothing is already indecent. I really need an overcoat. I will use 120 rubles for one with a collar, and the rest I want to use to get by until publication. Kraevsky himself has offered to help me. Ratkov and Kuvshinnikov publish things upon his recommendation. They have offered 4,000 rubles for a manuscript.

By January 1st I intend to write some kind of trifle for Kraevsky and then to get away from everyone. In order to get to Italy, I need to pay various debts (including what I owe you) to the tune of 1,600 paper rubles. Thus, I will have about 2,400 paper rubles left. I have asked about everything. The trip costs 500 (at most). In Vienna, I will have clothes and linen made for 300 rubles, things are cheap there. That means that 1,600 rubles will remain. I will get by for eight months. To *The Contemporary* I will send the first part of a novel,[4] get 1,200 [rubles], and from Rome go to Paris for two months and then back. When I arrive, I will publish the second part right away. I will be writing the novel until fall of 1848 and then publish its third or fourth parts. The first part will be published in *The Contemporary* in the form a prologue. I have both the plot and the idea in my head. I am now in almost a panicky fear over my health. Just like during the first part of my illness, the palpitations of my heart are terrible.

The Contemporary is being published by Nekrasov and Panaev on January 1st. The critic is Belinsky. Various journals and the devil knows what else are coming to the fore. But I am fleeing from everything because I want to be healthy to write something healthy. Nekrasov's shop is declining.[5] But Yazykov and company are flourishing. He also has commissions and books. I have already spoken to him about depositing copies with him for their management and dissemination.

Give my regards to everyone, especially to Emiliya Fyodorovna. The children, too, and for God's sake, answer me by the first mail. I am waiting for your letter. Write as soon as possible, because if you do not send money, then at least say so (for which, honest to God, I will not hold it against you), so that I can look elsewhere.

P.S. I will be writing letters very often now.

It will be a long time before we see each other now. But when I return from abroad, I will visit you directly, no matter where you are.

By October 20th, the time of finishing the raw material, that is, "Shaved Sideburns," my situation will become apparent in the clearest way, since on October 15, there will be the printing of *Poor Folk*.

October 14, 1846
Alexei Pleshcheev, from a review

This year is remarkable in our literature for the appearance of a new and bright star on its horizon—talent in the full artistic sense of the word: we are speaking about Mr. Dostoevsky, the author of *Poor Folk*, *The Double*, and "Mr. Prokharchin." Such talents appear rarely, and for this one can forgive the inadequacies of our fictional writing.

Before October 16, 1846
Avdotya Panaeva, from her memoirs

A particular master at jesting [in the salon] was Turgenev. On purpose, he dragged Dostoevsky into arguments and irritated him to the highest degree. In response, Dostoevsky often crawled over to the wall and defended in a passionate way absurd views about things he had blurted out in anger and which Turgenev seized upon to ridicule.

Before October 16, 1846
Avdotya Panaeva, from her memoirs

Belinsky, sometimes hearing how a flushed Dostoevsky argued with Turgenev, said quietly to Nekrasov . . . "What's with Dostoevsky! He is saying such absurdities, and with passion to boot." When later Turgenev told Belinsky about Dostoevsky's sharp and inaccurate judgments of some Russian writer, Belinsky responded:

"Well, you are one to talk! You pick on a sick individual, you egg him on as if you yourself do not see that he is irritated and does not understand what he is saying."

Before October 16, 1846
Agrafena Orlova, from her memoirs

> How passionately Belinsky . . . scolded Turgenev for irritating Dostoevsky, for egging on a sick man whom he loved, valued, and pitied.

Circa October 16, 1846
Isaak Pavlovsky, from his memoirs

> One time guests had gathered at Turgenev's home: Belinsky, Ogaryov, Herzen, and others. They were playing cards. Someone said something stupid just at the very moment when Dostoevsky entered. Everyone started laughing uproariously. Dostoevsky, turning pale, stopped on the threshold; then, without saying a word, he left the room.
>
> When Turgenev asked the valet about Fyodor Mikhailovich, he answered, "He has been pacing the courtyard for about an hour but without a hat on."
>
> It was terribly cold out. Turgenev ran into the courtyard.
>
> "What's with you, Dostoevsky?" he asked.
>
> "Good God! But this is impossible!" he answered. "Anywhere I go, people everywhere laugh at me. Unfortunately, I saw from the threshold how you had begun to snicker when you saw me. Are you not blushing now?"
>
> Despite Turgenev's assurances that no one had taken it into his head to laugh at Dostoevsky, the young man did not want to hear anything and, taking his hat, departed.

Circa October 16, 1846, and after
Avdotya Panaeva, from her memoirs

> Once in Dostoevsky's presence, Turgenev was describing his meeting in the provinces with one individual who imagined himself to be a genius and a masterly writer of human life. . . . Dostoevsky turned as white as a sheet and trembled all over. He ran out of the room without hearing Turgenev's story to the end. I said to everyone: What was the point of tormenting Dostoevsky so? But Turgenev was in the most merry mood and had so entertained the others that no one attached any significance to Dostoevsky's hasty departure. Turgenev then began to compose a humorous ditty on Devushkin, the hero of *Poor Folk*, as if grateful to Dostoevsky for having informed all of Russia of the work's existence and with lines that often included the word "mother."[6]

From that evening on, Dostoevsky no longer appeared at our place and even on the street avoided meetings with anyone from our circle.

After October 16, 1846
Avdotya Panaeva, from her memoirs

One time Panaev, having met Dostoevsky on the street, wanted to stop him and ask why he had not seen him in such a long time, but Dostoevsky ran quickly to the other side. He was seen with only one friend, who, when he visited the circle, reported that Dostoevsky was abusing everyone . . . as heartless, insignificant, and jealous of his success.[7]

After October 16, 1846
Dmitri Grigorovich, from his memoirs

After the scene with Turgenev there occurred a final break between Dostoevsky and the members of the Belinsky circle. He no longer visited them. About him there were scattered witticisms and caustic epigrams. He was accused of monstrous pride, as well as envy of Gogol, to whom he should have gone on his knees because in his much-celebrated *Poor Folk*, one felt the influence of Gogol on every page.

After October 16, 1846
Lyubov Dostoevskaya, from her memoirs

Father found it very painful that he had to bury his illusions of friendship. . . . Naively he assumed that his friends would be happy over his success, as he would have been over theirs. Especially painful to Father was the malice of Turgenev, who, beside himself over the success of *Poor Folk* . . . invented all kinds of things to harm him. . . . The enmity continued throughout their lives.

After October 16, 1846
Fyodor Dostoevsky, from his 1849 *Netochka Nezvanova*

Talent needs sympathy and understanding. But as soon as you have achieved the slightest success, you will see what kind of people flock to you. But they will not give [you] a second thought. They will look at you with contempt for what you have gained through hard work, self-denial, hunger, and sleepless nights. These future friends will neither encourage nor comfort you. They will not show what is good and true in you. Rather, with spite and glee, they will spot every one of your mistakes. They will point out all your faults and failings. With cold-blooded scorn, they will declare a holiday over every slip and blunder (as if anyone was perfect)!

October 17, 1846
Fyodor Dostoevsky, from a letter to Mikhail Dostoevsky

I hasten to inform you, dear brother, that I received your money, for which I am inexpressibly grateful, since I no longer feel the cold and other unpleasant things. I also hasten to tell you that all my hopes and calculations are seemingly postponed until a more convenient time.

At the very least, I myself still do not know very much. The conditions that people keep offering me are the likes of which one cannot accept. Either the money is too little; or the money is decent, but you do not get it all at once, but have to wait. It goes without saying that if I am to sell, I can do so only for cash. Finally, I am being advised to wait. That is both good and bad. It is bad for my health. It is good given the fact that if I wait, I can get a more significant sum. In the latter case, there is no chance of publishing before Christmas. Since I have to live on something, I need to sell stories to journals; and then I will have to wait. Therefore the earliest that the publication can occur is perhaps by May 1st. Moreover, I will have to exert myself to arrange everything. And publish two thick volumes and not for two rubles, fifty copecks as I had presumed. But for three, and perhaps more. And so, perhaps, we will see each other this summer, and the trip will not take place until the fall, if I have a lot of money.

All of this distresses me, brother, and I am like a crazy person. Oh, how much labor and difficulties of all kinds one has to endure at first in order to establish oneself. My health, for instance, I have to leave it to *luck*, and the devil knows whether I will have any security. I am writing you a short letter because I do not know anything certain for myself. But I am not entirely downcast. How are you getting along? You write that you are expecting a new guest in the family. God grant that all go well.[8] And may your circumstances also right themselves. I, brother, do not stop thinking about our goals. Our association can become a reality. I keep dreaming about it. I, brother, need to have a *complete success*, without which there will be nothing and I will be just barely getting by. All of this depends not on me but on my energy.

"Shaved Sideburns" is not quite finished. "Prokharchin" is being praised highly. I have been told a lot of judgments.[9] Belinsky still has not arrived yet. The gentlemen at *The Contemporary* keep on hiding.

So I am still hanging on to "Shaved Sideburns" and have not yet promised it to anyone. Perhaps Kraevsky will publish it. I do not know how I will manage with that, however. I will take advantage of circumstances and enter the story into the fray. Whoever fights harder for it will get it. Then I will surely pull down some decent money. But if it happens that I publish it separately, so that I am given a certain sum in advance, I will not give it to the journals.

Brother Andrei sends his regards to both you and Emiliya Fyodorovna. I visit them every so often. How they play cards! I kiss the children and I often think about them. If I do well in selling the story, I will without fail send them candy and various sweets for Christmas. Emiliya Fyodorovna can be assured of all my devotion. Let us be patient, brother, perhaps we will get rich. We need to work. But for God's sake, take care of your health. And I would advise and ask you not to work a great deal. Send it to the devil! Please take care of yourself. And most important, eat more healthily. Less coffee and meat. They are poison. Good-bye, brother. I will write again soon. It is so dark out.

P.S. October here is dry, clear, and cold. There have been few illnesses. Do not forget me and write.

October 18, 1846
Fyodor Dostoevsky, from a letter to Andrei Dostoevsky

Dear brother, I have long since arrived from Revel, and every Saturday circumstances of one sort or another prevent me from getting in touch with you. Forgive me. Come see me tomorrow about 10 a.m.

Late October 1846
Fyodor Dostoevsky, from a letter to Mikhail Dostoevsky

I want to write you a word or two, but no more, because I am running about and flapping about like a fish on ice. The problem is all my plans have collapsed. . . . The edition will not come to be. Because not a single one of the stories I told you about has become a reality. I am not writing "Shaved Sideburns" either. I have given up on everything: because it is all nothing but a repetition of old things that I have said long ago. Now more original, lively, and bright thoughts are begging to be put down on paper. . . . In my situation, monotony is ruin.

I am writing another story,[10] and the work is going as it did with *Poor Folk*, crisply, easily, and successfully. I intend it for Kraevsky. Let the folks at *The Contemporary* be angry with me. I do not care.[11]

Meanwhile, after finishing the story by January 1st, I will cease publishing entirely until next year and write a novel that is even now giving me no peace.[12]

But in order to live, I have made up my mind to publish *Poor Folk* and a revised *The Double* as separate books.[13] I will not put Part 1 and Part 2 on them, for instance, it will simply be *Poor Folk* separately and *The Double* too—all my work for the year. With my future novel I hope to do exactly the same thing. And finally, perhaps in 2 years or so I will put together a complete edition and in that way I will really luck out because I will get money twice and create renown for myself.

I will start to publish *Poor Folk* tomorrow or the day after. I will do this through Ratkov; he promises. Now I only curse fate that I do not have 700 paper rubles to publish it at my own expense. Publishing at your own expense is everything. With someone else means taking a risk; you can perish. Booksellers are scoundrels. They have scads of tricks which I do not know about and with which they can swindle you. But their most barbaric thing is the following: they publish an edition at their own expense, and for that they receive from me 350 or 400 copies (the price covering their expenses), they take 40 percent, i.e., 40 silver copecks per copy (I am selling them at a ruble each). That is for *the turnover of their capital* and for *the risk*. Let's say that a bookseller has in his hand 300 rubles. He is the one who sells them. I, however, do not have the right to sell a single copy until all of his are sold because I would be underselling him. He will sell them all and tell me that the public does not want any more and that the books will not sell. It is impossible to verify what he is saying. So that means quarreling with him. Such a thing is done only in extreme cases. I have copies lying around. I need money. Finally, after having made me starve, he will buy a couple hundred copies or so from me at half price.

Finally, there are rascals who hold back requests from other cities and do not release copies even to the Petersburg public who is asking for them. Now, if I publish myself, I suddenly sell to all the booksellers in Petersburg for hard cash. They take a certain percentage. Each one gives more than the other, trying to undercut each other if the book sells well, and finally, the main stockpile is set up in Yazykov's office.

Listen, brother: I request an immediate reply and here is what I propose. Only if you have the money, send me *200 silver rubles*. (I need more, but I can go slightly into debt.) Don't you want to do some speculation? If you are just saving money, then it is just lying around to no avail. I propose that you give me some money for the edition. I can have it published by November 15th. The edition will pay for itself by January 1st. I will send you your 200 silver rubles right away. Later, 1/4 of all the profits. The edition will pay for itself with 350 copies. There will then be 850 left at 75 silver copecks each = 635 paper rubles. I will give the profit to a bookseller. But I would be prepared to share it with you. My money will not be lost. Then, if there is a whiff of success, we would publish *The Double*. Finally, in any event, your money will be returned to you by January. I give you my word of honor that I will not drag you into a false position. Finally, I expect success even if it be slow in coming. It will take at least a year for the *entire* edition to sell out.[14] Here is an example: Osnovyanenko's *Mr. Kholyavsky* was published in *The Fatherland Notes* three years ago.[15] Then it was published separately, and now they want to do a third printing.

If you want, brother, answer me right away and with money. I will correct a few things, go to the censorship, and make arrangements with the printer. If you do not have that much, then for starters send at least 120 silver rubles, no less, for a deposit, and then the remaining 80 silver rubles without fail by November 15th.

Finally, if you cannot do all of this, you will not put me in straitened circumstances, at least as far as time. I will go to the booksellers, and we will publish *The Double* later.

In this matter cast aside all fraternal love, tactfulness, and other such things. Look at this matter as speculation. Do not rob yourself of the desire of doing me a good turn, even if only for a short time. You have a new child on the way. Good-bye, kiss everyone. Give my regards to everyone you should. I am still sick all the time. But after all, you know me.

P.S. Good-bye, dear brother. I await your reply immediately. For God's sake, do not put yourself in a false position, that is, if, for example, you will be giving me the last of your money. Then it is better not to. After all, I am only making a proposal to you. But if you are rich and *willing*, send the money by the first mail, for instance, by the 2nd or 3rd of this month.

Well, listen to me. I have written everything to you and I am saying for the last time: if you have money, do not be afraid and agree. If you do not have money or very little, for God's sake, do not enter into this venture. Answer right away.

Give my regards to Emiliya Fyodorovna. I wish you all happiness, my friends. Gogol died in Florence two years ago.[16]

November 1, 1846
Valerian Maykov, from a review

> With their masterly stories. . . . Pushkin, Lermontov, Gogol, and Dostoevsky . . . these self-seducers have stepped forth boldly into the field of novellas . . . to create works that are truly artistic!!!

November 9, 1846
Faddei Bulgarin, from a review

> The Cossack Lugansky is much higher than Gogol in education, his view on subjects, his exposition and his language, and we could not forgive ourselves if we dared to place Cossack Lugansky alongside Mr. Dostoevsky, whom [the people at] *The Fatherland Notes*, filling in the vacancy left by Gogol, have pronounced a genius!

November 17, 1846
Apollon Grigoriev, from a letter to Nikolai Gogol

> Have you read *The Double* by the talented Dostoevsky? Here for you is the realization of the fantastic basis of "The Portrait." From the work, one becomes oppressed spiritually, so exceedingly burdened as from "The Overcoat." Getting a grasp on this monstrous creation, you find yourself diminished and destroyed. You merge with its exceedingly insignificant hero, and you become sad that you are becoming such a person as well as amused that a person is and can only be that way. What guilt and responsibility are there here? What verdict hangs over you? A man lives likes a worm and dies like a worm, and the deal is done. *Une fois mort, on est bien mort.*[17]

November 23, 1846
Faddei Bulgarin, from a review

> Our honorable colleague[18] has, by mistake, placed Lermontov alongside Gogol, having named them as founders of a natural, that is, antigraceful school! *A Hero of Our Time* and all the fictional writings of Lermontov are much higher than *Dead Souls*, *Taras Bulba*, and all the fairy tales and old wives' stories of Mr. Gogol, as Eugène Sue, Victor Hugo, Alexander Dumas, and Pushkin are higher than the author of

"The Petersburg Corners,"[19] the author of *Poor Folk* . . . and other young writers who do not respect the literature of high art.

November 26, 1846
Fyodor Dostoevsky, from a letter to Mikhail Dostoevsky

Well, how could you, my priceless friend, write that I was seemingly angry with you for not having sent money and thus was silent? How could such an idea enter into your head? And finally, how could I have given you such a pretext to think that about me? If you love me, do me the favor of renouncing such ideas once and for all. Let us try to have everything between us be simple and direct. I will tell you aloud and straightforwardly that I am obliged to you for so much that for my part, not to admit such a thing would be ridiculous, swinish, and base. Now, enough about this. I will do better to write about my circumstances and try to make everything a bit clearer.

In the first place, all my editions have burst and come to nothing. It was not worth it, it took too much time, and it was too early. Perhaps also the public might not have gone for such a thing. I will do the edition toward next fall. By that time the public will have become better acquainted with me, and my position will be clearer. Furthermore, I am expecting several advances. *The Double* is already being illustrated by a Moscow artist. *Poor Folk* is being illustrated in two places here—whoever does the better job.[20]

Bernardsky[21] says that he is not opposed to beginning negotiations with me in February and to giving me a certain sum for the right to publish an illustrated edition. Until then he is busy with *Dead Souls*.[22] In a word, for the time being I have become indifferent to the edition. Besides, I do not have the time to bother with it. I have heaps of work and orders. I will tell you that I had the unpleasant experience of quarreling decisively with *The Contemporary* in the personage of Nekrasov. Annoyed at the fact that I am still giving my stories to Kraevsky, to whom I am in debt, and that I refused to declare publicly that I do not belong to *The Fatherland Notes*, and despairing of receiving a story from me in the future, he made a number of rude remarks to me and demanded money in an impudent way. I took him at his word and with an acknowledgment of debt, I promised to pay him a sum by December 15th. I want them to come to me themselves. They are all scoundrels and envious people. After I hauled off and let Nekrasov have it, he could only mince and try to escape, like a Jew who is having his money stolen. In a word, it is a dirty story. Now they are claiming that I have been infected by vanity, that I have conceived a high opinion of myself, and that I am going over to Kraevsky because Maykov praises me. Nekrasov is planning to criticize me. As for Belinsky, he is such a weak person that even in his literary opinions, he keeps changing his mind. It is only with him that I have kept my previous good relations. He is a noble person. Meanwhile Kraevsky, rejoicing over the chance, gave me some money and also promised to pay off all my debts for me by December 15th. In return I am working for him until the spring. You see what, brother: Out of all this, I have extracted a very wise rule. The first disadvantageous thing for a beginning talent is to be friends with proprietors of publications, from which, as an unavoidable consequence, proceed favoritism and then various obscenities. Then independence of position, work for Holy Art, work that is sacred and pure in the simplicity of a heart that has never before so trembled and moved in me as now before all the new images that are being created in my soul.[23]

Brother, I am being reborn, not only morally but also physically. Never before has there been in me such an abundance of clarity, such equilibrium in my character, such physical health. In this I am much obliged to my good friends the Beketovs . . . and others with whom I am living. They are practical, intelligent people, with an excellent heart, with nobility, with character. They have cured me with their company. Finally, I proposed that we all live together. A large apartment was found, and all the expenses for all the parts of the household do not exceed 1,200 paper rubles a year. How great are the boons of an association! I have my own room and I work days on end. . . .

I congratulate you, my dearest friend, on the arrival of my third nephew. I wish every blessing for both him and Emiliya Fyodorovna. I love you all now three times as much. But do not be angry at me, my priceless friend, for writing a scribbled-over wad of paper instead of a letter. There is no time, and people are waiting for me. But I will write again on Friday. Consider this letter unfinished.

December 17, 1846
Fyodor Dostoevsky, from a letter to Mikhail Dostoevsky

What has happened to you, dear brother, that you have fallen silent completely? With every mail I have been expecting something from you and not a word. I am worried, I think of you often, about the fact that you sometimes fall sick, and I am afraid to draw conclusions. For God's sake, write me at least a few lines. Please write and set my mind at ease. Perhaps you have been waiting for the continuation of my recent letter. Do not be angry at me for keeping my word so inaccurately. I am swamped with work now and I have pledged by January 5th to give Kraevsky the first part of the novel *Netochka Nezvanova*, about the publication of which you have read in *The Fatherland Notes*.[24] I am writing this letter in fits and starts because I am writing day and night except from 7 p.m. on, when, for entertainment, I go to the gallery at the Italian opera to listen to our incomparable singers. My health is good, so there is nothing more to write about it. I am writing with fervor. I keep feeling that I have started up a lawsuit against all of our literature, journals, and critics, and with the three parts of my novel in *The Fatherland Notes*, I am establishing my primacy for this year despite my ill-wishers. Kraevsky is discouraged.[25] He is almost perishing. *The Contemporary*, however, is performing brilliantly. They have already started up a crossfire.[26]

And, so, brother, I will not go abroad either this winter or summer, but will come again to see you in Revel.[27] I can hardly wait for the summer. In the summer I will redo my old things and prepare an edition for the fall. Then we will see what happens. Is your family well, brother? By any chance, is Emiliya Fyodorovna ill? I ask for an immediate response to this letter. As I have already written to you, brother, I am living with the Beketovs on Vasilievsky Island. It is not boring; it is also good and economical. I visit Belinsky sometimes. He is ill all the time, but he has hope. Mme. Belinskaya has given birth.

Thanks to Kraevsky, I am paying off all my debts. My entire task is to work and repay him everything over the winter and not owe a copeck for the summer. Sometime I will get out of debt. It is a bad thing to work as a day laborer. You will destroy everything, including talent and youth and hope, grow disgusted with work, and in the end become a pencil-pusher, not a writer.

Good-bye, brother. You have torn me from the most interesting page in my novel, and there is still a mountain of things ahead. Oh, my dear, if only you are successful. I would love to see you and, before I do, to settle and resolve my situation. I have bound myself with entrepreneurs hand and foot. Meanwhile, on the side, I am receiving brilliant offers. *The Contemporary*, which in the person of Nekrasov wishes to criticize me, will give me 60 silver rubles per signature page, which equals the 300 rubles at *The Fatherland Notes*. *The Library for Reading*—250 paper rubles per signature page, and so on, but I cannot give the people there anything. Kraevsky has taken everything for his 50 silver rubles given as an advance. By the way, Grigorovich has written a physiology, titled *The Village*, which is creating a furor here.[28] Well, good-bye, dear brother. Give my regards to Emiliya Fyodorovna, Fedenka, Mashenka, and Misha. Have the children forgotten me or not? . . . Regards to all the old friends.

P.S. Now, brother, here's what [to do]: come to Petersburg this year for Shrovetide. Even if it be for only two weeks. But definitely come. Room and board will not cost you anything. Nor will tea, sugar, and all your keep. You will not have to spend any pocket money at all. The entire trip will cost only a trifle. Well? What do you think? Think about it. Why not? I would be so glad to see you. And it would be pleasant for you to live while in Petersburg too. You do not need to take any money with you when you come here. I owe you and I will pay for everything. We will get hold of some money. For God's sake, brother, come. You are a stay-at-home. Can you really want to get to the point where you will have to be pulled out of Revel with tongs? Joking aside, come visit at Shrovetide.

Late 1846 and after
Stepan Yanovsky, from his memoirs

> Since by this time I was now close friends with Fyodor Mikhailovich, our conversations were most candid, familiar, and intimate. . . . We were almost the same age: I was twenty-eight; Fyodor Mikhailovich was twenty-four.[29] By nature I was a voracious reader and an individual who was extremely curious and enthusiastic about things. I was also a patriot to the marrow of my bones, as well as someone who believed in the Book of Revelation. Fyodor Mikhailovich was a similarly intense being, a profound thinker and observer. Perhaps it would be more accurate to say that he was a restless scientist-analyst, an extremely proud writer, a believer, and a patriot among patriots.[30] Fyodor Mikhailovich needed a friend who could understand his constantly analyzing mind, and who could esteem and empathize with the value of his work. In this, I as a doctor, together with the small circle of my colleagues and friends, satisfied him completely.
>
> From the very beginning, Fyodor Mikhailovich trusted me. He told me that he was an extremely poor individual who made his living as a writer.

Late 1846 and after
Stepan Yanovsky, from his memoirs

> The first illness for which Fyodor Mikhailovich appealed to me for help was purely local. In the course of treatment, though, he complained of

a mental nausea or faintness that is commonly associated with paralysis or strokes. After having examined him thoroughly, and taken into
account his physical build and temperament, and listened to him about
his symptoms since childhood, I diagnosed that he was suffering from
a nervous disorder.

Late 1846 and after
Stepan Yanovsky, from his memoirs

> Dostoevsky was a hypochondriac in the extreme (though undoubt-
> edly he had symptoms of such well-known brain dysfunctions . . . as
> "fainting sickness"). He also so feared strokes and paralysis that he did
> everything he could to shield himself from upset and distress. To outsid-
> ers, Dostoevsky's hypochondria often appeared laughable, and he often
> took great offense when people thought or told him that he was not
> sick. To tell the truth, there were times when one could not help but
> laugh at Dostoevsky's imagined illnesses. When someone happened to
> say, "What wonderful, fragrant tea!"—Fyodor Mikhailovich, who did
> not usually drink tea but warm water, would suddenly jump up from
> his chair, walk over to me, and whisper in my ear: "Will such a thing
> affect my pulse, doctor? After all, tea is made from leaves!" Each time
> I had to hide a smile, and to calm him in a serious way, assuring him that
> his pulse was fine, that his tongue was good, and that his head was clear.

Late 1846 and after
Stepan Yanovsky, from an 1884 letter to Anna Dostoevskaya

> Poverty in Fyodor Mikhailovich expressed itself in a way that was com-
> pletely analogous to his whining and complaints about his health. It
> often happened that after two or three comforting words, he himself
> pronounced himself completely well.

Late 1846 and after
Sergei Yanovsky, from an 1881 letter to Apollon Maykov

> The deceased Fyodor Mikhailovich Dostoevsky suffered from fall-
> ing sickness when he was still in Petersburg, three or even more
> years before his arrest in the Petrashevsky affair and his exile to
> Siberia. The fact of the matter is that this burdensome enemy, called
> *Epilepsia*—the falling illness—was observed in Fyodor Mikhailovich in
> 1846, '47, and '48 on an occasional basis.[31] [During that time] observers
> did not notice anything, but the sick man himself was aware—in truth,
> vaguely—of his illness and usually called it apoplexy with an aura or

a breeze.[32] (Notice this word aura or breeze.) To the extreme hypochondriac Fyodor Mikhailovich, it served to herald an attack, about
which he said later, "I always manage to get to Haymarket Square, to
my apartment"—even though such anticipation is a key characteristic
of *Epilepsia*.[33]

For me, as a doctor, it was clear that my dear friend suffered from
falling illness. Several times during those years his illness was seen not
only in its indubitable form but also to a life-threatening degree.

Late 1846 and after
Fyodor Dostoevsky, from an 1872 letter to Stepan Yanovsky

> You loved me and looked after me, with my great *spiritual illness* (after
> all, I understand that now).

Late 1846 and after
Lyubov Dostoevskaya, from her memoirs

> Doctor Yanovsky, who loved my father very much and often invited
> him to his place for consultations about his health, recalls that long
> before Dostoevsky's exile to Siberia, he suffered from a nervous illness
> akin to epilepsy.

Late 1846 and after
Yevgenya Rykacheva, from an 1881 letter to Andrei Dostoevsky

> Anna Grigorievna [Dostoevskaya] expressed her displeasure that
> Maykov published Yanovsky's letter without having shown it to her
> first, so that she could advise making several omissions regarding the
> family life of uncle [Fyodor].

Late 1846 and after
Andrei Dostoevsky, from an 1881 letter to Alexei Suvorin

> From 1843 to April 1849 (the time of his arrest), I, with rare exceptions,
> saw my brother [Fyodor] almost daily;[34] but never, in our protracted
> conversations, did I hear from him about this illness.
>
> One should also note that my brother did not hide his illnesses from
> me and often complained that he was feeling poorly.
>
> It is true that in this period (I do not recall the precise year), he was
> somewhat irritable and, it seems, suffered from some kind of nervous
> illness. I often came across notes which he had left behind for the night
> with this approximate content: "Tonight I might fall into a lethargic
> sleep, but do not bury me for several days."

I repeat: my brother never mentioned a "falling" [sickness] in this period. Finally I recall that I heard from him that he had acquired this illness when he was in Siberia.

Late 1846 and after
Stepan Yanovsky, from his memoirs

Not only did Dostoevsky not play cards, but also he did not understand a single hand of any game. In fact, he hated cards altogether. He was also a decisive enemy of wine, binges, and bouts.

Late 1846 and after
Stepan Yanovsky, from his memoirs

Fyodor Mikhailovich loved to arrange dinners at the Hôtel de France . . . with a group of close friends. Such gatherings usually cost less then two rubles each; but the merriment and fond memories of each affair lasted almost right up until the next. . . .

Before dinner everyone had a thimble-like glass of vodka (the sight of which always made Yakov Petrovich Butkov grimace wildly). There were also several bottles of champagne during the meal. At this time, Fyodor Mikhailovich did not drink vodka; and he usually took only a quarter of a glass of champagne, which he downed in one gulp after addresses to his guests, whom he loved to toast with great delight. Everyone also drank tea until late into the night.

Fyodor Mikhailovich enjoyed these dinners very much; and with his guests, he conducted the most sincere and intimate conversations. Indeed, the affairs were like a holiday for him. Fyodor Mikhailovich once told me the reason why he so loved these gatherings. "One's soul becomes light when one sees a poor proletarian, sitting in a nice room, eating a nice dinner and drinking both something fizzing and the real stuff." ("Proletarian" was what Fyodor Mikhailovich called anyone who did not have a regular income from a job, but who earned money on a daily basis.) At the end of a festive meal, a very pleased Fyodor Mikhailovich went up to each diner, shook his hand, and said, "The dinner was all right, but the fish and sauce were particularly good." He even sometimes kissed Yakov Petrovich Butkov.

Late 1846 and after
Stepan Yanovsky, from his memoirs

Fyodor Mikhailovich's love for society was so strong that even when he was sick or engaged in urgent work, he could not stay alone and invited one of his friends over to his place.

Late 1846 and after
Stepan Yanovsky, from an 1884 letter to Anna Dostoevskaya

> From 1846 to 1849, Fyodor Mikhailovich loved an audience and the couch upon which he spoke . . . as a teacher-virtuoso. We listened to him in a reverential way.

Late 1846 and after
Stepan Yanovsky, from an 1882 letter to Anna Dostoevskaya

> You cannot imagine how much I loved and respected your husband. He was not an unforgettable friend—no—this word is far from expressing the feelings which I nourished and nourish toward him. No, Fyodor Mikhailovich was my spiritual father. Every time he said sometime like "Ech, no, old man, Stepan Dmitrievich, that is not so or that is truly not so"—even now such things resound in my entire being as if am hearing them in real life. . . .
>
> I have had many good and honest friends . . . but no one was like Fyodor Mikhailovich. . . . To him went not only my heart but also my soul, both sustained by a profound humanity and by a striving for truth with which he himself had been endowed by God.

Late 1846 and after
Stepan Yanovsky, from an 1882 letter to Anna Dostoevskaya

> Here the image of Fyodor Mikhailovich rises up before me and my eyes, and I see his lips compressed from moral anguish. I notice the movement of his right hand first to smooth his hair and then curl his mustache. I even hear his voice, saying—"Ech, pal, how false it is, how bad it is"—and I also become truly burdened and sad.

Late 1846 and after
Stepan Yanovsky, from his memoirs

> Even as a joke, Fyodor Mikhailovich never allowed himself to lie. In fact, he also expressed disgust for the untruths that others uttered unexpectedly. I remember once an entire circle of individuals close to Fyodor Mikhailovich had gathered in the evening at the home of A. N. Pleshcheev. As usual, Fyodor Mikhailovich was in a good frame of mind and spoke a great deal. At dinner, though, the conversation focused on how one could ascertain that such publishers as Grech, Bulgarin, and P. I. Chichikov (our name for another editor) would never lie to us. During the discussion, someone began to defend Chichikov in a joking way.[35]

"Well, we can excuse him," this individual said, "since even though he squeezes our brother writers financially, he pays us and does not make mistakes with money. True, Chichikov lies sometimes, but what is the fault in that? After all, even the Gospels say that a lie can sometimes ensure one's salvation."

When Fyodor Mikhailovich heard these words, he grew quiet immediately. He also became withdrawn and he kept repeating to those who were sitting closest to him: "Isn't this something? He is even relying on the Bible. But it is not true what he is saying![36] After all, when one hears someone else lying, that is repulsive enough, but when this person lies and *slanders Christ at the same time, such a thing is repulsive and base.*"

Late 1846 and after
Stepan Yanovsky, from an 1884 letter to Anna Dostoevskaya

Truly Fyodor Dostoevsky was not a wealthy man, and before the publication of *Poor Folk*, he was so poor that he did not have a ruble for sugar and shoes, but when he retired [from state service] and set out on the literary enterprise, precisely when I first became acquainted with him and later became friends, Fyodor Mikhailovich not only was never hungry but also was never without tea or shoes. I know for sure that he helped many individuals who were close to him . . . although he himself talked constantly about his material needs and also constructed various fanciful plans for getting rich and to help the poor, not with pennies or tickets to a free dinner but with grandiose sums and schemes. And where is this in biographies of Fyodor Mikhailovich?

Late 1846 and after
Stepan Yanovsky, from an 1884 letter to Anna Dostoevskaya

Fyodor Mikhailovich complained about his lack of money, first because, being by birth a rentier, that is, an individual provided with a stable income from an estate—or as he loved to call himself, a person with a living labor—he throughout his entire life was not able to manage money; and second because by nature he was endowed with a heart that was so kind, empathetic, and generous that at the time he considered himself happy only when he could help a close friend. Furthermore, he forgot himself in a decisive way; and third, it is also important to note that in his very character was something exaggerated, as a result of which it seemed to him that he was very poor, although there was no extreme need.

Late 1846 and after
Stepan Yanovsky, from his memoirs

> Fyodor Mikhailovich was constantly in need of money. When one
> recalls, though, that he was very well paid for his work and that his life,
> especially as a bachelor, was extremely modest and without preten-
> sion, one has to ask the question: *What did Fyodor Mikhailovich do with
> his money?*
>
> This question I can answer truthfully, since, regarding monetary
> matters, Fyodor Mikhailovich was more open with me than with any-
> one else. Almost always he gave his money to someone who was poorer
> than he. Kindhearted soul that he was, though, he also gave money to
> people who were better off than he: individuals who swindled money
> from the infinitely good-natured individual that he was.

Circa 1847 and after
Vsevelod Solovyov, from his memoirs

> [Dostoevsky said]: "My nerves have been shot since youth. Two years
> before Siberia, during my various literary difficulties and quarrels,
> I was afflicted by some sort of strange and unbearably torturing ner-
> vous illness. I cannot tell you what these hideous sensations were; but
> I remember them vividly; it often seems to me that I was dying, and
> the truth is—real death came and then went away again. I also feared
> a lethargic sleep."

Circa 1847 and after
Fyodor Dostoevsvky, from *The Insulted and Injured*

> I must confess everything openly. At the beginning of dusk, first little
> by little and then gradually, whether from an upset in my nerves, or
> from impressions in a new apartment, or from a recent bout of depres-
> sion, I began to descend into that condition of the soul which comes
> to me now in my sickness and which I call *mystical terror*. It is a most
> oppressive, agonizing illness of something that I myself cannot define,
> something that is ungraspable and immaterial in the natural order of
> things, but also something that may yet take shape without fail, this
> very minute, something which mocks all the conclusions of reason and
> which stands before me as an undeniable fact that is terrible, horrible,
> and relentless.
>
> Usually, despite all the protests of reason, this illness becomes more
> and more powerful, so much so that although . . . the mind sometimes

acquires great clarity, it also loses all power to resist such sensations. It is unheeded, it becomes useless, and this division, this split intensifies the fearful angst of suspense. It [is] . . . something like the anguish of people who are afraid of the dead. But in my distress the vagueness of the danger intensifies my torment.

Circa 1847 and after
Lyubov Dostoevskaya, from her memoirs

Dostoevsky began to doubt his gifts. His health started to shatter and he became nervous and hysterical. Epilepsy had already taken hold of his organism, and although he still had no attacks, he felt himself oppressed. He now avoided visiting salons, locked himself up in his home for hours on end, or wandered through the darkest and most remote streets in Petersburg. During these walks, he talked with himself and gesticulated so that passers-by stared at him. His friends thought he was mad.

Circa 1847
Fyodor Dostoevsky, from an 1859 letter to Mikhail Dostoevsky

[The Double] had a splendid idea, a very great and socially important type, of whom I was the first to discover and be its proclaimer.

1847
Dmitri Grigorovich, from his memoirs

In the accusation [of Dostoevsky's imitation of Gogol]—if one could call it that, given that here was a beginning young writer—there was a grain of truth. Unwittingly, the face of the old man Devushkin in *Poor Folk* brings to mind the clerk Poprishchin in *Diary of a Madman;* the scene in which the director's daughter drops her handkerchief and Poprishchin, rushing to pick it up, slides and falls on the parquet floor and almost breaks his nose recalls the scene in which Devushkin, in the presence of his boss, has a button torn from his coat, and he, beside himself in distress, tries to pick it up. Not only in the frequent repetition of one and the same word but also in the construction of the very phrases, in their spirit one sees the remarkable influence of Gogol. . . .

Such influence, though, cannot serve as a great reproach to Dostoevsky. After all, for such a thing one could also indict the entire young literary generation of the time. In one and the same way, all were carried away by Gogol. Almost everything that was written in the narrative mode was a reflection of Gogol's stories, primarily "The Overcoat."

January–February 1847
Fyodor Dostoevsky, from a letter to Mikhail Dostoevsky

Again I beg your absolution that I did not keep my word and write
to you by the next mail. But . . . it has been impossible to write.
I have thought about you a great deal and agonizingly so. Your fate is a
burdensome one, dear brother! With your health, with your thoughts,
without people around, with depression instead of a holiday mood,
and with a family that, although a sacred and sweet worry, is still a
heavy burden—life is intolerable. But do not lose heart, brother. The
time will brighten. You see, the more spirit and inner content we have
in ourselves, the better is our corner and life. Of course, terrible are the
dissonance and disequilibrium that society presents to us. The *external* must be balanced with the *internal*. Otherwise, with the absence
of external phenomena, the internal will move too dangerously into
ascendancy. Nerves and fantasy will occupy too much space in a being.
For want of habit, any external phenomenon seems colossal and somehow frightening. You begin to fear life.

You are fortunate that nature has provided you abundantly with
love and a strong character. You also have great common sense and
flashes of brilliant humor and happiness. All of these things save you
too. I think about you a lot. But good God, how many repulsive, vilely
limited, and gray-bearded sages, authorities, and Pharisees of life are
there who *pride themselves* on their experience, that is, their lack of individuality (because they are all cut from the same cloth), useless people
who preach eternally about contentment with fate, belief in something,
limitation in life, and satisfaction with one's place, without penetrating
into the essence of these words—a contentment resembling monastic
torture and limitation, and with the inexhaustibly petty malice of those
who condemn the strong, ardent soul of one who cannot bear their
banal daily schedule and calendar of life. Such individuals are scoundrels with their earthly vaudeville-like happiness. . . . I come across
them sometimes and they infuriate me in a tormenting way. . . .

But time is getting away. I wanted to write you a great many things.
How irritating it is that everything has been interrupted. Thus I will
limit myself and write a thing or two about what I am doing. I am
working, brother, but I do not want to publish anything before I finish
it. In the meantime I have no money, and if it were not for kind people, I would perish. The decline of my fame in the journals is bringing
me more profit than loss. All the more quickly will I need things to be
seized upon by my admirers, who seem to be many and who will defend

me. I have been living poorly. Since I left you, I have spent only 250 silver
rubles; and I used up to 300 rubles on debts. I was clipped most badly by
Nekrasov, to whom I returned his 150 rubles because I do not want to
tie myself to him. Toward spring I will get a huge loan from Kraevsky
and without fail will send you 400 rubles. That is a sacred vow because
the thought of you tortures me more than anything else.

I doubt that I will come to Helsingfors early.[37] Because perhaps I will
try to cure myself completely with Priessznitz's method of cold water.[38]
Therefore I will not arrive any earlier than July 1. But I still do not know
anything, my dear. My future lies ahead. But even if thunder were to
crack over me, I will not move now. I know everything that I can do. I will
not spoil my work, and I will correct my financial circumstances with the
successful sale of my book that I will publish in the fall. . . .[39]

Take care of yourself, brother. Especially your health. Amuse yourself and wish me well in finishing my work quickly. After that I will
have money right away and I will visit you. I have Priessznitz's cure on
the brain. Perhaps the doctors will talk me out of it. How I would love
to see you. Sometimes I am tormented by such depression. Sometimes
I recall how awkward and difficult I was with you in Revel. I was ill,
brother. I remember that you once told me that my treatment of you
excluded mutual equality. My dear man, that was absolutely unjust.
But I do have such a vile and repulsive character. I have always valued
you higher and better than myself. I am ready to give my life for you
and your family; but sometimes when my heart is swimming in love,
you cannot get a tender word from me. In such moments my nerves
do not obey me. I am laughable and disgusting and because of that
I suffer constantly from an unfair conclusion about me. People say that
I am callous and lack a heart. How many times have I been rude to
Emiliya Fyodorovna, the most noble of women, who is a thousand
times better than I. I recall how purposely spiteful I was sometimes to
Fedya,[40] whom at the same time I loved even more than you. I can only
show that I am a person with a heart and love when the very exterior
of a circumstance, an incident, extracts me violently from my usual
banality. Until that point I am disgusting. That inequality I attribute to
illness. Have you read *Lucrezia Floriani*, take a look at *Carl*.[41] But soon
you will be reading *Netochka Nezvanova*. That will be a confession, like
Golyadkin,[42] although in a different tone and form.

On the sly (and from many people) I hear such rumors about Golyadkin that it is simply horrible. Some say straight out that the work is a
wonder and that it is has not been understood. . . . What if I had written

only Golyadkin? That would have been more than enough for me. For some it is more interesting than Dumas. Well, now my vanity has come gushing forth. But, brother! How nice it is to be understood. Brother, why do you love me so! I will try to embrace you soon. We will love each other passionately. Wish me success. I am writing "The Land-lady." It is already turning out better than *Poor Folk*. It is in the same style. My pen is being guided by a well of inspiration that springs forth directly from my soul. Not like "Prokharchin," with which I suffered all summer long. How much I would like to help you soon, brother. But, brother, rely on the money which I promised you as on a wall, as on a mountain. Kiss your family for me.

P.S. Will we get together in Petersburg sometime, brother? What would you say about a civilian job with a decent salary?

I do not know if Mme. Belinskaya gave birth to a son or a daughter, but it seems somehow strange and embarrassing to ask.

January 1847 and after
Lyubov Dostoevskaya, from her memoirs

The Double is far more endlessly valuable than *Poor Folk*. Here is the original, genuine Dostoevsky. Psychiatrists of our country praise this small masterpiece to an extreme; they are astounded how a young writer, who never studied medicine, could describe so well the last days of an insane person.

This second novel, though, did not have the success of the first. It was way too new; such a scrupulous analysis of the human heart . . . was still not understood. Madness still had not come into fashion;[43] and a novel without a hero or a heroine was found to be boring. The critics did not hide their disappointment. "We were mistaken," they wrote. "Dostoevsky's talent is far less significant than we thought."

If my father had been older, he would not have paid any attention to the critics. He would have continued in his new manner, he would have accustomed his readers . . . to an exclusively psychological inves-tigation. But at that time, he was too young. Criticism could deflect him from his path. My father was afraid to be deprived of the splendid success of his first novel; so he returned to the false genre of Gogol.

January 1847 and after
Avdotya Panaeva, from her memoirs

Dostoevsky had not visited us since the time when Belinsky published in *The Contemporary* his criticism of *The Double* and *Prokharchin*. Dostoevsky was offended by his analysis.[44] He even stopped seeing Nekrasov and Panaev, regarding them in a mocking and derisive way. They were quite surprised by the way Dostoevsky was acting toward them.

After January–February 1847
Fyodor Dostoevsky, from an 1861 article

Valerian Maykov undertook his task passionately, with enlightened conviction, with the first enthusiasm of youth. But he did not succeed in having his say. He died in the first year of his activities [as critic of *The Fatherland Notes*]. This fine personality promised much, and perhaps his passing deprived us of a good deal.

January 1, 1847
Vissarion Belinsky, from a review

Turning our attention to the remarkable works of belletristic prose that have appeared in anthologies and journals over the past year, our glance falls, first of all, on *Poor Folk*, a novel that has achieved great fame for an individual who, up until now, has been unknown in our literature. Incidentally, this work has been spoken about to such a great extent in all our journals that new similar opinions cannot be of interest to the public. Thus we will not expand upon it in any great detail.

No one has ever achieved fame so quickly in our literature as Mr. Dostoevsky. The power, depth, and originality of his talent has been recognized immediately by everyone. What is more important, the public has also shown an unrestrained appetite for Mr. Dostoevsky's giftedness, as well as an equally unrestrained impatience with his shortcomings. . . . Unanimously, almost everyone finds in Mr. Dostoevsky's *Poor Folk* the ability to tire the reader. . . . Some see such a thing as long-windedness, others as unrestrained fecundity.

Truly, one cannot but agree that if *Poor Folk* had appeared with only 10 percent fewer pages, and if the author had had the foresight to rid his novel of superfluous repetitions of one and the same phrases, *Poor Folk* would have been an irreproachably artistic work.

January 1, 1847
Vissarion Belinsky, from a review

Mr. Dostoevsky has submitted to the judgment of his interested public a second novel, titled *The Double. The Adventures of Mr. Golyadkin*. Although the initial debut of the young writer has smoothed his road to success, one must confess that *The Double* has not been a triumph with the public. But one still cannot judge the second work of Mr. Dostoevsky as unsuccessful or, even less, as not having any [good] qualities; still one must acknowledge that the verdict of the public is not completely unfounded.

In *The Double*, the author displays a great wealth of talent. His hero belongs to that group of the most profound, bold, and genuine conceptions, the type of which only Russian literature can boast. Here also is a deep wellspring of intelligence, truth, and artistic mastery. But together with such things, one can also see a terrible inability to possess and control an excess of personal powers in an economic way. Everything that was forgivable as shortcomings in *Poor Folk* appears as monstrous weaknesses in *The Double* . . . the inability of an extremely rich and powerful talent to determine, in a reasonable manner and within the limits of artistic development, the idea of the piece.

Let us attempt to explain our thought with an example. Gogol focused the idea of his Khlestakov in such a profound and lively way that it would have been easy to make him the hero of an entire dozen comedies in which he would appear as faithful to himself . . . as a fiancé, husband, father of a family, landowner, and so forth. Undoubtedly these comedies would be superb as *The Inspector General* . . . but they would tire the public . . . with one and the same thing. As soon as a poet expresses the idea of his work, he is done. He must leave it in peace, for fear of boring people with it.

Another example: What could be better than the two scenes that Gogol excluded from his comedy since they slowed the pace of his piece? Comparatively speaking, they ceded nothing in quality to any one of the scenes that remained. So why did Gogol exclude them? Because he, to the highest degree, possessed artistic measure. He knew not only with what to begin and when to end but also to develop his subject with no less or more than what was needed.

We know that Mr. Dostoevsky excluded from *The Double* one splendid scene, believing that it was extremely long;[45] and we are convinced that, at the very least, if he had shortened his *Double* by a third, without wondering if he had omitted something that was good, he would have had another success.

In *The Double*, also, there is still another key shortcoming: its fantastic coloring. In our time, the fantastic can have a place only in the homes of the mentally ill, not in literature; under the eye of doctors, not poets. For all these reasons, *The Double* has been valued only by several dilettantes of art,[46] for whom literary works are the subject not only of delight but also of study. The public is different . . . not thinking why they like a work, and immediately closing a book when it begins to tire them or without thinking why it is not to their taste. A work that is liked by connoisseurs and not the majority can have its strengths. But [what is] truly good is a work that can please both groups, or, at the least, [can be] liked by the first and read by the second. After all, Gogol was not liked by everyone, but he was read by all.

January 1, 1847
Vissarion Belinsky, from a review

Dostoevsky's story "Mr. Prokharchin" has caught all the admirers of his talent with an unpleasant surprise. The work flashes with bright sparks of great giftedness . . . but in such thick darkness that its light gives nothing for readers to discern. . . . Neither inspiration nor free and naive creativity has given birth to this strange story, but rather . . . how can one say? . . . something akin to feigned cleverness and pretense. . . . Perhaps we are mistaken, but why instead of a genuine . . . poetic creation . . . is there something so false, mannered, and incomprehensible . . . [so] muddled and strange? . . .

We should note in passing that Gogol contains no such contradictions. Of course, we have no right to demand from the works of Mr. Dostoevsky the perfection of the writings of Gogol, but nonetheless we think that it would be useful for a great talent to follow the example of an even greater one.

January 1, 1847
Valerian Maykov, from a review

Already in November and December 1845, all the literary dilettantes . . . were bandying about the comforting news about the appearance of a new and great literary talent. Some cried, "No worse than Gogol"; others took up the call, "Better than Gogol"; still others wailed, "Gogol has been killed." . . .

Having done such a good (or bad) turn to the author of *Poor Folk,* the town criers carried on so that the public expected a work of ideal perfection . . . but, having read the novel, it was astounded at having met, along with unusual strengths, several failings characteristic of the work of any young gifted writer, no matter how great his talent. . . .

Perhaps no one in this world has been judged so unreasonably harshly as Mr. Dostoevsky. People had assumed that *Poor Folk* would be the crown of literature, the prototype of an artistic work in both content and form, and that authors after him would be deprived even of the possibility of perfection. The result was that a large part of the public, after having read *Poor Folk*, talked primarily about the *long-windedness* of the novel but kept silent about everything else.

The same thing happened when *The Double* appeared. Indeed, one can say with assurance that it was only with a small circle of readers that these two works were a complete success. . . . [The reason why] most readers dislike Mr. Dostoevsky's works is that they are unaccustomed to the original way in which he depicts reality. . . . In vain do people say that novelty always influences the majority in a positive way. In the first place, the majority is not the same everywhere. In the second place, any majority has a well-established routine. There are examples of an immediate success for extremely mediocre literary works . . . a success founded primarily on nothing other than a novel content. Hence the reason why, in various times and places, genuinely original works are often met with coldness, but in time are acknowledged as first-class and praised to the skies! If Gogol was not understood and valued in the first years of his career, it was because he countered the romantic direction reigning in our literature at the time. It is not surprising that the popularity of Mr. Dostoevsky has met an obstacle, his manner opposing that of Gogol. . . .

The *manner* of Mr. Dostoevsky is original to the highest degree. He, less than anyone else, can be called an imitator of Gogol. Indeed, if anyone should tag him with such a name, the same person would have to call Gogol an imitator of Homer or Shakespeare. In this sense, all genuine artists imitate each other, because elegance is always and everywhere governed by the same rules.

Both Gogol and Mr. Dostoevsky depict genuine society as it exists in reality. But whereas Gogol is a poet who is primarily social, Mr. Dostoevsky is primarily psychological. For one, the individual is important as a representative of a well-known society or circle; for the other, society itself is interesting for its influence on the individual. Gogol is inspired by the individual only when he feels the possibility of using him to penetrate one of the wider spheres of society. With Chichikov, he travels all the corners and alleyways of the Russian provinces. The same thing can also be said about all his works, with the notable exception of *Diary of a Madman*. Gogol's collected works one can decisively call an artistic statistics of Russia.

In Dostoevsky one also meets strikingly artistic depictions of society, but they are for him the backdrop . . . drawn, for the most part, in such thin strokes that they are overwhelmed completely in vast psychological interest. Even in *Poor Folk*, the interest, brought about by the analysis of the characters . . . is incomparably more forceful than the sharp depiction of their surroundings. The more time one spends in reading *Poor Folk*, the more one discovers this feature of profound psychological analysis. We are convinced that any work of Mr. Dostoevsky will gain in the extreme if it is read a second or third time. We cannot explain in any other way the wealth of psychological details, the unusual depth and perception. For example, reading *Poor Folk* for the first time, one will wonder why, at the end of the novel, the author takes it into his head to force Varvara Alexeevna, with such cold despotism, to send Devushkin from store to store with repulsive orders. Such an incident, however, has great significance for the psychologist, and informs the work with an unusually faithful snapshot of human nature. It goes without saying that the love of Makar Devushkin cannot but arouse in Varvara Alexeevna a revulsion which she hides constantly and consistently, and perhaps also from herself. Is there anything more burdensome in the world than the necessity of restraining one's dislike of a person to whom for some reason we are obligated and who (God save us!) loves us! Whoever will take the trouble to sift through their past will most likely recall that they have felt the greatest antipathy not toward enemies but toward people who are devoted to them to the point of self-sacrifice and to whom, in the depths of their souls, they cannot respond in similar fashion.

Varvara Alexeevna (we are deeply convinced) is tortured by the devotion of Makar Alexeevich more than by her crushing poverty, but she cannot refuse the right to torture him . . . as a lackey so that she can be freed of his oppressive guardianship. . . . Reread *Poor Folk* after time has given you the chance to value all the details of this work, and you will find in it a wealth of virtues that, on first glance, you, we, and any reader or reviewer could see as faults.

The Double has had less success than *Poor Folk*. . . . In it, though, Mr. Dostoevsky expresses psychological analysis in all its fullness and originality. Here he has penetrated so deeply into the human soul. In fact, in *The Double*, so fearlessly and passionately has Mr. Dostoevsky looked into the treasured workings of human emotions, thoughts, and deeds . . . that he is like a curious person penetrating the chemical makeup of matter. It is a strange thing! What seemingly can be more positive than a chemical view of reality? But a picture of the world, enlightened by such a stance, always shows itself as enveloped also in a kind of mystical light. . . .

Before us *The Double* unfolds as the anatomy of a soul that has perished from being conscious of a lack of coordination of personal interests in a well-structured society. Recall the poor and sickly proud Golyadkin who lives in constant fear of himself, and who strives, tortuously, not to debase himself before anyone in any way; but who also destroys himself even before his rascal servant Petrushka, and who agrees to trim his pretensions to personhood, even to live *in his own right*. Recall how the slightest movement in nature seems to him to be an evil sign arranged by all kinds of enemies . . . who, fully and invisibly, devote themselves to doing him harm, who keep stubborn vigil over his unhappy persona, and who, stubbornly and without pause, undermine his trifling interests. . . .

We cannot help but say a few words about Mr. Dostoevsky's third work, "Mister Prokharchin." . . . Reading this piece, we were perturbed by a suspicion that until now we could not deny. It seems to us that the author has learned of complaints regarding the long-winded quality of his works, and that to please his readers, he is ready to cut out too many things for the sake of valued brevity, the scale of which no one has determined in a successful way. At the very least, we do not know how else to explain the vagueness of the idea of the piece.

January 5, 1847
Eduard Guber, from an article

What is our Russian literature? Where has it come from and where it is going? Where are its books and its writers? What does it demand, what does it want, and does it even want something? In reality, does it even exist, this literature without books and writers, this literature on the off chance, this literature of thick journals and little clerks. We read and write little. The new writer has become a phenomenon which people look at like a minor marvel. A good book becomes an event which enters into the line of careless gossip and our deeply thoughtful conversations, together with a new planet or a new vice.

Everything that is produced in our literature moves to journals. Individual books visit stores or go begging in libraries to be read. A writer who decides on a separate edition for his work does not like to talk about how many copies he has published or how they have been dispersed.

The number is limited to several hundred. From where comes this contradiction between the reader and the writer, between the book and the buyer? How can one reconcile the hungry head of a book concern with the growing number of literate people in Russia?

Poor Folk is a splendid work about the touching story of a poor worker with a pure and loving heart, who is condemned to humiliation, hunger, and sorrow. This is a simple tale from genuine life which is repeated, perhaps, every day in one of the dark back streets and corners of our noisy, cold, and indifferent city. The story is rendered with profound feeling and an accurate knowledge of life, but also with all the mistakes of a first attempt, with long repetitions, overblown diminutive names, and a tiresome monotony.

The new criticism has seized upon this book greedily, showering it with enthusiastic praises, welcoming this young writer into the ranks of first-class geniuses and raising him to such heights, willy-nilly, and as often happens in such a case, as to make his head spin. The blunders, forgivable in a first work, become coarse mistakes in a second. The inadequacies grow. What was at first monotonous has become so excruciatingly boring that, respected readers, it was only from a sense of duty that I finished reading to the end *Messers Golyadkin* and *Prokharchin.* This bitter but honest truth has to sadden an individual with such a decisive talent as Mr. Dostoevsky. Who knows how guilty in these failures is the careless criticism of the young generation? Who knows what influence they have had over the development of a young, powerful, but still unsteady and immature talent?

February 1, 1847
Vissarion Belinsky, from a review

According to Mr. Guber, it is the *new criticism* . . . which has raised the author of *Poor Folk* to head-spinning heights, and which has appeared in print exactly one month after *The Double.*[47] *The Adventures of Mr. Golyadkin* was published. Consequently, the author of *Poor Folk* has had no opportunity to spoil his second story as a result of the head-spinning from praise for his first. . . .

We also now consider Mr. Dostoevsky to be an individual with a decisive talent, and on the basis of this opinion, we think that neither praise nor abuse influences him in any way. . . . And truly, is it worthwhile to call attention to a talent that can be killed by the praise or censure of the critics? When Pushkin appeared, he was praised and abused without moderation; but he still went his own way; he always remained true to his poetic instinct, sometimes even in spite of the assertions of his own personal mind. Without instinct there is no artist, and so deprived, his talent is so insignificant that the sooner nothing comes from him, the better for literature and the public. Childishly unfounded is the opinion that criticism can kill talents, praising or abusing them, but such a view has lived on in our country since the arcadian period of our literature, when it drowned in the tears and sighs of sensitive writers. . . . But now such an opinion is laughable and wild.

February 19, 1847
Vissarion Belinsky, from a letter to Ivan Turgenev

To my surprise, I did not like Dostoevsky's correspondence between cardsharps.[48] I had to force myself to finish it.

By the way, here is an anecdote for you about one fine man. From Kraevsky this individual took more than four thousand paper rubles, being obligated under contract to deliver to him on December 5th the first part of his large novel, on January 5th the second, on February 5th the third, and on March 5th the fourth. December and January go by. Dostoevsky does not appear, and where to find him Kraevsky does not know. Finally one fine morning in February the doorbell rings in the foyer of Kraevsky's home. The servant opens [the door] and sees Dostoevsky. Taking his coat quickly, the servant rushes to inform Kraevsky. Kraevsky, it seems, is overjoyed. The servant rushes out to Dostoevsky to welcome him, but he sees neither galoshes nor overcoat nor Dostoevsky himself. He has vanished without a trace. Now, truly, is that not a point-by-point scene from *The Double*?[49]

February 21, 1847
Konstantin Aksakov, from a review

[In *Poor Folk*], Dostoevsky does not appear as a complete, artistic talent. Of course, this is his first work, but in the initial attempts of a genuine talent, one almost always sees . . . a sincerity of creation which belongs to him alone. But, generally speaking, such a thing we do not see in this work of Mr. Dostoevsky. . . . The pictures of poverty appear in all their randomness; they are neither refined nor extended to the general sphere. The impression is a burdensome one because the work does not remain in your soul forever. . . .

In Dostoevsky's story, though . . . several features of the poor girl [Varvara Dobroselova] are good; there is also much that is splendid in the story of the student Pokrovsky. . . . Also remarkable is Devushkin's opinion about Gogol's "The Overcoat" . . . even if it is drawn out. . . .

[In *The Double*] we do not see the influence of Gogol so much as an imitation of the writer . . . Mr. Dostoevsky does not understand that what in Gogol is splendid, original, and alive . . . is with him intolerably lifeless, dry, boring . . . and tiresome. . . . We simply do not understand how such a story could have come into being. Almost by heart . . . all of Russia knows Gogol. Before all, he stands as a person in his own right. Mr. Dostoevsky refashions and, as a whole, repeats Gogol's phrases. But it seems that these are only phrases, deprived of their own life. There is only the bare imitation of the externals of the great works of Gogol.

In *The Double* . . . there is neither sense nor content nor thought—there is nothing. From the scraps of the brilliant clothing of an artist, Mr. Dostoevsky has sewn a suit and steps out boldly before the public. . . .

Is he amusing himself at the public's expense? Such a thing is difficult to say.

Is this truly talent? What we have here is a pitiful parody [of Gogol]. Indeed, can *The Double* arouse anything other than boredom and repulsion? Does Mr. Dostoevsky really think that seizing another's devices for his own, he has somehow taken hold of this individual's poetic worth? Does he really think that he has rendered some kind of service [to society]?

Speaking about Mr. Dostoevsky's *The Double*, we can repeat the words that Mr. Goldyakin also often repeats:

"Oh, this is bad, bad! Oh, very bad, indeed! Oh, our affairs are bad! Oh, things have caught up with us!"

Yes, that is it exactly! *The Double* has caught up with all bad things and in a poor way at that!

If it were not for Dostoevsky's first story, in no way would we have the patience to read his second. But we did so from a sense of duty, wishing to find something in his piece, but did not. It is so boring that we set the work down many times only to force ourselves to pick it up and read it anew. . . . Where is the talent we saw in Dostoevsky's first piece? Or has he begun to leave it only there?

Circa March 1847 and after
Fyodor Dostoevsky, from testimony to the Investigatory Commission for the Petrashevsky affair

I first visited Petrashevsky's home during Lent 1847. . . . In the first two years of our acquaintance, I saw him rarely. Sometimes three or four months would pass before I came to his place.

March 5, 1847
Apollon Grigoriev, from a review

> Of works of the school of Gogol . . . worthy of attention is Dosto-
> evsky's superb story "A Novel in Nine Letters."

March 5, 1847
Ivan Goncharov, from a letter to Pyotr Yazykov

> As promised, I am being so bold as to send with this letter four copies
> of *A Common Story* . . . one for your personal library and the other
> three for the Committee for the Karamzin Library [in Simbirsk]. . . .
> I am also enclosing one copy of *Poor Folk* by F. M. Dostoevsky.

March 17, 1847
Apollon Grigoriev, from a review

> Writers . . . of the school that rather pitiful opponents call *natural* . . .
> see Gogol only as justifying and restoring any and all trifling personal-
> ity, any and all kind of microscopic entity. . . .
>
> In so doing . . . they have fallen into the sentimental generation of
> Makar Alexeevich Devushkin and Varvara Alexeevna Dobroselova (in
> the novel *Poor Folk*) . . . or they have focused on the individual to such
> a degree as to legitimate any and all pretenses in the pathological story
> of Golyadkin Senior, who appears fully as a slave with no escape from
> his bondage.

March 27, 1847
Vasily Botkin, from a letter to Vissarion Belinsky

> It is painful for me to recall the mannered, fanciful Dostoevsky,
> although one must confess that for all his closure and sedition, he has a
> deep sense of the tragic. But to dig down into such a thing, one has to
> go through entire piles of manure.

April–June 1847
Fyodor Dostoevsky, from a letter to Albert Starchevsky

> I am sending you your proofs, but I have not looked through
> them. I am unwell with a rush of blood to the head; on doctor's orders,
> I absolutely cannot work. When I am capable of doing so, I will start.
> If there is not any work for me, I will return the advance to you as soon
> as the *Dictionary* comes out.[50]

April–mid-May 1847
Fyodor Dostoevsky, from a letter to Albert Starchevsky

> I have sat down for five hours over the form that is being sent to you.
> The article about the Jesuits ought to be rewritten completely.

April 1, 1847
Ivan Panaev, from an article

> My glory is secure. People talk about me. They are interested to learn
> my name and rank. About town are so many anecdotes with me as the
> hero. One honorable writer grants me a laudatory word. Another, for
> several evenings in a row, talks about nothing but my lack of talent.
> A third gives a soiree and people come (although they never came
> previously) because deftly he wishes it to be known on what day, at
> what hour, he will show me at his home.
>
> I must confess that I got terribly cold feet when I appeared before a
> large and unfamiliar crowd; I was so scared that I almost died right then
> and there. But when I was led into a room and praised for my great
> talent, I was brought back to consciousness.
>
> Incidentally, I did not show right away that I needed medicine no
> longer. Having come to my senses completely, I, for a long time, did
> not show any signs of life, but, with closed eyes, kept listening, like a
> cat whose is tickled under its throat. . . .
>
> But you cannot imagine what a surprising delight it is when people
> talk about you, when they praise you so! . . .
>
> But now I am beginning to get angry and depressed when, for
> a long time now, people are talking about something else. . . . Pur-
> posely do I make the rounds of bookstores and taverns, sitting behind
> a journal, and looking and eavesdropping and choking from agita-
> tion. . . . But what is going on? . . . People are praising [me], good God,
> they are praising. . . . Of course, there are those who censure [me];
> but they are envious, undoubtedly envious, or they have a brother
> or some other relative who writes verse or they themselves do so.
> How can it be otherwise? You understand why else would they cen-
> sure [me]? . . . Oh, envy, cursed envy! . . . Oh, pride, which prevents
> deserving ones [from getting] what they deserve! . . . After all, am
> I at fault because chance has gifted me with the wings of an eagle but
> has forgotten to give others those of a raven? . . . What do you think?
> Guilty as charged!

After all, I have only just set out on my path, and already I have endured from you envy and pride, the zealous enemies of any kind of external success! Already on my heart are bruises (an expression borrowed from one well-known Russian poet) and various heavy sores. . . . But later, later. . . .

Soon, very soon I will present a complete picture of the horrors visited on me in my battle with human envy and pride. . . . Now, though, I wanted to present to you a more moving picture: a picture of glory and successes.

A first group, whom I have never seen, boast of their acquaintance with me; a second group gloat about what happened to me in a certain province; a third group, in surprising detail, describe my characters in such a way that when I go out, I resemble them like two peas in a pod; a fourth group are complete strangers to me, but when I meet them, act like they know me, bowing and smiling pleasantly. Finally, a certain publisher runs to my place, spreads his arms and legs, examines me from all sides, lisps, whistles, and at last explains that he wants my "poetry, if you please."

What do you think? Are all these facts seemingly sufficient to show that my glory is secure? Yes! My glory is secure: I am now a great person and no one can surpass me in anything! People should be honored to make my acquaintance. I have every right to put on airs before them—and I will put on airs!

How will I know what I am worth when my glory had already reached the furthermost corners of our country? . . . Just the other day I received a letter. . . . And what a letter it was! . . . From whom? . . . The hand of a woman.[51] She wrote to me that she was beautiful and young, and that in her earlier years she loved the mountains and valleys, hills and streams, and that I had begun to appear to her as an ideal. . . . "I am certain (she wrote to me!) that it was you! I knew your features . . . I knew you. Everywhere, for a long time, I felt you unseen alongside me. . . . Your genius. . . ." But I am telling you only a few words of what she said.

Finishing the letter, she asked for my picture and my verse. She herself wrote poetry, [crediting] an unnamed person who had inspired her inexperienced pen (an obvious reference to me, but again from modesty, I am only saying little). "Publish them," she said, "they are splendid." So I am doing so now. Read on:

In vain do people say I chase after glory
But no one knows what I hide

Suddenly my black curls are decked with myrtle
My mind takes all in stride. . . .

Why great thoughts, common sense,
Are the problems of the day?
They do not move or shake me
My fancy in a deadly way.
I need not the real world
but poetry, dreams, and fears
First salons, mazurkas, and polkas,
Then grottoes, moons, and tears!
In the blinding light of balls
Amidst roses of red and cream
I sit alone under a gloomy birch
With delight I dream and dream.
In vain do people say I chase after fame.
Tricked them have I one and all
No, in my black curly head, I think
and repeat: I'm having a ball.

April 12, 1847
Faddei Bulgarin, from a review

Young people do not understand that speculators denigrate them with
their ennobling views. The honorable Mr. Gogol who never rose higher
than Paul de Kock or Pigault-Lebrun, they proclaimed a Homer! . . .

After Mr. Gogol reduced these speculators to despair with his
silence, they put forth from the mob another young man, Mr. Dostoevsky, and call him a *genius, equal* to Gogol. They did so not to benefit
Mr. Dostoevsky but to call the attention of the public to that journal which has published the fairy tales of Mr. Dostoevsky. But their
attempts were not successful!

April 13, 1847
Fyodor Dostoevsky, from "The Petersburg Chronicle"

If you begin to feel like reading, take the two volumes of *The Con-
temporary* for March and April, and there, as you know, is *A Common
Story.* . . . The novel is good. In it is observation and much intelligence.
The idea seems to us bookish and belated, but it is done in a deft way.
Incidentally, the key wish of the author—to maintain his idea and to
explain it in as much detail as possible—imparts to the work some

kind of special dogmatism and dryness; it even stretches and strains it. Such a shortcoming does not also redeem the easy, almost flying style of Mr. Goncharov. The author believes in reality; he shows people how they are. The Petersburg women [in it] come out especially successfully. . . .

Mr. Goncharov's novel is extremely interesting.

April 21, 1847
Leopold Brandt, from a review

[Goncharov] is a worthy successor to both Messrs. Gogol and Dostoevsky, of whom, as is well known, one has refused glory, and the other has been denied such by both readers and reviewers.

April 27, 1847
Fyodor Dostoevsky, from "The Petersburg Chronicle"

Passionately do we love our fatherland, our native Petersburg, our love of play, wherever and whenever it happens. In a word, we have a great many public interests. But *circles* are even more useful in our country. Everyone knows that all of Petersburg is nothing more than a large collection of small circles, each with its own makeup, rules, laws, logic and oracle. . . . Such a thing is the result of our national character which still avoids social life . . . and looks homeward [for company]. For social life, one needs art. . . . Home is more natural and peaceful, there one does not need art at all.

In some circles, you are asked in a rousing way—*what's new?* Quickly the question takes on a personal cast, with answers as gossip, yawns or other things that make you also yawn in a cynical and patriarchal way. In these circles, between gossip and yawns, you can extend your useful life in a most serene and delight way . . . until you leave this pleasant and serene world and enter a better one.

In other circles . . . people talk business with force. With passion, there gather educated and well-intentioned individuals . . . who, cruelly, banish all innocent pleasures like gossip and preference (these are seemingly not literary circles); and who, with incomprehensible enthusiasm, talk about important things. When people in these circles finish talking, postulating, solving social questions, and convincing everyone of everything, they become irritated and unpleasantly tired. Everyone becomes angry with everyone else. Bitter truths are uttered, sharp and sweeping personalities are bared. In the end, all retreat to their corners and settle down . . . [making things] pleasant . . . but in the end, offensively annoying.

April 27, 1847
Fyodor Dostoevsky, from "The Petersburg Chronicle"

Good Lord! Where have they gone—the villains of old dramas and novels? How pleasant it was when they lived in the world . . . and to have alongside a most virtuous individual who defended good and punished evil. . . .

This villain, this *tirano ingrato* . . . was, for some secret and completely incomprehensible reason, predetermined by fate. He was a villain while still in his mother's womb. Even his ancestors . . . sensed his appearance in the world. Purposely, they chose *a family name* which accorded completely with the social situation of their descendant . . . and from which we knew that this individual went about with a knife and slashed people . . . without taking a copeck. . . . God knows why. . . . as if he were some kind of machine. . . . How good it was! At the very least, how understandable!

But now God knows what writers talk about. Now, suddenly, it turns out that the most virtuous person . . . and most incapable of wrongdoing, becomes a complete villain suddenly, without even himself noticing [such a change]. . . . Even more annoying is that no one notices or says [anything] . . . [since] he lives honorably and for a long time before he finally dies amidst such honors and praise that one becomes envious he is mourned so sincerely and tenderly.

April 27, 1847
Fyodor Dostoevsky, from "The Petersburg Chronicle"

Gogol's book created a great stir in early winter. Particularly noteworthy was the unanimous response from almost all the newspapers and journals, even as they contradicted one another constantly in their assessment.[52]

May 1847
Vera Dostoevskaya-Ivanova, from a letter to Andrei Dostoevsky

I do not know why brothers Misha and Fedinka are angry with me. I have sent two letters to them, but they have not answered either one. When you see brother Fedinka, ask him to write at least five lines to me. Such a thing will make me extremely happy.

May 1, 1847
Vissarion Belinsky, from a review

> Perhaps the talent of Mr. Dostoevsky was greeted with exaggerated
> praise. But why must one invariably put forth the verdict, a cabal, an
> assemblage, a speculation, and not an exaggeration, a mistake? No one
> from among people with intelligence and taste will not come to reject
> Mr. Dostoevsky's talent, even remarkable as it is. It must be that the
> entire question is the extent and volume of his talent. . . .
>
> We must avoid such praises as *"Pushkin, Lermontov, Gogol,
> Dostoevsky."*[53]

Circa May 7, 1847
Fyodor Dostoevsky, from a letter to Mikhail Dostoevsky

> I will write you only two lines because I am very busy. I do not know
> where my letter will find you. With all my might I will try to finish up
> my affairs so that I can visit you for a week even if it be in September.[54]
> As for money, I was a little mistaken in my calculations. I will have
> to write perhaps even two feuilletons a week,[55] that is, no more than
> 250–300 paper rubles' worth. Since I have to pay back the Maykovs,
> from whom I have borrowed a great deal (although they are not even
> asking for it back), and for the apartment, I do not know how much
> I will be sending to you. I am in such a state, brother, that if by October
> 1st I repay you only 100 silver rubles, I will consider myself to be most
> fortunate. But from the first of October or September (I will come to
> visit you then, on the last ship), things will change. After finishing my
> novel, I will take an advance of 1,000 silver rubles from Kraevsky and
> on no condition other than for *an indefinite period of time.* Since *The
> Contemporary* is making a go of it and luring contributors away from
> *The Fatherland Notes* in a fierce way, he, *Andrei Alexandrovich Kraevsky,*
> is very frightened. He will agree to anything. Furthermore, it is to his
> good fortune and *mine* that my novel is being published at the end
> of the year.[56] It will appear during the subscription period, and, most
> important, if I am not mistaken, it will be the capital thing of the year
> and will get the better of my friends, the "contemporaries," who are
> doing everything they can to bury me. But to hell with them. Then
> after receiving the 1,000 silver rubles, I will come to see you with the
> money and with the final decision regarding you. You can come to
> Petersburg even alone, taking a leave of 28 days, to find a position
> and—or continue to serve in the engineers or leave it forever. . . .

I do not know about a translation. I will work all summer and try to find one. In Petersburg we had a fool named Furmann (he's abroad now). He receives 20,000 a year just on translations! If you had even so much as a year of financial security, you could definitely make a go of it. You are young;[57] you could even make a literary career. Nowadays everyone is making one. In ten years or so you could even forget about translations.

I am writing very zealously; perhaps I will finish. Then we will see each other earlier than planned. What does Emiliya Fyodorovna have to say? I send her my humblest regards, the children also. Good-bye, brother. I have a slight fever. I caught a cold yesterday by going out at night without a frock coat and in just an overcoat, and it was sleeting ice along the Neva. It is as cold here as in November. But I have already caught cold up to six times—it is nothing! Generally speaking, my health has improved greatly.

Good-bye, brother. Wish me success. After the novel I will get down to publishing my three novels (*Poor Folk*, *The Double*, rewritten, and the last one) at my own expense, and perhaps my fate will clear up.

God grant you happiness, my dear.

P.S. You will not believe it. Here is it already the third year of my literary activity and it is as though I am in a daze. I do not see any life, and there is no time to come to my senses. Study disappears for lack of time. I want to establish myself. They have created a dubious renown for me, and I do not know how long this hell will continue. Here is poverty, rush work—if only there were some peace.

May 30, 1847
Apollon Grigoriev, from an article

> Akaky Akakievich of Gogol's "The Overcoat" has become the forefather for a multiplicity of microscopic personalities: For a long time, minuscule joys and trifling sufferings and sorrows have entered into the everyday habit of writers, but under the pen of Mr. Dostoevsky and Mr. Butkov, they have been carried to an extreme. . . . Such is "Prokharchin." . . .
>
> Dostoevsky and Butkov delve so deeply into the trifling appearances of an observed or moral disease that, consciously or unconsciously, they set aside any concern about the artistry of their descriptions, trying exclusively to render with all possible faithfulness and accuracy the charm of that corner where [a character like] Mr. Prokharchin lives, without taking hardly great responsibility for their writing.

June 1847
Vissarion Belinsky, from a review

> Mr. Imrek[58] calls *Poor Folk* . . . "an artistic work," and the author a "tal-
> ent that one cannot doubt." . . . But on that very same page . . . exactly
> nineteen lines later, he says: "But his (Mr. Dostoevsky's) story *decisively
> cannot be called an artistic work.*" Simple unhappiness! . . .
>
> From *Poor Folk* Mr. Imrek moves on to *The Double.* . . . The artificial,
> mannered style of this work is so strikingly manifest that even Mr.
> Imrek has rendered it with a rather successful parody:
>
> "It is not difficult to seize upon the devices [of the work]. The
> devices are not at all difficult to seize. It is not at all difficult or a dif-
> ficulty to seize upon devices such as these. But the matter is not thus
> done, ladies and gentlemen; the very matter, ladies and gentlemen, is
> not over; it is still not thus completed, my good people, this very mat-
> ter. And here, you know, one needs not only this but also that. It, you
> see, is something else that is demanded, this this, this that, and like it
> something else, too. And this this and this that is not to be had. Pre-
> cisely this very this is not to be had; a poetic talent, ladies and gentle-
> men, such an artistic thing is also not to be had. Yes, here it is, this very
> thing, that is genuine, so it is; so it really is."

June 1, 1847
Fyodor Dostoevsky, from "The Petersburg Chronicle"

> The study of a city . . . is not a useless thing. We do not recall when
> we happened to come across a French book which contained a bevy
> of views on contemporary Russia.[59] Of course, views by foreigners on
> contemporary Russia are well known; but for some reason, we have
> resisted measurement by European standards. . . .
>
> This book by a notorious tourist had been read greedily throughout
> Europe. In it he writes that there is nothing characteristic about Peters-
> burg architecture; that there is nothing particularly striking, or *nothing
> national* [about it], that the entire city is one ludicrous caricature of cer-
> tain European capitals; and that Petersburg, in its architecture alone,
> is such a strange mixture [of styles] that one cannot stop exclaiming
> "oh!" and "ah!" in surprise at every turn.
>
> Greek architecture, Roman architecture, Byzantine architecture,
> Dutch architecture, rococo architecture, the newest Italian architec-
> ture, our Orthodox architecture—all this, our traveler says, is thrown
> together in such an amusing way that . . . there is not a truly splendid
> building [in the city]!

Our tourist also waxes eloquent on Moscow, on its Kremlin. About the latter, he has several ornate, rhetorical phrases. He is proud of Muscovite nationality, but he curses droshkies and cabs for straying from ancient, patriarchal lines. . . . [He also laments] the disappearance of everything that is native and national in Russia. The idea here is that Russians are afraid of their national character and thus do not want to go about as before, fearing justly that somehow their patriarchal carriages will shake their souls.

So writes a Frenchman, that is, an intelligent individual who, like any Frenchman, is superficial and exceptionally stupid. Such an individual does not accept things that are not French whether they be literature, the arts, the sciences, or even native history. He can become angry that there are people who have their own history, ideas, native character, and development. But so adroitly, secretly, even subconsciously . . . does the Frenchman agree with certain—we will not say Russian— armchair, leisure-time ideas of ours. He sees Russian nationality in the same way that many of our time want to see it, that is, as a dead letter, as an idea that has outlived its time, as a heap of stones, as if recalling [the remains] of ancient Rus, and, finally, as a blind, wholehearted appeal to a dreamy native land.

Without a doubt, the Kremlin is an extremely honorable monument to our distant past. It is an antiquarian rarity to be regarded with special curiosity and great respect. But how the Kremlin is absolutely national—this is something we cannot understand! There exist national monuments that have outlived their time and have stopped being national. We will say further: the Russian folk knows the Kremlin . . . [as] a religious [monument] to which flow people from all corners of our country to kiss the relics of Russian miracle workers. Such a thing is good, but nothing special. Crowds of folk go to pray to Kiev, to the Solovetsky Islands,[60] to Lake Ladoga,[61] to Mount Athos,[62] everywhere. But do such individuals know the lives of the prelates, of Saints Peter and Philip?[63] Of course not. . . . They have not the slightest understanding of the most important periods of Russian history.

People will say: our folk venerate the memory of ancient tsars and princes . . . who are buried in the Archangel Cathedral.[64] That is good. But whom among Russian tsars and princes . . . do the folk know before the Romanovs [ascended the throne]? *By name*, they know three: Dmitri Donskoi, Ivan the Terrible, and Boris Godunov (the remains of the last one lying in the Holy Trinity Lavra). The people know Boris Godunov only because he built "Ivan the Great."[65] About Dmitri Donskoi and Ivan Vasilievich they will tell you wonders beyond belief. . . .

People will also say: Who is this folk? The folk is dark and illiterate. They will also point to society, to educated people. But the delight [of such people] for the native land . . . seemed to be airy and cerebral, armchair and romantic, for who in our country knows history?

Historical tales are very well known. But for some reason, history in our time is a most unpopular, armchair affair, the province of scholars who argue, serve up, and compare, but who . . . cannot agree on the most fundamental ideas. They seek to explain facts that, more than ever, remain riddles. We will not argue: Russians cannot remain indifferent to the history of their tribe, in whatever form it may appear. But to demand that everyone forget and reject their present for certain honored antiquarian subjects is, in the highest degree, both unjust and absurd.

June 1, 1847
Fyodor Dostoevsky, from "The Petersburg Chronicle"

Petersburg is not like [Moscow]. One does not move an inch without seeming to hear and feel the contemporary moment, its idea. Truly . . . here everything is chaos, everything is a mix. Many things are food for caricature, but so is all of moving life.

Petersburg is the head and heart of Russia. . . . Everything about its many-faceted character gives witness to unified thought and movement. The rows of Dutch buildings recall the time of Peter the Great. The structures of Rastrelli hark back to the era of Catherine [the Great]; those in the Greek and Roman style, to the present time. They all show the history of European life in Petersburg and in all of Russia.

These days Petersburg is dust and garbage. It is still building and becoming. Its future is still an idea—the idea of Peter I. With each day it is forming, growing, and taking root, not in a swamp but in all of Russia, which lives as one Petersburg. Already everyone has felt the power and the blessings of the Petrine direction. Already all of society has been summoned to realize this great idea. Everyone has begun to live. Everything—industry, trade, science, literature, education—has begun to organize social life. . . . In our contemporary striving, we see not the disappearance of national life but rather the triumph of nationality, which, contrary to what many people think, is not perishing under European influence. As we see it, whole and healthy is that folk which loves the genuine moment in a positive way, and which understands and lives by its principles.

June 1, 1847
Fyodor Dostoevsky, from "The Petersburg Chronicle"

Never have people talked about contemporary ideas and directions so much as now, in the present time. Never has literature, as well as all manifestations of social life, aroused such curiosity. . . .

Almost everyone is beginning to discern and analyze society, each other, and himself. Everyone is examining and measuring one another with curious glances. An overall confession is coming into place. People are talking about, quoting, and scrutinizing one another . . . often in torment and pain. A thousand points of view are opening up to people who never expected [to have] a personal view on anything. . . . They understand and espouse the view that analysis does not spare the analyzers, and that is better to know oneself than to get angry at writers who are a most quiet and submissive lot and who do not wish to offend anyone. . . .

There is nothing more unjust than reproaches as to the emptiness and the inertia of our literature in the past year. Several new stories and novels have appeared in various periodicals and have met with complete success.[66] There have appeared several remarkable articles, primarily in literary criticism.[67] . . . There has come to be an edition of Russian classics by Smirdin which also has enjoyed great success and will continue indefinitely.[68] There also has seen the light of day a complete edition of works by Krylov.[69] The number of subscribers to journals, newspapers, and other publications have increased greatly, and the demand for reading has begun to spread through all levels of society. The pencil and chisel of artists have also not remained idle. The splendid undertaking of Messrs. Bernardsky and Agin—the illustrations for *Dead Souls*—are coming to an end, but one cannot praise enough the conscientiousness of these two artists.[70] Several of their illustrations are so splendid that it would be difficult to want anything more. M. Nevakovich, for now our single best caricaturist, continues his *Jumble* in a constant and tireless way. From the very beginning, the newness and wonder of this publication has attracted fervent and widespread curiosity.[71] Truly it would be difficult to imagine a more convenient time than now for the appearance of a caricaturist-*artist*. Many are the ideas developed and experienced by society. It is nothing to crack heads for subjects [for stories], although we often seemingly hear [people saying]: "What is there to talk and write about?" But the more talented a writer, the richer are his methods for carrying this thought into society. For him there are neither barriers nor everyday difficulties. For him there are themes and subjects always and everywhere. In these times the artist can find food no matter where he wishes to speak about everything. Furthermore, people have the urge to speak their minds. They also have the urge to seize upon and to consider that which has been said.

June 13, 1847
Varvara Dostoevskaya-Karepina, from a letter to Andrei Dostoevsky

If you write to us, let me know if brother Fedinka is well and if he is in Petersburg. I have heard nothing about him regarding his literary activity.

June 15, 1847
Fyodor Dostoevsky, from "The Petersburg Chronicle"

A friend of mine has assured me that we [Russians] do not know how to be lazy, that we find such a thing burdensome, without delight and quiet, since rest for us is somehow feverish, angst-ridden, gloomy, and unsatisfying; and that at the same time, there [reigns] in our country analysis, comparison, skeptical glances, and secret thoughts that always before us is some eternal, never-ending, and mundane task. . . .

Such a claim reminds me of [the story of] the punctual German who, leaving Berlin, noted calmly in his roadbook: "Upon arriving in Nuremberg, don't forget to get married." Of course the German, first of all, always has some kind of system in his head. He never feels the ugliness of facts; he is grateful for such things.

In truth, though, one cannot help but acknowledge that sometimes our actions have no system and that things somehow move along according to some set Eastern order. . . . We drag our life harness by force, with burdensome effort, from responsibility and duty, and we are also ashamed to admit that we do not have the strength to do so and become tired. . . .

Is that why we have in our country a powerfully developed but extremely unpleasant habit (which, we do not deny, can also be somehow useful in our way of doing things) always . . . to believe and consider in an extremely precise way our impressions, to consider . . . a forthcoming future delight . . . [and] to value and enjoy it in advance, in dreams . . . even though it is ill-suited for the present? . . .

We always . . . tear apart a flower to understand it more forcefully and then complain when we have fumes, not scents. But it is difficult to say what will become of us if we do not devote even several days a year to quenching our eternal and endless thirst for immediate genuine life via the various manifestations of nature. . . .

How do we not become tired, how do we not fall into paralysis, always chasing impressions, as if finding rhythm in a poor line of verse; tortured by an external thirst for spontaneous life; and frightened, to the point of illness, of our very illusions, of the hungry chimera, of this very dreaminess, and all those auxiliary measures which in our time try somehow to fill the completely sluggish emptiness of every-day colorless life?

In our country, the thirst for life moves to such an unrestrained passion. Everyone wants a serious activity. Many wish passionately to do good, to be of use. Little by little they begin to understand that happiness consists not in sitting on your hands . . . [waiting] to become a knight when an opportunity presents itself, but in eternal tireless activity, in the development and practice of all our inclinations and talents.

But do we have in our country many who are engaged in such tasks, and who do them with desire, *con amore*?

People say that by nature we Russians are lazy and love to avoid matters at hand, but thrust something upon us and we will do it as never before. But is such a thing entirely true? What evidence is there for such an unenviable national trait? Generally speaking, people have been crying out far too many things about general laziness and lack of action. To one another they have also been talking a great deal about useful activity, although, one must confess, that is all they are doing. Not for anything, though, are they ready to accuse their colleagues, perhaps only because, as Gogol noted, such individuals do not bite.

But, ladies and gentlemen, try to take a first step forward toward a *better and useful activity* and imagine it in some form. You show us a *business or a cause* . . . you begin to interest us in such a thing, you give it to us to do, and you set in motion our personal individual creativity. But are you able to do such a thing, Messrs. Urgers-On? Yes or no? No. So there is nothing to accuse, only that you have wasted words in vain. So it is in our country that a business or cause somehow always happens by itself, that is somehow an external affair, and that it does not evoke a special empathy. Here appears a purely Russian ability: to carry out a business or cause by force is foolish, dishonorable, and, as they say, winds up going completely to pieces. This trait shows clearly our national habit and manifests itself in everything, even in the most insignificant facts of our common life.

For example, in our country, if one does not have the means to begin to live in palaces or to dress as respectable people should, to dress like *everyone* (that is, like the very few), then our corner often resembles a cowshed, and even our clothes lead to unpleasant cynicism. If a person is dissatisfied, and if he lacks the means to articulate and to manifest that which is a bit better in him (not as a matter of pride, but as a consequence of the most natural human necessity to acknowledge, realize, and bring about a personal I in real life), then he will fall immediately into the most improbable state. If one may be allowed to say so, he will drink heavily, yield first to card-playing and card-sharping, next to dueling, and finally go out of his mind from *ambition*. At the very same time, he will despise his ambition fully and even suffer that he has been pained by such trivialities as ambition. You look—and unwillingly come to a conclusion that is almost unjust, even offensive, but also *seemingly very likely* that in us is little sense of personal worth, little essential egoism, and that, finally, we are unaccustomed to do a good deed without some kind of reward.

For example, give a task to an exacting, systematic German, one that is contrary to all his strivings and inclinations, and explain to him that it will set him on his way, feed him and his family, introduce him to society, take him to a desired goal and so forth, and the German will set about the business right away. He will even complete it without question, and even introduce into the new task a special new system. But is this a good thing? In part no, because in this case the individual goes to another, terrible extreme, to phlegmatic immobility and sometimes excluding the individual and, in its place, taking in his system, responsibility, formula, as well as his absolute worship of old world customs even if they do not measure up to the current time.

The reforms of Peter the Great created in Russia free activity, but they would not have been possible with this element in the national character, naively splendid, but sometimes extremely comic.

We have seen that the German, until the age of fifty, remains a bachelor. He teaches the children of Russian businessmen, knocks together a copeck here and there, and copulates via a legal marriage with his Minchen, dried up from a long spinsterhood, but heroically faithful. A Russian will not endure such a situation. He will quit loving such an individual or *go completely to pieces* or do something else. Here one can truly quote the opposite of a well-known proverb: what is health to a German is death to a Russian.

Are there many among us Russians who have the means to carry out their business or cause with love as they should—because such a thing demands desire, love for an agent, the entire person. Have many have found their stride? . . . No, they wave their hands and let the matter slip from them. But in characters who yearn for action, for immediate life, and for reality, but who are also feminine, tender, and weak, there gradually comes to the fore what people call dreaminess, so much so that in the end, people become not people but strange entities of an average type—dreamers.

But do you know what dreamers are, ladies and gentlemen? They are Petersburg tragedies, personified sins, tragedies that are silent, mysterious, gloomy, and savage, with all frenzied tragedies, with all catastrophes, upheavals, beginnings and ends.

We are talking seriously here. You sometimes meet individuals who are absent-minded, with vacant looks and pale, haggard faces; who seem perpetually engaged in something that is terribly burdensome or some skull-cracking business; and who sometimes appear weary and wan from burdensome labors; but who essentially come up with exactly nothing. Such are dreamers from the outside. Dreams are always burdened because they are extremely unbalanced. They are first extremely happy, then extremely gloomy. They are first boors, then attentive and tender. They are first egoists, then capable of the most noble sentiments.

As far as jobs go, these people are not fit for anything. They work, but they accomplish nothing. Rather, they are only *pulled along* by their own business or cause, which, in essence, is almost as bad as doing nothing at all. Such individuals despise formalities . . . but especially because they are submissive, forgiving, and fear that life will pass them by, they themselves are premier formalists.

At home, though, dreamers are completely different. For the most part, they live in complete isolation, as if hiding from people and the world and even rushing off into something melodramatic at a first glance at them. They are gloomy and terse with servants, and withdraw deep into themselves; but they also very much love everything that is idle, easy, and contemplative, everything that affects, in a tender way, emotion or arousing sensations. They love to read, and relish all kinds of books, even serious and specialized ones, but typically, after the second or third page, they drop what they are reading or become dissatisfied with it completely. Their fantasies are lively, fleeting, and even arousing. Their impressions are in sync with their moods, and an entire dreamlike world, with joys and sorrows, with heavens and hells, with the most captivating women, with heroic gestures, with heroic activity, always with some heroic struggle, with crimes and all kinds of horrors, suddenly possesses the entire being of the dreamer. The room disappears. Space, too. Time stops or flies by so quickly that an hour becomes a minute. Sometimes entire nights pass by unnoticed, in indescribable delights. Often in the course of several hours, dreamers experience a paradise of love or an entire existence that is huge, gigantic, unheard of, marvelous like a dream, splendid and grandiose. From some unknown cause, the pulse quickens, tears well up, and pale, moist cheeks burn with feverish fire. When dawn bursts forth with rosy light into the windows of dreamers, they are pale, sick, tormented, and happy. They throw themselves on their bed without recalling anything and, nodding off, they still hear the sensation in their heart, physical and sickly. The minutes of sobering up are terrible. The unhappy ones cannot bear them and accept their hell quickly in new, increased doses. Again a book, a musical motif, some old, distant memory from actual life—in a word, one of a thousand reasons, the most insignificant, and hell rises to the fore. Again a fancy, in a bright and lavish way, stretches out along the patterned and whimsical canvas of a quite mysterious dream. On the street, he walks about, hanging his head, paying little attention to his surroundings, sometimes forgetting reality completely. But he will note that the most ordinary everyday trifle, the most empty mundane thing will quickly assume a fantastic coloring. Already his glance becomes so fixed as to see the fantastic in everything. Closed shutters in broad daylight, an old woman on her last legs, a gentleman off to a meeting, waving his arms and muttering aloud to himself—such types, incidentally, one meets often—a family picture in the window of a poor wooden home—all these things are almost adventures.

The imagination is set on fire. Suddenly there is born an entire story, a tale, a novel. Often reality makes a burdensome, hostile impression on the heart of dreamers. They rush off to take refuge in their cherished, golden corner, which in reality is often dusty, slovenly, disordered, and dirty. Little by little our pranksters begin to shun crowds and societal interests, and gradually, imperceptibly begins to lose the talent for genuine life. Naturally, it begins to seem to him that the delight attained by his willful fantasy is fuller, more lavish, and more alive than genuine existence. Finally, in his delusion, he loses completely the moral sense by which individuals are able to appreciate all genuine beauty. They become unhinged and lost. They let slip moments of genuine happiness. In their apathy, they lay down their hands in a lazy way. They do not want to know that human life is endless self-contemplation of nature and daily being. There are dreamers who even celebrate the anniversary of their fantastic sensations. They often note the days of the month when they are particularly happy and when their fantasies come into most pleasant focus. And if at that time they wander into some street, read some book, or see some woman, they, without fail, try to see them again on the anniversary of their impressions, copying and recollecting the slightest circumstances of their rotten, impotent happiness.

Is not such a life a tragedy! Is it not a horror and a sin? Is it not a caricature? And are we all not more or less dreamers!

June 17, 1847
Apollon Grigoriev, from an article

Mr. Imrek is displeased with Dostoevsky's *Poor Folk* particularly because it "leaves an unpleasant impression which is inadmissible in the creation of great art." . . . We do find faults in its extreme sentimentality, as well as the variations and variants in a single letter—but not because it leave a burdensome impression. Such a thing can arise from anything.

[But] *The Double* . . . Mr. Imrek laughs at in a very witty and, for the most part, accurate way.

Summer 1847
Mikhail Yazykov, from a letter to the editor

Two or three years before his exile, on a splendid summer evening sometime in July or August, F. M. Dostoevsky paid me one of his frequent visits. . . . Among the guests were I. I. Panaev . . . and, it seems, Nekrasov . . . as well as P. V. Annenkov and I. S. Turgenev.

As usual, the lively conversation continued far into the night. Suddenly at around two in the morning, when the room had already become filled with light, Dostoevsky's thoughtful and concentrated expression became somehow agitated . . . his eyes were frightened, and his voice anxious and hollow.

"Mikhailo Alexandrovich, where am I?" he asked.

I had no idea what to do when, suddenly, Dostoevsky jumped up from the couch and ran very quickly through the large room where we sitting and straight to the open window to get some fresh air.

My wife was not feeling well and in an adjoining room. All the other guests were taking their leave. Having seen them off quickly, I grabbed a carafe of water. . . . We were alone.

When I ran to the window, I saw Dostoevsky with a distorted expression on his face. His entire body was shaking, and his head was shuddering and leaning to one side.

Having never seen and not knowing the signs of falling sickness and not suspecting . . . also a mild epileptic attack, I decided to pour cold water over his head. Immediately, in a powerfully aroused condition . . . he ran headlong through the room . . . and, without a hat, onto the Fontanka in the direction of Anichkov Bridge.

Deciding to catch up with him, I ran out of the gates . . . of my home[,] . . . jumped into the first carriage that came my way and ordered the driver to head for Nevsky Prospekt. . . . I caught sight of Dostoevsky running toward Liteinyi Street. . . . Having finally caught up with him . . . I jumped out of the carriage and stopped him.

Dostoevsky had calmed down somewhat. He had come to his senses and began to thank me for my concern, adding, vaguely, that he was still far from his apartment and that it would be better to hurry on over to the Mariinsky Hospital . . . to find a doctor on duty.

Assured that the attack had passed, I seated him in the carriage headed toward my place; but after a few minutes, he was completely at peace, and continued on to his place.

July 7, 1847
Stepan Yanovsky, from an 1881 letter to Apollon Maykov

I ask you, Apollon Nikolaevich, to recall the time when, in July 1847, you found me at home in a complete uproar . . . and Fyodor Mikhailovich sitting on a chair with an uplifted arm from which blood [ran], as black as coal and flowing like a stream, and crying out to us, "I've been saved, pal, I've been saved!"

This was the first serious attack of the illness which was accompanied by a terrible rush of blood to the head and an unusual excitement of the entire nervous system.

Another time I accidentally met Fyodor Mikhailovich on St. Isaac Square. He was coming from Solonitsyn's place and was being led under his arm by some kind of clerk from a military department. Fyodor Mikhailovich was in a terribly aroused state. He was screaming that he was dying and that he be taken quickly to my place. His pulse was more than a hundred beats [per minute] and was extremely strong. His head was arched backward and convulsions had begun.

I sat him down alongside myself and the clerk in the first cab that came my way and took him to my place.

In this letter I will not describe to you more about the course of this illness. But several days after this paroxysm, you, your brother Vladimir Nikolaevich, and the deceased Alexander Ustinovich Poretsky, Pyotr Mikhailovich Tseidler, and Ivan Ivanovich Lkhovsky saw me in my apartment, and I remember well that I called this illness falling sickness and [said that I] had treated the ailing man with the appropriate measures.

July 7, 1847
Stepan Yanovsky, from his memoirs

Fyodor Mikhailovich and I agreed . . . that we would meet three times a week at my place from three to six in the afternoon. . . . But one time [Dostoevsky] having missed a meeting . . . I, instinctively and for no reason at all, was seized by an anxious feeling. . . . Walking toward Senate Square . . . I saw Fyodor Mikhailovich standing right in the middle of the place! He was not wearing a hat. His tie was loose and his coat and jacket unbuttoned. On his arm was a writer who wrote for the military. With all his might, Fyodor Mikhailovich was crying, "This is one who is saving me," and other things in that vein. . . . Later, whenever Fyodor Mikhailovich recalled our encounter, he always said, "After this, how can you not believe in premonitions?"

Mid-July 1847
Stepan Yanovsky, from his memoirs

Before his arrest [in 1849] Fyodor Mikhailovich did not write long letters. If and when he did write to someone, he did so on small scraps of paper. Of all the notes I received from Fyodor Mikhailovich, there is an interesting one . . . in which he informed me that, having lived in Pavlovsk,[72] he had been subject to paralysis. He had been very busy taking up a collection for a drunkard who did not have any money for drink, but who, when he did, got drunk . . . and went from cottage to cottage, demanding that someone beat him up for money.

Fyodor Mikhailovich told the story . . . not only with so much humanity for the drunkard that tears flowed down my face but also with the equally great humor and mercilessness that were part of his talent as well.

After July 15, 1847
Stepan Yanovsky, from a letter to Anna Dostoevskaya

> The Maykovs lived in a spacious apartment . . . with rooms that were large, high-ceilinged, and with furnishings that were extremely elegant and comfortable. Every Sunday . . . beginning at seven in the evening, there gathered youths with souls into which the good Lord had inserted a huge dose of talent, as well as with hearts that, from the very beginning, [were filled] with love for those close to them, with goodness and truth, and with minds that searched for light. . . .
>
> Here people read and discussed their articles and put forth projects and plans for works. . . . Everything was done in such an extremely serious and friendly way, without the slightest feeling of envy or malice, that one can say it was precisely here that would come the people who would write *The Frigate Pallada* and *Oblomov, Notes from the House of the Dead* and *The Diary of a Writer,*[73] and so many other things . . . works that would make up the treasured essence of Russian literature.
>
> In these groups . . . Fyodor Mikhailovich, with his personal atomic analysis, analyzed the writings of Gogol, Turgenev, and his own Prokharchin, a piece that remained unintelligible to most readers even though it was a subject taken directly from life. . . .
>
> Hosts and guests came together for dinner . . . for good music and singing . . . the gatherings lasting until three and even four in the morning.

After July 15, 1847
Dmitri Grigorovich, from his memoirs

> Once a week . . . in the Maykovs' home . . . one always met the leading lights of literature, many of them appearing with manuscripts.

After July 15, 1847
Stepan Yanovsky, from his memoirs

> From time to time, when the Maykovs hosted dances . . . Fyodor Mikhailovich not only loved to see people dance, but in such activities he also willingly took part. . . .
>
> Fyodor Mikhailovich loved dance as an expression of spiritual worth and a veritable sign of health. He regarded such activities, though, not as opportunities to become close to a woman physically but merely to exchange a lively word or two with his partner.

After July 15, 1847
Anna Dostoevskaya, from her memoirs

> [Dostoevsky] loved [Apollon] Maykov not only as a talented poet but
> also as the finest and most intelligent of men.

July 25, 1847
Nikolai Nekrasov, from a letter to Ivan Turgenev, Vissarion Belinsky, and
Pavel Annenkov

> *Illustrated Almanac* consists of small humorous articles in poetry and
> prose. . . . For it we have ordered and prepared articles from Goncharov,
> Dostoevsky, and Apollon Maykov.

August 1847
Ivan Goncharov, from an obituary

> Valerian Maykov studied history, politics, and economics. He adored
> philosophy and studied its latest trends, particularly in Germany. . . .
> He studied chemistry in spurts, as a person with a soul. He loved art
> passionately in all its manifestations and studied it in theory and prac-
> tice, both at home and abroad. Knowing three languages, he had access
> to all the great works in science and literature. His poor health allowed
> him to work only a few hours a day, but that did not prevent him from
> giving himself over to his favorite studies. Gifted with a mind that
> was enlightened, insightful, and receptive, he, with unusual facility,
> acquired knowledge unlike anyone else.
>
> When he studied, he did not hide from people or society. He
> shunned [even] the slightest pedantry and all external signs of erudi-
> tion. He found knowledge anywhere, anytime, in conversations, in
> books. Often a serious thought forced him into a friendly circle. There,
> in an easy and attractive way, he developed an idea, and possessing fully
> a gift for words, he could expound upon it in a way that was common
> and accessible to all. It was enough for him merely to latch on to a hint
> of a notion before he made it his own; subjected it immediately to an
> innate precise analysis; and from it drew an immediate, brilliant, often
> unexpected but always severely logical conclusion, avoiding, with
> unusual skill, paradox and sophistry. It was also sufficient for him to
> get hold of a bare outline of any system before, by virtue of his mental
> facilities, subjecting it to his own authority and bringing it to life. An
> important and profound work of a thinker or philosopher he read with
> such great enthusiasm, like a work of fiction, where and whenever he
> could, not hiding in his study or behind closed windows. . . .

Judging by his splendid beginnings [as a critic], his work ethic, his many-faceted education . . . one can say with assurance that he was fated to claim a great place among our genuine recognized talents of the first rank. . . .

Valerian Maykov always found the good in people . . . not with any design or advantage in mind, but even unconsciously . . . from an instinct that was tender, noble, and innate . . . [and] from impulses that were youthful and flowed from his splendid nature. . . .

His precise and observant mind did not overlook the failings of people . . . but the meekness and almost feminine softness of his heart caused him to be patient and indulgent of such things. No one ever heard from him a caustic or bilious word, or a sharp and decisive judgment or verdict at the expense of another. No one ever noticed in him a hostile disposition toward others. He . . . tried to excuse or mitigate a moral failing in a person . . . or to express an unfavorable expression with a regretful smile or a rare ironic word. One had to see his sense of calm . . . when he tried to arouse in himself dissatisfaction with someone, how he worried about how to erase any unpleasant trace from anyone who had offended him! It was also wondrous to see how he could right away call people to himself . . . that he attracted so many friends, and that his death called forth to them the double loss of a gifted, intelligent public figure and a kind, tender, and noble friend.

August 15, 1847
Alexei Pleshcheev, from an article

V. N. Maykov promised to be a critic whom our society awaited and who united in himself soundness, erudition, and aesthetic tact. By chance we have heard that this young critic was reproached for the length of his articles, his long-windedness, and his lack of journalistic liveliness. The first failing, if it existed at all, occurred solely from a desire to utter thoughts as clearly and demonstratively as possible. . . .

What a loss our literature has suffered! What a beneficial public figure society has lost! Such noble strivings and thoughts, so many broad concepts, so many bold and profound ideas have been carried with him to the grave! . . .

It was enough to meet Valerian Maykov only once to see how much love there was in his heart; how passionately it empathized with all that was noble and lofty; and how disturbed it was by the sight of anything that diminished human dignity.

Kindness and empathy incarnate, this man could not have enemies. He never offended anyone even with words, and if someone, in conversation with him, happened to have his pride hurt accidentally, Maykov redoubled his efforts right away to reach out to the offended party and to do anything he could to rectify the wrong.

Such an individual one could not help but love. . . . Valerian Maykov could find the good in anything. . . . He was ready to forgive all faults and failings. . . . He was there for everyone. Anyone who came his way with a confession, an inner doubt, or an unanswered question, he responded to with sympathy and comfort.

August 16, 1847
Mikhail Dostoevsky, from a letter to Fyodor Dostoevsky

I hasten to share with you, my treasured friend, some pleasant news. First of all, I am for the minute secure financially. I have received my salary, so if you still have not sent any money to me, then, at the very least, do not worry or grieve over me. You would not believe how often I think of you, my dear toiler. In the second place, Reingardt was in Helsinki. He dropped by our place but did not find us at home. We were at a summer cottage with acquaintances. The next day I went over to his place . . . and spent a half hour with him, i.e., right up to his very departure for Revel. He still had one or two people to visit, so it was only on the road to the ship that I managed to tell him that I had business with him and that . . . I wanted to write to him immediately. "But what is it? Can you not say it simply, in two words?" he said to me. So I allowed myself time to explain everything to him. This Reingardt is a rare individual. He did not hesitate and promised to send 300 rubles by the first mail. Nonetheless, I wrote to him because in my conversation with him there was much that was left unsaid. So if the Muscovites are swindling us,[74] this resource can be counted on. I say this . . . because I believe only in you and me. If there is money coming from Moscow, it will be addressed by me to repay Reingardt. He told me . . . that he would be glad to help me even more, that he agrees with me completely as to my business, and that there is nothing else for me to do.

So I will have 300 rubles. To his we will add 100 rubles from the sale of furniture and even an additional 100 rubles. So in a very short time, I will have gathered together 500 rubles. That is a significant sum, is it not? And 150 rubles to my wife for the two of us to live on for two months, and 100 rubles for equipment. So I can hope to bring with me about 200 rubles, which can serve for you and me as a deposit in our common bank. This money will be the beginning of that 350,000 rubles that, according to your words, we will be the happy possessors of in ten years. . . .

What kind of apartment do you have? Will it be suitable for both of us? Write and tell me how much you are paying for it. Does it come with wood? We definitely need an apartment with wood so as to spare us any vile fuss. . . .

Why don't you write, my dear? When I don't receive from you any news in a long time, I keep thinking that you are sick and I worry terribly. Just you wait—you will get better once I am there.

Brother, begin to busy yourself about work. We do not want to spend the day without something to do. How great it will be when we are living together. . . .

If you will begin to publish *Poor Folk* in the fall,[75] it will be for me a splendid occasion to strike up an acquaintance with the people who do typography and book production.

I fear that the Muscovites have written to Krivopishin. The fact of the matter is that my retirement will proceed through the Department of Inspection. But they might hold it up under a pretext, for example, that one of the forms is not correct. But you need not follow up on it. I will submit a petition on September 1st.

Late August–early September 1847
Fyodor Dostoevsky, from a letter to Nikolai Nekrasov

Of course the conditions that you were pleased to offer me at our last meeting at Maykov's [home] are quite advantageous. But at the present moment I find myself in such a difficult situation that the money you promised me will not bring me any benefit at all; it will only extend my desperation for no good purpose. Perhaps you may be partly aware of my circumstances.

In order to get on my feet at least a bit, I need 150 silver rubles. Therefore, Nikolai Alexeevich, if you do not wish to give me the money in a lump sum, then to my greatest regret, it will be impossible to deliver my story to you. Because I will not have the material means for writing it.[76] If, however, you agree to give me such a sum in advance,[77] then in the first place, the date by which you will receive the story will be January 1, 1848, no earlier. You probably would find it more pleasant for me to say *for certain, and not about.* Therefore, *for certain, by January 1, 1848.*

In the second place, I will ask you to pay out the money in the following way: 100 silver rubles on October 2, 1847, and 50 silver rubles, right now, that is, with *my* messenger.

Pardon me, Nikolai Alexeevich, for negotiating with you by means of a letter and not personally, as would be more convenient for us. I kept wanting to see you after I had completed my latest work in its entirety.[78] But now, at the present moment, I find myself in such a repulsive position that I decided to begin the business now about which I am writing to you openly.

I cannot leave the house because I caught a cold this morning and now it seems that I will have to stay home for about four days.

P.S. *In any event*, I ask you most humbly to send an answer with my messenger because afterwards I will not need him.

September 9, 1847
Fyodor Dostoevsky, from a letter to Mikhail Dostoevsky

I hasten to answer your letter. Well, do as you wish with your family, as you yourself think best, but you, in regard to yourself, do not change your disposition for anything. You are afraid that they will not grant you an extension; but can't you take a leave for 2 or 3 months? If you cannot, consult the district commander and simply ask him to see that there will be no delay with such a thing. After all . . . I do not think they want to squeeze someone who is retiring. But come anyway. . . . Your retirement may be issued in November.[79] You say that people are shaking their heads. I say to you—do not be upset over such a thing. You write that I have made a slow start too. But after all, that is only right now. Wait a bit, brother, things will improve. We have an association. It is impossible that we should both fail to make our way out onto the road. Nonsense! Just remember what sort of people are shaking their heads! What you are getting now, you will always get in Petersburg, but not without such hard work! I will stay in my apartment and wait for you. I am not well and am finishing a story so that it can be printed in October.[80] Thus I am hurrying.

You do not say on what day you are leaving for Revel. But it does not make any difference. My letter, perhaps, will reach you on the eve of your departure. How will you arrange things for your family there? 125 silver rubles is not a lot of money. I will write to the Muscovites, but you write too from Helsingfors and tell them to send the money to my address. It is clear that Karepin is a son of a bitch and a scoundrel of the first degree.

Come soon, brother. In a fit of terrible need, I can get some money. But do you know how much I need myself? At least 300 silver rubles by October 1st. Out of that sum, 200 rubles will be used for debts and 100 will be spent on me personally, and all of that is only if there is money. Just in case, I will write down for you everything that I can realize by the first days of October if some extreme need should present itself.

From Kraevsky	50 silver rubles
From Nekrasov	100 silver rubles
At a certain place	50 silver rubles
Selling the right to a printing of *Poor Folk*	200 silver rubles
	400 silver rubles

That is a goodly sum but it will ruin me, taking into consideration the sale of *Poor Folk*. I have no time to publish *Poor Folk*. But through a certain printer I hope to publish it without money. If you would turn up here, you could take care of all this; then all winter long we would keep getting money. You will not be making a mistake if you come here as soon as possible. I will tell you that perhaps there is hope that if you are in town, you will have the work about which I wrote you the last time. In addition, there is a certain publication toward the New Year, a colossal one, financed by huge capital, which will be able to furnish you with a great deal of work for translation-compilation. You can also get translations from Kraevsky or Nekrasov, with whom I will enter into a definite arrangement and which he wants awfully much. In addition, there is yet another publication toward the New Year, and still *another one* after that. All of them will come to be.[81] It is too bad that you did not finish translating Schiller's plays. If you had done them all, they could have been sold. Gather together everything you have. A few days ago, when I told Kraevsky that you could translate a book for the Geographic Society (in my last letter to him), and that you knew German and had translated all of Schiller, he suddenly asked rashly, "Where is his translation?" Then thinking the better of it, he fell silent suddenly. Even if it does not appear in *The Fatherland Notes*, Kraevsky could facilitate its acquisition.

Well, good-bye, my dear. I did not write much of what I wanted to. Honest to God, there is no time.

P.S. Do you know what an association means? If we work apart, we will collapse, become timid, and lose heart. But two people [working] together for a single goal—that is another matter. There you have a hearty person, boldness, love, and twice as much energy.

Write me about everything in as much detail as possible. Write me about figures (money, time, and so forth) carefully and precisely.

September 13, 1847
Mikhail Dostoevsky, from a letter to Fyodor Dostoevsky

> The Muscovites are not sending money. . . . We have 125 rubles which is
> terribly little. . . . Most likely I will arrive at your place without money.[82]
> But I am not downcast. We are healthy and will not perish. Our associa-
> tion is a matter that is sacred and great. . . .
>
> Do not think of selling *Poor Folk*. Somehow we will manage. . . . If
> only my retirement will not be delayed . . . this is what worries me.[83]
> Write to the people in Moscow. I will also write to them.

Fall 1847 and after
Fyodor Dostoevsky, from testimony to the Investigatory Commission for
the Petrashevsky affair

> It was through me that my brother, Mikhailo [Mikhail] . . . became
> acquainted with Petrashevsky when we lived together after his arrival
> from Revel. He met Petrashevsky for the first time at my place and
> was invited to gatherings at his place. I took my brother there to meet
> people and have fun, since he did not know anyone in Petersburg and
> missed his family.
>
> My brother, though, did not take any part in the conversations at
> Petrashevsky's place. I did not hear even two words from him. Every-
> one who came to Petrashevsky's home knows such a thing [to be true].
> Mikhail visited there more and more rarely, and when he did turn
> up there, it was from curiosity and because, being a working family
> man who was extremely poor . . . he denied himself almost all other
> pleasures.

Fall 1847 and after
Lyubov Dostoevskaya, from her memoirs

> Uncle Mikhail was also interested in this society [of Petrashevsky's],
> but since he was married and the father of a family, he considered it
> more sensible not to visit the gatherings at Petrashevsky's home too
> often. But he took advantage of the forbidden books from his library.
> At that time Uncle Mikhail was a great fan of Fourier and studied his
> utopian theories.

Fall 1847 and after
Lyubov Dostoevskaya, from her memoirs

> Uncle Andrei also visited the gatherings at Petrashevsky's.[84] At that
> time he was still too young and had begun to study at an institution of

higher learning. Several years younger than his brothers, he saw them more as heads of a family than friends. In their turn, the elder brothers treated him like a young boy. . . .

My father never spoke with his youngest brother about politics. As a result, Uncle Andrei did not suspect the role my father played in the Petrashevsky Circle. . . . He always surrounded himself with educated people. He heard about the interesting society that gathered at Petrashevsky's home and asked one of his friends to introduce him to its leader. . . .

One time there, he ran into my father, whose face was pale and distorted with anger.

"What are you doing here?" he asked Andrei in horror. "Leave right away so I can say that I never saw you here!"

My uncle was so frightened by my father's ire that he left the salon right away.[85]

Circa early October 1847
Stepan Yanovsky, from his memoirs

Still another incident [in readings with Dostoevsky] occurred with A. N. Pleshcheev, who was still a youth at the time, without a mustache or beard, seemingly no more than eighteen or nineteen.[86] As I now recall, Fyodor Mikhailovich left my place one Sunday, inviting me to a housewarming at his place. At that time, Mikhail Mikhailovich [Dostoevsky] was about to retire [from state service]. He arrived in Petersburg alone without his family and had moved in with Fyodor Mikhailovich. According to the invitation, I arrived at the Dostoevskys' with my friend Vlasovsky at five a.m. There I also found Pleshcheev, Kreshev, Butkov, an engineer-officer (whose name I forget), and Golovinsky. Also, acting as a servant and known to all was a noncommissioned officer named Yevstafy, whose name Fyodor Mikhailovich noted warmly in one of his stories.[87]

After Yevstafy gave each of us a glass of tea, Fyodor Mikhailovich turned to A. N. Pleshcheev and said, "Well, old boy, read to us what you did with the anecdote I gave you." Pleshcheev began to read his work immediately, but his story was so weak that we barely could listen through to the end. Although Pleshcheev was somehow pleased with his piece, Fyodor Mikhailovich said to him in a straightforward way, "In the first place, you did not understand me and came up with something different from what I told you to do; and in the second place, you expressed yourself in a very poor way." After such a verdict, Pleshcheev destroyed the story.

October 1847 and after
Lyubov Dostoevskaya, from her memoirs

> In colorless and limited Petersburg my father's talent burned itself
> out. . . . He did not have money for travel to Europe, the Caucasus, or
> the Crimea—travel at the time was very expensive. My father was per-
> ishing . . . and was happy only at the home of his brother Mikhail, who
> had settled in the capital and, having left his soldiering, had decided
> to devote himself entirely to literature. Mikhail was married to a Ger-
> man woman, Emiliya Ditmar, and they had several children. My father
> loved his nephews very much; their childlike laughter dispersed his
> melancholy.

October 1, 1847
Mikhail Dostoevsky, from a letter to Fyodor Dostoevsky

> I am very glad that [brother] Andryusha has left. Beyond the fact that
> he has a splendid job, he is finally getting accustomed to living with his
> mind. But you will not believe how weak his heart is.

November 4–8, 1847
Vissarion Belinsky, from a letter to Vasily Botkin

> Kraevsky is facing hard times, not because he does not have good sto-
> ries in hand, but because he publishes such vile things as . . . Dosto-
> evsky's "The Landlady"—a (nervous expletive) work, and without end
> to boot.

November 20–December 2, 1847
Vissarion Belinsky, from a letter to Pavel Annenkov.

> Dostoevsky did a really bad turn to Kraevsky, who published the first
> half of one of his stories [only to learn later] that he had not written
> the second half, nor would he ever do so. . . . The story is so extremely
> vulgar, stupid, and talentless. It starts off with absolutely nothing (and
> no matter how hard he tried) goes nowhere. The hero is a nervous
> (expletive deleted). No matter how the heroine looks at him, he flops
> down into a faint. Truly!

Conclusion

In 1846 and 1847 Fyodor Dostoevsky was decid-edly not on the straight and steady path that Pushkin and Gogol, Turgenev, and Tolstoy appeared to travel to glory and fame. Nothing was going right for the young writer. Indeed, the wrong turns were so manifest, multiple, and menacing that they threatened not just creative impasse but the end of his literary career. To everyone, including himself, Dostoevsky was not simply moving down slippery slopes; he was going off the rails in literature and life.

The threats were external and internal. The four works after *Poor Folk*—*The Double*, "Mr. Prokharchin," "The Landlady," and "A Novel in Nine Letters"—were seen as failures by readers and reviewers. Disturbed and deranged characters, complex and convoluted plots, and winding and windy prose caused former admirers and fans to lose faith in the young writer and to look elsewhere for solutions to national problems. Also, with his antics and shenanigans, Dostoevsky had so alienated the admittedly problematic and fickle members of the Belinsky circle that he soon found himself per-sona non grata, if not the laughingstock of the Russian literary world.

From within, Dostoevsky was beset by dark shadows of ongoing doubt. More than ever, he wondered if he had the stuff to be a writer. Anxiety and angst turned to depression, despair, even flirtations with death.

To be sure, there were bright spots for Dostoevsky in 1846 and 1847. There was Stepan Yanovsky, who assured him that he had a long while to live. There was brother Mikhail, who, more than ever, was ready to sacrifice everything for his younger sibling. There was Valerian Maykov, who understood what Dostoevsky was trying to do in his art. There were the other Maykovs, who, along with the Vielgorskys and the Beketovs, gave him friendship and family. There were dinners with Butkov, Pleschcheev, and other new acquaintances. At best, though, such people were temporary fixes for what ailed Dostoevsky. They were lulls in the gathering storm of his life.

With hindsight, it is tempting to posit numerous what-ifs for Dostoevsky during 1846 and 1847. What if he had handled the success of *Poor Folk* in a more humble and judicious way? What if he had gotten along with Nekrasov, Turgenev, and Panaev? What if he had taken Belinsky's advice and focused on sociopolitical themes? What if he had given readers and reviewers what they wanted in fiction? What if he had been more disciplined in his writing? What if he had had a more structured way of life? What if he had been faithful to his family and friends? What if he had adhered to the virtues and values of his childhood, adolescence, and youth? What if he had prayed to God? What if he had kept company with the philosophical and literary masters of the past?

Admittedly, if Dostoevsky had done all or any of these things, he would have had an easier time of things. In truth, though, the price the young writer would have paid for conformity would have been even higher than what he paid for going his own way. If Dostoevsky had listened to anyone but himself at this time, he would not have become the national and international figure he would be twenty years later. Most likely he would have been a footnote in Russian literature, a minor realist, akin to Grigorovich and Panaev, who wrote about "poor folk" in cities and villages throughout his homeland.

During this period, though, Dostoevsky was learning three valuable lessons. First, he was experiencing firsthand the perils of seeing himself as a genius, an extraordinary man. On good days, he soared on the success of *Poor Folk*. He was the self-appointed successor of Pushkin, Lermontov, and Gogol. No one could tell him anything. He knew it all. On bad days, he crashed with the failures of *The Double*, "Mr. Prokharchin," "The Landlady," and "A Novel in Nine Letters." Indeed, he seemed to be regressing as an artist. In response, Dostoevsky retreated into physical and spiritual "undergrounds," into self-canceling dualities. He was lord and louse. He was master and man.

Second, the young Dostoevsky was discovering the human penchant for putting idols and man-gods on pedestals one moment but tearing them down, suddenly and viciously, the next. It was a painful if invaluable lesson for the young writer to see that mobs made the man. The young Dostoevsky had been carried aloft by Belinsky and others who proclaimed him the savior of Russian literature. He was slammed against rocky shores when he failed to meet their expectations as a critic of national life. Even more shocking for the young Dostoevsky, perhaps, was not only how quickly he was abandoned by former friends and fans but also how he became the object of their relentless ridicule and scorn. Belinsky and company would not leave him in peace. Rather, among themselves and in poetry and prose, they took every opportunity to berate the young writer as a huckster and a fraud. Equally instructive, Belinsky and his circle were angrier with themselves than they were at him. No one, he learned, wanted to look foolish.

Third and most important, Dostoevsky was progressing as a writer. In *The Double*, "Mr. Prokharchin," "The Landlady," and "A Novel in Nine Letters," he was sketching heroes and heroines, images and ideas that would become mainstays of his later fiction. Indeed, in 1846 and 1847 Dostoevsky's topics and themes poured forth in a lava-like flow. If Belinsky and others censured the young artist for writing that was undisciplined, prolix, and repetitive, it was in part because he could not rein in the streams of impressions and observations that swept over him. Boldly he was transcending romantic and realist models to create his own poetics, his own rationale for his tortured path through existence. One wonders if in 1846 and 1847 the line between Dostoevsky and his heroes was too close for comfort. In the four works after *Poor Folk*, was Dostoevsky writing about himself or about others? Was he, in the depths of his soul, also a miser, a madman, a dreamer, a pervert, a huckster? In truth, he feared he was all of them.

In the long run, the blunders and slips that Dostoevsky made in 1846 and 1847 were minor and forgivable. He can be excused for vainglory and arrogance, as well as for anger and spite. He was, after all, only in his mid-twenties. Let others recall their sins in this period of their lives and cast the first stones.

Sadly, though, Dostoevsky did not learn from his mistakes. Within two years he would make a bad situation worse, committing such egregious errors that he descended into a personal and professional abyss. Refusing to indict himself for his ills, the young artist blamed the world. It was political, social, and economic systems, he believed, that caused human unhappiness. External not internal reform was the answer. A member of the Petrashevsky circle, Dostoevsky ran afoul of officialdom. The crime of seditious activity led to the punishment of exile in Siberia.

It may seem mere truism to say that if people did not make mistakes, there would be no literature. It is, perhaps, an even greater verity to note that if writers did not make mistakes, they would not be able to write about people who did. If Pushkin and Gogol, Turgenev and Tolstoy advanced slowly and steadily in their craft, Dostoevsky did not. He had more—a great deal more—living to do.

Directory of Prominent Names

Agin, Alexander Alexeevich (1817–1875), artist and illustrator

Aksakov, Konstantin Sergeevich (1817–1860), critic, writer, and Slavophile

Alexander III (1845–1894), tsar of Russia from 1881 to 1894

Alexandra Fyodorovna (1798–1860), wife of Nicholas I

Anna Ioannovna (1693–1740), empress of Russia from 1730 to 1740

Annenkov, Pavel Vasilievich (1813–1887), critic and memoirist

Babikov, Konstantin Ivanovich (1841–1873), poet, prose writer, and journalist

Bakunin, Mikhail Alexandrovich (1814–1876), revolutionary and anarchist

Balzac, Honoré de (1799–1850), French writer

Baratynsky, Yevgeny Abramovich (1800–1844), poet

Beketov, Alexei Nikolaevich (1823–?), classmate of Fyodor Dostoevsky and brother of Andrei and Nikolai Beketov

Beketov, Andrei Nikolaevich (1825–1902), botanist, rector, publicist, brother of Alexei and Nikolai Beketov, and grandfather of Alexander Blok

Beketov, Nikolai Nikolaevich (1827–1911), professor, academician, chemist, physicist, social figure, and brother of Alexei and Andrei Beketov

Belinskaya, Maria Vasilievna (1812–1890), wife of Vissarion Belinsky

Belinskaya, Olga Vissarionova (1845–1904), daughter of Vissarion Belinsky

Belinsky, Grigory Nikiforovich (1784–1835), doctor and father of Vissarion Belinsky

Belinsky, Vissarion Grigorievich (1811–1848), critic

Belinsky, Vladimir Vissarionovich (1846–1847), son of Vissarion Belinsky

Bellini, Vincenzo (1801–1835), Italian composer

Bernardsky, Yevstafy Yefimovich (1819–1889), engraver and illustrator

Bervi-Flerovsky, Vasily Vasilievich (1829–1918), writer, sociologist, publicist, and economist

Bilyarsky, Pyotr Spiridonovich (1817–1867), critic

Blanc, Louis (1811–1882), French politician, historian, and socialist

Blok, Alexander Alexandrovich (1880–1921), poet and grandson of Andrei Beketov

Bonaparte, Napoleon (1769–1821), French statesman and military leader

Botkin, Vasily Petrovich (1812–1869), essayist, critic, translator, and publicist

Brandt, Leopold Vasilievich (1813–1884), writer and critic

Bulavin, Kondraty Afanasievich (1660?–1708), revolutionary

Bulgarin, Faddei Veneviktovich (1789–1859), writer, journalist, and publisher

Butashevich-Petrashevsky, Mikhail Vasilievich (1821–1866), revolutionary and theorist

Butkov, Yakov Petrovich (1821–1856), writer

Byron, George Gordon (Lord) (1788–1824), English poet

Cabet, Étienne (1788–1856), French philosopher and socialist

Calderón de la Barca, Pedro (1600–1681), Spanish dramatist, poet, and writer

Catherine the Great (1729–1796), empress of Russia from 1762 to 1796

Cervantes, Miguel de (1547–1616), Spanish novelist

Custine, Marquis de (1790–1857), French aristocrat and writer

Dal', Vladimir Ivanovich (1801–1872), writer and lexicographer

Dickens, Charles (1812–1870), English writer

(von) Ditmar, Emiliya. See Emiliya Dostoevskaya

Donskoi, Dmitri (1350–1389), grand prince of Moscow from 1363 to 1389

Dostoevskaya, Anna. See Anna Snitkina-Dostoevskaya

Dostoevskaya, Emiliya Fyodorovna (1822–1879), wife of Mikhail Dostoevsky

Dostoevskaya, Lyubov Fyodorovna (1869–1926), daughter of Fyodor Dostoevsky

Dostoevskaya-Ivanova, Vera Mikhailovna (1829–1896), sister of Fyodor Dostoevsky

Dostoevskaya-Karepina, Varvara Mikhailovna (1822–1893), sister of Fyodor Dostoevsky

Dostoevskaya-Vladislavleva, Maria Mikhailovna (1844–1888), daughter of Mikhail Dostoevsky and niece of Fyodor Dostoevsky

Dostoevsky, Alexander Andreevich (1857–1894), son of Andrei Dostoevsky and nephew of Fyodor Dostoevsky

Dostoevsky, Andrei Mikhailovich (1825–1897), architect, engineer, and younger brother of Fyodor Dostoevsky

Dostoevsky, Fyodor Mikhailovich (1821–1881), novelist and short-story writer

Dostoevsky, Fyodor Mikhailovich (the Younger) (1842–1906), son of Mikhail Dostoevsky and nephew of Fyodor Dostoevsky

Dostoevsky, Mikhail Andreevich (1788–1839), father of Fyodor Dostoevsky

Dostoevsky, Mikhail Mikhailovich (1820–1864), writer, critic, journalist, translator, and older brother of Fyodor Dostoevsky

Druzhinin, Alexander Vasilievich (1824–1864), writer, translator, and editor

Dudyshkin, Stepan Semyonovich (1820–1866), critic and journalist

Dyadkovsky, Yustin Yevdokimovich (1784–1841), doctor

Fénelon, François (1651–1751), French archbishop, theologian, poet, and writer

Feuerbach, Ludwig von (1804–1872), German philosopher and anthropologist

Fonvizin, Denis Ivanovich (1744?–1792), dramatist

Fourier, Charles (1772–1837), French philosopher

Gagarin, Grigory Ivanovich (1782–1837), prince and brother of Sergei Gagarin

Gagarin, Ivan Sergeevich (1814–1882), Jesuit and son of Sergei Gagarin

Gagarin, Sergei Ivanovich (1777–1862), prince, brother of Grigory Gagarin, and father of Ivan Gagarin

Gall, Franz (1758–1828), German physiologist

Godunov, Boris Fyodorovich (1551–1605), tsar of Russia from 1598 to 1605

Goegg-Pouchoulin, Maria (1826–1899), Swiss feminist

Goethe, Johann Wolfgang von (1749–1832), German writer

Gogol, Nikolai Vasilievich (1809–1852), dramatist, novelist, and short story writer

Golovinsky, Vasily Andreevich (1829–1875), lawyer

Goncharov, Ivan Alexandrovich (1812–1891), writer

Granovsky, Timofei Nikolaevich (1813–1855), medievalist, professor, and Westernizer

Grech, Nikolai Ivanovich (1787–1867), grammarian and journalist

Grigoriev, Apollon Alexandrovich (1822–1864), poet, critic, translator, memoirist, and author

Grigorovich, Dmitri Vasilievich (1822–1899), writer

Grot, Yakov Karlovich (1812–1893), philologist

Guber, Eduard Ivanovich (1814–1847), poet and translator

Guizot, François (1787–1874), French historian, orator, and statesman

Hegel, Georg (1770–1831), German philosopher

Herzen, Alexander Ivanovich (1812–1870), writer and thinker

Hoffmann, E. T. A. (1776–1822), German writer, composer, and critic

Hugo, Victor (1802–1885), French writer

Ivan IV (the Terrible) (1530–1584), tsar of Russia from 1533 to 1547

Ivanov, Alexander Pavlovich (1813–1868), husband of Vera Dostoevskaya

Izler, Ivan Ivanovich (1811–1877), confectioner

Izmailov, Alexander Yefimovich (1779–1831), fabulist, poet, novelist, and publisher

Kalita, Ivan Daniilovich (Ivan I) (1288–1340?), grand duke of Moscow and Vladimir

Karamzin, Nikolai Mikhailovich (1766–1826), writer, poet, historian, and critic

Karepin, Pyotr Andreevich (1796–1850), husband of Varvara Dostoevskaya and guardian of the Dostoevsky children after the death of Mikhail Andreevich Dostoevsky

Katkov, Mikhail Nikiforovich (1818–1887), journalist

Kavelin, Konstantin Dmitrievich (1818–1885), historian, lawyer, and sociologist

Ketcher, Nikolai Khristoforovich (1809–1886), writer and translator

Khanykov, Nikolai Vladimirovich (1819–1878), historian, orientalist, ethnographer, and diplomat

Kirillov, Nikolai Sergeevich (dates unknown), captain and editor

Kock, Charles Paul de (1793–1871), French novelist

Koltsov, Alexei Vasilievich (1809–1842), poet

Kraevsky, Andrei Alexandrovich (1810–1889), editor and journalist

Kreshev, Ivan Petrovich (1824–1859), poet, translator, essayist, and journalist

Krivopishin, Ivan Grigorievich (1796–1867), general and lieutenant

Krylov, Ivan Andreevich (1769–1844), fabulist

Kukolnik, Nikolai Vasilievich (1809–1868), playwright and prose writer

Kumanin, Alexander Alexeevich (1792–1863), uncle of Fyodor Dostoevsky

Kuvshinnikov, Nikolai Ivanovich (1819–1893), publisher

Kvitka-Osnovyanenko, Hryhory (1778–1884), Ukrainian writer, journalist, and playwright

Lambert, Yelizaveta Yegorvna (1821–1883), countess

Lamennais, Robert de (1782–1854), priest and philosopher

Lermontov, Mikhail Yurievich (1814–1841), writer and poet

Leroux, Pierre (1797–1871), French philosopher and economist

Lichtenberg, Georg (1742–1799), German physicist and satirist

Lkhovsky, Ivan Ivanovich (1829–1867), collegiate assessor

Loeve, Ferdinand (1809–1899), German teacher and editor

Lomonosov, Mikhail Vasilievich (1711–1765), polymath, scientist, and writer

Louis Philippe I (1773–1850), king of France from 1830 to 1848

Lugansky. See Dal'

Maykov, Apollon Alexandrovich (1761–1836), father of Nikolai and Konstantin Maykov, and grandfather of Apollon, Valerian, and Leonid Maykov

Maykov, Apollon Nikolaevich (1821–1897), poet

Maykov, Konstantin Apollonovich (1811–1891), colonel and brother of Nikolai Maykov

Maykov, Leonid Nikolaevich (1839–1900), historian, bibliographer, ethnographer, and academician

Maykov, Nikolai Apollonovich (1794–1893), artist, academician, and father of Apollon, Valerian, and Leonid Maykov

Maykov, Valerian Nikolaevich (1823–1847), publicist and critic

Maykov, Vladimir Nikolaevich (1826–1885), journalist, translator, and editor

Maykova, Natalya Alexandrovna (1809–1871), daughter of Alexander Izmailov and wife of Valerian Maykov

Maykova, Yevgenya Petrovna (1803–1880), poet, prose writer, wife of Nikolai Maykov, and mother of Apollon, Valerian, and Leonid Maykov

Melgunov, Nikolai Alexandrovich (1804–1867), writer, publicist, translator, and critic

Meyerbeer, Giacomo (1791–1864), German composer

Miller, Orest Fyodorovich (1833–1889), folklorist, professor, and first biographer of Fyodor Dostoevsky

Mozart, Wolfgang Amadeus (1756–1791), Austrian composer

Nechaev, Sergei Gennadievich (1847–1882), revolutionary, terrorist, and nihilist

Nekrasov, Nikolai Alexeevich (1821–1878) poet, writer, critic, and publisher

Nevakovich, Mikhail Lvovich (1817–1850), artist, caricaturist, dramatist, and publisher

Nicholas I (1796–1855), tsar of Russia from 1825 to 1855

Odoevsky, Vladimir Fyodorovich (1803–1869), philosopher, writer, critic, philanthropist, and pedagogue

Ogaryov, Nikolai Platonovich (1813–1877), poet, historian, and activist

Orlova, Agrafena Vasilievna (1818–1901), sister-in-law of Vissarion Belinsky

Orlova-Belinskaya, Maria Vasilievna (1834–1902), wife of Vissarion Belinsky

Ozerov, Vladislav Alexandrovich (1769–1816), dramatist

Panaev, Ivan Ivanovich (1812–1862), writer and journalist

Panaeva, Avdotya Yakovlevna (1820–1893), writer and memoirist

Pavlov, Nikolai Filippovich (1803–1864), writer, dramatist, translator, publisher, and editor

Pavlovsky, Isaak Yakovlevich (1852–1924), journalist, dramatist, translator, and revolutionary

Peter (?–1326), metropolitan and saint

Peter the Great (1672–1725), tsar of Russia from 1682 to 1725

Petrashevsky. See Butashevich-Petrashevsky

Philip II (1507–1569), metropolitan and saint

Pigault-Lebrun, Charles (1753–1835), French novelist and playwright

Pleshcheev, Alexei Nikolaevich (1825–1893), poet

Pletnyov, Pyotr Alexandrovich (1792–1866), writer, poet, and critic

Pogodin, Mikhail Petrovich (1800–1875), historian and journalist

Poretsky, Alexander Ustinovich (1818–1879), writer, journalist, and undercover agent

Priessnitz, Vincenz (1799–1851), farmer and proponent of alternative medicine

Proudhon, Pierre-Joseph (1809–1865), politician and philosopher

Pushkin, Alexander Sergeevich (1799–1837), dramatist, novelist, poet, and short story writer

Pyat, Felix (1810–1889), French socialist, journalist, and politician

Pypin, Alexander Nikolaevich (1833–1904), academician and historian of
  literature

Rastrelli, Francesco (1700–1771), Italian architect

Ratkov, Pyotr Alexeevich (dates unknown), bookseller and publisher

Reingardt, Nikolai Ivanovich (dates unknown), friend of Mikhail Dostoevsky

Renan, Ernest (1823–1892), French linguist, philosopher, historian, and writer

Rossini, Gioachino (1792–1868), Italian composer

Rubenstein, Anton Grigorievich (1829–1894), pianist, composer, and conductor

Rykacheva, Yevgenya Andreevna (1853–1919), daughter of Andrei Dostoevsky
  and niece of Fyodor Dostoevsky

Saint-Simon, Henri de (1760–1825), French theorist and philosopher

Saltykov-Shchedrin, Mikhail Yefgrafovich (1826–1889), writer

Sand, George (1804–1876), French novelist and memoirist

Schelling, Friedrich (1755–1854), German philosopher

Schiller, Friedrich (1759–1805), German writer and poet

Scribe, Eugène (1791–1861), French dramatist and librettist

Senkovsky, Osip Ivanovich (1800–1858), orientalist, journalist, and entertainer

Senyavina, Alexandra Vasilievna (?–1862), society figure

Shakespeare, William (1564–1616), English dramatist

Shalikov, Pyotr Ivanovich (1767?–1852), writer and journalist

Shchepkin, Mikhail Semyonovich (1788–1863), actor

Shevyryov, Stepan Petrovich (1806–1864), literary historian, critic, and poet

Shidlovsky, Ivan Nikolaevich (1816–1872), friend of Fyodor Dostoevsky

Skabichevsky, Alexander Mikhailovich (1838–1910), historian, critic, and
  memoirist

Smirdin, Alexander Filippovich (1795–1857), publisher and editor

Snitkina-Dostoevskaya, Anna Grigorievna (1845–1918), second wife of Fyodor
  Dostoevsky

Socrates (470–399 BC), Greek philosopher

Sollogub, Vladimir Alexandrovich (1813–1882), writer

Solonitsyn (dates unknown), friend of Fyodor Dostoevsky

Soloviev, I. G. (dates unknown), bookseller

Solovyov, Vsevelod Sergeevich (1849–1903), writer

Starchevsky, Albert Vikentievich (1818–1901), Polish historian, journalist, editor,
  philologist, lexicographer, and encyclopedist

Stasyulevich, Mikhial Matveevich (1826–1911), writer, scholar, historian, journalist, editor, and publisher

Strakhov, Nikolai Nikolaevich (1828–1896), philosopher, publicist, and critic

Strauss, David (1808–1874), German theologian and writer

Studitsky, Alexander Yefimovich (1817?–?), journalist and translator

Suvorin, Alexei Sergeevich (1834–1912), publisher and journalist

Tissot, Samuel-Auguste (1728–1797), Swiss physician

Tolstoy, Lev (Leo) Nikolaevich (1828–1910), novelist and short story writer

Totleben, Eduard Ivanovich (1818–1884), engineer and general

Tredyakovsky, Vasily Kirillovich (1703–1769), poet, essayist, and playwright

Trutovsky, Konstantin Alexandrovich (1826–1893), painter and friend of Fyodor
    Dostoevsky

Tseidler, Pyotr Mikhailovich (1821–1873), pedagogue and writer

Turgenev, Ivan Sergeevich (1818–1883), novelist, short story writer, and
    playwright

Vielgorskaya, Anna Mikhailovna (1822–1861), daughter of Mikhail and Luisa
    Vielgorsky

Vielgorskaya, Luiza Karlovna (1791–1853), wife of Mikhail Vielgorsky

Vielgorsky, Mikhail Yurievich (1788–1856), author, composer, and musician

Vlasovsky, Nikolai Yefgrafovich (1818–1854), captain and friend of Stepan
    Yanovsky

Voltaire (1694–1778), French philosopher

Vyazemsky, Pyotr Andreevich (1792–1878), poet

Yanovsky, Stepan Dmitrievich (1815–1887), doctor

Yazykov, Mikhail Alexandrovich (1811–1875), friend of Fyodor Dostoevsky

Yazykov, Nikolai Mikhailovich (1803–1846), poet

Yevstafy (dates unknown), retired officer and Dostoevsky's servant in 1847

Zhukovsky, Vasily Andreevich (1783–1852), poet

Notes

Introduction

1. Claims as to Dostoevsky's alleged epilepsy had been made twice previously, also giving rise to suspicion and doubt.

The first was made by Dostoevsky's daughter Lyubov in her notoriously unreliable account of the writer's life. It was "family legend," she wrote, that "news about the death of Dostoevsky's father had brought about the first attack of his epilepsy."

The second claim was by Grigorovich circa 1844. "Intense work and constant sitting at home had been extremely harmful to Dostoevsky's health," he noted. Grigorovich continued: "Several times during our rare walks he experienced attacks. One time . . . we came across a funeral procession. Dostoevsky turned away quickly. He wanted to return home, but before we managed to take a few steps, he had an attack so powerful that with the help of passers-by, I carried him to the nearest bench. We brought him back to consciousness by force. After such attacks, Dostoevsky showed a usually oppressive spirit which lasted about two or three days."

Such a charge Grigorovich made in 1892, eleven years after Dostoevsky's death. Furthermore, given the fact that Grigorovich was a notorious gossip and scandalmonger who delighted in joining Belinsky, Turgenev, and others in poking fun at Dostoevsky, one wonders why he did not disclose this episode earlier, when he could have caused considerable harm to the writer, if not vanquished him completely.

See L. Dostoevskaia, *Dostoevskii v izobrazhenii svoei docheri,* 2nd ed. (St. Petersburg: Andreev i synov'ia, 1992), 39; and D. Grigorovich, *Vospominaniia* (Moscow: Zakharov, 2007), 71.

2. It should be noted that Nekrasov also claimed that Dostoevsky suffered from fainting spells, but in a little-known and unpublished document, titled *The Stone Heart,* thought to have been written in 1846–47 or 1855–56 but found among his papers long after his death and first published in 1917 (see the discussion later in the chapter).

3. I. Turgenev, "Vospominaniia o Belinskom," in *Polnoe sobranie sochinenii i pisem v dvadtsati tomakh. Sochineniia,* vol. 14 (Moscow: Nauka, 1967), 35. Turgenev also saw Maykov as Belinsky's successor. See Annenkov's letter to Alexander Pypin, dated July 12, 1874, in K. Bogaevkaia, "P. A. Annenkov o V. G. Belinskom," in *Literaturnoe nasledstvo. Revoliutsionnye demokraty. Novye materialy,* ed. V. Vinodradov et al., vol. 67 (Moscow: Izdatel'stvo Akademii nauk, 1959), 550.

Part One. Pride before the Fall

1. P. Annenkov, "Zamechatel'noe desiatiletie," in *Literaturnye vospominaniia* (Moscow: Pravda, 1989), 320–21.

2. See Belinsky's letter to K. Kavelin, dated November 22, 1847, in Belinskii, *Polnoe sobranie sochinenii v tridnadtsati tomakh*, vol. 12 (Moscow: Izdatel'stvo Akademii nauk, 1956), 433.

3. Ibid., 222 and 304.

4. Ibid., 128 and 257.

5. Ibid., 25, 128, and 252–53.

6. Ibid., 344 and 321.

7. Balzac wrote both *Cousin Pons* and *Cousin Bette* in 1846 under the collective name *Poor Relations*.

8. Dostoevsky's *Poor Folk* appeared in Nekrasov's anthology *The Petersburg Miscellany*, which went on sale in the imperial city on January 24, 1846.

9. *Leviathan*, an almanac of almost five hundred pages, was also to include prose by Turgenev, Panaev, and Herzen; poetry by Apollon Maykov; and criticism by Timofei Granovsky and others. Although *Leviathan* never came to be, most of the planned works appeared in *The Contemporary*.

10. Sologub has erred here. Kraevsky was editor of *The Contemporary*. As already noted, Dostoevsky's *Poor Folk* was published in Nekrasov's *Petersburg Miscellany*.

11. Brandt, of course, is referring to Belinsky and Nekrasov.

12. Makar's surname, Devushkin, is rooted in the Russian word *devushka*, or "girl."

13. That is, "without connection to anything."

14. Again, Belinsky and Nekrasov.

15. Brandt is quoting the Russian proverb "The first pancake is a lump" (*Pervyi blin komom*).

16. Sadly, the piece was never published. Anna Dostoevskaya writes: "The article suffered a mournful fate. Fyodor Mikhailovich had been asked to do the piece for an anthology [titled *The Chalice*] by the writer K. I. Babikov, who paid him an advance of two hundred rubles. The article was done by autumn and mailed to Hotel Rome in Moscow.

"Fearing that Babikov might have moved to another apartment, Fyodor Mikhailovich asked [Apollon] Maykov . . . to send the manuscript to the Moscow bookseller I. G. Solovyov to give to Babikov. In a letter dated November 3, 1867, Maykov informed us that he had carried out my husband's intentions.

"Living abroad, we did not know whether the article had appeared in print. It was only in 1872 that Fyodor Mikhailovich received a request from some bookseller to let him have the article . . . since Babikov had died and the volume had never been published.

"My husband was very upset over the loss of the article, all the more so because he had worked on it a great deal, and although dissatisfied with the piece, he valued it greatly. We began inquiring as to where it could have wound up, even asking the Moscow bookseller for help, but without any result. The article vanished without a trace.

"I still regret its loss. . . . It was a skillful and very interesting piece." See A. Dostoevskaia, *Vospominaniia* (Moscow: Khudozhestvennaia literatura, 1971), 159–60.

17. Znamensky Church, or the Church of the Sign, was built between 1794 and 1804 and is located in central St. Petersburg.

18. The Nikolaevsky station was completed in 1849. It is also likely that it is the station from which Tolstoy's Anna Karenina made her first trip to Moscow.

19. Dostoevsky's description is untrue for both men.

20. In an 1861 piece titled "Famous European Writers before the Judgment of Our Criticism," Grigoriev wrote: "Belinsky was, first of all, open—even sometime excessively open—to any new direction of truth. One can say without any special daring that in 1856 he would have become a Slavophile." See A. Grigoriev, "Znamenitye evropeiskie pisateli pered sudom nashei kritiki," *Vremia*, no. 3 (1861): otdeleniia 2, 47.

21. Maria Goegg-Pouchoulin was a founder of a women's boarding school in Geneva as well as editor of the journal *The United States of Europe* and secretary of the League of Peace and Freedom.

22. Dostoevsky is referring to Sergei Gagarin, grand master of the court, a member of the Council of the Empire, and a knight of Saint Alexander Nevsky and Saint Vladimir, first class; his brother Grigory Gagarin, prince, poet, diplomat, and patron of the arts; and Sergei's son Ivan, who converted to Catholicism and became a Jesuit.

23. Ernest Renan was the author of the enormously popular 1863 work *Life of Jesus*, in which he infused race into the theology and personhood of Jesus, specifically Renan's claim that Jesus had purified himself of his Jewishness and had become a Christian Aryan.

Also, by rejecting both Jesus as God as well as His miracles, Renan claimed not only that he was restoring Jesus to greater dignity as a human but also that Jesus's life should be written in the same way as any historical person's. He also insisted that the Bible could and should be subject to the same critical scrutiny as other historical documents.

Needless to say, with *Life of Jesus*, Renan angered many Christians. In particular, the work outraged Jews, since in it Renan depicted Judaism as foolish, illogical, and inferior to Christianity.

24. Belinsky reserved his vilification of Christ for a select few, but in letters to friends, he disparaged immortality, religion, and believers.

He wrote Botkin on September 5, 1840: "You say that you believe in immortality. But what is it really? One thing then another, anything you like—a glass with kvass, an apple, a horse. I congratulate you on your faith, but it is not for me." On June 27–28, 1841, he continued to Botkin that religion was a "strange idea that could arise only in the heads of cannibals."

To Herzen, Belinsky noted on January 26, 1845, "In words such as 'god' and 'religion,' I see obscurity and darkness, the chain, and the knout." And in his famous letter to Gogol, penned on July 15, 1847, Belinsky proclaimed that the "Russian utters the name of God when he scratches his ass." See Belinskii, *Polnoe sobranie sochinenii*, vol. 10 (1956), 215; vol. 11 (1956), 553; and vol. 12 (1956), 53 and 250.

25. In his 1867 *Literary and Life Reminiscences*, Turgenev wrote: "Belinsky's knowledge was not vast. He knew little and there is nothing surprising about this. Even his enemies did not accuse him of any lack of industry or laziness; but the poverty surrounding his childhood, his poor upbringing, his unfortunate circumstances, his early illnesses, and the necessity of earning a living by hurried work—all this prevented Belinsky from acquiring sound knowledge [of things]." See I. Turgenev, *Polnoe sobranie sochinenii v dvadtsati vos'mi tomakh. Sochineniia*, vol. 14 (Moscow: Akademiia nauk, 1967), 29–30.

26. Dostoevsky is referring to himself in the third person here.

27. The friend is thought to be Vasily Botkin, the young writer Turgenev.

28. George Sand, Belinsky wrote to Nikolai Bakunin on November 7, 1842, was "decidedly the Joan of Arc of our times, the star of salvation and prophetess of a great future." See Belinskii, *Polnoe sobranie sochinenii*, vol. 12, 115.

29. Annenkov recalled circa fall 1843: "In front of my eyes, Belinsky took up reading a history [of the French Revolution] . . . one that was remarkable for its complete lack of any verifications of the people and events, namely, Cabet's work *The People*, which found signs of a vast collective intelligence in all instances when the masses of the people took up action; and which explained . . . even the fall of the Republic in the moving and blessed unselfishness of these same masses who had sustained a victory over the foes, not for themselves, not for any immediate benefit to be derived from the event, but for the glorification of their principles—liberty, equality and fraternity."

The book in question is Cabet's 1841 *My Right Line or the True Path for the Salvation of the People*, in which Cabet argued that proletarians and bourgeoisie together establish both fellowship and communism. See Annenkov, "Zamechatel'noe desiatiletie," 185.

30. Doubtless Belinsky knew Pierre Leroux's 1837 essay "Cult," which, forbidden in Russia, argued for a national religion without spiritual despotism and theocracy. That said, Belinsky called Leroux an "insurgent Catholic priest." See Annenkov, "Zamechatel'noe desiatiletie," 213.

31. Belinsky was hardly alone in his passion for French socialists. Mikhail Saltykov-Shchedrin recalled in 1880: "From France—of course, not the France of Louis Philippe and Guizot, but the France of Saint-Simon, Cabet, Fourier, [and] Louis Blanc . . . —there flowed to us a *belief in humanity* . . . a shining conviction that the golden age was not behind us but before us." See M. Saltykov-Shchedrin, *Polnoe sobranie v dvadtsati tomakh*, vol. 14 (Moscow: Khudozhestvennaia literatura, 1972), 112.

32. Most likely, what appealed to Belinsky was Feuerbach's conception of men, women, and children as objects of their own worship. He took comfort from the fact that Feuerbach argued not only for the destruction of God but also for a theological foundation for a religion of humankind.

Belinsky knew Feuerbach's 1841 work *The Essence of Christianity*, a defense of materialism and of the anthropological essence of faith. No doubt he admired Feuerbach's claim that God did not create humankind in His own image and likeness so much as the opposite. It was humankind who had attributed its highest and most sublime attributes to a godhead, thereby alienating its very essence. Belinsky also had to applaud the task that Feuerbach outlined ahead: men and women were to reclaim from an imagined God or gods all the qualities that rightfully belonged to them and to incorporate such virtues and strengths into the very fabric of social life.

Annenkov recalled: "One of the almost inflammatory materials . . . [was] Feuerbach's famous work [*The Essence of Christianity*] which was then in everyone's hands. . . . No other work made such a powerful impression in our Western circle . . . obliterating so rapidly the remnants of all preceding outlooks."

"Herzen . . . was a fervent expositor of its propositions and conclusions . . . connecting the upheaval it revealed in metaphysical ideas with the political upheaval heralded by the socialists, and in which he once again coincided with Belinsky."

Annenkov adds: "One of Belinsky's friends had made a translation for him of a few chapters and crucial passages in Feuerbach's book. Belinsky was thus able to make . . . a palpable acquaintance with the process of criticism which overthrew his old mystical and philosophical idols. . . .

"Belinsky was so stupefied by [*The Essence*] that he remained completely mute in the face of the work and lost the ability to pose questions of his own, a feature that had always distinguished him." See Annenkov, "Zamechatel'noe desia-tiletie," 250.

33. In his 1835 work *The Life of Jesus*, a popular "forbidden" book in Russia, David Strauss criticized Christian dogma and denied both the authority and authenticity of the Gospels. In his view, the New Testament was the stuff not of divine revelation but of mythopoetic aspirations of the Jewish community during the time of Christ.

An early pioneer in the "quest for the historical Jesus," Strauss concluded that knowledge of a real-life Son of Man was buried hopelessly under layers of legend and myth, and that Jesus Christ, if He existed at all, was merely one of many self-proclaimed prophets of the period.

34. The French Commune was a radical socialist and revolutionary government that ruled Paris from March 18 to May 28, 1871. Felix Pyat was one of its most colorful members. He was also editor of *Avenger*, a widely read revolutionary journal.

In the first days of the Commune, Pyat advocated the end of national conscription, as well as the separation of church and state. Lies and missteps, the execution of enemies, the demolition of historical sites, and his stances as a firebrand revolutionary forced Pyat to flee France in late May and to be condemned to death in absentia by officials of the national government.

In 1880, however, Pyat was amnestied and allowed to return. Eight years later, he helped to prevent the overthrow of the Third Republic.

35. See the discussion of Pushkin later in this part of the book.

36. Gogol first published *Dead Souls* in 1842.

37. Dostoevsky has a point. In Gogol's works, Belinsky wrote, a "different definition of Art applies—that of a representation of reality in all its truth. Here everything is in types. The ideal is understood not as an embellishment (and consequently a lie), but as the relationships in which the author places the types he has created, along with the idea he wishes to express in his works." See Belinskii, *Polnoe sobranie sochinenii*, vol. 10 (1956), 294–95.

38. Pushkin published *The Tales of Belkin* in 1830. About this work, Belinsky wrote in 1846, "there is absolutely nothing good. . . . They are unworthy of Pushkin's talent and name. They are akin to stories by Karamzin, but with this difference. Karamzin's tales had a great significance in their day, but the *Tales of Belkin* are beneath their time. Especially pitiful is 'The Squire's Daughter,' untruthful and vaudeville-like in its portrayal of gentry life from an idyllic point of view." See Belinskii, *Polnoe sobranie sochinenii*, vol. 7 (1955), 577.

39. Gogol's "The Carriage" appeared in 1836. That same year Belinsky wrote, "'The Carriage' is nothing other than a joke, done in an extremely masterly way." See Belinsky, *Polnoe sobranie sochinenii*, vol. 2 (1953), 179–80.

40. Pushkin wrote *Eugene Onegin* between 1825 and 1832. As Belinsky wrote in his 1844 article titled "Eugene Onegin": "The novel ends with Tatyana's rebuke and the reader parts forever with Onegin in the most evil moment of his life. . . . But what is going on here? Where is the novel? What is its idea? What kind of novel lacks an ending? . . .

"What happened next to Onegin? Did he revive his passion for a new suffering, one that conforms better to human dignity? Or did he kill it with all the forces
of his soul, his cheerless angst having turned into deadly, cold apathy? We do not
know . . . since it is a *novel without an ending*." See Belinskii, *Polnoe sobranie sochinenii*,
vol. 7 (1955), 469.

41. As Belinsky wrote in his famous 1847 "Letter to N. Gogol," "Pushkin . . . had
to write only two or three loyal letters and to take on the livery of a chamber-Junker
to lose suddenly the love of the people." See Belinskii, *Polnoe sobranie sochinenii*, vol.
10 (1956), 217.

42. Turgenev penned "Three Portraits" in 1846. If Belinsky rejected "Three Portraits" in private, he extolled the work in public. "With its deft and lively exposition,"
he wrote in 1846, "Turgenev's 'Three Portraits' has the charm . . . of remembrances
of the good old days." He added a year later, "With 'Three Portraits,' it is apparent
that Turgenev has found his genuine path in prose." See Belinskii, *Polnoe sobranie
sochinenii*, vol. 9 (1955), 566, and vol. 10 (1956), 345.

43. In the ninth article in his cycle on the *Works of Alexander Pushkin*, Belinsky
used Tatyana's faithfulness to her husband to oppose despotism in families and to
defend the rights of women.

In his 1880 speech at the unveiling of Pushkin's statue in Moscow, Dostoevsky
saw Tatyana as a "pure Russian soul" who discerns that she cannot realize happiness
at the expense of another.

44. Since the 1830s, preference has been a popular card game in Russia.

45. Both Belinsky and Panaeva begged to differ. "In the evening, around ten,"
Panaeva recalled, "Belinsky visited us to play preference, for which he had a wild
passion. Talking forcefully throughout the game, he often sat next to me so that
I could see the game.

"'It would be much better to play preference with us than always reading
your George Sand,' Belinsky said. . . .

"'You and I always quarrel so, but at cards we simply will come to blows,'
I responded. 'Furthermore, it is harmful for you to play preference: you get
way too excited and then you need to rest.'

"'My excitement over cards is nothing; what really harms me is when, for
example today, I got upset when I was brought a page of my article which
had been bloodied by the censor. How can I allow [my editors] to publish
such a repulsive piece! From such distress the chest aches, and it is difficult
to breathe.'" See A. Panaeva, *Vospominaniia* (Moscow: Gosudarstvennoe
izdatel'stvo khudozhestvennoi literatury, 1956), 90.

About Belinsky and preference, Turgenev also remembered, "Belinsky
played cards poorly, but with the same sincerity and the same passion with which
he did everything." See Turgenev, *Polnoe sobranie sochinenii*, vol. 14, 47.

46. As has been noted, Dostoevskaya's assertion is incorrect.

47. This is not true. Before *Poor Folk*, Dostoevsky was a stranger to the Russian
literary world.

48. Gioachino Rossini's *William Tell* appeared in 1829, Wolfgang Amadeus
Mozart's *Don Giovanni* in 1787, Vincenzo Bellini's *Norma* in 1831, and Giacomo Meyerbeer's *Huguenots* in 1836.

49. Dostoevskaya is wrong again. *The Double* appeared in Kraevsky's *Fatherland
Notes* on January 30, 1846, two weeks after the appearance of *Poor Folk* in Nekrasov's

Petersburg Miscellany. Furthermore, the lie about borders concerned *Poor Folk*, not *The Double.*

50. The individual was Grigorovich.

51. Panaev's claim is suspect. As will be seen, Belinsky never believed that Dostoevsky would supersede Gogol.

52. Interestingly, Turgenev omitted the remark on Belinsky's failing powers as a critic in later editions of his memoirs.

53. The full text of this verse appears later in this part of the book.

54. Nekrasov's *The Stone Heart* is also known as *How Great I Am!* and *On That Day at Around Eleven O'Clock in the Morning.* In the piece, Mertsalov bears affinities to Belinsky, Glazhievsky to Dostoevsky, Trostnikov to Nekrasov, Balakleev to Grigorovich, Reshetilov to Turgenev, Razbegaev to Panaev; Sputnik to Annenkov, the Journalist to Kraevsky, and the All-Around (and Also Embracing) Nature to Botkin and Alexander Druzhinin.

55. Apparently Nekrasov knew that "to descend into nothingness" (*stushevat'sia*), was one of the young writer's favorite terms. As Dostoevsky wrote in *A Writer's Diary* in November 1877:

> "The verb *stushevat'sia* means to disappear, to perish, *to descend to nothingness,* so to speak. But *stushevat'sia* means to perish not immediately, not to be wiped off the face of the earth with thunder and crashing . . . but to sink gradually into nothingness. It is like a shadow on a drawing done in shaded lines that gradually moves from black into white until it disappears completely, *to nothingness.*
>
> "Although I was the first one to use the verb *stushevat'sia* . . . I was certainly not the one who invented it. The term was thought up by my classmates when I was at the Main School of Military Engineering. Perhaps I also took part in its invention . . . but somehow it came into being all by itself. In all six classes at the school, we had to draw various plans—fortifications, structures, and military buildings. The ability to draw a plan freehand and well was a strict requirement so that, like it or not, even students who had no inclination for drawing still had to attain a certain level in this art. . . . You might graduate . . . as an excellent mathematician, a builder of fortifications, or an engineer, but if your drawings were poor . . . you were deprived of such significant advantages as promotion to a higher rank. As a result, everyone tried hard to draw well.
>
> "All plans were drawn and shaded in India ink . . . and everyone tried to learn how to shade a given surface well, from dark to light to white—to nothingness; a good shading gave to the drawing a stylish look.
>
> "Suddenly people began to ask: 'Where's so-and-so?' 'Ah, he's disappeared [*stushevalsia*] somewhere.' Or, say, two friends were talking and one would say to the other that he had to get to work: 'Well, now you'd better disappear [*stushshiusia*].' Or a senior student would say to a new student, 'I called you; where did you manage to disappear to [*stushevat'sia*]'?
>
> "'*Stushevat'sia*' . . . was used only in our class . . . and when we graduated, it seemingly did so as well. Some three years later I remembered it and used it in my tale." See F. Dostoevskii, *Dnevnik pisatelia za 1877 god* (Berlin: Izdatel'stvo I. P. Ladyzhnikova, 1922), 456–59.

56. In truth, Dostoevsky had begun *Poor Folk* in early 1844—a year before its publication—and wrote no more than two redactions of the work.

57. The claim is wrong on both counts. Byron wrote *Manfred* from summer 1816 to winter 1817. He began *Don Juan* in July 1818, working on the piece until his death in 1824.

58. Such a piece is unknown.

59. Staraya Russa, famous for its mineral springs, is a town in northwest Russia, roughly sixty miles south of Novgorod.

60. This is not true. See Panaeva's excerpt from February 1846.

Part Two. Havens from the Storms

1. V. Sollogub, *Povesti. Vospominaniia* (Leningrad: Khudozhestvennaia literatura, 1988), 436 and 493.

2. Ibid., 435.

3. L. Dostoevskaia, *Dostoevskii v izobrazhenii svoei docheri*, 45.

4. St. Isaac's Cathedral is the largest Russian Orthodox cathedral in St. Petersburg. It is also the largest Orthodox basilica and the fourth-largest cathedral in the world.

5. V. Komarovich, "Iunost' Dostoevskogo," *Byloe*, no. 23 (1924): 17.

6. Maykov became the lead critic for *The Fatherland Notes* after Belinsky left the journal for *The Contemporary* in 1847.

7. The *Pocket Dictionary of Foreign Words,* edited by Mikhail Petrashevsky and Nikolai Kirillov in 1846, popularized materialist, democratic, socialist, and utopian views, and was thus, by the end of the decade, banned by the tsarist government.

8. The Catherine Institute was a school for girls of the nobility. Founded in 1798, it was closed after the October Revolution.

9. For whatever reason, Pavlov did not write the review.

10. Most likely Dostoevsky is referring to his final proofing of his story, *The Double*, which was published in *The Fatherland Notes* in February 1846.

11. Again, the work in question is *The Petersburg Miscellany*.

12. *Illustration* was a newspaper published weekly in St. Petersburg from 1845 to 1849, with Nikolai Kukolnik as its first editor.

13. *The Northern Bee* was a newspaper published in St. Petersburg, first three times a week and then weekly, and edited by Faddei Bulgarin, who, among others, attacked Pushkin, Gogol, and Belinsky.

14. *The Library for Reading* was a conservative monthly of literature, science, the arts, industry, news, and fashion published in St. Petersburg from 1834 to 1865. (Osip Senkovsky was its first editor.) It published works by Vasily Zhukovsky, Ivan Krylov, Vladimir Odoevsky, Yevgeny Baratynsky, and Pyotr Vyazemsky, as well as by Pushkin, Gogol, and Lermontov.

The Library for Reading reviewed and sometimes published in translation the works of such French writers as Honoré de Balzac, Victor Hugo, George Sand, and Eugène Scribe.

15. Neither Odoevsky nor Sollogub wrote an article about *Poor Folk.*

16. Dostoevsky is referring to Maykov's review, published in January 1846.

17. *The Fatherland Notes* was a literary and sociopolitical journal published in St. Petersburg from 1839 to 1867. It favored the ideas of the Westernizers, with Belinsky

playing a prominent role as editor of the literary, critical, and bibliographical sections of the publication. At this time, *The Fatherland Notes* had a huge circulation of some 2,500 copies monthly.

18. From 1769 to 1849, the tsarist officials allowed so-called assignat paper rubles to exist alongside silver rubles, with free convertability from paper to silver guaranteed by decree but limited to copper coins. By keeping silver in the state treasury and copper in circulation, they hoped to circulate money more rapidly, thereby strengthening the finances of government.

19. After having seen her fiancé only three times, the seventeen-year-old Vera Dostoevskaya married the thirty-three-year-old Alexander Pavlovich Ivanov, a professor at the Konstantinovsky Landmark Institute in Moscow, on January 7, 1846.

About Ivanov, Andrei Dostoevsky wrote: "I found Alexander Ivanov to be a very kind, merry, and sympathetic individual. From our first meeting, we got along well. I liked him a great deal and what feelings I had for him lasted to the end of his life."

Also, according to Anna Dostoevskaya, Dostoevsky loved Vera and her entire family in a special way. See M. Volotskoi, *Khronika roda Dostoevskogo, 1506–1933* (Moscow: Sever, 1933), 190; and Dostoevskaia, *Vospominaniia*, 126–27.

20. Bulgarin is referring to the so-called Natural School in Russian literature, a movement that embraced the youthful writings of such authors as Nekrasov, Dostoevsky, and Turgenev, which, beginning around 1840, sought to establish in native soil the content and form of European urban realism and which, as did Western writers of the city at this time, made everyday people the new heroes and heroines of literature.

21. Nekrasov's "On the Road" appeared in 1845.

22. About "Shaved Sideburns," see the discussion later in this part of the book.

23. Most likely Pletnyov is referring, tongue in cheek, to the so-called Nekrasovetsy, a religious sect of Old Believers who, as descendants of fugitives, Cossacks, runaways, and the participants in a civil uprising known as the Bulavin rebellion (1707–8), raided areas in southern Russia until 1737, when they resettled in territories of the Ottoman Empire.

24. Gogol wrote *Diary of a Madman* in 1835.

25. Gogol published "Nevsky Prospekt" in 1835.

26. *The Muscovite* was a monthly literary and historical journal published in Moscow from 1841 to 1856. Headed by Mikhail Pogodin and Stepan Shevyryov, *The Muscovite* espoused "official nationality," that is, conservative nationalism rooted in autocracy and monarchy.

27. Again, Belinsky, Nekrasov, and company.

28. Gogol's Popryshchin is the hero of his 1835 *Diary of a Madman*, Akaky Akakievich Bashmachkin of his story "The Overcoat."

29. Tatyana Larina is the heroine of Pushkin's *Eugene Onegin*.

30. The reference is to Ivan Krylov's 1813 fable "Demyan Fish Soup." When the "hot and red" Foka flees his host Demyan after repeated helpings of fish soup, Krylov concludes, "Author, if you have many gifts but do not know when to quit . . . then know that your verse and prose are more sickening than too much fish soup."

31. Eugène Sue wrote *The Mysteries of Paris* in 1842 and *The Wandering Jew* (not *Eternal*) in 1844; Alexander Dumas père wrote *The Count of Monte Cristo* also in 1844.

32. Izler's café-restaurant featured some thirty types of ice cream. In 1845 its owner, Ivan Izler, who was Swiss, was the first confectioner in Russia to receive a patent to make ice cream by machine. It exists today.

33. Robert Lovelace is the villain in Samuel Richardson's 1748 *Clarissa, or the History of a Young Lady.*

34. Chichikov, Petrushka, and Selifan are characters from Gogol's 1842 novel *Dead Souls.*

35. The Table of Ranks was established by 1722 by Peter the Great as a system for establishing equivalencies in titles and positions in the military, civil service, and court bureaucracy. It also provided a system of promotion for all governmental servitors vis-à-vis fourteen levels or steps.

The lowest or fourteenth rank included the army rank of ensign, the navy rank of ship commissar, and the civil service rank of assistant councilor. At the first or highest rank were such positions as field marshal, admiral general, and chancellor. Similar listings of ranks existed in both Denmark and Prussia.

36. Franz Joseph Gall was a physiologist and a pioneer in studying the localization of mental functions in the brain. He was also the founder of "cranioscopy" (later renamed "phrenology"), in which the external shape of the skull is seen as determining both the personality as well as the mental and moral faculties of the individual.

Needless to say, Gall's ideas were pronounced as invalid by both church and state in Germany and France. They were accepted in England, though especially among the ruling classes, who appealed to Gall to justify the presumed inferiority of colonial subjects. Gall's ideas were also popular in the United States from 1820 to 1850.

It should be noted, though, that Gall contributed significantly to the study of neurology. He was the first to suggest the then revolutionary idea that character, thoughts, and emotions were located in the brain, not the heart.

37. Khlestakov is the rogue hero of Gogol's *Dead Souls.*

38. In truth, Belinsky had notified Kraevsky of his move from *The Fatherland Notes* to *The Contemporary* on February 6, 1846. He did so not only because of his friendship with Nekrasov, editor of *The Contemporary,* but also because of the more radical political and social stance of the journal.

39. On May 12, 1846, Belinsky left for a two-week stay in Odessa to improve his failing health. The following year he traveled to cities in Germany, Belgium, and France to continue medical treatments.

40. The work in question is the already noted *Leviathan.*

41. Both stories remained unfinished. Sections from "A Tale about Destroyed Offices" appeared in Dostoevsky's 1846 story "Mr. Prokharchin" and echoes of "Shaved Sideburns" in his 1859 novel *The Village of Stepanchikovo and Its Inhabitants.*

42. Herzen had published "Dilletantism in Science" in 1842–43, "Letters on the Study of Nature" in 1845–46, and also during this time period *Who Is to Blame?* in *The Fatherland Notes.*

Goncharov made his literary debut with a translation of two chapters of Eugène Sue's novel *Atar-Gull,* in 1832; a story, titled "A Bad Ailment," in 1838; and another, named "A Lucky Error," in 1839.

43. Goethe wrote *Reynard the Fox* in 1793.

44. In fact, Dostoevsky visited Mikhail in Revel on May 25, 1846.

45. Mikhail Dostoevsky's translation of *Reynard the Fox* appeared in *The Fatherland Notes* in 1848.

46. Revel was the Russian name for Tallinn, the capital of Estonia.

47. Gapsal, more commonly known as Haapsalu, is a city in Estonia, roughly fifty miles southwest of Revel and 250 miles southwest of St. Petersburg.

48. Maria Belinskaya was thirty-four years old at the time. She died in 1890.

49. The story in question is "Mr. Prokharchin," which was published in *The Fatherland Notes* later that year.

50. Gogol wrote "Old-World Landowners" in 1835.

51. Maria Belinskaya, together with her daughter Olga and sister-in-law Agrafena Orlova, remained in Revel for the summer, where they were treated cordially by Mikhail Dostoevsky and his family. The two women, though, saw their hosts as highly impractical people.

52. Mikhail's children Fedya (Fyodor) and Masha (Maria) Dostoevsky would later become pianists and students of Anton Rubinstein, one of the great keyboard virtuosos of the nineteenth century.

53. The child in question is Olga Belinskaya, born on June 13, 1845. A son, Vladimir, died in infancy in 1847.

54. The reference is to Belinsky.

55. "Piter" is the affectionate name of the citizens of St. Petersburg for their city.

56. Goncharov published *The Precipice* in 1869.

57. Vasily Tredyakovsky published *Telemachus*, a translation of François Fénelon's 1669 *Adventures of Telemachus*, in 1766.

58. See the next note.

59. The Troitsky Izmailovsky Cathedral, also known as Trinity Cathedral, the Trinity-Izmailovsky Cathedral, and the Cathedral of the Holy Primary-Life Trinity of the Imperial Guard of the Izmailovsky Regiment, was built between 1828 and 1835. Dostoevsky married his second wife, Anna Grigorievna Snitkina, there in 1867.

60. The Small Church of the Winter Palace was built in 1768. Destroyed by fire in 1837, it was rebuilt in 1839.

61. The Izmailovsky Regiment was founded by Empress Anna Ioannovna on September 22, 1730, to support the throne. The regiment was particularly crucial during the Battle of Borodino against Napoleon Bonaparte on September 7, 1812.

62. Natalya Maykova was the wife of Valerian Maykov.

63. The individual in question is Alexander Izmailov.

64. Manilov is also a character in Gogol's *Dead Souls*.

65. Goethe wrote his loosely autobiographical epistolary novel *The Sorrows of Young Werther* in 1774.

66. In truth, Nekrasov was in a peaceful ménage à trois with Panaeva, who, for the next ten years, was his common-law wife.

67. Gogol's "Will" appeared in 1847 as part of his *Selected Passages from a Correspondence with Friends*.

68. Belinsky had left St. Petersburg for Moscow on April 26, 1846, and, after a trip to southern Russia, returned to the imperial capital around October 20.

69. Penza is a city located about four hundred miles southeast of Moscow. Kiev, capital of Ukraine, is about five hundred miles to the southwest of the Russian capital.

70. The work in question is Grigorovich's *The Village*.

71. The article in question is Valerian Maykov's article "Something about Russian Literature in 1846," published in *The Fatherland Notes* in January 1847.

72. Pargolovo is a municipal settlement, located roughly eleven miles north of St. Petersburg. Parnassus Hill, at a height of roughly 140 feet, is the highest point in the city.

73. Briefly, Fourierism is a philosophy of utopian reform that sought to recast society into independent, self-sufficient "phalanges" (phalanxes).

Fourier's phalanges were to consist of roughly 1,500 individuals of varying ages, aptitudes, intelligence, and wealth who would live and work harmoniously in rural settings, as well as in massive and sumptuous palace- and hotel-like structures, without government intervention.

Work was to be apportioned on a rational and rotating basis; goods produced were seen as the property of the group. Members of phalanges would receive hourly wages, scaled to the difficulty or disagreeableness of tasks; they could also lay claim to private property and inheritances.

The result, Fourier claimed, would be increased industry, social and sexual equality, as well as the end to indigence, fraud, oppression, and war.

74. The piece was "Mr. Prokharchin."

Part Three. The Psycho-Spiritual Turn

1. Panaev fails to note that Nekrasov did not wish to publish *Leviathan* but that he had offered to print all the materials in the anthology in *The Contemporary*.

2. At this time Dostoevsky did not realize his wish to go to France and Italy.

3. The work in question is *Netochka Nezvanova*.

4. Dostoevsky may be alluding to *Netochka Nezvanova*.

5. Dostoevsky may be referring to the sales of *The Petersburg Miscellany*.

6. Such a verse is unknown.

7. Again, the individual in question is Grigorovich. Consider Turgenev's remark in a letter to Yelizaveta Lambert, written on November 28, 1860, that Grigorovich was a "heartless gossip and liar." See I. Turgenev, *Polnoe sobranie sochinenii. Pis'ma*, vol. 4 (Moscow: Akademiia nauk, 1962), 166.

8. Mikhail Mikhailovich Dostoevsky was born on November 5, 1846.

9. What Dostoevsky fails to tell his brother Mikhail is that the reviewers were sharply critical of "Mr. Prokharchin."

10. Most likely the story in question is "The Landlady," which was published in the October–December 1847 issue of *The Fatherland Notes*.

11. Dostoevsky has in mind both Nekrasov and Panaev.

12. Most likely *Netochka Nezvanova*.

13. Dostoevsky was unable to publish *Poor Folk* as a separate book until 1847 and a revised edition of *The Double* until 1866.

14. Dostoevsky's plans were not realized.

15. Hryhory Kvitka-Osnovyanenko wrote *Mr. Kholyavsky*, a humorous portrait of life among the Ukrainian gentry, in 1839.

16. This is not true. Gogol died in Moscow on February 21, 1852. Dostoevsky may be referring to Gogol's death metaphorically, as the writer was no longer writing fiction.

17. "Once you're dead, you're really dead."

18. Bulgarin, of course, is referring to Belinsky.

19. "The Petersburg Corners" was written by Nekrasov in 1845.

20. As has been noted, Dostoevsky's revision of *The Double* was not published until 1866. Also, the edition of *Poor Folk* that appeared in November 1847 lacked illustrations.

21. Yevstafy Bernardsky was a wood engraver who began publishing illustrations for Gogol's *Dead Souls* in 1846.

22. Also, in his feuilleton "A Petersburg Chronicle," written on June 1, 1847, Dostoevsky wrote: "The splendid undertaking of Messers Bernardsky and Agin—the illustrations for *Dead Souls*—are coming to an end, and one cannot praise enough the conscientiousness of both artists. Several of their drawings are done so splendidly that it is difficult to want anything better." See Dostoevskii, *Polnoe sobranie sochinenii*, vol. 18, 28.

23. Dostoevsky was working on "The Landlady."

24. The publication of *Netochka Nezvanova* was announced in *The Fatherland Notes*, no. 12 (1846), but the work did not appear in print until issues 1, 2, and 5 of the journal in 1849.

25. As will be seen, Dostoevsky had not fulfilled his contractual obligations to Kraevsky, a situation that led Belinsky, for one, to conclude that the writer had taken advantage of the publisher.

26. Dostoevsky is referring to the polemic between Belinsky in *The Contemporary* and Maykov in *The Fatherland Notes* in 1846 and 1847, in part over the poetry of Koltsov.

27. Dostoevsky did not go to Revel in 1847.

28. As well it should have. Akulina, the heroine of Grigorovich's work, suffers an "education" of beatings and abuse by her husband, Grigory; but she retains her dignity and self-worth even as she dies in the process.

In the final scene, Grigory drives through a blinding snowstorm to bury his wife's body, accompanied by their distraught daughter, Dunka, who runs through deep snowdrifts to keep up with her father.

Grigorovich's *The Village* was praised by reviewers and readers because it showed not only a peasant woman with human emotions but also the changing tenor of serf life. (Grigory is corrupted by the idle life of a village factory.) It also garnered praise for depicting peasant mores, folklore, and vernacular language in a realistic way.

29. Yanovsky claims that he met Dostoevsky in 1846; if so, he was thirty-one, and the writer, twenty-five at the time.

30. As has already been noted, Yanovsky's claims as to Dostoevsky's religious and patriotic beliefs are without evidence in this period.

31. Doctors had called epilepsy "the falling sickness" for almost a century. Samuel-Auguste Tissot, in his 1771 work *Treatise on Epilepsy or the Falling Sickness*, saw the affliction as caused by brain tumors, head injuries, metabolic disturbances, or hypersensitivity of the brain. For victims of "falling sickness," valerian drops were a common remedy.

32. The Russian here is *kondrashka s veterkom*. At the time, *kondrashka* was a collo-quial term for apoplectic stroke or even sudden death—a darkly humorous expression derived, supposedly, from Kondrati (Kondrashka) Bulavin, who staged an uprising—the previously mentioned Bulavin rebellion—against tsarist forces in 1707–8. (The hero in Dostoevsky's "Mr. Prokharchin" also suffers from *kondrashka*.)

Russian textbooks of the 1840s translated "aura," the classic warning symp-tom for epilepsy, as "breeze," which conveys the literal meaning of the phenomenon. For instance, Yustin Dyadkovsky, in his 1847 work *Practical Medicine: Lectures,* noted, "Suddenly there appears a special sensation of rising hot or cold steam, well known as *epileptic breeze,* which runs through one nerve ending to the entire nervous system, immediately causing attacks." . . .

"[Such a condition] ends in *death* or a hemorrhage in the brain or a weakening of strength, the result of repeated attacks." See Iu. Diadkovskii, *Izbrannye sochineniia* (Moscow: Medgiz, 1958), 431.

Since Dyadkovsky's *Practical Medicine* appeared in early 1845, it is more than likely that Dostoevsky knew of the publication and even self-diagnosed his illness.

33. Haymarket Square was established in 1737 for the sale of wood, oats, and cattle. Known as the "belly of St. Petersburg," Haymarket Square became, by the mid-nineteenth century, the quarter for the lower classes of the city, as well as for prostitution and other dubious activities. Many of the old buildings in Haymarket Square, including the Church of the Assumption of the Mother of God, fell victim to urban planning in the Soviet era.

Haymarket Square was also the site where Raskolnikov in *Crime and Punish-ment* kissed the earth in a frenzied attempt to atone for the murder of the pawnbro-ker Alyona Ivanovna and her sister Lizaveta.

34. Andrei's claim is not true. As has been noted, he was not close to Fyodor and often did not see his brother for weeks on end.

35. Conceivably the individual is Senkovsky.

36. Dostoevsky is correct here: an incorrect interpretation of Psalm 32.

37. Helsingfors is the Swedish name for Helsinki. Mikhail was transferred to the city in 1847, but Fyodor never got to visit him there.

38. Dostoevsky is citing Vincenz Priessznitz, a German doctor and one of the founders of hydrotherapy, which became very popular in the 1830s.

39. Dostoevsky is referring to a book edition of *Poor Folk.*

40. Fyodor Mikhailovich Dostoevsky, son of Mikhail and Emiliya.

41. Carl von Roswald is the hero of George Sand's 1846 novel *Lucrezia Floriani.* He is also a partial prototype for the character of Ordynov in Dostoevsky's "The Landlady."

42. A reference to *The Double.*

43. Such an assertion is false.

44. Most likely Panaeva is referring to Belinsky's article "A Look at Russian Lit-erature for 1846," which was published in January 1847.

45. The scene is unknown.

46. Again, Belinsky has in mind Maykov's "Something about Russian Literature in 1846."

47. By the "new criticism," Guber means Belinsky's reviews of Dostoevsky's first two works. Dostoevsky finished *The Double* on January 28, 1846.

48. Belinsky is referring to Dostoevsky's "Novel in Nine Letters," which was published in the January 1847 issue of *The Contemporary*.

49. Belinsky had written a similar missive to Botkin two days earlier.

50. Desperate for money, Dostoevsky was editing the proofs of an article on the Jesuits for the fifth volume of the *Reference Encyclopedia Dictionary*, which, edited by Albert Starchevsky, came out in May 1847.

51. Panaev is referring to the previously mentioned Alexandra Senyavina.

52. The book in question is Gogol's *Selected Passages from My Correspondence with Friends*, which glorified autocracy, serfdom, and Orthodoxy as God-given and sacred, and which caused Belinsky to call the author a "proponent of the knout, an apostle of ignorance, a champion of obscurantism, and a panegyrist of Tartar ways." See Belinskii, *Polnoe sobranie sochinenii*, vol. 10 (1956), 214.

53. Belinsky is quoting from Maykov's April 1847 article in *The Fatherland Notes*.

54. In the summer of 1847 Dostoevsky did not go to visit Mikhail; instead, Mikhail came to St. Petersburg.

55. Dostoevsky surely means two feuilletons a month, not a week.

56. The reference is probably to *Netochka Nezvanova*.

57. Mikhail Dostoevsky was twenty-seven years old at the time.

58. Mr. Imrek was a pen name for Konstantin Aksakov.

59. The work in question is *Russia in 1839* by the Marquis de Custine about his time in St. Petersburg, Moscow, and Yaroslavl. First published in 1841, his less than flattering account of Russia and Russians went through six printings and was read widely in England, France, and Germany.

Lost to obscurity for a time, Custine's work became a favorite text for disgruntled American diplomats who, stationed in Moscow during Stalin's rule, plundered the book for the writer's insights into the national despotism, for example, on Russians as "voluntary automata" who, among other things, surrendered to "the police of the imagination."

60. The Solovetsky Islands, located in the White Sea in northern Russia, are the site of the famous Solovetsky Monastery, which was founded in 1436 by the monk Zosima. Between 1926 and 1939 the monastery was converted into a prison and a labor camp, serving as a prototype for the camps of the gulag system. During World War II, the monastery housed young sailors in training. Beginning in the late 1980s, the Solovetsky Monastery, together with other churches in the locale, was permitted to conduct religious services and underwent rebuilding and restoration. In 1992 it was placed on the list of UNESCO World Heritage Sites, and today it is a place for pilgrimage and prayer.

61. Lake Ladoga, just to the northwest of St. Petersburg, hosts three religious institutions: the Valaam Monastery, thought to have been founded sometime in the twelfth century; the Konovsky Monastery, established around 1393; and the Alexander-Svirsky Monastery, which came into being in 1487.

62. Mount Athos, both a mountain and a peninsula in northeastern Greece, is home to some twenty monasteries under the jurisdiction of the Ecumenical Patriarch of Constantinople.

63. Dostoevsky is referring to Saint Peter, the patron saint of Moscow, who, in 1325, at the request of Grand Prince Ivan Kalita, transferred the metropolitan

cathedral-church from Vladimir to Moscow, thereby strengthening the political position of Moscow and establishing it as the spiritual capital of a fragmented Russia.

Dostoevsky is also referring to Saint Philip II, who was metropolitan of Moscow during the reign of Ivan the Terrible, and who, having dared openly to contradict royal authority, is alleged to have been murdered by the tsar.

64. The Archangel Cathedral is a Russian Orthodox church dedicated to the Archangel Michael. Located in the Kremlin in Moscow and constructed between 1505 and 1508, it was the main necropolis of the tsars until the relocation of the capital to St. Petersburg.

65. Not quite. The bell tower of Ivan the Great has existed since 1508, having been raised by Boris Godunov to its present height in 1600.

66. Dostoevsky has in mind such works as Grigorovich's "The Village," Herzen's *Who Is at Fault?*, and Goncharov's *A Common Story*.

67. Most likely Dostoevsky is thinking about Belinsky's "A Look at Russian Literature in 1846" and "A Look at Russian Literature in 1847"; as well as Maykov's "The Poetry of Koltsov" and "Something about Russian Literature in 1847."

68. At the end of 1846 and the beginning of 1847, the bookseller Alexander Smirdin had published collections of the writings of Vladislav Ozerov, Denis Fonvizin, and Mikhail Lomonosov.

69. A three-volume edition of the works of Krylov appeared in 1847.

70. Dostoevsky has in mind Bernadsky and Agin's album *One Hundred Drawings from the Writings of N. V. Gogol: "Dead Souls,"* which appeared in 1846.

71. Mikhail Nevakovich's album *Jumble* appeared four times a year from 1846 to 1849.

72. Pavlovsk is a town located about twenty miles south of St. Petersburg, and is the site of the Pavlovsk Palace, a major residence of the Russian imperial family.

73. Goncharov wrote *The Frigate Pallada* in 1854–57 and *Oblomov* in 1859. Dostoevsky published *Notes from the House of the Dead* in 1862 and *The Diary of A Writer* in two volumes, the first between 1873 and 1876 and the second between 1877 and 1881.

74. The reference is to Pyotr Karepin, who was the husband of Dostoevsky's sister Varvara, the financial guardian of the family after the death of the writer's father, Mikhail, and a man with whom Dostoevsky warred constantly over money, property, and other matters.

75. Mikhail is referring to a new and separate edition of *Poor Folk*.

76. Most likely the story in question is "Polzunkov."

77. At the time of his arrest in 1849, Dostoevsky owed Nekrasov 165 rubles. So it is reasonable to assume that Nekrasov agreed to the writer's present request for 150 silver rubles.

78. Most likely Dostoevsky is referring to "The Landlady."

79. Dostoevsky is correct here. Mikhail Dostoevsky retired in that month.

80. Dostoevsky is again referring to "The Landlady."

81. In 1848 there came into existence three large journals: *The Geographic News of the Russian Geographic Society*, *The Northern Survey*, and *The Moscow Miscellany*. As Kraevsky was an influential member of the Geographic Society, Dostoevsky was counting on his connections and assistance.

82. Mikhail visited his brother on September 27, 1847.

83. Mikhail Dostoevsky retired from service to the state on October 14, 1847.

84. Such an assertion is false. Andrei Dostoevsky did not even know who Petrashevsky was.

85. Dostoevskaya's story here is again pure fiction.

86. In truth, Pleschcheev was a year or two older.

87. Specifically in Dostoevsky's 1848 story, "The Honest Thief."

SOURCE NOTES

Part One

1846 and after. F. Dostoevskii, *Dnevnik pisatelia za 1873 god* (Berlin: Izdatel'stvo I. P. Ladyzhnikova, 1922), 216.

1846 and after. F. Dostoevskii, *Polnoe sobranie sochinenii v tridtsati tomakh*, vol. 27 (Moscow: Khudozhestvennaia literatura, 1984), 120.

1846 and after. Dostoevskii, *Polnoe sobranie sochinenii*, vol. 28, bk. 1 (1985), 296.

1846 and after. Dostoevskii, *Polnoe sobranie sochinenii*, vol. 18 (1978), 122.

1846 and after. S. Ianovskii, "Vospominaniia o Dostoevskom," *Russkii vestnik*, no. 4 (1884), 814–15.

1846 and after. N. Grech, *Zapiski o moei zhizni* (Moscow: Kniga, 1990), 91–92.

1846. P. Annenkov, "Molodost' I. S. Turgeneva, 1840–1856 g.," *Vestnik Evropy*, no. 2 (1884): 467.

1846. A. Dostoevskaya, "God kak zhizn'. Iz zapisnoi knizhki," *Literaturnaia gazeta* (April 16, 1986): 3.

January–March 1846. Dostoevskii, *Polnoe sobranie sochinenii*, vol. 28, bk. 1, 525.

January 1, 1846. V. Belinskii, *Polnoe sobranie sochinenii v tridnadtsati tomakh*, vol. 9 (Moscow: Akademiia nauk, 1955), 407–8.

January 2, 1846. Belinsky, *Polnoe sobranie sochinenii*, vol. 12 (1956), 254.

Before January 24, 1846. D. Grigorovich, *Vospominaniia* (Moscow: Zakharov, 2007), 73.

After January 24, 1846. I. Panaev, *Literaturnye vospominaniia* (Moscow: Pravda, 1988), 162.

After January 24, 1846. V. Sollogub, *Vospominaniia* (Moscow: Academia, 1931), 413–14.

January 26, 1846. Belinskii, *Polnoe sobranie sochinenii*, 261.

January 26, 1846. A. Grigoriev, "Peterburgskii sbornik, izdannyi N. Nekrasovym," *Illiustratsiia* (January 26, 1846): 59.

January 26, 1846. N. Kukol'nik, "Peterburgskii sbornik, izdannyi N. Nekrasovym," *Severnaia pchela* (January 26, 1846): 59.

January 30, 1846. V. Pletnev, *Perepiska Ia. K. Grota s P. A. Pletnevym*, vol. 2 (St. Petersburg: Tipografiia ministerstva putei soobshcheniia, 1896), 663–64.

January 30, 1846. L. Brandt, "Peterburgskii sbornik, izdannyi N. Nekrasovym," *Severnaia pchela* (January 30, 1846): 99.

Late January 1846. L. Lanskii, "Dostoevskii v neizdannoi perepiske sovremennikov (1837–1881)," in *Literaturnoe nasledstvo. F. M. Dostoevskii. Novye materialy i issledovaniia*, ed. V. Shcherbina et al. (Moscow: Nauka, 1973), 370.

Circa February 1846 and after. A. Dolinin, ed., *F. M. Dostoevskii: Pis'ma v chetyrekh tomakh*, vol. 2 (Moscow: Khudozhestvennaia literatura, 1930), 36.

Circa February 1846 and after. A. Dostoevskaia, *Vospominaniia* (Moscow: Khudozhestvennaia literatura, 1971), 159.

Circa February 1846 and after. Dostoevskii, *Dnevnik pisatelia za 1873 god*, 216.

Circa February 1846 and after. Vs. Soloviev, "Vospominaniia o F. M. Dostoevskom," *Istoricheskii vestnik*, no. 3 (1881): 608.

Circa February 1846 and after. Dostoevskii, *Dnevnik pisatelia za 1876 god* (Berlin: Izdatel'stvo I. P. Ladyzhnikova, 1922), 85.

Circa February 1846 and after. Dostoevskii, *Polnoe sobranie sochinenii*, vol. 11 (1974), 73.

Circa February 1846 and after. Dostoevskii, *Dnevnik pisatelia za 1873 god*, 222.

Circa February 1846 and after. Dostoevskii, *Dnevnik pisatelia za 1873 god*, 219.

Circa February 1846 and after. Dostoevskii, *Dnevnik pisatelia za 1876 god*, 163.

Circa February 1846 and after. F. Dostoevskii, "Zapisnaia tetrad', 1876–1877 gg.," in *Literaturnoe nasledstvo. Neizdannyi Dostoevskii. Zapisnye knizhki i tetradi, 1876–1877 gg.*, ed. V. Shcherbina et al., vol. 83 (Moscow: Nauka, 1971), 526.

Circa February 1846 and after. Dostoevskii, *Dnevnik pisatelia za 1873 god*, 218.

Circa February 1846 and after. Dostoevskii, *Dnevnik pisatelia za 1873 god*, 221–22.

Circa February 1846 and after. Dolinin, ed., *F. M. Dostoevskii. Pis'ma*, vol. 2, 149.

Circa February 1846 and after. Dostoevsky, *Polnoe sobranie sochinenii*, vol. 29, bk. 1 (1986), 145.

Circa February 1846 and after. Dostoevskii, *Polnoe sobranie sochinenii*, vol. 29, bk. 1, 208.

Circa February 1846 and after. Dostoevskii, *Polnoe sobranie sochinenii*, vol. 28, bk. 2 (1985), 259.

Circa February 1846 and after. Dostoevskii, *Dnevnik pisatelia za 1876 god*, 278.

Circa February 1846 and after. Dostoevskii, *Dnevnik pisatelia za 1877 god* (Berlin: Izdatel'stvo I. P. Ladyzhnikova, 1922), 310.

Circa February 1846 and after. Dostoevskii, "Zapisnaia tetrad'," 530.

Circa February 1846 and after. Dostoevskii, "Zapisnaia tetrad'," 530–31.

Circa February 1846 and after. Dostoevskii, "Zapisnaia tetrad', 1880–1881 gg.," 672.

Circa February 1846 and after. Dostoevskii, *Dnevnik pisatelia za 1873 god*, 412–13.

Circa February 1846 and after. Dostoevskii, *Dnevnik pisatelia za 1873 god*, 218–19.

Circa February 1846 and after. Dostoevskii, *Dnevnik pisatelia za 1873 god*, 219–20.

Circa February 1846 and after. Dostoevskii, *Dnevnik pisatelia za 1873 god*, 220.

Circa February 1846 and after. Dolinin, *Dostoevskii, Pis'ma*, vol. 2, 364.

Circa February 1846 and after. Dostoevskii, *Polnoe sobranie sochinenii*, vol. 11 (1974), 73.

Circa February 1846 and after. Dostoevskii, *Polnoe sobranie sochinenii*, vol. 14 (1976), 500.

Circa February 1846 and after. Dostoevskii, *Dnevnik pisatelia za 1873 god*, 220–21.

Circa February 1846 and after. Dostoevskaia, *Vospominaniia*, 159.

Circa February 1846 and after. Dostoevskii, *Dnevnik pisatelia za 1873 god*, 221.

Circa February 1846 and after. Dolinin, *Dostoevskii, Pis'ma*, vol. 2, 364.

Circa February 1846 and after. Dostoevskii, *Polnoe sobranie sochinenii*, vol. 29, bk. 1, 260.

Circa February 1846 and after. Dolinin, *Dostoevskii. Pis'ma*, vol. 2, 364–65.

Circa February 1846 and after. Dostoevsky, *Polnoe sobranie sochinenii*, vol. 29, bk. 1, 146.

Circa February 1846 and after. Dostoevskii, *Polnoe sobranie sochinenii*, vol. 18 (1978), 127.

Circa February 1846 and after. Dostoevskii, *Polnoe sobranie sochinenii*, vol. 3 (1972), 193.

Circa February 1846 and after. Ianovskii, "Vospominaniia," 817.

Circa February 1846 and after. Turgenev, *Polnoe sobranie sochinenii. Sochineniia*, vol. 14 (1967), 52.

Circa February 1846 and after. A. Panaeva, *Vospominaniia* (Moscow: Gosudarstvennoe izdatel'stvo khudozhestvennoi literatury, 1956), 145.

Circa February 1846 and after. Ianovskii, "Vospominaniia," 817.

Circa February 1846 and after. P. Annenkov, *Literaturnye vospominaniia* (Moscow: Pravda, 1989), 259–60.

Circa February 1846 and after. Dostoevskii, *Polnoe sobranie sochinenii*, vol. 27 (1984), 198.

Circa February 1846 and after. Panaeva, *Vospominaniia*, 144–45.

Circa February 1846 and after. Dostoevskaia, *Vospominaniia*, 159.

Circa February 1846 and after. Dostoevskii, *Dnevnik pisatelia za 1873 god*, 39.

Circa February 1846 and after. Dostoevskaia, *Vospominaniia*, 60.

Circa February 1846 and after. Dostoevskaia, *Vospominaniia*, 316.

Circa February 1846 and after. L. Dostoevskaia, *Dostoevskii v izobrazhenii svoei docheri* (St. Petersburg: Andreev i sinov'ia, 1992), 45.

Circa February 1846 and after. Ianovskii, "Vospominaniia," 814.

Circa February 1846 and after. Dostoevskaia, *Vospominaniia*, 159.

Circa February 1846 and after. Dostoevskaia, *Dostoevskii*, 46.

Circa February 1846 and after. Grigorovich, *Vospominaniia*, 84–85.

Circa February 1846 and after. Panaeva, *Vospominaniia*, 144.

Circa February 1846 and after. I. Panaev, "Vospominaniia o Belinskom," *Sovremennik*, no. 1 (1860): 369.

Circa February 1846 and after. Turgenev, *Polnoe sobranie sochinenii*, vol. 14, 52.

Circa February 1846 and after. I. Panaev, "Zametki novogo poeta," *Sovremennik*, no. 12 (December 1855): 238–39.

Circa February 1846 and after. N. Nekrasov, "Kamennoe serdtse," in *Tonkii chelovek i drugie neizdannye proizvedeniia* (Moscow: Federatsiia, 1928), 231–38.

Circa February 1846 and after. Nekrasov, "Kamennoe serdtse," 238–40

Circa February 1846 and after. Nekrasov, "Kamennoe serdtse," 240–44.

Circa February 1846 and after. Nekrasov, "Kamennoe serdtse," 244–48.

Circa February 1846 and after. Nekrasov, "Kamennoe serdtse," 248–51.

Circa February 1846 and after. Nekrasov, "Kamennoe serdtse," 251–55.

Circa February 1846 and after. Nekrasov, "Kamennoe serdtse," 255–60.

Circa February 1846 and after. Nekrasov, "Kamennoe serdtse," 260–62.

Circa February 1846 and after. Nekrasov, "Kamennoe serdtse," 262–68.

Circa February 1846. Panaeva, *Vospominaniia*, 177–78.

Circa February 1846. I. Nikol'skii, *Turgenev i Dostoevskii. Istoriia odnoi vrazhdy* (Sofia: Rossisko-Bolgarskoe Knigoizdatel'stvo, 1921), 5–6.

Circa February 1846. D. Grigorovich, "Iz zapisnoi knizhki D. V. Grigorovicha," *Ezhemesiachnye literaturnye prilozheniia k "Nive,"* no. 11 (1901): 393–94.

Circa February 1846. Grigorovich, *Vospominaniia*, 139.

Circa February 1846. A. Suvorin, "Nabroski i melochi," *Novoe vremia* (May 18, 1880): 4.

Circa February 1846. M. Stasiulevich and M. Lemke, eds., *M. Stasiulevich i ego sovremenniki v ikh perepiske*, vol. 3 (St. Petersburg: M. Stasiulevich, 1912), 388.

Circa February 1846. N. Nekrasov, *Polnoe sobranie sochinenii i pisem v piatnadtsati tomakh*, vol. 4 (Leningrad: Nauka, 1982), 39.

Circa February 1846. A. Dolinin, ed., *F. M. Dostoevskii. Stat'i i materialy*, vol. 2 (Leningrad: Mysl', 1924), 387.

Circa February 1846. D. Grigorovich, "Otryvki iz zapisnoi knizhki D.V. Grigorovicha," *Niva*, no. 11 (1901): 393.

Circa February 1846. Dostoevskaia, *Dostoevskii*, 46.

Part Two

February 1846. Lanskii, "Dostoevskii," 370.

February 1846. Dostoevskaya, *Dostoevskii*, 47.

February 1, 1846. Dolinin, *Dostoevskii. Pis'ma*, vol. 1, 86–87.

February 1, 1846. Dostoevskii, *Dnevnik pistelia za 1877 god*, 456.

February 1, 1846. Belinskii, *Polnoe sobranie sochinenii*, vol. 9, 475–76.

February 1, 1846. Belinskii, *Polnoe sobranie sochinenii*, vol. 9, 493.

February 1, 1846. P. Pletnev, "Novye sochineniia," *Sovremennik*, no. 2 (1846), 273.

February 1, 1846. F. Bulgarin, "Zhurnal'naia vsiakaia vsiachina," *Severnaia pchela*, no. 27 (February 1, 1846): 107.

February 1, 1846. A. Grigoriev, *Literaturnaia kritika* (Moscow: Khudozhestvennia literatura, 1967), 459.

February 5, 1846. Ia. Grot, *Sochineniia i perepiska P.A. Pletneva*, vol. 3 (St. Petersburg: Tipografiia Imperatorskoi Akademii nauk, 1885), 570.

February 6, 1846. Belinskii, *Polnoe sobranie sochinenii*, vol. 12, 261.

February 6, 1846. K. Grot, ed., *Perepiska Ia. K. Grota s P. A. Pletnevym*, vol. 2 (St. Petersburg: Tipografiia Ministerstva putei soobshcheniia, 1896), 668–69.

February 9, 1846. Grot, ed., *Perepiska*, 671.

February 9, 1846. A. Grigoriev, "Novye knigi. Peterburgskii sbornik, izdannyi N. Nekrasovym," *Vedomosti Sankt-Peterburgskoi gorodskoi politsii*, no. 39 (February 9, 1846): 2.

February 10, 1846. Bez podpisi, "Peterburgskii sbornik, izdannyi N. Nekrasovym," *Russkii invalid* (February 10, 1846): 137–38.

February 12, 1846. Bez podpisi, "Peterburgskii sbornik, izdannyi N. Nekrasovym," *Russkii invalid* (February 12, 1846): 137.

February 15, 1846. Lanskii, "Dostoevskii," 370.

February 16, 1846. N. Barsukov, *Zhizn' i trudy M. P. Pogodina*, kn. 8 (St. Petersburg: Tipografiia M.M. Stasiulevicha, 1894), 349.

February 18, 1846. N. Iazykov, "Pis'ma N. M. Iaykova k N. V. Gogoliu," *Russkaia starina*, no. 12 (1896): 640–41.

February 19, 1846. Belinskii, *Polnoe sobranie sochinenii*, vol. 12, 265.

February 28, 1846. L. Brandt, "Russkaia literatura. Zhurnalistika," *Severnaia pchela* (February 18, 1846): 187.

February 28, 1846. L. Brandt, "Russkaia literatura. Zhurnalistika," *Severnaia pchela* (February 28, 1846): 187.

February 28, 1846. Bez podpisi, "Smes'. Literaturnye izvestiia i zametki," *Finskii vestnik*, vol. 8, pt. 5 (1846): 4.

March 1, 1846. Belinskii, *Polnoe sobranie sochinenii*, vol. 9, 543, 549, and 550–51.

March 1, 1846. Belinskii, *Polnoe sobranie sochinenii*, vol. 9, 551–52.

March 1, 1846. Belinskii, *Polnoe sobranie sochinenii*, vol. 9, 552–54.

March 1, 1846. Belinskii, *Polnoe sobranie sochinenii*, vol. 9, 554–55, and 563.

March 1, 1846. Belinskii, *Polnoe sobranie sochinenii*, vol. 9, 563–65.

March 1, 1846. Belinskii, *Polnoe sobranie sochinenii*, vol. 9, 565–66.

March 1, 1846. A. Nikitenko, "Peterburgskii sbornik, izdannyi N. Nekrasovm," *Biblioteka dlia chteniia*, no. 3, otd. 5 (1846), 18, 21, 26, and 30.

March 1, 1846. O. Senkovsky, "Literaturnaia letopis'," *Biblioteka dlia chteniia*, no. 3 (March 1846): 2–3.

March 1, 1846. L. Brandt, "Zhurnalistika," *Severnaia pchela* (March 1, 1846): 191.

March 1, 1846. L. Brandt, "Zhurnalistika," *Severnaia pchela* (March 1, 1846): 191.

March 1, 1846. A. Studitskii, "Russkie literaturnye zhurnaly za fevral' 1846-go goda," *Moskvitianin*, no. 3 (1846): 194.

March 3, 1846. S. Shevyrev, "Peterburgskii sbornik, izdannyi N. Nekrasovym," *Moskvitianin*, no. 2 (1846): 163–70.

March 3, 1846. Shevyrev, "Peterburgskii sbornik," 172–74.

March 4, 1846. K. Grot, "K perepiske N. V. Gogolia s P. A. Pletnevym. Neizdannye pis'ma 1832–1846 gg.," *Izvestiia otdeleniia russkogo iazyka i slovesnosti imperatorskoi Akademii nauk 5*, no. 1 (1900): 279.

March 9, 1846. F. Bulgarin, "Zhurnal'naia vsiakaia viachina," *Severnaia pchela*, no. 55 (March 9, 1846): 218.

March 18–21, 1846. V. Shenrok, "N. V. Gogol' i Viel'gorskie v ikh perepiske," *Vestnik Evropy*, no. 11 (1889): 105.

Circa early spring 1846. Grigorovich, *Vospominaniia*, 76.

April–May 1846 and after. Dostoevskii, *Polnoe sobranie sochinenii*, vol. 28, bk. 1, 224.

April–May 1846 and after. Dostoevskii, *Polnoe sobranie sochinenii*, vol. 28, bk. 1, 296.

April–early May 1846 and after. Ianovskii, "Vospominaniia," 796–99.

April–early May 1846 and after. Ianovskii, "Vospominaniia," 805–6.

April–early May 1846 and after. Dolinin, *F. M. Dostoevskii. Stat'i i materialy*, 380–81.

April 1, 1846. Dolinin, *F. M. Dostoevskii. Pis'ma*, vol. 1, 88.

April 1, 1846. Belinskii, *Polnoe sobranie sochinenii*, vol. 9 (1955), 612 and 650.

April 15, 1846. F. Bulgarin, "Russkaia literatura," *Severnaia pchela*, no. 81 (April 15, 1846): 522.

April 26, 1846. Dolinin, *F. M. Dostoevskii. Pis'ma*, vol. 1, 90–92.

April 30, 1846. A. Grigoriev, "Bibliograficheskaia khronika," *Finskii vestnik*, no. 9 (1846): 21 and 24–30.

May 1, 1846. Bez podpisi, "Moskovskaia letopis. Zhizn' v Moskve v aprele 1846 goda," *Moskvitianin*, no. 5 (1846): 212.

May 14, 1846. N. Gogol', *Polnoe sobranie sochinenii v semnadtsati tomakh*, vol. 13 (Moscow: Izdatel'stvo Moskovskoi Patriarchii, 2009), 319.

Circa mid-May 1846. I. Iakubovich, *Letopis' zhizni i tvorchestva F. M. Dostoevskogo v trekh tomakh*, vol. 1 (St. Petersburg: Gumanitarnoe agentstvo "Akademicheskii proekt," 1993), 117.

May 16, 1846. Dolinin, *F. M. Dostoevskii. Pis'ma*, 92–93.

After May 16, 1846. Dolinin, *F. M. Dostoevskii. Pis'ma*, 569.

After May 16, 1846. Dolinin, *F. M. Dostoevskii. Pis'ma*, 313–14.

May 24, 1846. Dostoevskii, *Polnoe sobranie sochinenii*, vol. 18, 138.

May 24, 1846. Dostoevskii, *Polnoe sobranie sochinenii*, vol. 28, 124.

June 14, 1846. Belinskii, *Polnoe sobranie sochinenii*, vol. 12, 287.

June 15, 1846. Bez podpisi, "Novosti zagranichnye," *Severnaia pchela*, no. 133 (June 15, 1846): 529.

June 24, 1846. N. Iazykov, "Pis'ma N. M. Iazykova k N. V. Gogoliu," *Russkaia starina*, no. 12 (1896): 644.

Circa July 1846 and after. M. Alekseev, ed., *Literaturnyi arkhiv. Materialy po istorii literatury i obshchestvennogo dvizheniia*, vol. 6 (Moscow: Akademiia nauk, 1961), 305.

Circa July 1846 and after. S. Derkach, "I. A. Goncharov i kruzhok Maikovykh," *Uchenye zapiski. Seriia filologicheskikh naukh* 355, no. 76 (1971): 21.

Circa July 1846 and after. A. Skabichevskii, *Literaturnye vospominaniia* (Moscow: Zemlia i fabrika, 1928), 113–15.

Circa July 1846 and after. A. Starchevskii, "Odin iz zabytkh zhurnalistov," *Istoricheskii vestinik*. no. 3 (1886): 374–76.

Circa July 1846 and after. Dolinin, *F. M. Dostoveskii. Stat'i i materialy*, 384.

July 1846. P. Bilyarskii, "Obozrenie russkikh gazet i zhurnalov za pervoe trekhmesiachie 1846 goda," *Zhurnal ministerstva narodnogo prosveshcheniia*, no. 7 (1846): 104.

July 1, 1846. V. Maykov, "Peterburgskie vershiny, opisannye Ia. Butkovym," *Otechestvennye zapiski*, no. 7 (1846): 12.

July 12, 1846. Belinskii, *Polnoe sobranie sochinenii*, vol. 12, 300–301.

August 15–18, 1846. F. Loeve, "'Die armen Leute,' Roman (In Briefen) von F. M. Dostojewski," *Sankt-Peterburgische Zeitung* (August 15–18, 1846): 737–51.

Early September 1846. K. Trutovskii, "Vospominaniia o Feodore Mikhailoviche Dostoevskom," *Russkoe obozrenie*, no. 1 (1893): 216.

September 1, 1846. V. Maykov, "Kratkoe nachertanie istorii russkoi literatury," *Otechestvennye zapiski*, no. 9 (1846): 10.

September 5, 1846. Dolinin, *F. M. Dostoevskii. Pis'ma*, vol. 1, 93–94.

September 11, 1846. Grot, ed., *Perepiska*, 882.

September 17, 1846. Dolinin, *F. M. Dostoevskii. Pis'ma*, 94–96.

September 17, 1846, and after. Grigorovich, *Vospominaniia*, 76–77.

September 17, 1846, and after. Grigorovich, *Vospominaniia*, 77–78.

September 17, 1846, and after. N. Piksanov, *Iz arkhiva F.M. Dostoevskogo. Pis'ma russkikh pisatelei* (Moscow: Gosizdat, 1923), 30.

September 17, 1846, and after. Dolinin, *F. M. Dostoevskii. Stat'i i materialy*, 382–83.

September 17, 1846, and after. V. Bervi-Flerovskii, "Petrashevskii," in *Sorokovye gody XIX veka: v memuarakh sovremennikov, dokumentakh, i khudozhestvennyikh proizvedeniiakh* (Moscow: Khudozhestvannia literatura, 1959), 191.

September 17, 1846, and after. V. Bervi-Flerovskii, "Vospominaniia," *Golos minuvshego*, no. 3 (1915): 143.

September 17, 1846, and after. V. Enisherlov, "Sem'ia moei materi," *Prometei* 13 (1983): 260.

September 17, 1846, and after. R. Poddubnaia, "Beketovskii krug v ideinykh iskaniiakh Dostoevskogo 1840 godov," *Osvobidetel'noe dvizhenie v Rossii* (Saratov) 8 (1978): 30.

Between 21 and 26, 1846. N. Nekrasov, *Polnoe sobranie sochinenii*, vol. 14, bk. 1 (1998), 58.

Part Three

October 1, 1846. E. Liatskii, ed., *Belinskii. Pis'ma*, vol. 3 (St. Petersburg: Tipografiia M. M. Stasiulevicha, 1914), 362.

October 5–8, 1846. A. Herzen, *Sobranie sochinenii v tridtsati tomakh*, vol. 22 (Moscow: Izdatel'stvo Akademiia nauk, 1961), 259.

October 7, 1846. Dolinin, *F. M. Dostoevskii. Pis'ma*, 96–98.

October 14, 1846. A. Pleshcheev, "Peterburgskaia khronika," *Russkii invalid* (October 13, 1846): 908.

Before October 16, 1846. Panaeva, *Vospominaniia*, 144.

Before October 16, 1846. Panaeva, *Vospominaniia*, 145.

Before October 16, 1846. A. Orlova, "Iz vospomaniii o semeinoi zhizni V. G. Belinskogo," in *V pol'zu golodaiushchikh. Lepta Belinskogo* (Moscow: Tipografiia D.I. In Inozemtseva, 1892), 30.

Circa October 16, 1846. I. Pavlovsky, *Souvenirs sur Tourgueneff* (Paris: A. Savine, 1887), 38–39.

Circa October 16, 1846, and after. Panaeva, *Vospominaniia*, 145–46.

After October 16, 1846. Panaeva, *Vospominaniia*, 146.

After October 16, 1846. Grigorovich, *Vospominaniia*, 90.

After October 16, 1846. Dostoevskaya, *Dostoevskii*, 46–47.

After October 16, 1846. Dostoevskii, *Polnoe sobranie sochinenii*, vol. 2 (1972), 152.

October 17, 1846. Dolinin, *F. M. Dostoevski. Pis'ma*, 98–99.

October 18, 1846. Dostoevskii, *Polnoe sobranie sochinenii*, vol. 28, bk. 1, 130.

Late October 1846. Dolinin, *F. M. Dostoevskii. Pis'ma*, 99–102.

November 1, 1846. V. Maykov, "Stikhotvoreniia Kol'tsova," *Otechestvennye zapiski*, no. 11 (1846): 21.

November 9, 1846. F. Bulgarin, "Pis'ma vechnostranstvuiushchago zhida k F. B," *Severnaia pchela*, no. 254 (November 9, 1846): 1015.

November 17, 1846. V. Kniazhin, ed., *Apollon Aleksandrovich Grigoriev. Materialy dlia biografii* (Petersburg: Izdanie Pushkinskogo Doma pri Akademii Nauk, 1917), 115–16.

November 23, 1846. F. Bulgarin, "Medintsinskaya literatura," *Severnaia pchela*, no. 265 (November 23, 1846): 1059.

November 26, 1846. Dolinin, *F. M. Dostoevskii. Pis'ma*, 102–3.

December 17, 1846. Dolinin, *F. M. Dostoevskii. Pis'ma*, 103–5.

Late 1846 and after. Ianovskii, "Vospominaniia," 799.

Late 1846 and after. Ianovskii, "Vospominaniia," 799–800.

Late 1846 and after. Ianovskii, "Vospominaniia," 802.

Late 1846 and after. Dolinin, *F. M. Dostoevskii. Pis'ma*, 394.

Late 1846 and after. S. Ianovskii, "Bolezn' F. M. Dostoevskogo," *Novoe vremia* (February 24, 1881): 1–2.

Late 1846 and after. Dolinin, *F. M. Dostoevskii, Pis'ma*, vol. 3, 23.

Late 1846 and after. Dostoevskaia, *Dostoevskii*, 49.

Late 1846 and after. G. Galagan, "Konchina i pokhorony F. M. Dostoevskogo (V pis'makh E. A. i M. A. Rykachevykh), in *Dostoevskii. Materialy i issledovaniia*, ed. V. Bazanov, vol. 1 (Leningrad: Nauka, 1974), 303.

Late 1846 and after. A. Dostoevskii, "O F. M. Dostoevskom. Pis'mo k izdatel'iu," *Novoe vremia* (February 8, 1881): 2.

Late 1846 and after. Ianovskii, "Vospominaniia," 802.

Late 1846 and after. Ianovskii, "Vospominaniia," 803.

Late 1846 and after. Ianovskii, "Vospominaniia," 812.

Late 1846 and after. Dolinin, *F. M. Dostoevskii. Pis'ma*, 395.

Late 1846 and after. Dolinin, *F. M. Dostoevskii. Stat'i i materialy*, 380–81.

Late 1846 and after. Dolinin, *F. M. Dostoevskii. Stat'i i materialy*, 381.

Late 1846 and after. Ianovskii, "Vospominaniia," 813–14.

Late 1846 and after. Dolinin, *F. M. Dostoevskii. Stat'i i materialy*, 393.

Late 1846 and after. Dolinin, *F. M. Dostoevskii. Stat'i i materialy*, 393–94.

Late 1846 and after. Ianovskii, "Vospominaniia," 802.

Circa 1847. Soloviev, "Vospominaniia," 609.

Circa 1847. Dostoevskii, *Polnoe sobranie sochinenii*, vol. 3 (1972), 208.

Circa 1847. Dostoevskaia, *Dostoevskii*, 49.

Circa 1847. Dolinin, *F. M. Dostoevskii. Pis'ma*, 257.

Circa 1847. Grigorovich, *Vospominaniia*, 75–76.

January–February 1847. Dolinin, *F. M. Dostoevskii. Pis'ma*, 105–8.

January 1847 and after. Dostoevskaya, *Dostoevskii*, 48.

January 1847 and after. Panaeva, *Vospominaniia*, 175.

After January–February 1847. Dostoevskii, *Polnoe sobranie sochinenii*, vol. 18, 70–71.

January 1, 1847. Belinskii, *Polnoe sobranie sochinenii*, vol. 10 (1956), 39–40.

January 1, 1847. Belinskii, *Polnoe sobranie sochinenii*, vol. 10, 40–41.

January 1, 1847. Belinskii, *Polnoe sobranie sochinenii*, vol. 10, 41–42.

January 1, 1847. V. Maikov, "Nechto o russkoi literature v 1846 godu," in V. Maikov, *Litereraturnaia kritika. Stat'i, retsenzii* (Leningrad: Khudozhestvennaia literatura, 1985), 179–83.

January 5, 1847. E. Guber, "Russkaia literatura v 1846 godu," *Sankt-Peterburgskie vedomosti* (January 5, 1847): 2.

February 1, 1847. Belinskii, *Polnoe sobranie sochinenii*, vol. 10, 98.

February 19, 1847. Belinskii, *Polnoe sobranie sochinenii*, vol. 12, 335–36.

February 21, 1847. K. Aksakov, "Peterburgskii sbornik, izdannyi Nekrasovym," in *Moskovskii literaturnyi i uchenyi sbornik* (Moscow: Tipografiia Semena, 1847), 29–36.

Circa March 1847 and after. Dostoevskii, *Polnoe sobranie sochinenii*, vol. 18, 138.

March 5, 1847. A. Grigoriev, "Obozrenie zhurnal'nykh iavlenii za ianvar' i fevral' tekushchago goda," *Moskovskii gorodskoi listok* (March 5, 1847): 2.

March 5, 1847. I. Goncharov, "Neizdannye pis'ma I. A. Goncharova," *Krasnyi arkhiv*, no. 2 (February 1923): 257.

March 17, 1847. A. Grigoriev, "Gogol i ego poslednaia kniga," *Moskovskii gorodskoi listok* (March 17, 1847): 250.

March 27, 1847. V. Botkin, *Literaturnaya mysl'. Al'manakh*, vol. 2 (Petrograd: Mysl', 1923), 190.

April–June 1847. Dolinin, *F. M. Dostoevskii. Pis'ma*, 113.

April–mid-May 1847. Dolinin, *F. M. Dostoevskii. Pis'ma*, 112.

April 1, 1847. I. Panaev, "Eshche neskol'ko stikhotvoreniia novogo poeta," *Sovremennik*, no. 4, otd. 4 (1847): 154–55.

April 12, 1847. F. Bulgarin, "Zhurnal'naia vsiakina vsiachina," *Severnaia pchela*, no. 84 (April 12, 1847): 322.

April 13, 1847. Dostoevskii, *Polnoe sobranie sochinenii*, vol. 18, 113–14.

April 21, 1847. L. Brandt, "Russkaia literatura," *Severnaia pchela*, no. 88 (April 21, 1847): 550–51.

April 27, 1847. F. Dostoevskii, *Polnoe sobranie khudozhestyennykh proizvedenii v tridnadtasti tomakh*, vol. 13 (Leningrad: Gosudarstevennoe izdatel'stvo, 1930), 9.

April 27, 1847. Dostoevskii, *Polnoe sobranie khudozhestyennykh proizvedenii*, 11.

April 27, 1847. Dostoevskii, *Polnoe sobranie khudozhestyennykh proizvedenii*, 15.

May 1847. Lanskii, "Dostoevskii," 372.

May 1, 1847. Belinskii, *Polnoe sobranie sochinenii*, vol. 10, 180 and 186.

Circa May 7, 1847. Dolinin, *F. M. Dostoevskii. Pis'ma*, 108–9.

May 30, 1847. A. Grigoriev, "Obozrenie za aprel'," *Moskovskii gorodskoi listok* (May 30, 1847): 465.

June 1847. Belinskii, *Polnoe sobranie sochinenii*, vol. 10, 206.

June 1, 1847. Dostoevskii, *Polnoe sobranie khudozhestyennykh proizvedenii*, 21–23.

June 1, 1847. Dostoevskii, *Polnoe sobranie khudozhestyennykh proizvedenii*, 23.

June 1, 1847. Dostoevskii, *Polnoe sobranie khudozhestyennykh proizvedenii*, 24–26.

June 13, 1847. Lanskii, "Dostoevskii," 372.

June 15, 1847. Dostoevskii, *Polnoe sobranie khudozhestyennykh proizvedenii*, 27–31.

June 17, 1847. A. Grigoriev, "Moskovskii literaturnyi i uchenyi sbornik na 1847 g.," *Moskovskii gorodskoi listok* (June 17, 1847): 524.

Summer 1847. M. Yazykov, "Pis'mo k redaktsiiu," *Novoe vremia* (March 2, 1881): 2.

July 7, 1847. Ianovskii, "Bolezn' F. M. Dostoevskogo," 1–2.

July 7, 1847. Ianovskii, "Vospominaniia," 800–801.

Mid-July 1847. Ianovskii, "Vospominaniia," 801–2.

After July 15, 1847. Dolinin, *F. M. Dostoevskii. Stat'i i materialy*, 383–84.

After July 15, 1847. Grigorovich, *Vospominaniia*, 100.

After July 15, 1847. Ianovskii, "Vospominaniia," 814.

After July 15, 1847. Dostoevskaia, *Vospominaniia*, 60.

July 25, 1847. Nekrasov, *Polnoe sobranie sochinenii*, vol. 14, bk. 1 (1998), 75.

August 1847. I. Goncharov, "V. N. Maikov (Nekrolog)," *Otechestvennye zapiski*, no. 8 (1847): 104–8.

August 15, 1847. Alexei Pleshcheev, "Fel'ton, Peterburgskaia khronika," *Russkii invalid*, no. 181 (August 15, 1847): 2.

August 16, 1847. M. Dostoevskii, "Pis'ma M. M. Dostoevskogo k F. M. Dostoevskomu," in *Iskusstvo*, vol. 3, kn. 1 (1927), 107–8.

Late August–early September 1847. F. Dostoevskii, *Polnoe sobranie sochinenii*, vol. 28, bk. 1, 142–43.

September 9, 1847. Dolinin, *F. M. Dostoevskii. Pis'ma*, vol. 1, 110–12.

September 13, 1847. Dostoevskii, "Pis'ma M. M. Dostoevskogo," 108–9.

Fall 1847 and after. Dostoevskii, *Polnoe sobranie sochinenii*, vol. 18, 139–40.

Fall 1847 and after. Dostoevskaya, *Dostoevskii*, 53.

Fall 1847 and after. Dostoevskaya, *Dostoevskii*, 53.

Circa early October 1847. Ianovskii, "Vospominaniia," 811.

October 1847 and after. Dostoevskaia, *Dostoevskii*, 49.

October 1, 1847. M. Volotskoi, *Khronika roda Dostoevskogo, 1506–1933* (Moscow: Sever, 1933), 173.

November 4–8, 1847. Belinskii, *Polnoe sobranie sochinenii*, vol. 12, 421.

November 20–December 2, 1847. Belinskii, *Polnoe sobranie sochinenii*, vol. 12, 430.

Index

Printed in the USA
CPSIA information can be obtained
at www.ICGtesting.com
LVHW091644250823
756268LV00025B/624/J

RECONCILIATION BY STEALTH

RECONCILIATION BY STEALTH

How People Talk about War Crimes

Denisa Kostovicova

CORNELL UNIVERSITY PRESS   **ITHACA AND LONDON**

First published 2023 by Cornell University Press

Library of Congress Cataloging-in-Publication Data

Names: Kostovicova, Denisa, author.
Title: Reconciliation by stealth : how people talk about war crimes /
    Denisa Kostovicova.
Description: Ithaca, [New York] : Cornell University Press, 2023. |
    Includes bibliographical references and index.
Identifiers: LCCN 2022040456 (print) | LCCN 2022040457 (ebook) |
    ISBN 9781501769030 (hardcover) | ISBN 9781501769054 (epub) |
    ISBN 9781501769047 (pdf)
Subjects: LCSH: Regionalna komisija za utvđivanje činjenica o ratnim zločinima
    i drugim teškim kršenjima ljudskih prava na području nekadašnje SFRJ. |
    Reconciliation—Former Yugoslav republics. | Yugoslav War, 1991–1995—Peace. |
    War crimes—Former Yugoslav republics. | Transitional justice—Former
    Yugoslav republics. | Ethnic conflict—Former Yugoslav republics. |
    Former Yugoslav republics—Ethnic relations.
Classification: LCC DR1313.7.P43 K67 2023 (print) | LCC DR1313.7.P43 (ebook) |
    DDC 949.703—dc23/eng/20221206
LC record available at https://lccn.loc.gov/2022040456
LC ebook record available at https://lccn.loc.gov/2022040457

To those seeking justice after violence and to those helping them with their search

Contents

Acknowledgments

For a long time I had a strong urge to study whether civil communication in discussions about the painful legacy of violence is possible in the Balkans. Throughout the 1990s and early 2000s, I witnessed and researched violence in the region, which is when disagreements about the past and the future took a toll on civil communication between ethnic groups. After the violence ended, the war of words continued—in the newspapers, on TV, and later on social media. Justice for war crimes has become one of the most contentious issues in the countries that emerged from the former Yugoslavia's bloody breakup. The voices of those who denied or minimized wrongdoing prevailed. These dominant public discourses seemed to foreclose any possibility of reconciliation—I wanted to test that.

This is how I got interested in the multiethnic civil society initiative advocating for the Regional Commission for Establishing the Facts about War Crimes and Other Gross Violations of Human Rights Committed on the Territory of the Former Yugoslavia from January 1, 1991 to December 31, 2001 (RECOM), that is the subject of this book. I was drawn particularly to studying transcripts of the discussions that RECOM organized. These discussions involved people from all ethnic groups in the region, who were brought together to help design a bespoke mechanism to address their justice needs. To a researcher, the transcripts of these discussions, which RECOM made publicly available, provided an invaluable source of original data on real-life interactions in a postconflict zone. The transcripts recorded every word spoken in the RECOM consultations, amounting to millions of words—each line deserving of close attention. I am deeply grateful to the Leverhulme Trust for awarding me a Research Fellowship, which allowed me to take time out of my daily teaching and administrative duties at the London School of Economics and Political Science (LSE) and to dedicate my time to research. I immersed myself in the coding of the RECOM corpus for nearly eight months, traveling to conduct fieldwork and analyzing the data. I am also indebted to the Arts and Humanities Research Council for the grant "Art and Reconciliation: Conflict, Culture and Community," awarded jointly to the LSE, King's College London, and the University of the Arts London. This support allowed me to press on with fieldwork, analysis, and writing. In addition, I am grateful for the support I received for methods training, travel, and research support at different stages of this book from LSE's Department of Government and, especially, from the European Institute.

I am indebted to colleagues who recognized the value of the contribution I strove to make with my research. I am especially grateful to James Gow for his support over the years, and for his incisive comments and useful suggestions. I also thank Helmut Anheier, John Gledhill, and Anne Phillips for their support and advice. I received valuable guidance when I was designing my empirical strategy. On the quantitative side of this research, I am thankful to André Bächtiger and Dominik Hangartner for fielding my questions about measuring the deliberative quality of discourse. On the qualitative side, I am grateful to Liz Stokoe, who connected me with the Discourse and Rhetoric Group at the University of Loughborough. I was inspired by my exchanges with their research community and benefited greatly from the training by Paul Drew and John Heritage in ethnomethodological and interactional approaches to the study of discourse. These colleagues opened my eyes to new ways of analyzing discourse and interactions. I am particularly grateful to Paul Drew for taking a keen interest in my research and for his useful insights.

I presented various parts of this book at many professional conferences: Association for the Study of Nationalities World Convention (New York); American Political Science Association Annual Meeting (Boston); Annual Conference of the Historical Dialogues, Justice, and Memory Network (Amsterdam); British International Studies Annual Conferences (Edinburgh, London, and Brighton); European Political Science Association Conference (Vienna); Central and East European International Studies Association-International Studies Association ISA Joint International Conference (Belgrade); Conflict Research Society Annual Conferences (Birmingham and Oxford); International Studies Association Annual Convention (Atlanta); Political Studies Association Political Methodology Group Annual Conference (University of Essex); WARM Festival (Sarajevo), and others. I thank the many discussants and audience members who asked questions and offered suggestions. Their and my colleagues' comments on various drafts and parts of the manuscript were immensely helpful to me as I refined and developed the arguments of this book. I thank Stefano Bianchini, Vesna Bojičić-Dželilović, Christine Chinkin, Marsha Henry, Anna Oltman, Mareike Schomerus, Eric Wiebelhaus-Brahm, and Reed Wood for their generous and constructive feedback. Collaboration within the "Arts and Reconciliation" project provided ample opportunity for critical and friendly exchanges. For these, I thank Tiffany Fairey, James Gow, Rachel Kerr, Paul Lowe, Milena Michalski, Nela Milić, Henry Redwood, and Ivor Sokolić. My colleagues at the European Institute made for an attentive audience. I am grateful for their intellectual curiosity, questions, and observations, including those from skeptics of deliberation.

Here I am particularly thankful to Chris Anderson, Simon Glendinning, Abby Innes, Waltraud Schelkle, and Jonathan White.

Reflexivity in the research and writing process is integral to projects addressing sensitive topics. I benefited a great deal from lively discussions with Eleanor Knott about questions related to research ethics. Comments and questions about the book by Vesna Bojičić-Dželilović and Mary Martin encouraged me to press on. Conversations and research collaborations with Mary Kaldor focused on the ambiguous role of civil society during conflict and in its aftermath were formative for my work. They revealed to me the particular significance of empirical evidence for the claims in this field, which is not only normatively contested but also highly politicized.

My engagement with policy makers helped guide my thinking about the practical challenges involving public policy approaches to reconciliation in divided postconflict societies. I thank my interlocutors working on the Balkans and on global postconflict reconstruction challenges from the European Union, the United Nations (the Department of Political and Peacebuilding Affairs and the United Nations Development Programme), and the British Parliament. Specifically, I learned from engagements with policy makers within the scope of the Balkans inquiry by the House of Lords Select Committee on International Relations. Numerous discussions with research analysts from the Foreign, Commonwealth and Development Office were especially useful.

In this book I explore ideas that were previously published in the articles "Seeking Justice in a Divided Region: Text Analysis of a Regional Civil Society Initiative in the Balkans," *International Journal of Transitional Justice* 11, no. 1 (2017): 154–75, https://doi.org/10.1093/ijtj/ijw023, and "Gender, Justice and Deliberation: Why Women Don't Influence Peacemaking," *International Studies Quarterly* 65, no. 2 (2021): 263–76, https://doi.org/10.1093/isq/sqab003, the latter of which I coauthored with Tom Paskhalis. I thank Oxford University Press for permission to reuse this material.

Above all, I owe special thanks to all participants in this research. Over the years I have benefited from extensive engagement with members of the RECOM Coalition and people who took part in the RECOM process as nonmembers. I thank them for the openness with which they met my questions, and for their answers in which they often revisited their difficult experiences. I am also grateful to them for tolerating my relentless focus on my research questions. I learned from my research participants—whom I consider collaborators in this research endeavor—in interviews and focus groups, during many informal conversations before and after these research interactions, and on the sidelines of RECOM's gatherings. I built my arguments on their insights, but the claims I make and responsibility for them are solely mine. Although I owe my gratitude equally to all who engaged with me, even briefly, here I single out by name Nataša Kandić and Vesna Teršelić. They have been generous with their views, insights, and self-criticism. More than that, it is they who sparked my interest, back in the early 2000s before RECOM was created, in what can happen when civil society activists recognize the necessity of connecting across borders to pursue justice for all victims.

I have others to thank as well, and for more than just their insights, though those on their own have been crucial to this book. From comments and book suggestions to recommendations for a venue for focus groups in different countries, the help I received from Nora Ahmetaj, Jelena Bjelica, Bekim Blakaj, Yllka Buzhala, Venera Çoçaj, Dženana Karup Druško, Orli Fridman, Eugen Jakovčić, Besa Kabashi, Nikola Mokrović, Ian O'Flynn, Vesna Popovski, Rebeka Qena, Tolga Sinmazdemir, Ellie Smith, and Ivor Sokolić was indispensable. I am indebted to Lush Krasniqi for his permission to start this book by recounting his search for justice. His and others' steely determination in pursuit of justice deeply impressed me. It is to them and those helping them in their pursuit, especially their civil society supporters, who risk a great deal to battle injustice, to whom I dedicate this book.

I am grateful for assistance with empirical analysis of deliberative quality to Helen Addison and to Tom Paskhalis for initial explorations. I am grateful to Ivona Lađevac, Aleksandra Filipović, and, in particular, to the late Svetlana Đurđević-Lukić for their assistance with various tasks that helped me transform the RECOM transcripts into data. I thank Aaron Glasserman for his methodical edits of the manuscript, and for his incisive questions about my arguments. I also thank Melina Ackermann for her assistance with the formatting.

Finally, I greatly appreciate support from the team at Cornell University Press. I am indebted to senior editor Jim Lance for supporting this book. I am grateful to him and Clare Jones for their patience and their guidance through the publication process. Pointed critique, insightful questions, and constructive suggestions by editors at the press and reviewers helped me better contextualize my argument and the wider message of this work. I am also grateful to Mary Kate Murphy, Irina Burns, Karen M. Laun, and Mia Renaud for their meticulous work and their professionalism in the production phase of this book.

I was not alone on this journey of research and writing. I especially thank Dave for his unwavering support, his probing engagement with my ideas and their execution, as the book became a part of our daily conversations, and, as importantly, for holding the fort when I was away. Our children's offers to help and curiosity about my work, even when too little to understand, have spurred me on all along. I am also thankful to them for not reproaching me for missing those important school plays and sports games because of fieldwork. I am grateful to my parents-in-law, Angela and Robert, and to my parents and my brother, for their keen interest in my work and their generous help when needed, and especially to my mother for her support and for teaching me perseverance and compassion.

Note on Transliteration

All names of places in the main text are in their anglicized form. All personal names in the main text are spelled as in the original language. All place names and personal names in the notes and the bibliography are as they appear in original references.

RECONCILIATION BY STEALTH

RECONCILIATION THROUGH PUBLIC COMMUNICATION

> **All around me I can see people who used to look at each other across a barrel of a gun. Now they are sitting together and discussing what needs to be done so that we can move forward.**
>
> —Participant in the RECOM consultation in Macedonia, December 18, 2010

> **We saw the exit out of the Balkan darkness.**
>
> —Participant in RECOM consultations from Montenegro, September 2, 2016

Shoes were all Lush Krasniqi found at the site where his two brothers and an uncle were killed.[1] The mass grave next to a pile of shoes belonging to them and other victims was empty. Lush's relatives were among over 350 Albanian civilians—men, women, and children—who perished at the hands of Serbian security forces in a single armed operation in the villages of western Kosovo in the spring of 1999.[2] Lush, a primary school teacher, escaped with his life but was expelled by Serbian forces from his village. After the North Atlantic Treaty Organization (NATO) military operation ended the Kosovo war, he returned home and embarked on a long search for the bodies of his relatives and for justice. The remains of his brothers and his uncle were eventually found in a secondary mass grave, hundreds of miles away from their Kosovo village where they were killed, on the grounds of a special police training center near Serbia's capital, Belgrade.[3]

To avoid being brought to justice for war crimes, Serbs organized a systematic cover-up of their atrocities committed during the 1998–99 Kosovo war that took over 10,000 lives, the vast majority of them Albanian.[4] They used diggers to excavate the bodies of Albanian victims from mass graves in Kosovo. Heaps of bodies, body parts, and personal belongings were then transported beyond Kosovo's borders. They were reburied in secondary mass graves in two locations not far from Belgrade, like the bodies of Lush's relatives.

A Serbian fisherman discovered the cover-up while fighting was still going on in Kosovo in the spring of 1999. He noticed a freezer truck in the River Danube, unaware that it contained the bodies of Albanian victims.[5] This discovery remained secret until the ousting of Serbia's strongman leader, Slobodan

Milošević, in the autumn of 2000. His nationalist policies stoked ethnic tensions, leading to the violent dissolution of the former Yugoslavia and a series of conflicts in the Balkan region in the 1990s and early 2000s, including in Kosovo.[6] A few months after Milošević's fall, gruesome details of the gravest crimes Serbs committed against Albanians in Kosovo and of the extent of their cover-up began to emerge.[7] A Serbian journalist, an author of an exclusive report on the cover-up, commented on the power of disclosed facts about the war crimes: "the problem with the dead is that they can shout very loudly and demand justice."[8] Lush was eventually able to identify his relatives and return their bodies home. Along with other Kosovo Albanian victims, they were given a dignified burial in their local village in 2005.[9]

In his search for justice for his relatives, Lush Krasniqi joined a multiethnic transitional justice initiative led by civil society in the Balkans. It is known by its acronym RECOM, which stands for its goal of the creation of an official record of all victims of the conflicts surrounding the breakup of the former Yugoslavia: the Regional Commission for Establishing the Facts about War Crimes and Other Gross Violations of Human Rights Committed on the Territory of the Former Yugoslavia from January 1, 1991 to December 31, 2001. RECOM's restorative, victim-oriented approach to transitional justice was motivated by weaknesses in addressing past wrongs through trials.

Justice pursued in the trial chambers of the International Criminal Tribunal for the Former Yugoslavia in The Hague (ICTY) left many victims across the region unsatisfied.[10] Despite the evidence uncovered by ICTY, all ethnic groups in the Balkans continued to emphasize and often exaggerate war crimes committed by the other side(s) while minimizing their wrongdoing. Empathy remained reserved for victims belonging to one's own ethnic group, while the suffering of victims from other ethnic groups was denied or, at best, contested.[11] RECOM's mission was driven by a need to acknowledge the suffering of all victims in the region, regardless of their ethnic identity.

There was no sense of justice for victims in Lush's family, even after ICTY found some Serbian military and police officers guilty of war crimes in Kosovo. Dozens of other members of Serbian security forces whose criminal involvement was alleged during the trial evaded accountability.[12] Lush told me that even the national authorities in Kosovo turned a deaf ear to his pleas to restore his relatives' dignity by preserving their personal effects and their memory.[13] With official avenues to justice closed, Lush turned to a civil society-led, justice-seeking process that involved people from all ethnic groups impacted by Balkan conflicts. Participants came together as representatives of various civil society groups, associations, and nongovernmental organizations (NGOs), or as individuals: human rights activists, lawyers, prosecutors, journalists, youth, and above all, victims and family members of the missing and the killed, like Lush Krasniqi. RECOM's regional approach to transitional justice was also uniquely tailored to the needs of victims affected by the cross-border violence in the region.[14] RECOM's regional fact-finding was a response to the regional dynamics of the Balkan conflicts, where fighters crossed borders to commit atrocities, people fled across borders in search of safety, and perpetrators transferred victims' remains, as was the case with the bodies of Lush's relatives, to evade accountability.

RECOM's mission crystallized through a unique regional process of public consultations from 2006 to 2011. This interethnic, civil society-led process aimed to identify an appropriate mechanism for addressing the violent past. It spawned an initiative to create a regional record of all victims.[15] The legitimacy of this strategy rested on the perceived credibility of facts, and their ability to help heal divisions in the region.[16] Eventually, the consultation process resulted in the adoption of the Draft Statute of the regional fact-finding commission. Some 6,000 people from all ethnic groups involved in the wars of Yugoslavia's dissolution took part in these discussions, which were organized at regional, national, and local levels in all former Yugoslav states.[17]

Civil society activists then sought to gain support from the leaderships of the post-Yugoslav states for the fact-finding commission, envisioned as an interstate body. Official state participation was deemed essential to bestowing legitimacy on the regional record of war dead. Soon, however, it became clear that support from post-Yugoslav states would not be forthcoming.[18] RECOM turned to the European Union (EU) for help. The EU endorsed RECOM's fact-based, victim-oriented approach to reconciliation in the region, but it too withheld strong political support. The founding of this interstate, regional fact-finding commission is still out of reach.

It is not surprising then that some scholars have seen in RECOM evidence of the failure of transitional justice and reconciliation in the Balkans, focusing on RECOM's inability to reach its goal of establishing the regional fact-finding commission. They have explained the failure of this grassroots justice-seeking effort as being a result of the imposition of a global norm of transitional justice and associated human rights language, which alienates local victim communities. Others have dismissed the need for regional justice-seeking altogether, or prioritized a national over a regional approach to addressing past wrongs.[19] An appraisal of the RECOM initiative as a failure fits neatly into the dominant research agenda in the field of transitional justice centered on the inability of transitional justice efforts to bring about either justice or reconciliation.

From the sidelines of the RECOM regional meetings, I listened to how people engaged with each other across ethnic lines. On one occasion, two veterans who had fought on opposing sides in the Bosnian war sat behind me in the audience.

They conversed quietly, leaning closely into each other to avoid disturbing the proceedings. I repeatedly heard from people who participated in the RECOM consultations how transformative it had been for them to engage with people from adversary ethnic groups in search of justice for past wrongs. For many, it was their first experience of talking across ethnic lines after the war. One woman described what took place in the consultations as "revolutionary."[20] I found scholarly assessments of the RECOM process a failure to be wide of the mark. Above all, they missed how the RECOM consultations had repaired torn interethnic relations.[21] The contentious issue of justice for war crimes discussed by people taking part in the RECOM consultations could have divided people further into already polarized ethnic groups. However, people engaged across ethnic lines, discussed their differences, and agreed on a transitional justice strategy. How they engaged with each other arguably constitutes one form of reconciliation.

This book relies on mixed method research, including the analysis of a new dataset I created by coding a large multilanguage corpus comprising the original transcripts of over half a million words of RECOM consultations and extensive fieldwork in five Balkan countries.[22] I systematically study how people talk about war crimes and advance the concept of *reconciliation by stealth*.[23] Reconciliation through public engagement with former adversaries has been overlooked because scholars have focused on what people say when they discuss past wrongs. This book is motivated by a need to understand and explain how the pursuit of transitional justice can deliver on its normative goal of advancing peace by promoting reconciliation.

Argument in Brief

In this book I employ the concept of reconciliation by stealth to explain the repair of interethnic relations. The concept denotes that reconciliation can occur but remain undetected by scholars because of their theoretical and methodological choices. Anchoring the concept of reconciliation in mutuality, which refers to norms of civility and recognition in public communication, this book directs attention to features of discourse in transitional justice consultations involving former adversaries. People's sense of ethnic identity is heightened after a conflict. I focus on how people enact their ethnic identities in interethnic interactions and show that reconciliation occurs through the combination of deliberative rationality and discursive solidarity.

Deliberative rationality, which refers to upholding deliberative virtues of equality, reason-giving, respect, common good orientation, and reciprocity in interethnic communication, can help advance the search for justice in postconflict societies. On its own, however, it cannot achieve reconciliation. To reconcile, people also need to show that their moral horizons, once narrowed by conflict, have expanded beyond a commitment to their own ethnic group. Reconciliation requires discursive solidarity, which entails granting recognition and dignity to members of adversary ethnic groups, and which we can infer from how people enact their identities during deliberation.

Using mixed methods research, including multicountry fieldwork in the Balkans and quantitative content analysis of the transcripts of real-world discussions about war crimes across ethnic lines, I show that a sense of difference along the ethnic identity axis figures prominently despite evidence of high quality of deliberation. If ethnicity forms a line of division in postconflict societies, how can deliberation about the legacy of interethnic violence promote reconciliation? Adopting an ethical perspective, I demonstrate that people enact their ethnic identity in ways conducive to the emergence of solidary bonds across ethnic lines. These discursive identity practices offset divisive identity politics and make way for reconciliation during deliberation about war crimes.

The evidence of reconciliation by stealth advances the study of deliberation in divided societies by demonstrating how identities matter during interethnic deliberation. This research connects with efforts focused on identifying and theorizing processes, places, and agents that can contribute to what Roger Mac Ginty calls "strong everyday peace."[24] As Joanna Quinn points out, thickening transitional justice by cultivating an understanding of the experiences of the Other in conflict is an integral part of peace and reconciliation.[25] By quantifying discourse in transitional justice, this book also adds to empirical efforts to measure the quality of peace from the perspective of citizens in postconflict contexts.[26] Lastly, reconciliation by stealth has implications for practitioners dedicated to assisting postconflict recovery of societies afflicted by mass atrocity. These lessons emerge after refocusing our efforts to understand how transitional justice can deliver on its normative goals.

Reversing the Puzzle in Transitional Justice

Transitional justice has developed as a distinctly normative field of study and practice. It rests on the foundational assumption that "countries should initiate a response to mass violence and repression to promote societal rebuilding."[27] The pursuit of justice in response to mass violence and brutality has become normalized.[28] The response encompasses legal instruments such as international, domestic, and hybrid war crimes trials, nonlegal restorative mechanisms embodied by truth commissions or reparations, as well as symbolic forms such as memorialization and artistic practice. Transitional justice is an emancipatory concept. The consensus that "societies must explicitly address their legacies of violence" in order to transition to democracy applies to states and societies transitioning from an illiberal regime to democracy and those emerging from war.[29] This "determined connection related to the normative goal[s]" has been the one constant in the study of postauthoritarian and postcommunist transitions, on the one hand, and postconflict transitions, on the other.[30]

Along the way, the study of postconflict justice as a form of peacebuilding has emerged as a subfield. This development recognizes that "the practical dilemmas actors face in peacebuilding can be quite different from those involved in the instauration of democratic citizenship and the transformation of an abusive state security apparatus."[31] Conceptualizing justice as integral to peace draws attention to the complexity of the postconflict context within which justice is pursued.[32] The postconflict environment is replete with political, economic, and social dynamics that can derail the pursuit of transitional justice and undermine its normative aspirations.

International and domestic war crimes trials, truth commissions, and traditional instruments of justice are often used to promote narrow political interests and marginalize victims. The discourse of division overtakes discourse of reconciliation, and further traumatization of victims takes the place of healing. What is intended to be transitional justice ends up being "transitional injustice."[33] Paradoxically, injustice in this sense is not a consequence of the lack of transitional justice practices. Rather, it results from the pursuit of transitional justice. Scholarly preoccupation with unmet normative expectations now defines the agenda in the field of transitional justice that has grown into a vibrant, multifaceted, and multidisciplinary research program.

This research agenda has also revealed a gap in our knowledge. Scholarship with various disciplinary viewpoints has enhanced our understanding of how the pursuit of postconflict justice through different mechanisms further antagonizes ethnic groups previously involved in a conflict and stymies postconflict reconciliation. By contrast, our grasp of how interethnic reconciliation can be achieved remains more limited. This book reverses the puzzle focused on unintended consequences of transitional justice and asks how a transitional justice process can promote reconciliation. The answer hinges on sharpening our conceptual and methodological tools to refine our evaluation of transitional justice and its effects in postconflict societies.[34] This endeavor starts with specifying what in this book is meant by reconciliation.

Reconciliation: Definition and Operationalization

Reconciliation marks the fulfillment of normative aspirations of postconflict transitional justice.[35] It commonly denotes overcoming past wrongs and the prospects for life in a future without violence. As a relational concept, reconciliation is invested with the capacity for change in the engagement with former adversaries on a journey from war to peace.[36] However, whether reconciliation should merely encompass behavioral change when interethnic contact becomes routinely nonviolent, or requires a change of a moral outlook toward wrongdoers, is a matter of debate. Although there is no resolution about the meaning of reconciliation, we have gained clarity about the lines of scholarly divisions on how to conceptualize reconciliation. This is helpful when it comes to making and justifying conceptual and methodological choices in our study of reconciliation.

Debates on reconciliation are framed by dichotomies that concern its breath, nature, and locus. Trudy Govier puts a range of possible conceptualizations of reconciliation on a spectrum. One end is characterized by emotional richness and the "thickness" of the concept, which incorporates notions of healing and forgiveness. At the other, "thinner" end of the spectrum, focus shifts from attitudes and feelings to institutional and behavioral factors related to institution-building and nonviolent coexistence.[37] Recognition of the values requisite for reconciliation has broadened discussions to include the role of remorse, repentance, and mercy in the process of reckoning with one's own wrongdoing, while the religious underpinnings of these attitudes have prompted debates about the role of religion in reconciliation.[38] Scholars are divided over whether to understand reconciliation as a process or an end-state. Reconciliation as a process assumes a series of steps that will eventually lead to a conclusion, whereas reconciliation as an outcome presupposes "the stage at which the relationship in question has been repaired."[39] Lastly, from the perspective of those harmed by violence, reconciliation as justice "aims to bring repair to persons and relationships that political injustices have wounded."[40] Another point of contention is whether reconciliation obtains at the individual or collective level.[41] This raises additional questions about whether the concept of reconciliation can be transposed from one level to another.[42] The matter is complicated by the recognition that reconciliation encompasses both intergroup and intragroup processes, and that these occur both at a community and institutional level.[43]

Scholars have bemoaned the lack of definitional and conceptual clarity, both for the theory and the practice of reconciliation. Different operationalizations of reconciliation have resulted in its different evaluations in societies that have suffered gross human rights violations.[44] These, in turn, have produced different understandings of obstacles and paths to reconciliation. Contested understandings of reconciliation by local actors in postconflict environments have further complicated the task of supporting reconciliation as a part of peacebuilding.[45] Given the lack of a consensus on the concept of reconciliation, how can the study of reconciliation be advanced? Vigorous debate in the extant scholarship

on reconciliation points to two needs: one is for a rigorous definition and operationalization of the concept of reconciliation; the other is to extend the evidence
base for claims about the effectiveness of transitional justice and apply appropriate methods to capture these effects.

How should scholars deal with the multiple definitions of reconciliation?
Should one definition be adopted over all others? I propose that it is counterpro-
ductive to do so when investigating a concept that takes shape in diverse political,
social, and cultural contexts as a response to various manifestations of violence
and its consequences. Rather than insisting on *the* concept of reconciliation,
I approach the task in this book by studying *a* conceptualization of reconciliation. To define reconciliation, I take as my starting point Jens Meierhenrich's
observation that "the problem of conceptualization has been neglected in the
study of reconciliation—to the detriment of theory and practice." Although there
is no single prescribed way to go about conceptualization, conceptual rigor is
paramount. Conceptual ambiguity has operational consequences that, in turn,
affect the measurement of reconciliation.[46]

This book grounds the concept of reconciliation in the principle of mutuality
in public communication. Understanding reconciliation as a particular kind of
public communication requires us to distinguish the concept from mere negative
peace, which refers to nothing more than the cessation of violence.[47] Reconciliation embodies Christian Davenport's idea of peace as mutuality, unlike conflict
conceptualized as the state of being in opposition.[48] Furthermore, communication is by definition interactive. Reconciliation rooted in mutuality in public
communication departs from minimalist perspectives that equate reconciliation
with nonlethal coexistence.

Communication must be more than simply an exchange of views in order
to be reconciliatory. Overcoming interethnic conflict, Donald Ellis points out,
requires arguing cooperatively rather than "oppositionally," which refers to
"a decision to be more adaptive to others and privilege argumentative practices
that show concern for satisfactory conclusions based in both interests."[49] From
this perspective, the principle of mutuality in which I ground the concept of
reconciliation requires "complex reasoning and important concessions." Such
communication guards against polarization and facilitates acknowledgment of
wrongdoing.[50]

When grounded in mutuality, reconciliation involves particular values associated with its "thicker" meaning. According to Daniel Philpott, "restoring the
persons and relationships wounded by political injustices requires a counter-
communication that nullifies this injustice and recognizes the dignity of the
wounded in the eyes of the political order."[51] Although this ethical requirement
falls short of demanding forgiveness and apology, it is conditional on reversing

the diminishing of a person by recognizing that "legitimacy may lie in more than one's own perspective."[52] Accordingly, healing can be understood as "the mutual respect and tolerance for fellow citizens who together deliberated and decided on the common good," which is a "tremendous accomplishment" in a divided postconflict society.[53]

Ultimately, reconciliation through public communication highlights the role of language in peacebuilding as mutuality-building, whereas "situations of mutuality put forward constant references to a shared sense of identity and a common mission."[54] Achievement of national unity in a postconflict society may be a utopian goal. As Louis Kriesberg notes, "reconciliation is never total, never including all members of antagonistic parties, not including every dimension of reconciliation completely, nor being fully reciprocal between parties."[55] Recognizing that the process of reconciliation is incomplete does not lessen its significance for peacebuilding. It still represents "a radical way of confronting the past."[56] A change in communication between former antagonists from negative to positive indicates a shift toward mutuality, and thus toward reconciliation as it is conceptualized in this book. Grounded in mutuality, the concept of reconciliation in this book is operationalized as deliberation.[57]

To explain reconciliation by analyzing how people talk about war crimes, I use the theory of deliberative democracy and extend its existing applications to divided societies. Transitional justice as a field of study without a unified theory has thrived by borrowing theories from related fields.[58] Such an eclectic approach to theory-building in transitional justice is appropriate for this multidisciplinary field. It has resulted in a great theoretical breadth of inquiry of transitional justice and its effects in postconflict societies. However, borrowing from cognate fields to study transitional justice has also had its pitfalls, including the descriptive use of the theory of deliberative democracy.

Scholars of peacebuilding have embraced the theory of deliberative democracy to envision reconstruction of societies divided by conflict. Specifically, they have put forth a deliberative conception of justice to address the divisive past and reconstruct postconflict societies.[59] These scholars have introduced the concept of democratic deliberation into the field of transitional justice and peacebuilding because of their faith in deliberative virtues: rational justification, reciprocity, respect, equality, and interest in the common good that overcomes self-interest. These normative cornerstones of deliberation, it is argued, promote societal healing and interethnic reconciliation. Yet, when applying a deliberative perspective to transitional justice, scholars have dropped these deliberative standards from the analysis.[60] The concept of deliberation to date has been used merely descriptively in the field of transitional justice.

Even when scholars have referred to deliberation over transitional justice, they have actually studied debates about transitional justice. A debate in this context is nondialogical communication. It is an exchange of monologues, where one side defends its positions, and the other attacks them. Debates do not primarily aim to change the preferences of interlocutors, even though they can influence the views of those listening to them.[61] If, as James Fearon points out, "deliberative" is taken to mean "that more people should be brought into a richer conversation about public policy and politics ... the term then becomes merely a site for fighting over what should be done and why."[62] The descriptive use of the concept of deliberation in transitional justice and peacebuilding has been consequential theoretically and empirically.

When using the concept of deliberation descriptively, scholars have shown that discourses about justice for past abuse are contested.[63] Robust debates that expose different views on redress for past wrongs are important in the recovery from war to peace. There is nothing wrong with arguing, Fearon adds. However, this sort of communication is not deliberation, because, he reminds us, deliberation is "a particular sort of discussion—one that involves the careful and serious weighing of reasons for and against some proposition."[64] Consequently, transitional justice scholars have not been able to show whether postconflict societies can discuss past wrongs deliberatively nor to assess empirically whether deliberation can lead to reconciliation. They have deployed the theory of democratic deliberation but slipped onto the well-trodden analytical path that focuses on what is being said about war crimes.

The theoretical premise in this book is that the phenomenon of reconciliation can be grasped by studying how people talk about war crimes in search of justice, which pivots on the fulfillment of deliberative virtues in interethnic communication. This book's focus on deliberative virtues and the measurement of the quality of discourse involving former adversaries discussing justice for war crimes overcomes the limitation of descriptive approaches to deliberation in transitional justice scholarship. However, by operationalizing reconciliation grounded in mutuality as deliberation, this book goes beyond "the give-and-take of deliberation."[65] It advances the scholarship on deliberation in divided societies by accounting for how ethnic identities matter during deliberation about war crimes. Unlike existing scholarship on deliberation in divided societies focused predominantly on issues that can unite communities, such as education or peace, the analysis in this book turns to discussions of wartime harm—usually the most polarizing issue in societies emerging from conflict. It needs to be addressed rationally and morally in order to lead to the repair of interethnic relations.[66]

This book shows how deliberative discussion involving former adversaries about the legacy of war crimes yields reconciliation. To infer reconciliation by studying *how* people talk about war crimes, we need to observe deliberative virtues in interethnic communication, alongside the ethics of solidarity, which recognizes and restores the dignity of the ethnic Other—the argument I lay out in chapter 2. At the same time, advancing the theories of reconciliation also involves extending the empirical evidence base for normative claims with appropriate methods. To this end, I investigate an understudied area of transitional justice practice: transitional justice consultations.

Reconciliation and Transitional Justice Consultations

Postconflict transitional justice is a matter of global public policy. All components of transitional justice specified by the United Nations (UN)—prosecutions, truth commissions, reparations, institutional reform, and national consultations—aim "to ensure accountability, serve justice and achieve reconciliation."[67] By contrast, the scholarship on reconciliation is narrowly based on the study of the effects of criminal prosecutions and truth commissions. Consultations are the least understood of the formal components of transitional justice.

The UN considers national consultations "a critical element of the human rights-based approach to transitional justice."[68] The exercise of this "right to be consulted" supports broader peacebuilding goals; consultations enable people affected by conflict to take ownership of the transitional justice strategy and contribute to designing a locally responsive approach to criminal legacy.[69] Consultations can also support postconflict democratization by creating opportunities for the freedom of expression and including marginalized voices such as those of the victims.[70] Consulting the opinions of conflict-affected populations is critical for ensuring the normative and political legitimacy of a transitional justice policy. Within the limited set of studies about consultations, scholars have been preoccupied with whether consultations legitimize the selection of a transitional justice instrument.[71] However, consultations can also plausibly promote reconciliation themselves.

According to the UN, "national consultations are a form of vigorous and respectful dialogue whereby the consulted parties are given the space to express themselves freely, in a secure environment, with a view to shaping or enhancing the design of transitional justice programmes." The UN specifies that "such processes must respect and promote the fundamental dignity of every human being, based on the principles of equality and nondiscrimination on the grounds of race, colour, gender, language, religion, opinion, national or social origin, property, birth or other status."[72] These are high aspirations for divided societies emerging from conflict. Nonetheless, if these values are upheld in consultations that represent "public deliberation on human rights," then they can also contribute to the repair of relations.[73] Participation in transitional justice practices holds "the prospect of transformation" of those involved and of the processes themselves.[74] Empirical assessment can demonstrate whether this applies to transitional justice consultations.

Before discussing the empirical approach of this book, it is important to distinguish consultations from what Nevin Aiken calls "instrumental reconciliation initiatives" centered on intercommunal contact and dialogue.[75] Interethnic dialogues aim to restore relations with the Other by enhancing the understanding of the Other and of the conflict "as a mutual problem," rather than directly attempting to resolve conflict.[76] They are distinct from transitional justice consultations that are aimed primarily at decision making on a transitional justice strategy in which ethnic groups have a high stake. Although consultations, like interethnic dialogues, foreground the deepest of moral disagreements, in consultations disagreement is accentuated by an imperative for parties to influence decision making.[77]

This book shows that people in divided societies can deliberate about the nuts and bolts of the transitional justice strategy, and that this process can bring them together even when they hold different views on the subject. It demonstrates that major benefits to postconflict societies derive not only from sharing the experiences of harm but also from discussing how those experiences should be addressed.

Research Design and Methods

This book uses a convergent, parallel, mixed method design.[78] In this type of research design, the same case or topic is investigated at each stage of the research process, with different methods used in parallel and given equal status in the analysis. I conducted a quantitative content analysis of a large corpus of over half a million words of multilanguage text data consisting of transcripts of the RECOM transitional justice consultations; and qualitative analysis drawing on my fieldwork in five Balkan countries, including semi-structured interviews, focus groups, participant observation of RECOM meetings, and a discussion-focused workshop with stakeholders.

In transitional justice research, a focus on methods is key to closing "a huge gap in our empirical knowledge with respect to what transitional justice may or may not do for reconciliation."[79] This gap reflects the enduring challenge of being "scientifically precise about the importance of the various [transitional justice] measures," including transitional justice consultations.[80] Using both quantitative and qualitative analytical tools provides a complete understanding of the research problem compared to either method individually.[81] It also allows for validation of the assumptions made in theory development.[82]

Quantifying discourse to examine reconciliation furthers the existing quantitative study of transitional justice, whose expansion has been largely based on surveys, survey experiments, and field experiments.[83] I use content analysis as a "means of measuring or quantifying dimensions of the content of messages," specifically, to measure the quality of deliberation about war crimes involving former adversaries, as discussed in chapter 3.[84] Content analysis uncovers patterns in the text and "offers the possibility of tapping complex, latent constructs," such as reconciliation.[85] Content analysis also enhances our understanding of the role of discourse in constructing the social "through its focus on being systematic and quantitative."[86] Qualitative research in this book is attuned to the discursive engagement with the ethnic Other and probes relations between actors, which are the staple of qualitative discourse analysis.[87] Discourse entails a set of practices implicated in the social production of reality that we can glean from the use of language in social settings.[88] This book focuses on the microlevel production of solidary relations during interethnic deliberation, presented in chapter 6.

Mixed method research needs to be explicit about the nature of mixing and integration, including its timing during the research process.[89] These decisions are reflected in how one approaches research questions.[90] This book's overarching question is: How do people talk about war crimes? This book aims to understand whether deliberative virtues can be attained in discussions across ethnic lines about war crimes in search of postconflict justice, and whether discursive identity practices offset the risks to reconciliation posed by identity politics. These aims map onto quantitative and qualitative subquestions: Can people deliberate about war crimes with members of adversary ethnic groups? And can people's enactment of ethnic identities during deliberation foster solidary bonds?

Lastly, the mixed method research design in this book relies on interpretive integration: insights that are generated by different methods and within the parameters of their own paradigm are "brought together at the level of analysis or theory to generate an overarching account of the phenomenon."[91] In line with this strategy, this book aspires to "expand insight of the phenomenon of interest."[92] Inferences based on the findings from quantitative and qualitative research are synthesized and form a meta-inference, which in this book points to a novel conceptualization of reconciliation.[93] An empirical micro-comparative analysis of discourse reveals how reconciliation can take place through public consultations about justice for war crimes. The discovery of reconciliation by stealth is strong evidence of the importance of sharpening our theoretical inquiry and methodological strategy to capture normative gains of transitional justice, lest they continue to elude us.

Chapter Summary

Chapter 1 grounds the RECOM initiative within its historical and political context. It first provides an overview of the wars fought in the former Yugoslavia in the 1990s and early 2000s. It then discusses postconflict transitional justice efforts, and how these promoted ethnocentric justice in the post-Yugoslav states in the Balkans. This distortion of transitional justice prompted the emergence of the RECOM initiative as a victim-focused, civil society-led, and regional transitional justice process. The chapter details the consultations held by RECOM, including its recruitment of a wide range of participants from all ethnic groups. It also analyzes the pressures that RECOM encountered from within the process and from outside, as well as its inability to establish a regional fact-finding commission. The chapter concludes by pointing out the gap in our understanding of the RECOM consultation process and its contribution to repairing interethnic relations.

Chapter 2 lays out the theoretical framework for the analysis. It argues that reconciliation after conflict results from good-quality deliberation and discursive solidarity during a transitional justice process involving ethnic adversaries. Alongside a deliberative discussion of past wrongs, characterized by equality, reason-giving, reciprocity, common good orientation, and respect, reconciliation also requires recognition of the ethnic Other and their wartime suffering. This ethical perspective highlights the need for ethnic adversaries to expand their moral horizons that were narrowed by conflict. The argument responds to our limited understanding of the role of ethnic identities in postconflict deliberation, which this chapter attributes to scholars' neglect of conflict dynamics, tendency to approach ethnic identity as a fixed attribute, and overlooking how identity politics bears on deliberation. In conclusion, an interactional approach to the study of identity during deliberation is presented. It shifts attention to how people enact their identities in interethnic interactions, which can provide insight into whether deliberators can forge solidary bonds across ethnic lines and offset divisive effects of identity politics, leading to reconciliation.

Chapter 3 presents the empirical strategy for studying the quality of deliberation and introduces the corpus comprised of the transcripts of the RECOM consultations in the Balkans. It elaborates on the refinement of one measurement instrument, the Discourse Quality Index (DQI), and the creation of the Discourse Quality Index for the Study of Transitional Justice (DQITJ), to evaluate the quality of cross-ethnic communication after a conflict. It also outlines the research design for the quantitative leg of this research, including the discussion of the textual data, sampling, and coding of 1,211 speech acts. Lastly, the chapter analyzes the deliberativeness of discourse based on the observed prevalence of deliberative virtues in the RECOM consultations. These empirical insights indicate an (unexpectedly) good quality of postconflict deliberation, despite the divisiveness of the subject and normative demands it makes of participants.

Chapter 4 assesses which factors predict good-quality deliberation about war crimes, focusing on how ethnic identities matter during deliberation. The analysis captures the effects of conflict dynamics and the linguistic features of discourse, a novel predictor of deliberativeness of interethnic discourse. The chapter first illustrates what good-quality deliberation about mass violence looks like by analyzing an excerpt from the RECOM corpus. It goes on to discuss predictors of good-quality deliberation and present the findings. They show that ethnically polarizing issues pertaining to redress for mass violence, ethnic diversity of discussions, and expressions of subjectivity in ethnic terms increase the quality of deliberation. These insights provide evidence that a discussion about justice for war crimes, the most divisive issue in divided societies, is compatible with a deliberative mode of communication. They also challenge the accepted assumption that the benefits of deliberation in divided societies accrue primarily from nonethnic and human rights-oriented discourse.

Chapter 5 investigates interactivity by focusing on the count and content of responses across ethnic lines. Certain tendencies can distort interethnic discourse and undermine the benefits of good-quality deliberation. If deliberators disagree with members from adversary ethnic groups and agree with their coethnics, and if they disagree with members from adversary ethnic groups disrespectfully, discourse can undermine prospects for reconciliation. The findings show, however, that there is no discursive ethnic enclavization, as greater interactivity exists across ethnic lines than between speakers belonging to the same ethnic group. Further probing the nature of interactivity reveals similar levels of agreement and disagreement in interethnic and intraethnic interactions, which is conducive to good-quality deliberation. Lastly, the results show no consistent pattern of disrespectful as opposed to respectful disagreement across ethnic lines, confirming the deliberative nature of transitional justice consultations.

Chapter 6 interrogates how people enact their identities during deliberation and whether this enactment can engender solidary bonds. It builds on the argument that to be reconciliatory, good-quality deliberation needs to be accompanied by recognition of the ethnic Other and their suffering. The qualitative analysis shows that discursive solidarity emerges from revealed differences between speakers, which dispel (mis)perceptions of opinion homogeneity of the

ethnic adversary group; from affective alignment, which leads to the acknowledgment of the suffering of ethnic Others by expression of empathy; and from
blame aversion, which involves restraint in apportioning blame in interethnic
engagement and prevents negative reciprocity in interethnic communication.
The chapter demonstrates how discursive identity practices counter divisive
effects of identity politics premised on the denigration of the ethnic Other during deliberation and lead to reconciliation.

The concluding chapter summarizes the book's main arguments and findings
about reconciliation through good-quality deliberation and discursive solidarity in transitional justice consultations. It reflects on the scope of the research
and charts directions for future research emerging from this book's contribution
to the scholarship on transitional justice and peacebuilding from a deliberation
perspective. In particular, it points to the role of identity talk in deliberation
and makes a case for the study of deliberative intergroup contact to advance
our understanding of interethnic communication in the reconstruction of postconflict societies. Lastly, it discusses policy implications, focusing on the role
of deliberation as a specific type of discussion-based approach to postconflict
reconciliation; the role of civil society actors in repairing interethnic relations;
and the value of regional transitional justice efforts as a policy space for addressing legacies of human rights violations resulting from cross-border dynamics of
violence in contemporary conflicts.

WARS, CRIMES, AND JUSTICE IN THE BALKANS

We killed each other regionally.

—Participant in RECOM consultations from Bosnia and Herzegovina, December 11, 2015

Nationalism is still exceptionally strong here, and influences how victims are perceived.

—Participant in RECOM consultations from Serbia, September 25, 2014

In the mid-2000s the regional civil society initiative known as RECOM launched consultations about justice for war crimes and grave human rights violations perpetrated during the Balkan wars. The consultations represented a great leap into the unknown. The organizers of the RECOM process, who brought together people from all ethnic groups in the region, had a clarity of purpose. It arose from their critical stance toward denigration of victims of war in all states in the region, where for the most part sympathy remained reserved for members of one's own ethnic group. The RECOM consultations were motivated by a need to recognize all victims of the conflicts associated with the former Yugoslavia's dissolution. This conviction stood in contrast to the many uncertainties surrounding the interethnic process the initiative set into motion. Would participants in the RECOM consultations who belonged to opposing ethnic groups defy the ethnic politics of their environments? Would RECOM withstand the political censure that its advocacy of inclusive justice provoked? Would this civil society-led initiative win states over to its de-ethnicized conception of justice? At every turn, the RECOM process had to contend with the ethnic politics that informed dominant approaches to justice in the region that emerged from a decade of wars.

The RECOM consultations, which took place from 2006 to 2011, spawned the idea of documenting war crimes committed against all victims in the region. They led to the adoption of the Draft Statute—a blueprint for a regional fact-finding commission. RECOM's strategy of regional justice-seeking challenged prevailing ethnocentric notions and practices of justice, which had "no understanding for, or feelings for, the suffering of others."[1] Following the breakup of the multiethnic

Yugoslav federation, nationalist narratives of conflict constructed a sense of collective martyrdom centered on the harms endured by one's own ethnic group. These narratives suppressed acknowledgment of events that might complicate the clear-cut attribution of blame and innocence and invented new symbols of suffering to reinforce exclusive ethnic identities.[2] Victims were denied recognition of their suffering by opposing ethnic groups, both within their countries and in neighboring ones.

The transitional justice process that unfolded under the auspices of RECOM hit a nerve with purveyors of postconflict nationalism in the Balkans. RECOM's guiding idea—recognition of all victims regardless of ethnicity—was the anathema to local nationalists, both among elites and significant sections of local publics. Pursuing ethnocentric justice kept nationalism alive and served as a distraction from governance failures. In challenging ethnocentric justice, RECOM pioneered a regional approach to transitional justice. Its goal—the establishment of the record of all victims of the wars in the former Yugoslavia—was a response to the regional nature of conflicts in the Balkans. For advocates of RECOM, this regional response was the way to "break the vicious circle of ethnic interpretations [of violence] used by states and nations to speak only about their own victims."[3] RECOM's efforts to fulfill its goal encountered challenges both inside and outside the RECOM initiative.

This chapter situates the RECOM initiative within its historical and political context. It first provides an overview of the wars fought in the former Yugoslavia in the 1990s and early 2000s. It then discusses postconflict transitional justice efforts and how they promoted ethnocentric notions of justice in the post-Yugoslav states. This distortion of transitional justice prompted the emergence of the RECOM initiative as a civil society-led, victim-focused, and regional transitional justice process. The chapter details the consultations held by the RECOM, including its recruitment of diverse participants from all ethnic groups involved in the conflicts. It also analyzes the pressures RECOM faced, both from participants within the process and from outside the process, including the representatives of post-Yugoslav states as well as members of broader civil societies. These pressures explain how ethnic politics in the Balkan states has stymied RECOM's goal of establishing a regional fact-finding commission. At the same time, my analysis clarifies how remarkable it is that these pressures did not stymie interethnic consultations—the least understood part of the RECOM process and the main subject of this book.

Ethnicity and Violence in the Balkans

The Socialist Federal Republic of Yugoslavia—a communist federation often described as a "mosaic" of ethnic groups—unraveled through a series of conflicts in the 1990s and early 2000s.[4] These conflicts pitted ethnic groups against each other. The new nation-states that took shape on the territory of the former Yugoslavia were homogenized along ethnic lines.[5] Violence separated ethnic groups within states, as in Bosnia and Herzegovina, and reduced the presence of minority ethnic group(s) in them, for instance, in Croatia.[6] As Ivo Banac notes, "ethnic cleansing and the construction of nationally homogenous states were not the consequence of but rather the aim of the war."[7] Ethnic nationalism fueled the violence. This kind of nationalism refuses to tolerate ethnic Others within the national state.[8] The ethnic mobilization that preceded the violence constructed the ethnic Other as an enemy. Consequently, ethnicity became "a matter of life or death."[9] Nonetheless, the ethnic logic of violence does not mean that ethnicity was a cause of conflicts.[10]

Voluminous scholarship has debunked essentialist and deterministic accounts of the Yugoslav wars as ethnic. Current debates concern the factors and contingencies that led to the mobilization of fear and grievances on an ethnic basis. Scholars have emphasized various historical, political, economic, and transnational dynamics within and beyond the former Yugoslavia.[11] Although debates about the causes of these wars persist, there is a broad consensus regarding their effects. The wars resulted in the primacy of ethnic identity, establishing its political currency in the countries faced with the challenge of providing justice for wartime harm.

A combination of human geography and federal administrative arrangements underpinned conflict in the former Yugoslavia. The Yugoslav federation, constituted after the end of the Second World War, comprised six republics: Slovenia, Croatia, Bosnia and Herzegovina, Serbia, Montenegro, and Macedonia.[12] A particular ethnic group dominated the population of each one. Serbia had an additional administrative layer, with two multiethnic autonomous provinces, Kosovo and Vojvodina. Yugoslavia's ethnic diversity was characterized by a misalignment of ethnic groups and administrative boundaries of constituent administrative units (republics and provinces) that help explain conflict dynamics. Yet this diversity also enabled the emergence of vibrant cosmopolitan culture and, to some extent, the anchoring of identities within an overarching framework of Yugoslavism.[13] However, cosmopolitan and narrowly nationalist currents and aspirations constantly competed with one another. Communist ideologues attempted to manage both trends, often with the brute force directed against nationalists and liberals.[14] Communist elites kept ethnic tensions in check as long as they believed their legitimacy and power rested on safeguarding the federal state.[15]

The demise of communism at the end of the Cold War changed the political calculation of elites in the former Yugoslavia. Nationalism rather than communism would give them legitimacy. Democracy was primarily understood as the freedom to advocate and implement nationalist programs. Their dictum, one nation in one state, offered no security guarantees to minority populations. Nationalist leaders ensured broad political appeal for their new ideology through carefully targeted manipulation and amplification of past political and economic grievances.[16] They also instrumentalized the divisive legacy of previous interethnic violence that had punctuated the history of this multiethnic region and, in particular, the violence that took place in the shadow of geopolitical and ideological confrontation during the Second World War.[17] Crimes committed in this period were airbrushed by the ruling ideology of "brotherhood and unity."[18] The communist government attempted to control the country's ethnic diversity by balancing identification with socialist self-management—a core tenet of Yugoslav communist ideology—with "scrupulous respect for the national sensitivities, linguistic rights, and cultural needs of all of Yugoslavia's groups."[19]

In the late 1980s, the communists-turned-nationalists were quick to seize the opportunity to use the legacy of past violence to whip up nationalist sentiment and shore up their power amidst the deepening economic crisis. The strategy was effective in rallying support from many ordinary people. It also resonated among some quarters of civil society; many historians, artists, and journalists helped construct and perpetuate the sense of historical grievance among their own ethnic groups.[20] Meanwhile, liberal parties and civil society groups, who sought a democratic alternative to nationalist solutions and growing interethnic tensions, were systematically delegitimized, marginalized, and repressed.[21] The region edged closer to war. Nationalists tied ethnic diversity to conflict. Division along ethnic lines appeared to be an appropriate response to growing insecurity.[22] Neighbors turned against each other in cities, towns, and villages.[23]

The former Yugoslavia became an arena of competing nationalisms. Led by their nationalist leader, Serbs began to implement a program of uniting all Serbs in the territory of the former Yugoslavia under a single state, the so-called Greater Serbia. They destroyed the constitutional structure of the federal state as a prelude to a decade of conflicts that engulfed the federation. Serbian nationalists framed Serbs, the largest identity group within the federation, as emasculated victims. Other groups, such as Croats in Croatia and Albanians in Kosovo, had their own historical and political grievances. These grievances supported nationalist narratives and arguments in favor of independence from what they saw as Serbia's domination within the federation. Their programs for national independence did not sufficiently guarantee security to Serb minorities living in Croatia and Kosovo. In the most ethnically diverse republic, Bosnia and Herzegovina, the nationalism of Bosnian Serbs and Croats was amplified by support from their kin states Serbia and Croatia that border Bosnia and Herzegovina. Meanwhile, the Bosnian Muslim leadership tried to balance support for multiethnic Bosnia's sovereignty with a Bosniak nationalist program preoccupied with Muslim issues and representation, which delegitimized its vision of multiculturalism for most of Bosnian Serbs and Croats.[24]

The violent dissolution of Yugoslavia unfolded in a series of conflicts: Slovenia in 1991, involving a conflict with the Serb-controlled Yugoslav Peoples' Army; Croatia in 1991–95, involving Croats and Serbs; Bosnia and Herzegovina in 1992–95, involving Bosnian Muslims, Bosnian Serbs, and Bosnian Croats; Kosovo in 1998–99, involving Serbs and Albanians; and Macedonia in 2001, involving Macedonians and Albanians. The severity of violence perpetrated by a range of state security forces, including the army and police, as well as non-state actors such as local paramilitaries and foreign mercenaries had not been seen on Europe's soil since the end of the Second World War. The scale of the suffering was massive. The brutality was incomprehensible. It is estimated that some 140,000 people lost their lives in the conflicts within the territory of former Yugoslavia.[25] This number includes many civilians—men, women, and children. Many were tortured and perished in forced detention. More than 35,000 people went missing, according to the International Committee of the Red Cross.[26] Millions were expelled from their homes and found refuge within the former republics and provinces or with their ethnic kin in the neighboring states; others fled abroad. Sexual and gender-based violence was unleashed to create ethnically homogenous states.

After peace accords mediated by the international community in the 1990s and early 2000s ended the conflicts, the peoples, politics, and spaces in the region were profoundly transformed. Having been targeted based on their ethnicity, people retained a heightened sense of belonging to a particular ethnic group.[27] The election of political leaders from one's own ethnic group legitimized ethnic politics fueled by the legacy of interethnic violence. Identity-based politics was also promoted through various consociational power-sharing arrangements implemented to manage ethnic pluralism in Bosnia and Herzegovina, Kosovo, and Macedonia.[28] The physical landscape changed, too. Symbolic erasure of ethnic groups from territories was accomplished by intentionally destroying their religious temples and cultural institutions. Postconflict societies in the Balkans confronted the enormity of past violence and began to seek justice for past wrongs in the context of deep, persisting divisions along ethnic lines.

The Logic of Ethnocentric Justice

Considering that there was no radical break with the nationalist politics that led to violence in the former Yugoslavia, it is noteworthy, as Jasna Dragović-Soso and Eric Gordy observe, that transitional justice initiatives ever occurred "on the meaningful scale" in the post-Yugoslav countries.[29] They developed incrementally after the ICTY in the Hague promoted accountability for past wrongs. Facing the past involved different retributive and restorative transitional justice initiatives. However, the pursuit of transitional justice resulted in a widespread sense of injustice. Ethnic groups viewed the question of justice for war crimes through the prism of ethnicity. The suffering of one's own ethnic group was prioritized.[30] In many ways these transitional justice practices widened divisions between ethnic groups, leaving victims bereft of the justice they sought. The RECOM transitional justice initiative challenged these prevailing ethnocentric conceptions of justice by seeking recognition of all victims.

Founded as an ad hoc international criminal tribunal during the Bosnian war in 1993, the ICTY was the sole transitional justice instrument when the fighting in the region ended. The European Union's ICTY conditionality policy made progress in the European integration process of the countries that emerged from the former Yugoslavia's dissolution conditional on cooperation with the ICTY. This policy accelerated the transitional justice process. Addressing impunity, albeit in a distant Hague court, made it impossible for political elites and societies in the Balkans to ignore past wrongdoing. However, coopted into collaboration with the ICTY through the European integration process, political elites were intent on undermining the court's legitimacy.[31]

Throughout the ICTY's twenty-four years of existence, elites attacked the tribunal for biasing particular ethnic groups.[32] The ICTY also struggled to win the endorsement of local victims' groups. Some were aligned with their ethnic elites' rejection of international justice, while others doubted the ICTY procedures. Evidence of fairness of the ICTY's legal process was overlooked.[33] Delegitimization of the ICTY relied on strategic misrepresentation of trials of individual war crimes suspects as trials of entire ethnic groups, and on people's suspicion of the foreign court combined with a lack of understanding of the legal process. The ICTY's ability to advance broader peacebuilding goals, including interethnic reconciliation, was undermined.[34]

Domestic war crimes trials were spurred by the transfer of cases from the ICTY after announcing of the international tribunal closing down. Ethnic politics also captured domestic prosecutions. This is illustrated by the prosecutorial strategy of disproportionately targeting Serbs in Croatia, or by the political strategy in Serbia of avoiding accountability for war crimes committed by Serbs.[35] In Kosovo and Bosnia, which were under international supervision, hybrid war crimes trials involved domestic and international legal practitioners. They were instituted to remedy the weaknesses of both international and domestic prosecutions, which they achieved with limited success.[36] Nonetheless, in all post-Yugoslav states political elites, with individual exceptions, and large sections of local publics dismissed domestic prosecutions of members of their own ethnic group as treacherous and unjust.

Retributive justice initiatives were gradually complemented with restorative transitional justice practices, but these too suffered from ethnocentrism. An attempt to establish a national truth commission in Bosnia and Herzegovina faltered after political elites representing their ethnic constituencies appropriated the project, further entrenching ethnic divisions.[37] In Serbia, the failed truth and reconciliation project was a nationalist scheme in all but in its name, and was widely seen as an attempt to justify Serb involvement in the conflicts in the 1990s.[38] Similarly, the so-called Srebrenica commission in Republika Srpska, one of the constituent units of postwar Bosnia, reinforced the sense of injustice shared by the Bosniaks when it declined to classify the massacre of Bosniaks in Srebrenica as genocide.[39]

Ethnic politics also framed other transitional justice initiatives such as commemorations and reparations. In particular, commemorations polarized ethnic groups with their focus on the suffering of one ethnic group. The local geography of violence may have warranted such focus. However, other groups contextualized these events within their ethnocentric narratives of conflict, turning commemorations into arenas of interethnic competition and confrontation.[40] Furthermore, political elites' nationalist grandstanding on these occasions resulted in further marginalization and manipulation of victims by their own ethnic group. Victims felt that politicians were quick to use their suffering to gain popularity, but ignored them when it came to action needed to support their quest for justice and recognition.[41] Commemorations acknowledging the suffering of all victims, including those from other ethnic groups, have been rare.[42]

Postconflict transitional justice practices in post-Yugoslav states gave rise to the conception of transitional justice as redress first and foremost for one's own ethnic group. The states' involvement in these transitional justice practices supported the view that states cannot be expected to produce "contributions of substance" to transitional justice.[43] As in many other postconflict contexts, the Balkan states' resistance to transitional justice propelled other actors to step in and engage with the legacy of human rights violations.[44] Civil society groups in the region fought to shift the ethnocentric paradigm of transitional injustice by providing inclusive justice narratives and practices. Nongovernmental human rights organizations exposed political elites' attempts to evade accountability and subvert justice, for example, by condemning celebrations of convicted war criminals as national heroes. They also scrutinized domestic war crimes trials and attempted to mitigate their failures by providing legal representation to victims.

Activism by civil society groups and human rights organizations was not without its challenges. There were profound differences of opinion over how to achieve justice for past wrongs. Competition for limited funding and inequality between organizations operating in urban and rural settings made reaching a consensus even more difficult.[45] Meanwhile, liberal civil society organizations also confronted ethnocentric narratives of conflict and demands for justice propagated by illiberal nonstate groups, just as they had to confront state-led nationalism.[46] Despite the restricted political space for their activism, human rights NGOs promoted critical engagement with one's own group's responsibility for war crimes and recognition of all victims of violence in the region.[47] Their inclusive views on transitional justice contrasted sharply with the dominant, ethnocentric conception of justice.

The Rise of RECOM

The RECOM initiative advocated the establishment of the regional fact-finding commission. It emerged as a response to ethnocentric transitional justice in the post-Yugoslav states. The historical continuity of civil society activism in defense of human rights paved the way for RECOM. Civil society organizations and groups that had opposed nationalism even before the violence continued their activism during the wars and called for justice for all victims after the wars ended.[48] Human rights NGOs maintained some cross-border links despite ongoing wars and renewed those that were severed by violence. New connections were created among groups that envisioned a different kind of future than that offered by nationalists. Aware of how transitional justice in the region was failing the victims of war crimes, RECOM developed a distinctively victim-centered, fact-based, and regional approach to transitional justice.

The RECOM initiative originated in discussions among three NGOs from the former Yugoslavia—Documenta in Croatia, the Research and Documentation Center in Bosnia and Herzegovina, and the Humanitarian Law Center in Serbia. These NGOs reached out to people from all ethnic groups in the region and started consulting them about an appropriate response to the legacy of mass atrocity. Out of the discussions emerged the idea of a regional fact-finding process. The subsequent founding of the Coalition for RECOM in 2008 formally launched the process of regional justice-seeking.[49] The Coalition attracted the membership of approximately 2,000 human rights groups and individuals throughout the region, including victims.[50] Many human rights organizations and victims in the region did not formally join the Coalition.[51] Nonetheless, some 6,000 people from all ethnic groups involved in the wars in the region took part in the RECOM consultation process. By reaching out to people who were not formally Coalition members and involving them in the consultations, RECOM ensured that these meetings were not limited to people who saw the issue of redress for past wrongs the same way. Interactions between people who came from different ethnic groups and held opposing views about justice for war crimes are of particular interest for this book. In 2011, the RECOM consultations produced the Draft Statute.[52] This document spelled out the mandate for the regional fact-finding commission.[53]

As a victim-centered model of transitional justice, RECOM attempted to remedy the shortcomings of retributive transitional justice. It provided a grass-roots approach to addressing past harm while being attuned to the cross-border nature of violence and suffering in the former Yugoslavia. The organizers took pride in the local origins of the RECOM initiative, which "did not originate either in Brussels, or in any of the governments in the region."[54] In their eyes, this was an important source of the initiative's legitimacy.[55] As a civil society network, RECOM was an alternative to state-led efforts associated with politicizing transitional justice. Like other human rights initiatives in the poor, post-conflict region, RECOM's activities were supported by foreign donations. But RECOM's members set the agenda.[56] As one participant put it, "we did not apply a pre-existing formula. We learnt from the experiences of others, and were inspired by them, but we were creating our own [approach]."[57] Critical evaluation of the applicability of other models to the Balkans resulted in the adoption of regional fact-finding as RECOM's transitional justice strategy. This approach also considered the context of ethnic politics in the post-Yugoslav states, where key aims of transitional justice, such as reconciliation, had been systematically discredited.

"Reconciliation" was not included in the name of the RECOM commission. This was not because RECOM "shunned reconciliation," as its organizers explained, but rather because "they wanted to be smarter, since there was a lot of manipulation in the region with the concept of reconciliation."[58] They referred to politicians' hollow rhetoric about reconciliation, with invocations of the term often followed by inaction or even measures that undermined the process.[59] Therefore, RECOM's approach to justice was narrow and focused on fact-finding. According to the initiators, the establishment of war crime facts would provide "a healthy foundation for reconciliation of future generations."[60] This justification echoes Frédéric Mégret's assessment of fact-finding as a response to a moral imperative in the aftermath of human rights violations, and a strategy that counteracts "the reign of opinion."[61] The lack of facts about war crimes in the Balkans allowed ethnocentric interpretations of violence and postconflict justice.

Participants in the RECOM process saw the facts as being linked to broader peacebuilding goals. They would be an obstacle to manipulation with figures of war dead by political elites. The elites resisted making an accurate record of victims of conflict "because this gave them political room to manipulate with the figures," minimizing the suffering of other ethnic groups and exaggerating the losses of one's own ethnic group. Creating the regional record of war dead, the first in the history of the conflicts in the former Yugoslavia, was expected to have a deterrent effect. It would prevent the "recurrence of future conflicts" by enabling debates based on documented facts.[62] The public record of named victims, along with the circumstances of the crimes they suffered, would also provide recognition of individual experiences, embodying a core principle of RECOM: "all victims are equal."[63]

The recognition of all victims could only be achieved through a regional process. This approach reflected the regional nature of conflict in the Balkans, where perpetrators crossed borders to commit crimes and civilians fled across borders to safety. When the conflicts in the region ended, the new state borders blocked justice. Perpetrators ended up in one county, and the evidence and the victims in another, exposing the limitations of a national approach to transitional justice.[64] Another regional dimension of the RECOM process was that it provided a platform that brought together people from all ethnic groups affected by the Balkan conflicts. This platform overcame structural barriers to interethnic engagement, which was needed to move beyond ethnocentric discussions about past wrongs. As one participant put it: "As long as we live in ethnically divided areas, even streets, we won't be able to speak more freely or realistically about the crimes committed by members of our ethnic groups."[65] Victims were denigrated by the denial of their suffering by other ethnic groups within their own and in neighboring states. The regional platform also addressed victims' need "for the other side that is responsible for what happened to hear about how they suffered."[66] The model of regional fact-finding was honed during the consultations RECOM organized in order to solicit views from people from all ethnic groups involved in the conflicts.

The RECOM Consultative Process

The RECOM consultations unfolded over five years, from 2006 to 2011. They solicited opinions about justice needs and how best to address them. After a proposal to establish a regional war crimes fact-finding commission had crystalized, the next step was to discuss and adopt a Draft Statute. This document, created in the multiethnic forum of regional consultations, was to be presented to the governments of the post-Yugoslav states. Their endorsement was sought for establishing this commission, which was to be an official interstate body and cease being a civil society initiative. The RECOM leadership believed that the official nature of the commission, where fact-finding is sponsored by the states in the region, would be key for the legitimacy of the established facts.

To consider the widest spectrum of opinions, the organizers' priority was to ensure that consultations were diverse and inclusive across different identity axes: people from all ethnic groups involved in the Balkan conflicts; men and women; as well as people from different constituencies, including victims, veterans, human rights activists, youth groups, and professionals, such as lawyers, journalists, and teachers, as well as religious leaders.[67] According to one organizer of the RECOM process, they encouraged the participation of people who did not usually join civil society initiatives.[68] They organized consultations in rural locations, not just in cities and towns. They also ensured representation of different experiences of conflict and views on redress for past harm. At a group level, people brought their distinct perspectives on violence and injustice as members of a particular ethnicity. At an individual level, their exposure to violence varied: some were victims and survivors of violence themselves, while others were not affected by it directly. Such diversity was summarized by an interviewee who participated in the RECOM process: "There were thousands of little stones in one place that were heterogeneous in every single respect, in terms of political views, education level, generationally, nationally, ethnically, and in terms of life-experience. Some watched their closest being killed, others watched their future being killed."[69]

The RECOM consultative process attracted people with interest in postconflict justice. But these individuals were not necessarily like-minded. Even participants who supported the idea of a regional fact-finding commission could hold opposed views on various issues. Some participants, an interviewee told me, "challenged absolutely everything."[70] Organizers welcomed the diversity of opinions and their free expression during the consultations. Their rationale was that exchanging different opinions would lead to a better-informed and more legitimate outcome of the consultation process.[71] The RECOM consultations were radically different from those interethnic activities organized by civil society organizations that were criticized for bringing together only those people who agreed with each other.[72]

The consultations resulted in the adoption of the Draft Statute of the regional fact-finding commission in 2011. It was an organic process, during which the idea of regional fact-finding took shape. Initially, from 2006 to 2010, discussions were open-ended, focusing on identifying an appropriate nonjudicial transitional justice mechanism. Some consultations also incorporated public hearings of victims, who spoke about their experience of violence to a multiethnic audience. These sessions foreshadowed the testimonial-based methodology of the fact-finding commission. Scholars noted their potential for generating understanding of the Other and their suffering.[73] However, the organizers soon realized the risk of potential retraumatization and criticized the hasty "experimentation" with this format without proper support for victims.[74] The consultation process subsequently focused on defining a transitional justice approach appropriate for this postconflict region.

The consultations about the Draft Statute of the regional commission, which took place from May 2010 to March 2011, were different in character. The participants in these consultations debated the articles of the Draft Statute and expressed their opinions about their wording and content. The Draft Statute defined the commission's mandate, which laid out the commission's functions, attributions, and responsibilities.[75] RECOM's document included provisions on its remit, objectives, competencies, protocols outlining the commission's power and operation (such as statement-taking, public hearings, and field visits), procedures for its establishment (including the appointment of commissioners along with their rights and obligations, and internal governance arrangements), financing of the commission, and the production of the commission's report.[76]

A Working Group comprised of a multiethnic team of legal experts from the former Yugoslavia was assembled to provide expert guidance. The Working Group drafted initial proposals after considering participants' views expressed during the consultations and analyzing the statutes of other national truth commissions in other postconflict cases, while considering the laws of all former Yugoslav countries. It accepted proposals that were "possible, realistic, relevant and applicable" and translated them into the contours of the future commission.[77] The length of consultations varied. Some lasted a day, and others took place over two days. Each consultation gathered a diverse range of participants. Participants had an opportunity to hear and consider the Working Group's proposals on each article of the Draft Statute and express their views, propose solutions, and debate them with other participants. All consultations were dedicated to the areas corresponding to the headings in the Draft Statute.

The process unfolded iteratively. The Working Group updated the drafts of the document based on participants' suggestions and proposals during the consultations.[78] These drafts were discussed in subsequent consultations. Often, there were disagreements within the Working Group on a particular proposal, and two versions of an article were presented to participants.[79] The final version of the Draft Statute was agreed on through this process of "chiseling."[80] The legitimacy of the process lay in its responsiveness to the participants' views, including their cultural sensibilities. For example, the Working Group used the term "members of the commission" and not the usual term "commissioners," considering the negative connotations the word "commissioner" or "komesar" had for participants owing to its association with political repression during the communist period.[81] The proceedings of each consultation were transcribed in their entirety and made publicly available on the RECOM website. A meticulous record of the consultations was kept in order to document the diversity of opinions before settling on the final version of the Draft Statute, and to ensure that this local transitional justice process was transparent.[82] The heated discussions during the RECOM consultations about the Draft Statute impressed the organizers, participants, and scholars who observed the process. To the organizers, it looked as though reaching a consensus would be impossible.[83] Similarly, scholars noted that "practically every aspect of a possible regional truth commission was the subject of heated debate."[84]

The Draft Statute was adopted at the Assembly of the RECOM Coalition on March 26, 2011. The Assembly is one of RECOM's governing bodies and comprises the members of the Coalition. Without a hard and fast rule on the membership of the Assembly, the Coalition considered members to be active participants in the consultation process while ensuring representation of all ethnic groups involved in the conflicts in the Balkans. In practice, according to one member of the Working Group, "the authors of the Draft Statute were all 6,000 people who took part in the consultation process."[85] Importantly, the Draft Statute did not reflect the views only of the members of the RECOM Coalition alone, who were a minority of participants in the consultation process.[86] The adoption of the Draft Statute of the regional fact-finding commission showed that "a common interest to put an end to the Balkan practice of nameless victims" prevailed.[87] The Draft Statute was the outcome agreed on after heated discussions about a difficult past involving people from all ethnic groups involved in the Balkan conflicts of the 1990s and the early 2000s.[88] It is also a testament to the resilience of the RECOM process in the face of many challenges.

Challenges to RECOM from Within and Without

The RECOM Coalition became a notable transitional justice actor in the region, promoting justice for all victims. Elites in different countries wanted to downplay its work because it challenged their framing of transitional justice as exclusive redress for their victims. The RECOM initiative had to find a way to operate as a transitional justice actor reliant on external support while it confronted the local powerholders' resistance to inclusive transitional justice. Challenges came both from within the initiative and from the surrounding political environment.

The initiative launched by the three nongovernmental human rights organizations grew into the RECOM Coalition, a network of civil society organizations and groups. It was governed by the Coordination Council, which served as an executive body, the Secretariat, which organized the events and planned activities, and the Assembly, which debated and steered its activism. At all levels of the organization, RECOM abided by the principle of multiethnic representation.

The leadership of the process by three NGOs from Serbia, Bosnia, and Croatia also presented a difficulty concerning the governance of the funds donated to RECOM. The partner from Sarajevo left the Coalition after a disagreement. According to reports, the Bosnian partner demanded that the administration of a particular grant awarded to the Belgrade partner be shared rather than it being administered by the recipient as awarded.[89] Along with the personal styles of the RECOM leaders and their relationships, this split has attracted significant scholarly attention.[90] It has led some to conclude that diverse ethnic interests could not be accommodated within a regional transitional justice process, overlooking the resilience of the consultative process that continued despite this disagreement.[91]

The split at the top disturbed but ultimately did not derail the RECOM process. Participants were affected by the perception that the lead organizations could not reach an agreement and concerned about the implications of the falling-out for representation of Bosnia in the process.[92] The remaining lead organizations from Serbia and Croatia, and the Bosnian organizations that stepped in, were transparent about the split. During the consultations they discussed with participants the constraints and importance of financial prudence in the administration of funds.[93] A handful of organizations left the Coalition, but most continued their involvement with RECOM. The process of justice-seeking proceeded apace.[94] The participants recognized the value of the RECOM consultations irrespective of organizational and perceived personal rivalries among the leaders. They considered RECOM to be the "key to success" for transitional justice in Bosnia, since the truth about "crimes in Bosnia and Herzegovina cannot be established without the truths and facts either from Montenegro, Serbia or Croatia, because many paramilitaries came from there to commit crimes in Bosnia."[95]

At the same time, opposition to the RECOM process and to the idea of regional justice-seeking swelled. Vehement criticism came from nationalist circles in all former Yugoslav states, targeting various aspects of the RECOM process. It was driven by the need to preserve dominant nationalist interpretations of conflict, and the conception of transitional justice as justice primarily for members of one's own ethnic group. To portray the RECOM initiative as a betrayal of ethnic interests, critics misrepresented RECOM's ideas. Supporters and advocates of the RECOM initiative engaged the critics.[96] The resulting public discussion revolved around some key themes.

Nationalists throughout the region dismissed the regional approach to transitional justice as a ploy for advancing the ethnic interests of others and a scheme by RECOM to delegitimize national transitional justice initiatives. In Croatia, RECOM was accused of trying to hide "Serb aggression," and in Kosovo, RECOM was accused of being a Serb ploy to deny Kosovo's independence.[97] Among the range of accusations leveled in Serbia was that it aimed at usurping court powers and dispensing summary justice, and that it was "organizing collective brainwashing about the causes of war."[98]

In response, supporters of the RECOM process underscored their commitment to recognizing all victims regardless of their ethnicity. They specified that the regional approach was not an alternative to national initiatives but should be understood as complementary. Similarly, they reaffirmed their commitment to restorative justice, insisting on its complementarity with other national-level transitional justice initiatives.[99] Public condemnation of RECOM, by both state and nonstate actors throughout the region, pointed to the potential power of an inclusive approach advocated by RECOM to unsettle the ethnic logic of justice-seeking. Bringing to light how elites failed their own victims from their same ethnic groups constituted a part of the threat that the RECOM posed. Opponents stigmatized participation in RECOM's interethnic process, enforcing ethnocentric justice.

During the RECOM consultations, the organizers openly spoke about the challenges of organizing interethnic consultations and about their "fear from the reactions of people in their surroundings." Local nationalists felt threatened by civil society initiatives that lifted the "smoke" and revealed their failure to recognize the victims.[100] Participants spoke about being called out by nationalists for "having engaged with the mercenaries," a reference to human rights organizations supported by external grants.[101] Liberal NGOs were criticized for their dependence on foreign funding and inclusive vision of transitional justice. People who joined these interethnic consultations were marked by some as "black sheep" upon return to their neighborhoods.[102] Despite such instrumentalist stigmatization, people joined the RECOM consultation process, motivated by the quest for justice.

Another challenge to RECOM was a lack of broader societal engagement. RECOM was "sandwiched between politicians who do not want to ruffle their electors and a great number of indifferent citizens."[103] To date, the RECOM initiative has not succeeded in obtaining lasting support from the leaderships of the post-Yugoslav states for the regional fact-finding process. RECOM's discussions with presidential envoys and joint scrutiny of the Draft Statute along with its subsequent amendments led to the creation of the legal framework for establishing the regional commission in 2014. Political support for RECOM disappeared in the next cycle of elections in the region.[104] Meanwhile, the efforts to bring about a domestic policy change by obtaining political support from the European Union for establishing the regional fact-finding commission have also faltered.[105]

Simultaneously, the RECOM Coalition confronted a problem of "a broad-based lack of interest in and receptiveness" to transitional justice mechanisms, which is common in postconflict societies.[106] RECOM's media campaign to collect one million signatures in support of the regional commission, the "Race for RECOM" in the Belgrade Marathon, and other traditional and social media campaigns engaged ordinary people, but their limitations were evident. RECOM has been unable to change dominant nationalist narratives or mobilize meaningful popular support for its cause. Nonetheless, its contribution to the pluralization of public discourses by presenting an alternative view of inclusive postconflict justice should not be dismissed. The inability of RECOM to fulfill its goal of establishing the regional fact-finding commission has informed scholarly assessments of this initiative as a failure of transitional justice. However, as Gordy has remarked, "everything RECOM didn't fail at, it succeeded at."[107] Above all, as one participant in the RECOM process poignantly put it in an interview in 2013, "the process [of consultations] was invaluable for the region, even at the cost of the commission never being established."[108]

Beyond Ethnocentrism

The ethnocentric practice of transitional justice followed interethnic violence during the Balkan wars. In this case, justice primarily meant justice for members of one's own group. The ethnocentric perspective defined nationalist narratives that reduced the complexity of the conflicts to "our" victims and "their" perpetrators. This was mirrored by discourses of denials or downplaying of wrongdoing by members of one's own ethnic group.[109] The dominance of ethnocentric narratives of war and justice in the post-Yugoslav states, purveyed both by nationalist elites and local nationalist civil society associations and groups, has been widely documented. However, the sole focus on these narratives risks misunderstanding these discourses as an omnipresent and totalizing force in postconflict societies.

Isabelle Delpla has argued that even "the victims' minds are not so enmeshed in collective 'ethnic' thinking so as to define perpetration and victimhood solely in collective, ethnic terms."[110] The ruptures and complexities of living in postatrocity societies can be easily overlooked. They undermine the parsimony of scholars' and practitioners' explanations for why justice and reconciliation remain elusive. In these accounts, ethnonational categories of analysis link the salience of ethnic identities and dominance of ethnic politics with the impossibility, even immorality, of postconflict reconciliation. But, as Aida Hozić warns, viewing postconflict polities solely through an ethnonationalist lens "plays into the hands of those who committed genocide."[111] Likewise, solely focusing on nonethnic categories of analysis, including civic identities, also misses the vicissitudes of postconflict life in the shadow of war crimes. As Torsten Kolind observes, counterdiscourses that mark the "shift away from ethnic towards nonethnic cultural and moral categories" exist alongside different ethnic identities carved by war that remain "complex, fragmented and inconsistent."[112] Daily life presents people with dilemmas about how to present and enact ethnic identities in interactions with the ethnic Other(s). Even in ethnically divided environments, these enactments challenge the uniformity of collective views promoted and enforced by nationalists.[113]

To understand the prospects for reconciliation after war crimes, we need to interrogate different expressions of identity in specific contexts along with positive and negative effects in concrete conversational settings. By doing so, we can account for an ethnic politics that dominates and constrains yet does not order all life and interactions in divided postconflict societies. The RECOM consultations involving people from opposing ethnic groups in the postconflict Balkans are a case in point.

The RECOM initiative pioneered an innovative format for regional consultations about the legacy of violence. It allowed for the exchange of different views across ethnic lines on postconflict justice. RECOM was a reaction to ethnic politics in the post-Yugoslav states in which official ethnocentric approaches to transitional justice were embedded. At the same time, ethnic politics also encroached on the process; it informed the views of some of its participants, while others rejected it. For many participants, the RECOM consultations stand out as a major achievement. They saw "success in gathering different interest, social, and victim groups together, and show[ing] that a dialogue is possible."[114] I put these anecdotal observations under scrutiny by identifying and analyzing the discourse patterns in this transitional justice process and their effect on interethnic relations. The next chapter lays out the theoretical framework for thinking about how reconciliation informed by mutuality in the context of peacebuilding flows from deliberative interactions across ethnic lines.

BRINGING IDENTITIES INTO POSTCONFLICT DELIBERATION

My point has nothing to do with ethnicity. It doesn't matter to me whether it concerns Serbs, Albanians, or extra-terrestrials.

—Participant in the RECOM consultation in Kosovo, February 21, 2011

I was very afraid of talking to Croats and Bosnians, who are closer to me, much more than I would fear talking to an American, Canadian, Brit, or Italian.

—Participant in the RECOM consultation in Montenegro, December 15, 2010

The prospect of coming face-to-face with former adversaries in a transitional justice process is daunting. The violence suffered during the conflict is revisited. The words that are spoken risk sharpening divisions between people along ethnic lines. An agreement on a joint pursuit of postconflict justice depends on people's ability to overcome ethnocentric perspectives and consider the views of ethnic Others. To date, we have not had evidence about whether this kind of deliberative communication can occur in postconflict contexts when members of adversary ethnic groups address the issue of war crimes.

Deliberation in societies divided by conflict faces formidable obstacles. Ethnocentric views are entrenched by ethnic targeting, a recurring element of contemporary conflicts. Even though mass killings are not necessarily aimed at specific individuals, they are not random; rather, as David Moshman argues, "they are crimes of group violence involving dichotomized social identities" that pit us against them.[1] These divisions can endure even after violence ends, as people are socialized into ethnocentric narratives about conflict and victimhood. A deliberative approach to conflict-resolution and peacebuilding recognizes the reality of deep ethnic divisions but also envisions their transcendence through discursive interaction.

This study of reconciliation embedded in mutuality in public communication recognizes the potential of deliberation involving former adversaries to contribute to peacebuilding in postconflict societies. Like deliberative democrats, I endorse the premise that reasoned, respectful, and other-regarding exchange of views across ethnic lines can help reconstruct societies torn apart by conflict.

However, I argue that fulfillment of deliberative virtues on its own cannot bring about a reconciliation of former adversaries, even if we establish that they can discuss redress for past wrongs in a deliberative manner. As André Bächtiger and John Parkinson point out, "exclusionary arguments can be couched in seemingly inclusive and respectful language."[2]

Although ethnic adversaries need to be able to discuss past wrongs deliberatively to appreciate each other's perspectives on justice for war crimes, repair of interethnic relations is conditional on granting recognition and dignity to the ethnic Other during deliberation. The bonds of solidarity that develop are the antithesis of divisive identity politics and denigration of the ethnic Other that bears on deliberation. I argue that reconciliation results from deliberative rationality and discursive solidarity when ethnic adversaries discuss war crimes during transitional justice consultations. The argument requires interrogation of how speakers deploy their identities in discourse, which James Paul Gee defines as "interactive identity-based communication using language."[3]

In this chapter, I lay out the theoretical framework for bringing identities into deliberation. It addresses the gap in the scholarship on deliberation in divided societies, which reflects our limited understanding of the role of ethnic identities at a microlevel of deliberative exchange. The gap has resulted from scholars' neglect of conflict dynamics and tendency to approach ethnic identities as speakers' fixed attributes while studying interethnic deliberation as if politics was not central to it. Bringing identities into the study of deliberation requires engaging with conflict dynamics. At the same time, an interactional perspective on how identities are enacted can provide insight into whether deliberators can counteract divisive identity politics by forging solidary bonds during good-quality deliberation about redress for war crimes.

The Case for Deliberation in Divided Societies

Appreciation of Jürgen Habermas's theory of communicative action has led scholars of critical peacebuilding to recognize nonconfrontational dialogue about the violent past as a means of reconstructing divided societies.[4] In contrast to strategic action, where actors are interested solely in achieving their interests, communicative action involves sharing knowledge in order to arrive at mutual understanding.[5] The theory of deliberation is a procedural theory and presupposes a certain quality of communication. As a mode of communication, deliberation is characterized by the realization of deliberative virtues. Peacebuilding and conflict resolution scholars contend that these deliberative virtues can mend relationships torn by conflict.

Common to all theoretical approaches to democratic deliberation is a requirement of reason-giving, while reasons in this context refer to "*propositions that can serve as premises in inferences that justify action.*"[6] Deliberators are expected to provide reasons for their positions and to respond to reasons offered by others.[7] To make decisions deliberatively, everyone should have an equal opportunity to contribute. Deliberation is also other-regarding communication; it entails respect for deliberative partners and openness to hearing their views. Other-regarding orientation of deliberation embodies the principles of reflexivity and reciprocity; deliberators reflect on their positions, weighing them in the light of counterarguments.[8] Reciprocity thus refers to the mutuality of reasons offered to reach a mutually binding decision.[9] Deliberation is thought to have a transformative effect on deliberators' views. Transformation of preferences occurs "when participants change their minds because they have adopted to some degree the perspective of another or taken the other's interests as their own."[10]

As a normative theory, deliberative democracy stipulates that deliberative virtues produce deliberative gains. Deliberation is beneficial because it produces legitimacy for deliberatively derived decisions. Legitimacy is related to the democratic dimension of deliberation, which entails free, equal, and inclusive participation. Deliberation also contributes to the justice of decisions by granting public discursive opportunities to all.[11] Opinions formed after deliberation are better informed, more thoroughly considered, more stable, and better aligned with deliberators' underlying values.[12] Lastly, as a form of social interaction and learning, deliberation also fosters solidarity and trust and creates social capital.[13]

Deliberative virtues, which include rational justification, equality, reciprocity, respect, common good orientation, and other-regarding logic, play a particularly important role in the transition from war to peace in ethnically divided societies. Manlio Cinalli and Ian O'Flynn remind us that a normative starting point in the study of deliberation is that in any modern, pluralistic society, different people have different views of the world.[14] However, these differences are amplified in societies emerging from violent conflict, not least because of ethnic groups' previous inability to resolve disagreements peacefully. Normative standards of deliberation can help moderate and overcome mistrust and polarization that prevent the development of an inclusive public sphere and effective public policy making in postconflict societies.[15] Donald Ellis specifies that "deliberation does not seek rationality in the strongest of terms." Rather, rationality has to be understood as correcting bias against the ethnic Other, which is especially critical in divided societies.[16] In addition, deliberation entails orientation toward the common good that transcends narrowly defined interests, which can help transcend the ethnic logic in interest formation in societies emerging from conflict.[17] Deliberation can promote postconflict transitional justice-seeking since it fosters consideration of the perspectives and needs of the ethnic Other.[18] Even if no decision is reached during deliberation and the requirement of decision making is removed, the very process of deliberation across ethnic lines can help repair interethnic ties.

The Case against Deliberation in Divided Societies

Reflective preference transformation that promotes the common good through noncoercive reason-giving and reciprocal dialogue lies at the heart of the theory of deliberative democracy. Procedural and outcome-oriented ideals delimit the theory. Against this benchmark, real-life deliberation is bound to be no more than an approximation of a theoretical ideal. At the same time, how close in practice deliberation will come to the ideal is highly context-dependent.[19] Divided societies often fail to meet many conditions for meaningful deliberation and are therefore unlikely to enjoy deliberative gains. Jürg Steiner captures the paradox succinctly, that deliberation is most difficult to achieve in divided societies, precisely "where deliberation is most needed."[20]

Differences of opinion are a precondition for initiating and sustaining deliberation. To be "situated in the circumstances of deliberation," participants should not be like-minded before the start of the discussion.[21] Likewise, the deliberation process entails a willingness to participate in a dialogical exercise across lines of division, adopt an accommodating stance, and be prepared to offer reasons and listen to others and their reasons.[22] However, the lack of trust that defines ethnically divided societies presents an obstacle to intergroup deliberation.[23] It takes shape in the form of ethnic segmentation of the public sphere.[24] Consequently, deliberation is unlikely to extend beyond ethnic spaces to include ethnic Others. At the same time, an emotionally charged environment of identity politics is at odds with the necessary deliberative exchange of reasons.[25] Positions are likely to be informed by ethnic allegiances and encourage turning a tin ear to others' perspectives.

Reservations about the possibility of deliberation in divided societies are attuned to critical arguments that, even in democratic contexts, deliberation deepens rather than bridges intergroup divisions. They are informed by Cass Sunstein's concept of "enclave deliberation" and the argument that opinions tend toward the extreme position and in the direction of the group opinion.[26] Enclave deliberation thus "encourages the conceptualization of values and policy in rivalrous" rather than in other-regarding and cooperative terms required for deliberative communication.[27] Scholars have also questioned people's general willingness to engage with different opinions, even in societies that are not torn apart by conflict-related identity issues.[28] In divided societies, positions can be expected to align with ethnic identities and reflect ethnic interests. Consequently, attempts at deliberation are likely to falter as group-specific interests dominate and passions flare, undermining prospects for attaining deliberative standards.[29] Furthermore, even if participants invoke universal principles, such as human rights, they may actually be used strategically to promote their group-specific interests and incite conflict between groups.[30] Interethnic communication in both institutional and informal settings poses unique challenges in societies divided by conflict. This raises the question of whether expectations of high deliberative standards and beneficial effects of exposure to different viewpoints must be adjusted when deliberation encounters identity politics.

Deliberation without Reconciliation?

Notwithstanding "the intuitive disjunct between the conditions of deliberative reason-giving and the precarious position of divided societies," scholars have tackled such tensions in thinking about deliberation in divided societies.[31] John Dryzek and O'Flynn, respectively, first theorized the possibility of deliberation in divided societies.[32] Both scholars engage with consociationalism as a political and normative framework for conflict-resolution in deeply divided societies, although they offered different perspectives on deliberative democracy in contexts politicized by identity conflicts.[33] Dryzek emphasizes the public sphere, separate from the state and embodied by networks as an organizational form conducive to negotiation across difference. O'Flynn also recognizes civil society's contribution to building interethnic trust and solidarity. Unlike Dryzek, he places the burden on the state for bringing about a deliberative democratic resolution of conflict, arguing that civil society's behavior ultimately depends on that of the political leadership.[34]

These theoretical forays were followed by empirical investigations of the procedural and outcome-oriented measures of deliberation in divided societies. Deliberative experiments in Belgium involving Dutch- and French-speaking participants found that the quality of interethnic deliberation was higher than that of intragroup deliberation and that intergroup deliberation led to intergroup appreciation.[35] Another set of deliberative experiments in Colombia, Bosnia and Herzegovina, Belgium, and Finland (as a control case) established that ordinary citizens were both able and willing to deliberate across lines of division in their local environments.[36] Similarly, a deliberative poll—an alternative analytical tool in the study of deliberation—pointed to knowledge gains, mutual respect, and perceptions of trustworthiness as outcomes of deliberation involving Protestants and Catholics in Northern Ireland.[37] However, further deliberative experiments in Colombia put a damper on the prospects for good-quality deliberation among antagonists in this postconflict society.[38]

This scholarship marked the empirical turn in the study of deliberation in divided societies.[39] The evidence supports the claim that deliberation across the identity divide is challenging but possible.[40] It also identifies institutional conditions for good-quality deliberation despite an adverse environment.[41] These insights from divided societies resonate with findings from the empirical study of deliberation in democratic contexts, which suggest "that cases approaching ideal deliberation are rare, but that group interaction sometimes works surprisingly well according to such ideals."[42] Empirical studies of deliberation in divided societies suggest possibilities for carefully calibrated deliberative problem-solving in societies emerging from conflict. They do not make a compelling case for reconciliation born out of deliberation. However, as James Fishkin shows, deliberation can change views in support of reconciliation, as was the case with a deliberative poll about the acknowledgment of the role of indigenous peoples in Australian history.[43]

The empirical study of deliberation in societies divided by conflict has refined normative requirements of the deliberative approach to conflict resolution and peacebuilding. The evidence it has produced speaks to "deliberative reconciliation" premised on inclusion and moderation as a foundation for institutional stability and improved governance in divided societies.[44] Nonetheless, this falls short of providing evidence for reconciliation through deliberation. Juan Ugarriza and Natalia Trujillo-Orrego contend that deliberation does not have built-in mechanisms for constraining extreme positions—constraints that are necessary for reconciliation. According to them, "antagonists run a high risk of polarization, understood as a worsening of their mutual attitudes toward each other, due to their contentious interactions, regardless of deliberative quality."[45] These risks cannot be assessed without more thorough scrutiny of deliberative discourse in postconflict societies. Specifically, the case against deliberative reconciliation falters in the face of a lack of evidence on how deliberators express their ethnic identities during postconflict deliberation.

Paradoxically, although the concepts of ethnic identity and identity politics are central to theorizing deliberation and its transformative effect in divided societies, the role of ethnic identities in the course of deliberation remains poorly understood at both the macro- and microlevel of interethnic interactions. Pathways that link interethnic deliberation with change in deliberants' identity from one defined by ethnicity to one defined by civicness—as an indicator of interethnic reconciliation—remain unclear in the scholarship on deliberation in divided societies.[46] While suggesting that deliberation has a political effect in broader societies where it can moderate ethnic division, scholars of deliberation in divided societies have written politics out of the very act of deliberation at the microlevel of interethnic interactions. Yet, even in contexts far removed from violent conflict, as Donatella della Porta shows, identity politics is closely "intertwined" with the deliberation process among citizens, threatening to contaminate the normative discourse.[47] Gaps in the scholarship on postconflict deliberation reflect our limited understanding of the use of ethnic identities during deliberation, weaken theoretical claims about a deliberative route to reconciliation, and point to the need to bring identities into the study of postconflict deliberation.

Deliberation and Conflict Dynamics

The narrowness of the theorization and operationalization of the concept of ethnic identity in the scholarship on deliberation in postconflict societies stems from the field's general lack of engagement with conflict, including its dynamics and legacies.[48] To infer reconciliation by studying how people talk about war crimes, we need to account for how conflict defines the scope of postconflict contention, draws the lines of societal division, and informs the use of identities during deliberation. As I argue below, even if it is attainable in discussions about war crimes involving all parties to a conflict, good-quality deliberation measured by fulfillment of deliberative standards of equality, reciprocity, common good orientation, and respect is necessary for discussing and agreeing on a transitional justice strategy among former foes. However, on its own it is not sufficient for interethnic reconciliation.

The arguments about good-quality deliberation do not shed light on how people use ethnic identities during postconflict deliberation and how it intersects with identity politics. By contrast, an ethical perspective can capture how people enact their ethnic identities during deliberation. It highlights the extent to which these discursive identity practices can address and counter divisive identity politics premised on the denigration of the ethnic Other and their wartime suffering. Foregrounding the role of ethnic identities in deliberation allows us to evaluate the transformative impact of deliberation in postconflict contexts, where the possibility for the deliberative repair of interethnic relations depends on addressing challenges to interethnic reconciliation posed by conflict and postconflict identity politics.

Hot Issues in Hot Settings

The case for deliberation despite deep divisions and for its contribution to a transition from war to peace rests on the ability of deliberative democracy to "process what are arguably the toughest kinds of political issues, the mutually contradictory assertions of identity that define a divided society."[49] Theoretically, the case for deliberation in hot settings is a push-back against skepticism that ethnic division will spoil the quality of deliberation. Empirical tests of deliberation in postconflict societies have produced limited insights into the possibility of deliberation (as a mode of communication distinct from debate) in divided societies.

These limitations result from a selective approach to issues presented as deliberation topics across deep divides. With a caveat that any topic can be controversial in societies polarized by conflict, scholars of deliberation in divided societies such as Northern Ireland, Belgium, Colombia, and Bosnia and Herzegovina have focused on issues that can unite communities.[50] We have learned that divided societies can deliberate about education and peace, for example.[51] However, we do not yet know whether the legacy of mass atrocity, which is the most divisive of all issues in postconflict societies, can lead to good-quality deliberation. National identity issues put a toll on deliberation both as a process and an outcome, as demonstrated by the engagement of Tibetans and ethnic Chinese over the issue of Tibet's self-determination.[52] Will discussion about war crimes involving former adversaries derail deliberation?

When people die or suffer in war because of their ethnic identity, wartime injury becomes a symbol of that identity. At the same time, transitional justice, and reconciliation as its prime normative goal, are premised on addressing past wrongs. Luigi Bobbio argues that prejudices surface more easily where what is at stake includes hot questions along which "explicit fracture lines exist in public opinion."[53] Deliberating about war crimes is akin to stress-testing the concept of deliberation in divided societies. To reconstruct postconflict societies during peacebuilding, deliberation must withstand the potentially detrimental effects of engaging with the root cause of identity polarization in postconflict societies: the commission of war crimes. Therefore, when grounding reconciliation in mutuality in interethnic discourse, we need to show that deliberation of a hot issue, such as the legacy of violence, can take place in the hot setting of divided societies. To avoid slipping into the descriptive study of deliberation, which overlooks normatively demanding features of a deliberative mode of communication, the empirical strategy must demonstrate the fulfillment of deliberative virtues when antagonists discuss past wrongs.

Deliberation and Ethnic Diversity

Scholars have approached deliberation in divided societies exclusively as a dyadic exchange between members of two ethnic groups. Focusing on how deliberation unfolds between two ethnic groups, for example, fits the conflict in Northern

Ireland, which has involved Catholics and Protestants. However, a model of dyadic deliberation is ill-suited for the study of many other contemporary conflicts. It does not reflect the ethnic complexity of intrastate conflicts, such as the one in Bosnia and Herzegovina, which involve more than two ethnic groups; neither does it account for challenges to deliberation posed by the regional character of contemporary conflicts that involve multiple ethnic communities straddling state borders.

Unlike scholars of deliberation, scholars of conflict processes have engaged with ethnic complexity and its consequences for conflict.[54] For example, David Cunningham shows that a greater number of parties in a conflict means that the conflict will last longer and involve graver harm.[55] The question of the extent of ethnic diversity and its effects on deliberation has not been addressed to date. If deliberation is to have a restorative impact on war-torn societies, a deliberative exercise should align with conflict dynamics and include all parties to a conflict. As we will see, a regional and ethnically complex conflict such as that surrounding the dissolution of Yugoslavia is a case in point.

Since the end of the Cold War, there has been an increase in intrastate wars that have a cross-border dimension.[56] In 2016, 38 percent of intrastate conflicts "were internationalized, in the sense that external states contributed troops to one or both sides in the conflict."[57] In regional conflicts, neighboring ethnic-kin states and substate groups of paramilitaries and rebels are directly or indirectly involved in violence across borders. Additionally, as illustrated by the disintegration of the former Yugoslavia and the former Soviet Union, state fragmentation changes the nature of borders, and with them, the nature of the cross-border actors' involvement. Regional and cross-border dimensions of conflict shape peace efforts.[58]

Recognizing the regional dynamics of conflicts and patterns of harm, scholars have called for the inclusion in transitional justice processes of all ethnic groups involved in a conflict.[59] Similarly, multiple lines of identity division need to be considered when a deliberative approach is applied to recovery in postconflict environments, which ought to align with conflict dynamics. We need to be precise when theorizing and evaluating the kind of ethnic diversity that supports or undermines good-quality deliberation.

We know that dyadic deliberation that includes members of two ethnic groups is possible in divided societies. However, deliberative gains achieved in dyadic interactions partially satisfy justice needs after conflicts that involve more than two ethnic groups. As Kathleen Gallagher Cunningham and Nils Weidmann note, "accommodation that is group-specific provides no benefit to other groups."[60] When reconciliation is at stake, multiethnic discussions that accurately reflect all ethnic groups involved in a conflict should also be deliberative. In line with the critique centered on theorizing identity in deliberation across ethnic lines, the question of identity will impinge on deliberation in terms not only of the number of ethnic identity groups involved but also, crucially, of how people involved express their ethnic identities in deliberation.

Enactment of Ethnic Identities in Deliberation

People have many identities, and certain identities become more salient in different contexts. Violence people suffer as members of an ethnic group can accentuate ethnic identity. Engagement with a former adversary entails a social context where people's sense of difference is likely to be accentuated further. The gap I have outlined—our limited grasp of how speakers use their ethnic identities when interacting with members from adversary ethnic groups about past wrongs—results from two related weaknesses of the study of deliberation in divided societies.

On the one hand, embracing a constructivist approach to identity as malleable, scholars have credited deliberation with a normative shift from exclusive ethnic identity to inclusive civic identity. This identity change is conceived at the macrolevel of a conflict-ridden polity, spurred by the reconfiguration of state-civil society relations within a consociational institutional context. This assertion raises a question about how the microlevel practice of deliberation, which may occur among citizens or within state institutions, such as parliaments, can produce macrolevel effects in a divided society, including identity transformation. It is a recognized dilemma in the scholarship on deliberative democracy, which scholars of deliberation across deep divisions have also left unaddressed. On the other hand, although the constructivist approach to identity is a lynchpin of theorizing the benefits of deliberation in divided societies, to test deliberation across deep divides empirically, scholars have operationalized ethnic identities as speakers' fixed identity categories (for example, Catholics and Protestants in Northern Ireland).[61] Positive outcomes for intergroup relations are inferred from the measurement of the quality of discourse during interethnic communication, or as a measure of attitudes toward antagonists as an outcome of interethnic deliberation. However, they do not speak directly to ethnic identity change of individuals and groups, posited as critical to the reconstruction of divided societies.

These theoretical and empirical challenges in importing a concept of identity into the study of deliberation in divided societies reflect the broader challenge of studying identity. The definitional anarchy and the related complexity of identity as a concept, evident across different disciplines, have impacted scholarly attempts to devise analytic frameworks for identity as a variable.[62] Although theorizing deliberation in divided societies pivots on the impact of deliberation on ethnic identities and vice versa, the scholarship generally glosses over these defi-nitional quandaries and their theoretical and empirical implications. This reveals the need to specify how a conceptualization of identity is "uniquely matched" to appropriate analytic approaches to overcome the disconnect between theo-retical propositions and empirical observations in the study of postconflict deliberation.[63]

To submit normative claims made by deliberative democrats to rigorous scru-tiny, it is useful to specify that envisaging a shift from ethnic to civic identity in divided societies reflects the understanding of identity as a type identity. Type identities, according to James Fearon, are "labels applied to persons who share or are thought to share some characteristics or characteristic, in appearance, behav-ioral traits, beliefs, attitudes, values, skills (e.g., language), knowledge, opinions, experience, historical commonalities (like region or place of birth), and so on."[64] Drawing on the scholarship on contact theory, which informs theories of delib-eration in divided societies, can help us illuminate how scholars have conceptual-ized identity change as a result of deliberation in divided societies.[65]

Recategorization implies the creation of a superordinate category, where in-group and out-group categories are merged under a more inclusive super-ordinate identity.[66] This is what deliberative democrats mean when they argue that deliberation in divided societies promotes an (inclusive) national identity, propped up by a change from ethnic to civic identity of groups that constitute the postconflict polity.[67] Pursuing a procedural understanding of deliberative democracy, O'Flynn argues that "deliberative democracy provides normative standards that, if appropriately institutionalised, can lead to a stronger sense of common national identity among citizens."[68] Recategorization implies the maxi-mum reduction of prejudice toward the out-group. It is not easy, but it is possible to achieve.[69] Such a conception of identity change, either at the macrolevel of groups or at the microlevel of individuals involved in interethnic discussions, has not been demonstrated to flow from the experience of deliberation, undermin-ing the normative claims made by scholars of deliberation in divided societies.[70]

Fresh perspectives on the role of ethnic identities in deliberation in societies divided by conflict can be gained by shifting our approach from recategorization of identities as a result of deliberation to the enactment of identities during delibera-tion. This approach broadly relates to the understanding of identity as role identity and locates the study of identity at the intersection of social interaction and dis-course. According to Peter Burke and Donald Reitzes, "identities are meanings one attributes to oneself in a role (and that others attribute to one)," which come to be known and understood by individuals through interactions with others.[71] Under-standing identity as an "interactional accomplishment" has a long history and spans multiple disciplines.[72] The notion of identity produced through interaction is an alternative to the operationalization of identity as a static category in the empirical scholarship on deliberation across deep divides. It directs our attention to the contingent and dynamic deployment of identity during deliberation.

How speakers enact their ethnic identities is an unexplored dimension of deliberation. One potential approach to study this question is the positioning perspective. This approach focuses on the discursive process of joint production of an(y) identity as it emerges in interaction.[73] The analytical focus on interaction leads to the possibility for conceptualizing how identities are enacted in interethnic communication. However, because the positioning perspective does not specify a priori which particular position or identity is of prime theoretical interest, it is of limited use to the study of postconflict deliberation. By contrast, an alternative approach that retains the focus on interaction and embraces the concept of role identities associated with predictable role performances is analytically more promising. Given the salience of ethnic identity in postconflict societies, leveraging the concept of role identity allows us to scrutinize how a sense of ethnic difference defined by victimization based on ethnicity is deployed in deliberation across ethnic lines.[74]

The enactment of ethnic identity as a role identity during deliberation across ethnic lines is both a conceptual and empirical question. As Hartmut Mokros points out, views of identity as interactively achieved rather than fixed "offer opportunities for personal liberation and social reorganization around principles of relational responsibility."[75] If we think of deliberation after conflict in terms of "social interaction" as a site where identities are enacted and negotiated, different enactments of ethnic identity can either promote or undermine reconciliation grounded in mutuality.[76] Examining how (and whether) ethnic identity is enacted provides a novel perspective on what "work" ethnic identities do during deliberation across ethnic lines.[77] This social interactional perspective on identity opens up new vistas for empirical research on reconciliation that are otherwise closed off by the "categorical essentialism" underlying the operationalization of static identities in extant scholarship.[78] An ethical perspective on deliberative interaction can reveal how these identity dynamics in public communication across ethnic lines overcome identity politics and what Bächtiger and Parkinson call the "competitive search for truth" during deliberation, which stands in the way of interethnic solidarity and reconciliation.[79]

Reconciliation and Discursive Solidarity

The next section turns to solidarity in interethnic interactions, which is necessary for reconciliation through deliberation about war crimes. Solidarity—a concept that denotes "the feeling of reciprocal sympathy and responsibility among members of a group which promotes mutual support"—has preoccupied scholars of transitional justice processes, who have a fundamental concern with reconstructing societies torn by conflict.[80] In postconflict societies where in-group solidarity has been cemented by war and violence, a shift toward solidarity that transcends group boundaries indicates a "certain amount of moral transformation."[81] Drawing on Habermas's theory of communicative action and Axel Honneth's theory of recognition, I develop a discursive perspective on solidarity in interethnic interactions in a transitional justice process. This perspective focuses on empathetic recognition of the ethnic Other in public discourse as a vehicle for counteracting divisive identity politics and its distorting effect on interethnic discourse. Like Stijn Oosterlynck et al., I am interested in shifting the analysis from macrolevel sources of solidarity toward "forms of solidarity in diversity [that] can emerge from concrete interpersonal practices."[82] Here I am particularly interested in discursive identity practices that capture various ways in which people enact their identity in interethnic interactions that are a source of solidarity. At this "microlevel of everyday interaction," identity-based grievances, Paige Arthur argues, have "important and varied effects."[83]

Habermas's theory of communicative action, which informs theorizing on deliberation in divided societies, is a dialogical theory. It "regards the identification of the correct principles of morality as a project that must be carried out collectively by all those potentially affected by their adoption."[84] Deliberation as an intersubjective communicative practice brings to the fore the relationship between deliberators. According to Habermas, "discourse ethics defends a morality of equal respect and solidaristic responsibility for everybody."[85] Such an ethical perspective on deliberation is sensitive to the risk that "there is always a possibility of communication getting distorted, especially when humans have to engage in situations of differences and conflicts," as is the case in societies divided by conflict.[86] The discourse-ethical model of deliberation requires operationalization that is responsive to deliberation in a concrete context and concerning different kinds of questions.[87] Albena Azmanova observes that "deliberations are inevitably permeated by real interests and ideological distortions."[88] A deliberative approach to reconciliation needs to show how distortions stemming from identity politics present during interethnic deliberation are overcome through solidary interactions.

Deliberation is widely understood to be transformative. It can yield respect and solidarity and thus reduce the differences between deliberators.[89] From this perspective, solidarity is an outcome of deliberation. However, addressing the character of the ethics of deliberation, Conrado Hübner Mendes contends that "a focus solely on the consequences does neither portray nor explain the proper actions that are likely to produce those cherished effects."[90] Rather, the ethics of deliberation is instantiated through practices during deliberation itself, as these practices are more than just means to coveted ends.[91] If we conceptualize post-conflict reconciliation through public communication grounded in mutuality, then the very process of deliberation ought to be a solidary interaction. Rosemary Nagy argues that in postconflict contexts solidarity needs to be "something deeper or more substantive" than democratic reciprocity.[92] Democratic reciprocity is a feature of good-quality deliberation that signals convergence or consensus on an issue but does not require the deeper commitment to moral values on which reconciliation depends.[93] Therefore, leveraging the ethical perspective clarifies the theoretical and practical importance of postconflict deliberation as an exercise of relationship-building between ethnic Others. When solidarity emerges through exposure to "the otherness of others," foregrounding the role of identity in postconflict deliberation entails asking how the ethnic Other is construed and engaged.[94] What is the role and effect of identities conceived as an individual versus a collective concept? I answer this question by considering how recognition of the ethnic Other can accommodate differences and offset divisive identity politics.

Solidarity as a practical exercise of the ethics of deliberation captures the dynamics of negotiation and transformation of human relations through communication.[95] As William Umphres points out, deliberative conflicts are conflicts between different identities within society. Different conceptions of justice reflect people's different life histories, race, gender, sexuality, or religion, and the reasons people give and claims they make to others are public expressions of their identity. Consequently, people engage in public deliberation because they seek affirmation of their claims: "we want our reasons to matter, not just for us, but for others." Ultimately, "successful deliberation forms a process of recognition that builds solidarity."[96]

Addressing the struggles for recognition, Habermas concedes that "the challenge becomes all the greater the more profound are the religious, racial, or ethnic differences, or the historical-cultural disjunctures."[97] Societies emerging from ethnic conflict present us with a case of the deepest sort of identity divisions. Bodily injury and harm, most commonly through ethnic targeting, intensify the sense of ethnic difference. In struggles for recognition, Honneth contends, physical injury such as torture and rape are the most fundamental sort of personal degradation and the most destructive type of humiliation.[98] Bodily injury represents an extreme type of disrespect and the antithesis of solidarity. Therefore, drawing on Honneth, during deliberation about war crimes in postconflict societies, solidarity arises at the intersection of newfound recognition and persistent ethnic identities defined by wartime injury. These "lifeworld solidarities depend on a mutual understanding that individuals can achieve and sustain" within a group.[99] In the deliberative quest for justice for war crimes, a group involves people from different ethnic groups affected by wartime violence. Solidarity hence entails a sense of community; or, as Nancy Fraser puts it, the privileged moral feeling is "social solidarity." This means that the norms governing interactions are not norms of intimacy such as love and care, or those of formal institutions such as rights and entitlement. Rather, in public communication, the norms of recognition and dignity are enshrined through social practices.[100] Communication is one such practice that can be empirically traced in discourse.

Furthermore, in a deliberative approach to reconciliation, it is important to elucidate the relationship between an individual (and their own ascriptive group) and a community of deliberators. From the perspective of discourse ethics, the sense of groupness that undergirds solidarity does not entail erasing one's own (group) identity. Habermas presents a moral universalism that is responsive to difference. He draws an explicit connection between justice and solidarity because "moral concern is owed equally to persons both as irreplaceable individuals and as members of the community."[101] At the same time, Habermas specifies that individuality is preserved within a solidary community in a moral universalism sensitive to difference by "tak[ing] the form of *nonleveling* and *nonappropriating* inclusion of the other *in his otherness*."[102] This intersubjective understanding of solidarity, according to Honneth, draws attention to the structure of relations of recognition.[103] Honneth argues that it is "the mechanism of symmetrical esteem" that can produce the relations of solidarity and sympathy across social boundaries, where "symmetrical" means that "every subject is free from being collectively denigrated, so that one is given the chance to experience oneself to be recognized."[104]

In deliberation about war crimes, solidary bonds ought to cross ethnic boundaries, and recognition of individuals should be accompanied by an acknowledgment of their "connectedness to specific human groups" with particular cultures, histories, social practices, values, habits, forms of life, vocabularies of self-interpretation, and narrative traditions.[105] The acknowledgment of an individual's sense of difference is of paramount importance in deliberations in postconflict societies, because although the individual injury for which justice is sought is experienced personally and intimately, it is embedded in the specific wartime experience of one's identity group. As Daniel Philpott argues, recognition of victims in the aftermath of mass violence entails "addressing the wound of social ignorance."[106] This moral act is also profoundly political in societies divided by conflict and identity politics, where the relationships between diversity and solidarity are "ultimately a matter of politics."[107] Determining whether solidary bonds based on recognition of the ethnic Other have formed during deliberation can tell us a great deal about whether the virtue of ethical communication between former adversaries can transcend divisive identity politics in face-to-face, interethnic interactions.

The study of deliberation in divided societies has established itself as a subfield in the scholarship on deliberation. The conceptual leap of locating deliberation in circumstances that are arguably the least conducive for deliberation is driven by the recognition of the potential contribution of deliberation to the transition from war to peace. Although identity politics features prominently in discussions both of impediments to deliberation and of its necessity in divided societies, theorizing on deliberation in divided societies has—paradoxically—neglected the role of identities, and with it the role of identity politics, in deliberation. To date, our understanding of how deliberation after conflict can be reconciliatory, and promote peace, has been constrained by a lack of consideration of how conflict shapes identities, and of how identities shaped by conflict affect deliberation. Identities, as Rogers Smith argues, "are among the most normatively significant and behaviorally consequential aspects of politics," especially so in the aftermath of mass atrocity.[108] Deliberation involving former adversaries needs to be more finely attuned to the role of identities underwritten by mutual victimization in order for deliberation to help build peace.

Drawing on deliberative approaches to the reconstruction of postconflict societies, I argue that reconciliation takes place through deliberative rationality and discursive solidarity in public communication about war crimes involving former adversaries. How people enact their ethnic identities at the microlevel of deliberative communication is distinct from how they fulfill deliberative virtues in communication across ethnic lines. With an eye toward ethnic identities defined by conflict, the key analytical question is not whether someone can be described in a particular way but whether and how an identity "is made relevant" in deliberation.[109] The enactment of ethnic identities when addressing the legacy of mass atrocity has to support the ethic of interethnic solidarity. Otherwise, deliberation about war crimes in postconflict societies may be well reasoned without being reconciliatory.

Engagement with conflict dynamics and their legacy frames the investigation of identity and its significance for deliberation in divided societies in three ways. First, deliberation should address war crimes as a cause of an identity divide. Second, ethnic diversity of deliberations needs to reflect the reality of ethnic conflict. Third, we need to understand whether and how people enact their ethnic identities in deliberative encounters with ethnic Others, and how that enactment affects identity politics. Recalibrating deliberation in divided societies by bringing identity into the study of deliberation raises several empirically verifiable questions: Can war crimes and their legacy be deliberated in societies divided by conflict? How does ethnic diversity impact deliberation? Is the enactment of ethnic identity compatible with the ethics of discursive solidarity? These questions turn on the microlevel dynamics of deliberation as a process and guide the empirical analysis in the ensuing chapters.

QUANTIFYING DISCOURSE IN TRANSITIONAL JUSTICE

> **Why do we always make transcripts of all these consultations? Because they show an evolution, starting with an initial idea, which was a beautiful but insufficiently clear vision, and its development to where we are today.**
>
> —Participant in the RECOM consultation in Serbia, October 10, 2008

The RECOM coalition meticulously recorded and transcribed the consultative sessions involving participants from all ethnic groups that fought in the Balkan conflicts. In the process, it generated some 4 million words of publicly available data, uniquely valuable for the empirical study of postconflict deliberation.[1] The transcripts served as a record of a wide range of positions expressed by the participants on their preferred approaches to transitional justice and as a guide for crafting proposals for a transitional justice mechanism. The first phase of consultations identified the focus on a regional approach to transitional justice through a fact-finding process. The transcripts were particularly important in the second phase, which focused on the Draft Statute and the codification of the agreed terms of the proposed regional fact-finding commission.

This book examines reconciliation after conflict by investigating how people talk about war crimes. As Paige Arthur points out, new normative perspectives require that "those working in transitional justice develop a new set of measures to address the specific justice concerns of transitions to peace."[2] This chapter lays out the empirical strategy for studying reconciliation by measuring the quality of deliberation in RECOM's discussions about war crimes across ethnic lines. Empirically establishing the quality of deliberation allows us to assess how speakers engage with each other. As I have argued, good-quality deliberation in discussions about past wrongs in search of justice is necessary for reconciliation. It indicates that former adversaries can address the divisive legacy through a reasoned, civil, and respectful discussion while considering the positions of ethnic Others. The measuring of the deliberativeness of discourse in this research builds on the empirical study of democratic deliberation in general, and of deliberation in divided societies in particular. The chapter discusses how the measurement instrument has been refined in order to capture the deliberativeness of discourse in postconflict societies.

While acknowledging that the effects of justice are difficult to measure, scholars have made strides in addressing a major weakness in the transitional justice literature: the lack of empirical evidence for its normative claims.[3] The growing body of empirical evidence about the effects of transitional justice relies almost exclusively on survey and experimental methods.[4] The full theoretical potential of the quantitative study of discourse is yet to be tapped.[5] The quantitative content analysis applied to the naturally occurring data of real-life discussions about war crimes presented in this book expands the scope of empirical evidence for normative claims in the study of transitional justice and reconciliation. The quantification of discourse in the field of transitional justice extends efforts to provide a novel empirical assessment of peace.[6] Framed in terms of mutuality, reconciliation is an integral part of peacebuilding. Empirical elucidation of how reconciliation among former adversaries unfolds enhances our understanding of the quality of peace. As Peter Wallensteen argues, "quality peace" is determined by the extent to which the postwar condition provides for justice, reflected "in the recognition of pain and creation of transparent structures" that address past wrongs.[7]

This chapter reviews the Discourse Quality Index (DQI), which is the measurement instrument that captures the deliberative quality of discourse, and outlines its adaptation for this book. The result is the construction of the Discourse Quality Index for the Study of Transitional Justice (DQITJ), fit for measuring the extent of fulfillment of deliberative virtues in postconflict civil society deliberations about war crimes.[8] The DQITJ's application provides insight into the deliberativeness of the discourse of the RECOM consultations.

The Measurement Instrument

The DQI measures the quality of deliberation. Jürg Steiner and his colleagues developed it in response to the need to supplement philosophical theorizing about deliberation with "empirical investigations of real-life deliberations."[9] Application of the DQI in various deliberative contexts contributed to the empirical turn in the scholarship on deliberation. Scholars of deliberation have applied different research designs (experimental vs. naturalistic-observational) and measurement strategies (DQI vs. outcome-based measures).[10] The DQI has become "the most encompassing and most widely used measure of deliberation," in formal and informal settings, predominantly in democratic contexts.[11] It has also been applied to deliberation in divided societies. As a measurement strategy, the DQI is fit for a process-based approach to deliberation because it captures the deliberativeness of discourse.[12] It lends itself to empirical evaluation of reconciliation as a communicative process, with the potential to provide granular insight into multiple dimensions of deliberative discourse.[13]

As a content analysis scheme aimed at assessing deliberation, the DQI begins "with categories based on political theory and measure[s] the extent to which these categories occur in the actual talk of participants."[14] The DQI is grounded in Jürgen Habermas's discourse ethics.[15] Given the complexity of the theoretical debate about the meaning and substance of deliberation, the creators of the DQI offered methodological and practical reasons for their decision to operationalize the Habermasian perspective on deliberation. According to them, taking into account all theories of deliberation would result in an unworkably complex and inconsistent measurement instrument. Grounding the DQI in Habermas's discourse ethics ensured the instrument would be more usable and reliable.[16]

The dimensions of DQI are defined by Habermas's notion of "communicative action," which stipulates that "individuals give and criticize reasons for holding or rejecting particular validity claims, so that universally valid norms can be discovered through reason."[17] Informed by Habermas's understanding of deliberation, which foregrounds the force of a better argument, the DQI consists of seven dimensions: participation, level of justification, content of justification, respect (for groups, demands of others, and counterarguments), and constructive politics.[18] Together, they represent the virtues of deliberation and capture procedural requirements that distinguish deliberation from other modes of communication.

Participation refers to the ability of speakers to participate freely in a debate, which is reflected in categories of the DQI that indicate whether a speaker has been interrupted.[19] The level of justification refers to the extent of justification offered for each demand, which represents a position articulated by a speaker. The level of justification ranges from no justification to sophisticated justification, and it is based on evaluating reasons offered by the speaker. The content of justification identifies whether appeals have been made in terms of a narrow group interest or in terms of the common good. This category of the DQI distinguishes two types of the common good: one expressed in utilitarian terms, derived from J. S. Mill's reference to "the greatest good for the greatest number," and the other expressed in terms of a difference principle, derived from Rawls, referring to helping the least advantaged in society.[20] The three categories of respect concern respect for groups affected by policies, respect for demands expressed by others, and respect for counterarguments, including specification of whether demands are expressed in a neutral, degrading, or respectful manner. Lastly, constructive politics gauges the extent to which speakers are prepared to build consensus, assessed in terms of whether speakers retain their positions, suggest alternative proposals beyond the given agenda, or offer mediating proposals that fit the given agenda.[21]

A subsequent revision of the original 2003 DQI, yielding DQI 2.0, retained the Habermasian underpinnings of deliberation, as well as a conception of deliberation occurring on a continuum from "no deliberation" to "ideal deliberation."[22] The DQI 2.0 addressed a need to adapt the index to the reality of citizens' deliberation (as opposed to its original application in parliamentary settings). Difference democrats—scholars preoccupied with differences and their implications for democratic politics—argued that the requirement for dispassionate argument in deliberation disadvantages some speakers. This criticism led to recognition of "alternate" forms of discourse, such as storytelling, narration, and testimony, as acceptable deliberative practice.[23] In the DQI 2.0, storytelling is another category of deliberative discourse.

In this research, I adapt and refine those measures of different dimensions of deliberative discourse that are consequential features of discourse in post-conflict societies. This adaptation of the DQI is guided by a need for maximum adherence to the DQI as specified by its creators. It entails carrying out critical, albeit minimal, adjustments, which is appropriate for studying postconflict civil society deliberations on the legacy of mass atrocity. This measurement strategy is motivated by considerations of democratic deliberative theory-building, which highlights the necessity to produce comparable findings with existing studies of citizens' deliberations in general, and of deliberation across deep divisions in particular.[24] A comparative dimension is critical so that "empirical research can provoke reflection on normative values" of democratic deliberation.[25]

The creators of the DQI have recognized that discourse is context-specific and that not all of their categories may be applicable all the time.[26] Scholarly applications of the DQI have been accompanied by revisions appropriate for studying deliberation in various contexts, contributing to theorizing about deliberation and its premises.

Constructing the DQI for the Study of Transitional Justice

The adaptation of the DQI for the study of reconciliation and transitional justice has adhered to the structure of DQI 2.0, which was modified for application to citizens' deliberation and included storytelling. Deliberative virtues expressed as DQI categories contained in the DQI for the Study of Transitional Justice are summarized in table 3.1. As in the original DQI and DQI 2.0, it includes the categories of participation and the rationality of justification, expressed in four categories: no justification, inferior justification, qualified justification, and sophisticated justification. The common good categories are disaggregated and include separate indicators for the common good expressed in terms of the group interest, in terms of the difference principle, an abstract good, and an individual interest.

In particular, the category of group interest is refined to capture how conflict refracts on interethnic communication involving multiple ethnic groups. Measuring the quality of deliberation about war crimes after a regional conflict raises the same questions of specification and disaggregation of group interest as applications of the DQI to transnational deliberations in the European context. On the one hand, the dilemma concerns the scale of reference: is group interest expressed in terms of, for example, the national, European, or global common good?[27] On the other hand, there is a question about which kind of group interests are invoked: should the group be defined by an identity-related concept, such as a nation or an ethnic group, or by a sectoral affiliation, for example an energy sector or an educational sector?[28] In cross-ethnic deliberations about transitional justice in the aftermath of regional conflict, public and group interests "cannot be seen only within the narrow borders of nation states."[29] It also should include common good framed in regional, that is multiethnic, terms. Furthermore, the conceptualization of a group interest in a region comprising states that are themselves multiethnic states requires an additional level of disaggregation below the level of the state. The DQITJ was adjusted to reflect nested group identities: ethnic group, country, and region or a larger multiethnic community.[30] For deliberations about war crimes, the specification of ethnic identity group as a basis of the common good is consequential. The casting of interests in ethnocentric terms represents a narrow, inward-looking definition of the common good, in contrast to when it is framed in multiethnic terms, where regard for the ethnic Other—a key procedural dimension of good-quality deliberation—is implicit. The latter captures the notion of mutuality into which the understanding of reconciliation is embedded. Existing studies of deliberation in divided societies that apply the DQI have used a common good category of "own group," which, on the one hand, conflates different forms of group identities, such as ethnic and national (i.e., related to one's country), and, on the other hand, overlooks the possibility that speakers can also appeal to the interests of a region or a broader multiethnic community, thus transcending a narrow ethnic interest.[31] These nuances have to be a part of the measurement strategy if we want to capture the quality of postconflict deliberation in a regional, albeit divided, context.

Further, the DQITJ incorporates a common good category in terms of the difference principle. This category pertains to groups such as victims, young people, and future generations. It is distinct from the group interest category defined by different levels of identity speakers invoke. In other words, the definition of a group in terms of the difference principle is nonascriptive and refers to a group singled out in cost-benefit reasoning. In addition, the DQITJ introduces the common good category in terms of abstract principles.[32] In divided postconflict societies, the common good category may be expressed without mentioning any groups and may refer to a general need for peace or social justice, for example.[33] Lastly, an additional category captures whether the common good is expressed in self-interested terms as an individual-centered justification. This indicator captures the opposite pole of the common good, which is expressed in terms of a group interest.

Respect categories in the DQITJ are adjusted for cross-ethnic deliberations. These categories capture whether there is respect toward participants (and their arguments), as well as groups, expressed in language, ranging from disrespectful to explicitly respectful.[34] The inclusion of respectful language as a DQI category reflects the adaptation of the DQI from institutional to citizen-centered settings.[35] If we are to glean the deliberativeness of discourse in societies divided by conflict, the distinction between (dis)respect that deliberators express toward individuals versus groups is relevant. The collective conception of the ethnic Other is considered an obstacle to interethnic relations and could be associated with distortion of discourse across ethnic lines. How respect is expressed toward both individuals and groups corresponds to critical dimensions of deliberativeness in interethnic contexts that have routinely been neglected in existing empirical studies of deliberation in divided societies.[36]

Lastly, DQITJ includes the storytelling category and specifies the relationships between it and the presented argument, whether a story figures as a sole justification or is used to reinforce an argument. This specification goes beyond binary identification of the presence or absence of stories during deliberation and captures their status in relation to rational justification.[37]

To analyze the quality of deliberation about the legacy of war crimes across ethnic lines, individual dimensions of deliberation need to be constructed as an index, which can be used as a measurement instrument. The guiding principle in constructing the DQI is that the index's components are scalable. As unidimensionality of scale-building is not a given, it is necessary to check whether components form a coherent set, measured by their correlations.[38] They then "can be combined to form a scale that can serve as an overall measure of discourse quality."[39] Following Marco Steenbergen et al. and Markus Spörndli, the DQITJ was created first by running the Principal Component Analysis on the polychoric correlations of the following categories: justification rationality, common good, two categories of respect (for participants and groups), and storytelling.[40] The results show that the first component represents more variance than other components and more variance than the original variables (i.e., DQI categories), and that all categories load positively on the first component.[41] These observations justify the construction of a single, additive index that can capture the quality of deliberation in the RECOM corpus.

RECOM's Consultations and Textual Data

Divided societies are characterized by sparse interaction and communication across ethnic divisions. Structural divisions further reduce possibilities for intergroup contact. Ethnic homogenization of territories due to wartime violence can often be enshrined in peace agreements. In addition, postconflict consociational governance arrangements rest on intergroup elite communication. As critics of consociationalism point out, these arrangements can simultaneously entrench segmentation at a societal level. The lack of communication across ethnic lines has also impacted research designs in the study of deliberation in divided societies, notably the use of experiments and deliberative polls. For example, Didier Caluwaerts and Kris Deschouwer cite the "absence of 'naturalistic' locations" as a reason for their opting for an experimental research design.[42] At the same time, Seraina Pedrini points out the rareness of transcripts of civic deliberation, such as the transcripts of the RECOM civil society consultations, which involved speakers from adversary ethnic groups who themselves belong to different stakeholder communities, including victims, teachers, human rights activities, legal professionals, and veterans. Unlike the transcripts of civil society deliberations, the transcripts of parliamentary debates are widely available.[43] The systematic analysis of the RECOM corpus can contribute to empirical validation and development of the tenets of deliberative democracy in divided societies by probing whether "hot deliberations" about hot issues, such as war crimes, in postconflict contexts are feasible.[44] In order to assess the validity of the findings, the following sections address the issue of selection. In this book, the selection issue concerns the rationale for selecting specific debates, that is consultations about the Draft Statute as opposed to all consultations, and the profile of participants in those consultations.

The text corpus comprises twenty transcripts of debates about the Draft Statute of the regional fact-finding commission held in 2010 and 2011.[45] These twenty transcripts represent all consultations about the Draft Statute. The procedural dimension of these consultations—speakers presenting their positions on the articles of the Draft Statute—approximates parliamentary debates about draft bills, although they represent citizens' deliberations. A researcher can track and evaluate positions on specific policy points, which makes the RECOM text corpus particularly suitable for the measurement of deliberativeness of discourse.[46] The form of communication and the issues discussed in these consultations about the Draft Statute differed from those of other consultations held under RECOM's auspices, where the discussion consisted of free-flowing expression of different views on how to pursue postconflict justice in the region. These unstructured consultations are not included in the corpus because they are not comparable with the consultations about the Draft Statute. Analyzing all cases of Statute deliberations in the universe of the RECOM consultations enhances the internal validity of the analysis, which aims to assess the relationship between a range of predictors of discourse quality and the deliberativeness of discourse.[47]

Next, I address the issue of participation in the RECOM process, because the findings can be driven by self-selection of participants into a deliberative process. For instance, Steiner observes that there was "most likely a bias toward moderation" in deliberative experiments in Bosnia and Herzegovina that included ordinary people.[48] Therefore, it is important to consider who took part in the RECOM consultations in order to ascertain the basis for the theoretical claims presented in this book. As discussed in chapter 1, participants in the RECOM consultations came from opposing ethnic groups and different stakeholder communities. Given the observational nature of this study, the selection of participants is not random. Even when conducting experiments, scholars of deliberation in divided societies have confronted the problem of random selection, particularly where it concerns the recruitment of research subjects directly affected by conflict.[49] In Colombia, where research involved ex-combatants from opposed sides in the conflict, the researchers faced the challenge of securing participation in experiments and could not assert that "the ex-combatants [they] studied were a random sample of the total population of ex-combatants."[50] The claims in this study are based on the informed assumption that participants in the process approximate typical fissures along different identity axes that affect how people address past harm in ethnically divided societies. All participants in the RECOM process had an interest in postconflict justice. Ian O'Flynn argues that shared intentions can facilitate deliberation in divided societies.[51] Postconflict justice had become a key fissure between ethnic groups in the Balkans. In the case of the RECOM process, it was by no means certain that participants in the RECOM would engage deliberatively with each other, despite their interest in postconflict justice. They were divided by multiple lines of division and, above all, by ethnicity. This identity-based cleavage could have been deepened by discussing the highly sensitive and politicized nature of the topic of postconflict justice.

The RECOM consultations can be considered a typical case that contributes to theory development by producing arguments that can explain some but not all cases.[52] One needs to be precise about its external validity. The value of a typical case is in "contingent generalizations that apply to the subclass of cases" similar to those studied.[53] The RECOM consultations are a case of multistakeholder discussions in divided societies focused on shaping the transitional justice policy instrument after a regional conflict. As such they are distinct both from discussions in postconflict societies involving ordinary people or a single stakeholder group, such as victims or ex-combatants; from citizens' reconciliatory dialogues or open-ended discussions, for example about the future, that do not involve decisions on a particular issue; and from parliamentary debates in divided societies. The RECOM consultations involved people who are invested in transitional justice after the conflict but divided by their views on the issue. As such they represent a type of case in which "deliberation is most needed," but, at the same time, it is "most difficult to achieve."[54] The viability of deliberation as a mode of communication in such conditions of acute diversity and about a divisive topic in a postconflict context is an empirical question addressed in this book. Further external validity checks need to consider precisely the basis of the claims made here as part of future advances in the empirical study of deliberation in divided societies in different postconflict contexts.

The findings about deliberation and reconciliation in this study are based on the coding of the text corpus and analysis of the patterns of discourse, including identification of its latent features related to characteristics of the data, by adapting and applying the DQI.[55] The nature of the data also entails some limitations to the observational research design. As opposed to experimental research design, naturalistic observation does not involve any intervention or interference by a researcher. The RECOM textual data, produced in its natural setting, is independent from a researcher's control or manipulation. Variation in contextual and speaker variables is given; it cannot be assigned or controlled as in the experimental design. In addition, a researcher working with observational data does not have the possibility of administering a pre- and postdeliberation questionnaire. Apart from expanding the number of speaker variables (such as age, education and income levels, and linguistic competence in the outgroup's language) to assess deliberation, these questionnaires allow a researcher to capture the transformative impact of deliberation by measuring, for example, the change of opinion on an issue, or the change of attitude toward the outgroup, as Robert Luskin et al. do.[56] Constraints inherent in observational research impact how the DQI will be used. The DQI can be used both as a predictor of policy outcomes and as a dependent variable. This study adopts the latter strategy and associates the variation in contextual conditions and speakers' characteristics with the quality of discourse.[57] The variation in this research pertains to the characteristics of speakers, issues, and consultations, as well as linguistic features of discourse, measured at the level of speech. These variables are presented in table 4.1, which discusses their theoretical relevance for measuring deliberativeness.

The unit of analysis in the DQI coding strategy is a "speech," defined as "the public discourses by a particular individual delivered at a particular point in a debate." The relevance of the speech for coding is determined by whether it contains a "demand," that is "a proposal on what decision should or should not be made." According to Steenbergen et al., the demand is at "the heart of deliberation."[58] In the RECOM corpus, a demand corresponds to a position expressed by a participant in the consultations on a specific article of the Draft Statute. For example, this can be a position concerning where the seat of the future fact-finding commission should be located. The possibility of multiple demands within a single speech—that is, within a speaker's single speaking turn—requires adaptation of the coding strategy. Following André Bächtiger, this is accomplished by coding multiple demands in parallel.[59] This is an appropriate strategy for the RECOM corpus because speakers expressed views on different articles of the Draft Statute during a single speaking turn. Every time a speaker formulates a demand, it is considered a speech act.[60] Such use of discourse as a unit of analysis is particularly "appropriate for answering questions about how the deliberative discussion works and what kinds of communication people engage in when they are brought together to deliberate."[61]

The RECOM textual data consists of 1,211 speech acts uttered during twenty consultations. The entire corpus was first parsed so that each speech act corresponded to a speaker's position directly linked to an article of the Draft Statute. These speech acts include utterances by discussants but exclude utterances by moderators, in line with the practice followed in the study of parliamentary debates as well as experiments. The moderators introduced the sessions, briefed other participants about the process, summarized the arguments, and managed the flow of communication during the RECOM consultations.[62] The coded transcripts were in Bosnian, Serbian, Croatian, and Montenegrin languages.[63] The RECOM corpus was coded independently by the author and another coder. They manually coded each speech act, that is the segment of text expressing a position about an article of the Draft Statute, by assigning to it the values for all categories, for example equality, justification rationality, common good, as specified in the DQITJ codebook. An example of applying the coding to one speech act is presented in chapter 4.

The application of categories in the DQI is a subjective exercise because it requires a judgment by a coder.[64] It is necessary to verify whether coding decisions can be replicated by another coder to ascertain that the produced measures are not idiosyncratic, and that they are reproducible.[65] The total word count of the corpus of the RECOM consultations amounts to over half a million words.[66] The coding took seven and a half months.[67] Time and effort are challenging for a microlevel content analysis, which is why systematic content analysis is not carried out more frequently.[68] According to Klaus Krippendorff, "there is no set answer" to the question of what the level of acceptable disagreement is.[69] Existing empirical studies of deliberation, which apply the DQI, are a guide for an acceptable level of agreement. The results of the intercoder reliability tests for coding the categories in the DQITJ demonstrate substantial agreement.[70] Having checked the validity of codes that capture dimensions of deliberativeness, the following section provides insight into the extent of deliberative virtues present in the RECOM transitional justice consultations.

Deliberative Virtues in Discourse about War Crimes

A descriptive overview of the quality of deliberation about the legacy of war crimes in the Balkans is based on the analysis of the frequency of the codes corresponding to categories of the DQITJ (as shown in table 3.1) assigned to the speech acts in the RECOM corpus. These findings, which indicate the deliberativeness of discourse about war crimes involving former adversaries, are discussed comparatively in relation to the existing scholarship on deliberation in divided societies. A comparative perspective allows us to tease out the pattern of talk in discussions about the hot issue of wartime harm within the broader universe of cases of deliberation in divided societies, which have not addressed this divisive topic.

This section first turns to the level of justification, which speaks to the challenge of providing reasons while engaging with past injustice in a transitional justice process that brings together ethnic communities who were on opposite sides during the conflict. Of all speech acts in the RECOM corpus, just under one-third, or 27.17 percent, offered no or only inferior justification, whereas a majority (54.34%) provided qualified justification. The percentage of speech acts with sophisticated justification is 18.5 percent, which is somewhat lower than the percentage with inferior justification (19.82%).[71] The results indicate that discussing justice for war crimes—a highly divisive issue—is not incompatible with reason-giving.

TABLE 3.1 Absolute and relative frequency of DQITJ categories (N = 1,211 speech acts)

DQITJ CATEGORY	DESCRIPTION	N	%
Equality of participation	Interruption of a speaker	45	3.72
	No interruption	1,166	96.28
Justification rationality	No justification	89	7.35
	Inferior justification	240	19.82
	Qualified justification	658	54.34
	Sophisticated justification	224	18.50
Common good			
Identity group	Ethnic group	54	4.46
	My country	46	3.80
	Neutral/no reference	1,076	88.85
	My region/multiethnic	35	2.89
Difference principle	No reference	986	81.42
	Reference	225	18.58
Abstract principles	No reference	1,086	89.68
	Reference	125	10.32
Individual principle	No reference	1,192	98.43
	Reference	19	1.57
Respect			
Toward participants	Negative (disrespectful, foul language)	75	6.19
and their arguments	No reference	3	.25
	Neutral reference	1,054	87.04
	Positive (explicitly respectful)	79	6.52
Toward groups	Other groups denigrated	28	2.31
	Other groups not mentioned	1,012	83.57
	Neutral (mentioned but not denigrated)	157	12.96
	Explicit respect toward other groups	14	1.16
Storytelling	No story	1,126	92.98
	Story unrelated to the argument	4	.33
	Story related to the argument, sole justification	5	.41
	Story related to the argument, supports rational justification	76	6.28

These findings, drawn from a transitional justice process in the Balkans that involves all ethnic groups impacted by conflicts in the region, differ from results generated by dyadic deliberative experiments in Bosnia and Herzegovina, and in Colombia, where speech acts with no justification prevailed. Steiner reports that 36 percent of speeches included no justification in Colombia, and as many as 79 percent in Srebrenica, in Bosnia and Herzegovina. The much lower percentage of 7.35 percent of speech acts with no justification in the RECOM process approximates the lower figure of speech acts with no justification in the Belgian experiments, which is 18 percent. In that case, the propensity for reason-giving is accounted for by the fact that Belgium is an advanced democracy, and that participants were not "traumatized by an internal armed struggle."[72] Following this logic, the results in the RECOM case from the Balkans, which took place in a democratizing (and not yet fully democratized) context, and in the shadow of wartime trauma, should have been in line with the findings from experiments conducted in Bosnia and Herzegovina, and in Colombia, rather than with those in Belgium. This pattern of deliberative discourse raises two questions. The first concerns the extent of ethnic diversity during deliberation, which needs to reflect conflict dynamics, and its effects on the quality of deliberation.[73] The second concerns the importance of the format of an interethnic dialogue in divided societies, given the focus on the RECOM Draft Statute within this civil society-led consultative process on a transitional justice strategy, as opposed to open-ended discussion of a relevant question (as in deliberative experiments) or unstructured interethnic dialogues aimed at reconciliation but not necessarily at achieving agreement or a decision on a given issue. I return to this second question in the conclusion.

The prevalence of reason-giving in deliberation about transitional justice in the Balkans is accompanied by the relative absence of stories, which constitute an alternative type of discourse with a recognized role in deliberation. Given that the RECOM process is a type of citizens' deliberation, one would expect storytelling to be more common. However, only 7.02 percent of speech acts in the RECOM corpus contain a story.[74] Importantly, when participants told a story articulating their position on an article of the RECOM Draft Statute, it was usually to reinforce rational justification. Seventy-six speech acts (out of eighty-five that use a story) related the story to the argument rather than using it in place of an argument.[75]

The common good category as a distinct deliberative virtue indicates deliberators' willingness to move beyond a (narrowly) self-interested position. The DQITJ disaggregates different conceptions of the common good in terms of common group interest, the difference principle, abstract principle, and individual orientation.[76] The values for the common good category where interest is expressed through the prism of group identity are my ethnic group, my country, and our region/multiethnic. Only 1.57 percent of speech acts in the common good category are articulated in terms of individual orientation (as opposed to any type of group identity orientation). In the category that captures the notion of interest in terms of a group identity, 4.46 percent (or fifty-four) speech acts frame interest in terms of the benefit to the ethnic group and 3.8 percent (or forty-six) in terms of benefit to one's country, compared to 2.89 percent (or thirty-five) speech acts that refer to a regional and/or multiethnic conception of the community.[77] However, the prevalence of "selfish" self-interest, expressed in terms of an ethnocentric orientation needs to be evaluated in the context of other types of expression of the common good. The most prevalent common good orientation in the RECOM corpus, with a total of 225 speech acts, or 18.58 percent in this category, invokes the difference principle that refers to disadvantaged groups. In the RECOM corpus, these include victims in general and specific categories of victims, such as victims of sexual violence, the disabled, and young people. Abstract principles such as peace and reconciliation are invoked in 125 speech acts, or 10.32 percent in this category.

Such a distribution of the common good categories indicates that in formulating their positions, participants in the RECOM process were mindful of groups that were most affected by war crimes and the prospects of justice, in addition to invoking justification defined by ethnic identity. This points to the relevance of nonethnic rather than ethnic classification of cost-benefit calculations during deliberation of war crimes, though it is important to note that when participants presented their arguments in identity terms, ethnocentrism prevailed. When viewed comparatively with the results from deliberative experiments in divided societies, proportionally there are fewer speech acts in the RECOM corpus that reference the benefits of a speaker's own group (operationalized as an ethnic group), as compared to 31 percent in Colombia.[78] There is a similar level of reference to abstract principles as in Belgium, that is 8.5 percent compared to 10.32 percent in the RECOM process, but double the 5 percent found in Colombia.[79] With 504 speech acts cumulatively considering some form of common good (of which 350 are not expressions in identity terms or in terms of individual interest), deliberators in the real-life interactions of the RECOM process were more attuned to the common good orientation than participants in experimental settings in divided societies who did not tackle the topic of past violence.

This granular insight into the formulation of the common good speaks to the viability of deliberation about past wrongs in adverse circumstances. The finding that expression of ethnic group interest does not predominate is counterintuitive, given the salience of ethnic identity in postconflict societies, which is defined by past violence and cultivated by identity politics. It requires further checks, in line with the aim of this research to better understand how ethnic identity matters and how it is enacted during deliberation.

In addition, relative frequencies of two categories of respect in the RECOM data (respect toward individuals and respect toward groups) demonstrate greater engagement with individuals than with groups in a cross-ethnic transitional justice process. A total of 12.71 percent of explicit references (respectful and disrespectful) pertain to fellow deliberators in the category of respect toward individuals, as opposed to only 3.47 percent of explicit references to ethnic groups to which these deliberators belong in the category of respect toward groups. A comparison within these categories is instructive; whereas there is broadly the same proportion of disrespectful (6.19%) and respectful references (6.52%) to participants, there are twice as many disrespectful (2.31%) as respectful references (1.16%) toward groups. These figures indicate that an enduring collective conception of identity in postconflict contexts is a challenge for deliberative engagement, even as deliberators avoid references to groups, preferring to engage both respectfully and disrespectfully with individuals.

Viewed comparatively with other measures of deliberation across the deep divide, the number of respectful references toward fellow deliberators is 6.52 percent in the RECOM consultations in the Balkans, as opposed to 10.2 percent in Belgium, with a caveat that the comparison to Belgium, a divided but democratized context, is of limited value.[80] In relation to other postconflict contexts, there are proportionally more speech acts in the RECOM corpus (79 out of 1,211) expressing respect than in Colombia (8 out of 1,027), and only two in Srebrenica in Bosnia and Herzegovina.[81]

Lastly, the low frequency of interruption of speakers (only 3.72% of speech acts were interrupted) in the RECOM transitional justice consultations can be attributed to the moderated nature of these sessions.[82]

Emerging empirical scholarship on deliberation in divided societies has helped refine the normative claims of the theory of deliberative democracy. Although limited to a handful of studies, a parallel development in the study of deliberation in divided societies has provided critical new evidence of the viability of deliberative communication under adverse conditions. This book's contribution to normative theory development is premised on the need to test the utility of postconflict deliberation as part of peacebuilding: to reconcile, these societies need to be able to address the issue of justice and wartime harm deliberatively, as this issue underpins all divisions in fractured postconflict societies. This aim calls for an appropriate empirical strategy, which has been presented in this chapter.

This empirical study of deliberation about war crimes across ethnic lines is motivated by a need for a bespoke but comparable assessment of deliberation, given the contextual constraints on "healthy deliberation" in postconflict societies.[83] Legacies and dynamics of conflict shape the contours of deliberative discourse in the transition from war to peace. Consequently, the measurement instrument, the DQITJ, is finely tuned to capture how these contextual constraints are reflected in deliberation across ethnic lines. Its contribution to the empirical study of deliberation lies in its responsiveness to contextual particularities of postconflict societies.[84]

The application of the DQI as a method to assess deliberativeness of discourse enables a microlevel analysis that "involves assessing the deliberative quality of discussion discourse through closely analyzing the content of people's comments during the deliberation."[85] Notably, the scrutiny of the content here reveals "the formal way" in which people engage with each other's discourses during deliberation.[86] This approach allows us to evaluate "the actual process of deliberation," which, when people from opposing ethnic groups come face to face to discuss justice after mass atrocity, can also reveal how they may or may not be reconciled.[87] The DQI, like any other measurement instrument, is not intended to capture all dimensions of discourse but only those of particular theoretical interest. In this case, what is of interest are the deliberative standards derived from Habermas's discourse ethics that can promote the search for justice in postconflict societies.

When focusing on nonideal contexts of deliberation, such as societies divided by violence, André Bächtiger and John Parkinson remark that we do not have to abandon the core concept of deliberation. Instead, according to them, we can concentrate on assessing the deliberativeness of discourse comparatively and identifying gross violations of deliberative standards.[88] The distribution of deliberative virtues in the RECOM transitional justice consultations, based on the frequencies of DQI categories, demonstrates the resilience of deliberativeness despite the divisive topic of war crimes and ethnic divisions inflicted by conflict. A fine-grained adjustment of the DQI categories in the DQITJ more richly captures the texture of deliberative claims in divided societies than was previously possible. From a comparative perspective, the descriptive statistics of the RECOM corpus of a real-world process compare favorably with the deliberativeness of discourse measured in deliberative experiments in divided societies that shied away from introducing the most divisive topic—mutual harm—into discussions across ethnic lines. The next chapter takes the analysis further and provides insight into conditions that predict good-quality deliberation about war crimes in divided societies.

WORDS OF REASON AND TALK OF PAIN

When you hear a different opinion, you see how entrenched your views are.

—Participant in the RECOM consultation in Croatia, October 22, 2010

The path to repair of interethnic relations after conflict leads through deliberative engagement with the legacy of mass violence. To gauge whether reconciliation is taking root, Priscilla Hayner remarks, we need to answer the question of whether people can talk about past conflicts and past abuses "if not easily, then at least in a civil manner—even with former opponents."[1] Grounding reconciliation in mutuality in public communication, I have argued that quality deliberation about wartime harm is necessary for interethnic reconciliation. The previous chapter has shown that deliberative virtues are attainable even when former adversaries tackle a divisive topic of past harm in the search for justice. The deliberativeness of discussions about interethnic violence is important. If the contentious issue of justice for past wrongs can be addressed through reason-giving and respectful engagement, and if people can discuss remedying wartime harm by taking account of others' opinions, then this mode of deliberative communication can contribute to overcoming divisions in postconflict societies.

However, the quality of deliberation is variable. It may rise and fall, depending on various factors associated with characteristics of speakers, issues, and contexts. Evaluation of the deliberativeness of discourse in divided societies has to consider the conflict dynamics that shape postconflict identities and the divisions based on them. Scholars of deliberation in divided societies have glossed over how the long shadow of conflict shapes deliberation across ethnic lines. In chapter 2, I developed a general theoretical framework for reconciliation through deliberation, premised on the assumption that ethnic identities matter during deliberation. To be reconciliatory, quality deliberation involving former adversaries in a postconflict setting needs to be demonstrated, while considering conflict dynamics and people's expression of their identities during these discussions.

Scholars have approached deliberation in divided societies as a question of communication between two opposing sides. A closer look at conflict dynamics offers a more complex picture of culpability and victimhood in many contemporary conflicts. For example, a dyadic paradigm within a national context does not capture the complexity of many conflicts, such as that of Bosnia and Herzegovina, which involved three parties in various configurations.[2] Further, the regional nature of certain conflicts, like those in the Balkans, implies the involvement of ethnic groups beyond national borders. Yet this regional aspect has been overlooked in the study of postconflict deliberation. The issue of ethnic diversity raises an important question for reconciliation after conflict: will greater ethnic diversity of deliberators lower the quality of deliberation and thereby undermine the prospects for reconciliation? At the same time, the role of ethnic identities during interethnic deliberation in divided societies has been neglected because scholars have operationalized ethnic identity as a fixed attribute of speakers. We need to investigate how the expression of people's ethnicness, which captures how people bring their subject perspectives into discussion, is associated with the deliberative quality of discourse.[3] The question is: will the ethnic dimension of discourse that reflects speakers' sense of ethnic difference undermine deliberativeness?

Informed by one of this book's larger arguments, that reconciliation takes place when the divisive impact of ethnic identities is overcome in deliberative communication about war crimes across ethnic lines, this chapter shows that ethnic identities matter during deliberation. This point may sound intuitive, but scholars of postconflict deliberation have not investigated it. The chapter evaluates the relationship between quality deliberation and three factors: ethnically polarizing issues in discussions about justice for war crimes; different types of ethnic divisions corresponding to various conflict dynamics; and the permeation of ethnic identity in discourse as manifested in its linguistic features.[4]

This chapter illustrates what good-quality deliberation about mass violence looks like. It also describes the variables in the model used to predict the quality of deliberation and relates them to the theoretical propositions in the framework developed in chapter 2. Statistical models are then estimated to explain the quality of deliberation as measured by the DQITJ applied to the RECOM corpus. The results show that ethnically polarizing issues addressed in a postconflict transitional justice process, the ethnic diversity of discussions (dyadic, involving two opposed sides; and multiethnic, involving all parties to a regional conflict), and a sense of ethnic subjectivity in speakers' positions increase the quality of deliberation. They provide robust evidence that a discussion of the legacy of violence,

which is the most divisive issue in divided societies, is compatible with a deliberative mode of communication. These insights refine our understanding of which
conditions of ethnic diversity are conducive to quality deliberation. Lastly, the
overlooked ethnic dimension of deliberative discourse in divided societies challenges conventional wisdom in scholarship on deliberation that holds that benefits of deliberation in divided societies accrue primarily from nonethnic, that is
human rights-oriented, discourse.

What Does Good-Quality Deliberation about War Crimes Look Like?

Before proceeding with the statistical analysis of predictors of deliberation quality, this chapter first illustrates what good-quality deliberation looks like in real-
life discussions about war crimes and their legacy. The excerpt below from the
RECOM transitional justice consultations has the highest score measured by
the DQITJ.[5]

At this point of discussion in the RECOM consultative process on the Draft
Statute of the proposed regional fact-finding commission, the participants were
asked to consider the commission's mandate. Besides helping shape the overall
transitional justice strategy, one of the key benefits of transitional justice consultations is stakeholders' input into the mandate of a transitional justice mechanism. The legitimacy of the designed transitional justice process will be bolstered
if the remit—whether of a war crimes trial or a truth commission—is seen to be
responsive to the needs of a postconflict society.[6] However, deciding which violations will be included in the mandate and how that inclusion will be worded is
a contentious process. Different positions are grounded in people's experience
of conflict, which is, in turn, shaped by their ethnic identity and the pattern of
violence to which they and their ethnic group were exposed. These differences
will overlay others that reflect people's moral outlook on law, justice, and peace,
their political and economic interests, or their gendered experience of conflict.

The excerpt from the RECOM corpus is drawn from a part of the discussion
when participants were presented with two options for the commission's remit:
to provide either a list of specific violations or a general reference to war crimes
and grave human rights violations (and consider all specific violations to be subsumed under this reference). Therefore, participants were asked to present their
positions on:

> the alternative a) war crimes and gross human rights violations within
> the commission's remit include but are not limited to genocide, pogroms,

killings, enslavement, illegal detention, torture, forced disappearances, deportation and forced displacement of population, rape and other grave forms of sexual abuse, large scale confiscation and destruction of property, hostage-taking, destruction of religious and cultural-historical objects, using civilians and war prisoners as human shields; and alternative b) the commission establishes the facts of war crimes as well as the facts related to other grave human rights violations.[7]

Defining the commission's remit concerning which abuses should be investigated was among the most divisive issues in the RECOM consultative process.[8] It prompted a lively discussion as participants presented different arguments for or against either option. The contention centered on the reference to genocide. Arguments for explicitly referencing genocide (alongside other human rights violations) reflected some participants' conviction that this wording would resonate with victims and survivors and engender their trust in the commission's work. Others opposed listing specific violations. They were concerned that the list risked not being comprehensive (considering the various forms of injury people suffered) and would undermine the stakeholders' faith in the commission. In addition, they favored the reference to war crimes and grave human rights violations to avoid any ambiguity. They reasoned that a reference to genocide might wrongly raise expectations that the RECOM fact-finding commission would be tasked with providing legal qualifications for acts of violence, including genocide; the latter was deemed to be the role of a due legal process. Yet others saw the question in a political light. They expressed concern that omitting a reference to genocide might signal an equivocal position on whether genocide in the region was committed or might even amount to a denial of genocide.[9]

Addressing the reference to genocide in the commission's mandate was a delicate undertaking. The consultative process was taking place in the shadow of divisive ethnic politics within and between countries in the Balkans. Such politics was fueled by the contestation of genocide verdicts passed by the International Criminal Tribunal for the Former Yugoslavia (ICTY) and other charges of genocide.[10] Such tensions permeate the broader political context in which deliberation takes place and refract on the deliberative process itself. They are therefore thought to constitute conditions that distort the deliberative quality of discourse in divided societies. However, the excerpt from the RECOM consultations shows that good-quality deliberation is achievable in discussions involving people from adversary ethnic groups despite challenging conditions for deliberation and a divisive topic:

> The alternative b. was not political. It is purely legal and comprehensive. It is not good for our task at hand to be setting conditions. If someone

sets conditions, this then invites others to respond with their condi-tions. We cannot accomplish this task successfully if we start setting conditions; especially if the article contains everything that the person who sets conditions wants. I hope I expressed myself clearly on this point. Especially let's not invoke victims. That is a very sensitive issue. There were victims on all sides. I can speak from my experience; peo-ple around me who lost family members say literally that their loss is the biggest genocide. Therefore, I completely understand victims from Srebrenica, and why they demand that [the term genocide be listed], because inside them they feel the enormous injustice done to them, and by using that term they want to express all the tragedy and injustice they suffered. Therefore, let's consider their request also within the alterna-tive b., but let's not complicate both the alternative a. and b. by adding something—they'll only be watered down.[11]

This statement by a male speaker, which constitutes a speech act to which the DQITJ is applied, demonstrates a sophisticated rational justification of the argu-ment. In line with the logic of the measurement instrument, the level of sophis-tication is established based on an in-depth examination of a problem and the completeness of the justifications.[12] At least two complete justifications are given. Justifications include a commentary on other speakers' setting conditions, the views of victims, and, ultimately, the wording of the article of the Draft Stat-ute. The consideration of victims' needs figures prominently in the construction of his position, as shown in his empathetic reflection on their suffering. This speaker of Serb ethnicity publicly shows empathy for Bosnian Muslim victims of the Srebrenica genocide, which reflects the other-regarding logic of his utterance. Lastly, the terse reference to his experience can also be understood as a personal story and reflection that supports the rational argument being made (rather than replacing an argument with storytelling).

The deliberative quality of this and other speech acts is a composite qual-ity that captures the attainment of discreet deliberative virtues. As discussed in chapter 3, the DQI is a measurement instrument that allows us to verify empiri-cally the variation of deliberation quality in any given discourse.

Factors Predicting Deliberative Quality in Transitional Justice Consultations

Drawing on the theoretical framework set out in chapter 2, I address the qual-ity of deliberation among people from different ethnic groups involved in

TABLE 4.1 Predictors of the quality of deliberation

VARIABLE	LABEL	VALUE
Speaker	Gender	Female Male
	Speaker type	Speaks once Speaks >1
Consultations	Ethnic diversity	Monoethnic Dyadic Triadic Multiethnic
	Stakeholder type	Victims Civil society activists Professionals
	Translation	Yes No
Issue	Polarization	High Medium Low
Identity in discourse	Subjectivity in rational justification	None Nonethnic Ethnic Multiethnic
	Storytelling positionality	None Own group Other group Personal

discussions about war crimes in the Balkan conflicts. I focus on how the quality of deliberation is associated with characteristics related to speakers, issues, and consultations, as well as linguistic and semantic features of discourse. The latter capture how identities are enacted during deliberation and provide insight into postconflict deliberation across ethnic lines. These predictors of the quality of deliberation are shown in table 4.1.

Gender

Attention to gender has helped broaden what was once a narrowly Habermasian focus on the requirement of rational reasoning in theorizing on deliberation. Lynn Sanders has noted that "the invitation to deliberation has strings attached," because it excludes any type of communication other than dispassionate and reasoned argument.[13] This normative threshold was seen to be particularly disadvantageous for women, as highlighted by difference democrats, since—it was argued—women are more likely to use other forms of discourse such as stories and narratives.[14] However, others have pointed out that women have a greater capacity for deliberation because of their propensity to be respectful and empathetic, which facilitates deliberative exchange.[15] Addressing the question of "gendered deliberation," empirical studies of democratic deliberation have found no difference in the quality of deliberation (when it is a composite measure) between men and women, for example, in national parliaments.[16] In the context of divided societies, the evidence is inconclusive.[17] At the same time, discrete dimensions of deliberation, such as understanding of the common good and respect for one's interlocutors, point to a gendered pattern of deliberation: women may be disadvantaged on a single dimension of deliberation, such as equality, but their speech may also be associated with a higher quality of deliberation, measured as respect for arguments of other deliberators.[18] Without persuasive empirical evidence that gender is significantly associated with the quality of deliberation, no effect of gender on the quality of deliberation is hypothesized.[19]

Speaker Type

Marlène Gerber et al. shed light on individual deliberators as "deliberative citizens."[20] Deliberation studies generally have used education level as an indicator of an individual's deliberative ability, producing mixed empirical findings.[21] Given the constraints of the observational nature of the RECOM data, speakers' deliberative competence is proxied by the frequency of their contributions to the debate. The speaker type variable distinguishes between those speakers who have spoken only once and those who have spoken more than once during a deliberative session.[22] It is hypothesized that speech acts of those speakers who take the floor more than once will have a higher quality of deliberation. Informing this assumption is that a postconflict context of war-to-peace transition is also a democratizing context.[23] Madeleine Fullard and Nicky Rousseau argued that transitional justice practices such as truth telling can create opportunities for many to perform publicly as citizens for the first time.[24] For many speakers, the RECOM transitional justice consultations were the first experience of democratic deliberation. Although other explanations related to a speaker's personality cannot be ruled out, taking the floor more than once indicates both confidence to contribute to a public exchange of views and an ability to do so effectively. Differential participation in communication and its association with good-quality deliberation will also be conditional on gender and a type of stakeholder community, respectively. On the one hand, such conditional effect of speaker type

reflects arguments about adverse effects of different patterns of women's participation in discourse and influence in public debates as opposed to men's.[25] On the
other hand, it considers scholarly arguments about victims' marginal contribution to shaping the transitional justice process, as opposed to the disproportion-
ate influence of human rights activists and professionals. In this sense, the quality
of deliberation in a transitional justice process may be one more manifestation of
the disempowerment of the victims.[26]

I now turn to contextual determinants. Their close examination is in line with
scholarly findings that "no massive socio-economic stratification of deliberative
behavior" is associated with speakers' characteristics.[27] Given the preponderance
of empirical studies of deliberation in parliamentary settings, contextual factors noted in the literature are mainly institutional and refer to consensus versus
competitive systems, presidential versus parliamentary systems, second versus
first chambers, and so on.[28] A parallel distinction concerns deliberation in institutional fora, such as parliaments, as opposed to citizens' deliberation alongside
virtual deliberation. This book about civil society-led, postconflict deliberation
across ethnic lines investigates the effects of variation in contextual features of
consultative sessions that are closely aligned with conflict dynamics. The dynamics include the ethnic diversity of consultations and the diversity of consultations
regarding stakeholder type.

Ethnic Diversity of Consultations

Deliberation as the communicative exchange is premised on engaging with difference by adhering to procedural standards, such as equality, reason-giving, reciprocity, equality, common good orientation, and respect. However, if the diversity
of opinion coincides with ethnic fault lines, as can be expected in divided postconflict contexts, deliberativeness of discourse will be harder to attain. Deliberation across ethnic lines entails coming into contact with former adversaries and
may therefore activate prejudices and stereotypes in deliberators' minds. Opinions will tend toward extremes and become polarized.[29] This tendency embodies
logic opposite to respectful and other-regarding communication and can further
divide ethnic communities. Introducing deliberative norms, such as discussion
rules and facilitation, can contribute to depolarization.[30]

The perils of ethnic polarization for deliberation quality have been tested in
the context of identity division in Belgium. Contrary to expectations, Didier
Caluwaerts and Kris Deschouwer found that ethnically divided groups are associated with higher deliberation quality than groups composed of members of the
same ethnic group.[31] Although Belgium is not a society divided by violent conflict, it is a valuable case for comparing a society riven by violent dyadic conflict

(albeit not a conflict involving more than two ethnic groups). This book seeks to extend our understanding of the effects of greater ethnic diversity on the quality of deliberation in postconflict contexts.

As I have argued, many contemporary conflicts involve more than two ethnic groups. Furthermore, conflict actors cross state boundaries, resulting in regional patterns of violence involving multiple identity groups. To anticipate how greater ethnic diversity of deliberators may affect deliberation quality, we can draw on the scholarship on deliberation both in the European Union—in the institutional setting of the European Parliament and a pan-European deliberative poll, the Europolis—and World Social Fora. This scholarship has explored the supranational arena as a deliberative setting, furthering the study of deliberation by identifying features involving participants from multiple national groups. However, their insights into the quality of deliberation inferred from the application of the DQI are limited, and not just because they do not occur in conflict-affected societies. These studies do not directly compare the quality of deliberation at a supranational level with the quality of deliberation at a national level on the same or similar issues.[32] By contrast, the ethnic diversity of the RECOM consultations varied: at different points they were monoethnic, dyadic, triadic, and multiethnic. Such a granular classification of predictors of deliberative quality pertaining to a type of societal division corresponds to differing conflict dynamics. It thus allows us to evaluate whether greater ethnic diversity of deliberations is conducive to deliberation quality and to assess comparatively the effect of different levels of diversity on deliberation. Drawing on the related extant research, we can hypothesize that dyadic sessions will be associated with higher DQI scores compared to monoethnic sessions. This hypothesis can be extended to triadic sessions, that is discussions involving members of three ethnic groups. Since increasing the ethnic diversity further can elicit a greater commitment to deliberative ideals, especially when it comes to openness to the ethnic Other, multiethnic sessions are also hypothesized to be associated with higher deliberative quality compared to monoethnic sessions.[33]

Stakeholder Type

Distinguishing types of consultations in terms of participating stakeholders allows us to probe how invested the deliberators are in the deliberation process and the effect of that investment. Evidence on this question is mixed. High investment in deliberation is thought to lead to heightened emotions, which is not conducive to cooperation.[34] By contrast, speakers are more likely to sustain deliberative reasoning when outcomes matter to them.[35] Arguing that high stakes will lead to better deliberation, Archon Fung contends that "participants will invest more of their psychic energy and resources into the process and so make it more thorough and creative."[36] The RECOM consultations included different types of stakeholders: professionals (such as lawyers, journalists, and teachers), civil society activists (coming from a variety of human rights and advocacy groups and associations), as well as victims. The perceived lack of justice and acknowledgment for the victims of the Yugoslav wars across ethnic groups motivated the launch of the RECOM initiative. The participation of victims in these real-world deliberations alongside professionals and civil society activists was a unique feature of this process. They brought to the sessions raw pain and emotion associated with the abuse they or their loved ones had suffered. In deliberative experiments where speakers discussed peace in Colombia, Juan Ugarriza and Enzo Nussio did not find a significant effect of a victim category as a socio-demographic control on the deliberative quality score assessed in relation to nonvictims. Notably, the topic in those discussions was peace.[37] By contrast, the RECOM transitional justice process was about wartime harm and how to address it. Since victimization occurred on an ethnic basis, it is plausible that a sense of grievance would be heightened in interethnic interactions about justice for war crimes, undermining the quality of deliberation.[38] We can hypothesize that victims' consultations will be associated with a lower DQI score than those involving professionals and civil society activists. Relative distance from war-related grief and grievance, coupled with a presumably higher educational level, especially for professionals such as lawyers, journalists, and teachers, adds further support to the hypothesis that sessions with civil society and professionals will be associated with higher DQI scores than sessions involving victims.

Translation

The study of deliberation in a multiethnic setting with participants from different linguistic backgrounds brings to the fore the role of translation in deliberation. In the European Social Forum study, Nicole Doerr finds that the requirement for translation was conducive to deliberation because it lengthened discussions and encouraged participants to listen to each other.[39] In the RECOM transitional justice consultations, the role of translation in discussions involving participants from different ethnic groups is of particular theoretical interest. The provision of translation during the RECOM process was intended to prevent the linguistic hegemony of a single working language. The possibility to speak in one's native tongue ensured an opportunity for equal participation. In the postconflict context, it also represented recognition and acceptance of ethnic difference. In the words of one participant in the RECOM process, "one should commend that all languages are treated as being official, and that everyone here feels equal; so that people from Kosovo can speak Albanian, people from Macedonia can speak Macedonian, and the people from Slovenia can speak Slovenian. The rest of us understand each other."[40] Like the European Social Forum, the RECOM process is one type in a range of "multilingual face-to-face arenas involving ordinary citizens in transnational public deliberations 'from below.'"[41] Therefore, it is anticipated that translation during transitional justice consultations will be associated with a higher level of deliberation. Moving on from consultation-related predictors, the next predictor concerns the type of issue under discussion.

Issue Polarization

Controversial topics stir passions and as such are not conducive to rational arguments.[42] This claim is particularly relevant for investigating transitional justice deliberations since debates about war crimes cut to the core of division in postconflict contexts. Issue polarization refers to the distance in the policy preference of actors, which Jürg Steiner et al. call "the ideational (or, more narrowly, ideological) dimension of policy issues."[43] The criterion of polarization and the potential distance of actors on a given issue in this research corresponds to the ethnic salience of issues. Ethnic issues are highly polarizing because they are considered to be indivisible.[44] The location of the seat of the regional commission in the RECOM corpus is one example of such indivisibility: the seat can be either in the Bosnian capital Sarajevo or the Serbian capital Belgrade (or any other regional capital). By contrast, the question of the regional commission's media strategy, which has no ethnic dimension, is an issue with low polarization.[45] Operationalization of issue polarization along the spectrum between ethnic and nonethnic allows us to indirectly capture the ethnic dimension of discourse. It provides an additional evaluation of the possibility of quality deliberation about contentious issues in postconflict contexts. Drawing on the existing evidence of the effects of issue polarization, we can hypothesize that highly polarizing issues will decrease the quality of deliberation.[46]

Lastly, this book aims to understand how ethnic identity matters during deliberation in societies divided by conflict by capturing and assessing its effects directly. This chapter turns to linguistic and semantic features of discourse that capture empirically identity-related dimensions of speakers' utterances. I focus on subject perspectives underlying deliberators' articulated positions on policy points. These predictors of the variability of the DQI score can capture quantitatively "more detailed, multi-dimensional and dynamic understandings of identity."[47] They can thus provide novel insights into how ethnic identities are enacted in interethnic deliberation in postconflict societies.

Subjectivity in Rational Justification

Subjectivity in rational justification refers to the subjectivity that a speaker artic- ulates when justifying a position on a given issue. In line with the theoretical interest in role identities and how they are enacted in discourse, this variable captures ethnicness in speakers' utterances. Drawing on the linguistic study of subjectivity and discourse, the assumption behind this variable is that there are systematic ways in which "the speaking subject manifests itself in language."[48] The "subjective realm" includes utterances to "which the personal pronouns 'I' and 'we' are or could be applied."[49] Subjectivity is always configured within but is never identical to the social-political order and its subjective productions such as myths, national histories, race, and so on.[50] Therefore, subjective senses can reflect the broader social order—which in this book is an ethnically divided society—or they can offer a possibility for the subversion of this order.[51] The empirical approach to studying subjectivity is guided by formal markers that inscribe the latter into textual data.[52] Scrutinizing subjectivity will reveal whether ethnicness, understood as ascriptively defined subjectivity, is present in speak- ers' utterances in cross-ethnic communication. When we study "communica- tion as a new space for subjectivation," the enunciation of ethnicness implies the expression of difference.[53] Following the arguments by scholars of deliberation in divided societies, which equate good-quality deliberation with nonethnic dis- course associated with human rights talk, we expect ethnicness to be associated with lower-quality deliberation.

Positionality in Storytelling

Positionality in storytelling has a rationale similar to that of the previous variable but pertains to subjectivity within stories. This variable also captures ethnicness in terms of one's personal experience or the experience of one's ethnic group or of other ethnic groups. It enables us to refine our understanding of whether stories are told from one's personal subject position as an individual or as a col- lective experience. Scholars of deliberation have obscured this difference because stories were considered to be a personal experience tout court. Granular analysis of how stories are constructed is particularly relevant in transitional justice pro- cesses. Communicating the experience of harm as an individual experience can cut through the logic of collective identities (as individuals are viewed through their groups in reference to victimhood and culpability) that has undermined the quest for justice in postconflict contexts. We can therefore hypothesize that stories of one's own experience will be associated with higher levels of delibera- tion, as they will elicit more empathetic and respectful engagement from fellow deliberators.

The Legacy of Mass Violence and the Quality of Deliberation

The chapter now proceeds with analyzing the power of the selected variables to explain the quality of deliberation in transitional justice consultations. The unit of analysis is a speech act. There are 1,211 speech acts in the RECOM corpus. The measure of the quality of deliberation, the dependent variable, is the DQI adapted for the study of transitional justice.[54] The data for the independent variables were obtained by coding the speech acts according to the given observational values on the speaker, consultation, and issue variables. The two variables that capture identity in discourse (subjectivity in rational justification and storytelling positionality), which required researcher judgment, were coded independently in all 1,211 speech acts by the author and a second coder at an acceptable level of intercoder reliability.[55]

Ordinary least squares (OLS) regression analysis was conducted to test the hypotheses. The results of four estimated models are reported in table 4.2. The first model includes only the predictors derived from the observational data of the RECOM transitional justice consultations. These are gender, speaker type, issue polarization, translation, stakeholder type (which distinguishes the victims' discourse from that of civil society activists and professionals), and the refined variable ethnic diversity (which reflects conflict dynamics by specifying the number of groups involved in a conflict). The analysis also includes terms to investigate a possible interaction of gender and speaker type and of stakeholder type and speaker type.

As table 4.2 shows, the value of R^2 in model 1 is .048, indicating that the variables explain about 5% of the variance in the DQI in this model. Model 2 illustrates the effect of adding the variable subjectivity in rational justification, and model 3 adds the second subject perspective variable, positionality in storytelling. The value of R^2 is .32 for model 2 and .519 for model 3, indicating that about 32 percent and 52 percent of the variance in the DQI is explained by the independent variables in these models, respectively. By including discourse's linguistic and semantic features, the model fit increases considerably, showing that these subject perspectives are powerful predictors of deliberative quality. The last model is the most parsimonious, run with all the variables significant at the 10 percent level.[56] It also includes the main effects of the variables included in statistically significant interactions. Only translation is dropped, as its effect is insignificant when the effects of both the subjectivity and positionality variables are estimated. This model achieves a similar R^2 value as model 3 (.518).[57] The analysis of the results below refers to model 4 in table 4.2.[58] Given the goal of explaining what determines the quality of discourse in transitional justice consultations, the

TABLE 4.2 OLS regression models analyzing the quality of deliberation

	MODEL			
EXPLANATORY VARIABLE	(1) BASE	(2) SUBJECTIVITY	(3) SUBJ.+POSITIONALITY	(4) FINAL
Gender (ref. Female): Male	-.337** (.171)	-.295* (.151)	-.171 (.115)	-.181 (.114)
Speaker type (ref. Speaks once): Speaks more than once	-.316 (.251)	-.218 (.223)	.112 (.183)	.117 (.183)
Gender x Speaker type: Male x Speaks more than once	.468** (.190)	.417** (.164)	.262** (.129)	.265** (.129)
Stakeholder type (ref. Victims):				
Civil society activists	-.255 (.198)	-.158 (.178)	.159 (.138)	.168 (.137)
Professionals	.035 (.194)	.034 (.177)	.414*** (.144)	.400*** (.143)
Stakeholder type x Speaker type:				
Civil society activists x Speaks more than once	-.143 (.253)	-.151 (.224)	-.281 (.181)	-.308* (.177)
Professionals x Speaks more than once	-.388 (.241)	-.279 (.218)	-.468*** (.178)	-.447** (.176)
Ethnic diversity (ref. Monoethnic):				
Multiethnic	.434*** (.168)	.385*** (.142)	.358*** (.113)	.308*** (.100)
Triadic	.309 (.230)	.331 (.211)	.294* (.161)	.291* (.161)
Dyadic	.521*** (.166)	.429*** (.136)	.398*** (.110)	.401*** (.110)
Translation (ref. Yes): No	.221** (.097)	.197** (.081)	.065 (.066)	
Issue polarization (ref. Low): Medium & high	.288*** (.073)	.193*** (.062)	.169*** (.053)	.164*** (.053)
Subjectivity (ref. None):				
Ethnic		2.264*** (.118)	2.114*** (.099)	2.115*** (.099)
Nonethnic		2.119*** (.070)	2.068*** (.060)	2.068*** (.060)
Multiethnic		2.782*** (.103)	2.677*** (.085)	2.678*** (.085)

Storytelling positionality (ref. No storytelling):

Own group's experience			1.883*** (.210)	1.894*** (.210)
Others' experience			2.248*** (.482)	2.262*** (.483)
Personal experience			2.365*** (.157)	2.371*** (.157)
Constant	4.436*** (.261)	2.296*** (.242)	1.883*** (.195)	1.962*** (.177)
R^2	.048	.320	.519	.518
Adj. R^2	.038	.311	.511	.511
F statistic	4.085	83.88	110.6	116.6
Model degrees of freedom	12	15	18	17

Note: Response variable is deliberative quality as DQI score. Robust standard errors in parentheses. $N = 1,211$. ***$p < .01$, **$p < .05$, *$p < .10$.

variables of particular theoretical interest here are issue polarization (with ethnic issues considered most divisive), ethnic diversity of consultation, and subjectivity in rational justifications and storytelling positionality.

We must first ascertain that the legacy of violence can be discussed deliberatively in postconflict societies searching for justice. Analysis of attainment of deliberative virtues presented in chapter 3 indicates that the divisive topic of redress for ethnically based violence does not stymie deliberation. However, not all aspects of a discussion about a criminal legacy are equally divisive. With that in mind, estimating how issue polarization—where polarization of issues related to war crimes, and their redress is conceived in ethnic terms—is associated with the quality of deliberation provides a stringent test of the feasibility of deliberation about justice for war crimes involving members of adversary ethnic groups.

The results show that an increase in issue polarization is associated with higher quality deliberation, with effects significant at $p < .01$. Speech acts about medium- or highly polarizing issues are associated with a DQI score that is .164 points higher than speech acts about less polarizing issues, controlling for all other variables.[59] Thus, the "hottest" issues evince high-quality deliberation in real-life discussions about war crimes.[60] This is a counterintuitive insight. It demonstrates that most ethnically divisive aspects of reckoning with past wrongs focus deliberators' minds on how to present, articulate, and argue their positions in transitional justice consultations when encountering an ethnic Other. The hypothesis that "highly polarized issues are likely to be less conducive to deliberation than less polarized issues" is rejected.[61] This finding is a powerful verification of the feasibility of deliberation about war crimes in divided societies. From the perspective of deliberative conceptions of peacebuilding, it indicates the capacity for cross-ethnic deliberative cooperation in postconflict societies, even on fractious issues related to past harm. Ethnically salient aspects of redress for past crimes indirectly tap into an ethnic dimension of discourse in a way that is not antithetical to high-quality deliberation. This result points to the need to better understand ethnic features of discourse and related identity dynamics during deliberation, examined in ensuing chapters.

Next, aiming to refine arguments about postconflict deliberation that have overlooked how different conflict dynamics shape deliberativeness, I turn to the effects of ethnic diversity on deliberative quality, while differentiating the effect of discussions involving members of all ethnic groups in a regional conflict (multiethnic), of three ethnic groups (triadic) and of two ethnic groups (dyadic) in comparison with discussions involving only members of one ethnic group (monoethnic). The results show that, compared to monoethnic sessions, ethnically diverse discussions have higher deliberative quality, holding all else equal. The estimated DQI scores of dyadic and multiethnic sessions are .401 and .308

higher, respectively, than those of monoethnic sessions, at the 1 percent signifi-cance level. Triadic sessions have an estimated DQI score .291 points higher than monoethnic sessions at the 10 percent significance level.

These findings provide fine-grained insight into deliberation in societies divided by conflict, with categories that capture the context of deliberation while precisely mirroring the conflict dynamics; that is whether a conflict was fought between two or three ethnic groups or is conceived as involving multiple groups across borders in a regional conflict. The deliberative quality of discussion in ethnically mixed consultations, involving two ethnic groups, is higher than in ethnically homogenous consultations, confirming Caluwaerts and Deschouwer's results.[62] However, the differential effects of ethnic diversity on the quality of deliberation are notable when comparing dyadic, triadic, and multiethnic ses-sions. Achieving deliberative quality after conflicts involving two sides is less demanding than in discussions involving three sides, as in Bosnia and Herzegov-ina (compared to monoethnic sessions). This insight refines our understanding of what type of ethnic diversity presents more adverse conditions for postcon-flict deliberation. It echoes findings from conflict research that the more sides are present to a national level conflict, the more challenging the peace-making becomes.[63] Further, considering multiethnicity at a regional level enhances our understanding of the effects of ethnic diversity. A regional space can be a deliber-ative space where people from adversarial groups can productively engage when addressing past wrongs in search of justice. The evidence points to the benefits of multiethnic deliberation in the context of transitional justice consultations at a regional level in response to regional dynamics of violence, and hence to its potential contribution to peacebuilding across borders in war-affected regions.

Lastly, this book tackles the question of how linguistic features of a speaker's utterances are related to the deliberativeness of discourse in postconflict contexts. This previously overlooked predictor of deliberative quality captures how people bring their identities into a deliberative exchange with an ethnic Other. The coef-ficients of the categories of subjectivity in rational justification and positionality in storytelling suggest a strong and significant ($p < .01$) relationship between subject perspectives and the quality of deliberation. Of particular interest is the effect of the presence of ethnicness in discourse, which captures the expression of ethnic identity. In comparison to speech acts in which no subjectivity is expressed, subjectivity in rational justification expressed in ethnic terms increases delibera-tive quality by 2.115 points; subjectivity expressed in nonethnic terms increases DQI by 2.068 points; whereas subjectivity expressed in multiethnic terms raises DQI by 2.678 points, controlling for all other variables.

These empirical findings have far-reaching theoretical implications. They indi-cate that the presence of an ethnic sense of self in argumentation is not anathema to deliberative quality. This finding invites skepticism toward the widely held and unquestioned premise of the necessity of nonethnic discourse in democratic deliberation in divided societies. Furthermore, these results shed new light on the relationship between subjectivity in terms of multiethnicity and high-quality deliberation. Projecting a sense of self in multiethnic or cosmopolitan terms is most conducive to high-quality deliberation.

In addition to a subject perspective in rational justification, the fitted model also includes a subject perspective in storytelling. In comparison to no storytelling, the estimated DQI is 2.371 points higher when speakers convey a personal perspective in their stories, 1.894 points higher when speakers refer to their own ethnic group experience, and 2.262 points higher when references are made to the experiences of other groups, controlling for all other variables. These coefficients are significant at $p < .01$. David Ryfe has argued that storytelling during deliberation creates "moral communities around the issues under discussion."[64] The findings show that storytelling that contains individualization, which is conducive to creating solidarities and empathy, is important in deliberation about wartime violence. It also shows that referring to other groups' experience is also consequential for deliberativeness. Doing so indicates a sense of mutual understanding across groups when discussing the legacy of past violence. Consideration of others and their views is a defining feature of deliberative discourse. In this case, the other-regarding logic concerns ethnic Others, which is normatively a tall order in societies divided by conflict along ethnic lines. From the perspective of transitional justice debates, bringing the experience of other ethnic groups into discussion does not distort the deliberativeness of ethnic discourse. This finding runs counter to the insights derived from the qualitative study of discourse in the field of transitional justice.[65] Scholars have shown that the effect of storytelling in relation to transitional justice depends on the context in which stories are told, for example, in official or unofficial spaces.[66] At the same time, little effort has been made to assess whether the stories are told from an individual or a collective perspective. This research thus furthers the study of storytelling and transitional justice by demonstrating that the impact of storytelling depends on what kind of subjectivity is present in the discourse.

The analysis now turns to the remaining controls, further illuminating post-conflict deliberation quality. The analysis of the effect of stakeholder type indicates that the quality of professionals' discourse is .400 points higher than that of victims ($p < .01$), as predicted. However, the result showing the higher deliberative quality of discourse of civil society activists than that of victims is not significant. It provides a novel comparative perspective on victims' participation in a transitional justice process and their ability to represent their views, especially as they may differ from those held by civil society representatives.[67] Further, gender is not significantly associated with the quality of deliberation in this data. The same applies to another speaker-related characteristic, that is speaker type: the frequency of contribution to the discussion, taken here to indicate a speaker's deliberative competence. However, we need to interrogate further whether there is "gendered deliberation."[68] This concept implies that the quality of women's deliberative discourse is different from men's, including the consideration that the discourse quality of women who belong to different stakeholder groups is different from the discourse quality of men in those groups, and how these differences are conditional on speaker's presumed deliberative competence.

In the final, selected regression model, model 4 in table 4.2, two interaction effects are significant: between speaker type and gender, and between speaker type and the two nonreferent categories of stakeholder type, that is civil society and professionals. Figure 4.1 depicts the effect of speaker type on the DQI as moderated by gender. Panel (a) represents predicted DQI values when all other variables are set to the mean of their observed values. Panels (b) to (d) do the same, except that stakeholder type is set to its three values. Since speaker type is

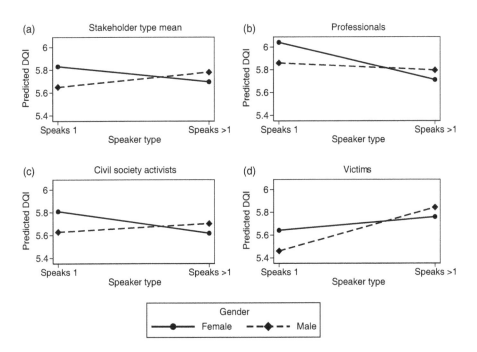

FIGURE 4.1. The effect of speaker type on DQI scores as moderated by gender
Note: (a) for the average stakeholder type in the sample and for consultations of (b) professionals, (c) civil society activists, and (d) victims for the selected model in table 4.2. The value of all other variables is set to their sample mean.

in both interactions, stakeholder type affects the strength of the interaction of speaker type and gender (represented by the slope of the lines).

When considering speakers who contribute once and those who contribute more than once to discussions, the same relative difference in quality exists between women and men, as shown by the distance between the intercepts of the lines with the respective axes. When not distinguishing among stakeholder types, as depicted in panel (a), we can observe that the deliberative quality of discourse of men who speak repeatedly is higher than the deliberative quality of discourse of both men who speak once and women who speak repeatedly. By contrast, the deliberative quality of discourse of women who speak once is higher than the deliberative quality of discourse of women who speak repeatedly and men, whether they speak just once or repeatedly.[69] However, when distinguishing among stakeholder types, professionals who engage repeatedly in the discussion evince a lower DQI score than one-time speakers, as seen in panel (b). This effect is stronger for women than for men. Victims who speak repeatedly have a higher DQI score than those who speak just once, an effect that is this time stronger for men, as seen in panel (d). The DQI score of civil society activists reflects that of the average profile, as seen in panel (c).

These findings provide evidence for women's unique deliberative style and the specific economy of women's discourse, which we can refine further by taking into account the profile of women, whether they are victims, professionals, or civil society activists. Women civil society activists and professionals attain higher deliberative scores than men when they contribute only once to the discussion, while their repeated contributions to debates are not conducive to increasing deliberative quality. By contrast, women victims (like men victims) who are repeat speakers have higher deliberative quality. These are important insights into women's contributions to transitional justice processes (as well as potentially to other political processes). They reveal that evaluations of women's input to discussions based on the number of their speaking turns proportional to those of men are a crude measure of women's influence on policies under deliberation.[70] As figure 4.1 shows, the occasions when women contribute to shaping policies are consequential, as measured by the DQI.

Figure 4.2 depicts the effect of speaker type on DQI as moderated by stakeholder type. Panel (a) represents predicted DQI scores when all other variables are set at the average of their observed values, and panels (b) and (c) do the same, except that gender is set at its two values. These plots illustrate again this nuanced set of interactions; here, depicting how the simple effect of stakeholder type on the relationship of speaker type to DQI scores is affected by gender.

These plots indicate that when considering one-time speakers and repeat speakers separately, the same relative difference in quality exists between victims,

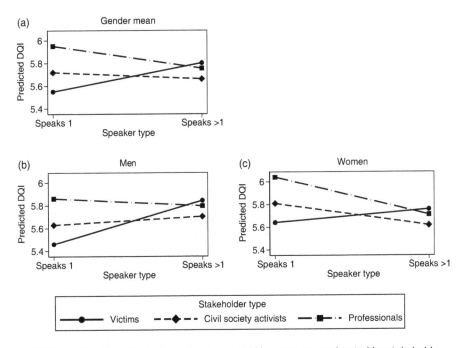

FIGURE 4.2.   The effect of speaker type on DQI scores as moderated by stakeholder type. *Note:* (a) for average gender in the sample, and for (b) men and (c) women for the selected model in table 4.2. The value of all other variables is set to their sample mean.

civil society activists, and professionals, as shown by the distance between the intercepts of the lines with the respective axes. As seen in panel (a), on average, the victims who are actively engaged in the discussion, that is speak more than once, have a higher quality of deliberation than more reticent victims, while professionals and civil society activists evince the opposite effect. Panel (b) reveals that male professionals and activists have largely the same quality of deliberation regardless of their frequency of contribution. Men victims, by contrast, have much higher deliberative quality when they speak repeatedly rather than just once; also, the deliberative quality of men victims who speak repeatedly is higher than that of professionals and civil society activists who speak repeatedly. However, as seen in panel (c), women professionals and civil society activists who speak repeatedly have a markedly lower quality of deliberation than those who contribute once, whereas women victims who speak repeatedly have a higher quality of deliberation than women victims who speak once; women professionals and civil society activists who speak repeatedly have a lower quality of deliberation than women victims who contribute repeatedly.

These findings are relevant for scholarly and policy-related discussions about victims' ability to articulate their own justice needs and interests and for the criticism of the monopolization of victims' voices and their agency by human rights organizations. New comparative evidence presented in this book shows that victims can articulate their views on transitional justice—a policy in which they are personally invested—deliberatively. Victims' investment in the issue translates into higher quality deliberation, for both men and women victims, among repeat speakers than is attained by civil society activists and professionals who are repeat speakers. This is perhaps surprising. It points to civil society activists' and professionals' lack of attention to the framing of arguments associated with repeated contributions to debates, assuming that civil society activists and professionals are (more) competent deliberators (than victims) by virtue of their professional background and presumably greater frequency of opportunities to engage in a public exchange of arguments. The results may signal civil society activists' and professionals' relative disengagement, especially when compared to the victims who are invested in the process and its outcome. But we should also note a gendered pattern of victims' discourse; male victims who contribute more than once are more effective speakers, in terms of higher deliberative quality of their speeches than women victims. Conversely, women victims have deliberative advantage over men when they speak once. Lastly, the evidence that victims (both men and women) who speak only once are not able to articulate their positions as deliberatively as they want or as would be desirable, if they are to be their own advocates, should be noted because their views and concerns can otherwise be marginalized.

The analysis shows that translation during consultations does not affect the deliberation quality and confirms findings that deliberation is not conditional on linguistic homogeneity.[71] With its focus on translation in transitional justice consultations, this finding expands our understanding of the role of translation in transitional justice processes.[72]

This chapter has measured the quality of deliberation of discussions about mass violence and other human rights violations in the search for justice. It explained variation in the quality of deliberation by refining common predictors of deliberativeness and incorporating novel covariates that capture linguistic and semantic features of language and their relationship with good-quality deliberation. The results presented and discussed here indicate the complexity of how ethnic identities matter during deliberation. These findings defy widely held assumptions that ethnicized discourse necessarily undermines the deliberativeness of discourse. It was found that higher deliberative quality was associated with highly polarizing issues defined in ethnic terms; with dyadic and multiethnic sessions (but not triadic ones) that mirror conflict dynamics; and with expressions of ethnicness in speeches during discussions with former adversaries. These three associations indicate the indirect and direct effects of ethnic identity and considerations based on enacting this identity on the quality of discourse, which has not been anticipated by scholars of deliberation or by scholars of transitional justice.

The necessity of recasting the discussion from ethnic to nonethnic terms as the way to overcome conflict in divided societies has been taken as a given by scholars of deliberation in divided societies. That change has been seen as dovetailing with a shift from ethnic to civic conceptions of identity and nationhood, as deliberation "transform[s] the hard parameter of ethnic identity into a soft parameter of diversity."[73] This is why scholars have generally overlooked various ethnic dimensions of deliberative discourse as they take shape in the lived environment of interethnic deliberation. The empirical analysis presented in this chapter shows multiple ways in which a sense of ethnic identity affects deliberation in divided societies where ethnicity is a salient and enduring identity marker. These results point to the need for a better understanding of how ethnic identity, a primary axis of difference and division in postconflict societies, is expressed in discussions involving former adversaries. The findings in this chapter raise the question of how these expressions of ethnicity can be compatible with deliberativeness. The possibility of reconciliation through deliberative engagement between formerly opposed ethnic groups rests on the answer to this question. I have argued that studying the enactment of ethnic identity in a way that overcomes treating ethnic identity as a static category can reveal the role of ethnic identity in deliberation across ethnic lines.

The insights from this chapter challenge the dichotomous logic of ethnic versus nonethnic discourse in scholarly discussions of deliberation and its benefits for divided societies. If we leverage a deliberative perspective on transitional justice, these findings open up a new vista for observing reconciliation after conflict. A deliberative engagement with the legacy of conflict involving previously opposed ethnic groups is necessary for reconciliation. Its prospects are not diminished by a sense of ethnic identities that permeates discussions. The measurement of deliberative quality shows that the sense of ethnic identification figures prominently in interethnic discussions without being antithetical to deliberativeness. This premise, however, needs to be tested further. We need to assess empirically how the deliberative quality of discourse, as measured by the DQITJ, relates to other features of talk that may distort interethnic discourse and hijack the benefits of deliberation. The next chapter investigates patterns of agreement and disagreement across ethnic lines.

5

WHO AGREES AND WHO DISAGREES

It would be illusory to expect everyone to speak in one voice—as if we were in North Korea.

—Participant in RECOM consultations from Kosovo, May 24, 2016

Sparks flew when someone opposed some suggestion.

—Participant in RECOM consultations from Serbia, September 26, 2014

A deliberative perspective on peacebuilding holds that a reasoned exchange of arguments that accommodate views of fellow deliberators can repair relationships broken by violence.[1] The exchange of arguments, in this case, entails interaction with people from other ethnic groups. In the context of ethnic segregation and homogenization in postconflict environments, where ethnic groups are separated in municipalities, towns, and even schools,[2] transitional justice consultations, like the ones held by the RECOM, can "transcend interpersonal geography and expose people to views unlike their own."[3] But we do not know how ethnic polarization at the societal level will impact microlevel dynamics in interethnic discussions. Will people disagree with fellow deliberators from other ethnic groups more than with speakers from their own ethnic group? Under what conditions will deliberators be respectful? As Max Pensky notes, deep disagreement has "desolidarizing effects."[4] Consistently dissenting behavior toward out-group members is particularly pernicious in ethnically divided societies. To understand the patterns of agreement and disagreement across ethnic lines, this chapter analyzes interactivity in discussions about war crimes.

Interactivity reflects both a behavioral and a substantive dimension of discourse. Deliberators choose to react and respond to other speakers and their arguments. Interactivity offers a new angle on the prospects for reconciliation as it reveals the nature of interactions across ethnic lines. From the perspective of deliberation, interactivity is a direct measure of patterns of communicative exchange, a critical element of Jürgen Habermas's theory of communicative action.[5] In divided societies, the reconciliatory potential of deliberation rests on the fulfillment of deliberative virtues such as equality, reason-giving, respect, common good orientation, and reciprocity.[6] As the analysis in chapters 3 and 4 shows, discussions about divisive wartime legacy can be deliberative as measured by the fulfillment of deliberative virtues. However, this measure does not capture other properties of discourse that can have normative implications, undermining the potential of good-quality deliberation to bridge the ethnic divide in postconflict societies.

If deliberators exclusively agree with members of their in-group and disagree with members of their out-groups, interactivity can prevent reconciliation. Donald Horowitz argues that in societies where ethnic identity is a salient marker, which is typical of divided societies, ethnicity is "often accompanied by hostility towards outgroups" and a sense of allegiance toward members of in-groups.[7] Conversely, the beneficial impact of agreement and civility across ethnic lines will be amplified in ethnically divided settings. The crux of Habermas's communicative action is that communicative actors share knowledge to arrive at mutual understanding.[8] For interethnic discussion about war crimes to be reconciliatory, the fulfillment of deliberative virtues must coexist with interactivity conducive to robust and constructive exchange across ethnic lines. We need to investigate empirically whether these aspects of discourse are complementary or at odds with each other. Excessive disagreement across ethnic lines can undermine the benefits of good-quality deliberation.

The chapter first defines the concept of interactivity. It proceeds by reviewing the study of interactivity in scholarship on deliberation in divided societies. Based on this, I argue that we need to go beyond a narrow operationalization of interactivity and consider the nature of responses (agreement and disagreement) alongside the tally of counts of interethnic responses. In addition, we need to understand whether deliberators are respectful when engaging individuals and groups across ethnic lines.

What Is Interactivity?

The concept of interactivity and its operation in practice are emerging areas of interest in the study of deliberation in divided societies. Scholars have derived the meaning of "interactivity" from the notion of deliberation as communicative exchange and used it interchangeably with "interaction." Here, my use of the term "interactivity" is informed by explications of this concept in communication studies.[9] These explications offer a deeper understanding of how interactivity enhances deliberation across identity lines, which is directly relevant for measuring reconciliation.

Interactivity "is not a monolithic concept."[10] It is a feature of communication in diverse fora, encompassing face-to-face interactivity as well as user-to-user interactivity in web-based and computer-mediated communication.[11] This distinction was originally made in communications studies, which spearheaded efforts to theorize the concept of interactivity in response to the rise of new technologies. At the same time, interest in online deliberation has spurred the study of interactivity in democratic deliberation.[12] The study of interactivity in face-to-face deliberation, as is the case in this book, can benefit from insights generated by scholars of online deliberation.

As Spiro Kiousis points out, at the core of many conceptions of interactivity is "the emphasis on *feedback*."[13] Referring to the tenets of Habermas's theory of communicative action, Jennifer Stromer-Galley underscores that "the free give and take of dynamic deliberation occurs when there is feedback offered by a discussant in an exchange."[14] It follows that interactivity is a relational concept that sheds light on the interdependence of messages.[15] Such interdependence goes beyond formal interactivity that merely records whether contributions are "a reply to another contribution."[16] Matthias Trénel specifies that substantive interactivity, which is "a substantive reference from one contribution to the other, . . . is essential for deliberation."[17] Feedback or reference, understood narrowly as a response to a previous utterance, provides only a limited insight into how deliberators interact and how the dialogic nature of deliberation is realized. Drawing on Mikhail Bakhtin's theory of dialogic communication, Danielle Endres and Barbara Warnick point to the role that style and language play in opening up a deliberative space and interactive engagement.[18] The pattern of agreement and disagreement, along with a scrutiny of how they are expressed, has a role in facilitating or undermining deliberative engagement.

To comprehensively capture interactivity as a feature of the deliberative process, we need to link the pattern of engagement, read from an overall interactivity score that tallies the number of responses to previous speeches, to the analysis of the kind of responses, which may be agreement or disagreement.[19] This distinction between understanding interactivity as a mechanical count of responses and operationalizing interactivity to consider the content of interactions allows us to identify a gap in scholarly approaches to interactivity in relation to overcoming identity conflict.

Interactivity and Ethnic Division

Discursive interaction lies at the heart of deliberation. Every dimension that captures the quality of deliberation, whether an interruption or an expression of reciprocity, is also an indicator of how that interaction unfolds. However, this conceptualization of deliberation as a communicative exchange only provides an indirect take on interactivity. It stops short of addressing explicitly and precisely the questions of who responds to whom and how. Interactivity is directly related to the quality of deliberation. How participants interact with each other is a fundamental question when assessing the deliberativeness of discourse. Given that "the only available resource for diverse opinions is the discussants themselves," interactivity allows us to capture how deliberators engage with diverse views.[20] In the context of recovery from conflict, people need to hear views of ethnic Others and engage with these views. During public deliberation, interactivity opens the space for "continuous renegotiation" and prevents monopolization of the interpretation of traumatic events, as illustrated by dominant ethnocentric understandings of the Balkan conflicts.[21] In postconflict societies, interactivity, as Jürg Steiner argues, "can help to build trust in the sense that the speaker acknowledges that the other side also has certain rationality, and this gives the other side a human face."[22]

Deliberation is a normatively demanding form of communication. It is about more than just expressing and hearing different views; it requires engagement with those views. As Ian Rowe puts it, "if commenters fail to take in to account the views, opinions, and arguments of other participants, the discussion can hardly be labelled deliberative."[23] He suggests that we can find out whether participants "actively engage with one another in this way is to determine the extent to which they interact."[24] An empirical measure of interactivity is of particular importance in diverse settings along identity lines, where deliberation involves divisive issues. By studying interactivity, we can assess whether a discussion is deliberative and how deliberation can help bring divided communities together. Unsurprisingly, "the black box of interaction" has been opened by scholars concerned with how the identities of deliberators, such as ethnicity and gender, affect deliberation.[25]

Cass Sunstein defines "enclave deliberation" as "that form of deliberation that occurs within groups that have engaged in self-sorting, or that have been sorted, through practices of discrimination or oppression, into relatively homogenous domains."[26] This concept has provided a theoretical entry point into the study of deliberation in divided societies. Sunstein does not explicitly associate an enclave with an identity group; rather, according to him, an enclave is a group of like-minded individuals. In divided societies, deliberative enclaves are understood as being coterminous with ethnic divisions in society at large and as such can lead to polarization of ethnic groups.[27] Scholars referred to the concept of enclave deliberation to question whether ethnic diversity is detrimental to deliberation in postconflict contexts. Subsequent empirical studies have explored the patterns of interactivity across ethnic lines in microlevel deliberations in experimental settings.

Didier Caluwaerts and Kris Deschouwer investigate whether a speech act is a reaction to a speech act uttered by an in-group or an out-group member. Their findings point to "a fair amount of discursive integration," as participants' interaction patterns do not constitute enclave deliberation in deliberative experiments involving the Dutch- and French-speaking Belgians.[28] Their measurement of interactivity captures whether deliberators interact, that is respond to members of an out-group. However, it does not capture how they interact, whether they agree or disagree with each other. By contrast, in their study of deliberation focused on the Muslim community in the United Kingdom (UK), Manlio Cinalli and Ian O'Flynn investigate a pattern of ties among deliberative actors qualified as supporting or dissenting. They apply Social Network Analysis to analyze the structure of ties and to find out how these patterns map onto deep divisions. Aiming to assess whether deliberation results in political integration of Muslims in the UK, they sum up the problem: "we should worry greatly if it turns out that Muslim actors talk only amongst themselves or, by corollary, only side with one another."[29] Cinalli and O'Flynn do not find evidence supporting group polarization: Muslim actors figure in diverse cliques of both support and dissent, which are comprised of different types of actors and do not overlap with ethnic cleavages. Their findings are based on attitudes expressed by British Muslims in newspapers, which raises the question of how the pattern would hold in a face-to-face discussion.

The salience of gender as an identity axis affirms the importance of studying interactivity as more than simply a reaction to a particular speech act or person. In their study of gender inequality and deliberation, Tali Mendelberg et al. operationalize interaction as an interruption, which they qualify as positive (expressing agreement) or negative (expressing disagreement). According to them, positive interruptions represent support for the speaker that does not undermine the speaker's effectiveness. By contrast, negative interruptions represent the demonstration of power, for example, the floor being taken away from a speaker, or a topic being changed unilaterally.[30] The rate of positive and negative interruptions of female speakers affects their status as speakers and weakens social solidarity among speakers during deliberation.[31]

Therefore, to further our understanding of interactivity in face-to-face deliberations across ethnic lines, we need to go beyond a narrow operationalization of interactivity and better grasp which factors are conducive to positive interactions. We still do not know how the patterns of agreement and disagreement align with ethnic divisions in ethnically diverse face-to-face discussions, even though the implications for deliberation and reconciliation are profound.

The Role of Disagreement in Deliberation

Disagreement plays a paradoxical role in deliberation. According to Kevin Esterling et al., "with no disagreement, reasons need not be offered nor considered, and
with too much disagreement reasons fall on deaf ears."[32] Deliberation depends
on the exposure to different viewpoints, which may spur reconsideration of one's
original position along with the appreciation of viewpoints held by others. As
Dennis Thompson puts it, "some basic disagreement is necessary to create the
problem that deliberative democracy is intended to solve."[33] However, more than
"some basic disagreement" can have the opposite effect. Too much disagreement
can undermine the benefits of a deliberative process. Given the importance of
contestation in a deliberative mode of communication, André Bächtiger and
Marlène Gerber contend that "the problem here is not one of presence or absence
of contestation but one of basic orientation and quantity."[34] In divided societies,
a legacy of conflict and distrust increases the potential for disagreement. In these
contexts, the pattern of disagreement matters because it can distort deliberative
discourse and deepen ethnic fissures.

Another important question is what disagreement means and does in social
interactions. Scholars have pointed out that disagreement can mean more than
just a discrepancy between one's views and those held by others. Thus, Andrew
Smith notes that disagreement and disapproval "reflect the judgement that *someone* must be in the wrong: us, our critic(s) or both."[35] Huw Price elaborates this
point by saying disagreement "is an indication of culpable error, on one side or
the other."[36] From this perspective, disagreement in deliberation matters because,
as Cheryl Misak argues, it aims to get "the right answers to our questions about
what we ought to do and about how we ought to treat others."[37] Disagreement
indicates exposure to views other than one's own, which may also close off the
possibility of accommodation. Mindful of bias in information processing during deliberation, Diana Mutz suggests that disagreeing may trigger greater ste-
reotyping of out-group members.[38] Other scholars highlight the positive effects
of disagreement; Michael Neblo points out that listening respectfully to views
with which one disagrees can build trust among deliberators.[39] Although "the
benefits of deliberation critically depend on the confrontation of opposing
arguments," how agreements and disagreements are expressed—respectfully
or disrespectfully—will also affect reconciliation in postconflict contexts.[40] In
a deliberative exchange, especially across ethnic lines, a distinction between a
respectful and disrespectful assertion of views needs to be made.[41]

Respectful engagement during a disagreement is a requirement for deliberation. According to Thompson, "the reasoning must show respect to the participants and their arguments, even if it challenges the validity of the claims."[42]

As this quote suggests, the expression of respect for arguments is bound up with respect for persons.[43] Consideration of respect figures prominently in the scholarship on deliberation in divided societies. On the one hand, the legacy of conflict presents an obstacle to respectful deliberation. On the other hand, respectful engagement across ethnic lines is critical to restoring relationships in conflict-affected communities.[44] Insofar as respect entails recognition of a person, and, conversely, disrespect entails denigration, rehabilitation of ethnic relations through deliberation in divided societies rests on civility in communicative interaction. However, greater theoretical attention is required in relation to the question of who is the target of respectful or disrespectful remarks.

A consequence of conflict-induced ethnic polarization is the blurring, even outright conflation, of individual and collective conceptions of ethnic identity. Individuals are killed in the conflict as members of an opposite ethnic group, which facilitates the conflation of individual and collective identification. As Peter Dahlgren contends, "to point to the interaction among citizens—whether or not it is formalized as deliberation—is to take a step into the social contexts of everyday life."[45] When citizens deliberate about overcoming harms caused by an identity conflict, the act of deliberation is simultaneously an encounter with members of ethnic groups that committed those wrongs. The study of interactivity can further our understanding of how individual and collective notions of identity are brought into deliberation at a microlevel of deliberation, and how these dynamics hinder or promote conflict resolution. Will a face-to-face encounter with an ethnic Other in a robust communicative exchange trigger individual or group identification dynamics?

In both the lab and the field, experimental studies of postconflict deliberation do not distinguish between individual and collective identities—even when inferences about mutual accommodation among ethnic groups through deliberation are being made. By contrast, transitional justice scholarship and practice are premised on the assumption that a collective understanding of responsibility for wartime violence underpinned by a collective construction of identity impedes justice and reconciliation. This construction means that "the 'other' is perceived as a whole, whose constituent parts are subsumed into the collective identity."[46] When identity is a collective construct, individual responsibility for war crimes and human rights violations is obscured and truth recovery is blocked.

One potential benefit of dialogical approaches to reconciliation in ethnically mixed settings is facilitating recognition of an individual as separate from the group. This mechanism humanizes the opposing side and engenders empathy toward the suffering of a human being from another ethnic group. Both individual and collective conceptualizations of identity are enacted in all deliberations.

How references to collective versus individual identities are associated with the pattern of agreement and disagreement across ethnic lines can further our understanding of the role identities play in postconflict deliberation and their effect on reconciliation. The next section details the empirical approach to interactivity.

Coding Interactivity

Interactivity is measured by coding 1,211 speech acts in the RECOM corpus, a record of real-life discussions about war crimes in the Balkans. In line with the empirical strategy applied in the study of quality of deliberation, a speech act is defined as a statement containing a position on an issue discussed. The author and another coder coded each speech act independently, applying a coding scheme presented in table 5.1. The intercoder reliability statistics demonstrate an acceptable level of agreement.[47]

The coding strategy for the study of interactivity registered the presence of interactive references, specifying whether they were interethnic, involving speakers from two different ethnic groups, or intraethnic, involving speakers from the same ethnic group. Another layer of information on the nature of these references was added by coding whether they were neutral or denoted agreement or disagreement, in line with Stromer-Galley's scheme.[48] Previous research on interactivity in divided societies applied a minimalist operationalization of interactivity across ethnic lines in face-to-face deliberations, such as "a response to a previous statement."[49] This operationalization reflects the sequence of speakers. What remains unclear with such operationalization of interactivity as simply a

TABLE 5.1 Interactivity variables

LABEL	VALUE
Reference to other participants	No reference Yes
Interethnic reference	No Yes (Disagreement) Yes (Neutral) Yes (Agreement)
Intraethnic reference	No Yes (Disagreement) Yes (Neutral) Yes (Agreement)

response is whether a response is triggered by a position expressed by a previous speaker or possibly by a point made earlier in a discussion. In sum, this operationalization does not (adequately) reflect the character of feedback, which is critical to defining interactivity. To address this lack of clarity, the coding in this research specifies a high standard for signaling interactivity, informed by the concept of social presence.

In line with research by Kiousis, "social presence" denotes clear recognition of the person to whom a speaker is responding.[50] Interactivity is coded when a speaker explicitly refers to another speaker by name, or otherwise unambiguously signals their identity, including by repeating verbatim what the previous speaker uttered.[51] For example, a deliberator may refer to someone by a surname, such as, "I agree with fellow discussant Jović."[52] Or, he or she may refer to a fellow speaker from Macedonia, a colleague from Belgrade, and so on. By using social presence as the benchmark for coding, interactivity in this book is determined neither by the flow of deliberation nor by the speaking order, which a moderator may impose. In deliberative settings, the discussion moves relatively fast. A particular named speaker may have presented her or his argument two or three speaking turns before another speaker has an opportunity to engage with that argument. Coding interactivity signaled by social presence comprehensively captures the relatedness of utterances, as it also includes the substantive content of the speech act. Furthermore, the requisite identification of a speaker whose point is responded to (and who may have spoken earlier during a discussion) allows for precise coding of the ethnicity of that speaker.[53]

Lastly, signaling social presence in the context of face-to-face deliberations across the deep divide in real-life discussions about war crimes and their legacy raises the stakes of deliberators' contributions to the deliberative process. This is particularly the case if they depart from what might be the expected line of argumentation associated with an ethnic identity. Such stepping out of line, especially to agree with a member from a different ethnic group, represents a strong indication of deliberativeness of interethnic communication along with its reconciliatory potential. During the RECOM consultations, the margin of error in recognizing someone's ethnic identity was minimal. The participants introduced themselves at the start of the consultative session, making their identities clear to fellow discussants. Absent that, their identity could be unambiguously inferred from their account of their circumstances and suffering during the conflict or of their activism. At the same time, the tacit knowledge that allowed fellow deliberators to identify interlocutors should not be underestimated. In these transitional justice consultations led by civil society, which gathered people from different sides of a regional conflict who were previously citizens of the same state (i.e., the former Yugoslavia) and exposed to one another's languages, all had an acute awareness of their participation in delicate communication across lines of division and the significance of their utterances.

The Patterns of Agreement and Disagreement

The following sections present the results of the analysis of interactivity with participants of the same ethnic group and of a different ethnic group. Interactivity is observed in terms not only of a formal count of responses to a named speaker and his or her arguments, but also in terms of the substantive content of those responses that contain a viewpoint (agreement, disagreement, and a neutral position toward another's argument). Also of interest is examining how respect toward individuals and toward groups expressed during deliberation are associated with agreement and disagreement across ethnic lines.

Interactivity and Ethnic Enclavization

The first set of results addresses whether ethnic enclavization has occurred and whether deliberative enclaves, following Sunstein, that are defined by ethnicity can be observed in interethnic deliberations about justice for past wrongs.[54] As scholars of deliberation in divided societies have specified, ethnic enclaves involve engagement with members of one's own ethnic group during interethnic deliberation. Such distortion of discourse in the direction of groupthink undermines the legitimacy of deliberative democracy and prospects for reconciliation.[55] Overlapping and intersecting loyalties of ethnic, religious, racial, and cultural groups are a feature of plural democratic societies.[56] These multiple loyalties are elided in the aftermath of a conflict and collapse into a single division that runs along the lines of an identity that becomes salient. After an ethnic conflict, this division is often institutionalized through consociational power-sharing arrangements on an ethnic basis. Further, the creation of new state borders, as occurred after the breakup of the former Yugoslavia, introduces another dimension of division. Even in heterogeneous communities that have not been directly affected by conflict, people "refrain from social opportunities that might lead to interactions with individuals from different racial, income, or ethnic groups."[57] If we consider the adverse impact of conflict on interethnic relations, including macrolevel political and social divisions in postconflict communities, we would expect to find a pattern of discursive ethnic enclavization at the microlevel as well.

Frequencies of speech acts indicating interethnic and intraethnic interactivity in the RECOM consultations are presented in table 5.2. Contrary to expectations, they show that there is no discursive ethnic enclavization in these consultations

TABLE 5.2   Absolute and relative frequency of interactions by ethnicity of speakers

	N	VALID PERCENT
Interaction with a speaker from another ethnic group	208	64.4
Interaction with a speaker from the same ethnic group	115	35.6
Missing	790	
Total	1,113	100

Note: The missing observations include speech acts that did not include interaction. Monoethnic sessions are excluded.

comprised of speakers from different ethnic groups discussing the legacy of war crimes. We can observe greater interactivity across ethnic lines than within the same ethnic group: 64.4 percent of all interactions in the RECOM consultations occurred across ethnic lines, as opposed to 35.6 percent that occurred between individuals belonging to the same ethnic group. Based on the unique observational data of real-world deliberations that constitute the RECOM consultations, these findings show that people are willing to engage across the ethnic divide to discuss how to address the legacy of war crimes and achieve justice for past wrongs.[58]

It is also worth recalling that the RECOM process was a regional civil society network that provided space for deliberation by bringing together people from all ethnic groups involved in the wars of Yugoslavia's dissolution. John Dryzek argues that networks are located at the informal end of an institutional spectrum and help disperse "control over the content and the weight of discourses, facilitating deliberation across difference."[59] His argument is informed by an oppositional stance toward a state in divided societies that enshrines and promotes narrow ethnic interests. The tally of interethnic interactions presented here indicates that a network appears to be conducive to engagement across ethnic lines, as deliberators overcome separation entrenched by ethnic segmentation in the context of reluctance by states to address the legacy of mass atrocity and justice for war crimes.[60]

Furthermore, the distribution of interethnic and intraethnic interactivity indicates a level of engagement with difference, conceived in terms of ascriptive difference along the ethnic identity axis, required for deliberation. However, this tally of interactive references does not reveal how people engage with difference when it is understood as engagement with different viewpoints. Given the impact of conflict on constructing exclusive ethnic identities and the power of those identities to shape both the understanding of conflict and the response to its painful legacy, ethnocentrism is a prominent feature of contentious discussions about transitional justice issues. If social identities in postconflict contexts act as "discursive weapons" and lead to the automatic refutation of arguments by out-group members, we would expect to observe more agreement in interactions with co-ethnics than with speakers from other ethnic groups.[61] Similarly, we would expect more disagreement in interactions across ethnic lines than in interactions with one's own ethnic group members. To distinguish engagement with difference across ethnic lines from engagement with different opinions, I measure interactive references in terms of occurrence and viewpoint, including agreement, disagreement, and a neutral position (neither agreement nor disagreement).[62] Proportions of interactive references across ethnic lines by agreement, disagreement, and a neutral position are presented in figure 5.1; proportions of interactive references with members of one's ethnic group by viewpoint are shown in figure 5.2.

We can observe a similar pattern of disagreement and agreement between interactions with speakers from different ethnic groups and interactions with speakers from one's own ethnic group.[63] Contrary to the expectation grounded in the scholarship on deliberation in divided societies, which warns of antagonism and contention in intergroup deliberation, figures 5.1 and 5.2 show that disagreement is not a defining feature of interactivity across ethnic lines. Rather,

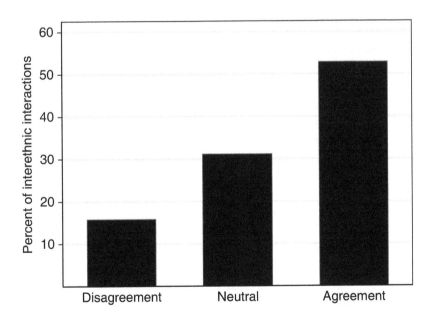

FIGURE 5.1. Relative frequency of interactive references across ethnic lines by viewpoint

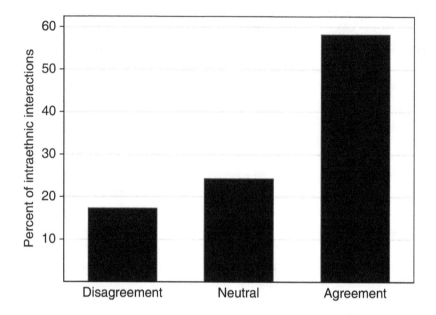

FIGURE 5.2. Relative frequency of interactive references within an ethnic group by viewpoint

we can observe that agreement is prevalent in interactions with members both of an out-group and the in-group—although the level of neutral interactions (indicating neither agreement nor disagreement) is somewhat higher when interacting across ethnic lines than when interacting with co-ethnics. These findings align with the pattern of face-to-face social interactions in democratic contexts.[64] They confirm people's tendency to select politically like-minded discussion partners, while being averse to disagreement.[65] Although interactivity is measured under the most adverse of conditions—after a conflict and when deliberating about war crimes across ethnic lines—the quantity and the pattern of disagreement provide evidence of a robust deliberative process without risk of derailment by what John Gastil calls "extreme disagreement."[66] Such a pattern of interactivity in a justice-seeking process captures the nature of engagement with different viewpoints and people from different ethnic groups. It points to the existence of normative preconditions that are needed for deliberation to deliver benefits for postconflict recovery, specifically, to repair interethnic relations.

Moving beyond describing interactivity in transitional justice consultations, the analysis turns to the determinants of interactivity across ethnic lines. This part of the empirical investigation queries how the expression of respect is associated with interactivity across ethnic lines.

Respectful or Disrespectful Disagreement?

When citizens deliberate in democratic societies, "they express and respect their status as political equals even as they continue to disagree about important matters of public policy."[67] Respectful engagement with individuals and groups across ethnic lines is a demanding ask of deliberators in a postconflict context. Offensive engagement across ethnic lines deepens division and distrust between ethnic adversaries, while public expression of respect for individuals and groups across ethnic lines can help repair social relations after a conflict. According to Amy Gutmann and Dennis Thompson, "mutual respect requires more than toleration or a benign attitude toward others. It requires a favorable attitude toward, and constructive interaction with, people with whom one reasonably disagrees when those persons are similarly willing and able to adopt such an attitude."[68] Such public expression of respect can be interpreted as a signal of reconciliation and encourage reciprocity.[69] In addition, assessments of whether deliberators are respectful toward individuals or groups of other ethnicities, and how such expressions are associated with patterns of agreement and disagreement in interacting across ethnic lines, indicate how the deployment of individual and collective identity categories facilitates reconciliation during deliberation.

A multinomial logistic regression model was fitted to assess what predicts interaction across ethnic lines measured as no interaction and three categories of viewpoint (agreement, disagreement, and neutrality), with a particular interest in the effect of respect for participants. The results are presented in table 5.3. To isolate the effects of respect toward participants and/or their arguments (hereafter, respect) on the occurrence and the nature of interactivity with ethnic Others, the analysis controlled for discussion length, as measured by the number of speech acts, and issue polarization.[70]

The speech acts were observed on the variable respect in terms of explicit respect, neutral respect (neither respect nor disrespect), and disrespect. Respectful speech acts contain a positive and explicitly respectful reference to a fellow deliberator. For example, a speaker makes a proposal in reference to the previous speaker's argument: "I would like to suggest to the Working Group to consider Mrs Jukić's suggestion very well because I think that it is extremely relevant."[71] Another example of respect for the argument of a previous speaker is: "In the context of what you've just said, I really like [the suggestion when] the mandate should start."[72] Speech acts are neutral if they mention participants' arguments in neutral terms, without explicit respect or disrespect. For example, a speaker

TABLE 5.3 Modeling interethnic interactivity using multinomial logistic regression

	COEFF.	STD. ERR.	*p*-VALUE	ODDS RATIO
	Indicating disagreement			
Number of speech acts in consultation	.007	.003	.029	1.007
Issue polarization (ref. Low): Medium & high	.919	.377	.015	2.507
Respect for participants (ref. Disrespect):				
Neutral	−1.482	.489	.002	.227
Respect	−.508	.752	.500	.602
(Constant)	−3.247			
	Indicating neutrality			
Number of speech acts in consultation	.007	.002	.002	1.007
Issue polarization (ref. Low): Medium & high	.442	.270	.101	1.556
Respect for participants (ref. Disrespect):				
Neutral	.476	.738	.519	1.609
Respect	2.017	.804	.012	7.514
(Constant)	−4.183			
	Indicating agreement			
Number of speech acts in consultation	.006	.002	< .001	1.007
Issue polarization (ref. Low): Medium & high	.435	.214	.042	1.545
Respect for participants (ref. Disrespect):				
Neutral	.989	.732	.176	2.689
Respect	2.657	.775	.001	14.258
(Constant)	−4.090			

Note: Pseudo R^2 = .052. N = 1,110. Response variable: Interethnic interaction. Base: No interaction. Speech acts in monoethnic consultations, and speech acts containing no expression of respect, neutrality, or disrespect to participants and/or their arguments, are omitted.

says, unambiguously engaging with a previous speaker's argument, "I wanted to say exactly the same thing."[73] By contrast, disrespectful references to the previous speaker's arguments include rude, unpleasant comments or foul language about participants or arguments, such as a speaker engaging with another speaker's argument by dismissing it as having "nothing do with a mathematical logic."[74] Another speaker qualified the proposition about an article of the Draft Statute as so "catastrophic" that it "made her go mad."[75] How is respect associated with interactivity across ethnic lines?

The analysis found that, holding discussion length and issue polarization constant, the odds of agreement with the ethnic Other (versus not interacting) are 14.258 times higher for speech acts expressing respect to participants than those expressing disrespect. Similarly, all else equal, the odds of a neutral viewpoint (neither agreement nor disagreement) in interacting with the ethnic Other (versus not interacting) are 7.514 times higher for speech acts expressing respect to participants than of those for speech acts expressing disrespect. This result is noteworthy. Agreeing with the named ethnic Other and making a respectful remark can be morally and politically demanding in a postconflict context, given the pressure for nonengagement with the ethnic Other and their denigration in the public discourse in postconflict societies. Considering that the RECOM consultations focused on the divisive issue of redress for wartime violence, the association of the expression of respect with agreement across ethnic lines in this context amplifies the sense of collaboration about this contentious issue regardless of the ethnicity of those with whom a speaker is engaging.

The analysis also found that, holding discussion length and issue polarization constant, neutral respect compared to disrespect toward a participant does not change the odds of agreement or a neutral viewpoint in interaction (versus not interacting) across ethnic lines (the results are insignificant). However, the odds of disagreeing with an ethnic Other (versus not interacting) for speech acts expressing neutral respect are .227 times those of speech acts showing disrespect toward participants, that is 77 percent lower. Thus, speakers who refer to participants or their arguments neutrally are more inclined not to interact with the ethnic Other rather than to explicitly disagree with them. This result could be indicative of people's propensity to avoid disagreement.[76] However, the same finding from the perspective of disrespect compared to neutral respect references indicates that those expressing disrespect are more likely to disagree with ethnic Others than not to interact at all.[77] How does this finding illuminate the nature of disagreement across ethnic lines?

Arguably, an equally important finding is that explicit respect compared to disrespect toward participants does not make disagreement (versus not interacting) with an ethnic Other less likely (the estimate is statistically insignificant). This result is noteworthy considering the prior finding that a neutral respect reference versus disrespect makes interethnic disagreement less likely. Those participants who are respectful do not differ from those who are disrespectful in their readiness to disagree. Therefore, we do not observe a clear and consistent pattern of disrespectful as opposed to respectful disagreement across ethnic lines. Hence, the measurement of the nature of agreement and disagreement in this transitional justice process indicates a robust exchange of opposed and concurring views across ethnic lines that is conducive to deliberation.

Lastly, an observation about the expression of respect toward groups is in order. Speech acts in which expression of respect is directed at individual fellow participants are significantly associated with interethnic interactivity, as opposed to speech acts in which expression of respect is directed at ethnic groups to which deliberators belong.[78] These contrasting results indicate the tendency of deliberators to interact in face-to-face discussions with members of other ethnic groups as individuals rather than focusing on their group membership. This tendency pushes against the collective conceptualization and construction of ethnic identities that, as scholars of transitional justice have shown, is an impediment to inclusively addressing the legacy of violence.[79] Interethnic deliberation in transitional justice consultations appears conducive to challenging the dominance of ethnocentric collective identification that underpins a collective construction of victimhood and culpability, unlike other transitional justice practices such as war crimes trials and memorializations.[80] Interethnic deliberation can contribute to the decoupling of collective identities from their association with antagonism toward the collective ethnic Other through the process of individuation that indicates the evaluation of a person as different from a group.[81] Ethnic enclavization is characteristic of societies emerging from conflict.[82] In postconflict societies, such as Bosnia's, ethnic segregation as a consequence of conflict has been referred to as "ethnic apartheid."[83] The ethnic configuration of territories explains a lack of interactions across ethnic lines.[84] Transitional justice consultations involving people belonging to opposing ethnic groups provide a possibility for overcoming ethnic enclavization. They provide an opportunity not only to meet people from other ethnic groups face-to-face but also to engage in discursive interaction. However, it is by no means certain that these opportunities will help people overcome mistrust and division. Deliberators may tend toward engaging with their co-ethnics as opposed to reaching across ethnic lines; alternatively, even if they reach across ethnic lines, they may do so to disagree with speakers from ethnic groups other than their own. Deliberation requires disagreement and consideration of views from different perspectives. However, if disagreement with ethnic Others is always disrespectful rather than respectful, it can undermine good-quality deliberation and reconciliation.

The normative appeal of deliberation rests on the benefits of this communicative exercise: exposure to the diversity of views, including across ethnic lines, enhances mutual understanding and tolerance.[85] In the context of conflict-resolution and peacebuilding, confronting multiple viewpoints about the route to justice opens the space for reconciliation through constructive engagement with the violent past. Active engagement with diverse viewpoints held by the "other" side highlights multiple perspectives on harm and suffering. But active engagement across ethnic lines also needs to be civil and respectful to reinforce deliberative quality and pave the way for the benefits of deliberation in divided societies. These benefits extend beyond the immediate effects of a specific discussion. Jennifer Stromer-Galley and Peter Muhlberger show that a positive evaluation of deliberation increases motivation to participate in future deliberations.[86] This conclusion is particularly important for divided postconflict societies, where routine interethnic deliberation on a range of issues of public interest can also contribute to the repair of interethnic relations.

As an aspect of deliberativeness of discourse, the patterns of interethnic interactivity identified in this book confound "the most pessimistic predictions for divided societies," that different ethnic groups cannot deliberate because of a prevailing sense of distrust and resentment between them.[87] Any engagement, especially respectful engagement, with members from other ethnic groups and endorsement of their views through agreement is costly in postconflict contexts where ethnocentric narratives of conflict and victimhood are maintained by elites and society at large. Numerous participants in the RECOM consultations were concerned that their engagement with this multiethnic process would be considered an act of treason by other members of their ethnic groups.[88] Showing respect publicly toward members of other ethnic groups defies the norms of nonengagement and noncooperation in ethnicized postconflict societies. It points to the possibility of reconciliation grounded in mutuality in public communication. This empirical evidence of people's civil engagement across ethnic lines, with the level of dissent conducive to rigorous scrutiny of issues, is consistent with various measures of good-quality deliberation presented in chapters 3 and 4. It reinforces the conclusion of the previous chapter about the resilience of deliberation as a mode of communication in postconflict contexts.

I have argued that good-quality deliberation is a necessary but insufficient condition for reconciliation through transitional justice consultations that address the legacy of mass atrocity. For deliberation to deliver its normative benefits, we need to observe deliberation quality, measured by the attainment of deliberative virtues in discourse, along with the pattern of interethnic interactivity that avoids ethnic enclavization and disagreement as the exclusive mode of engaging ethnic Others. Analysis of the RECOM corpus demonstrates that the two measured dimensions of discourse—deliberative quality and interactivity—safeguard deliberativeness of discourse in transitional justice consultations, although a sense of ethnic difference permeates interethnic discourse. If a sense of ethnic difference contributes to polarization in divided societies, this raises the question of how the discussion about war crimes can be reconciliatory. The next chapter demonstrates how people enact their ethnic identities during postconflict deliberation forging solidary bonds across ethnic lines.

DISCURSIVE SOLIDARITY AGAINST IDENTITY POLITICS

All dead are equal.

—Participant in RECOM consultations from Kosovo, May 25, 2016

Violence in identity conflicts locks in ethnocentric thinking. It makes it difficult for people in divided societies to transcend their ethnic perspectives after conflict ends. Such narrowing of ethical horizons hampers the search for justice for wartime wrongs. This contentious issue is likely to polarize communities along ethnic lines and foreclose the possibility of postconflict deliberation. Scholars have put faith in deliberation to address postconflict justice and bring divided societies together. However, we still lack empirical evidence on the deliberative repair of broken interethnic relations through discussion of redress for wartime harm. Presenting the argument for reconciliation through deliberation, this book has put deliberation in divided societies to the most stringent of tests. It has asked: can people engage with each other deliberatively across ethnic lines when discussing justice for mass violence?

The evidence presented in the preceding chapters shows that postconflict deliberation in practice is resilient. People can have comparatively high-quality deliberation across the ethnic divide even when they address the subject of wartime injury in a transitional justice process. However, deliberative interethnic discourse does not in itself necessarily indicate reconciliation. To be reconciliatory, deliberation across ethnic lines about wartime harm has to overcome the desolidarizing effects of identity politics; interethnic communication has to live up to the requirement of discursive solidarity that recognizes, dignifies, and respects the deliberative partner in their suffering and pain, regardless of their ethnicity.

Elaborating on the ethical goals of deliberation, André Bächtiger and John Parkinson specify that deliberation—a normatively demanding mode of communication—creates a moral "we-perspective." Alongside mutual recognition, this perspective entails a sense of collective enterprise, mutual interdependence, trust, and the creation of social bonds across group boundaries.[1] In divided societies, identity politics based on exclusive ethnic identities obstructs these ethical goals. For reconciliation to occur and to be evidenced in deliberative discourse, a nationalist "us first" orientation has to give way to a moral "we perspective."[2]

This ethical perspective leads us to explore how people enact their ethnic identities during deliberation in consultations on transitional justice. These identity dynamics cannot be captured by measuring the quality of deliberation alone, because this empirical strategy considers identities to be static—fixed attributes of speakers. Studies of identity in social interaction show that the identities people enact do not map neatly onto ethnic or other group membership categories. Moreover, people's enactment of identities cannot be understood merely in its microlevel interactional environment. The analysis must also take into account macrolevel ideologies and discourses.[3] Nationalist discourses in postconflict societies create normative pressure to enact exclusivist, ideologically prescribed ethnic identities. This pressure falls on microdeliberation and risks distorting interethnic communication, undermining the prospects for reconciliation.

This chapter investigates how people's enactment of their ethnic identities meets ethical goals of deliberation in order to reveal how people orient themselves discursively toward each other in public communication. I find that deliberators are involved in a delicate process of self-expression, negotiating their individual and collective identities as they encounter the ethnic Other. The expression of difference along the ascriptive axis of ethnicity remains prominent in interethnic deliberation about past wrongs. However, people calibrate the enactment of their ethnic identities in a way that is accepting of the ethnic Other and respectful of their suffering, offsetting the divisive impact of identity politics and thus facilitating reconciliation.

In what follows, I first show how identity politics bears on deliberation in civil society, which is why we need an ethical perspective to evaluate the enactment of ethnic identities during deliberation. The data and the qualitative method—the other strand alongside the quantitative analysis in this book's mixed-method research design—are then introduced. Lastly, I analyze discursive identity practices that reflect the enactment of ethnic identities in discourse and evaluate how they overcome divisive identity politics during deliberation.

Ethical Discourse, Identity Politics, and Civil Society in Postconflict Environments

William Rehg raises the question of how discourse ethics can be practiced in real social interaction processes, specifically in real conflict resolution. For Jürgen Habermas, everyday interactions are the locus of discourse ethics.[4] Interactions occur in different sites and different contexts, and each involves different priorities and expectations.[5] Habermas theorized communication processes both within institutions, such as parliamentary bodies and in informal networks of the public sphere.[6] Those informal communications in civil society are particularly important in postconflict environments because, as John Dryzek and Ian O'Flynn argue, they provide an opportunity to bypass institutionalized ethnic divisions.[7]

Similarly, peacebuilding scholars have singled out the discursive conception of civil society, informed by the ideas of public sphere and deliberation, as conducive to reconciliation.[8] When addressing the legacy of conflict, it is essential that civil society as a site of deliberation is autonomous from the state and the economic system.[9] Postconflict states are often defined by consociational governance arrangements that institutionalize ethnic divisions.[10] Civil society, as the "social underpinning of autonomous publics," and as a deliberative space, allows people from different ethnic groups, who often live in segmented, ethnically homogeneous communities, to meet.[11] Just as important, civil society provides "communicative freedom," as James Bohman points out.[12] Such freedom releases people from the pressure often exerted on them through official norms and discourses to comply with ethnocentric views on postconflict justice. Freedom from internal and external coercion ensures that people assess validity claims solely based on the rational force of better reasons.[13]

However, these normative assumptions about a civil society that can repair relationships broken by violence do not stand up to the realities of civic life in many postconflict environments. Civil society often exhibits the same malaise as formal institutions, a tendency overlooked by scholars of deliberation in divided societies. Postconflict civil societies, not unlike postconflict states, are often fragmented along ethnic lines, while segments of civil society are themselves purveyors of ethnically exclusionary nationalist ideology. These "uncivil" manifestations of civic life in organizational forms outside the state embody identity politics and present obstacles to reconciliation.[14] As a civil society process, the RECOM transitional justice consultations embodied the normative contradiction that marks postconflict civil societies. Spearheaded by a liberal segment of civil society, the RECOM process was open to democratic discussion and accepted perspectives of all ethnic groups as valid and equal. At the same time, it was fraught with exclusionary identity politics purveyed by civil society actors.

Both organizers and participants in the RECOM consultations were aware of the perils of politicized ethnic identity. The process was thought to be "contaminated" by an "identitarian nightmare" characteristic of the politics of Balkan states from which participants came.[15] In the words of one participant in the RECOM consultations, the politics "in our societies is forcing us into adversarial relations" with members of other ethnic groups.[16] Others voiced their concern that "messages coming from governments w[ould] influence how people engage with those with whom they communicate directly."[17] At the same time, participants were aware that they would be castigated as "traitors" within their own communities for engaging ethnic Others in search of justice for war crimes.[18] This insight shows that an engagement with ethnic adversaries, especially if it is an empathetic engagement that creates cross-group solidarities, can be costly. This obstacle to good-quality deliberation is found "at a microlevel by individuals and communities as a result of the societal norms and structures," including identities, beliefs, and ideologies.[19] Besides affecting individuals participating in the RECOM consultations, state-led nationalist discourse and ideology also shaped the agendas of civil society organizations in the Balkan region.

Many NGOs, including victims' associations, brought identity politics into the RECOM process. The organizers aimed to involve the widest range of stakeholders in consultations about justice for war crimes. As a result, they did not question the participation of such NGOs despite apprehension about their impact on interethnic communication. As one organizer put it: "We had learnt from our past engagement with them [these NGOs] that they have hard-line positions and that they view the other side, even the associations [of the victims' families from the other side] as their enemies."[20]

The multiethnic nature of the RECOM transitional justice process itself entailed another dilemma. One participant described it: "people were not quite sure whether they represented only their organization, or themselves personally, or, in a way, their ethnic or national community as well."[21] The transitional justice process, which involved members of all ethnic groups in a regional conflict, accentuated the distinction between individual and collective identities. The process heightened awareness of social sanction for publicly dissenting from the dominant views of one's ethnic group. An interviewee articulated the obligation to express a sense of group identity: "you have to see things collectively—as an individual you are nobody here still."[22]

Lastly, the legacy of ethnic targeting during conflict made it difficult for people to jettison an ethnic perspective on victimhood. An interviewee remarked that these ethnic identities were "the result of genocide." Because people identified with a group and the wartime harm it had suffered, they approached the ethnic Other in an adversarial manner, as "a warrior, not a human being."[23] Deeply shaped by identity politics, the RECOM civil society consultations embodied two notions of civil society: as a common space characterized by pluralism, where actors can negotiate their differences, and a fragmented space marked by identity politics. The study of discourse in the RECOM process allows us to evaluate how people enact their ethnic identities from an ethical perspective, and how these enactments shape the moral dimension of discourse and its impact on the prospect of reconciliation.

Identity Enactments and Discursive Solidarity

The circumstances in which deliberation can take place are varied and "request different ethical responses."[24] When addressing the legacy of war crimes in a postconflict transitional justice process, solidarity across ethnic lines has to counteract the distortions of discourse inherent in identity politics, even when deliberation takes place in the domain of civil society. Our empirical strategy needs to identify discursive identity practices that embody enactments of ethnic identity and demonstrate how these identity practices intersect with identity politics during a deliberative exchange. Guided by Habermas's and Axel Honneth's conceptualization of solidarity as a discursive act of recognition of the other, I analyze the following identity practices in discourse: identity disjunctures, affective alignment, and blame aversion.[25] I ask how they overcome key manifestations of divisive identity politics: perceived opinion homogeneity of adversary ethnic group(s), hierarchy of harm that gives moral priority to victims of one's own ethnic group, and negative reciprocity that entails blaming wartime injury exclusively on others (see table 6.1). The empirical investigation of the ethical dimension of interethnic discourse reveals the "integrative force of solidarity" in the RECOM transitional justice consultations as people's enactment of their ethnic identities counteracts identity politics within this civil society initiative.[26]

In line with the mixed-method research design, qualitative analysis is applied to field interview data (twenty-eight semi-structured interviews in five Balkan countries) and focus group data (three focus groups in Bosnia and Herzegovina, Kosovo, and Serbia) with participants in the RECOM process. The interviewees

TABLE 6.1 Discursive solidarity and identity politics

IDENTITY POLITICS	DISCURSIVE IDENTITY PRACTICES	EFFECTS ON IDENTITY POLITICS
Ethnic group opinion uniformity	Identity disjunctures	In-group and out-group differentiation
Ethnocentric hierarchy of harm	Affective alignment	Interethnic empathy
Negative reciprocity	Blame aversion	Commonness across ethnic divide

were selected based on a purposive sampling strategy to represent a variety of participants in the RECOM consultations and their views: the leadership, organizers, and participants (including victims, human rights activists, youth representatives, prosecutors, veterans, observers, and others). By contrast, focus groups only involved participants to gain a perspective independent of the leadership and organizers of the RECOM process. Informal interviews with focus group participants before and after discussions provided additional insights. Participant observation of four RECOM regional meetings (two in Bosnia and Herzegovina, one in Serbia, and one in Croatia from 2013 to 2019) provided an opportunity for observation of interactions across ethnic lines, and informal engagement with dozens of participants and observers of the RECOM process. In addition, a day-long discussion-focused workshop in Kosovo in 2018 with civil society representatives beyond the RECOM process was used as an out-of-sample data source about interethnic interactions and reconciliation to verify the findings. I coded the corpus of interview and focus group data qualitatively, using an iterative approach. My analysis was informed by the argument that "at heart of discourse ethics [is] an openness to others who are different or of different minds," a condition that is difficult to achieve in interethnic communication in divided societies.[27] The themes grounded in theory were complemented with the themes that emerged through iteration from the interview and focus group data, reflecting participants' experience of the RECOM process. To ensure the validity of the findings, I checked these themes against the evidence from the transcripts of the RECOM consultations, which represent the record of the actual process. I relied on data triangulation, which refers to the use of different data sources in a single study to inform theoretical claims, while being mindful of establishing whether and how the identified themes converge with the use of discourse to "build and sustain (or change or destroy) social relationships."[28] The analysis was guided by the need to understand how ethnic identities matter during deliberation about the legacy of past violence. Ultimately, the aim was to identify mechanisms in discourse that allow participants to counteract divisive identity politics and forge solidary bonds during face-to-face exchange with the ethnic Other.

Identity Disjunctures

The salience of ethnic identity, which refers to the degree to which individuals view their ethnicity as important, is heightened when encountering an ethnic Other.[29] The salience of ethnic identity is enhanced by conflict.[30] It is further heightened by nationalist discourses peddled by postconflict governments where actual interethnic contact is rare.[31] In such contexts, interactions across ethnic lines can also "engender enhanced prejudice" toward the ethnic Other rather than

reduce it.[32] The salience of ethnically exclusive identification manifests in political and social pressure for opinion homogeneity within an ethnic group about
ethnically salient issues related to conflict, such as culpability and victimhood.

Identity disjuncture refers to a rupture in the expected enactment of dominant ethnic identities in discourse and opinions informed by it. People navigate
face-to-face communication with people from other ethnic groups by choosing
how to enact their identity. As a result, they may resist explicit or implicit pressure within their own identity group to assert their identity in the prescribed way,
which indicates the political nature of identification.[33] Opinion uniformity within
one's own ethnic group is often justified with reference to perceived homogeneity
in an adversary ethnic group. However, enacting ethnic identities on a spectrum
from civic to exclusive-ethnic disrupts that perception; it becomes clear that an
adversary ethnic group has a range of opinions on war crimes. Demonstration
of differences within ethnic groups as a form of resistance to the imposition of
"a unity of views" creates space for solidary interactions across ethnic lines.[34]

In the RECOM consultations, diversity of participants from different ethnic
groups and with different opinions about how to achieve justice for war crimes
facilitated the discursive practice of identity disjunctures. Participants asserted
their civic identity, publicly resisting pressure to endorse ethnic self-identification,
side-by-side with those who presented themselves primarily in terms of their ethnic group membership. Some human rights activists were explicit about expressing a sense of identity that is not ascriptive, as illustrated by one participant:
"When I speak I do not represent Serbia. I have not come here as a representative
of my country. I am a human rights activist. Therefore, I also represent people
coming from other countries who are activists themselves or victims of human
rights violations."[35] Another one said: "I'm not representing Croatia. I just happen to be from Croatia."[36] These and other participants enacted their identities in
stark contrast to those expressing an exclusive sense of ethnic identity informed
by nationalist discourse. Leaders of some human rights NGOs from all the Balkan countries participating in the RECOM process were widely recognized by
others involved in the process as being particularly "skillful" in expressing this
exclusive sense of ethnic identity.[37]

The leaders of many human rights NGOs, specifically victims' associations,
had either been socialized to adopt this nationalist stance or were pressured
indirectly by their respective national states.[38] The participants in the RECOM
consultations understood that these hard-line NGO leaders lacked an "independent, autonomous approach" to postconflict justice and were seen as "acting out nationalist lesson given to them at home."[39] Participants in the RECOM
process were critical of these NGO leaders' enactment of exclusive ethnic identity, reflected in their nationalist positions vis-à-vis postconflict justice. One

interviewee wondered: "Are these political parties or human rights NGOs? How can we put this ethnicity thing in front of human rights NGOs?"[40] Ideological positions featured in the discourse of these "NGO professionals" seemed "irreconcilable" with their proclaimed human rights mission, reflecting the reality of identity politics in a civil society-led transitional justice process.[41]

In contrast to these nationalist views, expressions of dissent from ethnic "groupthink" by deliberators from adversary ethnic groups had a profound impact on all present.[42] One participant in the RECOM process remarked: "It was for the first time in my life that I heard someone from the Serb side, who is not supporting their side. I am not saying that they were against their own side, but simply the woman spoke on the basis of arguments, against what is her ethnicity."[43] People witnessed the differentiation of individual positions within each ethnic group represented in the RECOM consultations. One participant observed that "those who came from Kosovo did not hold the same view, neither were all Serbs the same."[44] Bearing witness to disagreement within adversary ethnic groups driven by civic versus ethnic enactments of identity dispelled the erroneous assumption of opinion homogeneity within an adversary ethnic group.[45]

An interviewee from Kosovo recalled a tense exchange between Croatian victims and another Croatian participant.[46] Before joining the RECOM process, people expected disagreements to occur only across ethnic lines. Hearing fellow deliberators express views that dissented from those of others within their own ethnic group prompted others to be more open to express their individual views, even when they differed from those dominant in their ethnic communities.[47] This led participants to accept fellow deliberators from adversary ethnic groups as "someone with whom one can have a polite discussion."[48]

In the context of deliberation across ethnic lines, such identity disjunctures were a powerful demonstration of opinion diversity, itself a reflection of the variability of self-identification. They exposed participants in the RECOM process to a range of views about justice for war crimes. Diversity of opinions within ethnic groups also affected interethnic deliberation in ways that scholars of deliberation in divided societies have not recognized. In the context of deep identity divisions, these identity disjunctures engendered trust in interlocutors from other ethnic groups.[49]

Enacting ethnic identity without alienating or antagonizing fellow participants required delicate negotiation. One Kosovo Albanian stated, "of course, that the war that I was able to speak about happened in Kosovo," indicating how much her immediate experience of conflict shaped her views. However, this interviewee also emphasized her autonomy to express her own identity rather than an identity "delegated" to her by state authorities.[50] Directly opposed, even antagonistic, enactments of identity were evident, especially between victims and NGO leaders. In these cases, victims demonstrated greater openness toward the ethnic Other than NGO leaders from their own ethnic group. This dynamic was a result of the "elitization of NGOs."[51] It reflected the paradox that some civil society organizations claiming to represent the victims and their families were the "farthest away from these affected communities."[52] The diversity of participants in the civil society-led process ensured that all voices were heard and allowed in-group and out-group differentiation to be displayed.

Criticism of nationalist NGOs from within the RECOM process echoed scholarship on the adverse impact of civil society on postconflict peacebuilding.[53] The loss of legitimacy of professionalized NGOs with their stakeholders and within societies has roots in their transformation into executioners of projects attuned primarily to foreign donors' interests and normative agendas.[54] However, the ideologies of local human rights NGOs who purvey nationalist views sanctioned by nationalist authorities, and these NGOs' role as civil society actors fueling identity politics and obstructing reconciliation, have been neglected by scholars of deliberation in divided societies and by scholars of peacebuilding and transitional justice more generally.

RECOM transitional justice consultations provided a public space for many stakeholders. Such diversity—in terms of both ascriptive identities corresponding to dynamics of the regional conflict and of opinions within groups—allowed for demonstration of identity disjunctures as people departed to various degrees from officially sanctioned, exclusive identities and from opinions based on them. Identity disjunctures transformed people's perceptions of adversary groups and the belief that all members of adversary ethnic groups harbor uniform views on postconflict justice.[55] Dispelling the belief that "everyone coming from the other sides thinks [about issues] contrary [to us]" allowed for the repair of relations across ethnic lines.[56]

Affective Alignment

Identity politics in postconflict societies thrives on ethnically defined hierarchies of harm, which are premised on the notion that some harms, commonly those suffered by one's own ethnic group, are more worthy of recognition than others.[57] An interviewee remarked that victimhood had become "a new identity" in the politicized societies of the Balkans.[58] Denying the recognition of suffering to victims from adversary ethnic groups is a pernicious aspect of identity politics in postconflict societies. This "ethnocentrism of death" denigrates the victims, robbing them of dignity in their pain.[59] Denial and impunity intensify the sense of injustice and increase the salience of ethnic identity. Consequently, discussing wartime harm in transitional justice consultations can contravene the ethical requirement of recognition and distort interethnic communication.

To counter the dimension of identity politics associated with the hierarchy of harm, alignment with people's suffering across ethnic lines must overcome the divisive impact of denigrating the ethnic Other. Empathy encompasses a cognitive element that entails taking the perspective of another and an emotional element that relates to the immediate experience of another person's emotions.[60] From the vantage point of the theory of democratic deliberation, the broad definition of empathy as "the capacity and willingness to put oneself in the shoes of others and to consider a situation from their perspective" captures the essence of deliberativeness.[61] The emotional dimension, which is prominent in interethnic contact, is underplayed in theorizing deliberation because it often contradicts the notion of deliberation as a rational exchange of views.[62] Michael Neblo has challenged this view, outlining some roles that emotions have in deliberation.[63] For example, emotions have an important role to play in "struggles for recognition," as defined by Habermas. In so far as these struggles occur *"within* discourse," emotions can signal that the claim of the aggrieved is recognized as morally relevant.[64] This highlights the important role of emotions in deliberation involving people affected by conflict and connects with the study of transitional justice and reconciliation, where the analysis of emotions is pivotal. Expressing empathy for people's suffering helps restore the dignity of the injured and opens up the possibility of repair of interethnic relations.[65] From the perspective of discourse ethics, the question is whether people's moral commitment can extend beyond the boundary of their own ethnic group and whether empathy for the suffering of ethnic Others can be expressed publicly in an interethnic context.

Awareness that members of the in-group are responsible for the suffering and pain of members of an out-group makes expressing empathy for out-groups particularly challenging, especially in a transitional justice process focused on justice for wartime harm.[66] According to one of the organizers, during the RECOM consultations, "people opened up in a peculiar and unpredictable ways, so that we could never predict how [the discussion] would unfold and what it would lead to."[67] This is why the study of discourse within the RECOM process allows us to understand how participants came to "see the 'other' as part of one's shared moral universe."[68] Specifically, it allows us to trace how the hierarchy of pain was dismantled through affective alignment.

In postconflict contexts overshadowed by identity politics, aligning with the suffering of ethnic Others involves a trade-off in people's minds. People involved in the RECOM process feared that regarding all victims of war crimes as equal regardless of their ethnicity would result in relativization or minimization of their own group's suffering.[69] Hence, the value of the RECOM consultations was that "people realized that suffering is universal, although the situations and the contexts in which their closest family members were killed or forcefully disappeared were different."[70] As with identity disjunctures, the diversity of people involved in the RECOM process, which also included victims, was consequential for the discursive manifestation of affective alignment. People perceived the RECOM gatherings as "a real civil society" in action, distinct from other civil society initiatives confined to a narrow circle of NGO professionals.[71]

Participants stressed the importance of a face-to-face encounter "of all those different people, those who were on one side, and those on the other," and its impact on all sides.[72] One interviewee explained that "mutual empathy was born out of an opportunity to talk across ethnic lines. If you never had an opportunity to share your experience with the Other, then you think that you and only you have been a victim."[73] The directness and authenticity of unmediated communication came into full view. The RECOM consultations gave people an "opportunity to meet and learn about the Other and their suffering, but not in a sense of rehashing [official] narratives; quite the contrary, you could see a person and hear them breathe."[74] The face-to-face encounter with the ethnic Other facilitated mutual recognition of suffering. When people heard the other side, even those who had previously not been receptive to others' suffering moderated their views so as not to "exaggerate at the expense of the other side."[75] The sincerity felt in face-to-face communication with an ethnic Other allowed people to "overcome narrow [ethnic] identities and view each other as human beings."[76] It also alleviated concerns that recognizing all victims of crimes would minimize the suffering of one's own group.

Public alignment with the suffering of other people had a profound impact on participants. For example, a Bosniak survivor of the genocide in Srebrenica where some 8,000 Bosniak men and boys were killed by Bosnian Serbs in 1995, said:

> I lost all male family members of my family, I was expelled. I have returned and now mostly live in Srebrenica. I still haven't found many male members of my family. So, allow me to—in advance—express my deep condolences and empathy for all those who have been expelled, who cannot return to their homes, all those who lost their closest family members, and still have not found their bodily remains, and all those who survived other forms of torture, and have not received satisfaction, either from the state, or through empathy by those who are most responsible for their suffering.[77]

Empathetic alignment was accompanied by perspective-taking, signaling the transition from an ethnocentric to universal moral commitment. People put themselves in each other's shoes. Impressed upon participants in the RECOM process was people's ability to transcend ethnocentric morality; what was observed was succinctly summarized by one participant as "empathy across borders."[78]

The shift from an ethnically bounded to the universal understanding of the ethnic Other was a gradual process, not an instantaneous switch. When first encountering the ethnic Other, participants "did not see everyone as belonging to one whole, i.e. a damaged whole, fighting for their rights." As a consultative session unfolded, ethnocentric positions gave way to recognition of the Other: "people empathized with those across the table, realizing that they suffered in similar ways. They began to feel that those people [from other ethnic groups] were closer to them than some people from their own ethnic group."[79] Notions of class also helped people affiliate with the ethnic Other, as one participant explained: "they could see before them a woman of the same social status as them, [and] could therefore not deny what was being said. This created an atmosphere of solidarity."[80] Apart from bestowing dignity to victims hitherto denied recognition for their suffering, the very act of empathizing with ethnic Others also impacted participants in the RECOM process. As one of them put it: "I am happy that I have shown empathy towards that person . . ., so that he can feel that I have listened to him actively and given him human support to overcome that pain in some way."[81]

Empathic alignment countered denigration of the victimhood of the Other, which characterized identity politics and nationalist discourses in the societies from which participants came.[82] Empathic alignment was made possible by sharing new information during the RECOM transitional justice consultations, as a result of which participants learned about what had happened in other countries and to victims on the other side.[83] Illustrative here is one Bosnian Croat participant's observation that they had an opportunity to hear a Bosniak and a Serb victim of Bosnia's conflict for the first time.[84] People gained a radically different perspective on past conflicts from those enshrined in ethnically biased nationalist narratives promoted by state-controlled media and education systems in the post-Yugoslav states.[85] A young woman from Montenegro reflected on the ethnocentric history taught at school, adding: "I did not know anything about what happened to the other side."[86]

Solidarity based on affective alignment with the suffering of the ethnic Other during the war was reinforced by recognition that all victims, regardless of their ethnic group, continued to suffer injustice after the war. This recognition was demonstrated by a woman addressing fellow participants during a RECOM consultation: "Don't you think my fellow co-sufferers, all of you present here, that the executioners of those criminal acts have already been pardoned by the fact that so many years have gone by and we still don't know the fate of our loved ones? Meanwhile, they walk the streets freely, they live with their families, like normal human beings; and we live with our sorrow, our desperation, and with uncertainty that marks our days."[87] Gathered in the RECOM consultations, an embodiment of a restorative approach to transitional justice, participants shared disappointment that war crimes proceedings at the ICTY and domestic war crimes trials had not adequately addressed the legacy of conflict.

As the excerpts from the transcripts of the RECOM consultations show, intragroup politics, dynamics, and discourses were critical to facilitating affective alignment across ethnic lines. Victims on all sides came to share the realization that their suffering had become political capital in the hands of their own nationalist elites. Verbal support of victims boosted the elites' nationalist credentials but was not followed with policies to deliver justice to victims or improve their economic and social welfare. One participant articulated the feeling on behalf of all: "We, the victims, are humiliated, on top of all that suffering and pain."[88]

In addition, a hierarchy of intragroup rather than intergroup harm engendered a deep sense of marginalization of victims within their ethnic groups. Many victims felt ignored because of selective public recognition of victims of certain crimes that had become symbols of an ethnic group's wartime suffering.[89] The RECOM process provided space for the recognition of suffering of all victims regardless of where their suffering was located in the hierarchy of harm within their own ethnic communities. Marginalization of victims by their coethnics was another important axis for affective alignment with victims from other ethnic groups, who were also recognized as being denigrated in their own communities. As one participant put it: "It is crucial that I can see here that there is no principle of ethnic belonging. There are two categories: one is a category of a perpetrator, and the other of equality of all victims who need to be helped."[90]

Participants' appreciation of a common need for justice was critical to bringing "the discussion to the civilized form without denying the victims of the other side." An affective perspective on deliberation across ethnic lines sheds light on the emergence of solidarity transcending ethnicity through recognition of suffering regardless of "a speaker's ethnic prefix."[91] As with identity disjunctures, affective alignment emerged through a complex interplay of interethnic and intraethnic identity dynamics. In postconflict contexts, both the wartime harm caused by mutual victimization of groups and harm caused by a lack of recognition of suffering within one's own identity group allowed deliberators to take the perspective of the Other and affiliate affectively with them.

Blame Aversion

In contrast to affective alignment, which centers on recognition of suffering, blame aversion concerns how participants in transitional justice consultations address the question of culpability for war crimes. Identity politics in post-conflict contexts is steeped in negative reciprocity. Unlike positive reciprocity, which is based on shared morality, negative reciprocity is "rooted in a break, transformation or suspension of the moral order."[92] It is manifested in negative mutuality, where the blame for the commission of war crimes is always directed against the ethnic Other. Negative reciprocity produces "predatory outcomes of social relations," such as ethnic divisions that hinder reconciliation.[93] Kieran McEvoy and Kirsten McConnachie contend that "locating blame in the 'other' also absolves 'us' of any semblance of guilt or responsibility."[94] Mutual recrimination within multiethnic societies and across borders maps onto geographies of conflict, distorts communication, and counters the ethics of discursive solidarity. How participants in interethnic discussions apportion blame for war crimes is reflected in discursive enactment of their ethnic identities, defined by a collective experience of conflict, in terms of both suffering endured and suffering caused.

The dominant feature of discussions about war crimes in the RECOM process was blame aversion. People focused on details of suffering without naming perpetrators, individually or collectively. As a result, people perceived the mode of communication within the RECOM process as nonaccusatory. A quote from one of the RECOM consultations illustrates how apportioning blame is avoided without calling into question the severity of the crime committed. Referring to children who were killed during the siege of Sarajevo in Bosnia and Herzegovina, a participant said:

> Children were killed by snipers. Children were mainly killed when there was a lull in the fighting; since there was fighting in Sarajevo almost every day, and the children were mainly in cellars and shelters, when the fighting stopped for a little while, the parents would let the children out of the cellars and shelters, to have a bit of a respite and to play; it was in those situations that 90 percent of the children were killed, on sleds, playing ball games, in their classrooms, in their bedrooms, at their desks, and so forth.[95]

Similarly, when articulating arguments to support specific articles of the Draft Statute, the speakers referred to their grievances and suffering but avoided pointing the finger at the other side. The ethnic identities of perpetrators were often not mentioned. A speaker from a Bosnian Muslim community said about the missing victims of Bosnia's war: "Today in Bosnia and Herzegovina our human rights are being violated by hiding mass graves, and the mandate of this commission should be to find out as soon as we can where those mass graves are."[96] On another occasion, a Kosovo Serb put forth his proposition:

> My father and seven others were deprived of their lives. They were brutally killed, burnt, and so on. This could not have been done by one person. He was not alone, there must have been a few of them. It would be invaluable if all of us could say that someone who is prepared to help to shed light on those events, that they as an individual can either be amnestied or be given mitigating circumstances, and that this should be one of RECOM's recommendations.[97]

A Serbian mother who had lost her son in the Kosovo conflict contributed to the discussion about the definition of a category of "victim" in the RECOM mandate. She argued that it should encompass army recruits: "There are several categories of military casualties. There are recruits who were conscripted, who had to join the army to respect the law of the country where they live. If they didn't, they would have gone to prison. My son and so many others were killed on the border [between Kosovo and Albania] as army recruits." She resisted replicating the pattern of always blaming the ethnic Other—a typical position in the public discourse in postconflict societies where discussion of past harm is animated by identity politics. As she elaborated her argument, she refrained from naming the ethnic adversary. Rather, she pointed at her compatriots in Serbia. "My son was killed along with three, four other soldiers, nineteen and twenty year-olds. He indeed was killed 150 meters away from the Albanian border while on patrol, but someone sent him there. I know that his death sentence was signed in Belgrade. They, over there, were only executioners."[98]

This discursive practice of blame aversion contributed to what one organizer called an "atmosphere of solidarity," in which people could speak out about their suffering and see their suffering being acknowledged.[99] Even when civil society provides a safe deliberative space, encountering members of adversary ethnic groups can still be daunting. Scholars of contact theory have shown that the prospect of meeting members of the out-group induces anxiety, especially where there is a history of intergroup conflict.[100] Similarly, people were apprehensive about participation in the RECOM process. A Kosovo Albanian remarked how the communication with Serbs (who were at war with Albanians in Kosovo) "was not as judgmental as I was expecting it to be; it was my first time in Belgrade [the capital of Serbia]." As a result, this participant gained confidence in the space provided by the RECOM consultations where one could "speak about the war as an Albanian."[101]

People involved in the RECOM consultations spoke about wartime violence while avoiding apportioning blame. The consultations increased awareness of the injury patterns and provided another avenue for forging a sense of commonness and understanding across ethnic lines. "They did not distinguish perpetrators by their ethnicity; the crime that was committed against them was used as a prism through which they were able to understand a woman sitting next to them, even though she came from a different ethnic group and suffered at someone else's hands," as one participant put it.[102] Negative reciprocity, which thrives in conditions of ethnic diversity and ethnic divisions, is a feature of identity politics marked by accusations and counter-accusations.[103] Avoiding mutual recrimination in the RECOM transitional justice consultations allowed people to overcome the "barricades" of state-sponsored nationalist narratives.[104]

Blame aversion involves demonstrating restraint in a polarizing enactment of ethnic identity. It entails raising the issue of responsibility for war crimes in a manner that does not alienate or antagonize communication partners. It should not be equated with impunity or forgiveness. The pattern of abuse in the Balkan conflicts involved "intimate enemies," as poignantly illustrated by common cases of abuse and violence meted out by former neighbors, teachers, or childhood friends.[105] Participants in the RECOM consultations had a tacit but unmistakable understanding of the perpetrators' ethnicity. Restraint from naming and blaming perpetrators explicitly as members of ethnic groups, which also included making a clear distinction between perpetrators and entire ethnic groups, was a discursive practice that helped people navigate a complex moral terrain of culpability and victimhood and steer interethnic communication away from the quagmire of divisive identity politics. This was poignantly illustrated at one of the regional RECOM meetings by an elderly father's account of the treatment he and his son, who were Croats, endured in a Serb-run detention camp in Serbia (in which they were transferred from neighboring Croatia). He drew a clear distinction between a Serb colonel, who treated them professionally and humanely, and Serb torturers, who abused detainees when the colonel was away.[106]

According to participants in the RECOM process, "intoning one's narrative in such a way so as not to accuse anyone" profoundly affected the kind of communication that took place. Because people did not make accusations against different ethnic groups, interlocutors did not feel "a need to respond in kind" and were able to focus on "arguments to address issues."[107] Blame aversion enabled positive mutuality with the ethnic Other. Such practices transformed the binary understanding of war crimes perpetration and victimhood on which postconflict identity politics thrives. People learned "of how complicated the situation was and about everything that took place."[108] Blame aversion had another unforeseen effect: people involved in the RECOM process began to reflect on the culpability of members of their own ethnic groups for war crimes. This was a radical departure from the typical blame game of identity politics, where people focus solely on the crimes committed against their own group. One Kosovo Albanian participant remarked bluntly: "it was a knock on our conscience."[109] The sentiment was shared across ethnic lines, as noted by a Serb participant in the process: "There is no doubt that war crimes are a part of our history and group identity, and we rely on each other to address them together."[110] Another one openly articulated that what was paramount was the truth that would emerge from establishing facts about past war crimes: "Whether it [the truth] is painful or not painful for the Serbian nation to which I belong, is not important. What is important is the truth, which is the whole truth."[111]

Although many participants did avoid making direct accusations against ethnic Others, engagement across ethnic lines was not entirely collaborative. Participants in the RECOM process felt pressured to compete rhetorically and make a persuasive argument about the suffering of their ethnic group to gain recognition for past wrongs from the ethnic Other.[112] They were keen to express themselves as articulately and competently as speakers from other ethnic groups.[113] Scholars note that competitive victimhood, which is a belief that one's own ethnic group has suffered more than the adversary group, is an obstacle to reconciliation because it leads to apportioning blame.[114] The insights from participants in the RECOM process point to the competitive nature of presenting one's suffering in a multiethnic transitional justice process. The toxic effect of competitive victimhood on interethnic interaction was avoided since participants addressed the commission of war crimes without apportioning blame and without minimizing the suffering of others.

Avoiding incrimination was a discursive practice whereby speakers enacted a sense of ethnic identity underpinned by wartime injury in a way that avoided the distortion of discourse and negative reciprocity typical of identity politics. One observer summed it up: "People paid special attention not to insult people on the other side, when they made arguments and how they said things, so as not to cause conflict with the [ethnic] Other."[115] How participants in this process expressed their injury allowed "the expansion of the space of common denominators through the process of consultations."[116] Its most prominent manifestation was the recognition of commonness despite ethnic divisions. Recognition of commonness, in terms of both crimes suffered and implication of members of one's ethnic group in the suffering of others embodied solidarity that transcended ethnicity.

Solidary Bonds in Interethnic Interactions

The ethical perspective adopted in this chapter reveals how people express their ethnic identities in deliberation about the legacy of war crimes. The chapter traced the emergence of solidary bonds that overcame the divisiveness of identity politics in situ during a deliberative exchange across ethnic lines. This analysis focused on distinct discursive identity practices—identity disjunctures, affective alignment, and blame aversion—that counter the desolidarizing effects of identity politics. Discursive solidarity emerges from revealed in-group and out-group differences, which dispel (mis)perceptions of opinion homogeneity within ethnic groups; from affective alignment, which leads to the acknowledgment of the suffering of ethnic Others by expression of empathy; and from blame aversion, which involves restraint in recrimination in interethnic engagement and prevents negative reciprocity in interethnic communication.

Discursive solidarity captures the effects of discursive identity practices observable in discourse and points to the complexity of people's expression of ethnic identity in an encounter with an ethnic adversary. As Jeffery Pittam remarks, enacting identities in social interaction can be "illogical and inconsistent," with equally unexpected outcomes.[117] There is no linear shift from an ethnic to civic identity, which deliberative democrats expect will result from good-quality deliberation and lead to the reconstruction of divided societies. Rather, two related dynamics underlie the emergence of solidary bonds at the microlevel of interethnic interactions in a transitional justice process. At an intragroup level, there is ongoing distinguishing, resisting, and negotiating individual versus collective ethnic identities. At an intergroup level, people calibrate the expression of ethnic identity, the salience of which is heightened by wartime injury and enduring impunity for war crimes. This calibration is done in a way that does not necessarily accentuate opposition to the ethnic Other. Kristin Davies et al. observe that cross-group interactions "can be complicated, psychologically demanding and fraught with potential for miscommunication and misunderstanding" and, above all, for distortion of communication.[118]

In-group identity distinctions between "doves" and "hawks" shape interethnic contact outcomes but have not received due scholarly attention.[119] This chapter shows that interethnic deliberation is also influenced by the diversity of identity enactments within an ethnic group, which map onto a range of exclusively ethnic to civic conceptions of identity. However, even when people hold on to their distinct sense of ethnic identity, underwritten by wartime harm, the way it is enacted is not inevitably either offensive or oppositional to the ethnic Other. Such diversity creates a moral space for discursive solidarity that crosses ethnic lines in relation to both wartime harm and postwar injustice. Above all, the detrimental effects of identity politics on interethnic communication are avoided when people express their sense of wartime injury, as both individuals and members of an ethnic group, without denigrating, diminishing, or disrespecting ethnic Others and their suffering.

These identity dynamics evaluated from the ethical perspective are facilitated by deliberation in the domain of civil society. When removed from ethnicized states, civil society is open to identity and opinion diversity, although, as this research has shown, it is not devoid of identity politics. Because diversity brings with it identity politics, we can investigate how the way people express their identities enables deliberators from opposed ethnic groups to transcend their divisions. The result is "a deeper level of solidarity," where solidarity is not "restricted to the substantive level of like interests and worldviews," which is the kind of solidarity that indicates good-quality deliberation.[120] Rather, people and their wartime suffering are recognized despite being ethnically different, as they forge solidary bonds across ethnic lines. This dimension of discourse ethics points to the possibility of moral restoration of the ethnic Other during a postconflict transitional justice process alongside good-quality deliberation in discussions about war crimes. It results in reconciliation embedded in mutuality in public communication.

Conclusion

RECONCILIATION AND DELIBERATIVE INTERETHNIC CONTACT

It has not been easy to participate in this process, but it has been honorable.

—A participant in the RECOM consultation in Slovenia, September 10, 2010

This book concludes by addressing the paradox of reconciliation. Although its connotation of life without violence is indisputable, reconciliation as an academic concept and a policy goal has been mired in growing skepticism.[1] This skepticism, even outright rejection of reconciliation, also comes from communities worldwide that have been brutalized by violence. These are the same communities that need solace, dignity, and peace that reconciliation is meant to confer. For some, reconciliation has become a "dirty word."[2] The provenance of the skepticism toward reconciliation as a scholarly concept and global policy practice is multifaceted. Difficulties plaguing the academic study of reconciliation are largely intertwined with challenges involved in practical efforts to promote reconciliation in postconflict societies.

At the scholarly level, there is a lack of consensus on the definition of reconciliation. The concept of reconciliation appears elastic and prone to misinterpretation. On the one hand, using "reconciliation" as a catch-all term has produced slippery evidence for the prospects for the repair of relations torn by war. On the other hand, reducing reconciliation to its particular aspects has provoked criticism that the term is often conflated with mere tolerance of adversaries, which does not amount to genuine repair of intergroup relations. At the policy level, despite vast amounts of funding funneled by international donors to reconciliation activities, there is no accepted methodology for evaluating the effectiveness of these various initiatives. Practitioners face the same challenge as scholars. Difficulties in evaluating reconciliation activities are bound up with the unresolved question of what exactly is meant when activities are funded under the heading of reconciliation.[3] Perspectives from war-affected communities also point to a lack of conceptual clarity. The injured refuse to join reconciliation initiatives because they equate reconciliation with blanket forgiveness of perpetrators or moral relativism and the belittling of their suffering. Alternatively, they dismiss reconciliation because to them it entails brushing aside rather than addressing past harms and, therefore, is no more than an unjust imposition. This has led to a damning appraisal of the politicized discourse of reconciliation as "profoundly immoral."[4]

Local communities see the efforts of external peacebuilders as exacting a high moral price. However, external state-builders have also struggled to translate this emancipatory idea into a legitimate program of action precisely because the concepts of reconciliation they employ are too unwieldy and policy instruments too rigid. Reconciliation thus joins an array of other concepts, such as democracy or local ownership, that form the backbone of liberal peacebuilding in postconflict societies, which has been criticized as insensitive to the specificities of local communities.[5] Moreover, external actors and their policies in postconflict contexts are not alone in eroding confidence in reconciliation, conceived as a form of therapeutic peacebuilding.[6] Reconciliation is also devalued systematically in postconflict societies. Local actors use reconciliation instrumentally, further alienating the injured. Nationalist politicians have learned to use reconciliation rhetoric to gain favorable appraisal by the international community without a genuine commitment to the most demanding of moral projects facing societies divided by conflict. At the same time, political elites commonly exclude or ignore ordinary people's understandings of reconciliation and what it entails for them, which, in turn, breeds popular resentment toward the concept and practice.[7] This is why it is increasingly common to qualify reconciliation efforts in various contexts as "elusive."[8] Elusive reconciliation, traced back to the inability of transitional justice to deliver on its normative goals, has become evidence of transitional "injustice."[9]

These adverse and unintended effects have become a dominant focus for research in transitional justice, restricting the breath of the theoretical inquiry. The questions of how transitional justice can work and how it can deliver on its foundational promise to promote peace remain poorly understood. Stasis in the field of transitional justice has prompted scholars to identify new spaces of postconflict justice, such as artistic interventions and social media interactions, to continue scrutinizing contextual factors that promote transitional justice and dissect the minutiae of transitional justice practices from within.

This book about reconciliation connects with these theoretical forays and data-driven efforts to advance the study of transitional justice.[10] Our conceptualization of reconciliation must meet the analytical challenges of the political, economic, and social complexities of the transition from war to peace. At the same time, because of these complexities, it is easy to substitute theoretical rigor and operationalization of our conception of reconciliation with loose normative benchmarks and vague moral coordinates. Aware of this pitfall, I anchored the concept of reconciliation in mutuality in a broader context of peacebuilding as mutuality building, drawing on Christian Davenport.[11]

The notion of reconciliation by stealth, advanced in this research, underscores that reconciliation as an emancipatory and intended effect of transitional justice can be easily overlooked. I examined how people talk about war crimes in search of justice, departing from the well-trodden path of studying only what people say when they discuss the legacy of past wrongs. I accepted the premise that differences in ethnically divided societies are "constituted partly through narratives and discourses, and consequently could be reconceived or transformed through sustained institutional dialogue among the various groups."[12] This book's insights into reconciliation through a deliberative engagement about past wrongs rest on three related arguments.

First, we need to take the foundational normative premise of the field as a starting point and focus on how transitional justice interventions can help repair broken relations and promote peace in postconflict communities. It is a lacuna in current transitional justice scholarship that scholars are just beginning to recognize. Joanna Quinn, for example, highlights the need to better understand how transitional justice can resonate among communities and heal divisions in postconflict societies.[13] I show that reconciliation after conflict occurs through deliberative rationality and discursive solidarity in transitional justice consultations. To find that transitional justice can promote reconciliation does not imply that we have to lower the bar normatively and settle for a minimalist understanding of reconciliation as nonlethal coexistence. Conceptualizing reconciliation as mutuality in interethnic communication is normatively demanding because it foregrounds the values of reason, embracing the perspective of the ethnic Other, and showing respect to former adversaries while engaging with the legacy of violence and suffering, the most divisive topic of all in postconflict societies.

Second, the evaluation of reconciliation is a matter of both theory and method. I have seized on previously untapped potential to advance our understanding of transitional justice and peacebuilding by leveraging the theory of democratic deliberation. Scholars of critical peacebuilding have latched onto "an inherent and significant relationship between discourse and reconciliation."[14] For them, the value of deliberation for peacebuilding lies in its mode of communication, which allows the discussion of the legacy of mass atrocity in search of justice involving ethnic adversaries. However, they have skirted the empirical question of whether standards of equality, reason-giving, reciprocity, respect, common good orientation, and perspective-taking that distinguish deliberative discourse from other forms of communication can be met in postconflict contexts. At the same time, empirical scholars of deliberation across deep divides have investigated discussions about issues of mutual interest that can unite opposed ethnic groups, such as education or peace, albeit with the caveat that no issues in divided societies are beyond contention. Whether opposed ethnic groups can discuss deliberatively the underlying causes of division, such as the legacy of mass atrocity, is the ultimate test of the theory of democratic deliberation given its normative benefits to postconflict societies. This empirical study of reconciliation from a deliberative perspective foregrounded deliberative standards while embracing social science research methods that can measure how these deliberative standards are realized in interethnic communication about the legacy of violence.

The analysis of transitional justice consultations has answered key questions that the scholarship on deliberation in divided societies thus far has overlooked. Can deliberation be a part of conflict resolution when people from adversary ethnic groups address war crimes? And will interethnic discussion about past wrongs spiral into mutual recrimination instead of fostering solidarity through the exchange of other-regarding arguments? Conducting mixed-method research, including the quantification of discourse, I have shown that the patterns of public discourse in interethnic interactions align normatively with reconciliation grounded in mutuality.

Third, reconciliation by stealth denotes the idea that reconciliation in some cases has escaped our recognition because we focus on the "obvious," formal transitional justice mechanisms expected to deliver reconciliation, such as war crimes trials and truth commissions, rather than transitional justice consultations. As one of the formal pillars of transitional justice and of global transitional justice policy, transitional justice consultations have been viewed primarily in terms of generating legitimacy for a chosen transitional justice strategy in postconflict societies by bringing in the voices of a range of stakeholders. By focusing on the process of consultation, this book has extended the empirical basis for the evaluation of reconciliation. It has pointed to the benefits of interethnic communication facilitated by transitional justice consultations.

By calibrating theoretical inquiry and methodological strategy, the notion of reconciliation by stealth points to the repair of relationships between former adversaries involved in a regional conflict through transitional justice consultations. Specifically interested in reconciliation through public communication, this research provides strategies for advancing discursive approaches to postconflict recovery. It also has policy implications for practitioners involved in peacebuilding. Before addressing the significance of the present research and its findings for a future research agenda, a discussion of the caveats concerning the scope of this research, and the questions they raise, is in order.

Reconciliation through deliberation about war crimes should be understood as one aspect of a long and complex reconstruction of a postconflict society. As Pablo de Greiff remarked, "it is a mistake to think that there are shortcuts to reconciliation."[15] Scholars have abandoned the binary thinking that marked early theorizing in the field about the appropriateness of some as opposed to other transitional justice mechanisms in different contexts. We now recognize that justice needs in societies recovering from violence can only be addressed by pursuing multiple approaches to transitional justice. Within this logic of complementarity, the question this research raises is how the study of public communication can help us better understand the precise conditions under which transitional justice can work.

From the perspective of democratic deliberation, this research is a study of a deliberative mini-public, understood in Robert Goodin and John Dryzek's terms as "groups small enough to be genuinely deliberative, and representative enough to be genuinely democratic (though rarely will they meet standards of statistical representativeness, and they are never representative in the electoral sense)."[16] A multiethnic, civil society-led deliberative process may differ from deliberation in formal settings such as national or supranational parliaments. Yet both types of deliberative domains, including virtual deliberation, comprise a part of the deliberative system in a postconflict environment. How deliberative processes at a micro- and macrolevel are connected is a question that has puzzled both scholars of transitional justice and scholars of democratic deliberation.[17] It is premature to assert that there are "scalar limits" to the benefits of microlevel interethnic deliberation about war crimes because of their presumed limited impact on macrolevel deliberation in postconflict societies.[18] As Katharina Ploss shows, the benefits of intercommunity dialogue meetings can transfer to a wider community.[19] We need a better understanding of the factors that facilitate this transfer. Further, this book contributes to discussions about the relationship between micro- and macrolevel deliberation by raising the question of the emergence of a regional public sphere after a regional conflict and its effects on peacebuilding. This book has shown how people bring their local, ethnic, and national perspectives into regional-level deliberation. Doing so raises a new question of reverse effects: how people's experiences of regional-level deliberation shape their discursive engagement at a subregional scale in national and local environments as well as in microlevel interactions.

Lastly, this book has explored how people talk rather than just what they say. In this sense, a systematic analysis of the content of people's speeches has been tailored to capture the deliberative nature of people's communicative engagement rather than their substantive views. A lack of focus on the substantial content of speech in the empirical study of deliberativeness of discourse is a standard point of criticism. It could plausibly be argued that a lack of focus on the substance of speech acts in the study of postconflict reconciliation can undermine the argument presented here. In this mixed-method research, the fine-grained qualitative analysis addresses this criticism. Although this research segment corresponds to the principal approach centered on the how (rather than the what) of people's engagement across ethnic lines, a focus on the enactment of ethnic identities can capture by proxy the effects of the substantive content of discourse. For example, a denial of harm will not be compatible with empathetic alignment with the ethnic Other. Nonetheless, this research does pose a question of how deliberative engagement across ethnic lines in a transitional justice process is associated with other moral dimensions of justice-seeking that center on the substance of what people say when they seek truth, show forgiveness, admit culpability, or express remorse.

These questions call for answers from future research. Still, they can be raised only after presenting empirical evidence that deliberation as a mode of communication is resilient even when people across ethnic lines get together to discuss the legacy of mass violence. This evidence helps us chart out how a deliberative approach to transitional justice and peacebuilding can be advanced.

Deliberative Contact across the Identity Divide

Puzzling over credible exercises of deliberative democracy "across the borders of nationality," James Fishkin has asked whether deliberation "can take root without much trust—and perhaps contribute to the development of trust and mutual respect?"[20] I have observed interethnic reconciliation anchored in mutuality in public communication. Reconciliation in a postconflict context that takes place through deliberation about justice for war crimes involving former adversaries turns on how people use their ethnic identities when engaging across the deep divide. By taking "a closer look at how groups and identities fare within a model" of deliberation, this research has addressed a lacuna that has loomed large both in scholarship on deliberation in divided societies and in the critical study of peacebuilding, of which transitional justice is a part.[21] Having recognized that identity politics in postconflict societies defines adverse conditions for achieving quality deliberation and inclusive peacebuilding, scholars have stopped short of exploring the role that identities play during deliberation and its effects.

As I have shown, a scholarly inquiry has been hamstrung by operationalizing identities as static and fixed in the empirical investigation of deliberation. Another problem arises from the fact that many scholars simply write identity politics out of the very act of deliberation. Overcoming these limitations in the study of deliberation in divided societies lays bare how a particular understanding of the conditions that impede deliberation have closed off productive avenues for theorizing and testing how deliberation can contribute to the reconstruction of postconflict societies. Specifically, a focus on interethnic division has overridden consideration of intraethnic divisions, and the primacy given to human rights talk has led to overlooking identity-based talk in deliberation across deep identity divides.

Deliberation and Intraethnic Division

Conflict can divide communities along ethnic lines. This division, produced and reproduced by identity politics, presents a major impediment to good-quality deliberation. Seyla Benhabib sums up the logic of ethnonationalism: "since every search for identity includes differentiating oneself from what one is not, identity politics is always and necessarily a politics of the creation of difference."[22] Scholars of deliberation in divided societies have overlooked enduring intraethnic divisions by focusing on interethnic ones.[23] Differences within groups persist beyond conflict despite increased group cohesion rooted in pre- and postconflict mobilization of identities. These intragroup divisions do not disappear in face-to-face deliberation with ethnic Others, despite strong pressure within ethnic communities for all to toe the group line. Quite the contrary, interethnic deliberation can bring to the fore the diversity within an adversary ethnic group and prove auspicious for deliberativeness. The revelation of intraethnic divisions, as this research has shown, is key to delivering normative benefits such as interethnic reconciliation.

Deliberative democrats engaged with difference democrats and became preoccupied with the question of inclusion and equality from the vantage point of recognition of difference. However, this engagement remained restricted to consideration of the role of discourse other than reasoned argumentation in deliberation, such as recognizing the role of storytelling in deliberation. An opportunity was missed to advance the study of deliberation in divided societies, particularly by not engaging with difference democrats' criticism of claims that identity politics flattens intragroup differences. Iris Young has challenged the understanding of identity politics "as either the assertion of a group interest without regard for the interests of others, and/or the demand that others in a polity recognize their group identity as such." The consequence of such hardening of the inside-outside distinction, according to her, is that it "both denies the similarities that many group members have with those not considered in the group, and denies the many shadings and differentiations within the group."[24]

Considering intraethnic differences minimizes neither differences between groups nor the salience of ascriptive identities, such as ethnicity. Both figure prominently, especially in postconflict contexts. Difference democrats embrace and theorize ascriptive identities. Rejecting that these ascriptive identities are essentialist, like scholars of deliberation in divided societies, difference democrats caution against equating group interests with group identity. Anne Phillips has argued that ethnicity can "become a short-hand which obscures other areas of difference and erases other aspects of political choice." Overlooking internal differentiation and putting too much emphasis on group difference "threatens to propel the citizens out of [the] realm of unifying ideas, and the prospects for cross-group cooperation then become more bleak."[25] This is an important lesson for scholars studying deliberation in deeply divided societies where cross-group cooperation entails the prospects of peace without violence.

This research has begun to illuminate how intragroup divisions pave the way for solidary interactions during interethnic deliberation. Still, how intragroup differentiation shapes deliberation across deep divides remains one of the least understood dimensions of postconflict deliberation. When opening this frontier of research, scholars of deliberation in societies divided by conflict can draw their inspiration from the scholars of conflict processes. On the one hand, intragroup dynamics provide a potent explanation of how conflict breaks out, how it is fought, and why peace is hard to achieve in divided societies. On the other hand, microcomparative perspectives on violence reveal that conflict has a differential impact on people belonging to the same ethnic group, compounded by differences in the experience of conflict along other identity axes, such as gender. As in the field of conflict studies, in the study of deliberation in divided societies there is a need for a better understanding of "the mutable character of group boundaries and the need for theory that moves beyond assumptions of fixed cleavages."[26]

A useful starting point is the premise elaborated by John Dryzek in his pioneering theorization of the path to deliberation in divided societies. He contends that cultures, identities, and civilizations are not "seamless wholes," and that internal contestation offers the possibility for "dialogue across boundaries."[27] Hence, the analytical straight-jacket imposed by foregrounding the interethnic division in the study of deliberation in divided societies can be overcome by recognizing the multiplicity of identities each person holds, various positions concerning one's ethnicity (from an inclusive-civic to exclusive-ethnic), and how they intersect with other identities a person holds to enable deliberative engagement across ethnic lines.[28] The role of identity expression in enabling the deliberativeness of interethnic discourse in both the process- and outcome-based study of deliberation needs to be taken into account. To the extent that politics is implicated both in the construction and expression of people's identities, the study of deliberation in divided societies needs to acknowledge individual autonomy and the power of deliberators to resist the homogenizing pressure of identity politics in postconflict environments—despite the high cost of social sanction by coethnics. Although ethnic identities are contested within and across groups, their prominence during deliberation raises an unexpected question concerning the value of ethnic identification during deliberation.

Deliberative Value of Identity Talk

The key to meaningful deliberation, as Dryzek argues, is "reframing issues away from identity," which can be achieved by expressing particular needs in terms of more general principles.[29] According to him, an exchange across "alleged civilizational boundaries" can be productive if it "focuses on the particular needs of individuals and groups, as opposed to general principles and markers of identity."[30] Dryzek developed his position on deliberation in divided societies in response to Chantal Mouffe's account of agonistic pluralism and, in particular, her argument that deep differences have to be addressed through passionate and continuous contestation as enemies become deliberative adversaries.[31] Dryzek maintains that "if identities themselves are highlighted, exchange is more likely to freeze identities than to convert them."[32] This perspective forms the lynchpin of arguments about the prospects and benefits of deliberation in divided societies. Discussion of issues in nonethnic terms, which avoids incendiary questions of ethnicity, nationalism, and religion, can foster trust and acceptance between deliberators and further promote broader processes of democratization and reconciliation.[33] Ultimately, deliberation can contribute to the transformation of identities in the direction of the common good, and mitigate their exclusionary and parochializing tendencies that underpin social division.[34]

Under the right conditions, deliberation can soften societal divisions by bringing reason and consideration to bear on decisions concerning specific issues or needs in place of instinctive views determined by ethnic or, more broadly, cultural considerations. It is accompanied by a willingness to open up to the perspectives of ethnic Others. A self-centered logic in decision making is countered by considering how a decision may affect others. As the onus is on deliberation to produce emancipatory outcomes, the notion of identity as difference figures in these accounts to the extent that it is overcome, transcended, or even suppressed. When a deliberative process is conceived in this way, Young sums up, the assertion of difference, such as ethnic identity, "only serves to divide people, produce unworkable conflict, and remove the possibility for a genuinely public discourse in which people look beyond their private interests and experience."[35] It is a guiding assumption in the empirical study of deliberation in divided societies that the assertion of difference is antithetical to deliberation. This assumption is reflected in how people are expected to talk deliberatively about issues that matter to them. Dryzek's illustration of this argument about war crimes in the Balkans is of particular interest in this book: "A harrowing story of (say) rape in a Bosnian village can be told in terms of guilt of one ethnic group and violated innocence of another—fuel for revenge. But the story can also be told in terms of violation of basic principles of humanity that apply to all ethnicities, making reconciliation at least conceivable (though not easy)." According to Dryzek, the focus on specific needs is less likely to end in hostility and may yield outcomes such as reconciliation and, related to it, change of identities, which are constructed by discourses.[36]

This research has shown that a deliberative discussion about war crimes cannot be easily "reframed away from identity and expressed in terms of more general principles," as deliberative democrats expect, to enable a deliberative dialogue in the presence of the ethnic Other.[37] As one interviewee told me with explicit reference to the RECOM transitional justice consultations, only in "rare cases would people speak about their experience of [violence] just on the basis of human nature."[38] People will bring their ethnic identities and ethnically defined experiences of violence into deliberation since discussion remains framed in terms of identities on issues bound up with who they are, such as the legacy of violence in ethnic conflicts. However, bringing ethnic identities into deliberation does not necessarily derail communicative exchange across the identity divide because they are not (always) used as "oppressive identities and discourses" on the opposite end of the progressive political spectrum.[39]

In this book I have shown that deliberation across a deep divide can accommodate the assertion of difference because people bring their identities to bear on discussion with the ethnic Other in an ethically considerate way. For example, they express a sense of harm but refrain from blaming the ethnic Other. They carefully navigate the tension between their particular, ethnically framed perspectives, experiences, and allegiances while maintaining a commitment to deliberative engagement across ethnic lines. These insights echo Katherine Cramer Walsh's findings that difference-focused communication plays a prominent role in inter-racial dialogues in ways that challenge the expectations charted out by theorists of deliberative democracy: the focus on difference does not stifle dialogue, nor is it incompatible with a quest for unity.[40] Her evidence contradicts claims that focusing on overarching identities in intergroup contact is the most productive way of reducing prejudice.[41] Cramer Walsh shows that appeals to difference are not just an integral part of dialogues across the racial divide, but counterintuitively contribute to finding and forging commonality and solidarity even when discussing the divisive issue of race. The evidence I presented in this book also suggests that difference-oriented communication is not incompatible

with good-quality deliberation in postconflict contexts. The expression of ethnicity in microlevel interethnic interactions can promote the repair of interethnic relations among participants involved in these processes. This opens up a new
frontier for research at the intersection of deliberation in divided societies and
transitional justice.[42]

The extant scholarship on deliberation in divided societies has shown that
talking "about issues related but not always reducible to the deep divide may
increase perceptions of the other side's trustworthiness and openness to reason."[43]
But, as Alain Noël warns, identity issues cannot be wished away.[44] Elisabeth King
and Cyrus Samii demonstrate that nonrecognition of ethnicity in constitutions
and peace settlements in ethnically divided postconflict societies does not dimin-
ish the salience of ethnicity in public life.[45] Moreover, Noël warns that "unaddressed issues of identity and recognition create and perpetuate injustice" in
divided societies.[46] Rather than softening the divisions, skirting issues that cut
to the core of the ethnic divide can widen the chasm between communities.
Scholars of deliberation in divided societies have proposed that divided societies need to address contentious issues, echoing arguments presented by scholars
of critical peacebuilding about the role of deliberative approaches in addressing
past wrongs.[47] While the most contentious issues in divided societies are usually
those bound up with identity-based grievances, deliberative approaches need to
consider that expression of difference will figure prominently in interethnic discussion on these subjects. The task will then be to ascertain what kinds of expressions of difference can do deliberative work across different formal and informal
communication domains and how they can help repair relations torn by conflict.

As Diana Mutz observes, "deliberative theory does make implicit empirical
predictions, and empirical research does incorporate implicit normative commitments."[48] The motivation behind this research was a pressing need to better
understand how we can promote postconflict recovery and peace. In this book
focused on a public transitional justice consultation process, I have addressed
whether deliberation can be harnessed to advance reconciliation and peacebuilding in societies torn apart by violence. Along with the emergence of the subfield of deliberation in divided societies, a deliberative perspective is becoming a
prominent part of discussion-based approaches to conflict resolution and peacebuilding. Common to all these approaches is attention to "discussion as means
to reduce conflict."[49] Specifically, scholars have been drawn to the restorative
power of intergroup dialogues to reconstruct postconflict societies, from which
comes the appeal of deliberation to peacebuilding scholars. However, recognizing the value of the dialogic nature of deliberation risks conflating a deliberative
approach to peacebuilding with other communication-based approaches premised on the restorative effects of intercultural encounters.

Deliberation is a distinct approach to overcoming divisions in postconflict societies. As a mode of communication, it requires the demonstration of certain normative features in discourse, such as equality, reason-giving, reciprocity, common good orientation, respect for deliberative partners, and consideration of their views. These features of discourse distinguish a deliberative exchange from other kinds of communication, such as debates or dialogues. Therefore, further theorizing of deliberative postconflict reconstruction and peacebuilding, as a part of communication-based approaches to postconflict recovery, needs to foreground normatively demanding deliberativeness of discourse, which it has hitherto neglected, while continuing to elucidate the conditions under which interethnic discourse can be deliberative. Considering that discussion—including deliberative discussion—that involves parties to a conflict is "a form of intergroup contact," engagement with contact theory constitutes unexplored terrain for future theorizing on ways to deliberate out of conflict.[50]

Gordon Allport's contact theory was used to theorize deliberation in divided societies.[51] Buoyed by compelling evidence that intergroup contact can reduce prejudice, scholars made a case for the emancipatory effect of deliberation in divided societies. Shifting their focus, theoretically and empirically, onto the feasibility of deliberation in divided societies, the effects of deliberation on attitudes of deliberators toward the ethnic Other, and the conditions that can deliver positive effects of deliberation, they have spearheaded the theoretical development of this subfield away from contact theory. As a consequence, existing explanations of deliberation in divided societies have neglected a range of determinants shown by scholars of intergroup contact to either facilitate or undermine positive experiences and effects of intergroup contact, which may also be hypothesized to be associated with good-quality deliberation.[52] Likewise, the scholarship on intergroup contact has neglected communication variables that can potentially mediate intergroup contact.[53] This void is particularly evident in investigations of intergroup contact in conflict and postconflict contexts.[54] Such analysis of the effects of intergroup contact is divorced from consideration of how communication and discourse at different levels of postconflict societies (with family and friends, local, and national) affect the expected, perceived, or actual experience of contact with the ethnic Other.[55] In this vein, how deliberative virtues, which define deliberativeness, are fulfilled in intergroup discussions in postconflict societies, and how they shape the perception of the quality of intergroup contact alongside predispositions to seek out future contact across ethnic lines is of immediate theoretical and practical interest. Bringing contact theory into the fold of theorizing deliberation can open up new horizons for the study of reconciliation and peacebuilding in divided societies. In line with the prominence of ethnic identities in the course of reconciliation through deliberation revealed in this book, future research should recognize the need for further theoretical elucidation and empirical verification of how ethnic identity and deliberation interact.

Engaging with the scholarship on intergroup contact relates to two questions that preoccupy transitional justice and reconciliation scholars. The first question concerns the need to grasp better when the sense of belonging to an ethnic group is compatible with deliberative cooperation with opposed ethnic groups on issues facing societies emerging from conflict. It is informed by Marilynn Brewer's "optimal distinctiveness theory," which proposes social identification at the equilibrium between individuals' contradictory needs for inclusion in a group and differentiation from others. Its wider implications aimed at providing multicultural polities with ways to "reap the benefits of diversity without the costs of intergroup conflict," are particularly relevant for divided postconflict societies.[56] The second question concerns collective versus individual conceptions of identity in a deliberative approach to peacebuilding. Scholarship on postconflict deliberation has focused on divided societies. By framing the problem of identity in collective terms, it assumes all individuals to be divided too. However, communication is "highly dependent on identities of its participants" and, specifically, on the type of identity that assumes prominence in interaction.[57] Distinguishing theoretically and empirically between personal and social (collective) identities, scholars of intergroup contact have studied individuation in interactions across identity lines.[58] It is of particular interest in deliberative approaches to peacebuilding, as this dynamic chips away at the (mis)perceptions of out-group members underpinned by collective identities. How this dynamic is associated with deliberative quality is a crucial question for deliberation when we aim to understand how intergroup interactions can promote reconciliation.

Engagement with contact theory can enhance theorizing on deliberation in divided societies and deliberative peacebuilding with it. By investigating deliberative intergroup contact and the role of identities therein, this new theoretical horizon stands to yield hypotheses the testing of which promises a better understanding of the prospects for transforming relationships in postconflict societies through deliberative engagement with former adversaries. Its practical value lies in identifying ways to counter identity politics, which relies on creating "false antinomies between closed wholes," perpetuates intergroup conflict, and undermines peacebuilding.[59]

An important research agenda lies before us. It can discover evidence and guidance for policies that grapple with one of the most intractable problems of our times: how to assist societies wrecked by conflict in transition from war to peace in a way that respects the dignity of the victims, acknowledges their suffering, and restores relationships across identity divides. That is a profoundly moral question. Its relevance to millions living in postconflict zones around the world whose lives have been blighted by violence is not diminished by the technical language of policy effectiveness. This book about reconciliation in a real-world search for justice in a civil society-led, multiethnic process in the Balkans provides some concrete lessons for how this moral quest can be supported in practice.

Lessons for Policy

The findings presented in this book offer insights that can guide policy approaches of practitioners, political leaders, and activists working to build peace and assist the recovery of postconflict societies.

The first lesson concerns the practical pursuit of and support for reconciliation in postconflict contexts. As I have argued, the policy and practice of reconciliation have become mired in confusion and misinterpretation. At the same time, transitional justice, with its premise that addressing past wrongs is a condition for the healing and reconciliation of postconflict societies, has become a global norm. It is enshrined in strategic documents by international and supranational organizations such as the United Nations and the European Union, espoused by regional actors such as the African Union, and promoted by a host of international, national, and local nonstate actors and activists.[60] However, despite the prioritization of reconciliation in policy documents and pronouncements, the question that hangs over policy commitments concerns its operationalization, which brings us back to the unresolved meaning of reconciliation and its effect both on what activities are supported and how they are understood by those involved. As is the case with the academic study of reconciliation, policies promoting reconciliation would benefit from precision and specificity when setting out the aims and modalities of activities. This is essential to reduce the misinterpretation of moral demands made of the aggrieved and avoid raising expectations that will not be fulfilled. Just as important, precision and specificity are critical for preventing political elites and spoilers from exploiting initiatives meant to address the legacy of past abuse.

The second lesson relates to discussion-based approaches to postconflict recovery. The value of the opportunity to simply meet and talk with people from adversary ethnic groups can easily be underestimated. The dilemma for policymakers and activists is how to engineer these opportunities in postconflict societies that are institutionally and socially segmented along identity lines while being mindful that not every contact between adversaries will be beneficial. Short of reversing policies that formalize and legitimize ethnic separation (which can be externally imposed or home-grown), the creation of civic spaces open to diversity is critical.

This lesson for policymaking pushes against ever more audible dismissal of liberal civil society activism in postconflict zones. Criticism of—as they are portrayed—self-interested foreign-funded NGOs in the local nonstate sphere has led to a dangerous delegitimization of local civil societies tout court. Civic society actors working on human rights in postconflict societies have been singled out, even as critics have overlooked how these NGOs embrace the needs of those most afflicted and marginalized in postconflict societies and facilitate engagement with difficult past.[61] When I put forward an argument for supporting civil society spaces that facilitate interethnic contact, I draw on rigorous scholarly appraisals of the conditions under which NGOs in postconflict contexts enjoy legitimacy among the local population whose needs they work to meet, regardless of whether foreign grants fund them. We must keep in mind that for local civil societies in impoverished postconflict countries, external support is a lifeline for a range of activities that the state is either unable to support or, more likely, rejects for political or ideological reasons. Activities by human rights NGOs that transcend divisive ethnic politics (perpetuated by political elites and nationalist NGOs) and that address the issue of responsibility for war crimes and reconciliation are a case in point, as in the Balkans. This book shows that liberal civil society actors and NGOs provide an otherwise scarce space for interethnic contact and discussions. These inclusive spaces that enable face-to-face communication across ethnic lines are critical to advancing peacebuilding in subtle but substantial ways. These may not be easily quantifiable, especially by policymakers. Nonetheless, as this book shows, civic spaces that allow deliberative interethnic interactions can help bring about a needed shift in perceptions of the ethnic Other and contribute to postconflict recovery.

More broadly, a deliberative perspective is of particular significance within discussion-based approaches to peacebuilding, which have been narrowly focused on reconciliatory interethnic dialogues. This book has demonstrated that major benefits to postconflict societies derive not only from sharing the experiences of harm, as people do in reconciliatory interethnic dialogues, but also from discussing how those experiences should be addressed. Focused on deliberative problem-solving that includes people from adversary identity groups, discussion-based interventions have yet to be embraced as an avenue for reconstructing postconflict societies and advancing postconflict reconciliation. Further, this book that analyzes deliberation about war crimes has shown that even the most sensitive issues are amenable to deliberative scrutiny in postconflict contexts. Although the exact conditions for high deliberative quality within the constraints of societies divided by conflict remain an open question, emerging evidence from the scholarship on deliberation in divided societies points to the untapped potential of deliberation for the betterment of postconflict environments. The experience of deliberation can provide wider benefits to the reconstruction of relations in war-torn societies, alongside legitimate solutions to issues that affect all people regardless of ethnicity.

The third and final policy lesson concerns the need for continued commitment to refining our understanding of the effects of transitional justice practices and sharpening policy tools in support of initiatives that promote justice and reconciliation in societies recovering from gross human rights violations. Understanding how the practice of transitional justice can overcome political, social, and ideological obstacles that subvert its normative aspirations is an enduring challenge for scholars and practitioners. Turning to the consultations with stakeholders—one of the least studied transitional justice mechanisms—and leveraging a new theoretical perspective, this research has shown how consultations promote reconciliation. Scholars and practitioners have not anticipated this impact of a public consultative process because of predetermined expectations and nearly exclusive focus on legitimacy as the benchmark of the effectiveness of this particular transitional justice instrument. This points to the possibility of additional unintended but normatively emancipatory effects of other transitional justice mechanisms, to which researchers and practitioners need to be open. Although more robust assessments of the work of transitional justice mechanisms remain the staple of scholarly efforts, the insights from the analysis of transitional justice consultations in this book indicate that reconciliation can start even before the instruments such as war crimes trials and truth commissions are put in place.

In addition, as a study of regional justice transitional justice consultations, this book points to the value and necessity of a cross-border justice response to a cross-border conflict. Justice initiatives can suffer from gaps if they do not match the nature of conflict and its dynamics. The findings in this book demonstrate how innovating a format of transitional justice consultations by adapting them from the national to the regional level better responds to the regional nature of the conflict they seek to address. This innovation contributes to transforming a region from a space of conflict into a space of reconciliation and peace. While regional transitional justice consultations point to opportunities for a deliberative pursuit of justice in practice, they are only one way of harnessing the regional dimension in pursuing justice and reconciliation in the aftermath of conflicts defined by cross-border violence. A fuller exploration of the possibilities for advancing peace through regional justice interventions is a matter for future policy innovation and research.

In this book, I sought to determine the conditions under which transitional justice can advance reconciliation, and how a discussion of the legacy of war crimes involving former adversaries can lead to the repair of relations. Using real-world data, the analysis presented above showed that focusing on how people talk to each other about war crimes reveals a previously undiscovered form of reconciliation after conflict—reconciliation by stealth. This investigation of deliberative interactions across ethnic lines contributes to empirical foundations for claims that transitional justice promotes quality peace. The new evidence of reconciliation after conflict points to the need for continued theoretical and methodological innovation in studying transitional justice effects—lest the prospects for identifying new ways of overcoming conflict be eclipsed by the growing disillusionment with elusive reconciliation and the goals of transitional justice be dismissed as normatively appealing but practically unattainable.

Appendix

Transcripts of RECOM Consultations about the Draft Statute

1. Regionalne konsultacije sa mladima i organizacijama mladih o Nacrtu statuta REKOM [Regional consultations with the youth and youth organizations about the Draft Statute of RECOM]. Podgorica, Montenegro, May 29, 2010.
2. Nacionalne konsultacije sa udruženjima žrtava o Nacrtu statuta REKOM [National consultations with victims' associations about the Draft Statute of RECOM]. Tuzla, Bosnia and Herzegovina, May 29, 2010.
3. Nacionalne konzultacije s organizacijama civilnog društva o Nacrtu statuta Regionalne komisije za ustanovljenje i javno iznošenje činjenica o ratnim zločinima i drugim teškim povredama ljudskih prava u bivšoj Jugoslaviji (REKOM) [National consultations with civil society organizations about the Draft Statute of the Regional Commission for the Establishment and Public Recording of Facts about War Crimes and Other Serious Violations of Human Rights in Former Yugoslavia (RECOM)]. Zagreb, Croatia, June 1, 2010.
4. Regionalne konsultacije sa nevladinim organizacijama o Nacrtu statuta REKOM [Regional consultations with nongovernmental organizations about the Draft Statute of RECOM]. Banja Luka, Bosnia and Herzegovina, June 5, 2010.

5. Nacionalne konsultacije s udruženjima žrtava i porodica žrtava o Nacrtu statuta REKOM [National consultations with the victims' associations and victims' families about the Draft Statute of RECOM]. Belgrade, Serbia, July 3, 2010.

6. Konzultacije s organizacijama civilnog društva u Osijeku i Osječko-baranjskoj županiji o Nacrtu statuta REKOM [Consultations with civil society organizations in Osijek and the Osijek-Baranja county about the Draft Statute of RECOM]. Osijek, Croatia, July 13, 2010.

7. Konzultacije s organizacijama civilnog društva u Vukovaru i Vukovarsko-srijemskoj županiji o Nacrtu statuta REKOM [Consultations with civil society organizations in Vukovar and Vukovar-Srijem County about the Draft Statute of RECOM]. Vukovar, Croatia, July 14, 2010.

8. Lokalne konzultacije s civilnim društvom o Nacrtu statuta REKOM [Local consultations with civil society about the Draft Statute of RECOM]. Knin, Croatia, September 2, 2010.

9. Regionalne konsultacije s novinarima/kama i urednicima/ama o Nacrtu statuta REKOM [Regional consultations with journalists and editors about the Draft Statute of RECOM]. Ljubljana, Slovenia, September 10, 2010.

10. Nacionalne konsultacije sa bivšim političkim zatvorenicima o Nacrtu statuta REKOM [National consultations with former political prisoners about the Draft Statute of RECOM]. Priština/Prishtinë, Kosovo, September 15, 2010.

11. Regionalne konsultacije sa udruženjima/udrugama žrtava i porodica žrtava o Nacrtu statuta REKOM [Regional consultations with victims' associations and victims' families about the Draft Statute of RECOM]. Sarajevo, Bosnia and Herzegovina, September 18, 2010.

12. Nacionalne konzultacije s lokalnim zajednicama o Nacrtu statuta REKOM [National consultations with the local communities about the Draft Statute of RECOM]. Pakrac, Croatia, October 22, 2010.

13. Regionalne konzultacije s pravosuđem o Nacrtu modela Regionalne komisije za ustanovljenje i javno iznošenje činjenica o ratnim zločinima i drugim teškim povredama ljudskih prava u bivšoj Jugoslaviji (REKOM) [Regional consultations with legal practitioners about the Draft model of the Regional Commission for the Establishment and Public Recording of Facts about War Crimes and Other Serious Violations of Human Rights in Former Yugoslavia (RECOM)]. Zagreb, Croatia, June 11, 2010.

14. Regionalne konsultacije sa pravničkom zajednicom o Nacrtu statuta REKOM [Regional consultations with the community of legal

practitioners about the Draft Statute of RECOM]. Belgrade, Serbia, December 4, 2010.

15. Regionalne konsultacije s višenacionalnim zajednicama o Inicijativi za osnivanje REKOM [Regional consultations with multiethnic communities about the Initiative for the establishment of RECOM]. Mostar, Bosnia and Herzegovina, August 28, 2010.

16. Regionalne konsultacije sa udruženjima žrtava i porodicama žrtava o Nacrtu statuta REKOM [Regional consultations with victims' associations and victims' families about the Draft Statute of RECOM]. Prishtina, Kosovo, December 17, 2010.

17. Regionalne konzultacije sa studentima i mladim znanstvenicima o Nacrtu statuta REKOM [Regional consultations with students and young scholars about the Draft Statute of RECOM]. Zagreb, Croatia, June 17, 2010.

18. Regionalne konsultacije sa veteranima o Nacrtu statuta REKOM [Regional consultations with veterans about the Draft Statute of RECOM]. Skopje, Macedonia, December 18, 2010.

19. Regionalne konsultacije sa pravnicima o Nacrtu statuta REKOM [Regional consultations with legal practitioners about the Draft Statute of RECOM]. Belgrade, Serbia, January 22–23, 2010.

20. Nacionalne konsultacije sa nevladinim organizacijama o Nacrtu statuta REKOM [National consultations with nongovernmental organizations about the Draft Statute of RECOM]. Sarajevo, Bosnia and Herzegovina, January 29, 2011.

Transcripts of Other RECOM Consultations and Meetings

21. Nacionalne konsultacije sa organizacijama za ljudska prava o inicijativi za osnivanje Regionalne komisije za utvrđivanje činjenica o ratnim zločinima u bivšoj Jugoslaviji [National consultations with the human rights organizations about the initiative for founding the regional commission for establishing facts about war crimes in the former Yugoslavia]. Fruška Gora, Serbia, October 10, 2008.

22. Regionalne konsultacije sa predstavnicima nevećinskih zajednica o Inicijativi za osnivanje REKOM [Regional consultations with the representatives of nonmajority communities about the

initiative for the establishment of RECOM]. Skopje, Macedonia, January 29, 2010.

23. Regionalne konsultacije s civilnim društvom o Inicijativi za osnivanje REKOM [Regional consultations with civil society about the initiative for the establishment of RECOM]. Skopje, Macedonia, July 3, 2010.

24. Nacionalne konsultacije sa lokalnim zajednicama o Inicijativi za osnivanje REKOM [National consultations with local communities about the initiative for the establishment of RECOM]. Podgorica, Montenegro, September 14, 2010.

25. Sedmi regionalni forum za tranzicijsku pravdu [The seventh regional forum for transitional justice]. Zagreb, October 16–17, 2010.

26. Nacionalne konsultacije sa prosvetnom zajednicom o Inicijativi za osnivanje REKOM [National consultations with educators about the initiative for the founding of RECOM]. Belgrade, Serbia, November 27, 2010.

27. Nacionalne konsultacije sa mladima o Inicijativi za osnivanje REKOM [National consultations with the youth about the RECOM initiative]. Podgorica, Montenengro, December 15, 2010.

28. Nacionalne konsultacije sa predstavnicima Kosovske strateško-akcione mreže (KSAM) o Inicijativi za osnivanje REKOM [National consultations with the representatives of the Kosovo strategic-action network (KSAM) about the RECOM initiative]. Gračanica/Graçanicë, Kosovo, February 21, 2011.

Fieldwork Overview

Author's Interviews

Interview 1, RECOM organizer and human rights activist, Serbia, November 26, 2013.

Interview 2, RECOM organizer, Serbia, April 18, 2014.

Interview 3, RECOM organizer, Serbia, September 16, 2014.

Interview 4, legal practitioner and observer, Serbia, September 24, 2014.

Interview 5, human rights activist, Serbia, September 24, 2014.

Interview 6, legal practitioner and human rights activist, Serbia, September 25, 2014.

Interview 7, RECOM organizer, Serbia, September 26, 2014.

Interview 8, human rights activist and artist, Serbia, September 26, 2014.

Interview 9, legal practitioner, Bosnia and Herzegovina, December 9, 2015.

Interview 10, journalist, Bosnia and Herzegovina, December 10, 2015.

Interview 11, academic and human rights activist, Bosnia and Herzegovina, December 10, 2015.

Interview 12, academic and human rights activist, Bosnia and Herzegovina, December 11, 2015.

Interview 13, human rights activist, Kosovo, May 23, 2016.

Interview 14, RECOM organizer, Kosovo, May 23, 2016.

Interview 15, legal practitioner and human rights activist, Kosovo, May 24, 2016.

Interview 16, RECOM organizer, Kosovo, May 24, 2016.

Interview 17, human rights activist, Kosovo, May 24, 2016.

Interview 18, human rights activist, Montenegro, September 2, 2016.

Interview 19, legal practitioner, Montenegro, September 2, 2016.

Interview 20, human rights activist, Montenegro, September 2, 2016.

Interview 21, victim and human rights activist, Serbia, November 14, 2016.

Interview 22, academic, Croatia, December 15, 2019.

Interview 23, RECOM organizer, December 16, 2019.

Interview 24, RECOM organizer and human rights activist, Croatia, December 16, 2019.

Interview 25, RECOM organizer, Croatia, December 16, 2019.

Interview 26, veteran, Croatia, December 16, 2019.

Interview 27, academic and human rights activist, December 16, 2016.

Interview 28, human rights activist, Croatia, December 17, 2016.

Focus Groups

Focus Group, Belgrade, Serbia, October 30, 2015.

Focus Group, Sarajevo, Bosnia and Herzegovina, December 11, 2015.

Focus Group, Prishtina, Kosovo, May 25, 2016.

Participant Observation

IX Međunarodni forum za tranzicionu pravdu: Pomirenje u postjugoslovenskim zemljama, u organizaciji Koalicije za REKOM [9th International Forum for Transitional Justice: Reconciliation in Post-Yugoslav Countries, organized by the RECOM Coalition]. Mount Jahorina, Bosnia and Herzegovina, May 17–18, 2013.

X Međunarodni forum za tranzicionu pravdu u postjugoslovenskim zemljama: Postignuća i prioriteti u postjugoslovenskim zemljama, u organizaciji Koalicije za REKOM [10th International Forum for Transitional Justice: Achievements and Priorities, organized by the RECOM Coalition]. Belgrade, Serbia, November 15–16, 2014.

XI Međunarodni forum za tranzicionu pravdu u postjugoslovenskim zemljama, u organizaciji Koalicije za REKOM [11th International Forum for Transitional Justice in Post-Yugoslav Countries, organized by the RECOM Coalition]. Sarajevo, Bosnia and Herzegovina, January 28–29, 2018.

XII Međunarodni forum za tranzicionu pravdu u postjugoslovenskim zemljama: „Da žrtve žive u pamćenju društva," u organizaciji Koalicije za REKOM [12th International Forum for Transitional Justice in post-Yugoslav Countries: "May victims live in the memory of the societies," organized by the RECOM Coalition]. Zagreb, Croatia, December 16, 2019.

Workshop

"Reconciliation as Activity." Workshop organized by the London School of Economics and Political Science in collaboration with the Centre for Research, Documentation and Publication. Prishtina, Kosovo, March 5, 2018.

Tables

TABLE A.3.1 Common good category as a composite measure

DQI CATEGORY: COMMON GOOD

Individual interest
Ethnic group interest
My country/national
Neutral/no reference to any form of common good
Region/multiethnic interest
Abstract principle
Difference principle

TABLE A.3.2 Correlation of DQI categories

	J	CG	P	G	S
Justification rationality (J)	1				
Common good (CG)	.185	1			
Respect for participants (P)	.123	.078	1		
Respect for groups (G)	.087	.183	−.001	1	
Storytelling (S)	.109	.143	.056	−.006	1

Note: Table entries are polychoric correlation coefficients. $N = 1,211$.

TABLE A.3.3 Principal component analysis of DQI categories

	COMPONENTS		
	1	2	3
Justification rationality	.717	−.098	.228
Common good	.508	.538	−.405
Respect for participants	.339	.540	.644
Respect for groups	.553	−.661	.194
Storytelling	.515	−.038	−.550
Eigenvalue	1.459	1.028	.970
% of variance	29.2	20.6	19.4

Note: First three principal components only, representing 69 percent of variance in the data. Main table entries are component loadings. N = 1,211.

TABLE A.3.4 Summary statistics of the RECOM corpus

RECOM CONSULTATION NUMBER	NUMBER OF WORDS	NUMBER OF SPEECH ACTS
1	15,568	27
2	24,214	31
3	33,085	103
4	29,523	88
5	32,931	61
6	18,905	67
7	20,389	27
8	19,616	18
9	22,806	12
10	41,320	31
11	23,302	38
12	20,694	34
13	37,390	142
14	26,158	101
15	29,992	66
16	20,052	40
17	22,057	68
18	27,166	28
19	59,164	194
20	20,738	35
Total	545,070	1,211

TABLE A.3.5 Intercoder reliability statistics for DQI categories

DQI CATEGORY	PA	κ	α	AC
Justification rationality	.958 (.003)	.758 (.016)	.757 (.016)	.905 (.007)
Common good	.955 (.003)	.686 (.023)	.685 (.023)	.899 (.008)
Respect for participants	.978 (.003)	.693 (.036)	.693 (.037)	.974 (.003)
Respect for groups	.980 (.002)	.645 (.034)	.645 (.034)	.973 (.003)
Storytelling	.990 (.003)	.916 (.024)	.916 (.024)	.989 (.003)

Note: PA = proportion of agreement; κ = Cohen's kappa; α = Krippendorff's alpha; AC = Gwet's agreement coefficient. Table entries are coefficients. Standard errors in parentheses. For all tests, *p* < .001. *N* = 1,211. All variables are ordinal.

TABLE A.4.1 Summary statistics of the unscaled and rescaled DQITJ

DQITJ VARIANT	MEAN	STD. DEV.	MIN. OBSERVED	MAX. OBSERVED	OBSERVED RANGE	MIN. POSSIBLE	MAX. POSSIBLE
DQI unsc.	6.003	1.597	.916	12.516	11.600	0	13.077
DQI	4.591	1.221	.701	9.571	8.871	0	10

Note: All figures rounded to three decimal places.

TABLE A.4.2 Intercoder reliability statistics for identity in discourse variables

VARIABLE	PA	κ	α	AC
Subjectivity	.825 (.011)	.663 (.020)	.662 (.020)	.788 (.014)
Positionality	.986 (.003)	.888 (.026)	.888 (.026)	.985 (.004)

Note: PA = proportion of agreement; κ = Cohen's kappa; α = Krippendorff's alpha; AC = Gwet's agreement coefficient. Table entries are coefficients. Standard errors in parentheses. For all tests, *p* < .001. *N* = 1,211. All variables are nominal.

TABLE A.5.1 Intercoder reliability statistics for interactivity variables

VARIABLE	PA	κ	α	AC
Ref. to other participants	.987 (.003)	.970 (.008)	.970 (.008)	.985 (.004)
Interethnic reference	.992 (.002)	.963 (.011)	.963 (.011)	.989 (.003)
Intraethnic reference	.994 (.002)	.962 (.012)	.962 (.012)	.993 (.002)

Note: PA = proportion of agreement; κ = Cohen's kappa; α = Krippendorff's alpha; AC = Gwet's agreement coefficient. Table entries are coefficients. Standard errors in parentheses. For all tests, *p* < .001 *N* = 1,211. Reference to other participants is a nominal variable; interethnic reference and intraethnic reference are ordinal variables.

Notes

INTRODUCTION

1. I spoke to Lush Krasniqi in Prishtina, Kosovo, on May 25, 2016. For an extensive account of Lush Krasniqi's personal loss, survival, and search for the bodies of his relatives, see "Outloud Podcast: The Story of Lush Krasniqi, Survivor of the Meja Massacre (27.04.1999)," in Dafina Halili, "The Struggle of a Survivor of One of the Largest Massacres in Kosovo," Kosovo 2.0, April 23, 2020, https://kosovotwopointzero.com/wp-content/uploads/2021/12/The-struggle-of-a-survivor-of-one-of-the-largest-massacres-in-Kosovo_POD_TRANSCRIPT.pdf.

2. The attack on the civilian population in western Kosovo is considered to be an instance of the single gravest crime against civilians in the Kosovo conflict. For the details of the operation conducted by the Serbian security forces, including the approximate figure of the killed, see *Dosije: Operacija Reka* (Belgrade: Fond za humanitarno pravo, October 2015). The report also specifies that the operation and its aftermath were reconstructed in two trials before the ICTY, the case against Vlastimir Đorđević, assistant minister of Internal Affairs of Serbia, and the case against Nikola Šainović, deputy prime minister of the Federal Republic of Yugoslavia (Serbia and Montenegro), and others. For the summaries of the cases and all trial documents, which quote 387 individuals killed in this operation, see International Criminal Tribunal for the Former Yugoslavia, Đorđević (IT-05-87/1), https://www.icty.org/en/case/djordjevic, and International Criminal Tribunal for the Former Yugoslavia, Šainović et al. (IT-05-87), https://www.icty.org/en/case/milutinovic, and particularly Prosecutor v. Nikola Šainović, Nebojša Pavković, Vladimir Lazarević, Sreten Lukić, Public Judgement, Case No. IT-05-87-A, International Criminal Tribunal for the Former Yugoslavia, January 23, 2014, https://www.icty.org/x/cases/milutinovic/acjug/en/140123.pdf. In 1999, under the terms of the 1244 United Nations Security Council resolution, Kosovo became a United Nations protectorate, having obtained de facto sovereignty. At the same time, the resolution restated the commitment to the territorial integrity and sovereignty of the Federal Republic of Yugoslavia (comprising Serbia and Montenegro). In 2008, Kosovo formally declared independence, which Serbia has continued to contest.

3. According to Jugo and Wastell, a primary mass grave refers to the site where bodies of the killed are originally buried, whereas a secondary mass grave is the site where the remains are reburied, usually for the purpose of concealing the crime. For implications of the destruction of bodies in the process of exhumation and reinternment for memory politics, see Admir Jugo and Sari Wastell, "Disassembling the Pieces, Reassembling the Social: The Forensic and Political Lives of Secondary Mass Graves in Bosnia and Herzegovina," in *Human Remains and Identification: Mass Violence, Genocide, and the "Forensic Turn,"* ed. Élisabeth Anstett and Jean-Marc Dreyfus (Manchester: Manchester University Press, 2015).

4. For assessments varying from some 10,000 to over 13,000 killed and disappeared in the Kosovo war, and for challenges involved in establishing the exact count, see Paul B. Spiegel and Peter Salama, "War and Mortality in Kosovo, 1998–99: An Epidemiological Testimony," *Lancet* 355 (2000): 2204–209, https://doi.org/10.1016/S0140-6736(00)02404-1; Patrick Ball, Wendy Betts, Fritz Scheuren, Jana Dudukovich, and Jana Asher, "Killings

and Refugee Flow in Kosovo March–June 1999: A Report to the International Crimi-nal Tribunal for the Former Yugoslavia," American Association for the Advancement of Science, January 3, 2002, New York, https://www.icty.org/x/file/About/OTP/War_Demo graphics/en/s_milosevic_kosovo_020103.pdf; Independent International Commission on Kosovo, "Annex 1: Documentation on Human Rights Violations," in *The Kosovo Report: Conflict, International Response, Lessons Learned* (Oxford: Oxford Univer-sity Press, 2000), 301–18; Humanitarian Law Center (Serbia) and Humanitarian Law Center Kosovo, "The Kosovo Memory Book 1998–2000," http://www.kosovomemory book.org/?page_id=29&lang=de.

5. Marlise Simons, "Danube's Grisly Tale, Staring Milosevic in the Face," *New York Times*, August 26, 2002, https://www.nytimes.com/2002/08/26/world/danube-s-grisly-tale-staring-milosevic-in-the-face.html.

6. I define ethnicity and the concept of an ethnic group related to it, following Horowitz, as an identity "based on a myth of collective ancestry, which usually carries with it traits believed to be innate." See Donald L. Horowitz, *Ethnic Groups in Con-flict*, 2nd ed. (Berkeley: University of California Press [1985] 2000), 52. For a range of features considered to represent descent, including a common culture, a common lan-guage, a common territory, and conceptual autonomy, see Kanchan Chandra, "What Is Ethnic Identity? A Minimalist Definition," in *Constructivist Theories of Ethnic Politics*, ed. Kanchan Chandra (Oxford: Oxford University Press, 2012), 71. The concepts of nation and national identity overlap with the concept of ethnicity but accentuate a "sense of political community" which, according to Smith, implies "at least some com-mon institutions and a single code of rights and duties for all members of the commu-nity." Anthony D. Smith, *National Identity* (London: Penguin, 1991), 9. Nationalism, therefore, following Gellner, is "primarily a political principle, which holds that the political and the national unit should be congruent." Ernest Gellner, *Nations and Nationalism* (Oxford: Blackwell, 1983), 1. For a discussion of different types of nationalism, ranging from civic nationalism to ethnic nationalism, see Harris Mylonas and Maya Tudor, "Nationalism: What We Know and What We still Need to Know," *Annual Review of Political Science* 24, no. 1 (2021): 109–32, https://doi.org/10.1146/ annurev-polisci-041719-101841. In this book, I refer interchangeably to the conflicts that accompanied the dissolution of the former Yugoslavia and the Balkan conflicts. The use of the term "Balkan conflicts" highlights the regional nature of the violence. Here, as in other scholarly literature on post–Cold War conflicts, the term specifically refers to the conflicts on the territory of the former Yugoslavia in the 1990s and early 2000s; it does not apply to the broader Balkan region beyond the former Yugoslavia's borders.

7. Some bodily remains were first discovered in trucks dumped in the River Danube and in a lake in Serbia before being transferred for reburial to two locations in Serbia. Bodies of other Albanian victims in Kosovo were transported directly to Serbia, either immediately following the killing or after their excavation from primary mass graves. For a detailed account of the Serbian state cover-up, see The Prosecutor v. Vlastimir Đorđević, Case No. IT-05-87/1-A and Case No. IT-05-87/1-A, International Criminal Tribunal for the Former Yugoslavia, December 20, 2011, https://www.icty.org/x/cases/djordjevic/ custom5/en/111220-1.pdf, 128–44. See also *Dosije*, 50–59.

8. Miloš Vasić, "Mrtvi putuju . . .", *Vreme*, June 21, 2001. https://www.vreme.com/ vreme/mrtvi-putuju/.

9. Several reburial ceremonies took place in the villages in western Kosovo as vic-tims' bodies were located, identified, and transferred to relatives in Kosovo. See "27 prilli," *Periodik informativ*, Meje-Gjakovë, 2, no. 6–7 (October 2005). However, more remain missing.

10. The trials before the ICTY were the main transitional justice mechanism after the wars in the region ended. On the inability of the ICTY to deliver justice to victims in Kosovo, see Aidan Hehir and Furtuna Sheremeti, eds., *Kosovo and Transitional Justice: The Pursuit of Justice after Large-Scale Conflict* (Abingdon: Routledge, 2022).

11. Antonija Petričušić and Cyril Blondel, "Reconciliation in the Western Balkans: New Perspectives and Proposals," *Journal of Ethnopolitics and Minority Issues in Europe* 11, no. 4 (2012).

12. Serbeze Haxhiaj and Milica Stojanovic, "Evidence Reveals Serbian Officers' Role in Kosovo Massacre was Ignored," *Balkan Investigative Reporting Network*, April 27, 2020, https://balkaninsight.com/2020/04/27/massacre-in-meja-evidence-of-serbian-officers-involvement-ignored/.

13. On the marginalization of civilian victims in Kosovo in nationalist discourses within the Kosovo Albanian community, see Gëzim Visoka, "Arrested Truth: Transitional Justice and the Politics of Remembrance in Kosovo," *Journal of Human Rights Practice* 8, no. 1 (2016): 67–68, https://doi.org/10.1093/jhuman/huv017.

14. "Victims" in this book refers to those who perished in the conflicts and those who survived violence. It is a term that resonates with the political and cultural context in the postconflict Balkans. The term has been habituated in the region in reference to war crimes and gross human rights violations, as opposed to the local translations of the term "survivors," as it is commonly used in English-language scholarship on transitional justice. Therefore, the reference to victims of violence in this book should not be equated with a linguistic and social construction of those who suffered violence as powerless, passive, and without agency. On difficulties caused by constructions of victims as passive and survivors as active agents for assessing transitional justice in specific contexts, see Mijke de Waardt and Sanne Webe, "Beyond Victims' Mere Presence: An Empirical Analysis of Victim Participation in Transitional Justice in Colombia," *Journal of Human Rights Practice* 11, no. 1 (2019), https://doi.org/10.1093/jhuman/huz002.

15. Nataša Kandić, "RECOM: A New Approach to Reconciliation and a Corrective for Criminal Justice," *Forum for Transitional Justice* 4 (2012).

16. RECOM Consultation no. 26.

17. *Proces REKOM: Konsultativni process o utvrđivanju činjenica o ratnim zločinima i drugim teškim kršenjima ljudskih prava počinjenim na području nekadašnje SFRJ* (Beograd: Fond za humanitarno pravo, 2011).

18. Some political leaders of the post-Yugoslav states supported RECOM. However, this support was either lost during the electoral cycle and the change of leadership or was always merely a matter of public declarations. Faced with a lack of support from states in the region, RECOM decided at an assembly meeting in 2019 that civil society should take on the responsibility for documenting war crimes in the former Yugoslavia. RECOM Reconciliation Network, "Coalition for RECOM Takes Charge of Creating List of War Victims on the Territory of Former Yugoslavia," Press Release (May 29, 2020), https://www.recom.link/en/coalition-for-recom-takes-charge-of-creating-list-of-war-victims-on-the-territory-of-the-former-yugoslavia/.

19. Jamie Rowen, "Mobilizing Truth: Agenda Setting in a Transnational Social Movement," *Law & Social Inquiry* 37, no. 3 (2012), https://doi.org/10.1111/j.1747-4469.2012.01317.x; Arnaud Kurze and Iva Vukusic, "Afraid to Cry Wolf: Human Rights Activists' Struggle of Transnational Accountability Efforts in the Balkans," in *Transitional Justice and Civil Society in the Balkans*, ed. Olivera Simić and Zala Volčič (New York: Springer, 2013); Jill A. Irvine and Patrice C. McMahon, "From International Courts to Grassroots Organizing: Obstacles to Transitional Justice in the Balkans," in Simić and Volčič, *Transitional Justice*; Anna Di Lellio and Caitlin McCunn, "Engineering Grassroots Transitional Justice in the Balkans: The Case of Kosovo," *East European Politics and Societies* 27,

no. 1 (2013), https://doi.org/10.1177/0888325412464550; Jelena Obradovic-Wochnik, "Serbian Civil Society as an Exclusionary Space: NGOs, the Public and 'Coming to Terms with the Past,'" in *Civil Society and Transitions in the Western Balkans*, ed. Vesna Bojicic-Dzelilovic, James Ker-Lindsay, and Denisa Kostovicova (Basingstoke: Palgrave Macmillan, 2013); Janine Natalya Clark, "Does Bosnia Need a Truth and Reconciliation Commission? Some Reflections on Its Possible Design," *Ethnopolitics* 12, no. 3 (2013), https://doi.org/10.1080/17449057.2012.688374.

20. Focus Group, Prishtina, Kosovo, May 25, 2016.

21. This omission is partly due to these scholars' cursory engagement with the process of the RECOM consultations. For example, see Rowen, "Mobilizing Truth"; Irvine and McMahon, "From International Courts"; Di Lellio and McCunn, "Engineering Grassroots"; Obradovic-Wochnik, "Serbian Civil Society." By contrast, Nießer argues that this process resulted in interethnic understanding based on a systematic study of victims' testimonies during the RECOM consultations. Jacqueline Nießer, *Die Wahrheit der Anderen: Transnationale Vergangenheitsaufarbeitung in Post-Jugoslawien am Beispiel der REKOM Initiative* (Göttingen: Vandenhoeck & Ruprecht, 2020).

22. The list of RECOM consultations whose transcripts are used in this research is in the appendix. The RECOM corpus can be accessed at Denisa Kostovicova, "Replication Data For: Gender, Justice and Deliberation: Why Women Don't Influence Peace-Making," *Harvard Dataverse V1*, 2020. https://doi.org/https://doi.org/10.7910/DVN/FC6WAO. For the fieldwork details, see the appendix.

23. I am indebted for this phrase to a participant contributing to a discussion about reconciliation at the workshop with representatives of civil society in Kosovo, "Reconciliation as Activity," organized by the London School of Economics and Political Science in collaboration with the Centre for Research, Documentation and Publication, Prishtina, Kosovo, March 5, 2018.

24. Roger Mac Ginty, *Everyday Peace: How So-Called Ordinary People Can Disrupt Violent Conflict* (Oxford: Oxford University Press, 2021), 212.

25. Joanna R. Quinn, *Thin Sympathy: A Strategy to Thicken Transitional Justice* (Philadelphia: University of Pennsylvania Press, 2021).

26. Richard Caplan *Measuring Peace: Principles, Practices, and Politics* (Oxford: Oxford University Press, 2019); Pamina Firchow, *Reclaiming Everyday Peace: Local Voices in Measurement and Evaluation after War* (Cambridge: Cambridge University Press, 2018).

27. Laurel E. Fletcher and Harvey M. Weinstein, "Writing Transitional Justice: An Empirical Evaluation of Transitional Justice Scholarship in Academic Journals," *Journal of Human Rights Practice* 7, no. 2 (2015): 189, https://doi.org/10.1093/jhuman/huv006.

28. Ruti Teitel, *Transitional Justice* (Oxford: Oxford University Press, 2000).

29. Colleen Murphy, *The Conceptual Foundations of Transitional Justice* (Cambridge: Cambridge University Press, 2017), 1.

30. Paige Arthur, "How 'Transitions' Reshaped Human Rights: A Conceptual History of Transitional Justice," *Human Rights Quarterly* 31, no 2 (2009): 334, https://doi.org/10.1353/hrq.0.0069.

31. Paige, "How 'Transitions,'" 360. Pablo de Grieff, "Transitional Justice Gets Its Own Encyclopedia: Vitamins or Steroids for a Developing Field," *International Journal of Transitional Justice* 7, no. 3 (2013): 552, https://doi.org/10.1093/ijtj/ijt023.

32. Dustin N. Sharp, "Emancipating Transitional Justice from the Bonds of the Paradigmatic Transition," *International Journal of Transitional Justice* 9, no. 1 (2015): 152, https://doi.org/10.1093/ijtj/iju021. For further elaboration on anchoring transitional justice in positive peace, see Dustin N. Sharp, *Rethinking Transitional Justice for the Twenty-First Century: Beyond the End of History* (Cambridge: Cambridge University Press, 2018),

137–54, and on the local perspective, see Oliver Richmond, *Peace Formation and Political Order in Conflict Affected Societies* (Oxford: Oxford University Press, 2016).

33. Cyanne E. Loyle and Christian Davenport, "Transitional Injustice: Subverting Justice in Transition and Postconflict Societies," *Journal of Human Rights* 15, no. 1 (2016): 126, https://doi.org/10.1080/14754835.2015.1052897; Sidney Leclercq, "Injustice through Transitional Justice? Subversion Strategies in Burundi's Peace Process and Postconflict Developments," *International Journal of Transitional Justice* 11, no. 3 (2017), https://doi.org/10.1093/ijtj/ijx017; Jacqueline H.R. deMeritt, "Transitional Justice: Prospects for Postwar Peace and Human Rights," in *What Do We Know about Civil Wars?*, ed. T. David Mason and Sara McLaughlin Mitchell (Lanham, MD: Rowman & Littlefield, 2016), 180.

34. On the need for greater conceptual clarity and methodological rigor, see Hugo van der Merwe, "Delivering Justice during Transition: Research Challenges," in *Assessing the Impact of Transitional Justice: Challenges for Empirical Research*, ed. Hugo van der Merwe, Victoria Baxter, and Audrey R. Chapman (Washington, DC: United States Institute of Peace Press, 2009); Oskar N. T. Thoms, James Ron, and Roland Paris, "State-Level Effects of Transitional Justice: What Do We Know?," *International Journal of Transitional Justice* 4, no. 3 (2010), https://doi.org/10.1093/ijtj/ijq012; Melissa Nobles, "The Prosecution of Human Rights Violations," *Annual Review of Political Science* 13 (2010), https://doi.org/10.1146/annurev.polisci.040108.110013; Tricia D. Olsen, Leigh A. Payne, and Andrew G. Reiter, "The Justice Balance: When Transitional Justice Improves Human Rights and Democracy," *Human Rights Quarterly* 32, no. 4 (2010), https://www.jstor.org/stable/40930342; Fletcher and Weinstein, "Writing Transitional Justice."

35. Rachel Kerr and Eirin Mobekk, *Peace & Justice: Seeking Accountability after War* (Cambridge: Polity, 2007), 6.

36. John Paul Lederach, *Building Peace: Sustainable Reconciliation in Divided Societies* (Washington, DC: United States Institute for Peace Press, 1997), 24–31.

37. Trudy Govier, *Taking Wrongs Seriously: Acknowledgment, Reconciliation and the Politics of Sustainable Peace* (Amherst: Humanity Books, 2006), 13. Other scholars have referred to the two poles of reconciliation as "shallow" and "deep," or "minimalist" or "maximalist" conceptions. On evaluating coexistence as a minimalist form of reconciliation, see Antonia Chayes and Martha Minow, eds., *Imagine Coexistence: Restoring Humanity after Violent Ethnic Conflict* (San Francisco: Jossey-Bass, 2003). Alternatively, for a discussion of reconciliation at a broader end of the spectrum, see Erin Daly and Jeremy Sarkin, *Reconciliation in Divided Societies: Finding Common Ground* (Philadelphia: University of Pennsylvania Press, 2007). For a comprehensive review of different approaches to reconciliation, see Audrey R. Chapman, "Approaches to Studying Reconciliation," in *Assessing the Impact of Transitional Justice: Challenges for Empirical Research*, ed. Hugo van der Merwe, Victoria Baxter, and Audrey R. Chapman (Washington, DC: United States Institute of Peace Press, 2009); James Hughes and Denisa Kostovicova, eds., *Rethinking Reconciliation and Transitional Justice after Conflict* (London: Routledge 2018); Lina Strupinskienė, "'What Is Reconciliation and Are We There Yet?' Different Types and Levels of Reconciliation: A Case Study of Bosnia and Herzegovina," *Journal of Human Rights* 16, no. 4 (2017), https://doi.org/10.1080/14754835.2016.1197771; David Bloomfield, *On Good Terms: Clarifying Reconciliation*, Berghof Report no. 14, Berghof Research Center for Constructive Conflict Management, 2006.

38. Brandon D. Lundy, Akanmu G. Adebayo, and Sherrill Hayes, eds., *Atone: Religion, Conflict, and Reconciliation* (Lanham, MD: Lexington Books, 2018).

39. Joanna R. Quinn, "Introduction," in *Reconciliation(s): Transitional Justice in Postconflict Societies*, ed. Joanna R. Quinn (Montreal: McGill-Queens University Press, 2009), 5. For a process-based perspective on reconciliation, see also Kimberly Theidon, *Intimate*

Enemies: Violence and Reconciliation in Peru (Philadelphia: University of Pennsylvania Press, 2012).

40. Daniel Philpott, *Just and Unjust Peace: The Ethic of Political Reconciliation* (Oxford: Oxford University Press, 2012), 31.

41. Herman Kelman, "Reconciliation as Identity Change: A Social-Psychological Perspective," in *From Conflict Resolution to Reconciliation*, ed. Yaacov Bar-Siman-Tov (Oxford: Oxford University Press, 2004).

42. Donna Pankhurst, "Issues of Justice and Reconciliation in Complex Political Emergencies: Conceptualising Reconciliation, Justice and Peace," *Third World Quarterly* 20, no. 1 (1999): 240–41, https://www.jstor.org/stable/3993193.

43. Alternatively, Staub identifies various levels at which reconciliation needs to take place, such as the psychological, political, institutional/structural, and cultural. Ervin Staub, "Reconciliation after Genocide, Mass Killing, or Intractable Conflict: Understanding the Roots of Violence, Psychological Recovery, and Steps toward a General Theory," *Political Psychology* 27, no. 6 (2006): 880, https://www.jstor.org/stable/20447006.

44. Elin Skaar, "Reconciliation in a Transitional Justice Perspective," *Transitional Justice Review* 1, no. 1 (2013), http://dx.doi.org/10.5206/tjr.2012.1.1.4.

45. Brandon Hamber and Gráinne Kelly, "Beyond Coexistence: Towards a Working Definition of Reconciliation," in *Reconciliation(s)*, ed. Quinn, 300–301; Heleen Touquet and Peter Vermeersch, "Changing Frames of Reconciliation: The Politics of Peace-Building in the Former Yugoslavia," *East European Politics and Societies* 30, no. 1 (2015), https://doi.org/10.1177/0888325415584048; Angelika Rettberg and Juan E. Ugarriza, "Reconciliation: A Comprehensive Framework for Empirical Analysis," *Security Dialogue* 47, no. 6 (2016), https://doi.org/10.1177/0967010616671858; Ivor Sokolić, "Reconciliation Rising: The Roles of the Everyday and the Informal in Successful Post-Conflict Reconciliation," *Ethnopolitics* 19, no. 2 (2020), https://doi.org/10.1080/17449057.2019.1653015.

46. Jens Meierhenrich, "Varieties of Reconciliation," *Law & Social Inquiry* 33 no. 1 (2008): 224, 195, 220, https://doi.org/10.1111/j.1747-4469.2008.00098.x.

47. Johan Galtung, "Violence, Peace, and Peace Research," *Journal of Peace Research* 6, no. 3 (1969), https://www.jstor.org/stable/422690.

48. Christian Davenport, "A Relational Approach to Quality Peace," in *The Peace Continuum: What It Is and How to Study It*, ed. Christian Davenport, Erick Melander, and Patrick M. Regan (Oxford: Oxford University Press, 2018).

49. Donald G. Ellis, *Deliberative Communication and Ethnopolitical Conflict* (New York: Peter Lang, 2012), 181.

50. Govier, *Taking Wrongs Seriously*, 124–25.

51. Philpott, *Just and Unjust Peace*, 56–57.

52. Ronnie Janoff-Bulman and Amelie Werther, "The Social Psychology of Respect: Implications for Delegitimization and Reconciliation," in *The Social Psychology of Intergroup Reconciliation*, ed. Arie Nadler, Thomas E. Malloy and Jeffrey D. Fisher (Oxford: Oxford University Press, 2008), 159.

53. David A. Crocker, "Punishment, Reconciliation, and Democratic Deliberation," in *Taking Wrongs Seriously: Apologies and Reconciliation*, ed. Elazar Barkan and Alexander Karn (Stanford: Stanford University Press, 2006), 71.

54. Davenport's model also includes values, behavior, and organizations. Davenport, "A Relational Approach," 163.

55. Louis Kriesberg, "Changing Forms of Coexistence," in *Reconciliation, Justice and Coexistence: Theory and Practice*, ed. Mohammed Abu-Nimer (Lanham, MD: Lexington Books, 2001), 60.

56. Stanley Cohen, *States of Denial: Knowing about Atrocities and Suffering* (Cambridge: Polity, 2001), 239.

57. Davenport, "A Relational Approach," 154–58.

58. Susanne Buckley-Zistel, Teresa Koloma Beck, Christian Braun, and Friederike Mieth, eds., *Transitional Justice Theories* (Abingdon: Routledge, 2014).

59. Kora Andrieu, "Political Liberalism after Mass Violence: John Rawls and a 'Theory' of Transitional Justice," in *Transitional Justice*, ed. Buckley-Zistel, Koloma Beck, Braun and Mieth, 98; Kirk Simpson, "Victims of Political Violence: A Habermasian Model of Truth Recovery," *Journal of Human Rights* 6, no. 3 (2007): 326, https://doi.org/10.1080/14754830701531120; Carlos L. Yordán, "Towards Deliberative Peace: A Habermasian Critique of Contemporary Peace Operations," *Journal of International Relations and Development* 12, no. 1 (2009), https://doi.org/10.1057/jird.2008.26; Michael Barnett, "Building a Republican Peace: Stabilizing States after War," *International Security* 30, no. 4 (2006), https://www.jstor.org/stable/4137530. Conversely, Pukallus argues in relation to "communicative peacebuilding" that discursive civility, implying politeness and respect in conversation, is necessary for civil peace, without engaging with the deliberative conception of discursive civility. Stefanie Pukallus, *Communication in Peacebuilding: Civil Wars, Civility and Safe Spaces* (Cham: Palgrave Macmillan, 2022), 137–79.

60. Iavor Rangelov, *Nationalism and the Rule of Law: Lessons from the Balkans and Beyond* (Cambridge: Cambridge University Press, 2014); Ivor Sokolić, *International Courts and Mass Atrocity: Narratives of War and Justice in Croatia* (Basingstoke: Palgrave Macmillan, 2019); Katherine Elizabeth Mack, *From Apartheid to Democracy: Deliberating Truth and Reconciliation in South Africa* (University Park: Pennsylvania University Press, 2014); Xolela Mangcu, ed., *Becoming Worthy Ancestors: Archive, Public Deliberation and Identity in South Africa* (Johannesburg: Wits University Press, 2011).

61. Claudia Landwehr and Katharina Holzinger, "Institutional Determinants of Deliberative Interaction," *European Political Science Review* 3 no. 2 (2010): 378–79, https://doi.org/10.1017/S1755773910000226.

62. James D. Fearon, "Deliberation as Discussion," in *Deliberative Democracy*, ed. John Elster (Cambridge: Cambridge University Press, 1998), 63.

63. For instance, see Rangelov, *Nationalism*.

64. Fearon, "Deliberation as Discussion," 63.

65. Crocker, "Punishment," 68.

66. For a selection of empirical scholarship on deliberation in divided societies, see Jürg Steiner, *The Foundations of Deliberative Democracy: Empirical Research and Normative Implications* (Cambridge: Cambridge University Press, 2012); Didier Caluwaerts and Kris Deschouwer, "Building Bridges across Political Divides: Experiments on Deliberative Democracy in Deeply Divided Belgium," *European Political Science Review* 6 no. 3 (2014), https://doi.org/10.1017/S1755393913000179; Robert C. Luskin, Ian O'Flynn, James S. Fishkin, and David Russell, "Deliberating Across Deep Divides," *Political Studies* 62, no. 1 (2014), https://doi.org/10.1111/j.1467-9248.2012.01005.x; Juan E. Ugarriza, "When War Adversaries Talk: The Experimental Effect of Engagement Rules on Postconflict Deliberation," *Latin American Politics and Society* 58, no. 3 (2016), https://doi.org/10.1111/j/1548-2456.2016.00319.x; Manlio Cinalli and Ian O'Flynn, "Public Deliberation, Network Analysis and the Political Integration of Muslims in Britain," *British Journal of Politics and International Relations* 16, no. 3 (2014), https://doi.org/10.1111/1467-856X.12003. Gutmann and Thompson argue that a deliberative perspective is promising for judging the work of truth commissions; however, a gap still exists in our understanding of whether former adversaries can discuss deliberatively which justice strategy to opt for in the first instance. Amy Gutmann and Dennis Thompson, "The Moral Foundations of

Truth Commissions," in *Truth v. Justice: The Morality of Truth Commissions,* eds. Robert I. Rotberg and Dennis Thompson (Princeton: Princeton University Press, 2010), 34.

67. *The Rule of Law and Transitional Justice in Conflict and Post-Conflict Societies: Report of the Secretary-General,* S/2004/616, United Nations Security Council, August 23, 2004, https://digitallibrary.un.org/record/527647?ln=en, 4.

68. *Annual Report of the United Nations High Commissioner for Human Rights and Reports of the Office of the High Commissioner and the Secretary-General.* Analytical study on human rights and transitional justice, United Nations, A/HRC/12/18, August 6, 2009, https://www.un.org/ruleoflaw/files/96696_A-HRC-12-18_E.pdf, 14.

69. Enshrined in Article 25 of the International Covenant on Civil and Political Rights, see *Rule-of-law Tools for Post-Conflict States: National Consultations on Transitional Justice* (New York: United Nations, 2009), https://www.ohchr.org/Documents/Publications/NationalConsultationsTJ_EN.pdf, 29.

70. *Rule-of-law Tools,* 2–3; Wendy Lambourne, "What Are the Pillars of Transitional Justice? The United Nations, Civil Society and the Justice Cascade in Burundi," *Macquarie Law Journal* 13 (2014), 50.

71. Sandra Rubli, "Transitional Justice: Justice by Bureaucratic Means?," *Swisspeace,* Working Paper no. 4 (2012); Domenica Preysling, *Transitional Justice in Post-Revolutionary Tunisia (2011–2013): How the Past Shapes the Future* (Wiesbaden: Springer, 2016), 107–12; Eric Stover, Hanny Megally, and Hania Mufti, "Bremer's 'Gordian Knot': Transitional Justice and the US Occupation of Iraq," *Human Rights Quarterly* 27, no. 3 (2005), https://doi.org/10.1353/hrq.2005.0044.

72. *Rule-of-law Tools,* 5.

73. Eduardo González and Howard Varney, eds., *Truth Seeking: Elements of Creating an Effective Truth Commission* (Brasilia: Amnesty Commission of the Ministry of Justice of Brazil; New York: International Center for Transitional Justice, 2013), 15.

74. Simon Robins, "Failing Victims? The Limits of Transitional Justice in Addressing the Needs of Victims of Violations," *Human Rights and International Legal Discourse* 17, no. 2 (2017): 54.

75. Nevin T. Aiken, "Learning to Live Together: Transitional Justice and Intergroup Reconciliation in Northern Ireland," *International Journal of Transitional Justice* 4 no. 2 (2010): 186, https://doi.org/10.1093/ijtj/ijq002.

76. On the history, rationale, and methodology of intercommunal dialogues, see Ronald J. Fisher, *Interactive Conflict Resolution* (Syracuse: Syracuse University Press, 1997), 137; Irfat Moaz, "An Experiment in Peace: Reconciliation-Aimed Workshops of Jewish-Israeli and Palestinian Youth," *Journal of Peace Research* 37, no. 6 (2000): 722, https://doi.org/10.1177/0022343300037006004.

77. Amy Gutmann and Dennis Thompson, *Why Deliberative Democracy?* (Princeton: Princeton University Press, 2004).

78. John W. Creswell and Vicki L. Plano Clark, *Designing and Conducting Mixed Methods Research,* 3rd ed. (Los Angeles: Sage, 2018).

79. Skaar, "Reconciliation," 57.

80. David P. Forsythe, "Human Rights and Mass Atrocities: Revisiting Transitional Justice," *International Studies Review* 13, no. 3 (2011): 92, https://www.jstor.org/stable/23016143; Victoria Baxter, "Critical Challenges for the Development of the Transitional Justice Research Field," in *Assessing the Impact,* van der Merwe, Baxter, and Chapman, 328; Nicola Palmer, Briony Jones, and Julia Viebach, "Introduction: Ways of Knowing Atrocity: A Methodological Enquiry into the Formulation, Implementation, and Assessment of Transitional Justice," *Canadian Journal of Law and Society* 30, no. 2 (2015): 180, https://doi.org/10.1017/cls.2015.19; Phuong Pham and Patrick Vinck, "Empirical Research and the Development and Assessment of Transitional Justice Mechanisms," *International*

Journal of Transitional Justice 1 (2007): 248. On the methodological underpinnings and measurement of reconciliation, see James L. Gibson, "'Truth' and 'Reconciliation' as Social Indicators," *Social Indicators Research* 81 no. 2 (2007), https://www.jstor.org/stable/20734426; Karen Brounéus, "Analyzing Reconciliation: A Structured Method for Measuring National Reconciliation Initiatives," *Peace and Conflict* 14, no. 3 (2008), https://doi.org/10.1080/10781910802017354; Ian S. McIntosh, "Reconciliation, You've Got to Be Dreaming: Exploring Methodologies for Monitoring and Achieving Aboriginal Reconciliation in Australia by 2030," *Conflict Resolution Quarterly* 32, no. 1 (2014), https://doi.org/10.1002/crq.21101.

81. John W. Creswell, "Mixed Methods Research," in *The SAGE Encyclopedia of Qualitative Research Methods*, ed. Lisa M. Given (Thousand Oaks: Sage, 2008). On the analytical benefits of mixed method research design in transitional justice, see Hugo van der Merwe, Richard Chelin, and Masana Ndiga-Kanga, "'Measuring' Transitional Justice," in *Transitional Justice: Theories, Mechanism and Debates*, ed. Hakeem O. Yusuf and Hugo van der Merwe (London: Routledge, 2022).

82. Dimiter Toshkov, *Research Design in Political Science* (Basingstoke: Palgrave Macmillan, 2016), 314.

83. Brandon Stewart and Eric Wiebelhaus-Brahm, "The Quantitative Turn in Transitional Justice Research: What Have We Learned About Impact?," *Transitional Justice Review* 1, no. 5 (2017), https://ir.lib.uwo.ca/tjreview/vol1/iss5/4; Roman David, "What We Know about Transitional Justice: Survey and Experimental Evidence," *Political Psychology* 38, no. 1 (2017), http://dx.doi.org/10.1111/pops.12395.

84. William L. Benoit, "Content Analysis in Political Communication," in *The Sourcebook for Political Communication Research: Methods, Measures, and Analytical Techniques*, ed. Erik P. Bucy and R. Lance Holbert (New York: Routledge, 2011), 268. Cf. Will Lowe, "Content Analysis and its Place in the (Methodological) Scheme of Things," *Qualitative Methods* 2 (2004).

85. Kimberley A. Neuendorf, "Content Analysis—A Contrast and Complement to Discourse Analysis," *Qualitative Methods* 2 (2004): 33.

86. Cynthia Hardy, Bill Harley, and Nelson Phillips, "Discourse Analysis and Content Analysis: Two Solitudes?," *Qualitative Methods* 2 (2004): 20.

87. Norman Fairclough, "Critical Discourse Analysis," in *The Routledge Handbook of Discourse Analysis*, ed. James Paul Gee and Michael Handford (London: Routledge, 2014). Cf. Mark Laffey and Jutta Weldes, "Methodological Reflections on Discourse Analysis," *Qualitative Methods* 2 (2004): 28.

88. Neta C. Crawford, "Understanding Discourse: A Method of Ethical Argument Analysis," *Qualitative Methods* 2 (2004): 24.

89. Abbas Tashakkori and John W. Creswell, "Exploring the Nature of Research Questions in Mixed Methods Research," *Journal of Mixed Methods Research* 1, no. 3 (2007): 208, https://doi.org/10.1177/1558689807302814.

90. Vicki L. Plano Clark and Manijeh Badiee, "Research Questions in Mixed Methods Research," in *SAGE Handbook of Mixed Methods in Social & Behavioral Research*, ed. Abbas Tashakkori and Charles Teddlie (Thousand Oaks: Sage, 2015); Abbas Tashakkori and John W. Creswell, "Exploring the Nature of Research Questions in Mixed Methods Research," *Journal of Mixed Methods Research* 1, no. 3 (2007): 208, https://doi.org/10.1177/1558689807302814.

91. Jo Moran-Ellis et al., "Triangulation and Integration: Processes, Claims and Implications," *Qualitative Research* 6, no. 1 (2006): 56, https://doi.org/10.1177/1468794106058870.

92. Michael D. Fetters, Leslie A. Curry, and John W. Creswell, "Achieving Integration in Mixed Methods Designs—Principles and Practices," *Health Services Research* 48,

no. 6 (2013): 2144, https://doi.org/10.1111/1475-6773.12117. Cf. Creswell and Plano Clark, *Designing and Conducting*, 224.

93. Charles Teddlie and Abbas Tashakkori, "A General Typology of Research Designs Featuring Mixed Methods," *Research in the Schools* 13, no. 1 (2006): 20.

1. WARS, CRIMES, AND JUSTICE IN THE BALKANS

1. RECOM Consultation no. 29.

2. Ger Duijzings, "Commemorating Srebrenica: Histories of Violence and the Politics of Memory in Eastern Bosnia," in *The New Bosnian Mosaic: Identities, Memories and Moral Claims in a Post-War Society*, ed. Xavier Bougarel, Elissa Helms, and Ger Duijzings (Farnham: Ashgate, 2007), 155; Ivor Sokolić, *International Courts and Mass Atrocity: Narratives of War and Justice in Croatia* (Basingstoke: Palgrave Macmillan, 2019), 207; Nicholas Moll, "Promoting 'Positive Stories' of Help and Rescue from the 1992–1995 War in Bosnia and Herzegovina," *Südosteuropa* 67, no. 4 (2019), https://doi.org/10.1515/soeu-2019-0036.

3. RECOM Consultation no. 24.

4. Vesna Pesic, *Serbian Nationalism and the Origins of the Yugoslav Crisis*, Peaceworks no. 8, United States Institute of Peace, April 1, 1996, https://www.usip.org/publications/1996/04/serbian-nationalism-and-origins-yugoslav-crisis.

5. For example, the number of ethnically mixed municipalities in Bosnia and Herzegovina decreased after the war. John O'Loughlin, "Inter-Ethnic Friendships in Post-War Bosnia-Herzegovina: Sociodemographic and Place Influences," *Ethnicities* 10, no. 1 (2010): 36, https://doi.org/10.1177/1468796809354153.

6. For example, the percentage of a Serb minority in the Croatian population went down from nearly 15 percent before the conflict to 4 percent after the conflict, see Dustin Tsai, "Navigating Exclusion as Enemies of the State: The Case of Serbs in Croatia and Croats in Serbia," *Geopolitics* (2021), https://doi.org/10.1080/14650045.2021.1881488.

7. Ivo Banac, "The Politics of National Homogeneity," in *War and Change in the Balkans: Nationalism, Conflict and Cooperation*, ed. Brad K. Blitz (Cambridge: Cambridge University Press, 2006), 30. Cf. James Gow, *Serbian Project and Its Adversaries: A Strategy of War Crimes* (London: Hurst & Company, 2003).

8. Harris Mylonas and Maya Tudor, "Nationalism: What We Know and What We still Need to Know," *Annual Review of Political Science* 24 (2021), https://doi.org/20.1146/annurev-polisci-041719-101841.

9. Torsten Kolind, "In Search of 'Decent' People: Resistance to Ethnicization of Everyday Life among the Muslims of Stolac," in Bougarel, Helms, and Duijzings, *The New Bosnian Mosaic*, 138. At the microlevel the incidence of interethnic violence varied in war-torn territories. The absence of mass violence and targeting of civilians in communities is attributed to the separation between their political and ethnic identities, see Mila Dragojević, *Amoral Communities: Collective Crimes in Time of War* (Ithaca: Cornell University Press, 2019), 47–49, or to the strength of historically anti-nationalist and class identities, as in Tuzla in Bosnia, see Goran Filic, "Rejection of Radical Nationalism in Wartime Yugoslavia: The Case of Tuzla (1990–1995)," *Journal of Peacebuilding and Development* 13, no. 3 (2019), https://doi.org/10.1080/15423166.2018.1516158.

10. V. P. Gagnon Jr., *The Myth of Ethnic War: Serbia and Croatia in the 1990s* (Ithaca: Cornell University Press, 2004).

11. For a selection of scholarly works on these debates, see Dejan Jovic, "The Disintegration of Yugoslavia: A Critical Review of Explanatory Approaches," *European Journal of Social Theory* 4, no. 1 (2001), https://doi.org/10.1177/13684310122225037; Sabrina P. Ramet, *Thinking about Yugoslavia: Scholarly Debates about the Yugoslav Breakup and the Wars*

in Bosnia and Kosovo (Cambridge: Cambridge University Press, 2005); Roger D. Petersen, *Western Intervention in the Balkans: The Strategic Use of Emotion in Conflict* (Cambridge: Cambridge University Press, 2011); Susan Woodward, *Balkan Tragedy: Chaos and Dissolution after the Cold War* (Washington, DC: Brookings Institution, 1995); Mary Kaldor, *New and Old Wars: Organised Violence in a Global Era* (Cambridge: Polity Press, 1999).

12. Henceforth, Bosnia is used as a shortened form for Bosnia and Herzegovina. After Yugoslavia's breakup, Macedonia was referred to as the Former Yugoslav Republic of Macedonia because of the name dispute with Greece. Following the UN-brokered agreement in 2018, its name became North Macedonia.

13. Cosmopolitan and consumerist culture in former Yugoslavia evolved in connection with global developments. Marie-Janine Calic, *The Great Cauldron: A History of Southeastern Europe* (Cambridge, MA: Harvard University Press: 2019), 491–502.

14. On nationalism reinforced by administrative arrangements and nationalist tensions, see Sabrina P. Ramet, *Nationalism and Federalism in Yugoslavia, 1962–1991* (Bloomington: Indiana University Press, 1992), 2nd ed., 176–213; on the role of national identification in mundane, everyday practices, see Stef Jansen, "National Numbers in Context: Maps and Stats in Representations of the Post-Yugoslav Wars," *Identities* 12 no. 1 (2005), https://doi.org/10.1080/10702890590914311.

15. On Yugoslav nationalities policy and nationalism, see Ramet, *Nationalism and Federalism*, 40–58.

16. Perunovic challenges claims of intense ethnic attachments among ordinary people in former Yugoslavia, drawing on prewar ethnic/national social distance survey results. Sreca Perunovic, "Animosities in Former Yugoslavia before Its Demise: Revelations of an Opinion Poll Survey," *Ethnicities* 16, no. 6 (2016), https://doi.org/10.1177/1468796815576059.

17. Tomislav Dulić, "Ethnic Violence in Occupied Yugoslavia: Mass Killing from Above and Below," in *New Perspectives on Yugoslavia: Key Issues and Controversies*, ed. Dejan Djokić and James Ker-Lindsay (London: Routledge, 2011).

18. In practice, this approach also exacerbated ethnic grievances related to victimization in the Second World War, see Duijzings, "Commemorating Srebrenica." The disconnect between official and vernacular mnemonic practices in former Yugoslavia, which revealed and reinforced an ethnic dimension of wartime violence, paved the way for political manipulation in the late 1980s. Jelena Đureinović, *The Politics of Memory of the Second World War in Contemporary Serbia: Collaboration, Resistance and Retribution* (Abingdon: Routledge, 2020), 35–51. Political motivations undermined the compilation of a comprehensive record of victims of the Second World War in the former Yugoslavia, paving the way for the manipulation of past grievances in the run-up to the country's violent disintegration in the 1990s. Srđan Bogosavljević, "Nerasvetljeni genocid," in *Srpska strana rata: Trauma i katarza u istorijskom pamćenju*, ed. Nebojša Popov (Beograd: BIGZ, 1996).

19. Ramet, *Nationalism and Federalism*, 55.

20. Jasna Dragović-Soso, *"Saviours of the Nation": Serbia's Intellectual Opposition and the Revival of Nationalism* (London: Hurst & Company, 2002); Nebojša Vladisavljević, *Serbia's Antibureaucratic Revolution: Milošević, the Fall of Communism and Nationalist Mobilization* (Basingstoke: Palgrave Macmillan, 2008).

21. Orli Fridman, "'It Was Like Fighting a War with Our Own People': Anti—War Activism in Serbia during the 1990s," *Nationalities Papers* 39, no. 4 (2011), https://doi.org/10.1080/00905992.2011.579953.

22. David Campbell, *National Deconstruction: Violence, Identity, and Justice in Bosnia* (Minneapolis: University of Minnesota Press, 1998); Gerard Toal and Carl T. Dahlman, *Bosnia Remade: Ethnic Cleansing and Its Reversal* (Cambridge: Cambridge University Press, 2011), 84–111; Jansen, "National Numbers," 48.

23. Tone Bringa, *Being Muslim the Bosnian Way: Identity and Community in a Central Bosnian Village* (Princeton: Princeton University Press, 1995). On everyday ethnicization, defined as "the fusion of ethnic or cultural and political identity," following from top-down elite ethnicization, see Dragojević, *Amoral Communities*, 19, 33–91.

24. A group name—Bosnian Muslims—refers to one of the three dominant ethnic groups who were constituent nations in Bosnia and Herzegovina. Although the name refers to a religion, not all Bosnian Muslims are religious. In the early 1990s, the Bosnian Muslim political and intellectual elite changed the group's name to Bosniaks (which should not be confused with Bosnians, the term that refers to all citizens of Bosnia and Herzegovina). Neven Andjelic, *Bosnia-Herzegovina: The End of a Legacy* (London: Frank Cass, 2003), 147 and 188–211. Bosnian Muslim and Bosniak are used interchangeably in this book.

25. For a detailed discussion of the complexities involved in establishing the death toll, see Ewa Tabeau, ed., *Conflict in Numbers: Casualties of the 1990s Wars in the Former Yugoslavia (1991–1999)* (Belgrade: Helsinki Committee for Human Rights, 2009). Human rights NGOs in the region have made a major contribution to recording war casualties. For example, see Istraživačko Dokumentacioni Centar, "Bosanska knjiga mrtvih," http://www.mnemos.ba/ba/home/Download, and Humanitarian Law Center (Serbia) and Humanitarian Law Center Kosovo, "The Kosovo Memory Book 1998–2000," http://www.kosovomemorybook.org/?page_id=29&lang=de.

26. There are still some 10,000 people still missing from the conflicts in the region. For the breakdown by country tracking the progress of identification since the end of the wars, see International Committee of the Red Cross, "ICRC Five-Year Strategy on the Missing in former Yugoslavia" (November 26, 2020), https://www.icrc.org/en/document/missing-bosnia-herzegovina-croatia-serbia-kosovo.

27. Ivana Maček, *Sarajevo under Siege: Anthropology in Wartime* (Philadelphia: University of Pennsylvania Press, 2009), 208.

28. For example, in Bosnia and Herzegovina, see Denisa Kostovicova, "Republika Srpska and its Boundaries in Bosnian Serb Geographical Narratives in the Post-Dayton Period," *Space and Polity* 8, no. 3 (2004), https://doi.org/10.1080/1356257042000309616.

29. Jasna Dragović-Soso and Eric Gordy, "Coming to Terms with the Past: Transitional Justice and Reconciliation in the Post-Yugoslav Lands," in *New Perspectives on Yugoslavia: Key Issues and Controversies*, ed. Dejan Djokić and James Ker-Lindsay (London: Routledge, 2011), 193.

30. For a comprehensive analysis of public perceptions of victimhood in the Balkans, see Marko Milanović, "The Impact of the ICTY on the Former Yugoslavia: An Anticipatory Postmortem," *American Journal of International Law* 110, no. 2 (2016): 243–45, https://doi.org/10.5305/amerjintelaw.110.2.0233.

31. Jelena Subotić, *Hijacked Justice: Dealing with the Past in the Balkans* (Ithaca: Cornell University Press, 2009).

32. After its closure, the functions of the ICTY were taken over by the International Residual Mechanism for Criminal Tribunals. For example, see Vjeran Pavlaković, "Croatia, the International Criminal Tribunal for the Former Yugoslavia, and General Gotovina as a Political Symbol," *Europe-Asia Studies* 62, no. 10 (2010), https://doi.org/10.1080/09668136.2010.522426.

33. James Meernik, "Victor's Justice or the Law?: Judging and Punishing at the International Criminal Tribunal for the Former Yugoslavia," *Journal of Conflict Resolution* 47, no. 2 (2003), https://doi.org/10.1177/0022002702251024.

34. Janine Natalya Clark, *International Trials and Reconciliation: Assessing the Impact of the International Criminal Tribunal for the Former Yugoslavia* (London: Routledge, 2014). For a selection of comprehensive evaluations of the ICTY and its legacy, see Carsten

Stahn, Carmel Agius, Serge Brammerz, and Colleen Rohan, eds., *Legacies of the International Criminal Tribunal for the Former Yugoslavia: A Multidisciplinary Approach* (Oxford: Oxford University Press, 2020); James Gow, Rachel Kerr, and Zoran Pajić, eds., *Prosecuting War Crimes: Lessons and Legacies of the International Criminal Tribunal for the Former Yugoslavia* (London: Routledge, 2013); Timothy William Waters, ed., *The Milošević Trial: An Autopsy* (New York: Oxford University Press, 2014).

35. Maja Munivrana Vajda, "Domestic Trials for International Crimes—A Critical Analysis of Croatian War Crimes Sentencing Jurisprudence," *International Criminal Law Review* 19, no. 1 (2019), https://doi.org/10.1163/15718123-01901002. See also *Četvrti izveštaj o sprovođenju Nacionalne strategije za procesuiranje ratnih zločina* (Beograd: Fond za humanitarno pravo, 2019).

36. Bogdan Ivanišević, *The War Crimes Chamber in Bosnia and Herzegovina: From Hybrid to Domestic Court* (New York: International Center for Transitional Justice, 2008), 10; *Tranziciona pravda u postjugoslavenskim zemljama: Izvještaj za 2010–2011. godinu* (Sarajevo: Udruženje "Tranzicijska pravda, odgovornost i sjećanje u BiH," 2012).

37. Jasna Dragovic-Soso, "History of a Failure: Attempts to Create a National Truth and Reconciliation Commission in Bosnia and Herzegovina, 1997–2006," *International Journal of Transitional Justice* 10, no. 2 (2016), https://doi.org/10.1093/ijtj/ijw005.

38. Brian Grodsky, "International Prosecutions and Domestic Politics: The Use of Truth Commissions as Compromise Justice in Serbia and Croatia," *International Studies Review* 11, no 4 (2009), http://www.jstor.org/stable/40389162.

39. Dragović-Soso and Gordy, "Coming to Terms."

40. Catherine Baker, *The Yugoslav Wars of the 1990s* (London: Palgrave Macmillan, 2015), 96.

41. Hariz Halilovich, *Places of Pain: Forced Displacement, Popular Memory and Trans-Local Identities in Bosnian War-Torn Communities* (New York: Berghahn Books, 2013), 94.

42. Orli Fridman, "Alternative Calendars and Memory Work in Serbia: Anti-War Activism after Milošević," *Memory Studies* 8, no. 2 (2015), https://doi.org/10.1177/1750698014558661.

43. Eric Gordy, *Guilt, Responsibility, and Denial: The Past at Stake in Post-Milošević Serbia* (Philadelphia: University of Pennsylvania Press, 2013), 68.

44. Adam Kochanski and Joanna R. Quinn, "Letting the State off the Hook? Dilemmas of Holding the State to Account in Times of Transition," *Peacebuilding* 9, no. 2 (2021), https://doi.org/10.1080/21647259.2021.1895616.

45. Eunice Castro Seixas, "How Activists See Civil Society and the Political Elite in Bosnia: Relevance to Prospects of Transitional Justice," in *Transitional Justice and Civil Society in the Balkans*, ed. Olivera Simić and Zara Volčič (New York: Springer, 2013).

46. On nationalist opposition to transitional justice from civil society groups in Serbia and Croatia, respectively, see Denisa Kostovicova, "Civil Society and Post-Communist Democratization: Facing a Double Challenge in Post-Milošević Serbia," *Journal of Civil Society* 2, no. 1 (2006), https://doi.org/10.1080/17448680600730918, and Ivor Sokolić, Denisa Kostovicova, and Adam Fagan, "Civil Society in Post-Yugoslav Space: The Test of Discontinuity and Democratization," in *The Legacy of Yugoslavia: Politics, Economics and Society in the Modern Balkans*, ed. Othon Anastasakis, Adam Bennett, David Madden, and Adis Merdzanovic (London: I.B. Taurus, 2020).

47. On the paucity of research on antiwar civil society activism in former Yugoslavia, see Bojan Bilić, "(Post-)Yugoslav Anti-War Engagement: A Research Topic Awaiting Attention," *Filozofija i društvo* 22, no. 4 (2011), https://doi.org/10.2298/FID1104083B.

48. Boris Kanzleiter, "Anti-War Activism, Yugoslavia, 1990s," in *The International Encyclopedia of Revolution and Protest*, ed. Immanuel Ness (Chichester: Blackwell, 2009); Mary Kaldor and Denisa Kostovicova, "Global Civil Society and Illiberal Regimes," in *Global*

Civil Society 2007/8: Communicative Power and Democracy, ed. Martin Albrow, Helmut K. Anheier, Marlies Glasius, Monroe E. Price, and Mary Kaldor (London: Sage, 2007).

49. Nataša Kandić, "RECOM: A New Approach to Reconciliation and a Corrective for Criminal Justice," *Forum for Transitional Justice* 4 (2012).

50. According to the Coalition, the membership included 461 NGOs, associations, civic groups, and 1,357 individuals. See Coalition Members, *Documents*, Inicijativa za REKOM, http://www.zarekom.org/documents/Coalition-members.en.html?page=1, quoted in Denisa Kostovicova, "Airing Crimes, Marginalizing Victims: Political Expectations and Transitional Justice in Kosovo," in *The Milošević Trial: An Autopsy*, ed. Timothy William Waters (Oxford: Oxford University Press, 2013), 252. Some human rights organizations were not formally members of the Coalition, but their representatives participated in the RECOM consultation process.

51. Anna Di Lellio and Caitlin McCunn, "Engineering Grassroots Transitional Justice in the Balkans: The Case of Kosovo," *East European Politics and Societies* 27, no. 1 (2013), https://doi.org/10.1177/0888325412464550.

52. See *Statut Koalicije za REKOM* (June 26, 2011), http://recom.link/wp-content/uploads/2011/06/Statut-Koalicije-za-REKOM-26.06.2011-SRB.pdf.

53. For detailed justification of terminology and provisions of the Draft Statute, see Koalicija za REKOM, *Obrazloženja uz Predlog Statuta regionalne komisije za utvrđivanje činjenica o ratnim zločinima i drugim teškim kršenjima ljudskih prava na području nekadašnje SFRJ* (March 26, 2011).

54. RECOM Consultation no. 23.

55. RECOM Consultation no. 24.

56. Iavor Rangelov and Ruti Teitel, "Transitional Justice," in *The Handbook of Global Security Policy*, ed. Mary Kaldor and Iavor Rangelov (Chichester: John Wiley & Sons, 2014).

57. Author's interview no. 8, Serbia, September 16, 2014.

58. RECOM Consultation no. 23.

59. For example, a commentator described Serbia's transitional justice policy as "schizophrenic" because it "supports both war crimes and war criminals, and reconciliation in the region." Safeta Biševac, "Kazani i mural," *Danas*, November 17, 2021, https://www.danas.rs/kolumna/safeta-bisevac/kazani-i-mural/.

60. RECOM Consultation no. 23.

61. Frédéric Mégret, "Do Facts Exist, Can They Be 'Found,' and Does It Matter?," in *The Transformation of Human Rights Fact-Finding*, ed. Philip Aston and Sarah Knuckey (Oxford: Oxford University Press, 2016), 30.

62. RECOM Consultation no. 26.

63. RECOM Consultation no. 24.

64. RECOM Consultation no. 23. For a comprehensive examination of justifications for RECOM's regional approach, see Denisa Kostovicova, "Seeking Justice in a Divided Region: Text Analysis of a Regional Civil Society Initiative in the Balkans," *International Journal of Transitional Justice* 11, no. 1 (2017), https://doi.org/10.1093/ijtj/ijw023.

65. RECOM Consultation no. 24.

66. RECOM Consultation no. 23.

67. Caterina Bonora, "The Question of Gender Inclusiveness of Bottom-Up Strategies in Bosnia and Herzegovina," in *New Critical Spaces in Transitional Justice*, ed. Arnaud Kurze and Christopher K. Lamont (Bloomington: Indiana University Press, 2019), 145.

68. Author's interview no. 24, Croatia, December 16, 2019.

69. Author's interview no. 19, Montenegro, September 2, 2016.

70. Author's interview no. 22, Croatia, December 15, 2019.

71. As one participant said, diversity was evident even in the "accents and dialects of the people who came from different parts of the former Yugoslavia." RECOM Consultation no. 26.

72. Nicholas R. Micinski, "NGO Frequent Flyers: Youth Organisations and the Undermining of Reconciliation in Bosnia and Herzegovina," *Journal of Peacebuilding & Development* 11, no. 1 (2016): 102, https://dx.doi.org/10.1080/15423166.2016.1143789.

73. Jacqueline Nießer, *Die Wahrheit der Anderen: Transnationale Vergangenheitsaufarbeitung in Post-Jugoslawien am Beispiel der REKOM Initiative* (Göttingen: Vandenhoeck & Ruprecht, 2020).

74. Author's interview no. 7, Serbia, September 26, 2014.

75. For a detailed discussion of the mandates of truth commissions, see Pablo de Greiff, "'Truth without Facts': On the Erosion of the Fact-Finding Function of Truth Commissions," in *The Transformation*, ed. Philip Alston and Sarah Knuckey (Oxford: Oxford University Press, 2016), 284.

76. *Statut Koalicije za REKOM.*

77. Author's interview no. 7, Serbia, September 26, 2014.

78. RECOM Consultation no. 27.

79. Author's interview no. 1, Serbia, November 16, 2013.

80. Author's interview no. 7, Serbia, September 26, 2014.

81. RECOM Consultation no. 24.

82. RECOM Consultation no. 1.

83. *Proces REKOM: Izvještaj*, May 2006–August 2011, https://recom.link/wp-content/uploads/2011/08/Proces_REKOM-Izvestaj-maj_2006-avgust_2011-15_09_2011-logo-BiH.pdf.

84. Jill A. Irvine and Patrice C. McMahon, "From International Courts to Grassroots Organizing: Obstacles to Transitional Justice in the Balkans," in *Transitional Justice and Civil Society in the Balkans*, ed. Olivera Simić and Zara Volčič (New York: Springer: 2013), 222–27. For example, for details of a discussion that revolved around how to define a "victim" for the purpose of regional fact-finding, see Arnaud Kurze and Iva Vukusic, "Afraid to Cry Wolf: Human Rights Activists' Struggle of Transnational Accountability Efforts in the Balkans," in Simić and Volčič, *Transitional Justice*, 210–11.

85. Author's interview no. 1, Serbia, November 16, 2013.

86. Author's interview no. 24, Croatia, December 16, 2019.

87. *Proces REKOM: Izvještaj*. For criticism of the gender dimension of the consultation process and the Draft Statute, see Denisa Kostovicova and Tom Paskhalis, "Gender, Justice and Deliberation: Why Women Don't Influence Peace-Making," *International Studies Quarterly* 65, no. 2 (2021), https://doi.org/10.1093/isq/sqab003. Cf. Bonora, "The Question."

88. The Draft Statute subsequently underwent minor amendments at the RECOM Assembly meeting in 2014. *Izmene Statuta REKOM* (November 14, 2014), http://recom.link/sr/izmene-statuta-rekom-28-oktobar-2014-2/. These amendments were part of the institutionalization process of the RECOM initiative through engagement with envoys from the former Yugoslav states.

89. Irvine and McMahon, "From International," 226.

90. See Bojan Bilić, *Borile smo se za vazduh: (Post)jugoslovenski antiratni aktivizam i njegovo nasleđe* (Zagreb: Documenta, Kuća ljudskih prava Zagreb & Naklada Jesenski i Turk, 2015), 162–65, originally published as *We Were Gasping for Air: [Post-]Yugoslav Anti-War Activism and Its Legacy* (Baden-Baden: Nomos, 2012). See also Jacqueline Nießer, *Die Wahrheit der Anderen: Transnationale Vergangenheitsaufarbeitung in Post-Jugoslawien am Beispiel der REKOM Initiative* (Göttingen: Vandenhoeck & Ruprecht, 2020), 260–64.

91. Jamie Rowen, "Mobilizing Truth: Agenda Setting in a Transnational Social Movement," *Law & Social Inquiry* 37, no. 3 (2012), https://doi.org/10.1111/j.1747-4469.2012.01317.x.

92. Focus Group, Sarajevo, Bosnia and Herzegovina, December 11, 2015.

93. They explained, in relation to the rules about discharging the grants, that the "European Commission has such strict rules that not a single Euro, or a Dinar [Serbian currency] can be spent except how it is stipulated and all spending has to be accounted for in the audit by an independent international company." RECOM Consultation no. 5.

94. In some cases organizations formally left the RECOM Coalition, but their representatives continued to participate in the consultation process.

95. Focus Group, Sarajevo, Bosnia and Herzegovina, December 11, 2015.

96. For a comprehensive overview of the criticism and RECOM's response, see Igor Mekina, "Analiza javne kritike i podrške Inicijative za osnivanje REKOM," 2011, accessed September 19, 2021, https://documenta.hr/wp-content/uploads/2019/11/rekom_javno_zagovaranje_08_f_2826_hr.pdf.

97. Zvonimir Despot, "REKOM-regionalna komisija koja želi zamagliti istinu o srbijanskoj agresiji," *Večernji list*, October 20, 2010, https://blog.vecernji.hr/zvonimir-despot/rekom-regionalna-komisija-koja-zeli-zamagliti-istinu-o-srbijanskoj-agresiji-925. Kostovicova, "Airing Crimes."

98. Branislav Ristivojević, "Nacrt statuta REKOM-a iz ugla Ustava RS i njenih krivičnopravnih propisa," *Nova srpska politička misao*, May 21, 2011, http://www.nspm.rs/istina-i-pomirenje-na-ex-yu-prostorima/nacrt-statuta-rekom-a-iz-ugla-ustava-rs-i-njenih-krivicnopravnih-propisa.html/.

99. Mekina, "Analiza."

100. RECOM Consultation no. 3.

101. Author's interview no. 21, Serbia, November 14, 2016.

102. Focus Group, Sarajevo, Bosnia and Herzegovina, December 11, 2015.

103. RECOM Consultation no. 25.

104. RECOM Reconciliation Network, "What Is RECOM Process?," 2021, https://www.recom.link/en/what-is-recom-process-3/.

105. The EU has been reluctant to use its leverage to compel the post-Yugoslav states to commit to the regional commission. Furthermore, Croatia's accession to the EU was used by the authorities to disassociate Croatia from the legacy of the war, further hindering regional justice-seeking promoted by RECOM.

106. Joanna R. Quinn, *Thin Sympathy: A Strategy to Thicken Transitional Justice* (Philadelphia: University of Pennsylvania Press, 2021), 40.

107. Eric Gordy's comment at "Reconciliation Policies and Their Results in the Western Balkans: A 30-Year Perspective," Foreign Policy Forum, Zagreb, October 20, 2021, https://www.youtube.com/watch?v=PWFN-oEnEXw.

108. Author's interview no. 1, Serbia, November 16, 2013.

109. On contestation of forensic facts and denial narratives in Bosnia and Herzegovina, see Victor Toom, "Ontologically Dirty Knots: The Production of Numbers after the Srebrenica Genocide," *Security Dialogue* 51, no. 4 (2020), https://doi.org/10.1177/0967010620902008.

110. Isabelle Delpla, "In the Midst of Injustice: The ICTY from the Perspective of Some Victim Associations," in Bougarel, Helms, and Duijzings, *The New Bosnian Mosaic*, 234.

111. Aida A. Hozić, "Writing after the Genocide: Lessons from Srebrenica and the Meaning of Community after Violence," *Journal of Muslim Minority Affairs* 35 no 3 (2015): 426, https://doi.org/10.1080/13602004.2015.1073957.

112. Kolind, "In Search," 137–38.

113. For example, in ethnically divided Kosovo, see Francesco Trupia, "'Good Person-hood' in Kosovo: A Serbian Perspective from Below," *Peacebuilding* 9, no. 4 (2021): 425–40, https://doi.org/10.1080/21647259.2021.1895605.

114. Zdravko Grebo, "!Uspjećemo," *!Glas Inicijative za REKOM*, February 20, 2015, 2.

2. BRINGING IDENTITIES INTO POSTCONFLICT DELIBERATION

1. David Moshman, "Identity, Genocide, and Group Violence," in *Handbook of Identity Theory and Research*, ed. Seth J. Schwartz, Koen Luyckx, and Vivian L. Vignoles, vol. 5, *Domains and Categories* (New York: Springer, 2012), 928.

2. André Bächtiger and John Parkinson, *Mapping and Measuring Deliberation: Towards a New Deliberative Quality* (Oxford: Oxford University Press, 2019), 56. Gutmann and Thompson also highlight the inadequacy of an exclusively procedural approach to deliberation in the face of the moral complexity of democratic politics. Amy Gutmann and Dennis Thompson, *Why Deliberative Democracy?* (Princeton: Princeton University Press, 2004), 119–24.

3. James Paul Gee, *An Introduction to Discourse Analysis: Theory and Method*, 4th ed. (London: Routledge, 2014), 24.

4. Jürgen Habermas, *The Theory of Communicative Action*. vol. 1, *Reason and the Rationalization of Society* (Cambridge: Polity Press, [1984] 2004).

5. Zsuzsanna Chappell, *Deliberative Democracy: A Critical Introduction* (Basingstoke: Palgrave Macmillan, 2012), 26.

6. Dennis F. Thompson, "Deliberative Democratic Theory and Empirical Political Science," *Annual Review of Political Science* 11, no. 1 (2008), https://doi.org/10.1146/annurev.polisci.11.081306.070555; Michael A. Neblo, "Impassioned Democracy: The Roles of Emotion in Deliberative Theory," *American Political Science Review* 114, no. 3 (2020): 923, https://doi.org/10.1017/S0003055420000210.

7. Robert Talisse, "Deliberation," in *The Oxford Handbook of Political Philosophy*, ed. David Estlund (Oxford: Oxford University Press, 2012).

8. André Bächtiger and Jürgen Steiner, "Introduction," *Acta Politica* 40, no. 2 (2005): 156, https://doi.org/10.1057/palgrave.ap.5500108.

9. Amy Gutmann and Dennis F. Thomson, *Democracy and Disagreement* (Cambridge: Harvard University Press, 1996).

10. Jane Mansbridge et al., "The Place of Self-Interest and the Role of Power in Deliberative Democracy," *Journal of Political Philosophy* 18, no. 1 (2010): 78–79, https://doi.org/10.1111/j.1467-9760.2009.00344.x.

11. Michael Neblo, "Thinking through Democracy: Between the Theory and Practice of Deliberative Politics," *Acta Politica* 40 (2005): 175, https://doi.org/10.1057/palgrave.ap.5500102.

12. Robert E. Goodin, "How Can Deliberative Democracy Get a Grip?," *Political Quarterly* 83, no. 4 (2012): 806, https://doi.org/10.1111/j.1467-923X.2012.02356.x.

13. Diana C. Mutz, "Is Deliberative Democracy a Falsifiable Theory?," *Annual Review of Political Science* 11 (2008): 523, https://doi.org/10.1146/annurev.polisci.11.081306.070308.

14. Manlio Cinalli and Ian O'Flynn, "Public Deliberation, Network Analysis and the Political Integration of Muslims in Britain," *British Journal of Politics and International Relations* 16, no. 3 (2014): 431, https://doi.org/10.1111/1467-856X.12003.

15. John S. Dryzek, "Deliberative Democracy in Divided Societies: Alternatives to Agonism and Analgesia," *Political Theory* 33, no. 2 (2005), https://doi.org/10.1177/0090591704268372; Ian O'Flynn, *Deliberative Democracy and Divided Societies*

(Edinburgh: Edinburgh University Press, 2006); Jürg Steiner, *The Foundations of Deliberative Democracy: Empirical Research and Normative Implications* (Cambridge: Cambridge University Press, 2012); Didier Caluwaerts and Kris Deschouwer, "Building Bridges across Political Divides: Experiments on Deliberative Democracy in Deeply Divided Belgium," *European Political Science Review* 6, no. 3 (2014), https://doi.org/10.1017/ S17553913000179.

16. Donald G. Ellis, *Deliberative Communication and Ethnopolitical Conflict* (New York, Washington, DC: Peter Lang, 2012), 17.

17. Gutmann and Thompson, *Democracy and Disagreement*, 9, 89; Magdalena Dembinska and Françoise Montambeault, "Deliberation for Reconciliation in Divided Societies," *Journal of Public Deliberation* 11, no. 1 (2015), https://doi.org/10.16997/jdd.226; Bashir Bashir, "Accommodating Historically Oppressed Social Groups: Deliberative Democracy and the Politics of Reconciliation," in *The Politics of Reconciliation in Multicultural Societies*, ed. Will Kymlicka and Bashir Bashir (Oxford: Oxford University Press, 2008).

18. James Bohman, "Transnationalizing Peacebuilding: Transitional Justice as a Deliberative Process," in *Jus Post Bellum and Transitional Justice*, ed. Larry May and Elizabeth Edenberg (Cambridge: Cambridge University Press, 2013); Kora Andrieu, "Political Liberalism after Mass Violence: John Rawls and a 'Theory' of Transitional Justice," in *Transitional Justice Theories*, ed. Susane Buckley-Zistel, Teresa Koloma Beck, Christian Braun, and Friederike Mieth (New York: Routledge, 2014).

19. Bächtiger and Steiner, "Introduction," 40.

20. Steiner, *The Foundations*, 14.

21. Thompson, "Deliberative Democratic Theory," 502.

22. Jane J. Mansbridge, *Beyond Adversary Democracy* (New York: Basic Books, 1980); Katherine Cramer Walsh, *Talking about Politics: Informal Groups and Social Identity in American Life* (Chicago: University of Chicago Press, 2004).

23. Caluwaerts and Deschouwer, "Building Bridges," 446.

24. Alain Noël, "Democratic Deliberation in Multinational Federation," *Critical Review of International Social and Political Philosophy* 9, no. 3 (2006), https://doi. org/10.1080/13698230600901212; Dryzek, "Deliberative Democracy."

25. Dryzek, "Deliberative Democracy"; Juan E. Ugarriza, "When War Adversaries Talk: The Experimental Effect of Engagement Rules on Postconflict Deliberation," *Latin American Politics and Society* 58, no. 3 (2016): 78. https://doi.org//10.1111/j.1548-2456.2016.00319.x.

26. Cass R. Sunstein, "Deliberative Trouble? Why Groups Go to Extremes," *Yale Law Journal* 110, no. 71 (2000), https://www.yalelawjournal.org/essay/deliberative-trouble-why-groups-go-to-extremes.

27. Ron Levy, Ian O'Flynn, and Hoi L. Kong, *Deliberative Peace Referendums* (Oxford: Oxford University Press, 2021), 12.

28. Robert Huckfeldt and John Sprague, *Citizens, Politics, and Social Communication: Information and Influence in an Election Campaign* (Cambridge: Cambridge University Press, 1995); Bernard Manin, "Democratic Deliberation: Why We Should Promote Debate Rather Than Discussion" (paper presented at the Program in Ethics and Public Affairs Seminar, Princeton University, October 13, 2005), 20, https://nyuscholars.nyu.edu/en/ publications/deliberation-why-we-should-focus-on-debate-rather-than-discussion.

29. Neblo has challenged the claim that reason and emotion are incompatible, outlining different ways in which emotion can facilitate democratic deliberation; see Neblo, "Impassioned Democracy." When deliberative democrats consider adverse effects of emotions on deliberation in postconflict societies, they specifically refer to negative emotions related to the experience of intergroup violence, such as hatred and anger toward outgroup members.

30. Tali Mendelberg and John Oleske, "Race and Public Deliberation," *Political Communication* 17, no. 2 (2000): 173, https://doi.org/10.1080/105846000198468.

31. Anna Drake and Allison McCulloch, "Deliberative Consociationalism in Deeply Divided Societies," *Contemporary Political Theory* 10, no. 3 (2011): 373, https://doi.org/10.1057/cpt.2010.22.

32. Dryzek, "Deliberative Democracy"; O'Flynn, *Deliberative Democracy*.

33. Addressing the puzzle of pluralism and stability, consociationalism, conceptualized by Arendt Lijphart, institutionalizes power-sharing among elites and segmental autonomy between divided groups. Arendt Lijphart, *Democracy in Plural Societies: A Comparative Exploration* (New Haven: Yale University Press, 1977).

34. O'Flynn, *Deliberative Democracy*, 141–42, 151.

35. Didier Caluwaerts and Min Reuchamps, "Does Inter-Group Deliberation Foster Inter-Group Appreciation? Evidence from Two Experiments in Belgium," *Politics* 34, no. 2 (2014), https://doi.org/10.1111/1467-9256.12043.

36. Steiner, *The Foundations*, 247.

37. James S. Fishkin, *When the People Speak: Deliberative Democracy and Public Consultation* (Oxford: Oxford University Press, 2009); Robert C. Luskin, Ian O'Flynn, James S. Fishkin, and David Russell, "Deliberating across Deep Divides," *Political Studies* 62, no. 1 (2014), https://doi.org/10.1111/j.1467-9248.2012.01005.x. Cf. Cinalli and O'Flynn, "Public Deliberation."

38. Juan E. Ugarriza and Enzo Nussio, "There Is No Pill for Deliberation: Explaining Discourse Quality in Post-Conflict Communities," *Swiss Political Science Review* 22, no. 1 (2015), https://doi.org/10.1111/spsr.12195. However, further research is needed to establish how different types of conflict and division impact postconflict deliberation, specifically distinguishing divisions based on ethnicity as opposed to a division based on ideology.

39. Dryzek, "Deliberative Democracy"; O'Flynn, *Deliberative Democracy*, 31; Steiner, *The Foundations*.

40. Caluwaerts and Deschouwer, "Building Bridges," 448. See also Jürg Steiner, Maria Clara Jaramillo, Rousiley C. M. Maia, and Simona Mameli, *Deliberation across Deeply Divided Societies: Transformative Moments* (Cambridge: Cambridge University Press, 2017), 253.

41. As in the study of parliaments where democratic deliberation originated, these conditions point to the effect of decision rules (a consensus and a majority vote). Juan E. Ugarriza, "When War Adversaries Talk: The Experimental Effect of Engagement Rules on Postconflict Deliberation," *Latin American Politics and Society* 58, no. 3 (2016), https://doi.org/10.1111/j/1548-2456.2016.00319.x.

42. André Bächtiger et al., "Disentangling Diversity in Deliberative Democracy: Competing Theories, Their Blindspots and Complementarities," *Journal of Political Philosophy* 18, no. 1 (2010): 32, https://doi.org/10.1111/j.1467-9760.2009.00342.x.

43. Fishkin, *When the People Speak*, 161–63.

44. Ian O'Flynn, "Review Article: Divided Societies and Deliberative Democracy," *British Journal of Political Science* 37, no. 4 (2007): 731, https://doi.org/10.1017/S0007123407000397.

45. Juan E. Ugarriza and Natalia Trujillo-Orrego, "The Ironic Effect of Deliberation: What We Can (and Cannot) Expect in Deeply Divided Societies," *Acta Politica* 55 (2020): 223, https://doi.org/10.1057/s41269-018-0113-1.

46. For an attempt to specify the diffusion of deliberative outcomes, see Dembinska and Montambeault, "Deliberation for Reconciliation."

47. Donatella della Porta, "Deliberation in Movement: Why and How to Study Deliberative Democracy and Social Movements," *Acta Politica* 40 (2005): 348, https://doi.org/10.1057/palgrave.ap.5500116.

48. Exceptionally, Levy, O'Flynn, and Kong's discussion of deliberative peace referendums engages with different categories of conflicts, including group sovereignty conflict, secessionist conflict, and indigenous settler conflict. Levy, O'Flynn, and Kong, *Deliberative Peace*. For lack of engagement with conflict studies by transitional justice scholars, see Denisa Kostovicova, "Transitional Justice and Conflict Studies: Bridging the Divide," *Journal of Global Security Studies* 4, no. 2 (2019), https://doi.org/10.1093/jogss/ogz003. For the siloed nature of peace and conflict studies, characterized by the lack of dialogue between the scholars of peace and the scholars of conflict, see John Gledhill and Jonathan Bright, "A Divided Discipline? Mapping Peace and Conflict Studies," *International Studies Perspectives* 19, no. 2 (2018), https://doi.org/10.1093/isp/ekx009.

49. Dryzek, "Deliberative Democracy," 219.

50. Horowitz writes about "the permeative propensity of ethnic affiliations in divided societies" to find their way in the discussion of a range of issues from education to tax policy. Donald L. Horowitz, *Ethnic Groups in Conflict*, 2nd ed. (Berkeley: University of California Press, [1985] 2000), 8.

51. Luskin et al., "Deliberating across Deep Divides"; Steiner, *The Foundations*; Ugarriza, "When War Adversaries."

52. Baogang He, "A Deliberative Approach to the Tibet Autonomy Issue: Promoting Mutual Trust through Dialogue," *Asian Survey* 50, no. 4 (2010), https://doi.org/10.1525/as.2010.50.4.709. Others argued that deliberation in divided societies should avoid divisive issues and focus on "a common future rather than a violent past"; see Juan E. Ugarriza and Enzo Nussio, "The Effect of Perspective-Giving on Postconflict Reconciliation. An Experimental Approach," *Political Psychology* 38, no. 1 (2017): 15, https://www.jstor.org/stable/45094336. Others suggest topics such as "constructing bridges or arranging for water supply," see Dembinska and Montambeault, "Deliberation for Reconciliation," 17.

53. Luigi Bobbio, "Types of Deliberation," *Journal of Public Deliberation* 6, no. 2 (2010): 14, https://doi.org/10.16997/jdd.105.

54. For effects on conflict onset, duration, and termination, see Kathleen Gallagher Cunningham and Nils B. Weidmann, "Shared Space: Ethnic Groups, State Accommodation, and Localized Conflict," *International Studies Quarterly* 54, no. 4 (2010), https://doi.org/10.1111/j.1468-2478.2010.00625.x; Jose G. Montalvo and Marta Reynal-Querol, "Ethnic Polarization and the Duration of Civil Wars," *Economics of Governance* 11, no. 2 (2010), https://doi.org/10.1007/s10101-010-0077-8.

55. David E. Cunningham, *Barriers to Peace in Civil War* (Cambridge: Cambridge University Press, 2011), 197.

56. Jeffrey T. Checkel, "Transnational Dynamics of Civil War," in *Transnational Dynamics of Civil War*, ed. Jeffrey T. Checkel (Cambridge: Cambridge University Press, 2013).

57. Marie Allansson, Erik Melander, and Lotta Themnér, "Organized Violence, 1989–2016," *Journal of Peace Research* 54, no. 4 (2017): 576, https://doi.org/10.1177/0022343317718773; Peter Wallensteen and Margareta Sollenberg, "Armed Conflict and Regional Conflict Complexes, 1989–97," *Journal of Peace Research* 35, no. 5 (1998): 624, https://doi.org/10.1177/0022343398035005005; Nadine Ansorg, "How Does Militant Violence Diffuse in Regions? Regional Conflict Systems in International Relations and Peace and Conflict Studies," *International Journal of Conflict and Violence* 5, no. 1 (2011): 173, https://doi.org/10.4119/ijcv-2853.

58. Mary Kaldor, *New and Old Wars: Organized Violence in a Global Era* (Cambridge: Polity Press, 1999); Wallensteen and Sollenberg, "Armed Conflict," 625.

59. Vesna Bojicic-Dzelilovic and Denisa Kostovicova, "Introduction," in *Austrian Presidency of the EU: Regional Approaches to the Balkans*, ed. Denisa Kostovicova and Vesna Bojicic-Dzelilovic (Vienna: Centre for the Study of Global Governance, LSE, and

the Center for European Integration Strategies, 2006), 21–22; Chandra Lekha Sriram and Amy Ross, "Geographies of Crime and Justice: Contemporary Transitional Justice and the Creation of 'Zones of Impunity,'" *International Journal of Transitional Justice* 1, no. 1 (2007), https://doi.org/10.1093/ijtj/ijm001; Iavor Rangelov and Ruti Teitel, "Transitional Justice," in *The Handbook of Global Security Policy,* eds. Mary Kaldor and Iavor Rangelov (Chichester: Wiley Blackwell, 2014): 348.

60. Gallagher Cunningham and Weidmann, "Shared Space," 1040.

61. Conceiving identities as fixed attributes also neglects the possibility that some differences in attitudes can be explained by differences in the gradation of ethnic identities, see Henry E. Brady and Cynthia S. Kaplan, "Categorically Wrong? Nominal Versus Graded Measures of Ethnic Identity," *Studies in Comparative International Development* 35, no. 3 (2000), https://doi.org/10.0007/bf02699766. Similar problems beset the empirical study of reconciliation that rely on surveys; see James L. Gibson, *Overcoming Apartheid: Can Truth Reconcile a Divided Nation?* (New York: Russel Sage Foundation, 2004).

62. Rawi Abdelal, Yoshiko M. Herrera, Alastair Iain Johnston, and Rose McDermott, "Identity as a Variable," in *Measuring Identity: A Guide for Social Scientists*, ed. Rawi Abdelal, Yoshiko M. Herrera, Alastair Iain Johnston, and Rose McDermott (Cambridge: Cambridge University Press: 2009), 18. On a range of identity concepts in comparative politics, see Peter Brunland and Michael Horowitz, "Research Report on the Use of Identity Concepts in Comparative Politics" (unpublished manuscript, Harvard Identity Project, April 2003); James D. Fearon, "What Is Identity (as We Now Use the Word?)" (unpublished manuscript, Stanford University, California, November 3, 1999), https://web.stanford. edu/group/fearon-research/cgi-bin/wordpress/wp-content/uploads/2013/10/What-is-Identity-as-we-now-use-the-word-.pdf.

63. Seth J. Schwartz et al., "Methodological Issues in Ethnic and Racial Identity Research with Ethnic Minority Populations: Theoretical Precision, Measurement Issues, and Research Designs," *Child Development* 85, no. 1 (2014): 58, https://doi.org/10.1111/cdev.12201.

64. Fearon, "What Is Identity," 17.

65. Based on Allport's proposition that intergroup contact benefits intergroup relations; see Gordon W. Allport, *The Nature of Prejudice*, 25th ed. (New York: Basic Books: 1954).

66. Samuel L. Gaertner, Jeffrey Mann, Audrey Murrell, and John F. Dovidio, "Reducing Intergroup Bias: The Benefits of Recategorization," *Journal of Personality and Social Psychology* 57, no. 2 (1989), https://doi.org/10.1037/0022-3514.57.2.239; Samuel L. Gaertner et al., "The Common Ingroup Identity Model: Recategorization and the Reduction of Intergroup Bias," *European Review of Social Psychology* 4, no. 1 (1993), https://doi.org/10.1080/14792779343000004.

67. Chandra points to the stickiness of descent based-attitudes; see Kanchan Chandra, "How Ethnic Identities Change," *Constructivist Theories of Ethnic Politics*, ed. Kanchan Chandra (Oxford: Oxford University Press, 2012): 132–78. Similarly, Horowitz observes that "some notion of ascription, however diluted and affinity deriving from it are inseparable from the concept of ethnicity." Horowitz, *Ethnic Groups*, 52.

68. O'Flynn, *Deliberative Democracy*, 36. On difficulties in constructing a shared identity and resistance of group boundaries to change in conflict-affected societies, see Levy, O'Flynn, and Kong, *Deliberative Peace*, 134–41.

69. Thomas F. Pettigrew, "Intergroup Contact Theory," *Annual Review of Psychology* 49 (1998): 77, https://doi.org/10.1146/annurev.psych.49.1.65.

70. Moreover, Walker queries whether ethnic identity can and should be modified at all in efforts to reconstruct societies after conflict, because "for the victims of past injustice, their claim to identity may be precisely what is at stake" and should, therefore, be

"bolstered, not erased or mitigated under the banner of a collective citizenship identity." Kathryn Walker, "Resolving Debates over the Status of Ethnic Identities during Transitional Justice," *Contemporary Political Theory* 11, no. 1 (2012): 74, https://doi.org/10.1057/cpt.2011.7.

71. Peter J. Burke and Donald C. Reitzes, "The Link between Identity and Role Performance," *Social Psychology Quarterly* 44, no. 2 (1981): 84, https://doi.org/10.2307/3033704. For a broader discussion of whether identity and role are synonymous, see Robin Williams, *Making Identity Matter: Identity, Society and Social Interaction* (Durham: Sociologypress, 2000), 4.

72. Williams, *Making Identity*, 92. Cf. Hartmut B. Mokros, ed., *Interaction and Identity* (New Brunswick, NJ: Transaction Publishers, 1996). Interactionist perspectives on identity straddle the boundaries of sociology, social and discursive psychology, and ethnomethodology. For a seminal reconceptualization in the sociology of identity as an act explicable in relation to the interaction between the self and others, see Erving Goffman, *The Presentation of Self in Everyday Life* (Garden City: Doubleday, 1959). On symbolic and structural symbolic interactionism, see Richard T. Serpe and Sheldon Stryker, "The Symbolic Interactionist Perspective and Identity Theory," in *Handbook of Identity Theory and Research*, ed. Seth J. Schwartz, Koen Luyckx, and Vivian L. Vignoles, vol. 1, *Structures and Processes* (New York: Springer, 2012). On discourse, identity, and interaction, see Bethan Benwell and Elizabeth Stokoe, *Discourse and Identity* (Edinburgh: Edinburgh University Press, 2006), and Derek Edwards and Jonathan Potter, *Discursive Psychology* (London: Sage, 1992). Comprehensive theoretical and methodological accounts of identity studies are outlined in Charles Antaki and Sue Widdicombe, eds., *Identities in Talk* (London: Sage, 1998); Stephen Hester and William Housley, eds., *Language, Interaction and National Identity: Studies in the Social Organisation of National Identity in Talk-in-Interaction* (Aldershot: Ashgate, 2017).

73. Bronwyn Davies and Rom Harré, "Positioning: The Discursive Production of Selves," *Journal for the Theory of Social Behaviour* 20, no. 1 (1990), https://doi.org/10.1111/j.1468-5914.1990.tb00174.x. According to O'Doherty and Davidson, participants based their claims during deliberation on a range of "subject positions" that reflect different aspects of their identity (e.g., as an expert or a patient); see Kieran C. O'Doherty and Helen J. Davidson, "Subject Positioning and Deliberative Democracy: Understanding Social Processes Underlying Deliberation," *Journal for the Theory of Social Behaviour* 40, no. 2 (2010), https://doi.org/10.1111/j.1468-5914.2009.00429.x.

74. On the effect of conflict on constructing ethnic groups as victims, see Masi Noor, Nurit Shnabel, Samer Halabi, and Arie Nadler, "When Suffering Begets Suffering: The Psychology of Competitive Victimhood between Adversarial Groups in Violent Conflicts," *Personality and Social Psychology Review* 16, no. 4 (2012), https://doi.org/10.1177/1088868312440048. On salience of ethnic identification among groups in the Balkans, see Felicia Pratto et al., eds., *Shaping Social Identities after Violent Conflict: Youth in the Western Balkans* (Basingstoke: Palgrave Macmillan, 2017).

75. Mokros, "Introduction: From Information and Behavior to Interaction and Identity," in *Interaction and Identity*, 13.

76. Ann Weatherall, Cynthia Gallois, and Jeffery Pittam, "Language and Social Interaction: Taking Stock and Looking Forward," *Annals of the International Communication Association* 24, no. 1 (2001): 372, https://doi.org/10.1080/23808985.2001.11678994; Katherine Smits, "Deliberation and Past Injustice: Recognition and the Reasonableness of Apology in the Australian Case," *Constellations* 15, no. 2 (2008): 237, https://doi.org/10.1111/j.1467-8675.2008.00487.x.

77. Benwell and Stokoe, *Discourse*, 34.

78. Wayne H. Brekhus, "Trends in the Qualitative Study of Social Identities," *Sociology Compass* 2, no. 3 (2008): 1061, https://doi.org/10.1111/j.1751-9020.2008.00107.x.

79. Bächtiger and Parkinson, *Mapping and Measuring*, 32.

80. Lawrence Wilde, "The Concept of Solidarity: Emerging from the Theoretical Shadows?," *British Journal of Politics and International Relations* 9, no. 1 (2007): 171, https://doi.org/10.1111/j.1467-856x.2007.00275.x. Transitional justice scholars' interest in the concept of solidarity, first brought to prominence in the social sciences by the sociologist Émile Durkheim in the late nineteenth century, has tracked the emergence of transitional justice as a multidisciplinary field. See Émile Durkheim, *The Division of Labour in Society* (London: Collier Macmillan: [1893] 1964). Cf. Wilde, "The Concept of Solidarity." Political scientists, sociologists, anthropologists, linguists, legal scholars, and others have studied political, affective, cognitive, and performative aspects of solidarity and their role in overcoming interethnic divisions in various empirical contexts marked by the legacy of violence and human rights violations. Rosemary Nagy, "Reconciliation in Post-Commission South Africa: Thick and Thin Accounts of Solidarity," *Canadian Journal of Political Science* 35, no. 2 (2002): 340, https://www.jstor.org/stable/3233430; Michele Lamb, "Ethno-Nationalist Conflict, Participation and Human Rights-Based Solidarity in Northern Ireland," *The International Journal of Human Rights* 17, nos. 7–8 (2013), https://doi.org/10.1080/13642987.2013.823271; Sharon Stanley, "Toward a Reconciliation of Integration and Racial Solidarity," *Contemporary Political Theory* 13, no. 1 (2014), http//doi.org/10.1057/cpt.2013.13; Alla V. Tovares, "Going Off-Script and Reframing the Frame: The Dialogic Intertwining of the Centripetal and Centrifugal Voices in the Truth and Reconciliation Commission Hearings," *Discourse & Society* 27, no. 5 (2016), https://doi.org/10.1177/0957926516651365; Scott D. Neufeld and Michael T. Schmitt, "Solidarity Not Homogeneity: Constructing a Superordinate Aboriginal Identity That Protects Subgroup Identities," *Political Psychology* 40, no. 3 (2019), https://doi.org/10.1111/pops.12530; Chi Adanna Mgbako, "Ingando Solidarity Camps: Reconciliation and Political Indoctrination in Post-Genocide Rwanda," *Harvard Human Rights Journal* 18 (2005); Alexander Koensler, "Acts of Solidarity: Crossing and Reiterating Israeli—Palestinian Frontiers," *International Journal of Urban and Regional Research* 40, no. 2 (2016), https://doi.org/10.1111/1468-2427.12380; Lea David, *The Past Can't Heal Us: The Dangers of Mandating Memory in the Name of Human Rights* (Cambridge: Cambridge University Press, 2020).

81. Siniša Malešević, *The Sociology of War and Violence* (Cambridge: Cambridge University Press, 2010); Nagy, "Reconciliation," 340.

82. Stijn Oosterlynck, Maarten Loopmans, Nick Schuermans, Joke Vandenbeele, and Sami Zemni, "Putting Flesh to the Bone: Looking for Solidarity in Diversity, Here and Now," *Ethnic and Racial Studies* 39, no. 5 (2016): 776, https://doi.org/10.1080/01419870.2015.1080380.

83. Paige Arthur, "Introduction: Identities in Transition," in *Identities in Transition: Challenges for Justice in Divided Societies*, ed. Paige Arthur (Cambridge: Cambridge University Press, 2011), 4.

84. Christopher McMahon, "Discourse and Morality," *Ethics* 110, no. 3 (2000): 514, https://doi.org/10.1086/233322.

85. Jürgen Habermas, *The Inclusion of the Other: Studies in Political Theory*, eds. Ciaran Cronin and Pablo De Greiff (Cambridge: Polity Press, 1999), 39.

86. John Cameron and Hemant Ojha, "A Deliberative Ethic for Development: A Nepalese Journey from Bourdieu through Kant to Dewey and Habermas," *International Journal of Social Economics* 34, nos. 1–2 (2007): 77, https://doi.org/10.1108/03068290710723372.

87. Habermas, *The Inclusion*, 46.

88. Albena Azmanova, "Deliberative Conflict and 'The Better Argument' Mystique," *Good Society* 19, no. 1 (2010): 50, https://doi.org/10.1353/gso.0.0098.

89. Christopher F. Karpowitz and Jane Mansbridge, "Disagreement and Consensus: The Need for Dynamic Updating in Public Deliberation," *Journal of Public Deliberation* 1, no. 1 (2005): 354, https://doi.org/10.16997/jdd.25. Cf. Stefan Rummens, "Staging Deliberation: The Role of Representative Institutions in the Deliberative Democratic Process," *Journal of Political Philosophy* 20, no 1 (2012): 28, https://doi.org/10.1111/j.1467-9760.2010.00384.x.

90. Conrado Hübner Mendes, *Constitutional Courts and Deliberative Democracy* (Oxford: Oxford University Press, 2013), 123.

91. Hübner Mendes, *Constitutional Courts*, 123.

92. Nagy, "Reconciliation," 340.

93. Nagy criticizes Gutmann and Thompson's argument that democratic reciprocity is the fundamental moral value required in the work of truth commissions because such a procedural approach to deliberation in postviolence contexts falls short of the required moral transformation that internalizes democratic reciprocity. Nagy, "Reconciliation," 338–42. For a similar critique, see Bashir, "Accommodating Historically Oppressed." Although Gutmann and Thompson also point to the limits of the procedural principle to advance reconciliation, their solution is premised on the need for its integration with the substantive principle in dealing with deep moral disagreements. Gutmann and Thompson, *Why Deliberative Democracy*.

94. Oosterlynck et al., "Putting Flesh," 776.

95. Cameron and Ojha, "A Deliberative Ethic," 77.

96. William P. Umphres, "Beyond Good Reasons: Solidarity, Open Texture, and the Ethics of Deliberation," *Constellations* 25, no. 4 (2018): 565, https://doi.org/10.1111/1467-8675.12344.

97. Habermas, *The Inclusion*, 212.

98. Axel Honneth, *The Struggle for Recognition: The Moral Grammar of Social Conflicts* (Cambridge: Polity Press, 1995), 132.

99. William Rehg, "Solidarity and the Common Good: An Analytic Framework," *Journal of Social Philosophy* 38, no. 1 (2007): 13, https://doi.org/10.1111/j.1467-9833.2007.00363.x.

100. Nancy Fraser, "Toward a Discourse Ethic of Solidarity," *Praxis International* 5, no. 4 (1986): 428.

101. Habermas, *The Inclusion*, 40. On Habermas's contribution to reconciling the communitarian premises with a deontological theory of justice and universal human rights, see Andrew J. Pierce, "Justice without Solidarity? Collective Identity and the Fate of the 'Ethical' in Habermas' Recent Political Theory," *European Journal of Philosophy* 26, no. 1 (2018): 548–49, https://doi.org/10.1111/ejop.12273.

102. Habermas, *The Inclusion*, 40. For a discussion of justice with solidarity as its reverse side, where a requirement of equal treatment and equal respect for the dignity of everyone exists together with the solidarity of individual members of their community, see Jürgen Habermas, "Justice and Solidarity: On the Discussion Concerning Stage 6," in *The Moral Domain: Essays in the Ongoing Discussion between Philosophy and the Social Sciences*, ed. Thomas E. Wren (Cambridge: MIT Press, 1990), 244.

103. Honneth, *The Struggle*, 128; Habermas, *The Inclusion*, 108.

104. Honneth, *The Struggle*, 128, 130. This idea echoes Habermas's notion of "symmetrical relations of recognition." Habermas, *The Inclusion*, 242.

105. Fraser, "Toward a Discourse Ethic," 428.

106. Daniel Philpott, "Reconciliation, Politics, and Transitional Justice," in *The Oxford Handbook of Religion, Conflict, and Peacebuilding*, ed. Atalia Omer, R. Scott Appleby, and David Little (Oxford: Oxford University Press, 2015): 346.

107. Keith Banting and Will Kymlicka, "Introduction: The Political Sources of Solidarity in Diverse Societies," in *The Strains of Commitment: The Political Sources of Solidarity in Diverse Societies*, ed. Keith Banting and Will Kymlicka (Oxford: Oxford University Press, 2017), 14.

108. Rogers M. Smith, "Identities, Interests and the Future of Political Science," *Perspectives on Politics* 2, no. 2 (2004): 305, https://10.1017/S1537592704040174.

109. Sue Widdicombe, "Identity as an Analysts' and a Participants' Resource," in *Identities in Talk*, ed. Charles Antaki and Sue Widdicombe (London: Sage, 1998), 191.

3. QUANTIFYING DISCOURSE IN TRANSITIONAL JUSTICE

1. The author's estimate is based on the sample of textual data used in this research.

2. Paige Arthur, "How 'Transitions' Reshaped Human Rights: A Conceptual History of Transitional Justice," *Human Rights Quarterly* 31, no. 2 (2009): 360, https://doi.org/10.1353/hrq.0.0069.

3. Thorsten Bonacker and Susanne Buckley-Zistel, "Introduction: Transitions from Violence. Analysing the Effects of Transitional Justice," *International Journal of Conflict and Violence* 7, no. 1 (2013): 6, https://doi.org/10.4119/ijcv-2945; Paige Arthur, "Notes from the Field: Global Indicators for Transitional Justice and Challenges in Measurement for Policy Actors," *Transitional Justice Review* 1, no. 4 (2016), http://dx.doi.org/10.5206/tjr.2016.1.4.9.

4. Roman David, "What We Know about Transitional Justice: Survey and Experimental Evidence," *Supplement: Advances in Political Psychology* 38, no. S1 (2017): 151–77, https://doi.org/10.1111/pops.12395. Game theoretic models have also been applied, see Sam Whitt and Rick K. Wilson, "The Dictator Game, Fairness and Ethnicity in Postwar Bosnia," *American Journal of Political Science* 51, no. 3 (2007), https://www.jstor.org/stable/4620090.

5. Chapman and van der Merwe have demonstrated the analytical value of a quantitative study of discourse using the South African truth and reconciliation commission's transcripts. Audrey R. Chapman and Hugo van der Merwe, eds., *Truth and Reconciliation in South Africa: Did the TRC Deliver?* (Philadelphia: University of Pennsylvania Press, 2008). Computer-assisted text analysis has presented new possibilities for advancing theoretical claims in the field of transitional justice, see Denisa Kostovicova and Aude Bicquelet, "Norm Contestation and Reconciliation: Evidence from a Regional Transitional Justice Process in the Balkans." *Ethnic and Racial Studies* 41. No. 4 (2018): 681–700, https://doi.org/10.1080/01419870.2018.1380211. Denisa Kostovicova and Tom Paskhalis, "Gender, Justice and Deliberation: Why Women Don't Influence Peacemaking," *International Studies Quarterly* 65 no. 2 (2021), https://doi.org/10.1093/isq/sqab003, and Juan-Luis Suárez and Yadira Lizama-Mué, "Victims of Language: Language as a Pre-condition of Transitional Justice in Colombia's Peace Agreement," in *Transitional Justice in Comparative Perspective: Preconditions for Success*, ed. Samar El-Masri, Tammy Lambert, and Joanna R. Quinn (Cham: Palgrave Macmillan, 2020).

6. Richard Caplan, *Measuring Peace: Principles, Practices, and Politics* (Oxford: Oxford University Press, 2019), 7.

7. Peter Wallensteen, *Quality Peace: Peacebuilding, Victory, and World Order* (Oxford: Oxford University Press, 2015), 156.

8. The construction of the DQITJ was first outlined in Kostovicova and Paskhalis, "Gender, Justice and Deliberation."

9. Jürg Steiner, André Bächtiger, Markus Spörndli, and Marco R. Steenbergen, *Deliberative Politics in Action: Analysing Parliamentary Discourse* (Cambridge: Cambridge University Press, 2004), 43.

10. Michael A. Neblo, "Family Disputes: Diversity in Defining and Measuring Deliberation," *Swiss Political Science Review* 13, no. 4 (2007): 527–28, https://doi.org/10.1002.j.1662-6370.2007.tb00088.x. On the proliferation of methods to study deliberation, see Christopher Lord and Dionysia Tamvaki, "The Politics of Justification? Applying the 'Discourse Quality Index' to the Study of the European Parliament," *European Political Science Review* 5, no. 1 (2013), https://doi.org/10.1017/S1755773911000300; Laura W. Black, Stepanie Burkhalter, John Gastil, and Jennifer Stromer-Galley, "Methods for Analyzing and Measuring Group Deliberation," in *The Sourcebook for Political Communication Research: Methods, Measures, and Analytical Techniques*, ed. Erik P. Bucy and R. Lance Holbert (New York: Routledge, 2011), 329.

11. André Bächtiger, Susumu Shikano, Seraina Pedrini, and Mirjam Ryser, "Measuring Deliberation 2.0: Standards, Discourse Types, and Sequentialization" (unpublished paper, University of Konstanz and University of Bern, 2009), 2, https://ash.harvard.edu/files/ash/files/baechtiger_0.pdf. The DQI has not been without its critics, including one of its creators. Steiner et al. have criticized the static nature of the measurement instrument. Jürg Steiner, Maria Clara Jaramillo, and Simona Mameli, "The Dynamics of Deliberation," *Belgrade Philosophical Annual* 27 (2014): 40, https://scindeks-clanci.ceon.rs/data/pdf/0353-3891/2014/0353-38911427039S.pdf. Others criticized the reliance on Habermas as the approach to deliberation, resulting in the prioritization of its procedural dimension at the expense of the substance of arguments. For a summary of these arguments, see Marco R. Steenbergen, André Bächtiger, Markus Spörndli, and Jürg Steiner, "Measuring Political Deliberation: A Discourse Quality Index," *Comparative European Politics* 1, no. 1 (2003): 43, https://doi.org/10.1057.palgrave.cep.6110002; André Bächtiger and John Parkinson, *Mapping and Measuring Deliberation: Towards a New Deliberative Quality* (Oxford: Oxford University Press, 2019), 54–56.

12. Bächtiger and Parkinson, *Mapping and Measuring*, 49.

13. This is in contrast to other studies that reduce deliberativeness of discourse to one dimension; for example, to interruptions, see Tali Mendelberg, Christopher F. Karpowitz, and J. Baxter Oliphant, "Gender Inequality in Deliberation: Unpacking the Black Box of Interaction," *Perspectives on Politics* 12, no. 1 (2014), https://doi.org/10.1017/S1537592713003691; to reciprocity, see Ramya Parthasarathy, Vijayendra Rao and Nethra Palaniswamy, "Deliberative Democracy in an Unequal World: A Text-as-Data Study of South India's Village Assemblies," *American Political Science Review* 113, no. 3 (2019), https://doi.org/10.1017/S0003055419000182; to reason-giving, see Cheryl Schonhardt-Bailey, *Deliberating American Monetary Policy: A Textual Analysis* (Cambridge: MIT Press, 2013).

14. Black et al., "Methods for Analyzing," 328.

15. Jürgen Habermas, *The Theory of Communicative Action*, vol. 1: *Reason and the Rationalization of Society* (Cambridge: Polity Press, [1984] 2004).

16. Steenbergen et al., "Measuring Political Deliberation," 23.

17. Steenbergen et al., "Measuring Political Deliberation," 25.

18. Habermas, *The Theory*; Stephen Elstub, "The Third Generation of Deliberative Democracy," *Political Studies* 8, no. 3 (2010), https://doi.org/10.1111/j.1478-9302.2010.00216.x; Steenbergen et al., "Measuring Political Deliberation," 25–26.

19. For an extensive account of how categorical variables capture the quality of deliberation, see Steenbergen at al., "Measuring Political Deliberation" (2003), and Steiner et al., *Deliberative Politics*, 43–73. For a comprehensive review of other measurements of deliberation, in part driven by a lack of an agreed definition of deliberation, see Black et al., "Methods for Analyzing," 326–38.

20. J. S. Mill, *Utilitarianism* (Oxford: Oxford University Press, 1998), qtd. in Steenbergen et al., "Measuring Political Deliberation," 28; John Rawls, *A Theory of Justice*

(Cambridge: Belknap Press of Harvard University Press, 1971), argument quoted in Steenbergen et al., "Measuring Political Deliberation," 28.

21. Steenbergen et al., "Measuring Political Deliberation," 26.

22. Steiner et al., *Deliberative Politics*, qtd. in Soo-Hye Han, William Schenck-Hamlin and Donna Schenck-Hamlin, "Inclusion, Equality, and Discourse Quality in Citizen Deliberation on Broadband," *Journal of Public Deliberation* 11, no. 1 (2015): 4–5, https://doi.org/10.16997/jdd.220; cf. Ugarriza, "When War Adversaries," 80.

23. Lynn M. Sanders, "Against Deliberation," *Political Theory* 25, no. 3 (1997), https://www.jstor.org/stable/191984. Cf. Iris Marion Young, "Activist Challenges to Deliberative Democracy," *Political Theory* 29, no. 5 (2001), https://www.jstor.org/stable/3072534. See also Marlène Gerber et al., "Deliberative Abilities and Influence in a Transnational Deliberative Poll (EuroPolis)," *British Journal of Political Science* 48, no. 4 (2016): 1100, https://doi.org/10.1017/S0007123416000144; Elstub, "The Third Generation."

24. Lord and Tamvaki make this point about deliberation in parliamentary settings. Lord and Tamvaki, "The Politics," 32.

25. Jürg Steiner, *The Foundations of Deliberative Democracy: Empirical Research and Normative Implications* (Cambridge: Cambridge University Press, 2012), 2.

26. Steiner et al., *Deliberative Politics*, 60.

27. Lord and Tamvaki, "The Politics," 40.

28. For example, Roger and Schaal subsume both types of interest under a single common good category. Léa Roger and Gary S. Schaal, "The Quality of Deliberation in Two Committees of the European Parliament: The Neglected Influence of the Situational Context and the Policymaking Stage," *Politics and Governance* 1, no. 2 (2013): 168, Appendix 2, https://doi.org/10.17645/pag.v1i2.101.

29. Steiner, *The Foundations*, 10.

30. Guntram H. Herb and David H. Kaplan, eds., *Nested Identities: Nationalism, Territory, and Scale* (Lanham, MD: Rowman & Littlefield, 1999).

31. This is in line with the existing literature's dyadic approach to conflict. For example, see Steiner, *The Foundations*, appendix, 270.

32. Following Steiner, *The Foundations*, appendix, 271.

33. Steiner, *The Foundations*, appendix, 271.

34. Didier Caluwaerts and Kris Deschouwer, "Building Bridges across Political Divides: Experiments on Deliberative Democracy in Deeply Divided Belgium," *European Political Science Review* 6, no. 3 (2014), https://doi.org/10.1017/S17553913000179; Steiner, *The Foundations*, appendix, 269; Gerber et al., "Deliberative Abilities."

35. Caluwaerts and Deschouwer, "Building Bridges," 436.

36. For example, in their application of the DQI, Ugarriza and Trujillo-Orrego define respect as the "use of explicitly respectful expressions," without specifying toward whom (groups or individuals). Juan E. Ugarriza and Natalia Trujillo-Orrego, "The Ironic Effect of Deliberation: What We Can (and Cannot) Expect in Deeply Divided Societies," *Acta Politica* 55 (2020): 228n12, https://doi.org/10.1057/s41269-018-0112-1. Cf. Juan E. Ugarriza, "When War Adversaries Talk: The Experimental Effect of Engagement Rules on Postconflict Deliberation," *Latin American Politics and Society* 58, no. 3 (2016), https://doi.org//10.1111/j.1548-2456.2016.00319.x; Juan E. Ugarriza and Enzo Nussio, "There Is No Pill for Deliberation: Explaining Discourse Quality in Post-Conflict Communities," *Swiss Political Science Review* 22, no. 1 (2015): 154n10, https://doi.org/10.1111/spsr.12195; Didier Caluwaerts and Min Reuchamps, "Does Inter-Group Deliberation Foster Inter-Group Appreciation? Evidence from Two Experiments in Belgium," *Politics* 34, no. 2 (2014): 106–7, https://doi.org/10.1111/1467-9256.12043; Caluwaerts and Deschouwer, "Building Bridges"; Steiner, *The Foundations*.

37. Following Steiner, *The Foundations*, appendix, 271.

38. Markus Spörndli, "Discourse Quality and Political Decisions: An Empirical Analysis of Debates in the German Conference Committee" (Wisssenschaftszentrum Berlin für Sozialforschung discussion paper, SP IV 2003-101, WZB, Berlin, 2003), 15. Steenbergen et al., "Measuring Political Deliberation," 39.

39. Steiner et al., *Deliberative Politics*, 60.

40. Steenbergen et al., "Measuring Political Deliberation"; Spörndli, "Discourse Quality." In line with André Bächtiger, Dominik Hangartner, Pia Hess, and Céline Fraefel, "Patterns of Parliamentary Discourse: How 'Deliberative' Are German Legislative Debates?," *German Politics* 17, no. 3 (2008): 282, https://doi.org/10.1080/09644000802300486. A composite measure is used for the common good dimension because the categories and respective values form a theoretical whole that incorporates a refined set of indicators of this deliberative dimension in postconflict contexts. See table A.3.1 in the appendix. There is no requirement for all categories to be combined all the time, as these will depend on the specific discourse. Steiner et al., *Deliberative Politics*, 60. For example, Caluwaerts and Deschouwer exclude interruptions and a common good category expressed in terms of abstract principles. Caluwaerts and Deschouwer, "Building Bridges," 438. Cf. Steenbergen, "Measuring Political Deliberation," 39. Participation (i.e., interruptions) is excluded from the DQITJ because it has insufficient variation. In the DQITJ, numeric values of all the DQI category items are scaled to have an equal range, between 0 and 6. Polychoric correlations are reported as they account for both the categorical and ordinal nature of the categories of the DQITJ. Steenbergen at al., "Measuring Political Deliberation," 40; Francisco Holgado-Tello, Salvador Chacón-Moscoso, Isabel Barbero-García, and Enrique Vila-Abad, "Polychoric versus Pearson Correlations in Exploratory and Confirmatory Factor Analysis with Ordinal Variables," *Quality and Quantity* 44, no. 1 (2010), https://doi.org/10.1007/s11135-008-9190-y. Cf. Spörndli, "Discourse Quality," 15–16. See table A.3.2 in the appendix.

41. Steenbergen et al., "Measuring Political Deliberation," 41. See table A.3.3 in the appendix.

42. Caluwaerts and Deschouwer, "Building Bridges," 433.

43. Seraina Pedrini, "Deliberative Capacity in the Political and Civic Sphere," *Swiss Political Science Review* 20, no. 2 (2014): 263–64, https://doi.org/10.1111/spsr.12074.

44. Fung defines "hot deliberations" as high-stakes deliberations. Archon Fung, "Recipes for Public Spheres: Eight Institutional Design Choices and Their Consequences," *Journal of Political Philosophy* 11, no. 3 (2003): 345, https://doi.org/10.1111/1467-9760.00181.

45. They were selected out of the 134 transcripts of the consultation sessions that constitute the RECOM data. See the appendix detailing all consultations analyzed in this book. After 2011, RECOM continued to organize regional fora, that is multiethnic gatherings at a regional level dedicated to discussing a theme related to postconflict justice. Textual data used in this book is accessible at Denisa Kostovicova, "Replication Data For: Gender, Justice and Deliberation: Why Women Don't Influence Peace-Making," *Harvard Dataverse* V1, 2020, https://doi.org/10.7910/DVN/FC6WAO.

46. This feature of discourse of the RECOM consultations distinguishes them from other discussions in divided societies in which exchanges fell into the quick interactive pattern with many shortcuts, including the utterance of a single word, as in deliberative experiments in Bosnia and Herzegovina and in Colombia, see Steiner et al., "The Dynamics of Deliberation," 41.

47. It replicates the approach that controls for the same type of case as elaborated in Steiner et al., *Deliberative Politics*, 99–100.

48. Steiner, *The Foundations*, 21.

49. For a discussion of the issues of representation and recruitment in public deliberation in nonconflict contexts, see Kieran C. O'Doherty and Karla Stroud, "Public

Deliberation and Social Psychology: Integrating Theories of Participation with Social Psychological Research and Practice," in *The Sage Handbook of Applied Social Psychology*, ed. Kieran C. O'Doherty and Darrin Hodgetts (Los Angeles: Sage, 2019): 424–25.

50. Steiner, *The Foundations*, 17. On randomization in deliberative experiments, see John Gastil, "The Lessons and Limitations of Experiments in Democratic Deliberation," *Annual Review of Law and Social Science* 14 (2018), https://doi.org.10.1146/annurev-lawsocsci-110316-113639. For limitations in quasi-experimental research, see Eoin O'Malley, David M. Farrell, and Jane Suiter, "Does Talking Matter? A Quasi-Experiment Assessing the Impact of Deliberation and Information on Opinion Change," *International Political Science Review* 41, no. 3 (2020), https://doi.org/10.1177/0192512118824459.

51. Ian O'Flynn, "Pulling Together: Shared Intentions, Deliberative Democracy and Deeply Divided Societies," *British Journal of Political Science* 47, no. 1 (2017), https://doi.org/10.1017/S0007123415000459.

52. Dimiter Toshkov, *Research Design in Political Science* (Basingstoke: Palgrave Macmillan, 2016), 292.

53. Alexander L. George and Andre Bennett, *Case Studies and Theory Development in the Social Sciences* (Cambridge: MIT Press, 2005), 32.

54. Steiner, *The Foundations*, 14.

55. Kenneth Benoit, "Text as Data: An Overview," in *Handbook of Research Methods in Political Science and International Relations*, ed. Luigi Curini and Robert Franzese (Thousand Oaks: Sage, 2020).

56. Robert C. Luskin, Ian O'Flynn, James S. Fishkin, and David Russell, "Deliberating Across Deep Divides," *Political Studies* 62 no. 1 (2014), https://doi.org/10.1111/j.1467-9248.2012.01005.x.

57. Steenbergen et al., "Measuring Political Deliberation," 42.

58. Steenbergen et al., "Measuring Political Deliberation," 27.

59. See communication with André Bächtiger in Vebjørn Roald and Linda Sangolt, *Deliberation, Rhetoric and Emotion in the Discourse on Climate Change in the European Parliament* (Delft: Eburon, 2012), 66–67n47.

60. Caluwaerts and Deschouwer, "Building Bridges," 436. In line with the empirical scholarship on deliberation, speeches that are clarifying questions or general comments are not considered relevant from the standpoint of measuring the quality of deliberation; see Steenbergen et al., "Measuring Political Deliberation," 27; Soo-Hye Han, Schenck-Hamlin, William and Schenck-Hamlin, Donna, "Inclusion, Equality and Discourse Quality in Citizen Deliberation on Broadband," *Journal of Public Deliberation* 11, no.1 (2015): 11n10, https://doi.org/10.16997/jdd.220.

61. Black et al., "Methods for Analyzing," 326.

62. For a discussion about a need for the presence of neutral facilitators for group deliberation to attain deliberative norms, as opposed to unstructured group discussion, see Black et al., "Methods for Analyzing," 338.

63. The RECOM Coalition made available the transcripts of consultations in all languages spoken in former Yugoslavia (Serbian, Bosnian, Croatian, and Montenegrin, which are mutually intelligible variants of the Serbo-Croat language spoken in the former Yugoslavia, as well as Albanian, Macedonian, and Slovenian). Coding was applied to the Bosnian, Serbian, Croatian, and Montenegrin versions of the transcripts (including those that were originally in Albanian, Macedonian, and Slovenian) after the author verified that the finesses of argumentation were retained in the translated version, relying on her fluency in Albanian and research competence in Slovenian and Macedonian. In this manner, both coders coded the RECOM transcripts in the same languages. On translation and coding of transcripts of deliberations, see Gerber at al., "Deliberative Abilities."

64. Kimberly A. Neuendorf, *The Content Analysis Guidebook* (Thousand Oaks: Sage, 2002), 131–32; Black et al., "Methods for Analyzing," 328.

65. Steiner et al., *Deliberative Politics*; Neuendorf, *The Content Analysis*, 131–32; Black et al., "Methods for Analyzing," 328. The reliability of coding can be ensured by providing comprehensive, theoretically informed coding instructions in combination with a training program, including rigorous discussion to avoid applying unspecified and informal rules. Tony Hak and Ton Bernts, "Coder Training: Explicit Instruction and Implicit Socialization?," in *The Content Analysis Reader*, ed. Klaus Krippendorff and Mary Angela Bock (Los Angeles: Sage, 2009), 220–23. Accordingly, the author compiled the DQITJ codebook informed by scholarship on deliberation. The codebook contains comprehensive coding instructions. The induction into the theory and the method were part of the training before coding. Both datasets—one coded by the author and one by a research assistant—used in this research are accessible, see Kostovicova, "Replication Data."

66. Descriptive statistics of the RECOM corpus are presented in table A.3.4 in the appendix.

67. From September 2015 to mid-April 2016.

68. Black et al., "Methods for Analyzing," 329.

69. Klaus Krippendorff, *Content Analysis: An Introduction to Its Methodology*, 3rd ed. (Thousand Oaks, CA: Sage, 2013), 241; Klaus Krippendorff, "Testing the Reliablity of Content Analysis Data," in Krippendorff and Bock, *The Content Analysis*, 354.

70. Results of intercoder reliability tests are reported in table A.3.5 in the appendix.

71. Figures are rounded to two decimal places.

72. Steiner, *The Foundations*, 75, 80, 81.

73. I introduced this argument in chapter 2. It is elaborated and supported with empirical evidence in chapter 4.

74. For example, Pedrini finds that ordinary citizens rely less on storytelling than elites. Pedrini, "Deliberative Capacity," 277.

75. Rather than being an alternative to rational discourse, this pattern shows that storytelling is intertwined with reason-giving.

76. Henceforth, when referring to the scores of deliberative quality the DQITJ and the DQI will be used interchangeably to indicate comparability with other studies.

77. The reference to one's country does not represent a restatement of an ethnic interest in a different form. Most speakers invoked the countries' interests given their unique circumstances, including a dimension of ethnic diversity that survived the conflict. It is notable that participants oriented toward an ethnic group identity when framing a narrow conception of common good rather than toward an ethnic nation(-state).

78. These experiments involved ex-guerrillas and ex-paramilitaries, see Steiner, *The Foundations*, 16–17 and 98. Similarly, Ugarriza and Trujillo-Orrego, in their studies of Colombia, find "rather selfish justifications," with very few references to the good of other groups, the common good or abstract principles. Ugarriza and Trujillo-Orrego, "The Ironic Effect," 229. According to Steiner, in deliberative experiments in Bosnia and Herzegovina, stories told by participants about stray dogs, wild pigs, the polluted river, and so on made it difficult to make judgments about explicit expression of common good and self-interest. This was reflected in their findings that 5 percent of speech acts referred to the common good, 1 percent to abstract/moral principles, and none (unexpectedly, for example, in Srebrenica) to one's own ethnic group. Steiner, *The Foundations*, 99. Caluwaerts and Deschouwer report a variation of less than 5 percent in the common good category in the Belgian experiments. Caluwaerts and Deschouwer, "Building Bridges," 436.

79. Caluwaerts and Deschouwer, "Building Bridges," 11; Steiner, *The Foundations*, 98.

80. Caluwaerts and Deschouwer, "Building Bridges," 437.

81. Steiner, *The Foundations*, 114. It is not specified out of how many; see Steiner, *The Foundations*, 116.

82. With less than 5 percent variation, this category was excluded from further analyses in this study.

83. Simone Chambers, "Deliberative Democratic Theory," *Annual Review of Political Science* 6, no. 1 (2003): 309, https://doi.org/https://doi.org/annurev.polisci.6/121901.085538.

84. Cf. Bächtiger and Parkinson, *Mapping and Measuring*, 2.

85. Black et al., "Methods for Analyzing," 327.

86. Ugarriza, "When War Adversaries," 80.

87. Bächtiger and Parkinson, *Mapping and Measuring*, 3.

88. Bächtiger and Parkinson, *Mapping and Measuring*, 39–40.

4. WORDS OF REASON AND TALK OF PAIN

1. Priscilla B. Hayner, *Unspeakable Truths: Confronting State Terror and Atrocity* (New York and London: Routledge, 2000), 161–62.

2. Steven L. Burg and Paul S. Shoup, *The War in Bosnia-Herzegovina: Ethnic Conflict and International Intervention* (Armonk, NY: M.E. Sharpe, 1999).

3. Following Riddle, the notion of ethnicness is used here to denote an embodied attribute of the discourse, in contrast to ethnicity, which refers to a characteristic in a generic sense. Elizabeth M. Riddle, "A Historical Perspective on the Productivity of the Suffixes -ness and -ity," in *Historical Semantics—Historical Word-Formation*, ed. Jacek Fisiak (Berlin: Mouton, 1985), 437.

4. On the lack of application of applied linguistics in deliberation, see André Bächtiger and John Parkinson, *Mapping and Measuring Deliberation: Towards a New Deliberative Quality* (Oxford: Oxford University Press, 2019), 75.

5. Summary statistics of DQITJ scores are presented in table A.4.1 in the appendix. The scaling of DQITJ to range from 0 to 10 assists interpretation of the expected change in the DQI score associated with the change in the value of an explanatory variable.

6. For a comprehensive review of different ways a truth commission's restrictive mandate can undermine its legitimacy, see Onur Bakiner, *Truth Commissions: Memory, Power, and Legitimacy* (Philadelphia: University of Pennsylvania Press, 2016), 76–80; cf. Hayner, *Unspeakable Truths*, 77–80. Bakiner highlights the adverse effects of inclusion and exclusion of specific violations in the commission's mandates, whereas the RECOM process points to the more subtle but no less contentious repercussions of the wording of a commission's mandate.

7. RECOM Consultation no. 19. The first alternative (with some amendments) was included in the adopted Draft Statute of the fact-finding commission, under Article 16, titled "Violations of Laws in the Commission's Remit." See *Statut Koalicije za REKOM* (June 26, 2011), http://recom.link/wp-content/uploads/2011/06/Statut-Koalicije-za-REKOM-26.06.2011-SRB.pdf.

8. A comprehensive summary of arguments for the commission's mandate can be found in *Proces REKOM: Konsultativni process o utvrđivanju činjenica o ratnim zločinima i drugim teškim kršenjima ljudskih prava počinjenim na području nekadašnje SFRJ* (Beograd: Fond za humanitarno pravo, 2011), 255–57 and 331–86; also see Arnaud Kurze, "Justice Beyond Borders? The Politics to Democratize HumanIghts in the Post-Conflict Balkans" (PhD diss., George Mason University, 2012), 144–63.

9. RECOM Consultation no. 19.

10. Gordy argues in reference to Serbia that the discourse of denial changed in the period of the ICTY's work, from "denial of facts to dispute over their meaning." See Eric

Gordy, *Guilt, Responsibility, and Denial: The Past at Stake in Post-Milošević Serbia* (Philadelphia: University of Pennsylvania Press, 2013), xiii.

11. When addressing the issue of setting conditions, the speaker referred to reports that some victims' associations reportedly said they would not support the regional fact-finding commission unless the term genocide was explicitly included in the wording concerning its remit. See RECOM Consultation no. 19.

12. Jürg Steiner, André Bächtiger, Markus Spörndli, and Marco R. Steenbergen, *Deliberative Politics in Action: Analysing Parliamentary Discourse* (Cambridge: Cambridge University Press, 2004), 57.

13. Lynn M. Sanders, "Against Deliberation," *Political Theory* 25, no. 3 (1997): 370, https://www.jstor.org/stable/191984.

14. Iris Marion Young, *Inclusion and Democracy* (Oxford: Oxford University Press, 2002); cf. Sanders, "Against Deliberation," 370.

15. Pippa Norris, "Women Politicians: Transforming Westminster?," *Parliamentary Affairs* 49, no. 1 (1996): 91, https://doi.org/10.1093/oxfordjournals.pa.a028675.

16. Rita Grünenfelder and André Bächtiger, "Gendered Deliberation? How Men and Women Deliberate in Legislatures" (paper presented at the European Consortium for Political Research Joint Sessions, Helsinki, May 2007). André Bächtiger and Dominik Hangartner, "When Deliberative Theory Meets Empirical Political Science: Theoretical and Methodological Challenges in Political Deliberation," *Political Studies* 58, no. 4 (2010), https://doi.org/10.1111/j.1467-9248.2010.00835.x.

17. Juan Esteban Ugarriza and Enzo Nussio, "There Is No Pill for Deliberation: Explaining Discourse Quality in Post-Conflict Communities," *Swiss Political Science Review* 22, no. 1 (2015), https://doi.org/10.1111/spsr.12195. Cf. Didier Caluwaerts and Kris Deschouwer, "Building Bridges across Political Divides: Experiments on Deliberative Democracy in Deeply Divided Belgium," *European Political Science Review* 6, no. 3 (2014), https://doi.org/10.1017/S17553913000179, and Didier Caluwaerts and Min Reuchamps, "Does Inter-Group Deliberation Foster Inter-Group Appreciation? Evidence from Two Experiments in Belgium," *Politics* 34, no. 2 (2014), https://doi.org/10.1111/1467-9256.12043.

18. Karpowitz and Mendelberg found that women speak markedly less than men in terms of time and speaking opportunities. Christopher F. Karpowitz, Tali Mendelberg, and Lee Shaker, "Gender Inequality in Deliberative Participation," *American Political Science Review* 106, no. 3 (2012): 545, https://doi.org/10.1017/S0003055412000329. See also Staffan Himmelroos, Lauri Rapeli, and Kimmo Grönlund, "Talking with Like-minded People—Equality and Efficacy in Enclave Deliberation," *Social Science Journal* 54 no. 2 (2017), https://doi.org/10.1016/j.soscij.2016.10.006; Francesca Polletta and John Lee, "Is Telling Stories Good for Democracy? Rhetoric in Public Deliberation after 9/11," *American Sociological Review* 71, no. 5 (2006), https://doi.org/10.1177/000312240607100501. Also, women use personal experiences more than men. Seraina Pedrini, "Deliberative Capacity in the Political and Civic Sphere," *Swiss Political Science Review* 20, no. 2 (2014), https://doi.org/10.1111/spsr.12074; cf. Marlène Gerber et al., "Deliberative Abilities and Influence in a Transnational Deliberative Poll (EuroPolis)," *British Journal of Political Science* 48, no. 4 (2018), https://doi.org/10.1017/S0007123416000144; Christopher Lord and Dionysia Tamvaki, "The Politics of Justification? Applying the 'Discourse Quality Index' to the Study of the European Parliament," *European Political Science Review* 5, no. 1 (2013), https://doi.org/10.1017/S1755773911000300.

19. Gerber et al., "Deliberative Abilities"; Pedrini, "Deliberative Capacity."

20. Gerber et al., "Deliberative Abilities," 1110.

21. Soo-Hye Han, William Schenck-Hamlin, and Donna Schenck-Hamlin, "Inclusion, Equality and Discourse Quality in Citizen Deliberation on Broadband," *Journal of Public*

Deliberation 11, no. 1 (2015): 12, https://doi.org/10.16997/jdd.220. Some find a significant association between education and quality deliberation, see Ugarriza and Nussio, "There Is No Pill," and Caluwaerts and Deschouwer, "Building Bridges," while others do not, see, for example, Pedrini, "Deliberative Capacity," and Gerber et al., "Deliberative Abilities."

22. This variable captures the number of speaking turns rather than the number of demands made in a single speaking turn.

23. On multiple transitions, see Vesna Bojicic-Dzelilovic, James Kerr-Lindsay, and Denisa Kostovicova, eds., *Civil Society and Transitions in the Western Balkans* (Basingstoke: Palgrave Macmillan, 2013).

24. Madeleine Fullard and Nicky Rousseau, "Truth Telling, Identities, and Power in South Africa and Guatemala," in *Identities in Transition: Challenges for Justice in Divided Societies*, ed. Paige Arthur (Cambridge: Cambridge University Press, 2011), 55–56.

25. For example, women are less successful than men at taking and holding the floor. Linsey M. Grob, Renee A. Meyers, and Renee Schuh, "Powerful/ Powerless Language Use in Group Interactions: Sex Differences or Similarities?," *Communication Quarterly* 45, no. 3 (1997), https://doi.org/10.1080/01463379709370066.

26. Tshepo Mandligozi, "On Transitional Justice Entrepreneurs and the Production of Victims," *Journal of Human Rights Practice* 2, no. 2 (2010): 225, https://doi.org/10.1093/jhuman/huq005.

27. Gerber et al., "Deliberative Abilities," 1098; Staffan Himmelroos, "Discourse Quality in Deliberative Citizen Forums—A Comparison of Four Deliberative Mini-Publics," *Journal of Public Deliberation* 13, no. 1 (2017): 16, https://doi.org/10.16997/jdd.269. For divided societies, in particular, see Caluwaerts and Deschouwer, "Building Bridges," 440; Caluwaerts and Reuchamps, "Does Inter-Group," 110–11.

28. Steiner et al., *Deliberative Politics*, 78–91.

29. Cas Sunstein, "Deliberative Trouble? Why Groups Go to Extremes," *Yale Law Journal* 110, no. 71 (2000).

30. Kim Strandberg, Staffan Himmelroos, and Kimmo Grönlund, "Do Discussions in Like-minded Groups Necessarily Lead to More Extreme Opinions? Deliberative Democracy and Group Polarization," *International Political Science Review* 40, no. 1 (2019), https://doi.org/10.1177/0192512117692136.

31. Caluwaerts and Deschouwer, "Building Bridges," 443.

32. Lord and Tamvaki, "The Politics," 42; however, Doerr finds from interviews and surveys of participants that the meetings of the Social Forum held at a European level were more inclusive, democratic, transparent, and respectful than preparatory meetings held at a national level. Nicole Doerr, "Language and Democracy 'in Movement': Multilingualism and the Case of the European Social Forum Process," *Social Movement Studies* 8, no. 2 (2009): 154–55, https://doi.org/10.1080/14742830902770290.

33. Cf. Doerr, "Language and Democracy," 159; Irena Fiket, Espen D. H. Olsen, and Hans-Jörg Trenz, "Confronting European Diversity: Deliberation in a Transnational and Pluri-Lingual Setting," *Javnost—The Public* 21, no. 2 (2014), https://doi.org/10.1080/13183222.2014.11009145.

34. Jane Mansbridge, "'Deliberative Democracy' or 'Democratic Deliberation?,'" in *Deliberation, Participation and Democracy: Can the People Govern?*, in ed. Shawn W. Rosenberg (Basingstoke: Palgrave Macmillan, 2007), 262.

35. David M. Ryfe, "Does Deliberative Democracy Work?," *Annual Review of Political Science* 8 (2005): 57, https://doi.org/10.1146/annurev.polisci.8.032904.154633.

36. Archon Fung, "Minipublics: Deliberative Designs and Their Consequences," in *Deliberation, Participation and Democracy: Can the People Govern?*, ed. Shawn W. Rosenberg (Basingstoke: Palgrave Macmillan, 2007), 165.

37. Ugarriza and Nussio, "There is No Pill," 158, table 2, 152.

38. Scholars have shown that the experience of war impedes reconciliation, tolerance, and forgiveness. For example, see Sara Kijewski and Carolin Rapp, "Moving Forward? How War Experiences, Interethnic Attitudes, and Intergroup Forgiveness Affect the Prospects of Political Tolerance in Postwar Sri Lanka," *Journal of Peace Research* 56, no. 6 (2019), https://doi.org/10.1177/0022343319849274; James Meernik and Jose Raul Guerrero, "Can International Criminal Justice Advance Ethnic Reconciliation? The ICTY and Ethnic Relations in Bosnia-Herzegovina," *Southeast European and Black Sea Studies* 14, no. 3 (2014), https://doi.org/10.1080/14683857.2014.924675.

39. Doerr, "Language and Democracy," 154–55.

40. This refers to the fact that Serbian, Croatian, Bosnian, and Montenegrin languages are mutually intelligible; see RECOM Consultation no. 17.

41. Nicole Doerr, "Translating Democracy: How Activists in the European Social Forum Practice Multilingual Deliberation," *European Political Science Review* 4, no. 3 (2012): 363, https://doi.org/10.1017/S1755773911000312.

42. Caluwaerts and Deschouwer, "Building Bridges," 441.

43. Steiner et al., *Deliberative Politics*, 88–89.

44. On the effects of how issues are framed in negotiations, see Cornelia Ulbert and Thomas Risse, "Deliberatively Changing the Discourse: What Does Make Arguing Effective?" *Acta Politica* 40 (2005): 364–65, https//doi.org/10/1057/palgrave.ap.5500117.

45. Issue polarization can also proxy the topics under discussion as different issues map onto different aspects of the commission's mandate. Specifically, for an analysis of topics discussed in the RECOM consultations, see Denisa Kostovicova and Tom Paskhalis, "Gender, Justice and Deliberation: Why Women Don't Influence Peacemaking," *International Studies Quarterly* 65, no. 2 (2021), https://doi.org/10.1093/isq/sqab003.

46. Steiner et al., *Deliberative Politics*, 131–35; Paul Magnette and Kalypso Nicolaïdis, "The European Convention: Bargaining in the Shadow of Rhetoric," *West European Politics* 27, no. 3 (2004), https://doi.org/10.1080/0140238042000228068.

47. Daniel Bochsler et al., "Exchange on the Quantitative Measurement of Ethnic and National identity," *Nations and Nationalism* 27 (2021): 24, https://doi.org/10.1111/nana.12688.

48. Jan Nuyts, "Subjectivity: Between Discourse and Conceptualization," *Journal of Pragmatics* 86 (2015): 106, https://doi.org/10.1016/j.pragma.2015.05.015.

49. For a more extensive psychological account, see Philip Bell, "Subjectivity and Identity: Semiotics as Psychological Explanation," *Social Semiotics* 12, no. 2 (2002): 203, https://doi.org/10.1080/103503302760212104. Cf. Johannes Angermüller, *Poststructuralist Discourse Analysis: Subjectivity in Enunciative Pragmatics* (Houndmills: Palgrave Macmillan, 2014), 59. This variable differs from a common good category expressed in group terms that captures self-interest (such as ethnic group interest). For example, a speaker may contextualize his or her proposal by referring to an experience of victims in Croatia, which captures the sense of ethnicness in discourse (linguistically, using the "we" form), but justify that proposal by invoking the benefit of all victims, that is common good based on the difference principle. RECOM Consultation no. 1.

50. Fernando L. González Rey, "Subjectivity and Discourse: Complementary Topics of a Critical Psychology," *Culture & Psychology* 25, no. 2 (2019): 191, https://doi.org/10.1177/1354067X18754338.

51. González Rey, "Subjectivity," 191.

52. Johannes Angermüller, "From the Many Voices to the Subject Positions in Anti-Globalization Discourse: Enuciative Pragmatics and the Polyphonic Organization of Subjectivity," *Journal of Pragmatics* 43, no. 12 (2011): 2998, https://doi.org/10.1016/j.pragma.2011.05.013.

53. Gonzáles Rey, "Subjectivity," 185.

54. Cf. Marco R. Steenbergen, André Bächtiger, Markus Spörndli, and Jürg Steiner, "Measuring Political Deliberation: A Discourse Quality Index," *Comparative European Politics* 1, no. 1 (2003): 42, https://doi.org/10.1057/palgrave.cep.6110002.

55. Intercoder reliability statistics are presented in table A.4.2 in the appendix.

56. Model 4 was derived by comparing nested models in the backward direction, dropping iteratively the variable with the largest *p*-value. Model specification tests indicated that model 4 is specified correctly and has no omitted variables.

57. It has fewer predictors and thus has a higher F-test statistic.

58. Other covariates investigated in the study, but not reported here, include the temporality of speech acts, whether they are present-, future- or past-oriented. The effect of the temporal orientation is of theoretical interest in the study of transitional justice, where past orientation as a feature of speech can reflect core grievances related to past violence and reflect the logic of ethnic identity at work in discourse, albeit indirectly. This dimension was captured by focusing on linguistic and semantic features of discourse (tense and temporal adverbials used in the speech acts) in the RECOM corpus, drawing on Michel Charolles, Anne Le Draoulec, Marie-Paule Pery-Woodley, and Laure Sarda, "Temporal and Spatial Dimensions of Discourse Organisation," *French Language Studies* 15, no. 2 (2005), https://doi.org/10.1017/S0959269505002036. All 1,211 speech acts were coded independently by the author and another coder, and intercoder reliability was checked. This variable was dropped from the models because of collinearity with ethnic subjectivity. Nonetheless, speakers' temporal orientation when addressing the criminal legacy is of theoretical interest for future transitional justice studies. See also Selvanathan et al., "Wedialog.net: A Quantitative Field Test of the Effects of Online Intergroup Dialogue in Promoting Justice- Versus Harmony-Oriented Outcomes in Bosnia and Serbia," *Peace and Conflict: Journal of Peace Psychology* 25, no. 4 (2019), https://doi.org/10.1037/pac0000395. Not reported here is the variable length of deliberation in each session, using the number of speech acts in each consultation as a proxy. This variable had very small and insignificant effects on the quality of deliberation.

59. This variable is dichotomized since higher- and medium-level polarization capture an ethnic dimension of an issue, unlike lower-level polarization.

60. By contrast, Caluwaerts and Deschouwer find no effect of issue polarization in discussions about peace. Caluwaerts and Deschouwer, "Building Bridges," 442, table 5.

61. Mark E. Warren, "Institutionalizing Deliberative Democracy," in *Deliberation, Participation and Democracy: Can the People Govern?*, ed. Shawn W. Rosenberg (Basingstoke: Palgrave Macmillan, 2007), 283. On the association between issue polarization and distinct categories of deliberation, such as level of justification or respect, see Steiner at al., *Deliberative Politics*, 131–34.

62. Caluwaerts and Deschouwer, "Building Bridges."

63. David E. Cunningham, *Barriers to Peace in Civil War* (Cambridge: Cambridge University Press, 2011), 197.

64. David M. Ryfe, "Narrative and Deliberation in Small Group Forums," *Journal of Applied Communication Research* 34, no. 1 (2006): 74, https://doi.org/10.1080/00909880500420226. Similarly, Steiner observes that storytelling is compatible with the model of deliberation, contributing to greater reciprocity and equality and reducing anonymity. Jürg Steiner, *The Foundations of Deliberative Democracy: Empirical Research and Normative Implications* (Cambridge: Cambridge University Press, 2012), 84–86.

65. For example, these studies have focused on how people contest harms suffered by other groups and denigrate their suffering, see Gordy, *Guilt, Responsibility, and Denial.*

66. Nevin T. Aiken, "Learning to Live Together: Transitional Justice and Intergroup Reconciliation in Northern Ireland," *International Journal of Transitional Justice* 4, no. 2

(2010), https://doi.org/10.1093/ijtj/ijq002; Claire Hackett and Bill Rolston, "The Burden of Memory: Victims, Storytelling and Resistance in Northern Ireland," *Memory Studies* 2, no. 3 (2009), https://doi.org/10.1177/1750698008337560.

67. Pamina Firchow and Yvette Selim, "Meaningful Engagement from the Bottom-Up? Taking Stock of Participation in Transitional Justice Processes," *International Journal of Transitional Justice*, February 2 (2022), https://doi.org/10.1093/ijtj/ijab031.

68. Grünenfelder and Bächtiger, "Gendered Deliberation." For further analysis of the patterns of women's participation, as compared to men's, in the RECOM consultations, including their representation, participation in turn-taking and in making arguments, and the length of their speeches, see Kostovicova and Paskhalis, "Gender, Justice and Deliberation."

69. This depicts a so-called crossover effect, which explains why the interaction term is statistically significant while the main effects of gender and speaker type are not.

70. For example, see Ramya Parthasarathy, Vijayendra Rao, and Nethra Palaniswamy, "Deliberative Democracy in an Unequal World: A Text-as-Data Study of South India's Village Assemblies," *American Political Science Review* 113, no. 3 (2019), https://doi.org/10.1017/S0003055419000182.

71. Doerr, "Translating Democracy," 381.

72. For a discussion of the linguistic challenges of translating legal terms and evidence in the ICTY proceedings and their effects on the administration of justice, see Ellen Elias-Bursać, *Translating Evidence and Interpreting Testimony at a War Crimes Tribunal: Working in a Tug of War* (Basingstoke: Palgrave Macmillan, 2015).

73. Adeno Addis, "Deliberative Democracy in Severely Fractured Societies," *Indiana Journal of Global Legal Studies* 16, no. 1 (2009): 69, https://doi.org/10.2979/GLS.2009.16.1.59.

5. WHO AGREES AND WHO DISAGREES

1. Kora Andrieu, "Civilizing Peacebuilding: Transitional Justice, Civil Society and the Liberal Paradigm," *Security Dialogue* 41, no. 5 (2010), https://doi.org/10.1177/0967010610382109; James Bohman, "Transnationalizing Peacebuidling: Transitional Justice as a Deliberative Process," in *Jus Post Bellum and Transitional Justice*, ed. Larry May and Elizabeth Edenberg (Cambridge: Cambridge University Press, 2013).

2. For example, on ethnic segregation in Bosnia, see John O'Loughlin, "Inter-Ethnic Friendships in Post-War Bosnia-Herzegovina: Sociodemographic and Place Influences," *Ethnicities* 10, no. 1 (2010): 36, https://www.jstor.org/stable/23890856; in Kosovo, see Denisa Kostovicova, *Kosovo: The Politics of Identity and Space* (London: Routledge, 2005), and in Croatia, see Tania Gosselin, "Info-Klub: Creating a Common Public Sphere for Citizens of Vukovar," in *Managing Hatred and Distrust: The Prognosis for Post-Conflict Settlement in Multiethnic Communities in the Former Yugoslavia*, ed. Nenad Dimitrijević and Petra Kovács (Budapest: Open Society Institute, 2004).

3. Diana C. Mutz and Paul S. Martin, "Facilitating Communication across Lines of Political Difference: The Role of Mass Media," *American Political Science Review* 95, no. 1 (2001): 110, https://doi.org/10/1017/S0003055401000223.

4. Max Pensky, *Ends of Solidarity: The Discourse Theory in Ethics and Politics* (Albany: State University of New York Press, 2009), 161.

5. Jürgen Habermas, *The Theory of Communicative Action*, vol. 1: *Reason and the Rationalization of Society* (Cambridge: Polity Press, [1984] 2004).

6. John S. Dryzek, "Deliberative Democracy in Divided Societies: Alternatives to Agonism and Analgesia," *Political Theory* 33, no. 2 (2005), https://doi.org/10.1177/009059170426 8372; Ian O'Flynn, *Deliberative Democracy and Divided Societies* (Edinburgh: Edinburgh

University Press, 2006); Jürg Steiner, *The Foundations of Deliberative Democracy: Empirical Research and Normative Implications* (Cambridge: Cambridge University Press, 2012); Didier Caluwaerts and Kris Deschouwer, "Building Bridges across Political Divides: Experiments on Deliberative Democracy in Deeply Divided Belgium," *European Political Science Review* 6, no. 3 (2014), https://doi.org/10.1017/S17553913000179; Juan Ugarriza and Didier Caluwaerts, eds., *Democratic Deliberation in Deeply Divided Societies: From Conflict to Common Ground* (Basingstoke: Palgrave Macmillan, 2014); Robert C. Luskin, Ian O'Flynn, James S. Fishkin, and David Russell, "Deliberating across Deep Divides," *Political Studies* 62, no. 1 (2014), https://doi.org/10.1111/j.1467-9248.2012.01005.x.

7. Donald L. Horowitz, *Ethnic Groups in Conflict* (Berkeley: University of California Press, 1985), 7.

8. Zsuzsanna Chappell, *Deliberative Democracy: A Critical Introduction* (Basingstoke: Palgrave Macmillan, 2012), 26.

9. Spiro Kiousis, "Interactivity: A Concept Explication," *New Media & Society*, 4 no. 3 (2002), https://doi.org/10.1177/146144480200400303.

10. Edward J. Downes and Sally J. McMillan, "Defining Interactivity," *New Media & Society* 2, no. 2 (2000): 159, https://doi.org/10.1177/14614440022225751.

11. Interactivity should be further differentiated from "human interaction," which is technologically mediated, and from "media interaction," which refers to interaction with the media. Jens F. Jensen, "'Interactivity': Tracking a New Concept in Media and Communication Studies," *Nordicom Review* 19, no. 1 (1998); Jennifer Stromer-Galley, "On-Line Interaction and Why Candidates Avoid It," *Journal of Communication* 50, no. 4 (2000): 117–18, https://doi.org/10.1111/j.1460-2466.2000.tb02865.x.

12. For a review of scholarship on online deliberation, see Dennis Friess and Christiane Eilders, "A Systematic Review of Online Deliberation Research," *Policy and Internet* 7, no. 3 (2015), https://doi.org/10.1002/poi3.95; Daniel Halpern and Jennifer Gibbs, "Social Media as a Catalyst for Online Deliberation? Exploring the Affordances of Facebook and YouTube for Political Expression," *Computers in Human Behaviour* 29, no. 3 (2013), https://doi.org/10.1016/j.chb.2012.10.008.

13. Kiousis, "Interactivity," 359.

14. Stromer-Galley, "On-Line Interaction," 117.

15. Rudy Bretz, *Media for Interactive Communication* (Beverly Hills: Sage, 1983), qtd. in Kiousis, "Interactivity," 357.

16. Matthias Trénel, "Measuring the Deliberativeness of Online Discussions. Coding Scheme 2.0" (unpublished paper, Social Science Research Center, Berlin, August 10, 2004), 21, http://www.wzberlin.de/~trenel/tools/quod_2_4.pdf.

17. Trénel, "Measuring," 21.

18. M. M. Bakhtin, *The Dialogic Imagination: Four Essays*, trans. C. Emerson and M. Holquist (Austin: University of Texas Press, 1981), 282, quoted in Danielle Endres and Barbara Warnick, "Effects of Campaign-to-User and Text-Based Interactivity in Candidate Campaign Web Sites: A Case Study from the 2002 Elections," *Western Journal of Communication* 68, no. 3 (2004): 328–29, https://doi.org/10.1080/10570310409374804. On the role of language in eliciting interaction, see Darren G. Lilleker and Casilda Malagón, "Levels of Interactivity in the 2007 French Presidential Candidates' Websites," *European Journal of Communication* 25, no. 1 (2010), https://doi.org/10.1177/0267323109354231.

19. Sheizaf Rafaeli, "Interactivity: From New Media to Communication," in *Advancing Communication Science: Merging Mass and Interpersonal Processes*, ed. Robert P. Hawkins, John M. Wiemann, and Suzanne Pingree (Newbury Park, CA: Sage, 1988).

20. Edith Manosevitch, Nili Steinfeld, and Azi Lev-On, "Promoting Online Deliberation Quality: Cognitive Cues Matter," *Information, Communication and Society* 17, no. 10 (2014): 1182, https://doi.org/10.1080/1369118X.2014.899610.

21. E. Johanna Hartelius, "'Leave a Message of Hope or Tribute': Digital Memorializing as Public Deliberation," *Argumentation and Advocacy* 47, no. 2 (2010): 80, https://doi.org/10.1080/00028533.2010.11821739.

22. Jürg Steiner, *The Foundations of Deliberative Democracy: Empirical Research and Normative Implications* (Cambridge: Cambridge University Press, 2012), 148.

23. Ian Rowe, "Deliberation 2.0: Comparing the Deliberative Quality of Online News User Comments Across Platforms," *Journal of Broadcasting & Electronic Media* 59, no. 4 (2015): 549, https://doi.org/10.1080/08838151.2015.1093482.

24. Rowe, "Deliberation 2.0," 549.

25. Tali Mendelberg, Christopher F. Karpowitz, and J. Baxter Oliphant, "Gender Inequality in Deliberation: Unpacking the Black Box of Interaction," *Perspectives on Politics* 12, no. 1 (2014), https://doi.org/10.1017/S1537592713003691.

26. Cass R. Sunstein, "Ideological Amplification," *Constellations* 14, no. 2 (2007): 277, https://doi.org/10.1111/j.1467-8675.2007.00439.x.

27. Manlio Cinalli and Ian O'Flynn, "Public Deliberation, Network Analysis and the Political Integration of Muslims in Britain," *British Journal of Politics and International Relations* 16, no. 3 (2014): 433, https://doi.org/10.1111/1467-856X.12003.

28. Caluwaerts and Deschouwer, "Building Bridges," 439; Similarly, see Steiner, *The Foundations*, 118–19.

29. Cinalli and O'Flynn, "Public Deliberation," 435.

30. Mendelberg, Karpowitz, and Oliphant, "Gender Inequality," 22–23.

31. Mendelberg, Karpowitz, and Oliphant, "Gender Inequality," 21. The study of interactivity provides a novel perspective on women's disadvantaged position in deliberation reflected in "the patterns of talking and listening." Lynn M. Sanders, "Against Deliberation," *Political Theory* 25, no. 3 (1997): 370, https://www.jstor.org/stable/191984.

32. Kevin M. Esterling, Archon Fung, and Taeku Lee, "How Much Disagreement Is Good for Democratic Deliberation?," *Political Communication* 32, no. 4 (2015): 530, https://doi.org/10.1080/10584609.2014.969466.

33. Dennis F. Thompson, "Deliberative Democratic Theory and Empirical Political Science," *Annual Review of Political Science* 11 no. 1 (2008): 502, https://doi.org/10.1146/annurev.polisci.11.081306.070555.

34. André Bächtiger and Marlène Gerber, "'Gentlemanly Conversation' or Vigorous Contestation? An Exploratory Analysis of Communication Modes in a Transnational Deliberative Poll (Europolis)," in *Deliberative Mini-Publics: Involving Citizens in the Democratic Process*, ed. Kimmo Grönlund, André Bächtiger and Maija Setälä (Colchester: ECPR Press, 2014), 118.

35. Andrew F. Smith, *The Deliberative Impulse: Motivating Discourse in Divided Societies* (Lanham, MD: Lexington Books, 2011), 73.

36. Huw Price, "Truth as Convenient Fiction," in *The Pragmatism Reader: From Peirce through the Present*, ed. Robert B. Talisse and Scott F. Aikin (Princeton: Princeton University Press, 2011), 464.

37. Cheryl Misak, "Making Disagreement Matter: Pragmatism and Deliberative Democracy," *Journal of Speculative Philosophy* 18, no. 1 (2004): 20, https://www.jstor.org/stable/25670494.

38. Diana C. Mutz, "Is Deliberative Democracy a Falsifiable Theory?," *Annual Review of Political Science* 11 (2008): 535, https://doi.org/10.1146/annurev.polisci.11.081306.070308; Probing the impact of contentious deliberation, Wojcieszak finds that perceived disagreement decreases communicative participation. Magdalena Wojcieszak "Pulling toward or Pulling Away: Deliberation, Disagreement, and Opinion Extremity in Political Participation," *Social Science Quarterly* 92, no. 1 (2011): 219, https://www.jstor.org/stable/42956481.

39. This, Neblo specifies, will legitimize deliberation even when there are no epistemic benefits to accrue. Michael A. Neblo, "Family Disputes: Diversity in Defining and Measuring Deliberation," *Swiss Political Science Review* 13, no. 4 (2007): 537, https://doi.org/10.1002/j.1662-6370.tb00088.x.

40. Bernard Manin, "Democratic Deliberation: Why We Should Promote Debate Rather Than Discussion" (paper presented at the Program in Ethics and Public Affairs Seminar, Princeton University, October 13, 2005), 20, https://nyuscholars.nyu.edu/en/publications/deliberation-why-we-should-focus-on-debate-rather-than-discussion.

41. Steiner, *The Foundations*, 122–23.

42. Thompson, "Deliberative Democratic," 504.

43. A contrary argument is presented by Testa, who distinguishes respect for persons from respect for what they say. Italo Testa, "The Respect Fallacy: Limits of Respect in Public Dialogue," in *Rhetorical Citizenship and Public Deliberation*, ed. Christian Kock and Lisa Villadsen (Philadelphia: Pennsylvania State University Press, 2012).

44. Didier Caluwaerts and Juan E. Ugarriza, "Beating the Odds: Confrontational Deliberative Democracy," in *Democratic Deliberation in Deeply Divided Societies: From Conflict to Common Ground*, ed. Juan Ugarriza and Didier Caluwaerts (Basingstoke: Palgrave Macmillan, 2014), 221.

45. Peter Dahlgren, "The Internet, Public Spheres, and Political Communication: Dispersion and Deliberation," *Political Communication* 22, no. 2 (2005): 149, https://doi.org/10.1080/10584600590933160.

46. Yehudith Auerbach, "The Reconciliation Pyramid—A Narrative-Based Framework for Analyzing Identity Conflicts," *Political Psychology* 30, no. 2 (2009): 299, https://doi.org/10.1111/j.1467-9221.2008.00692.x.

47. See table A.5.1 in the appendix for intercoder reliability statistics for interactivity variables.

48. Stromer-Galley, "On-Line Interaction."

49. See Caluwaerts and Deschouwer, "Building Bridges," 439.

50. Kiousis, "Interactivity," 376. Similarly, Manosevitch and Walker consider the form of address by referring to a contributor's username as an indicator of explicit acknowledgment of other comments and ideas mentioned therein. See Edith Manosevitch and Dana Walker, "Reader Comments to Online Opinion Journalism: A Space of Public Deliberation," *International Symposium on Online Journalism* 10 (2009).

51. I applied this strategy because the words are traced precisely to the speaker who uttered them. Some discussants reacted to the moderator's comments. These instances are included in the coding of interactivity along with reactions to discussants. Since moderators also came from different ethnic groups and restated positions, for example by the Working Group, on the Draft Statute in the course of the discussion, accounting for them contributes to understanding the pattern of interactivity across ethnic lines.

52. The last name is fictitious.

53. On the need for caution in inferring ethnicity from a surname, see Angus Nicoll, Karen Bassett, and Stanley J. Ulijaszek, "What's in a Name? Accuracy of Using Surnames and Forenames in Ascribing Asian Ethnic Identity in English Populations," *Journal of Epidemiology and Community Health* 40, no. 4 (1986), https://doi.org/10.1136/jech.40.4.364. Multiple strategies were used and triangulated to code deliberators' ethnicity. In those cases where speakers did not identify their ethnic background in the introductory part of the consultation session or at any other point during their participation in deliberation, the author conducted extensive research to establish the speaker's ethnicity, which was also verified by the second coder. The strategies used include consulting reports by local human rights NGOs in all post-Yugoslav countries; media reports related to advocacy for wartime human rights violations; and transcripts of war crimes trials, both domestic and

at the ICTY. Research into the genealogy of family names and their geographic distribution in former Yugoslavia was also conducted.

54. Sunstein, "Ideological Amplification."

55. James S. Fishkin, *When the People Speak: Deliberative Democracy and Public Consultation* (Oxford: Oxford University Press, 2009), 101.

56. Will Kymlicka, *Multicultural Citizenship: A Liberal Theory of Minority Rights* (Oxford: Oxford University Press, 1996).

57. Dietram A. Scheufele et al., "Democracy Based on Difference: Examining the Links Between Structural Heterogeneity, Heterogeneity of Discussion Networks, and Democratic Citizenship," *Journal of Communication* 56, no. 4 (2006): 733, https://doi.org/10.1111/j.1460-2466.2006.00317.x.

58. These results differ from Caluwaerts and Deschouwer's findings, which are based on experimental research in Belgium that shows more responses to an in-group than to an out-group, and whose claim of discursive integration is based on the claim that the difference between two types of responses is negligible. Caluwaerts and Deschouwer, "Building Bridges," 439.

59. Dryzek, "Deliberative Democracy," 230.

60. Additional analyses were conducted to investigate whether speakers from certain ethnic groups interact more with speakers from particular ethnic groups, for example a Croat responding to a Serb and vice versa as compared to an Albanian responding to a Serb and vice versa. All combinations of ethnicities represented in the RECOM process were considered. However, no particular pattern of interactivity involving speakers from specific groups was observed based on the available data. Future research can advance the study of interactivity in postconflict contexts by investigating how different pairs of speakers from different ethnic groups interact.

61. Caluwaerts and Deschouwer, "Building Bridges," 430.

62. Friess and Eilders, "A Systematic," 329.

63. Given the coding strategy of interactivity that includes moderators, this pattern of proportionally fewer interactions indicating disagreement than those indicating agreement holds when applied to discussants only.

64. For example, Europolis, a 2009 pan-European deliberative poll that included deliberators from different national backgrounds, see Bächtiger and Gerber, "'Gentlemanly Conversation.'"

65. It is noteworthy that the observed pattern of disagreement is the opposite of that in online deliberation, where there is a tendency to disagree rather than to agree. Stromer-Galley, "On-Line Interaction"; Manosevitch, Steinfeld, and Lev-On, "Promoting," 1189; Harold J. Jansen and Royce Koop, "Pundits, Ideologues, and Ranters: The British Columbia Election Online," *Canadian Journal of Communication* 30, no. 4 (2005): 624, https://doi.org/10.22230/cjc.2005v30n4a1483; Carlo Hagemann, "Participation in and Contents of Two Dutch Political Party Discussion Lists on the Internet," *Javnost-The Public* 9, no. 2 (2002): 72, https://doi.org/10.1080/13183222.2002.11008800.

66. John Gastil, "The Lessons and Limitations of Experiments in Democratic Deliberation," *Annual Review of Law and Social Science* 14, no. 1 (2018): 284 https://doi.org/10.1146/annurev-lawsocsci-110316-113639.

67. Amy Gutmann and Dennis Thompson, *Democracy and Disagreement* (Cambridge: Harvard University Press, 1996), 18.

68. Amy Gutmann and Dennis Thompson, *Why Deliberative Democracy?* (Princeton: Princeton University Press, 2004), 151.

69. William J. Long and Peter Brecke, *War and Reconciliation: Reason and Emotion in Conflict Resolution* (Cambridge: MIT Press), 18–19.

70. With these controls held constant, respect is a key predictor of interethnic interactivity. The likelihood ratio test of the hypothesis that all respect coefficients are 0 gives a test statistic of 47.38 for 6 *df*, which returns a *p*-value <.001. Other relevant variables were investigated as potential predictors of interactivity, namely, gender, speaker type, stakeholder type, ethnic diversity of the consultation, whether translation was required, and respect toward other ethnic groups and countries. A backward selection procedure was conducted, in which variables were iteratively dropped according to the largest *p*-value of the likelihood ratio test statistic. The procedure included combining and testing alternate theoretically justified combinations of variable categories at stages in the process determined by the largest *p*-value. Respect for groups was highly insignificant and dropped early in the process. The ethnic diversity of the consultation was dropped during the process because the only statistically significant partial effect was the dyadic vs. multiethnic consultation type, which lowered the probability of neutral interethnic interaction. The Wald test statistics of all other estimates (on all consultation types at all levels of interactivity) were insignificant. Because the research question of interest is explaining disagreement and agreement and not neutral interactions *per se*, and in the interest of model parsimony, consultation diversity was not included in the final model. Based on the RECOM data, we can conclude that dyadic deliberation, which we may assume has a sharper focus on division, is not associated with more disagreement across ethnic lines than deliberation between people from multiple ethnic groups.

71. Name changed. RECOM Consultation no. 3.

72. RECOM Consultation no. 2.

73. RECOM Consultation no. 3.

74. RECOM Consultation no. 4.

75. RECOM Consultation no. 1.

76. On most people's tendency to avoid conflict and disagreement, see John R. Hibbing and Elizabeth Theiss-Morse, *Stealth Democracy: Americans' Beliefs about How Government Should Work* (Cambridge: Cambridge University Press, 2002); Diana C. Mutz, *Hearing the Other Side: Deliberative versus Participatory Democracy* (Cambridge: Cambridge University Press, 2006).

77. Compared to a neutral respect reference, a disrespectful reference increases the odds of disagreement by a factor of 4.405 compared to not interacting across ethnic lines, i.e., 1/0.227.

78. As shown by the model selection process.

79. For a comprehensive discussion, see Nevin T. Aiken, "Rethinking Reconciliation in Divided Societies: A Social Learning Theory of Transitional Justice," in *Transitional Justice Theories*, ed. Susane Buckley-Zistel, Teresa Koloma Beck, Christian Braun, and Friederike Mieth (New York: Routledge, 2014), 40–65.

80. On elaboration of how the politicization of transitional justice in postconflict contexts contributes to these dynamics, see Christopher K. Lamont, *International Criminal Justice and the Politics of Compliance* (London: Routledge, 2010); Bekim Baliqi, "Contested War Remembrance and Ethnopolitical Identities in Kosovo," *Nationalities Papers* 46, no. 3 (2018), https://doi.org/10.1080/00905992.2017.1375906.

81. Christina Maslach, Joy Strapp, and Richard T. Santee, "Individuation: Conceptual Analysis and Assessment," *Journal of Personality and Social Psychology* 49, no. 3 (1985), https://doi.org/10.1037/0022-3514.49.3.729.

82. For Kosovo, see Denisa Kostovicova, "Legitimacy and International Administration: The Ahtisaari Settlement for Kosovo from a Human Security Perspective," *International Peacekeeping* 15, no. 5 (2008), https://doi.org/10.1080/13533310802396160.

83. Steven Majstorovic, "Ancient Hatreds or Elite Manipulation?: Memory and Politics in the Former Yugoslavia," *World Affairs* 159, no. 4 (1997): 170, https://www.jstor.org/stable/20672499.

84. O'Loughlin, "Inter-Ethnic Friendships."

85. Jack Knight and James Johnson, "Aggregation and Deliberation: On the Possibility of Democratic Legitimacy," *Political Theory* 22, no. 2 (1994), https://www.jstor.org/stable/192147; Tali Mandelberg and John Oleske, "Race and Public Deliberation," *Political Communication* 17, no. 2 (2000), https://doi.org/10.1080/105846000198468.

86. Jennifer Stromer-Galley and Peter Muhlberger, "Agreement and Disagreement in Group Deliberation: Effects on Deliberation Satisfaction, Future Engagement, and Decision Legitimacy," *Political Communication* 26, no. 2 (2009), https://doi.org/10.1080/10584600902850775.

87. Caluwaerts and Ugarriza, "Beating," 213.

88. This label is commonly attributed to civil society activists crossing ethnic lines in postconflict contexts, see Mary Kaldor, Yahia Said, and Denisa Kostovicova, "War and Peace: The Role of Global Civil Society," in *Global Civil Society 2006/7*, ed. Mary Kaldor, Martin Albrow, Helmut Anheier, and Marlies Glasius (London: Sage, 2006); Alexander Koensler, "Acts of Solidarity: Crossing and Reiterating Israeli—Palestinian Frontiers," *International Journal of Urban and Regional Research* 40 no. 2 (2016): 342, https://doi.org/10.1111/1468-2427.12380.

6. DISCURSIVE SOLIDARITY AGAINST IDENTITY POLITICS

1. André Bächtiger and John Parkinson, *Mapping and Measuring Deliberation: Towards a New Deliberative Quality* (Oxford: Oxford University Press, 2019), 32.

2. Rick Kosterman and Seymour Feshbach, "Toward a Measure of Patriotic and Nationalistic Attitudes," *Political Psychology* 10, no. 2 (1980), https://doi.org/10.2307/3791647; Bächtiger and Parkinson, *Mapping*, 32.

3. Mary Bucholtz and Kira Hall, "Identity and Interaction: A Sociocultural Linguistic Approach," *Discourse Studies* 7, no. 4–5 (2005): 607, https://doi.org/10.1177/1461445605054407.

4. William Rehg, *Insight and Solidarity: The Discourse Ethics of Jürgen Habermas* (Berkeley: University of California Press, 1994), 211, 176, 212–13.

5. Conrado Hübner Mendes, *Constitutional Courts and Deliberative Democracy* (Oxford: Oxford University Press, 2013), 122–23.

6. Jürgen Habermas, *The Inclusion of the Other: Studies in Political Theory*, eds. Ciaran Cronin and Pablo De Greiff (Cambridge: Polity Press, 1999), 248.

7. John S. Dryzek, *Deliberative Democracy and Beyond: Liberals, Critics, Contestations* (Oxford: Oxford University Press, 2000); Ian O'Flynn, *Deliberative Democracy and Divided Societies* (Edinburgh: Edinburgh University Press, 2006).

8. David Crocker, "Transitional Justice and International Civil Society: Toward a Normative Framework," *Constellations* 5, no. 4 (1998): 492, https://doi.org/10.1111/1467-8675.00110; Ernesto Verdeja, *Unchopping a Tree: Reconciliation in the Aftermath of Political Violence* (Philadelphia: Temple University Press, 2009), 143–47; Kora Andrieu, "Civilizing Peacebuilding: Transitional Justice, Civil Society and the Liberal Paradigm," *Security Dialogue* 41, no. 5 (2010): 567, https://doi.org/10.1177/0967010610382109.

9. Jürgen Habermas, *The Theory of Communicative Action*. vol. 1. *Reason and the Rationalization of Society* (Cambridge: Polity Press, [1984] 2004), 359–79.

10. Ian O'Flynn, *Deliberative Democracy*, 141–62.

11. Habermas, *The Inclusion*, 249.

12. James Bohman, "Transnationalizing Peacebuilding: Transitional Justice as a Deliberative Process," in *Jus Post Bellum and Transitional Justice*, ed. Larry May and Elizabeth Edenberg (Cambridge: Cambridge University Press, 2013), 298.

13. Habermas, *The Inclusion*, 44.

14. Petr Kopecký and Cass Mudde, eds., *Uncivil Society? Contentious Politics in Post-Communist Europe* (London: Routledge, 2003). On the relationship between illiberal civil society actors and conflict, see Mary Kaldor, Yahia Said, and Denisa Kostovicova, "War and Peace: The Role of Global Civil Society," in *Global Civil Society 2006/7*, ed. Mary Kaldor, Martin Albrow, Helmut Anheier, and Marlies Glasius (London: Sage, 2006), and on illiberal civil society and transitional justice, see Denisa Kostovicova, "Civil Society and Post-Communist Democratization: Facing a Double Challenge in Post-Milošević Serbia," *Journal of Civil Society* 2, no. 1 (2006), https://doi.org/10.1080/17448680600730918.

15. Author's interview no. 5, Serbia, September 24, 2014.

16. Author's interview no. 26, Croatia, December 16, 2019.

17. Author's interview no. 24, Croatia, December 16, 2019.

18. Focus Group, Bosnia and Herzegovina, December 11, 2015.

19. Naomi Head, "Costly Encounters of the Empathic Kind: A Typology," *International Theory* 8, no. 1 (2016): 173, https://doi.org.10.1017/S1752971915000238.

20. Author's interview no. 16, Kosovo, May 24, 2016.

21. Author's interview no. 24, Croatia, December 16, 2019.

22. Author's interview no. 14, Kosovo, May 23, 2016.

23. Author's interview no. 8, Serbia, September 26, 2014.

24. Hübner Mendes, *Constitutional Courts*, 122.

25. Habermas, *The Theory*; Axel Honneth, *The Struggle for Recognition: The Moral Grammar of Social Conflicts* (Cambridge: Polity Press, 1995).

26. Habermas, *The Inclusion*, 249.

27. Rehg, *Insight*, 169.

28. Nigel King and Christine Horrocks, *Interviews in Qualitative Research* (London: Sage, 2010), 164. See also James Paul Gee, *An Introduction to Discourse Analysis: Theory and Method*, 4th ed. (London: Routledge, 2014), 140.

29. Stella Ting-Toomey et al., "Ethnic/Cultural Identity Salience and Conflict Styles in Four US Ethnic Groups," *International Journal of Intercultural Relations* 24, no. 1 (2000), https://doi.org/10.1016/S0147-1767(99)00023-1.

30. The ethnic dimension of identity is heightened in the context of an intergroup conflict involving groups within a state and coethnics in a bordering state. Nicholas Sambanis and Moses Shayo, "Social Identification and Ethnic Conflict," *American Political Science Review* 107, no. 2 (2013), https://doi.org/10.2139/ssrn.1955111; Gautam Nair and Nicholas Sambanis, "Violence Exposure and Ethnic Identification: Evidence from Kashmir," *International Organization* 73, no. 2 (2019), https://doi.org/10.1017/s0020818318000498.

31. Conversely, governments can also manipulate and reduce the salience of ethnic identity. Arthur Bloun and Sharun W. Mukand, "Erasing Ethnicity? Propaganda, Nation Building, and Identity in Rwanda," *Journal of Political Economy* 127, no. 3 (2019), https://doi.org/10.1086/701441.

32. Thomas F. Pettigrew, Linda R. Tropp, Ulrich Wagner, and Oliver Christ, "Recent Advances in Intergroup Theory," *International Journal of Intercultural Relations* 35, no. 3 (2011): 277, https://doi.org/10.1016/j.ijintrel.2011.03.001.

33. Joanna Anneke Rummens, "Conceptualising Identity and Diversity: Overlaps, Intersections, and Processes," *Canadian Ethnic Studies Journal* 35, no. 3 (2003).

34. Bikhu Parekh, *A New Politics of Identity: Political Principles for an Interdependent World* (Basingstoke: Palgrave Macmillan, 2008), 35.

35. Author's interview no. 8, Serbia, September 26, 2014.

36. Author's interview no. 22, Croatia, December 15, 2019.

37. Author's interview no. 20, Montenegro, September 2, 2016.

38. According to one interviewee, the pressure included a threat, open or insinuated, of the withdrawal of state funding for activities of these NGOs. Author's interview no. 20, Montenegro, September 2, 2016.

39. Author's interview no. 2, Serbia, April 18, 2014; author's interview no. 9, Bosnia and Herzegovina, December 9, 2015.

40. Author's interview no. 15, Kosovo, May 24, 2016.

41. Author's interview no. 9, Bosnia and Herzegovina, December 9, 2015.

42. I refer to what Janis identified as overriding and excessive concurrence-seeking among group members, which in this case applies to an identity group; see Irving L. Janis, *Victims of Groupthink: A Psychological Study of Foreign Policy Decisions and Fiascoes* (Boston: Houghton Mifflin, 1972).

43. Author's interview no. 18, Montenegro, September 2, 2016; I heard this view repeatedly in informal discussions with participants from other countries.

44. Author's interview no. 19, Montenegro, September 2, 2016.

45. On people expressing positions they erroneously believe to be held by others, see Diane Rucinski, "The Centrality of Reciprocity to Communication and Democracy," *Critical Studies in Mass Communication* 8, no. 2 (1991): 189, https://doi.org/10.1080/15295039109366790.

46. Author's interview no. 16, Kosovo, May 24, 2016.

47. Author's interview no. 24, Croatia, December 16, 2019.

48. Author's interview no. 27, December 16, 2016.

49. Author's interview no. 27, December 16, 2016; author's interview no. 20, Montenegro, September 2, 2016.

50. Author's interview no. 17, Kosovo, May 24, 2016.

51. Author's interview no. 5, Serbia, September 24, 2014.

52. Author's interview no. 8, Serbia, September 26, 2014; author's interview no. 17, Kosovo, May 24, 2016; author's interview no. 20, Montenegro, September 2, 2016.

53. On the disempowerment of victims by NGOs purportedly representing them, see Tshepo Madligozi, "On Transitional Justice Entrepreneurs and the Production of Victims," *Journal of Human Rights Practice* 2, no. 2 (2010), https://doi.org/10.1093/jhuman/huq005.

54. This has become uniform mainstream criticism of externally funded NGOs in peacebuilding contexts. It restates similar arguments previously made by scholars of development, such as Jude Howell and Jenny Pearce, *Civil Society and Development: A Critical Exploration* (Boulder: Lynne Rienner, 2001). For criticism of foreign-funded NGOs and how they undermine peacebuilding, see Patrice C. McMahon, *The NGO Game: Post-Conflict Peacebuilding in the Balkans and Beyond* (Ithaca: Cornell University Press, 2017). For a discussion about transitional justice, see Paige Arthur and Christalla Yakinthou, eds., *Transitional Justice, International Assistance, and Civil Society: Missed Connections* (Cambridge: Cambridge University Press, 2018), and Olivera Simić and Zala Volčič, eds., *Transitional Justice and Civil Society in the Balkans* (New York: Springer, 2013). Emerging research goes beyond a wholesale dismissal of externally funded NGOs and their activities. It identifies when and how NGO activities enjoy local legitimacy and further justice and peacebuilding despite being foreign-funded, see Randall Puljek-Shank, "Civil Agency in Governance: The Role of Legitimacy with Citizens vs. Donors," *Voluntas: Journal of Voluntary and Nonprofit Organizations* 29, no. 4 (2018), https://doi.org/10.1007/s11266-018-0020-0; Milli Lake, *Strong NGOs and Weak States: Pursuing Gender Justice in the Democratic Republic of Congo and South Africa* (Cambridge: Cambridge University Press, 2018).

55. On a positive impact of out-group differentiation in overcoming identity division in the context of migration, see Ana Guinote, "The Perception of Group Variability in a Non-Minority and a Minority Context: When Adaptation Leads to Out-Group

Differentiation," *British Journal of Social Psychology* 40 (2001), https://doi.org/10.1348/014466601164722.

56. Author's interview no. 24, Croatia, December 16, 2019.

57. On deserving and undeserving victims, see Kieran McEvoy and Kirsten McConnachie, "Victims and Transitional Justice: Voice, Agency and Blame," *Social and Legal Studies* 22 no. 4 (2013): 504, https://doi.org/10.1177/0964663913499062. For example, Berry argues that Bosniak nationalists created a victim hierarchy that recognized Bosniak women victims of wartime rape alongside widows and mothers of men and boys who perished in the Srebrenica genocide above all other Bosniak victims and above victims of other ethnic groups. Marie E. Berry, "Barriers to Women's Progress After Atrocity: Evidence from Rwanda and Bosnia-Herzegovina," *Gender and Society* 31, no. 6 (2017): 841, https://doi.org/10.1177/0891243217737060. Similarly, for an "unjust favouring of some" over other victims, see Adriana Rudling, "'I'm Not That Chained-Up Little Person': Four Paragons of Victimhood in Transitional Justice Discourse," *Human Rights Quarterly* 41, no. 2 (2019), https://doi.org/10.1353/hrq.2019.0032. For differential treatment of victims in Bosnia, see Jessie Barton-Hronešová, *The Struggle for Redress: Victim Capital in Bosnia and Herzegovina* (Cham: Palgrave Macmillan, 2020).

58. Author's interview no. 8, Serbia, September 26, 2014.

59. Mark A. Wolfgram, *Antigone's Ghosts: The Long Legacy of War and Genocide in Five Countries* (Lewisburg, PA: Bucknell University Press, 2019), 8.

60. Duan and Hill refer to intellectual empathy and empathic emotions to distinguish these two aspects of empathy. Changming Duan and Clara E. Hill, "The Current State of Empathy Research," *Journal of Counseling Psychology* 43, no. 3 (1996): 263, https://doi.org/10.1037/0022-0167.43.3.261.

61. While foregrounding perspective-taking in consideration of empathy, neither Steiner et al. nor Ugarizza and Trujillo-Orrego investigate the expression of explicit affiliation with the suffering of members of the out-group caused by members of the in-group; see Jürg Steiner, André Bächtiger, Markus Spörndli, and Marco R. Steenbergen, *Deliberative Politics in Action: Analysing Parliamentary Discourse* (Cambridge: Cambridge University Press, 2004), 22; Ugarizza and Trujillo-Orrego consider messages that are expected to arouse empathy toward the speaker, as illustrated by an ex-combatant's statement, "our rights have been violent, we have nobody's support," but do not investigate how speakers empathize with the suffering of others. Juan E. Ugarizza and Natalia Trujillo-Orrego, "The Ironic Effect of Deliberation: What We Can (and Cannot) Expect in Deeply Divided Societies," *Acta Politica* 55 (2020): 233n18, https://doi.org/10.1057/s41269-018-0113-1.

62. Jake Harwood, Miles Hewstone, Yair Amichai-Hamburger, and Nicole Tausch, "Intergroup Contact: An Integration of Social Psychological and Communication Perspectives," *Annals of the International Communication Association* 36 no. 1 (2013): 62, 10.1080/23808985.2013.11679126; Esra Cuhadar and Bruce Dayton, "The Social Psychology of Identity and Inter-Group Conflict: From Theory to Practice," *International Studies Perspectives* 12, no. 3 (2011): 285–86, https://www.jstor.org/stable/44218664. A participant in RECOM consultations recalled there being "a lot of emotions" in the RECOM meetings, "which to [her] was touching." Author's interview no. 14, Kosovo, May 23, 2016. For example, on the juxtaposition between rational (deliberative) and emotional (empathetic) communication, see Ugarriza and Trujillo-Orrego, "The Ironic Effect of Deliberation."

63. Michael A. Neblo, "Impassioned Democracy: The Roles of Emotion in Deliberative Theory," *American Political Science Review* 114, no. 3 (2020), https://doi.org/10.1017/S0003055420000210.

64. Neblo, "Impassioned Democracy," 926n5; 926.

65. Head, "Costly Encounters." Scholars of intergroup contact show that empathy toward an out-group mediates forgiveness after conflict. Sabina Cehajic, Rupert Brown,

and Emanuele Castano, "Forgive and Forget? Antecedents and Consequences of Inter-group Forgiveness in Bosnia and Herzegovina," *Political Psychology* 29, no. 3 (2008), https://doi.org/10.1111/j.1467-9221.2008.00634.x.

66. Krystina A. Finlay and Walter G. Stephan, "Improving Intergroup Relations: The Effects of Empathy on Racial Attitudes," *Journal of Applied Social Psychology* 30, no. 8 (2000), https://doi.org/10.1111/j.1559-1816.2000.tb02464.x.

67. Author's interview no. 23, Croatia, December 16, 2019.

68. Stanley Cohen, *States of Denial: Knowing about Atrocities and Suffering* (Cambridge: Polity, 2001), 216.

69. Author's interview no. 6, Serbia, September 25, 2014.

70. Author's interview no. 25, Croatia, December 16, 2019.

71. Author's interview no. 15, Kosovo, May 24, 2016.

72. Author's interview no. 20, Montenegro, September 2, 2016.

73. Focus Group, Bosnia and Herzegovina, December 11, 2015.

74. Author's interview no. 23, Croatia, December 16, 2019.

75. Author's interview no. 16, Kosovo, May 24, 2016.

76. Author's interview no. 10, Bosnia and Herzegovina, December 10, 2015.

77. RECOM Consultation no. 11.

78. Author's interview no. 22, Croatia, December 15, 2019.

79. Author's interview no. 10, Bosnia and Herzegovina, December 10, 2015.

80. Author's interview no. 23, Croatia, December 16, 2019.

81. Author's interview no. 26, Croatia, December 16, 2019.

82. Roland Kostić, "Transnational Justice and Reconciliation in Bosnia-Herzegovina: Whose Memories, Whose Justice?," *Sociologija* 54, no. 4 (2012): 662, https://doi.org/10.2298/SOC1204649K.

83. Author's interview no. 16, Kosovo, May 24, 2016.

84. Focus Group, Bosnia and Herzegovina, December 11, 2015.

85. Tamara Pavasović Trošt, "Ruptures and Continuities in Nationhood Narratives: Reconstructing the Nation through History Textbooks in Serbia and Croatia," *Nations and Nationalism* 24, no. 3 (2018), https://doi.org/10.1111/nana.12433. On ethnocentric history in Serbian and Albanian textbooks before and after the 1998–99 Kosovo conflict, see Denisa Kostovicova, *Kosovo: The Politics of Identity and Space* (London: Routledge, 2005), 127–81.

86. Author's interview no. 18, Montenegro, September 2, 2016.

87. RECOM Consultation no. 5.

88. Focus Group, Serbia, October 30, 2015.

89. Author's interview no. 22, Croatia, December 15, 2019.

90. RECOM Consultation no. 24.

91. Author's interview no. 24, Croatia, December 16, 2019.

92. Susana Narotzky and Paz Moreno, "Reciprocity's Dark Side: Negative Reciprocity, Morality and Social Reproduction," *Anthropological Theory* 2, no. 3 (2000): 301, https://doi.org/10.1177/1463499602002003801. For a fine-grained breakdown of negative reciprocity beliefs, see Robert Eisenberger, Patrick Lynch, Justin Aselage, and Stephanie Rohdieck, "Who Takes the Most Revenge? Individual Differences in Negative Reciprocity Norm Endorsement," *Personality and Social Psychology Bulletin* 30, no. 6 (2004), https://doi.org/10.1177/0146167204264047.

93. Narotzky and Moreno, "Reciprocity's Dark Side," 301.

94. McEvoy and McConnachie, "Victims," 504.

95. Sedmi regionalni forum za tranzicijsku pravdu, Zagreb, October 16–17, 2010.

96. RECOM Consultation no. 2.

97. RECOM Consultation no. 5.

98. RECOM Consultation no. 17.

99. RECOM Consultation no. 8.

100. Walter G. Stephan and Cookie White Stephan, "Intergroup Anxiety," *Journal of Social Issues* 41, no. 3 (1985), https://doi.org/10.1111/j.1540-4560.1985.tb01134.x; J. Nicole Shelton, "Interpersonal Concerns in Social Encounters between Majority and Minority Group Members," *Group Processes & Intergroup Relations* 6, no. 2 (2003), https://doi.org/10.1177/1368430203006002003. Kristin Davies, Stephen C. Wright, Arthur Aron, and Joseph Comeau, "Intergroup Contact through Friendship: Intimacy and Norms," in *Advances in Intergroup Contact*, ed. Gordon Hodson and Miles Hewstone (London: Psychology Press, 2013): 203; Pettigrew, Tropp, Wagner, and Christ, "Recent Advances in Intergroup Contact Theory," 277. Such anxiety may be unfounded; see Robyn K. Mallett and Timothy D. Wilson, "Increasing Positive Intergroup Contact," *Journal of Experimental Social Psychology* 46, no. 2 (2010), https://doi.org/10.1016/j.jesp.2009.11.006.

101. Author's interview no. 17, Kosovo, May 24, 2016.

102. Author's interview no. 9, Bosnia and Herzegovina, December 9, 2015.

103. See Marianna Bicskei, Matthias Lankau, and Kilian Bizer, "Negative Reciprocity and Its Relation to Anger-Like Emotions in Identity-Homogeneous and Heterogeneous Groups," *Journal of Economic Psychology* 54 (2016), https://doi.org/10.1016/j.joep.2016.02.008.

104. Author's interview no. 23, Croatia, December 16, 2019.

105. Kimberly Theidon, *Intimate Enemies: Violence and Reconciliation in Peru* (Philadelphia: University of Pennsylvania Press, 2012); Focus Group, Serbia, October 30, 2015.

106. IX Međunarodni forum za tranzicionu pravdu: Pomirenje u post-jugoslovenskim zemljama, Koalicija za REKOM, Mount Jahorina, Bosnia and Herzegovina, May 17–18, 2013. For a full account, see Mirko Kovačić, "Dijalog u logoru," in *Tranziciona pravda i pomirenje u postjugoslovenskim zemljama: Glasovi institucija, verskih zajednica, aktivista, akademije, kulture i žrtava*, ed. Svetlana Slapšak and Nataša Kandić (Beograd: Koalicija za REKOM, 2015), 96–97.

107. Author's interview no. 26, Croatia, December 16, 2019.

108. Author's interview no. 18, Montenegro, September 2, 2016.

109. Focus Group, Kosovo, May 25, 2016.

110. Focus Group, Serbia, October 30, 2015.

111. RECOM Consultation no. 5.

112. Author's interview no. 17, Kosovo, May 24, 2016.

113. Focus Group, Serbia, October 30, 2015.

114. Masi Noor, Nurit Shnabel, Samer Halabi, and Arie Nadler, "When Suffering Begets Suffering: The Psychology of Competitive Victimhood Between Adversarial Groups in Violent Conflicts," *Personality and Social Psychology Review* 16, no. 4 (2012), https://doi.org/10.1177/1088868312440048. For a typology of victimhood on a spectrum from competitive to inclusive victimhood, see Cagla Demirel, "Re-Conceptualising Competitive Victimhood in Reconciliation Processes: The Case of Northern Ireland," *Peacebuilding*, September 2 (2021), https://doi.org/10.1080/21647259.2021.1977.

115. Author's interview no. 28, Croatia, December 17, 2016.

116. Author's interview no. 8, Serbia, September 26, 2014.

117. Jeffery Pittam, "The Historical and Emergent Enactment of Identity in Language," *Research on Language and Social Interaction* 32, no. 1–2 (1999): 113, https://doi.org/10.1080/08351813.1999.9683614.

118. Davies et al., "Intergroup Contact," 203.

119. Cuhadar and Dayton, "The Social Psychology," 290.

120. Rehg, *Insight*, 170.

CONCLUSION

1. Matthew Evans, "A Future without Forgiveness: Beyond Reconciliation in Transitional Justice," *International Politics* 55, no, 5 (2018), https://doi.org/10.1057/s41311-017-0091-3.

2. Lesley McEvoy, Kieran McEvoy, and Kirsten McConnachie, "Reconciliation as a Dirty Word: Conflict, Community Relations and Education in Northern Ireland," *Journal of International Affairs* 60, no. 1 (2006), https://www.jstor.org/stable/24358014; Furthermore, practitioners who work on reconciliation projects report people's hostility toward the term, see Ivor Sokolić and Denisa Kostovicova, *Reconciliation as Activity: Opportunities for Action*, Policy Brief (Prishtina: Centre for Research, Documentation and Publication), London School of Economics and Political Science, King's College London, University of the Arts London, 18), https://artreconciliation.org/wp-content/uploads/sites/181/2018/07/Reconciliation-as-Activity-Policy-Brief.pdf.

3. For an extensive discussion of the problems involved in evaluating reconciliation activities, see Tiffany Fairey, Rachel Kerr, Jelena Petrović, and James Gow, *New Bearings in Post-Conflict Evaluation: A Principle Based Approach* (London: King's College London, 2020), https://doi.org/10.18742/pub01-041.

4. Priscilla B. Hayner, *Unspeakable Truths: Confronting State Terror and Atrocity* (New York: Routledge, 2000), 160, quoting a journalist from Argentina.

5. James Hughes and Denisa Kostovicova, "Introduction: Rethinking Reconciliation and Transitional Justice After Conflict," *Ethnic and Racial Studies* 41, no. 4 (2018): 620, https://doi.org/10.1080/01419870.2017.1406129.

6. Vanessa Pupavac, "Therapeutic Governance: Psycho-social Intervention and Trauma Risk Management," *Disasters* 25, no. 4 (2001), https://doi.org/10.1111/1467-77 17.00184.

7. Nora Ahmetaj et al., *Zbërthimi i Konceptit të Pajtimit në Kontekstin e Kosovës* (Prishtine: Centre for Research, Documentation and Publication, 2017), http://www.new-perspektiva.com/wp-content/uploads/2017/07/Zb-rthimi-i-konceptit-t-pajtimit-n-kontekstin-e-Kosov-s-Deconstructing-Reconciliation-Qershor-2017.pdf.

8. This discourse permeates scholarship, policy analysis, and news reports; see Norman Porter, *The Elusive Quest: Reconciliation in Northern Ireland* (Belfast: Blackstaff, 2003); Mary Nolan, "The Elusive Pursuit of Truth and Justice: A Review Essay," *Radical History Review* 97 (2007), https://doi.org/10.1215/01636545-2006-020; "Somalia: Reconciliation is as Elusive as Ever," *Economist*, July 21, 2007, 54, https://www.econo mist.com/middle-east-and-africa/2007/07/19/reconciliation-is-as-elusive-as-ever; Julie McCarthy, "Sri Lanka's War Is Long Over: But Reconciliation Remains Elusive," *National Public Radio*, June 29, 2015, https://www.npr.org/sections/parallels/2015/06/29/418518\510/sri-lankas-war-is-long-over-but-reconciliation-remains-elusive?t=1646476282633.

9. Cyanne E. Loyle and Christian Davenport, "Transitional Injustice: Subverting Justice in Transition and Postconflict Societies," *Journal of Human Rights* 15, no. 1 (2016), https://doi.org/10.1080/14754835.2015.1052897.

10. For example, see Transitional Justice Research Collaborative, https://transitionaljusticedata.com/about.

11. Christian Davenport, "A Relational Approach to Quality Peace," in *The Peace Continuum: What It Is and How to Study It*, ed. Christian Davenport, Erick Melander, and Patrick M. Regan (Oxford: Oxford University Press, 2018).

12. Adeno Addis, "Deliberative Democracy in Severely Fractured Societies," *Indiana Journal of Global Legal Studies* 16, no. 1 (2009): 82, https://www.muse.jhu.edu/article/259582.

13. Joanna R. Quinn, *Thin Sympathy: A Strategy to Thicken Transitional Justice* (Philadelphia: University of Pennsylvania Press, 2021).

14. Julie M. Mazzei, "Finding Shame in Truth: The Importance of Public Engagement in Truth Commissions," *Human Rights Quarterly* 33, no. 2 (2011): 439, https://www.jstor.org/stable/23016021.

15. Pablo de Greiff, "'Truth without Facts': On the Erosion of the Fact-Finding Function of Truth Commissions," in *The Transformation of Human Rights Fact-Finding*, ed. Philip Alston and Sarah Knuckey (Oxford: Oxford University Press, 2016), 290.

16. Robert E. Goodin and John S. Dryzek, "Deliberative Impacts: The Macro-Political Uptake of Mini-Publics," *Politics and Society* 34, no. 2 (2006), https://doi.org/10.1177/0032329206288152. For a comprehensive overview of alternative definitions, see Matthew Ryan and Graham Smith, "Defining Mini-Publics," in *Deliberative Mini-Publics: Involving Citizens in the Democratic Process*, ed. Kimmo Grönlund, André Bächtiger and Maija Setälä (Colchester: ECPR Press, 2014).

17. Martina Fischer, "Transitional Justice and Reconciliation: Theory and Practice," in *Advancing Conflict Transformation: The Berghof Handbook II*, ed. Beatrix Austin, Martina Fischer, and Hans J. Giessmann (Opladen: Barbara Budrich Publishers, 2011); James Bohman, "Transnationalizing Peacebuilding: Transitional Justice as a Deliberative Process," in *Jus Post Bellum and Transitional Justice*, ed. Larry May and Elizabeth Edenberg (Cambridge: Cambridge University Press, 2013): 292; André Bächtiger and John Parkinson, *Mapping and Measuring Deliberation: Towards a New Deliberative Quality* (Oxford: Oxford University Press, 2019); Goodin and Dryzek, "Deliberative Impacts."

18. Jane Wills, "Identity Making for Action: The Example of London Citizens," in *Theorizing Identities and Social Action*, ed. Margaret Wetherell (Basingstoke: Palgrave Macmillan, 2009), 163.

19. Katharina Ploss, "Beyond the Meeting: How Community Activists Construe Idea Transfer from Intercommunity Encounters—The Cases of Northern Ireland and Kosovo," *International Negotiation* 16, no. 2 (2011), https://doi.org/10.1163/138234011X573066.

20. James S. Fishkin, *When the People Speak: Deliberative Democracy and Public Consultation* (Oxford: Oxford University Press, 2009), 105.

21. Simone Chambers, "Deliberative Democratic Theory," *Annual Review of Political Science* 6, no. 1 (2003): 321, https://doi.org/annurev.polisci.6/121901.085538.

22. Seyla Benhabib, "Introduction: The Democratic Moment and the Problem of Difference," in *Democracy and Difference: Contesting the Boundaries of the Political,* ed. Seyla Benhabib (Princeton: Princeton University Press, 1996), 3.

23. I use the term "division" rather than "diversity" because the former reflects more accurately the ideological chasm within groups when it comes to wartime harm and responsibility for the wrongdoing by members of one's identity group.

24. Iris Marion Young, *Inclusion and Democracy* (Oxford: Oxford University Press, 2002), 86, 89.

25. Anne Phillips, *The Politics of Presence: The Political Representation of Gender, Ethnicity, and Race* (Oxford: Oxford University Press, 1995), 100, 23.

26. T. Camber Warren and Kevin K. Troy, "Explaining Violent Intra-Ethnic Conflict: Group Fragmentation in the Shadow of State Power," *Journal of Conflict Resolution* 59, no. 3 (2015): 485, https://doi.org/10.1177/0022002713515400.

27. John S. Dryzek, *Deliberative Global Politics: Discourse and Democracy in a Divided World* (Cambridge: Polity, 2006), 42.

28. Phillips, *The Politics of Presence*, 52. Cf. Esra Cuhadar and Bruce Dayton, "The Social Psychology of Identity and Inter-Group Conflict: From Theory to Practice," *International Studies Perspectives* 12, no. 3 (2011): 290, https://www.jstor.org/stable/44218664.

29. John S. Dryzek, "Deliberative Democracy in Divided Societies: Alternatives to Agonism and Analgesia," *Political Theory* 33, no. 2 (2005): 225, https://doi.org/10.1177/0090591704268372.

30. Dryzek, *Deliberative Global Politics*, 43.

31. Chantal Mouffe, *Deliberative Democracy or Agonistic Pluralism* (Vienna: Institute for Advanced Studies, 2000).

32. Dryzek, "Deliberative Democracy," 221. Cf. Katherine Cramer Walsh, *Talking about Politics: Informal Groups and Social Identity in American Life* (Chicago: University of Chicago Press, 2004), 250.

33. Ian O'Flynn, "Review Article: Divided Societies and Deliberative Democracy," *British Journal of Political Science* 37, no. 4 (2007): 743, https://www.jstor.org/stable/4497320; Dryzek, *Deliberative Global Politics*, 61; Robert C. Luskin, Ian O'Flynn, James S. Fishkin, and David Russell, "Deliberating Across Deep Divides," *Political Studies* 62, no. 1 (2014), https://doi.org/10.1111/j.1467-9248.2012.01005.x; O'Flynn, "Review Article," 743; Dryzek, *Deliberative Global Politics*.

34. Jane Mansbridge et al., "The Place of Self-Interest and the Role of Power in Deliberative Democracy," *Journal of Political Philosophy* 18, no. 1 (2010): 78–79, https://doi.org/10.1111/j.1467-9760.2009.00344.x; Dryzek, *Deliberative Global Politics*. O'Flynn conceptualizes such a discursive shift as that from an ethnic to a civic identity. Ian O'Flynn, *Deliberative Democracy and Divided Societies* (Edinburgh: Edinburgh University Press, 2006).

35. Young, *Inclusion and Democracy*, 43.

36. Dryzek, "Deliberative Democracy," 224, 63, 4.

37. Dryzek, "Deliberative Democracy," 225.

38. Author's interview no. 17, Kosovo, May 24, 2016.

39. John S. Dryzek, *Deliberative Democracy and Beyond: Liberals, Critics, Contestations* (Oxford: Oxford University Press, 2000), 75.

40. Cramer Walsh considers dialogue as being constitutive of deliberative democracy in action. Cramer Walsh, *Talking about Politics*, 4.

41. Cramer Walsh, *Talking about Politics*, 138. For difference democrats' criticism that communal or civic identity may include dimensions of dominance, see Lynn M. Sanders, "Against Deliberation," *Political Theory* 25, no. 3 (1997), https://www.jstor.org/stable/191984.

42. These insights challenge suggestions to the contrary, for example by Koensler, who argues that interethnic dialogues and acts of solidarity during these dialogues have a paradoxical effect of entrenching sectarian identities and narratives of conflict. Alexander Koensler, "Acts of Solidarity: Crossing and Reiterating Israeli—Palestinian Frontiers," *International Journal of Urban and Regional Research* 40, no. 2 (2016), https://doi.org/10.1111/1468-2427.12380. For a similar argument, see Lea David, *The Past Can't Heal Us: The Dangers of Mandating Memory in the Name of Human Rights* (Cambridge: Cambridge University Press, 2020).

43. Luskin et al., "Deliberating Across," 121.

44. Alain Noël, "Democratic Deliberation in Multinational Federation," *Critical Review of International Social and Political Philosophy* 9, no. 3 (2006): 420, https://doi.org/10.1080/13698230600901212.

45. Elisabeth King and Cyrus Samii, *Diversity, Violence, and Recognition: How Recognizing Ethnic Identity Promotes Peace* (Oxford: Oxford University Press, 2020).

46. Noël, "Democratic Deliberation," 420.

47. Ian O'Flynn and Didier Caluwaerts, "Deliberation in Deeply Divided Societies," in *The Oxford Handbook of Deliberative Democracy*, ed. André Bächtiger, John S. Dryzek, Jane Mansbridge, and Mark Warren (Oxford: Oxford University Press, 2018), 750.

48. Diana C. Mutz, "Is Deliberative Democracy a Falsifiable Theory?," *Annual Review of Political Science* 11 (2008), https://doi.org/10.1146/annurev.polisci.11.081306.070308.

49. Elizabeth Levy Paluck, "Is It Better Not to Talk? Group Polarization, Extended Contact, and Perspective Taking in Eastern Democratic Republic of Congo," *Personality and Social Psychology Bulletin* 36, no. 9 (2010): 1170, https://doi.org/10.1177/0146167210 379868.

50. Paluck, "Is It Better," 1171.

51. Gordon W. Allport, *The Nature of Prejudice*, 25th ed. (New York: Basic Books: 1954).

52. Exceptionally, Ugarriza and Nussio test the effect of the perspective-giving protocols that encouraged participants to share personal stories compared to the effect of the instructions to deliberate about the future on attitudes toward discussion partners who are ex-combatants and community members in Colombia. However, they do not investigate moderating effects of a range of identity variables relevant for understanding intergroup contact in postconflict contexts, for example identity salience or nature of victimization. Juan E. Ugarriza and Enzo Nussio, "The Effect of Perspective-Giving on Postconflict Reconciliation. An Experimental Approach," *Political Psychology* 38, no. 1 (2017), https://www.jstor.org/stable/45094336.

53. Jake Harwood, Miles Hewstone, Yair Amichai-Hamburger, and Nicole Tausch, "Intergroup Contact: An Integration of Social Psychological and Communication Perspectives," *Annals of the International Communication Association* 36, no. 1 (2013): 64–66, https://doi.org/10.1080/23808985.2013.11679126. On social-psychological contributions to advancing the empirical study of deliberation, see Kieran C. O'Doherty and Karla Stroud, "Public Deliberation and Social Psychology: Integrating Theories of Participation with Social Psychological Research and Practice," in *The Sage Handbook of Applied Social Psychology*, ed. Kieran C. O'Doherty and Darrin Hodgetts (Los Angeles: Sage, 2019): 430–36.

54. Cf. Alberto Voci, Miles Hewstone, Hermann Swart, and Chiara A. Veneziani, "Refining the Association between Intergroup Contact and Forgiveness in Northern Ireland: Type of Contact, Prior Conflict Experience, and Group Identification," *Group Processes and Intergroup Relations* 1, no. 5 (2015), https://doi.org/10.1177/1368430215577001; Sabina Cehajic, Rupert Brown, and Emanuele Castano, "Forgive and Forget? Antecedents and Consequences of Intergroup Forgiveness in Bosnia and Herzegovina," *Political Psychology* 29, no. 3 (2008), https://doi.org/10.1111/j.1467-9221.2008.00634.x.

55. For example, on the effects of parasocial contact and the role of media in shaping attitudes toward out-group members, see Jake Harwood, "The Contact Space: A Novel Framework for Intergroup Contact Research," *Journal of Language and Social Psychology* 29, no. 2 (2010): 151, https://doi.org/10.1177/0261927X09359520. Cf. Harwood et al., "Intergroup Contact," 87.

56. Cf. Marilynn B. Brewer, "When Contact Is Not Enough: Social Identity and Intergroup Cooperation," *International Journal of Intercultural Relations* 20, no. 3–4 (1996): 295–300, 301, https://doi.org/10.1016/0147-1767(96)00020-X.

57. Tamara Rakić and Anne Maass, "Communicating between Groups, Communicating about Groups," in *Language, Communication, and Intergroup Relations*, ed. Jake Harwood et al. (New York: Routledge, 2019), 69.

58. Edward E. Sampson, *Dealing with Differences: An Introduction to the Social Psychology of Prejudice* (Forth Worth: Harcourt, Brace & Company, 1999), 147–61.

59. Bikhu Parekh, *A New Politics of Identity: Political Principles for an Interdependent World* (Basingstoke: Palgrave Macmillan, 2008), 36.

60. *Transitional Justice Policy*, African Union, February 2019, https://au.int/sites/default/files/documents/36541-doc-au_tj_policy_eng_web.pdf.

61. For example, see David, *The Past*. By contrast, for a more nuanced appraisal of NGOs and their contribution to reconciliation in postconflict societies, see Patrice C. McMahon, *The NGO Game: Post-Conflict Peacebuilding in the Balkans and Beyond* (Ithaca: Cornell University Press, 2017), and Quinn, *Thin Sympathy*.

Bibliography

"27 prilli" [April 27]. *Periodik informativ*, Këshili drejtues i familjarëve të zhdukur. Meje-Gjakovë, 2, no. 6–7. October 2005.

Abdelal, Rawi, Yoshiko M. Herrera, Alaistair Iain Johnston, and Rose McDermott. "Identity as a Variable." In *Measuring Identity: A Guide for Social Scientists*, edited by Rawi Abdelal, Yoshiko M. Herrera, Alastair Iain Johnston, and Rose McDermott, 17–32. Cambridge: Cambridge University Press, 2009.

Addis, Adeno. "Deliberative Democracy in Severely Fractured Societies." *Indiana Journal of Global Legal Studies* 16, no. 1 (2009): 59–83. https://doi.org/10.2979/gls.2009.16.1.59.

Ahmetaj, Nora, Besa Kabashi-Ramaj, Morgane Jacquot, Yllka Buzhala, and Adnan Hoxha. *Zbërthimi i Konceptit të Pajtimit në Kontekstin e Kosovës* [Deconstructing Reconciliation in Kosovo]. Centre for Research, Documentation and Publication, Prishtine, 2017. http://www.new-perspektiva.com/wp-content/uploads/2017/07/Zb-rthimi-i-konceptit-t-pajtimit-n-kontekstin-e-Kosov-s-Deconstructing-Reconciliation-Qershor-2017.pdf.

Aiken, Nevin T. "Learning to Live Together: Transitional Justice and Intergroup Reconciliation in Northern Ireland." *International Journal of Transitional Justice* 4, no. 2 (2010): 166–88. https://doi.org/10.1093/ijtj/ijq002.

———. "Rethinking Reconciliation in Divided Societies: A Social Learning Theory of Transitional Justice." In *Transitional Justice Theories*, edited by Susanne Buckley-Zistel, Teresa Koloma Beck, Christian Braun, and Friederike Mieth, 40–65. New York: Routledge, 2014.

Allansson, Marie, Erik Melander, and Lotta Themnér. "Organized Violence, 1989–2016." *Journal of Peace Research* 54, no. 4 (2017): 574–87. https://doi.org/10.1177/0022343317718773.

Allport, Gordon W. *The Nature of Prejudice*. 25th ed. New York: Basic Books, 1954.

Andjelic, Neven. *Bosnia-Herzegovina: The End of a Legacy*. London: Frank Cass, 2003.

Andrieu, Kora. "Civilizing Peacebuilding: Transitional Justice, Civil Society and the Liberal Paradigm." *Security Dialogue* 41, no. 5 (2010): 537–58. https://doi.org/10.1177/0967010610382109.

———. "Political Liberalism after Mass Violence: John Rawls and a 'Theory' of Transitional Justice." In *Transitional Justice Theories*, edited by Susanne Buckley-Zistel, Teresa Koloma Beck, Christian Braun, and Friederike Mieth, 85–104. Abingdon: Routledge, 2014.

Angermüller, Johannes. "From the Many Voices to the Subject Positions in Anti-Globalization Discourse: Enunciative Pragmatics and the Polyphonic Organization of Subjectivity." *Journal of Pragmatics* 43, no. 12 (2011): 2992–3000. https://doi.org/10.1016/j.pragma.2011.05.013.

———. *Poststructuralist Discourse Analysis: Subjectivity in Enunciative Pragmatics*. Houndmills: Palgrave Macmillan, 2014.

Annual Report of the United Nations High Commissioner for Human Rights and Reports of the Office of the High Commissioner and the Secretary-General. Analytical study on human rights and transitional justice, United Nations, A/HRC/12/18. August 6, 2009. https://www.un.org/ruleoflaw/files/96696_A-HRC-12-18_E.pdf.

Ansorg, Nadine. "How Does Militant Violence Diffuse in Regions? Regional Conflict Systems in International Relations and Peace and Conflict Studies." *International Journal of Conflict and Violence* 5, no. 1 (2011): 173–87. https://doi.org/10.4119/ijcv-2853.

Antaki, Charles, and Sue Widdicombe, eds. *Identities in Talk.* London: Sage, 1998.

Arnaud Kurze, "Justice Beyond Borders? The Politics to Democratize Human Rights in the Post-Conflict Balkans." PhD diss., George Mason University, 2012.

Arthur, Paige. "How 'Transitions' Reshaped Human Rights: A Conceptual History of Transitional Justice." *Human Rights Quarterly* 31, no. 2 (2009): 321–67. https://doi.org/10.1353/hrq.0.0069.

——. "Identities in Transition." In *Identities in Transition: Challenges for Justice in Divided Societies,* edited by Paige Arthur, 1–14. Cambridge: Cambridge University Press, 2011.

——. "Notes from the Field: Global Indicators for Transitional Justice and Challenges in Measurement for Policy Actors." *Transitional Justice Review* 1, no. 4 (2016): 283–308. https://doi.org/10.5206/tjr.2016.1.4.9.

Arthur, Paige, and Christalla Yakinthou. *Transitional Justice, International Assistance, and Civil Society: Missed Connections.* Cambridge: Cambridge University Press, 2018.

Auerbach, Yehudith. "The Reconciliation Pyramid—A Narrative-Based Framework for Analyzing Identity Conflicts." *Political Psychology* 30, no. 2 (2009): 291–318. https://doi.org/10.1111/j.1467-9221.2008.00692.x.

Azmanova, Albena. "Deliberative Conflict and 'The Better Argument' Mystique." *The Good Society* 19, no. 1 (2010): 48–54. https://doi.org/10.1353/gso.0.0098.

Ball, Patrick, Wendy Betts, Fritz Scheuren, Jana Dudukovich, and Jana Asher. "Killings and Refugee Flow in Kosovo March–June 1999: A Report to the International Criminal Tribunal for the Former Yugoslavia." American Association for the Advancement of Science, January 3, 2002, New York, https://www.icty.org/x/file/About/OTP/War_Demographics/en/s_milosevic_kosovo_020103.pdf.

Baker, Catherine. *The Yugoslav Wars of the 1990s.* London: Palgrave Macmillan, 2015.

Bakhtin, M. M. *The Dialogic Imagination: Four Essays.* Edited by Michael Holquist. Translated by Michael Holquist and Caryl Emerson. Austin: University of Texas Press, 1981.

Bakiner, Onur. *Truth Commissions: Memory, Power, and Legitimacy.* Philadelphia: University of Pennsylvania Press, 2016.

Baliqi, Bekim. "Contested War Remembrance and Ethnopolitical Identities in Kosovo." *Nationalities Papers* 46, no. 3 (2018): 471–83. https://doi.org/10.1080/00905992.2017.1375906.

Banac, Ivo. "The Politics of National Homogeneity." In *War and Change in the Balkans: Nationalism, Conflict and Cooperation,* edited by Brad K. Blitz, 30–43. Cambridge: Cambridge University Press, 2006.

Banting, Keith, and Will Kymlicka. "Introduction: The Political Sources of Solidarity in Diverse Societies." In *The Strains of Commitment: The Political Sources of Solidarity in Diverse Societies,* edited by Keith Banting and Will Kymlicka, 1–57. Oxford: Oxford University Press, 2017.

Barnett, Michael. "Building a Republican Peace: Stabilizing States after War." *International Security* 30, no. 4 (2006): 87–112. https://doi.org/https://www.jstor.org/stable/4137530.

Barton-Hronešová, Jessie. *The Struggle for Redress: Victim Capital in Bosnia and Herzegovina*. Cham: Palgrave Macmillan, 2020.

Bashir, Bashir. "Accommodating Historically Oppressed Social Groups: Deliberative Democracy and the Politics of Reconciliation." In *The Politics of Reconciliation in Multicultural Societies*, edited by Bashir Bashir and Will Kymlicka, 48–69. Oxford: Oxford University Press, 2008.

Baxter, Victoria. "Critical Challenges for the Development of the Transitional Justice Research Field." In *Assessing the Impact of Transitional Justice: Challenges for Empirical Research*, edited by Hugo van der Merwe, Audrey R. Chapman, and Victoria Baxter, 325–34. Washington, DC: United States Institute of Peace Press, 2009.

Bächtiger, André, and Dominik Hangartner. "When Deliberative Theory Meets Empirical Political Science: Theoretical and Methodological Challenges in Political Deliberation." *Political Studies* 58, no. 4 (2010): 609–29. https://doi.org/10.1111/j.1467-9248.2010.00835.x.

Bächtiger, André, and Marlène Gerber. "'Gentlemanly Conversation' or Vigorous Contestation? An Exploratory Analysis of Communication Modes in a Transnational Deliberative Poll (Europolis)." In *Deliberative Mini-Publics: Involving Citizens in the Democratic Process*, edited by Kimmo Grönlund, André Bächtiger, and Maija Setälä, 115–34. Colchester: ECPR Press, 2014.

Bächtiger André, and John Parkinson. *Mapping and Measuring Deliberation: Towards a New Deliberative Quality*. Oxford: Oxford University Press, 2019.

Bächtiger, André, and Jürg Steiner. "Introduction." *Acta Politica* 40, no. 2 (2005): 153–68. https://doi.org/10.1057/palgrave.ap.5500108.

Bächtiger, André, Dominik Hangartner, Pia Hess, and Céline Fraefel. "Patterns of Parliamentary Discourse: How 'Deliberative' Are German Legislative Debates?" *German Politics* 17, no. 3 (2008): 270–92. https://doi.org/10.1080/09644000802300486.

Bächtiger, André, Simon Niemeyer, Michael Neblo, Marco R. Steenbergen, and Jürg Steiner. "Disentangling Diversity in Deliberative Democracy: Competing Theories, Their Blindspots and Complementarities." *Journal of Political Philosophy* 18, no. 1 (2010): 32–63. https://doi.org/10.1111/j.1467-9760.2009.00342.x.

Bächtiger, André, Susumu Shikano, Seraina Pedrini, and Mirjam Ryser. "Measuring Deliberation 2.0: Standards, Discourse Types, and Sequentialization." Unpublished paper, University of Konstanz and University of Bern, 2009. https://ash.harvard.edu/files/ash/files/baechtiger_0.pdf.

Bell, Philip. "Subjectivity and Identity: Semiotics as Psychological Explanation." *Social Semiotics* 12, no. 2 (2002): 201–17. https://doi.org/10.1080/10350330276021204.

Benhabib, Seyla. "Introduction: The Democratic Moment and the Problem of Difference." In *Democracy and Difference: Contesting the Boundaries of the Political*, edited by Seyla Benhabib, 3–18. Princeton: Princeton University Press, 1996.

Bennett, Andrew. *Case Studies and Theory Development in the Social Sciences*. Cambridge: MIT Press, 2005.

Benoit, Kenneth. "Text as Data: An Overview." In *Handbook of Research Methods in Political Science and International Relations*, edited by Luigi Curini and Robert J. Franzese, 461–97. Thousand Oaks: Sage, 2020.

Benoit, William L. "Content Analysis in Political Communication." In *The Sourcebook for Political Communication Research: Methods, Measures, and Analytical*

Techniques, edited by Erik P. Bucy and R. Lance Holbert, 268–79. New York: Routledge, 2011.

Benwell, Bethan, and Elizabeth Stokoe. *Discourse and Identity*. Edinburgh: Edinburgh University Press, 2006.

Berry, Marie E. "Barriers to Women's Progress After Atrocity: Evidence from Rwanda and Bosnia-Herzegovina." *Gender and Society* 31, no. 6 (2017): 830–53. https://doi.org/10.1177/0891243217737060.

Bicskei, Marianna, Matthias Lankau, and Kilian Bizer. "Negative Reciprocity and Its Relation to Anger-Like Emotions in Identity-Homogeneous and -Heterogeneous Groups." *Journal of Economic Psychology* 54 (2016): 17–34. https://doi.org/10.1016/j.joep.2016.02.008.

Bilić, Bojan. *Borile smo se za vazduh: (Post)jugoslovenski antiratni aktivizam i njegovo nasleđe*. Zagreb: Dokumenta, Kuća ljudskih prava Zagreb & Naklada Jesenski i Turk, 2015. [Originally published as *We Were Gasping for Air: [Post-]Yugoslav Anti-War Activism and Its Legacy* (Baden-Baden: Nomos, 2012).]

———. "(Post-)Yugoslav Anti-War Engagement: A Research Topic Awaiting Attention." *Filozofija i društvo* 22, no. 4 (2011): 83–107. https://doi.org/10.2298/fid1104083b.

Biševac, Safeta. "Kazani i mural" [Kazani and the mural]. *Danas*, November 17, 2021. https://www.danas.rs/kolumna/safeta-bisevac/kazani-i-mural/.

Black, Laura W., Stephanie Burkhalter, John Gastil, and Jennifer Stromer-Galley. "Methods for Analyzing and Measuring Group Deliberation." In *The Sourcebook for Political Communication Research: Methods, Measures, and Analytical Techniques*, edited by Erik P. Bucy and R. Lance Holbert, 323–45. New York: Routledge, 2011.

Bloomfield, David. *On Good Terms: Clarifying Reconciliation*. Berghof Report no. 14. Berghof Research Center for Constructive Conflict Management, 2006.

Blouin, Arthur, and Sharun W. Mukand. "Erasing Ethnicity? Propaganda, Nation Building, and Identity in Rwanda." *Journal of Political Economy* 127, no. 3 (2019): 1008–62. https://doi.org/10.1086/701441.

Bobbio, Luigi. "Types of Deliberation." *Journal of Public Deliberation* 6, no. 2 (2010): 1–24. https://doi.org/10.16997/jdd.105.

Bochsler, Daniel, Elliott Green, Erin Jenne, Harris Mylonas, and Andreas Wimmer. "Exchange on the Quantitative Measurement of Ethnic and National Identity." *Nations and Nationalism* 27 (2021): 24–40. https://doi.org/10.1111/nana.12688.

Bogosavljević, Srđan. "Nerasvetljeni genocid" [Unexplained Genocide]. In *Srpska strana rata: Trauma i katarza u istorijskom pamćenju* [The Serbian Side of the War: Trauma and Catharsis in the Historical Memory], edited by Nebojša Popov, 159–70. Beograd: BIGZ, 1996.

Bohman, James. "Transnationalizing Peacebuilding: Transitional Justice as a Deliberative Process." In *Jus Post Bellum and Transitional Justice*, edited by Larry May and Elizabeth Edenberg, 285–304. Cambridge: Cambridge University Press, 2013.

Bojicic-Dzelilovic, Vesna, James Ker-Lindsay, and Denisa Kostovicova, eds. *Civil Society and Transitions in the Western Balkans*. Basingstoke: Palgrave Macmillan, 2013.

Bonacker, Thorsten, and Susanne Buckley-Zistel. "Introduction: Transitions from Violence. Analysing the Effects of Transitional Justice." *International Journal of Conflict and Violence* 7, no. 1 (2013): 4–9. https://doi.org/https://doi.org/10.4119/ijcv-2945.

Bonora, Catherina. "The Question of Gender Inclusiveness of Bottom-Up Strategies in Bosnia and Herzegovina." In *New Critical Spaces in Transitional Justice: Gender, Art, and Memory*, edited by Arnaud Kurze and Christopher K. Lamont, 135–56. Bloomington: Indiana University Press, 2019.

Brady, Henry E., and Cynthia S. Kaplan. "Categorically Wrong? Nominal Versus Graded Measures of Ethnic Identity." *Studies in Comparative International Development* 35, no. 3 (2000): 56–91. https://doi.org/10.1007/bf02699766.

Brekhus, Wayne H. "Trends in the Qualitative Study of Social Identities." *Sociology Compass* 2, no. 3 (2008): 1059–78. https://doi.org/10.1111/j.1751-9020.2008.00107.x.

Bretz, Rudy, and Michael Schmidbauer. *Media for Interactive Communication*. Beverly Hills: Sage, 1983.

Brewer, Marilynn B. "When Contact Is Not Enough: Social Identity and Intergroup Cooperation." *International Journal of Intercultural Relations* 20, no. 3–4 (1996): 291–303. https://doi.org/10.1016/0147-1767(96)00020-x.

Bright, Jonathan, and John Gledhill. "A Divided Discipline? Mapping Peace and Conflict Studies." *International Studies Perspectives* 19, no. 2 (2018): 128–47. https://doi.org/10.1093/isp/ekx009.

Bringa, Tone. *Being Muslim the Bosnian Way: Identity and Community in a Central Bosnian Village*. Princeton: Princeton University Press, 1995.

Brounéus, Karen. "Analyzing Reconciliation: A Structured Method for Measuring National Reconciliation Initiatives." *Peace and Conflict: Journal of Peace Psychology* 14, no. 3 (2008): 291–313. https://doi.org/10.1080/10781910802017354.

Brunland, Peter, and Michael Horowitz. "Research Report on the Use of Identity Concepts in Comparative Politics." Unpublished manuscript, Harvard Identity Project, April 2003.

Bucholtz, Mary, and Kira Hall. "Identity and Interaction: A Sociocultural Linguistic Approach." *Discourse Studies* 7, no. 4–5 (2005): 585–614. https://doi.org/10.1177/1461445605054407.

Buckley-Zistel, Susanne, Teresa Koloma Beck, Christian Braun, and Friederike Mieth, eds. *Transitional Justice Theories*. Abingdon: Routledge, 2014.

Burg, Steven L., and Paul S. Shoup. *The War in Bosnia-Herzegovina: Ethnic Conflict and International Intervention*. Armonk, NY: M.E. Sharpe, 1999.

Burke, Peter J., and Donald C. Reitzes. "The Link between Identity and Role Performance." *Social Psychology Quarterly* 44, no. 2 (1981): 83–92. https://doi.org/10.2307/3033704.

Calic, Marie-Janine. *The Great Cauldron: A History of Southeastern Europe*. Translated by Elizabeth Janik. Cambridge: Harvard University Press, 2019.

Caluwaerts, Didier, and Kris Deschouwer. "Building Bridges across Political Divides: Experiments on Deliberative Democracy in Deeply Divided Belgium." *European Political Science Review* 6, no. 3 (2014): 427–50. https://doi.org/10.1017/s1755773913000179.

Caluwaerts, Didier, and Min Reuchamps. "Does Inter-Group Deliberation Foster Inter-Group Appreciation? Evidence from Two Experiments in Belgium." *Politics* 34, no. 2 (2014): 101–15. https://doi.org/10.1111/1467-9256.12043.

Caluwaerts, Didier, and Juan E. Ugarriza. "Beating the Odds: Confrontational Deliberative Democracy." In *Democratic Deliberation in Deeply Divided Societies: From Conflict to Common Ground*, edited by Juan Ugarriza and Didier Caluwaerts, 206–17. Basingstoke: Palgrave Macmillan, 2014.

Cameron, John, and Hemant Ojha. "A Deliberative Ethic for Development: A Nepalese Journey from Bourdieu through Kant to Dewey and Habermas." *International Journal of Social Economics* 34, no. 1/2 (2007): 66–87. https://doi.org/10.1108/03068290710723372.

Campbell, David. *National Deconstruction: Violence, Identity, and Justice in Bosnia.* Minneapolis: University of Minnesota Press, 1998.

Caplan, Richard. *Measuring Peace: Principles, Practices, and Politics.* Oxford: Oxford University Press, 2019.

Cehajic, Sabina, Rupert Brown, and Emanuele Castano. "Forgive and Forget? Antecedents and Consequences of Intergroup Forgiveness in Bosnia and Herzegovina." *Political Psychology* 29, no. 3 (2008): 351–67. https://doi.org/10.1111/j.1467-9221.2008.00634.x.

Četvrti izveštaj o sprovođenju Nacionalne strategije za procesuiranje ratnih zločina [The Fourth Report on the Implementation of the National Strategy for Processing of War Crimes]. Beograd: Fond za humanitarno pravo, 2019.

Chambers, Simone. "Deliberative Democratic Theory." *Annual Review of Political Science* 6, no. 1 (2003): 307–26. https://doi.org/https://doi.org/annurev.polisci.6/121901.085538.

Chandra, Kanchan. "How Ethnic Identities Change." In *Constructivist Theories of Ethnic Politics*, edited by Kanchan Chandra, 132–78. Oxford: Oxford University Press, 2012.

——. "What Is Ethnic Identity? A Minimalist Definition." In *Constructivist Theories of Ethnic Politics*, edited by Kanchan Chandra, 51–96. Oxford: Oxford University Press, 2012.

Chapman, Audrey R. "Approaches to Studying Reconciliation." In *Assessing the Impact of Transitional Justice: Challenges for Empirical Research*, edited by Hugo van der Merwe, Audrey R. Chapman, and Victoria Baxter, 143–72. Washington, DC: United States Institute of Peace Press, 2009.

Chapman, Audrey R., and Hugo van der Merwe, eds. *Truth and Reconciliation in South Africa: Did the TRC Deliver?* Philadelphia: University of Pennsylvania Press, 2008.

Chappell, Zsuzsanna. *Deliberative Democracy: A Critical Introduction.* Basingstoke: Palgrave Macmillan, 2012.

Charolles, Michel, Anne Le Draoulec, Marie-Paule Pery-Woodley, and Laure Sarda. "Temporal and Spatial Dimensions of Discourse Organisation." *Journal of French Language Studies* 15, no. 2 (2005): 115–30. https://doi.org/10.1017/s0959269505002036.

Chayes, Antonia, and Martha Minow, eds. *Imagine Coexistence: Restoring Humanity After Violent Ethnic Conflict.* San Francisco: Jossey-Bass, 2003.

Checkel, Jeffrey T. "Transnational Dynamics of Civil War." In *Transnational Dynamics of Civil War*, edited by Jeffrey T. Checkel, 3–27. Cambridge: Cambridge University Press, 2013.

Cinalli, Manlio, and Ian O'Flynn. "Public Deliberation, Network Analysis and the Political Integration of Muslims in Britain." *British Journal of Politics and International Relations* 16, no. 3 (2014): 428–51. https://doi.org/10.1111/1467-856x.12003.

Clark, Janine Natalya. "Does Bosnia Need a Truth and Reconciliation Commission? Some Reflections on Its Possible Design." *Ethnopolitics* 12, no. 3 (2013): 225–46. https://doi.org/10.1080/17449057.2012.688374.

——. *International Trials and Reconciliation: Assessing the Impact of the International Criminal Tribunal for the Former Yugoslavia.* London: Routledge, 2014.

Cohen, Stanley. *States of Denial: Knowing about Atrocities and Suffering*. Cambridge: Polity, 2001.

Cramer Walsh, Katherine. *Talking about Politics: Informal Groups and Social Identity in American Life*. Chicago: University of Chicago Press, 2004.

Crawford, Neta C. "Understanding Discourse: A Method of Ethical Argument Analysis." *Qualitative Methods* 2 (2004): 23–25.

Creswell, John W. "Mixed Methods Research." In *The SAGE Encyclopedia of Qualitative Research Methods*, edited by Lisa M. Given, 526–29. Thousand Oaks: Sage, 2008.

Creswell, John W., and Vicki L. Plano Clark. *Designing and Conducting Mixed Methods Research*. 3rd ed. Los Angeles: Sage, 2018.

Crocker, David A. "Punishment, Reconciliation, and Democratic Deliberation." In *Taking Wrongs Seriously: Apologies and Reconciliation*, edited by Elazar Barkan and Alexander Karn, 50–82. Stanford: Stanford University Press, 2006.

———. "Transitional Justice and International Civil Society: Toward a Normative Framework." *Constellations* 5, no. 4 (1998): 492–517. https://doi.org/10.1111/1467-8675.00110.

Cuhadar, Esra, and Bruce Dayton. "The Social Psychology of Identity and Inter-Group Conflict: From Theory to Practice." *International Studies Perspectives* 12, no. 3 (2011): 273–93. https://www.jstor.org/stable/44218664.

Cunningham, David E. *Barriers to Peace in Civil War*. Cambridge: Cambridge University Press, 2011.

Dahlgren, Peter. "The Internet, Public Spheres, and Political Communication: Dispersion and Deliberation." *Political Communication* 22, no. 2 (2005): 147–62. https://doi.org/10.1080/10584600590933160.

Daly, Erin, and Jeremy Sarkin. *Reconciliation in Divided Societies: Finding Common Ground*. Philadelphia: University of Pennsylvania Press, 2007.

Davenport, Christian. "A Relational Approach to Quality Peace." In *The Peace Continuum: What It Is and How to Study It*, edited by Christian Davenport, Erik Melander, and Patrick M. Regan, 145–83. Oxford: Oxford University Press, 2018.

David, Lea. *The Past Can't Heal Us: The Dangers of Mandating Memory in the Name of Human Rights*. Cambridge: Cambridge University Press, 2020.

David, Roman. "What We Know about Transitional Justice: Survey and Experimental Evidence." *Political Psychology* 38, no. 1 (2017): 151–77. https://doi.org/10.1111/pops.12395.

Davies, Bronwyn, and Rom Harré. "Positioning: The Discursive Production of Selves." *Journal for the Theory of Social Behaviour* 20, no. 1 (1990): 43–63. https://doi.org/10.1111/j.1468-5914.1990.tb00174.x.

Davies, Kristin, Stephen C. Wright, Arthur Aron, and Joseph Comeau. "Intergroup Contact through Friendship: Intimacy and Norms." In *Advances in Intergroup Contact*, edited by Gordon Hodson and Miles Hewstone, 200–29. London: Psychology Press, 2013.

de Greiff, Pablo. "Transitional Justice Gets Its Own Encyclopedia: Vitamins or Steroids for a Developing Field." *International Journal of Transitional Justice* 7, no. 3 (2013): 547–53. https://doi.org/10.1093/ijtj/ijt023.

———. "'Truth without Facts': On the Erosion of the Fact-Finding Function of Truth Commissions." In *The Transformation of Human Rights Fact-Finding*, edited by Philip Alston and Sarah Knuckey, 281–301. Oxford: Oxford University Press, 2016.

de Waardt, Mijke, and Sanne Weber. "Beyond Victims' Mere Presence: An Empirical Analysis of Victim Participation in Transitional Justice in Colombia." *Journal*

of Human Rights Practice 11, no. 1 (2019): 209–28. https://doi.org/10.1093/
jhuman/huz002.

della Porta, Donatella. "Deliberation in Movement: Why and How to Study
Deliberative Democracy and Social Movements." *Acta Politica* 40 (2005):
336–50. https://doi.org/10.1057/palgrave.ap.5500116.

Delpla, Isabelle. "In the Midst of Injustice: The ICTY from the Perspective of Some
Victim Associations." In *The New Bosnian Mosaic: Identities, Memories and
Moral Claims in a Post-War Society*, edited by Xavier Bougarel, Elissa Helms,
and Ger Duijzings, 211–34. Farnham: Ashgate, 2007.

deMeritt, Jacqueline H. R. "Transitional Justice: Prospects for Postwar Peace and Human
Rights." In *What Do We Know about Civil Wars?*, edited by T. David Mason and
Sara McLaughlin Mitchell, 179–95. Lanham, MD: Rowman & Littlefield, 2016.

Despot, Zvonimir. "REKOM-regionalna komisija koja želi zamagliti istinu o
srbijanskoj agresiji" [The RECOM-regional Commission that Wants to Obscure
the Truth about the Serbian Aggression]. *Večernji list*, October 20, 2010. https://
blog.vecernji.hr/zvonimir-despot/rekom-regionalna-komisija-koja-zeli-
zamagliti-istinu-o-srbijanskoj-agresiji-925.

Dembinska, Magdalena and Françoise Montambeault. "Deliberation for
Reconciliation in Divided Societies." *Journal of Public Deliberation* 11, no. 1
(2015): 1–35. https://doi.org/10.16997/jdd.226.

Demirel, Cagla. "Re-Conceptualising Competitive Victimhood in Reconciliation
Processes: The Case of Northern Ireland." *Peacebuilding*, 2021, 1–17. https://doi.
org/10.1080/21647259.2021.1977016.

Di Lellio, Anna, and Caitlin McCurn. "Engineering Grassroots Transitional Justice in
the Balkans: The Case of Kosovo." *East European Politics and Societies* 27, no. 1
(2013): 129–48. https://doi.org/10.1177/0888325412464550.

Doerr, Nicole. "Language and Democracy 'in Movement': Multilingualism and the
Case of the European Social Forum Process." *Social Movement Studies* 8, no. 2
(2009): 149–65. https://doi.org/10.1080/14742830902770290.

——. "Translating Democracy: How Activists in the European Social Forum Practice
Multilingual Deliberation." *European Political Science Review* 4, no. 3 (2012):
361–84. https://doi.org/10.1017/s1755773911000312.

Dosije: Operacija Reka [Dossier: The Operation Reka]. Beograd: Fond za humanitarno
pravo, October 2015.

Downes, Edward J., and Sally J. McMillan. "Defining Interactivity." *New Media and
Society* 2, no. 2 (2000): 157–79, 159. https://doi.org/10.1177/
14614440022225751.

Dragojević, Mila. *Amoral Communities: Collective Crimes in Time of War*. Ithaca:
Cornell University Press, 2019.

Dragović-Soso, Jasna. "History of a Failure: Attempts to Create a National Truth
and Reconciliation Commission in Bosnia and Herzegovina, 1997–2006."
International Journal of Transitional Justice 10, no. 2 (2016): 292–310. https://
doi.org/10.1093/ijtj/ijw005.

——. *"Saviours of the Nation": Serbia's Intellectual Opposition and the Revival of
Nationalism*. London: Hurst & Company, 2002.

Dragović-Soso, Jasna, and Eric Gordy. "Coming to Terms with the Past: Transitional
Justice and Reconciliation in the Post-Yugoslav Lands." In *New Perspectives on
Yugoslavia: Key Issues and Controversies*, edited by Dejan Djokić and James Ker-
Lindsay, 193–212. London: Routledge, 2011.

Drake, Anna, and Allison McCulloch. "Deliberative Consociationalism in Deeply Divided Societies." *Contemporary Political Theory* 10, no. 3 (2011): 372–92. https://doi.org/10.1057/cpt.2010.22.

Dryzek, John S. *Deliberative Democracy and Beyond: Liberals, Critics, Contestations.* Oxford: Oxford University Press, 2000.

——. "Deliberative Democracy in Divided Societies: Alternatives to Agonism and Analgesia." *Political Theory* 33, no. 2 (2005): 218–42. https://doi.org/10.1177/0090591704268372.

——. *Deliberative Global Politics: Discourse and Democracy in a Divided World.* Cambridge: Polity, 2006.

Duan, Changming, and Clara E. Hill. "The Current State of Empathy Research." *Journal of Counseling Psychology* 43, no. 3 (1996): 261–74. https://doi.org/10.1037/0022-0167.43.3.261.

Duijzings, Ger. "Commemorating Srebrenica: Histories of Violence and the Politics of Memory in Eastern Bosnia." In *The New Bosnian Mosaic: Identities, Memories and Moral Claims in a Post-War Society,* edited by Xavier Bougarel, Elissa Helms, and Ger Duijzings, 141–66. Farnham: Ashgate, 2007.

Dulić, Tomislav. "Ethnic Violence in Occupied Yugoslavia: Mass Killing from Above and Below." In *New Perspectives on Yugoslavia: Key Issues and Controversies,* edited by Dejan Djokić and James Ker-Lindsay, 82–99. London: Routledge, 2011.

Đureinović, Jelena. *The Politics of Memory of the Second World War in Contemporary Serbia: Collaboration, Resistance and Retribution.* Abingdon: Routledge, 2020.

Durkheim, Émile. *The Division of Labour in Society.* London: Collier Macmillan, [1893] 1964.

Edwards, Derek, and Jonathan Potter. *Discursive Psychology.* London: Sage, 1992.

Eisenberger, Robert, Patrick Lynch, Justin Aselage, and Stephanie Rohdieck. "Who Takes the Most Revenge? Individual Differences in Negative Reciprocity Norm Endorsement." *Personality and Social Psychology Bulletin* 30, no. 6 (2004): 787–99. https://doi.org/10.1177/0146167204264047.

Elias-Bursać, Ellen. *Translating Evidence and Interpreting Testimony at a War Crimes Tribunal: Working in a Tug of War.* Basingstoke: Palgrave Macmillan, 2015.

Ellis, Donald G. *Deliberative Communication and Ethnopolitical Conflict.* New York: Peter Lang, 2012.

Elstub, Stephen. "The Third Generation of Deliberative Democracy." *Political Studies Review* 8, no. 3 (2010): 291–307. https://doi.org/10.1111/j.1478-9302.2010.00216.x.

Endres, Danielle, and Barbara Warnick. "Effects of Campaign-to-User and Text-Based Interactivity in Candidate Campaign Web Sites: A Case Study from the 2002 Elections." *Western Journal of Communication* 68, no. 3 (2004): 322–42. https://doi.org/10.1080/10570310409374804.

Esterling, Kevin M., Archon Fung, and Taeku Lee. "How Much Disagreement Is Good for Democratic Deliberation?" *Political Communication* 32, no. 4 (2015): 529–51. https://doi.org/10.1080/10584609.2014.969466.

Evans, Matthew. "A Future without Forgiveness: Beyond Reconciliation in Transitional Justice." *International Politics* 55, no. 5 (2018): 678–92. https://doi.org/10.1057/s41311-017-0091-3.

Fairclough, Norman. "Critical Discourse Analysis." In *The Routledge Handbook of Discourse Analysis,* edited by James Paul Gee and Michael Handford, 9–20. London: Routledge, 2014.

Fairey, Tiffany, Rachel Kerr, Jelena Petrović, and James Gow. *New Bearings in Post-Conflict Evaluation: A Principle Based Approach.* London: King's College London, 2020. https://doi.org/10.18742/pub01-041.

Fearon, James D. "Deliberation as Discussion." In *Deliberative Democracy*, edited by Jon Elster, 44–68. Cambridge: Cambridge University Press, 1998.

———. "What Is Identity (as We Now Use the Word?)." Unpublished manuscript, Stanford University, California, November 3, 1999. https://web.stanford.edu/group/fearon-research/cgi-bin/wordpress/wp-content/uploads/2013/10/What-is-Identity-as-we-now-use-the-word-.pdf

Fetters, Michael D., Leslie A. Curry, and John W. Creswell. "Achieving Integration in Mixed Methods Designs—Principles and Practices." *Health Services Research* 48, no. 6 (2013): 2134–56. https://doi.org/10.1111/1475-6773.12117.

Fiket, Irena, Espen D. H. Olsen, and Hans-Jörg Trenz. "Confronting European Diversity: Deliberation in a Transnational and Pluri-Lingual Setting." *Javnost—The Public* 21, no. 2 (2014): 57–73. https://doi.org/10.1080/13183222.2014.110 09145.

Filic, Goran. "Rejection of Radical Nationalism in Wartime Yugoslavia: The Case of Tuzla (1990–1995)." *Journal of Peacebuilding and Development* 13, no. 3 (2019): 55–69. https://doi.org/10.1080/15423166.2018.1516158.

Finlay, Krystina A., and Walter G. Stephan. "Improving Intergroup Relations: The Effects of Empathy on Racial Attitudes." *Journal of Applied Social Psychology* 30, no. 8 (2000): 1720–37. https://doi.org/10.1111/j.1559-1816.2000.tb02464.x.

Firchow, Pamina. *Reclaiming Everyday Peace: Local Voices in Measurement and Evaluation After War.* Cambridge: Cambridge University Press, 2018.

Firchow, Pamina, and Yvette Selim. "Meaningful Engagement from the Bottom-Up? Taking Stock of Participation in Transitional Justice Processes." *International Journal of Transitional Justice.* February 5, 2022. https://doi.org/10.1093/ijtj/ijab031.

Fischer, Martina. "Transitional Justice and Reconciliation: Theory and Practice." In *Advancing Conflict Transformation. The Berghof Handbook II*, edited by Beatrix Austin, Martina Fischer, and Hans J. Giessmann, 288–313. Opladen: Barbara Budrich Publishers, 2011.

Fisher, Ronald J. *Interactive Conflict Resolution.* Syracuse: Syracuse University Press, 1997.

Fishkin, James S. *When the People Speak: Deliberative Democracy and Public Consultation.* Oxford: Oxford University Press, 2009.

Fletcher, Laurel E., and Harvey M. Weinstein. "Writing Transitional Justice: An Empirical Evaluation of Transitional Justice Scholarship in Academic Journals." *Journal of Human Rights Practice* 7, no. 2 (2015): 177–98. https://doi.org/10.1093/jhuman/huv006.

Forsythe, David P. "Human Rights and Mass Atrocities: Revisiting Transitional Justice." *International Studies Review* 13, no. 1 (2011): 85–95. https://doi.org/https://www.jstor.org/stable/23016143.

Fraser, Nancy. "Toward a Discourse Ethic of Solidarity." *Praxis International* 5, no. 4 (1986): 425–29.

Fridman, Orli. "Alternative Calendars and Memory Work in Serbia: Anti-War Activism after Milošević." *Memory Studies* 8, no. 2 (2015): 212–26. https://doi.org/10.1177/1750698014558661.

———. "'It Was Like Fighting a War with Our Own People': Anti-War Activism in Serbia during the 1990s." *Nationalities Papers* 39, no. 4 (2011): 507–22. https://doi.org/10.1080/00905992.2011.579953.

Friess, Dennis, and Christiane Eilders. "A Systematic Review of Online Deliberation Research." *Policy and Internet* 7, no. 3 (2015): 319–39. https://doi.org/10.1002/poi3.95.

Fullard, Madeleine, and Nicky Rousseau. "Truth Telling, Identities, and Power in South Africa and Guatemala." In *Identities in Transition: Challenges for Justice in Divided Societies*, edited by Paige Arthur, 54–86. Cambridge: Cambridge University Press, 2011.

Fung, Archon. "Minipublics: Deliberative Designs and Their Consequences." In *Deliberation, Participation and Democracy: Can the People Govern?*, edited by Shawn W. Rosenberg, 159–83. Basingstoke: Palgrave Macmillan, 2007.

——. "Recipes for Public Spheres: Eight Institutional Design Choices and Their Consequences." *Journal of Political Philosophy* 11, no. 3 (2003): 338–67. https://doi.org/10.1111/1467-9760.00181.

Gaertner, Samuel L., Jeffrey Mann, Audrey Murrell, and John F. Dovidio. "Reducing Intergroup Bias: The Benefits of Recategorization." *Journal of Personality and Social Psychology* 57, no. 2 (1989): 239–49. https://doi.org/10.1037/0022-3514.57.2.239.

Gaertner, Samuel L., John F. Dovidio, Phyllis A. Anastasio, Betty A. Bachman, and Mary C. Rust. "The Common Ingroup Identity Model: Recategorization and the Reduction of Intergroup Bias." *European Review of Social Psychology* 4, no. 1 (1993): 1–26. https://doi.org/10.1080/14792779343000004.

Gagnon Jr., V. P. *The Myth of Ethnic War: Serbia and Croatia in the 1990s*. Ithaca: Cornell University Press, 2004.

Gallagher Cunningham, Kathleen, and Nils B. Weidmann. "Shared Space: Ethnic Groups, State Accommodation, and Localized Conflict." *International Studies Quarterly* 54, no. 4 (2010): 1035–54. https://doi.org/10.1111/j.1468-2478.2010.00625.x.

Galtung, Johan. "Violence, Peace, and Peace Research." *Journal of Peace Research* 6, no. 3 (1969): 167–91. https://doi.org/10.1177/002234336900600301.

Gastil, John. "The Lessons and Limitations of Experiments in Democratic Deliberation." *Annual Review of Law and Social Science* 14, no. 1 (2018): 271–91. https://doi.org/10.1146/annurev-lawsocsci-110316-113639.

Gee, James Paul. *An Introduction to Discourse Analysis: Theory and Method*. 4th ed. London: Routledge, 2014.

Gellner, Ernest. *Nations and Nationalism*. Oxford: Blackwell, 1983.

Gerber, Marlène, André Bächtiger, Susumu Shikano, Simon Reber, and Samuel Rohr. "Deliberative Abilities and Influence in a Transnational Deliberative Poll (EuroPolis)." *British Journal of Political Science* 48, no. 4 (2018): 1093–118. https://doi.org/10.1017/s0007123416000144.

Gibson, James L. *Overcoming Apartheid: Can Truth Reconcile a Divided Nation?* New York: Russell Sage Foundation, 2004.

——. "'Truth' and 'Reconciliation' as Social Indicators." *Social Indicators Research* 81, no. 2 (2007): 257–81. https://doi.org/https://www.jstor.org/stable/20734426.

Goffman, Erving. *The Presentation of Self in Everyday Life*. Garden City: Doubleday, 1959.

González, Eduardo, and Howard Varney, eds. *Truth Seeking: Elements of Creating an Effective Truth Commission*. Brasilia: Amnesty Commission of the Ministry of Justice of Brazil; New York: International Center for Transitional Justice, 2013.

González Rey, Fernando L. "Subjectivity and Discourse: Complementary Topics of a Critical Psychology." *Culture and Psychology* 25, no. 2 (2019): 178–94. https://doi.org/10.1177/1354067x18754338.

Goodin, Robert E. "How Can Deliberative Democracy Get a Grip?" *Political Quarterly* 83, no. 4 (2012): 806–11. https://doi.org/10.1111/j.1467-923x.2012.02356.x.

Goodin, Robert E., and John S. Dryzek. "Deliberative Impacts: The Macro-Political Uptake of Mini-Publics." *Politics and Society* 34, no. 2 (2006): 219–44. https://doi.org/10.1177/0032329206288152.

Gordy, Eric. *Guilt, Responsibility, and Denial: The Past at Stake in Post-Milošević Serbia.* Philadelphia: University of Pennsylvania Press, 2013.

———. "Reconciliation Policies and Their Results in the Western Balkans: A 30-Year Perspective." Foreign Policy Forum, Zagreb. October 20, 2021. https://www.youtube.com/watch?v=PWFN-oEnEXw.

Gosselin, Tania. "Info-Klub: Creating a Common Public Sphere for Citizens of Vukovar." In *Managing Hatred and Distrust: The Prognosis for Post-Conflict Settlement in Multiethnic Communities in the Former Yugoslavia,* edited by Nenad Dimitrijević and Kovács Petra, 65–79. Budapest: Open Society Institute, 2004.

Govier, Trudy. *Taking Wrongs Seriously: Acknowledgment, Reconciliation and the Politics of Sustainable Peace.* Amherst: Humanity Books, 2006.

Gow, James. *Serbian Project and Its Adversaries: A Strategy of War Crimes.* London: Hurst & Company, 2003.

Gow, James, Rachel Kerr, and Pajić Zoran, eds. *Prosecuting War Crimes: Lessons and Legacies of the International Criminal Tribunal for the Former Yugoslavia.* London: Routledge, 2013.

Grodsky, Brian. "International Prosecutions and Domestic Politics: The Use of Truth Commissions as Compromise Justice in Serbia and Croatia." *International Studies Review* 11, no. 4 (2009): 687–706. https://doi.org/http://www.jstor.org/stable/40389162.

Grebo, Zdravko. "!Uspjećemo" [We Will Succeed!]. *!Glas Inicijative za REKOM,* February 20, 2015.

Grünenfelder, Rita, and André Bächtiger. "Gendered Deliberation? How Men and Women Deliberate in Legislatures." Paper presented at the European Consortium for Political Research Joint Sessions, Helsinki, May 2007.

Guinote, Ana. "The Perception of Group Variability in a Non-Minority and a Minority Context: When Adaptation Leads to Out-Group Differentiation." *British Journal of Social Psychology* 40, no. 1 (2001): 117–32. ttps://doi.org/10.1348/014466601164722.

Gutmann, Amy, and Dennis Thompson. *Democracy and Disagreement.* Cambridge: Harvard University Press, 1996.

———. "The Moral Foundations of Truth Commissions." In *Truth v. Justice: The Morality of Truth Commissions,* edited by Robert I. Rotberg and Dennis Thompson, 22–44. Princeton: Princeton University Press, 2010.

———. *Why Deliberative Democracy?* Princeton: Princeton University Press, 2004.

Habermas, Jürgen. *The Inclusion of the Other: Studies in Political Theory.* Edited by Ciaran Cronin and Pablo De Greiff. Cambridge: Polity Press, 1999.

———. "Justice and Solidarity: On the Discussion Concerning Stage 6." In *The Moral Domain: Essays in the Ongoing Discussion between Philosophy and the Social Sciences,* edited by Thomas E. Wren, 224–52. Cambridge: MIT Press, 1990.

———. *The Theory of Communicative Action.* Vol. 1, *Reason and the Rationalization of Society.* Cambridge: Polity Press, [1984] 2004.

Hackett, Claire, and Bill Rolston. "The Burden of Memory: Victims, Storytelling and Resistance in Northern Ireland." *Memory Studies* 2, no. 3 (2009): 355–76. https://doi.org/10.1177/1750698008337560.

Hagemann, Carlo. "Participation in and Contents of Two Dutch Political Party Discussion Lists on the Internet." *Javnost—The Public* 9, no. 2 (2002): 61–76. https://doi.org/10.1080/13183222.2002.11008800.

Hak, Tony, and Ton Bernts. "Coder Training: Explicit Instruction and Implicit Socialization?" In *The Content Analysis Reader*, edited by Klaus Krippendorff and Mary Angela Bock, 220–33. Los Angeles: Sage, 2009.

Halilovich, Hariz. *Places of Pain: Forced Displacement, Popular Memory and Trans-Local Identities in Bosnian War-Torn Communities.* New York: Berghahn Books, 2013.

Halpern, Daniel, and Jennifer Gibbs. "Social Media as a Catalyst for Online Deliberation? Exploring the Affordances of Facebook and YouTube for Political Expression." *Computers in Human Behavior* 29, no. 3 (2013): 1159–68. https://doi.org/10.1016/j.chb.2012.10.008.

Hamber, Brandon, and Gráinne Kelly. "Beyond Coexistence: Towards a Working Definition of Reconciliation." In *Reconciliation(s): Transitional Justice in Postconflict Societies*, edited by Joanna R. Quinn, 286–310. Montréal: McGill-Queen's University Press, 2009.

Han, Soo-Hye, William Schenck-Hamlin and Donna Schenck-Hamlin. "Inclusion, Equality and Discourse Quality in Citizen Deliberation on Broadband." *Journal of Public Deliberation* 11, no. 1 (2015): 1–24. https://doi.org/10.16997/jdd.220.

Hardy, Cynthia, Bill Harley, and Nelson Phillips. "Discourse Analysis and Content Analysis: Two Solitudes?" *Qualitative Methods* 2 (2004): 19–22.

Hartelius, E. Johanna. "'Leave a Message of Hope or Tribute': Digital Memorializing as Public Deliberation." *Argumentation and Advocacy* 47, no. 2 (2010): 67–85. https://doi.org/10.1080/00028533.2010.11821739.

Harwood, Jake. "The Contact Space: A Novel Framework for Intergroup Contact Research." *Journal of Language and Social Psychology* 29, no. 2 (2010): 147–77. https://doi.org/10.1177/0261927x09359520.

Harwood, Jake, Miles Hewstone, Yair Amichai-Hamburger, and Nicole Tausch. "Intergroup Contact: An Integration of Social Psychological and Communication Perspectives." *Annals of the International Communication Association* 36, no. 1 (2013): 55–102. https://doi.org/10.1080/23808985.2013.11 679126.

Haxhiaj, Serbeze, and Milica Stojanovic, "Evidence Reveals Serbian Officers' Role in Kosovo Massacre was Ignored." *Balkan Investigative Reporting Network*, April 27, 2020. https://balkaninsight.com/2020/04/27/massacre-in-meja-evidence-of-serbian-officers-involvement-ignored/.

Hayner, Priscilla B. *Unspeakable Truths: Confronting State Terror and Atrocity.* New York: Routledge, 2000.

He, Baogang. "A Deliberative Approach to the Tibet Autonomy Issue: Promoting Mutual Trust through Dialogue." *Asian Survey* 50, no. 4 (2010): 709–34. https://doi.org/10.1525/as.2010.50.4.709.

Head, Naomi. "Costly Encounters of the Empathic Kind: A Typology." *International Theory* 8, no. 1 (2016): 171–99. https://doi.org/10.1017/s1752971915000238.

Hehir, Aidan, and Furtuna Sheremeti. *Kosovo and Transitional Justice: The Pursuit of Justice after Large-Scale Conflict.* Abingdon: Routledge, 2022.

Herb, Guntram H., and David H. Kaplan, eds. *Nested Identities: Nationalism, Territory, and Scale.* Lanham, MD: Rowman & Littlefield, 1999.

Hester, Stephen, and William Housley. *Language, Interaction and National Identity: Studies in the Social Organisation of National Identity in Talk-in-Interaction.* Aldershot: Ashgate, 2017.

Hibbing, John R., and Elizabeth Theiss-Morse. *Stealth Democracy: Americans' Beliefs about How Government Should Work*. Cambridge: Cambridge University Press, 2002.

Himmelroos, Staffan. "Discourse Quality in Deliberative Citizen Forums—A Comparison of Four Deliberative Mini-Publics." *Journal of Public Deliberation* 13, no. 1 (2017): 1–28. https://doi.org/10.16997/jdd.269.

Himmelroos, Staffan, Lauri Rapeli, and Kimmo Grönlund. "Talking with Like-Minded People—Equality and Efficacy in Enclave Deliberation." *Social Science Journal* 54, no. 2 (2017): 148–58. https://doi.org/10.1016/j.soscij.2016.10.006.

Holgado-Tello, Francisco Pablo, Salvador Chacón-Moscoso, Isabel Barbero-García, and Enrique Vila-Abad. "Polychoric versus Pearson Correlations in Exploratory and Confirmatory Factor Analysis with Ordinal Variables." *Quality and Quantity* 44, no. 1 (2010): 153–66. https://doi.org/10.1007/s11135-008-9190-y.

Honneth, Axel. *The Struggle for Recognition: The Moral Grammar of Social Conflicts*. Cambridge: Polity Press, 1995.

Horowitz, Donald L. *Ethnic Groups in Conflict*. 2nd ed. Berkeley: University of California Press, [1985] 2000.

Howell, Jude, and Jenny Pearce. *Civil Society and Development: A Critical Exploration*. Boulder: Lynne Rienner, 2001.

Hozić, Aida A. "Writing After the Genocide: Lessons from Srebrenica and the Meaning of Community After Violence." *Journal of Muslim Minority Affairs* 35, no. 3 (2015): 423–27. https://doi.org/10.1080/13602004.2015.1073957.

Hübner Mendes, Conrado. *Constitutional Courts and Deliberative Democracy*. Oxford: Oxford University Press, 2013.

Huckfeldt, Robert, and John Sprague. *Citizens, Politics, and Social Communication: Information and Influence in an Election Campaign*. Cambridge: Cambridge University Press, 1995.

Hughes, James, and Denisa Kostovicova. "Introduction: Rethinking Reconciliation and Transitional Justice after Conflict." *Ethnic and Racial Studies* 41, no. 4 (2018): 617–23. https://doi.org/10.1080/01419870.2017.1406129.

——, eds. *Rethinking Reconciliation and Transitional Justice after Conflict*. London: Routledge, 2018.

Humanitarian Law Center (Serbia) and Humanitarian Law Center Kosovo. "The Kosovo Memory Book 1998–2000." http://www.kosovomemorybook.org/?page_id=29&lang=de.

Independent International Commission on Kosovo. "Annex 1: Documentation on Human Rights Violations," In *The Kosovo Report: Conflict, International Response, Lessons Learned*, 301–18. Oxford: Oxford University Press, 2000.

International Committee of the Red Cross. "ICRC Five-Year Strategy on the Missing in former Yugoslavia." November 26, 2020. https://www.icrc.org/en/document/missing-bosnia-herzegovina-croatia-serbia-kosovo.

International Criminal Tribunal for the Former Yugoslavia. Đorđević (IT-05-87/1). https://www.icty.org/en/case/djordjevic.

——. Šainović et al. (IT-05-87). https://www.icty.org/en/case/milutinovic.

——. The Prosecutor v. Vlastimir Đorđević. Case no. IT-05-87/1-A and Case no. IT-05-87/1-A. December 20, 2011. https://www.icty.org/x/cases/djordjevic/custom5/en/111220-1.pdf.

——. Prosecutor v. Nikola Šainović, Nebojša Pavković, Vladimir Lazarević, Sreten Lukić, Public Judgement, Case No. IT-05-87-A. January 23, 2014. https://www.icty.org/x/cases/milutinovic/acjug/en/140123.pdf.

Istraživačko Dokumentacioni Centar. "Bosanska knjiga mrtvih" [The Bosnian Book of the Dead]. http://www.mnemos.ba/ba/home/Download.

Irvine, Jill A., and Patrice C. McMahon. "From International Courts to Grassroots Organizing: Obstacles to Transitional Justice in the Balkans." In *Transitional Justice and Civil Society in the Balkans*, edited by Olivera Simić and Zala Volčič, 217–39. New York: Springer, 2013.

Ivanišević, Bogdan. *The War Crimes Chamber in Bosnia and Herzegovina: From Hybrid to Domestic Court*. New York: International Center for Transitional Justice, 2008.

Izmene Statuta REKOM [The Amendments to the RECOM Statute]. November 14, 2014. http://recom.link/sr/izmene-statuta-rekom-28-oktobar-2014-2/.

Janis, Irving L. *Victims of Groupthink: A Psychological Study of Foreign Policy Decisions and Fiascoes*. Boston: Houghton Mifflin, 1972.

Janoff-Bulman, Ronnie, and Amelie Werther. "The Social Psychology of Respect: Implications for Delegitimization and Reconciliation." In *The Social Psychology of Intergroup Reconciliation*, edited by Arie Nadler, Thomas E. Malloy, and Jeffrey D. Fisher, 145–70. Oxford: Oxford University Press, 2008.

Jansen, Harold J., and Royce Koop. "Pundits, Ideologues, and the Ranters: The British Columbia Election Online." *Canadian Journal of Communication* 30, no. 4 (2005): 613–32. https://doi.org/10.22230/cjc.2005v30n4a1483.

Jansen, Stef. "National Numbers in Context: Maps and Stats in Representations of the Post-Yugoslav Wars." *Identities* 12, no. 1 (2005): 45–68. https://doi.org/10.1080/10702890590914311.

Jensen, Jens F. "'Interactivity': Tracking a New Concept in Media and Communication Studies." *Nordicom Review* 19, no. 1 (1998): 185–204.

Jovic, Dejan. "The Disintegration of Yugoslavia: A Critical Review of Explanatory Approaches." *European Journal of Social Theory* 4, no. 1 (2001): 101–20. https://doi.org/10.1177/13684310122225037.

Jugo, Admir, and Sari Wastell. "Disassembling the Pieces, Reassembling the Social: The Forensic and Political Lives of Secondary Mass Graves in Bosnia and Herzegovina." In *Human Remains and Identification: Mass Violence, Genocide, and the "Forensic Turn,"* edited by Élisabeth Anstett and Jean-Marc Dreyfus, 142–74. Manchester: Manchester University Press, 2015.

Kaldor, Mary. *New and Old Wars: Organized Violence in a Global Era*. Cambridge: Polity Press, 1999.

Kaldor, Mary, and Denisa Kostovicova. "Global Civil Society and Illiberal Regimes." In *Global Civil Society 2007/8: Communicative Power and Democracy*, edited by Martin Albrow, Helmut K. Anheier, Marlies Glasius, Monroe E. Price, and Mary Kaldor, 86–113. London: Sage, 2007.

Kaldor, Mary, Yahia Said, and Denisa Kostovicova. "War and Peace: The Role of Global Civil Society." In *Global Civil Society 2006/7*, edited by Mary Kaldor, Martin Albrow, Helmut Anheier, and Marlies Glasius, 94–119. London: Sage, 2006.

Kandić, Nataša. "RECOM: A New Approach to Reconciliation and a Corrective for Criminal Justice." *Forum for Transitional Justice* 4 (2012): 78–80.

Kanzleiter, Boris. "Anti-War Activism, Yugoslavia, 1990s." In *The International Encyclopedia of Revolution and Protest: 1500 to the Present*, edited by Immanuel Ness, vol. 1, 223–24. Chichester: Blackwell, 2009.

Karpowitz, Christopher F., and Jane Mansbridge. "Disagreement and Consensus: The Need for Dynamic Updating in Public Deliberation." *Journal of Public Deliberation* 1, no. 1 (2005): 348–64. https://doi.org/10.16997/jdd.25.

Karpowitz, Christopher F., Tali Mendelberg, and Lee Shaker. "Gender Inequality in Deliberative Participation." *American Political Science Review* 106, no. 3 (2012): 533–47. https://doi.org/10.1017/s0003055412000329.

Kelman, Herman. "Reconciliation as Identity Change: A Social-Psychological Perspective." In *From Conflict Resolution to Reconciliation*, edited by Yaacov Bar-Siman-Tov, 111–24. Oxford: Oxford University Press, 2004.

Kerr, Rachel, and Eirin Mobekk. *Peace & Justice: Seeking Accountability after War.* Cambridge: Polity, 2007.

Kijewski, Sara, and Carolin Rapp. "Moving Forward? How War Experiences, Interethnic Attitudes, and Intergroup Forgiveness Affect the Prospects of Political Tolerance in Postwar Sri Lanka." *Journal of Peace Research* 56, no. 6 (2019): 845–59. https://doi.org/10.1177/0022343319849274.

King, Elisabeth, and Cyrus Samii. *Diversity, Violence, and Recognition: How Recognizing Ethnic Identity Promotes Peace.* Oxford: Oxford University Press, 2020.

King, Nigel, Christine Horrocks, and Joanna Brooks. *Interviews in Qualitative Research.* London: Sage, 2010.

Kiousis, Spiro. "Interactivity: A Concept Explication." *New Media and Society* 4, no. 3 (2002): 355–83. https://doi.org/10.1177/146144480200400303.

Knight, Jack, and James Johnson. "Aggregation and Deliberation: On the Possibility of Democratic Legitimacy." *Political Theory* 22, no. 2 (1994): 277–96. https://doi.org/https://www.jstor.org/stable/192147.

Koalicija za REKOM. *Obrazloženja uz Predlog Statuta regionalne komisije za utvrđivanje činjenica o ratnim zločinima i drugim teškim kršenjima ljudskih prava na području nekadašnje SFRJ* [The RECOM Coalition: The Justification Accompanying the Draft Statute of the Regional Commission for Establishing the Facts about War Crimes and other Gross Violations of Human Rights Committed on the Territory of the SFRY]. March 26, 2011.

———. *Statut: Predlog Regionalne komisije za utvrdjivanje činjenica o ratnim zločinima i drugim teškim kršenjima ljudskih prava počinjenim na području nekadašnje SFRJ.* [The Statute: The Draft Proposal of the Regional Commission for Establishing the Facts about War Crimes and other Gross Violations of Human Rights Committed on the Territory of the SFRY]. March 26, 2011.

Kochanski, Adam, and Joanna R. Quinn. "Letting the State off the Hook? Dilemmas of Holding the State to Account in Times of Transition." *Peacebuilding* 9, no. 2 (2021): 103–13. https://doi.org/10.1080/21647259.2021.1895616.

Koensler, Alexander. "Acts of Solidarity: Crossing and Reiterating Israeli-Palestinian Frontiers." *International Journal of Urban and Regional Research* 40, no. 2 (2016): 340–56. https://doi.org/10.1111/1468-2427.12380.

Kolind, Torsten. "In Search of 'Decent' People: Resistance to Ethnicization of Everyday Life among the Muslims of Stolac." In *The New Bosnian Mosaic: Identities, Memories and Moral Claims in a Post-War Society*, edited by Xavier Bougarel, Elissa Helms, and Ger Duijzings, 123–38. Farnham: Ashgate, 2007.

Kopecký, Petr, and Cas Mudde, eds. *Uncivil Society? Contentious Politics in Post-Communist Europe.* London: Routledge, 2003.

Kosterman, Rick, and Seymour Feshbach. "Toward a Measure of Patriotic and Nationalistic Attitudes." *Political Psychology* 10, no. 2 (1980): 257–74. https://doi.org/10.2307/3791647.

Kostić, Roland. "Transnational Justice and Reconciliation in Bosnia-Herzegovina: Whose Memories, Whose Justice?" *Sociologija* 54, no. 4 (2012): 649–66. https://doi.org/10.2298/soc1204649k.

Kostovicova, Denisa. "Airing Crimes, Marginalizing Victims: Political Expectations and Transitional Justice in Kosovo." In *The Milošević Trial: An Autopsy,* edited by Timothy William Waters, 249–59. Oxford: Oxford University Press, 2013.

———. "Civil Society and Post-Communist Democratization: Facing a Double Challenge in Post-Milošević Serbia." *Journal of Civil Society* 2, no. 1 (2006): 21–37. https://doi.org/10.1080/17448680600730918.

———. *Kosovo: The Politics of Identity and Space.* London: Routledge, 2005.

———. "Legitimacy and International Administration: The Ahtisaari Settlement for Kosovo from a Human Security Perspective." *International Peacekeeping* 15, no. 5 (2008): 631–47. https://doi.org/10.1080/13533310802396160.

———. "Republika Srpska and Its Boundaries in Bosnian Serb Geographical Narratives in the Post-Dayton Period." *Space and Polity* 8, no. 3 (2004): 267–87. https://doi.org/10.1080/1356257042000309616.

———. "Replication Data For: Gender, Justice and Deliberation: Why Women Don't Influence Peace-Making." *Harvard Dataverse V1*, 2020. https://doi.org/https://doi.org/10.7910/DVN/FC6WAO

———. "Seeking Justice in a Divided Region: Text Analysis of a Regional Civil Society Initiative in the Balkans." *International Journal of Transitional Justice* 11, no. 1 (2017): 154–75. https://doi.org/10.1093/ijtj/ijw023.

———. "Transitional Justice and Conflict Studies: Bridging the Divide." *Journal of Global Security Studies* 4, no. 2 (2019): 273–78. https://doi.org/10.1093/jogss/ogz003.

Kostovicova, Denisa, and Aude Bicquelet. "Norm Contestation and Reconciliation: Evidence from a Regional Transitional Justice Process in the Balkans." *Ethnic and Racial Studies* 41, no. 4 (2018): 681–700. https://doi.org/10.1080/01419870.2018.1380211.

Kostovicova, Denisa, and Vesna Bojicic-Dzelilovic. "Introduction." In *Austrian Presidency of the EU: Regional Approaches to the Balkans*, 21–22. Vienna: Center for the Study of Global Governance, LSE, and the Center for European Integration Strategies, 2006.

Kostovicova, Denisa, and Tom Paskhalis. "Gender, Justice and Deliberation: Why Women Don't Influence Peacemaking." *International Studies Quarterly* 65, no. 2 (2021): 263–76. https://doi.org/10.1093/isq/sqab003.

Kovačić, Mirko. "Dijalog u logoru." In *Tranziciona pravda i pomirenje u postjugoslovenskim zemljama: Glasovi institucija, verskih zajednica, aktivista, akademije, kulture i žrtava* [Transitional Justice and Reconciliation in Post-Yugoslav Countries: The Voices of Institutions, Religious Communities, Activists, Academics, Cultural Figures and Victims], edited by Svetlana Slapšak and Nataša Kandić, 96–97. Beograd: Koalicija za REKOM, 2015.

Kriesberg, Louis. "Changing Forms of Coexistence." In *Reconciliation, Justice and Coexistence: Theory and Practice*, edited by Mohammed Abu-Nimer, 49–66. Lanham, MD: Lexington Books, 2001.

Krippendorff, Klaus. *Content Analysis: An Introduction to Its Methodology.* 3rd ed. Thousand Oaks: Sage, 2013.

———. "Testing the Reliablity of Content Analysis Data." In *The Content Analysis Reader*, edited by Klaus Krippendorff and Mary Angela Bock, 350–57. Los Angeles: Sage, 2009.

Kurze, Arnaud. "Justice beyond Borders? The Politics to Democratize Human Rights in the Post-Conflict Balkans." PhD diss., George Mason University, 2012.

Kurze, Arnaud, and Iva Vukusic. "Afraid to Cry Wolf: Human Rights Activists' Struggle of Transnational Accountability Efforts in the Balkans." In *Transitional Justice and Civil Society in the Balkans*, edited by Olivera Simić and Zala Volčič, 210–11. New York: Springer, 2013.

Kymlicka, Will. *Multicultural Citizenship: A Liberal Theory of Minority Rights*. Oxford: Oxford University Press, 1996.

Laffey, Mark, and Jutta Weldes. "Methodological Reflections on Discourse Analysis." *Qualitative Methods* 2 (2004): 28–30.

Lake, Milli. *Strong NGOs and Weak States: Pursuing Gender Justice in the Democratic Republic of Congo and South Africa*. Cambridge: Cambridge University Press, 2018.

Lamb, Michele. "Ethno-Nationalist Conflict, Participation and Human Rights-Based Solidarity in Northern Ireland." *International Journal of Human Rights* 17, no. 7–8 (2013): 723–38. https://doi.org/10.1080/13642987.2013.823271.

Lambourne, Wendy. "What Are the Pillars of Transitional Justice? The United Nations, Civil Society and the Justice Cascade in Burundi." *Macquarie Law Journal* 13 (2014): 41–60.

Lamont, Christopher K. *International Criminal Justice and the Politics of Compliance*. London: Routledge, 2010.

Landwehr, Claudia, and Katharina Holzinger. "Institutional Determinants of Deliberative Interaction." *European Political Science Review* 2, no. 3 (2010): 373–400. https://doi.org/10.1017/s1755773910000226.

Leclercq, Sidney. "Injustice through Transitional Justice? Subversion Strategies in Burundi's Peace Process and Postconflict Developments." *International Journal of Transitional Justice* 11, no. 3 (2017): 525–44. https://doi.org/10.1093/ijtj/ijx017.

Lederach, John Paul. *Building Peace: Sustainable Reconciliation in Divided Societies*. Washington, DC: United States Institute of Peace Press, 1997.

Levy, Ron, Ian O'Flynn, and Hoi L. Kong. *Deliberative Peace Referendums*. Oxford: Oxford University Press, 2021.

Lijphart, Arendt. *Democracy in Plural Societies: A Comparative Exploration*. New Haven: Yale University Press, 1977.

Lilleker, Darren G., and Casilda Malagón. "Levels of Interactivity in the 2007 French Presidential Candidates' Websites." *European Journal of Communication* 25, no. 1 (2010): 25–42. https://doi.org/10.1177/0267323109354231.

Long, William J., and Peter Brecke. *War and Reconciliation: Reason and Emotion in Conflict Resolution*. Cambridge: MIT Press, 2003.

Lord, Christopher, and Dionysia Tamvaki. "The Politics of Justification? Applying the 'Discourse Quality Index' to the Study of the European Parliament." *European Political Science Review* 5, no. 1 (2013): 27–54. https://doi.org/10.1017/s1755773911000300.

Lowe, Will. "Content Analysis and Its Place in the (Methodological) Scheme of Things." *Qualitative Methods* 2 (2004): 25–27.

Loyle, Cyanne E., and Christian Davenport. "Transitional Injustice: Subverting Justice in Transition and Postconflict Societies." *Journal of Human Rights* 15, no. 1 (2016): 126–49. https://doi.org/10.1080/14754835.2015.1052897.

Lundy, Brandon D., Akanmu G. Adebayo, and Sherrill Hayes, eds. *Atone: Religion, Conflict, and Reconciliation*. Lanham, MD: Lexington Books, 2018.

Luskin, Robert C., Ian O'Flynn, James S. Fishkin, and David Russell. "Deliberating across Deep Divides." *Political Studies* 62, no. 1 (2012): 116–35. https://doi.org/10.1111/j.1467-9248.2012.01005.x.

Mac Ginty, Roger. *Everyday Peace: How So-Called Ordinary People Can Disrupt Violent Conflict*. Oxford: Oxford University Press, 2021.

McCarthy, Julie. "Sri Lanka's War Is Long Over: But Reconciliation Remains Elusive." *National Public Radio*. June 29, 2015. https://www.npr.org/sections/parallels/2015/06/29/418518510/sri-lankas-war-is-long-over-but-reconciliation-remains-elusive?t=1646476282633.

Mack, Katherine Elizabeth. *From Apartheid to Democracy: Deliberating Truth and Reconciliation in South Africa*. University Park: Pennsylvania State University Press, 2014.

Maček, Ivana. *Sarajevo Under Siege: Anthropology in Wartime*. Philadelphia: University of Pennsylvania Press, 2009.

Madlingozi, Tshepo. "On Transitional Justice Entrepreneurs and the Production of Victims." *Journal of Human Rights Practice* 2, no. 2 (2010): 208–28. https://doi.org/10.1093/jhuman/huq005.

Magnette, Paul, and Kalypso Nicolaïdis. "The European Convention: Bargaining in the Shadow of Rhetoric." *West European Politics* 27, no. 3 (2004): 381–404. https://doi.org/10.1080/0140238042000228068.

Majstorovic, Steven. "Ancient Hatreds or Elite Manipulation?: Memory and Politics in the Former Yugoslavia." *Word Affairs* 159, no. 4 (1997): 170–82. https://doi.org/https://www.jstor.org/stable/20672499.

Malešević, Siniša. *The Sociology of War and Violence*. Cambridge: Cambridge University Press, 2010.

Mallett, Robyn K., and Timothy D. Wilson. "Increasing Positive Intergroup Contact." *Journal of Experimental Social Psychology* 46, no. 2 (2010): 382–87. https://doi.org/10.1016/j.jesp.2009.11.006.

Mangcu, Xolela, ed. *Becoming Worthy Ancestors: Archive, Public Deliberation and Identity in South Africa*. Johannesburg: Wits University Press, 2011.

Manin, Bernard. "Democratic Deliberation: Why We Should Promote Debate Rather Than Discussion." Paper presented at the Program in Ethics and Public Affairs Seminar, Princeton University, October 13, 2005. https://nyuscholars.nyu.edu/en/publications/deliberation-why-we-should-focus-on-debate-rather-than-discussion.

Manosevitch, Edith, and Dana Walker. "Reader Comments to Online Opinion Journalism: A Space of Public Deliberation." *International Symposium on Online Journalism* 10 (2009): 1–30.

Manosevitch, Edith, Nili Steinfeld, and Azi Lev-On. "Promoting Online Deliberation Quality: Cognitive Cues Matter." *Information, Communication and Society* 17, no. 10 (2014): 1177–95. https://doi.org/10.1080/1369118x.2014.899610.

Mansbridge, Jane J. *Beyond Adversary Democracy*. New York: Basic Books, 1980.

———. "'Deliberative Democracy' or 'Democratic Deliberation'?" In *Deliberation, Participation and Democracy: Can the People Govern?*, edited by Shawn W. Rosenberg, 251–71. Palgrave Macmillan, 2007.

Mansbridge, Jane, James Bohman, Simone Chambers, David Estlund, Andreas Føllesdal, Archon Fung, Cristina Lafont, Bernard Manin, and José luis Martí. "The Place of Self-Interest and the Role of Power in Deliberative Democracy." *Journal of Political Philosophy* 18, no. 1 (2010): 64–100. https://doi.org/10.1111/j.1467-9760.2009.00344.x.

Maoz, Ifat. "An Experiment in Peace: Reconciliation-Aimed Workshops of Jewish-Israeli and Palestinian Youth." *Journal of Peace Research* 37, no. 6 (2000): 721–36. https://doi.org/10.1177/0022343300037006004.

Maslach, Christina, Joy Stapp, and Richard T. Santee. "Individuation: Conceptual Analysis and Assessment." *Journal of Personality and Social Psychology* 49, no. 3 (1985): 729–38. https://doi.org/10.1037/0022-3514.49.3.729.

Mazzei, Julie M. "Finding Shame in Truth: The Importance of Public Engagement in Truth Commissions." *Human Rights Quarterly* 33, no. 2 (2011): 431–52. https://www.jstor.org/stable/2301602.

McEvoy, Kieran, and Kirsten McConnachie. "Victims and Transitional Justice: Voice, Agency and Blame." *Social and Legal Studies* 22, no. 4 (2013): 489–513. https://doi.org/10.1177/0964663913499062.

McEvoy, Leslie, Kieran McEvoy, and Kirsten McConnachie. "Reconciliation as a Dirty Word: Conflict, Community Relations and Education in Northern Ireland." *Journal of International Affairs* 60, no. 1 (2006): 81–106. https://doi.org/https://www.jstor.org/stable/24358014.

McIntosh, Ian S. "Reconciliation, You've Got to Be Dreaming: Exploring Methodologies for Monitoring and Achieving Aboriginal Reconciliation in Australia by 2030." *Conflict Resolution Quarterly* 32, no. 1 (2014): 55–81. https://doi.org/10.1002/crq.21101.

McMahon, Christopher. "Discourse and Morality." *Ethics* 110, no. 3 (2000): 514–36. https://doi.org/10.1086/233322.

McMahon, Patrice C. *The NGO Game: Post-Conflict Peacebuilding in the Balkans and Beyond*. Ithaca: Cornell University Press, 2017.

Meernik, James. "Victor's Justice or the Law?: Judging and Punishing at the International Criminal Tribunal for the Former Yugoslavia." *Journal of Conflict Resolution* 47, no. 2 (2003): 140–62. https://doi.org/10.1177/0022002702251024.

Meernik, James, and Jose Raul Guerrero. "Can International Criminal Justice Advance Ethnic Reconciliation? The ICTY and Ethnic Relations in Bosnia-Herzegovina." *Southeast European and Black Sea Studies* 14, no. 3 (2014): 383–407. https://doi.org/10.1080/14683857.2014.924675.

Meierhenrich, Jens. "Varieties of Reconciliation." *Law and Social Inquiry* 33, no. 1 (2008): 195–231. https://doi.org/10.1111/j.1747-4469.2008.00098.x.

Mekina, Igor. "Analiza javne kritike i podrške Inicijative za osnivanje REKOM" [The Analysis of Public Criticism of and Support for the Initiative for Establishing RECOM]. 2011. https://documenta.hr/wp-content/uploads/2019/11/rekom_javno_zagovaranje_08_f_2826_hr.pdf.

Mendelberg, Tali, and John Oleske. "Race and Public Deliberation." *Political Communication* 17, no. 2 (2000): 169–91. https://doi.org/10.1080/105846000198468.

Mendelberg, Tali, Christopher F. Karpowitz, and J. Baxter Oliphant. "Gender Inequality in Deliberation: Unpacking the Black Box of Interaction." *Perspectives on Politics* 12, no. 1 (2014): 18–44. https://doi.org/10.1017/s1537592713003691.

Mégret, Frédéric. "Do Facts Exist, Can They Be 'Found,' and Does It Matter?" In *The Transformation of Human Rights Fact-Finding*, edited by Philip Alston and Sarah Knuckey, 28–47. Oxford: Oxford University Press, 2016.

Mgbako, Chi Adanna. "Ingando Solidarity Camps: Reconciliation and Political Indoctrination in Post-Genocide Rwanda." *Harvard Human Rights Journal* 18 (2005): 201–24.

Micinski, Nicholas R. "NGO Frequent Flyers: Youth Organisations and the Undermining of Reconciliation in Bosnia and Herzegovina." *Journal of Peacebuilding & Development* 11, no. 1 (2016): 99–104. https://dx.doi.org/10.1080/15423166.2016.1143789.

Milanović, Marko. "The Impact of the ICTY on the Former Yugoslavia: An Anticipatory Postmortem." *American Journal of International Law* 110, no. 2 (2016): 233–59. https://doi.org/10.5305/amerjintelaw.110.2.0233.

Mill, John Stuart. *Utilitarianism*. Oxford: Oxford University Press, 1998.

Misak, Cheryl. "Making Disagreement Matter: Pragmatism and Deliberative Democracy." *Journal of Speculative Philosophy* 18, no. 1 (2004): 9–22. https://doi.org/https://www.jstor.org/stable/25670494.

Mokros, Hartmut B. "From Information and Behavior to Interaction and Identity." In *Interaction and Identity*, edited by Hartmut B. Mokros, 1–22. New Brunswick, NJ: Transaction Publishers, 1996.

———, ed. *Interaction and Identity*. New Brunswick, NJ: Transaction Publishers, 1996.

Moll, Nicolas. "Promoting 'Positive Stories' of Help and Rescue from the 1992–1995 War in Bosnia and Herzegovina." *Comparative Southeast European Studies* 67, no. 4 (2019): 447–75. https://doi.org/10.1515/soeu-2019-0036.

Montalvo, Jose G., and Marta Reynal-Querol. "Ethnic Polarization and the Duration of Civil Wars." *Economics of Governance* 11, no. 2 (2010): 123–43. https://doi.org/10.1007/s10101-010-0077-8.

Moran-Ellis, Jo, Victoria D. Alexander, Ann Cronin, Mary Dickinson, Jane Fielding, Judith Sleney, and Hilary Thomas. "Triangulation and Integration: Processes, Claims and Implications." *Qualitative Research* 6, no. 1 (2006): 45–59. https://doi.org/10.1177/1468794106058870.

Moshman, David. "Identity, Genocide, and Group Violence." In *Handbook of Identity Theory and Research*, edited by Seth J. Schwartz, Koen Luyckx, and Vivian L. Vignoles. Vol. 2, *Domains and Categories*, 917–32. New York: Springer, 2012.

Mouffe, Chantal. *Deliberative Democracy or Agonistic Pluralism*. Vienna: Institute for Advanced Studies, 2000.

Murphy, Colleen. *The Conceptual Foundations of Transitional Justice*. Cambridge: Cambridge University Press, 2017.

Mutz, Diana C. *Hearing the Other Side: Deliberative versus Participatory Democracy*. Cambridge: Cambridge University Press, 2006.

———. "Is Deliberative Democracy a Falsifiable Theory?" *Annual Review of Political Science* 11, no. 1 (2008): 521–38. https://doi.org/10.1146/annurev.polisci.11.081306.070308.

———. "Facilitating Communication across Lines of Political Difference: The Role of Mass Media." *American Political Science Review* 95, no. 1 (2001): 97–114. https://doi.org/10.1017/s0003055401000223.

Mylonas, Harris, and Maya Tudor. "Nationalism: What We Know and What We Still Need to Know." *Annual Review of Political Science* 24, no. 1 (2021): 109–32. https://doi.org/10.1146/annurev-polisci-041719-101841.

Nagy, Rosemary. "Reconciliation in Post-Commission South Africa: Thick and Thin Accounts of Solidarity." *Canadian Journal of Political Science* 35, no. 2 (2002): 323–46. https://doi.org/10.1017/S0008423902778268.

Nair, Gautam, and Nicholas Sambanis. "Violence Exposure and Ethnic Identification: Evidence from Kashmir." *International Organization* 73, no. 2 (2019): 329–63. https://doi.org/10.1017/s0020818318000498.

Narotzky, Susana, and Paz Moreno. "Reciprocity's Dark Side: Negative Reciprocity, Morality and Social Reproduction." *Anthropological Theory* 2, no. 3 (2000): 281–305. https://doi.org/10.1177/1463499602002003801.

Neblo, Michael A. "Family Disputes: Diversity in Defining and Measuring Deliberation." *Swiss Political Science Review* 13, no. 4 (2007): 527–57. https://doi.org/10.1002/j.1662-6370.2007.tb00088.x.

——. "Impassioned Democracy: The Roles of Emotion in Deliberative Theory." *American Political Science Review* 114, no. 3 (2020): 923–27. https://doi. org/10.1017/S0003055420000210.

——. "Thinking through Democracy: Between the Theory and Practice of Deliberative Politics." *Acta Politica* 40 (2005): 169–81. https://doi.org/10.1057/ palgrave.ap.5500102.

Neuendorf, Kimberly A. "Content Analysis—A Contrast and Complement to Discourse Analysis." *Qualitative Methods* 2 (2004): 33–35.

——. *The Content Analysis Guidebook.* Thousand Oaks: Sage, 2002.

Neufeld, Scott D., and Michael T. Schmitt. "Solidarity Not Homogeneity: Constructing a Superordinate Aboriginal Identity That Protects Subgroup Identities." *Political Psychology* 40, no. 3 (2009): 599–616. https://doi.org/10.1111/pops.12530.

Nicoll, Angus, Karen Bassett, and Stanley J. Ulijaszek. "What's in a Name? Accuracy of Using Surnames and Forenames in Ascribing Asian Ethnic Identity in English Populations." *Journal of Epidemiology and Community Health* 40, no. 4 (1986): 364–68. https://doi.org/10.1136/jech.40.4.364.

Nießer, Jacqueline. *Die Wahrheit Der Anderen: Transnationale Vergangenheitsaufarbeitung in Post-Jugoslawien Am Beispiel Der REKOM Initiative* [The others' truth: Transnational reckoning with the past in post-Yugoslavia on the example of the RECOM initiative]. Göttingen: Vandenhoeck & Ruprecht, 2020.

Nobles, Melissa. "The Prosecution of Human Rights Violations." *Annual Review of Political Science* 13, no. 1 (2010): 165–82. https://doi.org/10.1146/annurev. polisci.040108.110013.

Noël, Alain. "Democratic Deliberation in a Multinational Federation." *Critical Review of International Social and Political Philosophy* 9, no. 3 (2006): 419–44. https:// doi.org/10.1080/13698230600901212.

Nolan, Mary. "The Elusive Pursuit of Truth and Justice: A Review Essay." *Radical History Review* 97 (2007): 143–54. https://doi.org/10.1215/01636545-2006-020.

Noor, Masi, Nurit Shnabel, Samer Halabi, and Arie Nadler. "When Suffering Begets Suffering: The Psychology of Competitive Victimhood between Adversarial Groups in Violent Conflicts." *Personality and Social Psychology Review* 16, no. 4 (2012): 351–74. https://doi.org/10.1177/1088868312440048.

Norris, Pippa. "Women Politicians: Transforming Westminster?" *Parliamentary Affairs* 49, no. 1 (1996): 89–102. https://doi.org/10.1093/oxfordjournals.pa.a028675.

Nuyts, Jan. "Subjectivity: Between Discourse and Conceptualization." *Journal of Pragmatics* 86 (2015): 106–10. https://doi.org/10.1016/j.pragma.2015.05.015.

Obradovic-Wochnik, Jelena. "Serbian Civil Society as an Exclusionary Space: NGOs, the Public and 'Coming to Terms with the Past.'" In *Civil Society and Transitions in the Western Balkans,* edited by Vesna Bojicic-Dzelilovic, James Ker-Lindsay, and Denisa Kostovicova, 210–29. Basingstoke: Palgrave Macmillan, 2013.

O'Doherty, Kieran C., and Helen J. Davidson. "Subject Positioning and Deliberative Democracy: Understanding Social Processes Underlying Deliberation." *Journal for the Theory of Social Behaviour* 40, no. 2 (2010): 224–45. https://doi. org/10.1111/j.1468-5914.2009.00429.x.

O'Doherty, Kieran C., and Karla Stroud. "Public Deliberation and Social Psychology: Integrating Theories of Participation with Social Psychological Research and Practice." In *The Sage Handbook of Applied Social Psychology,* edited by Kieran C. O'Doherty and Darrin Hodgetts, 419–41. Los Angeles: Sage, 2019.

O'Flynn, Ian. *Deliberative Democracy and Divided Societies.* Edinburgh: Edinburgh University Press, 2006.

——. "Pulling Together: Shared Intentions, Deliberative Democracy and Deeply Divided Societies." *British Journal of Political Science* 47, no. 1 (2017): 187–202. https://doi.org/10.1017/s0007123415000459.

——. "Review Article: Divided Societies and Deliberative Democracy." *British Journal of Political Science* 37, no. 4 (2007): 731–51. https://www.jstor.org/stable/4497320.

O'Flynn, Ian, and Didier Caluwaerts. "Deliberation in Deeply Divided Societies." In *The Oxford Handbook of Deliberative Democracy*, edited by Bächtiger André, John S. Dryzek, Jane Mansbridge, and Mark Warren, 742–54. Oxford: Oxford University Press, 2018.

O'Loughlin, John. "Inter-Ethnic Friendships in Post-War Bosnia-Herzegovina: Sociodemographic and Place Influences." *Ethnicities* 10, no. 1 (2010): 26–53. https://doi.org/10.1177/1468796809354153.

O'Malley, Eoin, David M. Farrell, and Jane Suiter. "Does Talking Matter? A Quasi-Experiment Assessing the Impact of Deliberation and Information on Opinion Change." *International Political Science Review* 41, no. 3 (2020): 321–34. https://doi.org/10.1177/0192512118824459.

Olsen, Tricia D., Leigh A. Payne, and Andrew G. Reiter. "The Justice Balance: When Transitional Justice Improves Human Rights and Democracy." *Human Rights Quarterly* 32, no. 4 (2010): 980–1007. https://doi.org/10.1353/hrq.2010.0021.

Oosterlynck, Stijn, Maarten Loopmans, Nick Schuermans, Joke Vandenabeele, and Sami Zemni. "Putting Flesh to the Bone: Looking for Solidarity in Diversity, Here and Now." *Ethnic and Racial Studies* 39, no. 5 (2016): 764–82. https://doi.org/10.1080/01419870.2015.1080380.

"Outloud Podcast: The Story of Lush Krasniqi, Survivor of the Meja Massacre (27.04.1999)." In Dafina Halili, "The Struggle of a Survivor of One of the Largest Massacres in Kosovo," Kosovo 2.0, April 23, 2020. https://kosovotwopointzero.com/wp-content/uploads/2021/12/The-struggle-of-a-survivor-of-one-of-the-largest-massacres-in-Kosovo_POD_TRANSCRIPT.pdf.

Palmer, Nicola, Briony Jones, and Julia Viebach. "Introduction: Ways of Knowing Atrocity: A Methodological Enquiry into the Formulation, Implementation, and Assessment of Transitional Justice." *Canadian Journal of Law and Society* 30, no. 2 (2015): 173–82. https://doi.org/10.1017/cls.2015.19.

Paluck, Elizabeth Levy. "Is It Better Not to Talk? Group Polarization, Extended Contact, and Perspective Taking in Eastern Democratic Republic of Congo." *Personality and Social Psychology Bulletin* 36, no. 9 (2010): 1170–85. https://doi.org/10.1177/0146167210379868.

Pankhurst, Donna. "Issues of Justice and Reconciliation in Complex Political Emergencies: Conceptualising Reconciliation, Justice and Peace." *Third World Quarterly* 20, no. 1 (1999): 239–56. https://www.jstor.org/stable/3993193.

Parekh, Bhikhu. *A New Politics of Identity: Political Principles for an Interdependent World*. Basingstoke: Palgrave Macmillan, 2008.

Parthasarathy, Ramya, Vijayendra Rao, and Nethra Palaniswamy. "Deliberative Democracy in an Unequal World: A Text-as-Data Study of South India's Village Assemblies." *American Political Science Review* 113, no. 3 (2019): 623–40. https://doi.org/10.1017/s0003055419000182.

Pavasović Trošt, Tamara. "Ruptures and Continuities in Nationhood Narratives: Reconstructing the Nation through History Textbooks in Serbia and Croatia." *Nations and Nationalism* 24, no. 3 (2018): 716–40. https://doi.org/10.1111/nana.12433.

Pavlaković, Vjeran. "Croatia, the International Criminal Tribunal for the Former Yugoslavia, and General Gotovina as a Political Symbol." *Europe-Asia Studies* 62, no. 10 (2010): 1707–40. https://doi.org/10.1080/09668136.2010.522426.

Pedrini, Seraina. "Deliberative Capacity in the Political and Civic Sphere." *Swiss Political Science Review* 20, no. 2 (2014): 263–86. https://doi.org/10.1111/spsr.12074.

Pensky, Max. *The Ends of Solidarity: Discourse Theory in Ethics and Politics*. Albany: State University of New York Press, 2009.

Perunovic, Sreca. "Animosities in Yugoslavia before Its Demise: Revelations of an Opinion Poll Survey." *Ethnicities* 16, no. 6 (2016): 819–41. https://doi.org/10.1177/1468796815576059.

Pesic, Vesna. "Serbian Nationalism and the Origins of the Yugoslav Crisis." Peaceworks no. 8, United States Institute of Peace, April 1, 1996. https://www.usip.org/publications/1996/04/serbian-nationalism-and-origins-yugoslav-crisis.

Petersen, Roger D. *Western Intervention in the Balkans: The Strategic Use of Emotion in Conflict*. Cambridge: Cambridge University Press, 2011.

Petričušić, Antonija, and Cyril Blondel. "Reconciliation in the Western Balkans: New Perspectives and Proposals." *Journal of Ethnopolitics and Minority Issues in Europe* 11, no. 4 (2012): 1–6.

Pettigrew, Thomas F. "Intergroup Contact Theory." *Annual Review of Psychology* 49, no. 1 (1998): 65–85. https://doi.org/10.1146/annurev.psych.49.1.65.

Pettigrew, Thomas F., Linda R. Tropp, Ulrich Wagner, and Oliver Christ. "Recent Advances in Intergroup Contact Theory." *International Journal of Intercultural Relations* 35, no. 3 (2011): 271–80. https://doi.org/10.1016/j.ijintrel.2011.03.001.

Pham, Phuong, and Patrick Vinck. "Empirical Research and the Development and Assessment of Transitional Justice Mechanisms." *International Journal of Transitional Justice* 1, no. 2 (2007): 231–48. https://doi.org/10.1093/ijtj/ijm017.

Phillips, Anne. *The Politics of Presence: The Political Representation of Gender, Ethnicity, and Race*. Oxford: Oxford University Press, 1995.

Philpott, Daniel. "Reconciliation, Politics, and Transitional Justice." In *The Oxford Handbook of Religion, Conflict, and Peacebuilding*, edited by Atalia Omer, R. Scott Appleby, and David Little, 335–54. Oxford: Oxford University Press, 2015.

——. *Just and Unjust Peace: The Ethic of Political Reconciliation*. Oxford: Oxford University Press, 2012.

Pierce, Andrew J. "Justice without Solidarity? Collective Identity and the Fate of the 'Ethical' in Habermas' Recent Political Theory." *European Journal of Philosophy* 26, no. 1 (2018): 546–68. https://doi.org/10.1111/ejop.12273.

Pittam, Jeffery. "The Historical and Emergent Enactment of Identity in Language." *Research on Language & Social Interaction* 32, no. 1–2 (1999): 111–17. https://doi.org/10.1080/08351813.1999.9683614.

Plano Clark, Vicki L., and Manijeh Badiee. "Research Questions in Mixed Methods Research." In *SAGE Handbook of Mixed Methods in Social & Behavioral Research*, edited by Abbas Tashakkori and Charles Teddlie, 275–304. Thousand Oaks: Sage, 2015.

Ploss, Katharina. "Beyond the Meeting: How Community Activists Construe Idea Transfer from Intercommunity Encounters—The Cases of Northern Ireland and Kosovo." *International Negotiation* 16, no. 2 (2011): 319–46. https://doi.org/10.1163/138234011x573066.

Polletta, Francesca, and John Lee. "Is Telling Stories Good for Democracy? Rhetoric in Public Deliberation after 9/11." *American Sociological Review* 71, no. 5 (2006): 699–723. https://doi.org/10.1177/000312240607100501.

Porter, Norman. *The Elusive Quest: Reconciliation in Northern Ireland.* Belfast: Blackstaff Press, 2003.

Pratto, Felicia, Žeželj Iris, Edona Maloku, Vladimir Turjačanin, and Marija Branković, eds. *Shaping Social Identities after Violent Conflict: Youth in the Western Balkans.* Basingstoke: Palgrave Macmillan, 2017.

Preysing, Domenica. *Transitional Justice in Post-Revolutionary Tunisia (2011–2013): How the Past Shapes the Future.* Wiesbaden: Springer VS, 2016.

Price, Huw. "Truth as Convenient Fiction." In *The Pragmatism Reader: From Peirce through the Present,* edited by Robert B. Talisse and Scott F. Aikin, 451–70. Princeton: Princeton University Press, 2011.

Proces REKOM: Izvještaj [The RECOM Process: The Report]. May 2006–August 2011. https://recom.link/wp-content/uploads/2011/08/Proces_REKOM-Izvestaj-maj_2006-avgust_2011-15_09_2011-logo-BiH.pdf.

Proces REKOM: Konsultativni process o utvrđivanju činjenica o ratnim zločinima i drugim teškim kršenjima ljudskih prava počinjenim na području nekadašnje SFRJ [The RECOM Process: The Consultation Process about Establishing the Facts about War Crimes and other Gross Violations of Human Rights Committed on the Territory of the SFRY]. Beograd: Fond za humanitarno pravo, 2011.

Pukallus, Stefanie. *Communication in Peacebuilding: Civil Wars, Civility and Safe Spaces.* Cham: Palgrave Macmillan, 2022.

Puljek-Shank, Randall. "Civic Agency in Governance: The Role of Legitimacy with Citizens vs. Donors." *Voluntas: International Journal of Voluntary and Nonprofit Organizations* 29, no. 4 (2018): 870–83. https://doi.org/10.1007/s11266-018-0020-0.

Pupavac, Vanessa. "Therapeutic Governance: Psycho-Social Intervention and Trauma Risk Management." *Disasters* 25, no. 4 (2001): 358–72. https://doi.org/10.1111/1467-7717.00184.

Quinn, Joanna R. "Introduction." In *Reconciliation(s): Transitional Justice in Postconflict Societies,* edited by Joanna R. Quinn, 3–13. Montréal: McGill-Queen's University Press, 2009.

———. *Thin Sympathy: A Strategy to Thicken Transitional Justice.* Philadelphia: University of Pennsylvania Press, 2021.

Rafaeli, Sheizaf. "Interactivity: From New Media to Communication." In *Advancing Communication Science: Merging Mass and Interpersonal Processes,* edited by Robert P. Hawkins, John M. Wiemann, and Suzanne Pingree, 110–34. Newbury Park: Sage, 1988.

Rakić, Tamara, and Anne Maass. "Communicating between Groups, Communicating about Groups." In *Language, Communication, and Intergroup Relations: A Celebration of the Scholarship of Howard Giles,* edited by Jake Harwood, Jessica Gasiorek, Herbert Pierson, John F. Nussbaum, and Cynthia Gallois, 66–97. New York: Routledge, 2019.

Ramet, Sabrina P. *Nationalism and Federalism in Yugoslavia,* 1962–1991. 2nd ed. Bloomington: Indiana University Press, 1992.

———. *Thinking about Yugoslavia: Scholarly Debates about the Yugoslav Breakup and the Wars in Bosnia and Kosovo.* Cambridge: Cambridge University Press, 2005.

Rangelov, Iavor. *Nationalism and the Rule of Law: Lessons from the Balkans and Beyond.* Cambridge: Cambridge University Press, 2014.

Rangelov, Iavor, and Ruti Teitel. "Transitional Justice." In *The Handbook of Global Security Policy*, edited by Mary Kaldor and Iavor Rangelov, 338–52. Chichester: John Wiley & Sons, 2014.

Rawls, John. *A Theory of Justice*. Cambridge: Belknap Press of Harvard University Press, 1971.

RECOM Reconciliation Network. "Coalition for RECOM Takes Charge of Creating List of War Victims on the Territory of Former Yugoslavia." Press Release, May 29, 2020. https://www.recom.link/en/coalition-for-recom-takes-charge-of-creating-list-of-war-victims-on-the-territory-of-the-former-yugoslavia/.

———. "What Is RECOM Process?" https://www.recom.link/en/what-is-recom-process-3/.

Rehg, William. *Insight and Solidarity: The Discourse Ethics of Jürgen Habermas*. Berkeley: University of California Press, 1994.

———. "Solidarity and the Common Good: An Analytic Framework." *Journal of Social Philosophy* 38, no. 1 (2007): 7–21. https://doi.org/10.1111/j.1467-9833.2007.00363.x.

Rettberg, Angelika, and Juan Esteban Ugarriza. "Reconciliation: A Comprehensive Framework for Empirical Analysis." *Security Dialogue* 47, no. 6 (2016): 517–40. https://doi.org/10.1177/0967010616671858.

Richmond, Oliver P. *Peace Formation and Political Order in Conflict Affected Societies*. Oxford: Oxford University Press, 2016.

Riddle, Elizabeth M. "A Historical Perspective on the Productivity of the Suffixes -ness and -ity." In *Historical Semantics—Historical Word-Formation*, edited by Jacek Fisiak, 435–62. Berlin: Mouton, 1985.

Ristivojević, Branislav. "Nacrt statuta REKOM-a iz ugla Ustava RS i njenih krivičnopravnih propisa" [The Draft Statute of RECOM from the Perspective of the RS (Republic of Serbia) Constitutions and its Criminal Law]. *Nova srpska politička misao*, May 21, 2011. http://www.nspm.rs/istina-i-pomirenje-na-ex-yu-prostorima/nacrt-statuta-rekom-a-iz-ugla-ustava-rs-i-njenih-krivicnopravnih-propisa.html/.

Roald, Vebjørn, and Linda Sangolt. *Deliberation, Rhetoric and Emotion in the Discourse on Climate Change in the European Parliament*. Delft: Eburon, 2012.

Robins, Simon. "Failing Victims? The Limits of Transitional Justice in Addressing the Needs of Victims of Violations." *Human Rights and International Legal Discourse* 17, no. 2 (2017): 41–58.

Roger, Léa, and Gary S. Schaal. "The Quality of Deliberation in Two Committees of the European Parliament: The Neglected Influence of the Situational Context and the Policymaking Stage." *Politics and Governance* 1, no. 2 (2013): 151–69. https://doi.org/10.17645/pag.v1i2.101.

Rowe, Ian. "Deliberation 2.0: Comparing the Deliberative Quality of Online News User Comments Across Platforms." *Journal of Broadcasting and Electronic Media* 59, no. 4 (2015): 539–55. https://doi.org/10.1080/08838151.2015.1093482.

Rowen, Jamie. "Mobilizing Truth: Agenda Setting in a Transnational Social Movement." *Law and Social Inquiry* 37, no. 3 (2012): 686–718. https://doi.org/10.1111/j.1747-4469.2012.01317.x.

Rubli, Sandra. "Transitional Justice: Justice by Bureaucratic Means?" *Swisspeace*, Working Paper no. 4 (2012).

Rucinski, Dianne. "The Centrality of Reciprocity to Communication and Democracy." *Critical Studies in Mass Communication* 8, no. 2 (1991): 184–94. https://doi.org/10.1080/15295039109366790.

Rudling, Adriana. "'I'm Not That Chained-Up Little Person': Four Paragons of Victimhood in Transitional Justice Discourse." *Human Rights Quarterly* 41, no. 2 (2019): 421–40. https://doi.org/10.1353/hrq.2019.0032.

Rummens, Joanna Anneke. "Conceptualising Identity and Diversity: Overlaps, Intersections, and Processes." *Canadian Ethnic Studies Journal* 35, no. 3 (2003): 10–25.

Rummens, Stefan. "Staging Deliberation: The Role of Representative Institutions in the Deliberative Democratic Process." *Journal of Political Philosophy* 20, no. 1 (2012): 23–44. https://doi.org/10.1111/j.1467-9760.2010.00384.x.

The Rule of Law and Transitional Justice in Conflict and Post-conflict Societies: Report of the Secretary-General. S/2004/616, United Nations Security Council, August 23, 2004. https://digitallibrary.un.org/record/527647?ln=en.

Rule-of-law Tools for Post-Conflict States: National Consultations on Transitional Justice. Office of the United Nations High Commissioner for Human Rights. New York: United Nations, 2009). https://www.ohchr.org/Documents/Publications/ National ConsultationsTJ_EN.pdf.

Ryan, Matthew, and Graham Smith. "Defining Mini-Publics." In *Deliberative Mini-Publics: Involving Citizens in the Democratic Process,* edited by Grönlund Kimmo, Bächtiger André, and Setälä Maija, 9–26. Colchester: ECPR Press, 2014.

Ryfe, David M. "Does Deliberative Democracy Work?" *Annual Review of Political Science* 8, no. 1 (2005): 49–71. https://doi.org/10.1146/annurev. polisci.8.032904.154633.

———. "Narrative and Deliberation in Small Group Forums." *Journal of Applied Communication Research* 34, no. 1 (2006): 72–93. https://doi. org/10.1080/00909880500420226.

Sambanis, Nicholas, and Moses Shayo. "Social Identification and Ethnic Conflict." *American Political Science Review* 107, no. 2 (2013): 294–325. https://doi. org/10.2139/ssrn.1955111.

Sampson, Edward E. *Dealing with Differences: An Introduction to the Social Psychology of Prejudice.* Fort Worth: Harcourt, Brace & Company, 1999.147–161.

Sanders, Lynn M. "Against Deliberation." *Political Theory* 25, no. 3 (1997): 347–76. https://www.jstor.org/stable/191984.

Scheufele, Dietram A., Bruce W. Hardy, Dominique Brossard, Israel S. Waismel-Manor, and Erik Nisbet. "Democracy Based on Difference: Examining the Links Between Structural Heterogeneity, Heterogeneity of Discussion Networks, and Democratic Citizenship." *Journal of Communication* 56, no. 4 (2006): 728–53. https://doi.org/10.1111/j.1460-2466.2006.00317.x.

Schonhardt-Bailey, Cheryl. *Deliberating American Monetary Policy: A Textual Analysis.* Cambridge: MIT Press, 2013.

Schwartz, Seth J., Moin Syed, Tiffany Yip, George P. Knight, Adriana J. Umaña-Taylor, Deborah Rivas-Drake, and Richard M. Lee. "Methodological Issues in Ethnic and Racial Identity Research with Ethnic Minority Populations: Theoretical Precision, Measurement Issues, and Research Designs." *Child Development* 85, no. 1 (2014): 58–76. https://doi.org/10.1111/cdev.12201.

Seixas, Eunice Castro. "How Activists See Civil Society and the Political Elite in Bosnia: Relevance to Prospects of Transitional Justice." In *Transitional Justice and Civil Society in the Balkans,* edited by Simić Olivera and Zala Volčič, 69–85. New York: Springer, 2013.

Selvanathan, Hema Preya, Bernhard Leidner, Nebojša Petrović, Nedim Prelić, Ivan Ivanek, Johannes Krugel, and Jovana Bjekić. "Wedialog.net: A Quantitative Field Test of the Effects of Online Intergroup Dialogue in Promoting Justice-Versus Harmony-Oriented Outcomes in Bosnia and Serbia." *Peace and Conflict: Journal of Peace Psychology* 25, no. 4 (2019): 287–99. https://doi.org/10.1037/ pac0000395.

Serpe, Richard T., and Sheldon Stryker. "The Symbolic Interactionist Perspective and Identity Theory." In *Handbook of Identity Theory and Research,* edited by Seth J.

Schwartz, Koen Luyckx, and Vivian L. Vignoles. Vol 1, *Structures and Processes*, 225–48. New York: Springer, 2012.

Sharp, Dustin N. "Emancipating Transitional Justice from the Bonds of the Paradigmatic Transition." *International Journal of Transitional Justice* 9, no. 1 (2015): 150–69. https://doi.org/10.1093/ijtj/iju021.

——. *Rethinking Transitional Justice for the Twenty-First Century: Beyond the End of History*. Cambridge: Cambridge University Press, 2018.

Shelton, J. Nicole. "Interpersonal Concerns in Social Encounters between Majority and Minority Group Members." *Group Processes and Intergroup Relations* 6, no. 2 (2003): 171–85. https://doi.org/10.1177/1368430203006002003.

Simić, Olivera, and Zala Volčič, eds. *Transitional Justice and Civil Society in the Balkans*. New York: Springer, 2013.

Simons, Marlies. "Danube's Grisly Tale, Staring Milosevic in the Face." *New York Times*, August 26, 2002. https://www.nytimes.com/2002/08/26/world/danube-s-grisly-tale-staring-milosevic-in-the-face.html.

Simpson, Kirk. "Victims of Political Violence: A Habermasian Model of Truth Recovery." *Journal of Human Rights* 6, no. 3 (2007): 325–43. https://doi.org/10.1080/14754830701531120.

Skaar, Elin. "Reconciliation in a Transitional Justice Perspective." *Transitional Justice Review* 1, no. 1 (2013): 54–103. https://doi.org/10.5206/tjr.2012.1.1.4.

Smith, Anthony D. *National Identity*. London: Penguin, 1991.

Smith, Andrew F. *The Deliberative Impulse: Motivating Discourse in Divided Societies*. Lanham, MD: Lexington Books, 2011.

Smith, Rogers M. "Identities, Interests and the Future of Political Science." *Perspectives on Politics* 2, no. 2 (2004): 301–12. https://doi.org/10.1017/S1537592704040174.

Smits, Katherine. "Deliberation and Past Injustice: Recognition and the Reasonableness of Apology in the Australian Case." *Constellations* 15 no. 2 (2008): 236–48. https://doi.org/10.1111/j.1467-8675.2008.00487.x.

Sokolić, Ivor. *International Courts and Mass Atrocity: Narratives of War and Justice in Croatia*. Basingstoke: Palgrave Macmillan, 2019.

——. "Reconciliation Rising: The Roles of the Everyday and the Informal in Successful Post-Conflict Reconciliation." *Ethnopolitics* 19, no. 2 (2020): 162–67. https://doi.org/10.1080/17449057.2019.1653015.

Sokolić, Ivor, and Denisa Kostovicova. *Reconciliation as Activity: Opportunities for Action*. Policy Brief (Prishtina: Centre for Research, Documentation and Publication; London School of Economics and Political Science, King's College London, University of the Arts London, 2018). https://artreconciliation.org/wp-content/uploads/sites/181/2018/07/Reconciliation-as-Activity-Policy-Brief.pdf.

Sokolić, Ivor, Denisa Kostovicova, and Adam Fagan. "Civil Society in Post-Yugoslav Space: The Test of Discontinuity and Democratization." In *The Legacy of Yugoslavia: Politics, Economics and Society in the Modern Balkans*, edited by Othon Anastasakis, Adam Bennett, David Madden, and Adis Merdzanovic, 39–57. London: I.B. Tauris, 2020.

"Somalia: Reconciliation Is as Elusive as Ever." *Economist*, July 21, 2007. https://www.economist.com/middle-east-and-africa/2007/07/19/reconciliation-is-as-elusive-as-ever.

Spiegel, Paul B., and Peter Salama. "War and Mortality in Kosovo, 1998–99: An Epidemiological Testimony." *Lancet* 355 (2000): 2204–209. https://doi.org/10.1016/S0140-6736(00)02404-1.

Spörndli, Markus. "Discourse Quality and Political Decisions: An Empirical Analysis of Debates in the German Conference Committee." WZB Discussion Paper, SP IV 2003–101, Wisssenschaftszentrum Berlin für Sozialforschung, Berlin, 2003.

Sriram, Chandra Lekha, and Amy Ross. "Geographies of Crime and Justice: Contemporary Transitional Justice and the Creation of 'Zones of Impunity.'" *International Journal of Transitional Justice* 1, no. 1 (2007): 45–65. https://doi.org/10.1093/ijtj/ijm001.

Stahn, Carsten, Carmel Agius, Serge Brammertz, and Colleen Rohan, eds. *Legacies of the International Criminal Tribunal for the Former Yugoslavia: A Multidisciplinary Approach.* Oxford: Oxford University Press, 2020.

Stanley, Sharon. "Toward a Reconciliation of Integration and Racial Solidarity." *Contemporary Political Theory* 13, no. 1 (2014): 46–63. https://doi.org/10.1057/cpt.2013.13.

Statut Koalicije za REKOM [The Statute of the RECOM Coalition]. June 26, 2011. http://recom.link/wp-content/uploads/2011/06/Statut-Koalicije-za-REKOM-26.06.2011-SRB.pdf.

Staub, Ervin. "Reconciliation after Genocide, Mass Killing, or Intractable Conflict: Understanding the Roots of Violence, Psychological Recovery, and Steps Toward a General Theory." *Political Psychology* 27, no. 6 (2006): 867–94. https://doi.org/ https://www.jstor.org/stable/20447006.

Steenbergen, Marco R., André Bächtiger, Markus Spörndli, and Jürg Steiner. "Measuring Political Deliberation: A Discourse Quality Index." *Comparative European Politics* 1, no. 1 (2003): 21–48. https://doi.org/10.1057/palgrave.cep.6110002.

Steiner, Jürg. *The Foundations of Deliberative Democracy: Empirical Research and Normative Implications.* Cambridge: Cambridge University Press, 2012.

Steiner, Jürg, André Bächtiger, Markus Spörndli, and Marco R. Steenbergen. *Deliberative Politics in Action: Analysing Parliamentary Discourse.* Cambridge: Cambridge University Press, 2004.

Steiner, Jürg, Maria Clara Jaramillo, and Simona Mameli. "The Dynamics of Deliberation." *Belgrade Philosophical Annual* 27 (2014): 39–47. https://doi.org/ https://scindeks-clanci.ceon.rs/data/pdf/0353-3891/2014/0353-38911427039S.pdf.

Steiner, Jürg, Maria Clara Jaramillo, Rousiley C. M. Maia, and Simona Mameli. *Deliberation across Deeply Divided Societies: Transformative Moments.* Cambridge: Cambridge University Press, 2017.

Stephan, Walter G., and Cookie White Stephan. "Intergroup Anxiety." *Journal of Social Issues* 41, no. 3 (1985): 157–75. https://doi.org/10.1111/j.1540-4560.1985.tb01134.x.

Stewart, Brandon, and Eric Wiebelhaus-Brahm. "The Quantitative Turn in Transitional Justice Research: What Have We Learned about Impact?" *Transitional Justice Review* 1, no. 5 (2017): 97–133. https://ir.lib.uwo.ca/tjreview/vol1/iss5/4.

Stover, Eric, Hanny Megally, and Hania Mufti. "Bremer's 'Gordian Knot': Transitional Justice and the US Occupation of Iraq." *Human Rights Quarterly* 27, no. 3 (2005): 830–57. https://doi.org/10.1353/hrq.2005.0044.

Strandberg, Kim, Staffan Himmelroos, and Kimmo Grönlund. "Do Discussions in Like-Minded Groups Necessarily Lead to More Extreme Opinions? Deliberative Democracy and Group Polarization." *International Political Science Review* 40, no. 1 (2019): 41–57. https://doi.org/10.1177/0192512117692136.

Stromer-Galley, Jennifer. "On-Line Interaction and Why Candidates Avoid It." *Journal of Communication* 50, no. 4 (2000): 111–32. https://doi.org/10.1111/j.1460-2466.2000.tb02865.x.

Stromer-Galley, Jennifer, and Peter Muhlberger. "Agreement and Disagreement in Group Deliberation: Effects on Deliberation Satisfaction, Future Engagement, and Decision Legitimacy." *Political Communication* 26, no. 2 (2009): 173–92. https://doi.org/10.1080/10584600902850775.

Strupinskienė, Lina. "'What Is Reconciliation and Are We There Yet?' Different Types and Levels of Reconciliation: A Case Study of Bosnia and Herzegovina." *Journal of Human Rights* 16, no. 4 (2017): 452–72. https://doi.org/10.1080/14754835.2016.1197771.

Suárez, Jean-Luis, and Yadira Lizama-Mué. "Victims of Language: Language as a Pre-Condition of Transitional Justice in Colombia's Peace Agreement." In *Transitional Justice in Comparative Perspective: Preconditions for Success*, edited by Samar El-Masri, Tammy Lambert, and Joanna R. Quinn, 97–127. Cham: Palgrave Macmillan, 2020.

Subotić, Jelena. *Hijacked Justice: Dealing with the Past in the Balkans*. Ithaca: Cornell University Press, 2009.

Sunstein, Cass R. "Deliberative Trouble? Why Groups Go to Extremes." *Yale Law Journal* 110, no. 1 (2000): 71–119. https://doi.org/10.2307/797587.

——. "Ideological Amplification." *Constellations* 14, no. 2 (2007): 273–79. https://doi.org/10.1111/j.1467-8675.2007.00439.x.

Tabeau, Ewa, ed. *Conflict in Numbers: Casualties of the 1990s Wars in the Former Yugoslavia (1991–1999): Major Reports by Demographic Experts of the Prosecution in the Trials Before the International Criminal Tribunal for the Former Yugoslavia*. Belgrade: Helsinki Committee for Human Rights, 2009.

Talisse, Robert. "Deliberation." In *The Oxford Handbook of Political Philosophy*, edited by David M. Estlund, 205–22. Oxford: Oxford University Press, 2012.

Tashakkori, Abbas, and John W. Creswell. "Exploring the Nature of Research Questions in Mixed Methods Research." *Journal of Mixed Methods Research* 1, no. 3 (2007): 207–11. https://doi.org/10.1177/1558689807302814.

Teddlie, Charles, and Abbas Tashakkori. "A General Typology of Research Designs Featuring Mixed Methods." *Research in the Schools* 13, no. 1 (2006): 12–28.

Teitel, Ruti G. *Transitional Justice*. Oxford: Oxford University Press, 2000.

Testa, Italo. "The Respect Fallacy: Limits of Respect in Public Dialogue." In *Rhetorical Citizenship and Public Deliberation*, edited by Christian Kock and Lisa S. Villadsen, 77–92. Philadelphia: Pennsylvania State University Press, 2012.

Theidon, Kimberly. *Intimate Enemies: Violence and Reconciliation in Peru*. Philadelphia: University of Pennsylvania Press, 2012.

Thompson, Dennis F. "Deliberative Democratic Theory and Empirical Political Science." *Annual Review of Political Science* 11, no. 1 (2008): 497–520. https://doi.org/10.1146/annurev.polisci.11.081306.070555.

Thoms, Oskar N. T., James Ron, and Roland Paris. "State-Level Effects of Transitional Justice: What Do We Know?" *International Journal of Transitional Justice* 4, no. 3 (2010): 329–54. https://doi.org/10.1093/ijtj/ijq012.

Ting-Toomey, Stella, Kimberlie K. Yee-Jung, Robin B. Shapiro, Wintilo Garcia, Trina J. Wright, and John G. Oetzel. "Ethnic/Cultural Identity Salience and Conflict Styles in Four US Ethnic Groups." *International Journal of Intercultural Relations* 24, no. 1 (2000): 47–81. https://doi.org/10.1016/s0147-1767(99)00023-1.

Toal, Gerard, and Carl T. Dahlman. *Bosnia Remade: Ethnic Cleansing and Its Reversal.* Oxford: Oxford University Press, 2011.

Toom, Victor. "Ontologically Dirty Knots: The Production of Numbers after the Srebrenica Genocide." *Security Dialogue* 51, no. 4 (2020): 358–76. https://doi.org/10.1177/0967010620902008.

Toshkov, Dimiter. *Research Design in Political Science.* Basingstoke: Palgrave Macmillan, 2016.

Touquet, Heleen, and Peter Vermeersch. "Changing Frames of Reconciliation: The Politics of Peace-Building in the Former Yugoslavia." *East European Politics and Societies* 30, no. 1 (2015): 55–73. https://doi.org/10.1177/0888325415584048.

Tovares, Alla V. "Going Off-Script and Reframing the Frame: The Dialogic Intertwining of the Centripetal and Centrifugal Voices in the Truth and Reconciliation Commission Hearings." *Discourse and Society* 27, no. 5 (2016): 554–73. https://doi.org/10.1177/0957926516651365.

Transitional Justice Policy. African Union. February 2019. https://au.int/sites/default/files/documents/36541-doc-au_tj_policy_eng_web.pdf.

Transitional Justice Research Collaborative. November 15, 2020. https://transitionaljusticedata.com/about.

Tranziciona pravda u postjugoslavenskim zemljama: Izvještaj za 2010–2011. godinu [Transitional Justice in post-Yugoslav Countries: The Report for 2010–2011]. Sarajevo: Udruženje "Tranzicijska pravda, odgovornost i sjećanje u BiH," 2012.

Trénel, Matthias. "Measuring the Deliberativeness of Online Discussions. Coding Scheme 2.0." Unpublished Paper. Social Science Research Center, Berlin, August 10, 2004. http://www.wzberlin.de/~trenel/tools/qod_2_04.pdf.

Trupia, Francesco. "'Good Personhood' in Kosovo: A Serbian Perspective from Below." *Peacebuilding* 9, no. 4 (2021): 425–40. https://doi.org/10.1080/21647259.2021.1895605.

Tsai, Dustin. "Navigating Exclusion as Enemies of the State: The Case of Serbs in Croatia and Croats in Serbia." *Geopolitics*, 2021, 1–20. https://doi.org/10.1080/14650045.2021.1881488.

Ugarriza, Juan Esteban "When War Adversaries Talk: The Experimental Effect of Engagement Rules on Postconflict Deliberation." *Latin American Politics and Society* 58, no. 3 (2016): 77–98. https://doi.org/10.1111/j.1548-2456.2016.00319.x.

Ugarriza, Juan, and Didier Caluwaerts, eds. *Democratic Deliberation in Deeply Divided Societies: From Conflict to Common Ground.* Basingstoke: Palgrave Macmillan, 2014.

Ugarriza, Juan E., and Enzo Nussio. "The Effect of Perspective-Giving on Postconflict Reconciliation. An Experimental Approach." *Political Psychology* 38, no. 1 (2017): 3–19. https://www.jstor.org/stable/45094336.

———. "There Is No Pill for Deliberation: Explaining Discourse Quality in Post-Conflict Communities." *Swiss Political Science Review* 22, no. 1 (2015): 145–66. https://doi.org/10.1111/spsr.12195.

Ugarriza, Juan E., and Natalia Trujillo-Orrego. "The Ironic Effect of Deliberation: What We Can (and Cannot) Expect in Deeply Divided Societies." *Acta Politica* 55, no. 2 (2020): 221–41. https://doi.org/10.1057/s41269-018-0113-1.

Ulbert, Cornelia, and Thomas Risse. "Deliberatively Changing the Discourse: What Does Make Arguing Effective?" *Acta Politica* 40, no. 3 (2005): 351–67. https://doi.org/10.1057/palgrave.ap.5500117.

Umphres, William P. "Beyond Good Reasons: Solidarity, Open Texture, and the Ethics of Deliberation." *Constellations* 25, no. 4 (2018): 556–69. https://doi.org/10.1111/1467-8675.12344.

Vajda, Maja Munivrana. "Domestic Trials for International Crimes—A Critical Analysis of Croatian War Crimes Sentencing Jurisprudence." *International Criminal Law Review* 19, no. 1 (2019): 15–38. https://doi.org/10.1163/15718123-01901002.

van der Merwe, Hugo. "Delivering Justice during Transition: Research Challenges." In *Assessing the Impact of Transitional Justice: Challenges for Empirical Research*, edited by Hugo van der Merve, Audrey R. Chapman, and Victoria Baxter, 115–42. Washington, DC: United States Institute of Peace Press, 2009.

van der Merwe, Hugo., Richard Chelin, and Masana Ndinga-Kanga. "'Measuring' Transitional Justice." In *Transitional Justice: Theories, Mechanism and Debates*, edited by Hakeem O. Yusuf and Hugo van der Merwe, 281–300. London: Routledge, 2022.

Vasić, Miloš. "Mrtvi putuju . . ." [The Dead Are Traveling . . .]. *Vreme*, June 21, 2001. https://www.vreme.com/vreme/mrtvi-putuju/.

Verdeja, Ernesto. *Unchopping a Tree: Reconciliation in the Aftermath of Political Violence*. Philadelphia: Temple University Press, 2009.

Visoka, Gëzim. "Arrested Truth: Transitional Justice and the Politics of Remembrance in Kosovo." *Journal of Human Rights Practice* 8, no. 1 (2016): 62–80. https://doi.org/10.1093/jhuman/huv017.

Vladisavljević, Nebojša. *Serbia's Antibureaucratic Revolution: Milošević, the Fall of Communism and Nationalist Mobilization*. Basingstoke: Palgrave Macmillan, 2008.

Voci, Alberto, Miles Hewstone, Hermann Swart, and Chiara A. Veneziani. "Refining the Association between Intergroup Contact and Forgiveness in Northern Ireland: Type of Contact, Prior Conflict Experience, and Group Identification." *Group Processes and Intergroup Relations* 18, no. 5 (2015): 589–608. https://doi.org/10.1177/1368430215577001.

Walker, Kathryn. "Resolving Debates over the Status of Ethnic Identities during Transitional Justice." *Contemporary Political Theory* 11, no. 1 (2012): 68–87. https://doi.org/10.1057/cpt.2011.7.

Wallensteen, Peter. *Quality Peace: Peacebuilding, Victory, and World Order*. Oxford: Oxford University Press, 2015.

Wallensteen, Peter, and Margareta Sollenberg. "Armed Conflict and Regional Conflict Complexes, 1989–97." *Journal of Peace Research* 35, no. 5 (1998): 621–34. https://doi.org/10.1177/0022343398035005005.

Warren, Mark E. "Institutionalizing Deliberative Democracy." In *Deliberation, Participation and Democracy: Can the People Govern?*, edited by Shawn W. Rosenberg, 272–88. Basingstoke: Palgrave Macmillan, 2007.

Warren, T. Camber, and Kevin K. Troy. "Explaining Violent Intra-Ethnic Conflict: Group Fragmentation in the Shadow of State Power." *Journal of Conflict Resolution* 59, no. 3 (2015): 484–509. https://doi.org/10.1177/0022002713515400.

Waters, Timothy William, ed. *The Milošević Trial: An Autopsy*. New York: Oxford University Press, 2014.

Weatherall, Ann, Cynthia Gallois, and Jeffery Pittam. "Language and Social Interaction: Taking Stock and Looking Forward." *Annals of the International Communication Association* 24, no. 1 (2001): 363–84. https://doi.org/10.1080/23808985.2001.11678994.

Whitt, Sam, and Rick K. Wilson. "The Dictator Game, Fairness and Ethnicity in Postwar Bosnia." *American Journal of Political Science* 51, no. 3 (2007): 655–68. https://www.jstor.org/stable/4620090.

Widdicombe, Sue. "Identity as an Analysts' and a Participants' Resource." In *Identities in Talk*, edited by Charles Antaki and Sue Widdicombe, 191–206. London: Sage, 1998.

Wilde, Lawrence. "The Concept of Solidarity: Emerging from the Theoretical Shadows?" *British Journal of Politics and International Relations* 9, no. 1 (2007): 171–81. https://doi.org/10.1111/j.1467-856x.2007.00275.x.

Williams, Robin. *Making Identity Matter: Identity, Society and Social Interaction.* Durham: Sociologypress, 2000.

Wills, Jane. "Identity Making for Action: The Example of London Citizens." In *Theorizing Identities and Social Action*, edited by Margaret Wetherell, 157–76. Basingstoke: Palgrave Macmillan, 2009.

Wojcieszak, Magdalena. "Pulling Toward or Pulling Away: Deliberation, Disagreement, and Opinion Extremity in Political Participation." *Social Science Quarterly* 92, no. 1 (2011): 206–25. https://www.jstor.org/stable/42956481.

Wolfgram, Mark A. *Antigone's Ghosts: The Long Legacy of War and Genocide in Five Countries.* Lewisburg: Bucknell University Press, 2019.

Woodward, Susan L. *Balkan Tragedy: Chaos and Dissolution after the Cold War.* Washington, DC: Brookings Institution, 1995.

Yordán, Carlos L. "Towards Deliberative Peace: A Habermasian Critique of Contemporary Peace Operations." *Journal of International Relations and Development* 12, no. 1 (2009): 58–89. https://doi.org/10.1057/jird.2008.26.

Young, Iris Marion. "Activist Challenges to Deliberative Democracy." *Political Theory* 29, no. 5 (2001): 670–90. https://www.jstor.org/stable/3072534.

——. *Inclusion and Democracy.* Oxford: Oxford University Press, 2002.

Index

Page numbers in *italics* refer to tables.

pluralism in, 21; RECOM and, 31, 112–13; status as United Nations protectorate, 153n2; war crimes trials, 22
Kosovo Albanians, 1–2, 20, 115, 122, 124
Kosovo War (1998–99), 1, 21
Krasniqi, Lush, 1–3
Kriesberg, Louis, 9
Krippendorff, Klaus, 61

language, 9, 13, 88; translation of, 76–77, 80. See also discourse; mutuality in public communication
Levy, Ron, 172n48
liberals, 19–20, 24, 31, 110, 128, 141
Lord, Christopher, 179n24
Luskin, Robert, 59

Macedonia, 19; conflict in (2001), 21; name changes, 163n12. See also North Macedonia
Mac Ginty, Roger, 5
Manosevitch, Edith, 191n50
marginalization, 20, 120
mass graves, 1–2, 122
McConnachie, Kirsten, 121
McEvoy, Kieran, 121
Mégret, Frédéric, 25
Meierhenrich, Jens, 8
Mendelberg, Tali, 94, 184n18
Mill, J. S., 53
Milošević, Slobodan, 1–2
Misak, Cheryl, 95
Mokros, Hartmut, 45
Montenegro, 19, 119, 153n2
morality: deliberation and, 46–47; postconflict reconciliation and, 33. See also discourse ethics
moral universalism, 48
Moshman, David, 34
Mouffe, Chantal, 135
Muhlberger, Peter, 106
Muslims, Bosnian. See Bosniaks
mutuality in public communication: blame avoidance and, 123–24; reconciliation and, 4, 8, 67, 107, 126, 129, 130, 132; regard for ethnic Other and, 55
mutual understanding, 35, 48, 84, 91, 106
Mutz, Diana, 95, 137

Nagy, Rosemary, 47, 176n93
national identity, 44, 154n6
nationalism and ethnic identities, 109, 133; civil society and, 111; national unity, 9; political

elites and, 19–20, 120; postconflict, 17–18; regional approaches to transitional justice and, 30–31; victims' associations and NGOs, 114–16; violence and, 2, 19
Neblo, Michael A., 95, 117, 170n29, 191n39
negative reciprocity, 121, 123, 125
Nießer, Jacqueline, 156n21
Noël, Alain, 137
nongovernmental organizations (NGOs). See civil society activism; human rights NGOs
Northern Ireland, 41–43
North Macedonia, 163n12. See also Macedonia
Nussio, Enzo, 76, 203n52

O'Doherty, Kieran C., 174n73
O'Flynn, Ian, 36, 38, 44, 58, 94, 110, 172n48, 202n34
Oosterlynck, Stijn, 46
opinion diversity, 27, 126; deliberation and, 37–38; in RECOM consultations, 3–4, 27–29, 114–16
opinion homogeneity (within ethnic groups), 105, 109–11, 114–16, 125, 133, 135, 196n38
optimal distinctiveness theory, 139

Parkinson, John, 35, 45, 66, 109
parliaments, deliberation in, 43, 54, 57–60, 73–75, 110, 131, 171n41
participation, 53, 58, 62
peacebuilding: deliberation and, 34–35, 39, 65, 90, 106, 137–38 (see also deliberation in divided societies); discussion-based approaches, 138, 140–41; by external actors, 128; fact-finding and, 26; policy approaches, 140–43; postconflict justice as form of, 6 (see also transitional justice). See also reconciliation
Pedrini, Seraina, 57
Pensky, Max, 90
perspective-taking, 45, 119, 130, 203n52; empathy and, 197n61; "we-perspective," 109
Perunovic, Sreca, 163n16
Phillips, Anne, 134
Philpott, Daniel, 8, 48
Pittam, Jeffery, 125
Ploss, Katharina, 131
positioning perspective, 45. See also identities
postconflict societies: complexities of, 32–33. See also conflict resolution; deliberation in divided societies; peacebuilding; reconciliation; transitional justice; truth commissions

Printed in the USA
CPSIA information can be obtained
at www.ICGtesting.com
LVHW091644250823
756268LV00025B/625/J